The Awakening of Muslim Democracy

Why and how did Islam become such a political force in so many Muslim-majority countries? Will it impinge on the political transitions of the Arab Spring? In this book, Jocelyne Cesari investigates the relationship between modernization and Islam in Muslim-majority countries such as Egypt, Iraq, Pakistan, Tunisia, and Turkey – countries founded by secular rulers that have since undergone secularized politics. Cesari argues that nation-building processes in these states have not created Western types of regimes, but have instead spurred the politicization of Islam by turning it into a modern national ideology. Looking closely at examples of Islamic dominance in political modernization – nationalization of Islamic institutions and personnel under state ministries, religiously motivated social unrest or violence, and internationalization of Islam-aligned political movements or conflicts – this study provides a unique overview of the historical and political developments from the end of World War II to the Arab Spring that have made Islam a dominant political force. It also discusses Islam's impact on emerging democracies in the contemporary Middle East and contends that if new democracies emerge, they will probably be unsecular – that is, limiting the rights of the individual on religious grounds. This book offers a unique and original approach to the relationships between religion, politics, and secularism that is also relevant to non-Western political experience outside Muslim countries.

Jocelyne Cesari is director of the Islam in the West program at Harvard University and senior research Fellow at the Berkley Center for Religion, Peace and World Affairs at Georgetown University. Her most recent publication is *Why the West Fears Islam: Exploration of Muslims in Liberal Democracies.*

The Awakening of Muslim Democracy

Religion, Modernity, and the State

JOCELYNE CESARI

Harvard University and Georgetown University

CAMBRIDGE
UNIVERSITY PRESS

CAMBRIDGE
UNIVERSITY PRESS

32 Avenue of the Americas, New York NY 10013-2473, USA

Cambridge University Press is part of the University of Cambridge.

It furthers the University's mission by disseminating knowledge in the pursuit of education, learning and research at the highest international levels of excellence.

www.cambridge.org
Information on this title: www.cambridge.org/9781107664821

First published 2014

A catalogue record for this publication is available from the British Library

Library of Congress Cataloguing in Publication data
Cesari, Jocelyne.
The Awakening of Muslim Democracy / Jocelyne Cesari.
pages   cm
Includes bibliographical references and index.
ISBN 978-1-107-04418-0 (hardback) – ISBN 978-1-107-66482-1 (paperback)
1. Middle East – Politics and government – 1945– 2. Islam and politics – Middle East – History – 20th century. 3. Islam and state – Middle East – History – 20th century. 4. Democratization – Middle East – History – 20th century. 5. Arab Spring, 2010– I. Title.
DS63.1.C47 2013
909´.097492708312–dc23 2013018646

ISBN 978-1-107-04418-0 Hardback
ISBN 978-1-107-66482-1 Paperback

Contents

Acknowledgments

This volume is the result of two years of research conducted during my tenure at the National War College in 2011 and 2012 under the auspices of the Minerva Research Initiative of the Office of the Secretary of Defense (2011–12).

I am grateful to the National Defense University faculty members for their feedback and engaging conversations: John Ballard at the National War College (NWC), Judith Yaphe at the Institute of National Strategic Studies (INSS), and colleagues of the Conflicts Records Research Center (CRRC).

Jose Casanova and Tom Banchoff at the Berkley Center for Peace, Religion and International Affairs at Georgetown University have included me in their research team and supported my efforts to broaden my research on the role of religion in world politics.

The works of Charles Taylor, Vali Nasr, and Peter Katzenstein have been an inspiration for this book. I am particularly grateful to Peter for his feedback and guidance on numerous versions of this project.

Two wonderful research assistants, Stacey Lee and Sara Szeiger, worked enthusiastically and zealously with me during the long processes of data analysis and editing the manuscript.

The dedication of the Islamopedia Online team has been critical in creating country profiles on "Islam and Governance," from which I have benefited tremendously in the writing of this book. Thank you, Feriel Abouhafa, Elise Alexander, Bushra Asif, Mohamed Atta, Roger Bauman, Bentley Brown, Samah Chaudry, Shelby Condray, Conor Dube, Nelly Golson, Faisal Husain, and Tova Reznik.

The English transliteration of Arabic terms follows the guide of the *International Journal of Middle East Studies*.

Preface

On June 24, 2012, Mohamed Morsi of the Muslim Brotherhood's Freedom and Justice Party (FJP) won the first free Egyptian presidential elections since the end of the Mubarak regime. On July 3 of the following year, he was dismissed from power by the military after a year of unprecedented social unrest and growing popular discontent against his government. His political misfortune captures the contradictory meanings of what has been called the "Arab Spring."

At first came surprise and enthusiasm for the "democratic" power of the masses that brought down the authoritarian regimes of Mubarak in Egypt and Ben Ali in Tunisia. Then came doubt and concern when the demise of these powers resulted in the election of Islamist governments in both Egypt and Tunisia.

Steven A. Cook, in his December 19, 2011, piece for *Foreign Policy*, wrote about the "Frankenstein of Tahrir Square."[1] The Tahririans, once heralded as revolutionaries with "a cacophony of ideas, projects, initiatives, and manifestos," later morphed in the public eye into vagabond street protestors with "no moral leadership to give the best of ideas national political meaning and content." In contrast, in both Tunisia and Egypt, the Islamists, who did not instigate the ousters and laid low during the beginning of the massive protests, are the only ones who played post–Ben Ali and post-Mubarak politics well and surfaced as the elected postrevolutionary leaders.[2]

When the 2011 revolution took everybody by surprise, many eagerly proclaimed the end of Arab exceptionalism.[3] Throughout the rest of the year,

---

[1] Steven A. Cook, "The Frankenstein of Tahrir Square," *Foreign Policy,* December 19, 2011, accessed December 24, 2011, http://www.foreignpolicy.com/articles/2011/12/19/the_frankenstein_of_tahrir_square.

[2] Wiem Melki, "'Ennahda Played It Well' – Defeated Parties Learn from Ennahda's Success," *Tunisia Live*, October 28, 2011, accessed November 24, 2011, http://www.tunisia-live.net/2011/10/28/ennahda-played-it-well-defeated-parties-learn-from-ennahdas-success/.

[3] Omer Taspinar, "The End of Arab Exceptionalism," *Zaman Amerika*, February 14, 2011, accessed February 14, 2011, http://www.zamanusa.com/us-tr/columnistDetail_getNewsById.action?newsId=45952&columnistId=100.

rapid relays of information through satellite television and the Internet gave the international audience a front-row view into an Arab spring of high hopes, then into a stagnant yet restless Arab summer, and finally into an Arab winter filled with deep setbacks and protracted violence in Syria – and, for the Western viewer, slimmer prospects for democratization, especially with the rise to power of Islamist parties.[4] At the time, Daniel Brumberg wrote: "We must reckon with a process of authoritarian extraction that could last well into the next decade – one that promises as many if not more disappointments than successes."[5]

How do we make sense of such an apparently contradictory succession of events? It is a contradiction or an aberration only because most of the observers are prisoners of the dominant narrative, which pitches religion in general, and Islam in particular, as the alternative to secular politics. In other words, the first protesters in Tahrir Square did not use Islamic slogans, and that was interpreted as the end of Islam in politics. But because Islamist parties are emerging as the winners of the revolutions, the prospects of democratization are once again in question. The downfall of President Morsi in 2013 after two days of mass protest and the return of the military to the forefront of Egyptian politics have added to the confusion and raised renewed swift conclusions that Islamism is over.

Such a binary vision is closely related to the dominant approach to political Islam or Islamism defined as a set of ideas and beliefs, which are instrumentalized by political activists to bring down the secular state. At the core of such an approach are (1) the assumed definition of religion as a set of beliefs, values, and norms distinct from politics; and (2) the misnomer of previous regimes as "secular."

Anthropologist Talal Asad and philosopher Michael Connolly have strongly questioned such a limited approach of religion[6] and demonstrated that this understanding, far from being universal, is the direct outcome of the historical evolution of Christianity in the West.[7] Yet, interestingly, the

---

[4] Daniel Byman, "After the Hope of the Arab Spring, the Chill of an Arab Winter," *Washington Post*, December 1, 2011, accessed July 9, 2012, http://www.washingtonpost.com/opinions/after-the-hope-of-the-arab-spring-the-chill-of-an-arab-winter/2011/11/28/gIQABGqHIO_story.html.

[5] Daniel Brumberg, "Sustaining Mechanics of Arab Autocracies," *Foreign Policy*, December 19, 2011, accessed December 20, 2011, http://mideast.foreignpolicy.com/posts/2011/12/19/sustaining_mechanics_of_arab_autocracies.

[6] Talal Asad, *Genealogies of Religion: Discipline and Reasons of Power in Christianity and Islam* (Baltimore, MD: Johns Hopkins University Press, 1993), 40–44.

[7] In *Genealogies of Religion*, Talal Asad describes the status of religion in medieval society as very different from the place religion holds in the modern age. He argues that during this period Christianity functioned as a "great cloak" that defined an adherent's entire experience of the world. It possessed an "all-embracing capacity" – a distinctive practice and belief system – that disciplined the religious subject and nurtured certain virtues. Religion was not some essentially distinct form of culture, process of reasoning, or experiential state that existed apart from other cultural experiences. It encompassed the cultural horizon of the subject's practices and assumptions about the world.

historical and political conditions that led to the imposition on Islam of such a Western category of religion have not been systematically explored.[8] This book is an attempt to shed light on the political mechanisms that underlie the transformation of Islam into a modern religion. It shows that the state (not only Islamists) has been a central if not the primary agent in politicizing Islam.

Therefore, in this book, the term *political Islam* does not refer to the common definition of religiously based political opposition to the state. Instead it is broadened to include nationalization of Islamic institutions and personnel under state ministries; usage of Islamic references in political competition by both state actors and opponents (Islamism); religiously motivated social unrest or violence; and internationalization of Islam-orientated political movements or conflicts.

Such an exploration questions two major assumptions of the scholarly work on political Islam: the dichotomies between state and religion and between modernization and Islamization (see Chapter 1).

The main assertion of this book is that the modernization of Muslim societies, unlike Western ones, did not lead to privatization of religion but to the opposite, that is, the politicization of Islam in a way unprecedented in premodern Muslim polities. This is not because Islam does not separate religion and politics (which is, by the way, historically false), but because the Islamic tradition was integrated in the nation-state building that took place at the end of the Ottoman Empire. And by Islamic tradition, I refer not only to ideas or creeds but also to institutions of education and learning as well as religious personnel. For this reason, I advance new operational definitions of *religion* and *secularism*.

Islam is not only a set of beliefs; it is not a way of life either (in the sense that Islamists define it). It is better defined by the never-ending dialectics between believing, belonging, and behaving, which explains why Islam was woven into the social fabrics of modern Muslim societies throughout the nation-building process. In other words, religious belonging became entangled with national belonging.

In this regard, the state has played a central role in redefining and politicizing Islam. Strangely, the analysis of the state has been remarkably absent from any evaluation of political Islam and its capacity to influence political liberalization.

In light of the Arab Spring, the objective of this book is to explore this unexamined dimension of the politicization of Islam – that is, state actions and policies vis-à-vis religion in general and Islam in particular. My analytical eclecticism[9] combines institutional and norm diffusion

---

[8] For a parallel imposition of the Western category of religion on Judaism, see Leora Batnitzky, *How Judaism Became a Modern Religion* (Princeton, NJ: Princeton University Press, 2011).

[9] Rudra Sil and Peter J. Katzenstein, *Beyond Paradigms: Analytic Eclecticism in the Study of World Politics* (Houndmills, Basingstoke, Hampshire: Palgrave Macmillan, 2010).

approaches to propound several counterintuitive propositions. First, it is crucial to bring state actions and policies back into the study of cultural and religious changes. Second, an institutional approach to state-Islam dynamics substantially broadens the analysis beyond polarized state-religion relations, revealing a complex set of interactions between the two entities, including adaptation, cooperation, and competition. Third, the approach to secularization goes beyond state and religion in institutional arrangements to encompass social and individual aspects. Although the institutional level of state-religion relations is very important, as we will show in Part I of the book, it is not sufficient to efficiently differentiate regimes of secularity. For this reason, we introduce the social and individual levels and discuss how these three levels – institutional, social, and individual – interact to produce unique forms of secularity for each country.

In the case of Muslim countries, the building of the state led to a situation I call *hegemonic Islam*, in which the religion is not only absorbed within state institutions but also is fused with national identity and with the norms of the public space. This fusion has influenced the social status of Islam as well as the development of individualism. Interestingly, in contrast to the European and (to some extent) American experiences, we are witnessing a combination between, on one hand, the acceptance of free and fair elections, institutional stability, and social and political equality of citizens and, on the other hand, the acknowledgment of religion in politics. The latter translates into multiple initiatives to preserve the status of Islam as the religion of the nation through a discriminatory use of law, detrimental not only to religious minorities but also to Muslim citizens who wish to assert freedom of speech. Concretely, it means that the places of worship, clerics, and institutions of the dominant religion are part of the state institutions and, in addition, that the central status of religion in public space is secured by blasphemy laws and limitations on conversion.

Therefore a differentiation between legitimate and illegitimate individual rights is at play, with direct consequences on the nature of democracy that Muslim countries will attain. More specifically, I will demonstrate that the recognition of the rights concerning the spiritual and sexual actions of the person is a major challenge for democratization, even in cases of recognized democracies like Indonesia. I have called the recognition of this specific set of rights the principle of self, which translates into freedom of speech and sexuality independently of religious norms.

In these circumstances, if there is an effective transition to democracy (which at the time of this writing is uncertain), the plausible political evolution of Muslim countries is what I call *unsecular democracy*. I borrow the term *unsecular* from Kalyvas[10] but give it a more institutional meaning by

---

[10] Stathis Kalyvas, "Unsecular Politics and Religious Mobilization," in T. Kselman and J. A. Buttigieg (eds.), *European Christian Democracy* (Notre Dame, IN: University of Notre Dame Press, 2003), 293–320.

basing it on the *limitation by law* of the rights of the person on two levels – spiritual and sexual – through criminalizing blasphemy, homosexuality, and indecency. These limitations do not automatically coincide with discrimination against religious minorities. When religious minorities are discriminated against, as in Turkey, the regimes are better defined as competitive authoritarianism, as will be discussed in Part III. Unsecular democracy, on the other hand, refers to countries such as Indonesia or Senegal where religious minorities are recognized but limitations still apply to the spiritual and sexual rights of all individuals.

LAYOUT AND METHODOLOGY OF THE BOOK

In sum, the claim of this book goes against the dominant consensus that modernization projects are correlated with the social and political decline of religion. In other words, I challenge the underlying assumption that modernization, secularization, and democratization go hand in hand.[11]

It is worth emphasizing that the connection between modernization and secularization is not as common and systematic as the narrative of modernity would have us believe. Part I of this book sheds light on the role of the state in major domains of nation and institution building that have contributed to the politicization of Islam, even in the case of strong secular projects in Turkey, Egypt, Tunisia, and Iraq before the rise of Islamist opposition. These chapters specifically describe the construction of Islam as the hegemonic religion (i.e., a religion that not only is dominant but also enjoys legal privileges) as an inherent part of the nation building. To illustrate how the construction of hegemonic religion occurs in most Muslim-majority countries, I focus on those that have been defined as secular according to Western standards, meaning countries ruled by a secular elite educated or otherwise openly influenced by the West, such as Egypt, Iraq, Tunisia, Turkey, and Pakistan. Given that Egypt and Tunisia experienced drastic regime changes in 2011, the possibilities of political evolution under the Arab Spring conditions will be analyzed in light of Islam's status as a hegemonic religion. Particular attention will also be paid to the situation of Iraq since 2003 because, unlike Tunisia or Egypt, it illustrates the particular challenge of sectarian tensions on democratization.

In brief, the first part of the book demonstrates that state-generated norms of Islam are highly institutionalized. They are constructed and at the same time reflected in several facets of the state, including the constitution, the

---

[11] I am, of course, following the path opened by scholars such as Talal Asad, Jose Casanova, and Shmuel Einsenstadt, whose work will be discussed in the next chapters. While their work questions the dyads modernization-secularization or modernization-democratization, my specific objective was to deconstruct the triad modernity-secularism-democracy taken for granted in many analyses of Islam and politics.

religious state institutions, the legal system, and religious education in public schools. I have conducted this investigation by systematically collecting and analyzing original documents: constitutions, administrative materials, platforms of political parties, and Islamic textbooks as well as by tracing all political events and reforms relevant to state-Islam relations from the time of independence until now.

The building of Islam as a hegemonic religion under the authoritarian regime explains why and how Islamism became the major political opposition under authoritarian rule (Part II). It also provides hints on the future of political Islam in democratic transitions.

In this regard, the institutional approach to religion also holds implications for the direction Islam-state relationships will take in the post-Mubarak and post–Ben Ali contexts, as discussed in Part III. It is worth emphasizing that the goal of this part of the book is not to assess the overall democratic transition of these countries but only the role of Islam in it. The probability that Tunisians, and even more so Egyptians, will move toward questioning the legal privileges conferred upon Islam seems very thin, and the failure to do so may impinge on the future democratization of these regimes. However, it does not mean that the Islamic tradition per se is the cause for the lack of democratization.[12]

As I am putting the last touches to this book in September 2013, the Egyptian military has launched a fierce initiative to annihilate the Muslim Brotherhood by repressing and jailing its followers and main leaders. At the same time, the Ennahada government in Tunisia has agreed to step down in an attempt to put an end to long months of political crisis. As events are unfolding, it would be premature to draw any definitive conclusion on the near future of Islamism. But if any lesson can be learned from the recent political history of these countries and from their political culture as analyzed in the next chapters, it is reasonable to assume that political Islam will not disappear anytime soon.

---

[12] After all, the major ranking systems of degree of democracy concur that Muslim-dominated Senegal and Indonesia are relatively advanced on the democratic scale. From Ted Robert Gurr's *Polity IV Project: Political Regime Characteristics and Transitions, 1800–2010*, accessed July 9, 2012, http://www.systemicpeace.org/polity/polity4.htm. *Polity IV Country Report 2010: Senegal*, accessed July 9, 2012, http://www.systemicpeace.org/polity/Senegal2010.pdf. *Polity IV Country Report 2010: Indonesia*, accessed July 9, 2012, http://www.systemicpeace.org/polity/Indonesia2010.pdf. Also see Freedom House, "Country Ratings and Status by Region, FIW 1973–2012 (EXCEL)," *Freedom in the World Index: 1973–2012*, accessed July 9, 2012, http://www.freedomhouse.org/report-types/freedom-world?gclid=CLO5hNLaj7ECFUlN4A odTwq3Cw.

PART I

THE MAKING OF ISLAM AS A MODERN RELIGION

I

Modernization and Politicization of Religion

The data presented in this section challenge the assumed connection between modernization and secularization that is at the core of most scholarship on political development. More precisely, two factors – separation of church and state and privatization of religion – have been central in measuring the conditions for political development and democratization.[1]

Drawing on the historical experience of Western countries, an academic consensus has emerged that modernization, democratization, and secularization are inextricably linked in any process of political development. However, recent sociological data show that democratization is not dependent on the separation of church and state – and that in fact, government involvement in religion often increases as democracy grows, especially in Christian nations.[2]

In the same vein, scholars such as Benjamin Kaplan have argued that democratization and secularization, even in the West, were not actually as smooth and linear as the narrative wants us to believe, and setbacks were inevitable.[3] For example, the European experience of democratization was part of a reaction to the religiously induced Thirty Years' War and to the rise of Enlightenment principles, which resulted in various forms of church and state separation. In other words, the differentiation of church and state experienced throughout Europe was the solution to several decades of bloody

---

[1] See Daniel Bell, "The Return of the Sacred? The Argument on the Future of Religion," *British Journal of Sociology* 28.4 (1977): 420–49; Peter Berger (ed.), *The Desecularization of the World: Resurgent Religion and World Politics* (Washington, DC: Ethics and Public Policy Center, 1999); and Thomas Luckmann, *Invisible Religion: The Problem of Religion in Modern Society* (New York: Macmillan, 1967).

[2] See Jonathan Fox, "World Separation of Religion and State in the 21st Century," *Comparative Political Studies*, no. 39 (2006): 537–69.

[3] See Benjamin Kaplan, "Enlightenment?" in *Divided by Faith: Religious Conflict and the Practice of Toleration in Early Modern Europe* (Cambridge: Harvard University Press, 2007), 333–58.

3

religious wars during the sixteenth and seventeenth centuries. Ultimately, the matrix of long-term ideas – such as the necessity of separating religion and politics, the perception of religion as a disturbance in public spaces, and the idea that intertwining politics and religion creates absolute power – shapes political imagery and cultures. This imagery is continuously utilized by European political actors to build ideological arguments that secularization goes hand in hand with a decline of religion in the public space.

In the American republic, on the other hand, the separation of church and state was addressed very early on because of the initial European settlers' experiences of religious persecution. As a result, since its inception, American secularization was influenced by toleration, which at the time was defined as equality for all religious groups without political hierarchy between various religious beliefs. Such a perception of toleration, however, was very far from the modern conception that focuses on the individual freedom of belief or nonbelief, which is now considered one of the gold standards of democracy although it came to be only during nineteenth-century American democracy.

When it comes to modernization outside the West, political analysis of the historical role of religion is rare.[4] Instead, priority is given to unhistorical democracy models that are forged on the basis of the Western experience and therefore operate on the assumption of a uniform causality for secularization, which does not hold strong explanatory value. Surely, there have been remarkable scholarly attempts in the last twenty years to reevaluate secularization[5] by emphasizing that it does not automatically mean privatization of religion. Even those, however, rarely take into account political experiences outside the West.

It is not surprising then that most non-Western experiences of secularization have been measured and evaluated in comparison to *secularism*, which in this book refers to Western models of *secularity*. In other words, I define secularism as the various Western political cultures that contextualize and historicize two major defining principles of secularity: protection by law of all religions and equidistance of the state vis-à-vis all religions.[6] These

[4] See Yoshiko Ashiwa and David L. Wank, "Making Religion, Making the State in Modern China: An Introductory Essay," in *Making Religion, Making the State: The Politics of Religion in Modern China* (Palo Alto: Stanford University Press, 2009), 1–21.
[5] See José Casanova, "Religion, European Secular Identities, and European Integration," *Transit*, July 27, 2004, accessed June 8, 2011, http://www.bpb.de/files/XLKRLX.pdf; Grace Davie, Paul Heelas, and Linda Woodhead (eds.), *Predicting Religion: Christian, Secular and Alternative Futures* (Burlington, VT: Ashgate Publishing Company, 2003); José Casanova, "Beyond European and American Exceptionalisms: Towards a Global Perspective," in Grace Davie, Paul Heelas, and Linda Woodhead (eds.), *Predicting Religion: Christian, Secular and Alternative Futures* (Burlington, VT: Ashgate Publishing Company, 2003).
[6] Undeniably, these principles have their origin in the political history of the West, but they can be adapted in multiple cultural contexts.

two principles are continuously interpreted within specific political cultures that ultimately frame social expectations about the role of religion in public space and society. In the case of the West, these expectations are the separation of church and state and the privatization of religion, leading to its social decline. This Western experience is at the foundation of most secularization theories applied to non-Western countries.

As a case in point, Turkey, Tunisia under Ben Ali, and Iraq under Saddam Hussein have been defined as secular, as opposed to Saudi Arabia or the Islamic Republic of Iran, with the implicit assumption that the former are or were aligning themselves to the Western experience. These "secular" states have certainly attempted to diminish the role of religion in the public sphere. However, an irreversible decline of the social and political presence of Islam did not occur in any of these countries. Moreover, none of these states properly implemented separation of Islam and state or protection of religious diversity, which is the most critical factor of a secularization process. As described by Alfred Stepan, secularization entails a dual process of differentiation, in which "the minimal boundaries of freedom of action must somehow be crafted for political institutions vis-à-vis religious authorities, for religious individuals and groups vis-à-vis political institutions."[7] In other words, states would not use religions for political purposes and would grant equality to all religions, while religious groups would refrain from capturing state institutions and politics for their specific religious purposes. While such equilibrium is never completely achieved even in Western nations,[8] it can serve as a criterion to evaluate processes of secularization. Almost all Muslim countries, even the ones dubbed secular, fail on both accounts – that is, state equidistance vis-à-vis all religions and no encroachment of religion on politics. We are therefore in dire need of reconsidering or at least broadening the existing approaches to regimes of secularity in order to make sense of their particular political experience.

In this regard, an important aspect to consider is the role of the state. Ahmet T. Kuru's book *Secularism and State Policies toward Religion*[9] aims in this direction, as he points out the challenges and critiques of the secularization and modernization theories that relegate religion to a "'traditional' phenomenon, which will eventually be marginalized by the modernization

---

[7] Alfred Stepan, "Religion, Democracy and the 'Twin Tolerations,'" *Journal of Democracy* 11.4 (October 2000): 37–57, p. 37.

[8] For instance, see Jocelyne Cesari, *Why the West Fears Islam, Exploring Muslims in Liberal Democracies* (New York: Palgrave Macmillan, 2013), for the current debates on the status of Islam in Europe. For the ongoing debate in the United States on the First Amendment, see, for example, Barbara A. McGraw and Jo-Renee Formicola, *Taking Religious Pluralism Seriously: Spiritual Politics on American Sacred Ground* (Waco, TX: Baylor University Press, 2005), or Michael Corbett and Julia Corbett Mitchell, *Politics and Religion in the United States* (Abingdon: Taylor and Francis, 1999).

[9] Ahmet T. Kuru, *Secularism and State Policies toward Religion: France, Turkey and the United States* (New York: Cambridge University Press, 2009).

process."[10] Kuru specifically focuses on the ideological influence of state policies on religion. He differentiates them as "assertive secularism" (where the state plays an active role to exclude religion from the public sphere and relegate it to the private domain) or "passive secularism" (where religion is allowed to play a public role). He also presents two characteristics of secular states: "(1) their legislative and judicial processes are secular in the sense of being out of institutional religious control, and (2) they constitutionally declare neutrality toward religions; they establish neither an official religion nor atheism."[11] In contrast, "other states have established religious laws and courts as the basis of their legislative and judicial systems ('religious states'), [and/or] recognized an official religion ('states with an established religion')."[12]

The way Kuru defines secularism follows the taken-for-granted approach, which is a separation of state and religion as well as use of nonreligious norms in the legal system. In these conditions, Turkey is defined as secular, but as we will show in the subsequent chapters, the status of citizens, family life, and the definition of the nation involve a dominant religious element imposed on all members of the political community, Muslims and non-Muslims alike. In other words, protection of all religions as a major principle of secularity is not applicable to Turkey or to the majority of Muslim-majority countries. Furthermore, it can be argued that in the "secular" ones, like Tunisia and Turkey, Islam was indeed confined to private spaces, but it is not sufficient to make them secular because state actions did not translate into the neutrality and equidistance of the state vis-à-vis all religions. In this regard, it is true that France and the United States differ, as demonstrated by Ahmet Kuru, because the United States has a much friendlier approach to religion by allowing for its public visibility and by permitting God in the Pledge of Allegiance. In this way, the United States implements what Kuru calls "passive secularism." However, contrary to his approach, France and the United States still have more in common than France and Turkey. This is reflected in the different French and Turkish stances on legal protection of freedom of expression and freedom of speech. Certainly both France and Turkey have adopted very aggressive policies to remove religion from social life and public space. But Turkey, as we shall see in the following chapters, puts the dominant Islamic institutions under state control and does not grant the same status to other religions. Similarly, in both French and Turkish public education, religious symbols are banned.[13] At the same time, the French state does not allow for religious instruction in public schools,

[10] Ibid., 1.
[11] Ibid., 7.
[12] Ibid.
[13] Ibid., 9.

whereas Turkey (after 1949) not only allows but requires Muslim students to participate in Islamic education in public schools without providing the same right for other minorities (e.g., the Alevis). In other words, the paradox is that even if the Turkish state applies "assertive secularism" as a political ideology, Turkey, because of its compulsory religious education and its discriminatory treatment of religious minorities cannot be considered a secular state.

Thus, the use of Western terms or Western ideologies should not trick us into thinking that some of these countries went through a differentiation between Islam and politics similar to the one experienced in Western democracies. Actually, quite the opposite occurred. The use of Western secular techniques in law and constitutions created a strong connection between Islam and politics and contributed to the redefinition of Islam *as a political norm* in ways unknown under the Muslim empires.[14] My position, therefore, is that the making of Islam into a modern religion, whereby norms, organizations, and actors have been defined as Islamic, has been closely related to the making of the modern state.

One of my major conclusions drawn from the data analysis presented in this chapter is that modern religion in Muslim countries is positioned on the platform of the state. The institutionalization of religion occurs through the reconfiguration of relationships between people, property, and organizations that were "religious" but formerly outside the political control of the state apparatus.[15] The state actions described in the following chapters highlight efforts by the modern nation-state to make Islam both an organizational framework and an ideology of practice.[16] Modernity is thus constituted not by a one-sided, state-driven project to discipline people's thoughts but by "multiple projects or, rather a series of interlinked projects"[17] whereby state and religion reshape each other and, in the process, redefine themselves.

---

[14] In the Turkish case, Hakan Yavuz explains, "As a result of nation-building and militant secularization, society came to be divided along the now familiar cleavages of Turkish versus Kurdish and state versus society. In contrast, the caliphate, abolished in 1924, had represented an Islamicly sanctioned union of multiethnic groups and had recognized ethnic diversity without assigning it any political role. In other words, the caliphate was the symbol of a multiethnic polity and authority; it symbolized the unity of Muslims as a faith-based community and allowed space for diverse loyalties and local autonomy for the periphery." M. Hakan Yavuz, *Islamic Political Identity in Turkey* (New York and London: Oxford University Press, 2003), 52.

[15] Yoshiko Ashiwa and David L. Wank, *Making Religion, Making the State: The Politics of Religion in Modern China* (Palo Alto: Stanford University Press, 2009), 45.

[16] Ibid., 70.

[17] Ibid., 45.

Of course, this recalibration of religion by the modern state happened everywhere; in the West, its outcome was autonomy of religious institutions from political power, whereas in most Muslim countries, the trajectory has gone in the opposite direction. This counter-trajectory is a challenge for the dominant Western theories of secularization and democratization.

The difference between the Western experience and that of Muslim countries lies in the institutional arrangement of state-religion relations. In the West, secularism has translated into a legal order that preserves both the right to believe and to not believe, in essence defending their practical equality. This legal order is continuously evolving and at some moments can be difficult to maintain, as illustrated by the claims of Christian fundamentalists in the United States to take their religious convictions into account in secular law or by European tensions around Islamic dress codes in public spaces. In most Muslim countries, secularization of Islam has not led to a similar legal order. As a consequence, the "secular age" came to be embodied in ubiquitous hegemonic versions of Islam, even in countries like Turkey.

DEFINING HEGEMONIC ISLAM

In both domestic and international politics, Islam is often depicted as a tool of political opposition. At the national level, Islam is presented as an alternative ideological repertoire to the failed secular state. For example, the state-centered approach to the politicization of Islam, arising from the comparative politics discourse, demonstrates the influence of authoritarianism on the instrumentalization of Islam as a resource for political opposition.[18] The cultural duality theory and state culture theory also envision a parallel power structure of state and religion and expand upon this model by proposing that a dualist power structure occurs when an Islamist movement is formed in reaction to state ideology and policies.[19] These theories posit the existence of a rigid, stark opposition between the state and religious groups (as in Iran) or religious values (as in Egypt). Similarly, at the international level, most studies frame Islam as a resurgent ideology used almost exclusively as a tool for supranational political opposition. The concept of post-Islamism, promoted by Olivier Roy[20] and Asef Bayat,[21] is another version

[18] Seyyed Vali Nasr, *Islamic Leviathan: Islam and the Making of State Power* (New York: Oxford University Press, 2001), 3.

[19] Mansoor Moaddel, *Jordanian Exceptionalism: A Comparative Analysis of State-religion Relationships in Egypt, Iran, Jordan, and Syria* (Houndmills, Basingstoke, Hampshire: Palgrave, 2002), 373–4.

[20] See "Post-Islamic Revolution," *The European Institute*, 2011, accessed January 21, 2013, http://www.europeaninstitute.org/February-2011/qpost-islamic-revolutionq-events-in-egypt-analyzed-by-french-expert-on-political-islam.html.

[21] See "The Coming of a Post-Islamist Society," *Critique: Critical Middle East Studies*, 1996, accessed January 21, 2013, https://openaccess.leidenuniv.nl/bitstream/handle/1887/9768/12_606_020.pdf?sequence=1.

of the binary approach. The term qualifies political movements based on Islam that do not make the Islamic state their ultimate political goal.[22] While these approaches explain *how* Islam is efficiently constructed as an ideological tool for political opposition, they rarely explain *why*.

Most strikingly, the 2011 Arab Spring revolts are not decipherable within the polarized framework described earlier, as the Islamist parties were nearly absent in the initial phases of the protests. At the same time, Islam is likely to remain consequential in Arab countries' future political evolution. This is evidenced *inter alia* by the Islamists' electoral victories in the transitional phases in Egypt and Tunisia. On October 23, 2011, the Islamist party Ennahda won the majority of seats in Tunisia by a significant margin of nearly 40 percent. The Muslim Brotherhood's Freedom and Justice Party (FJP) also won Egypt's three stages of parliamentary elections, earning 38 percent of the votes in the final round in January 2012, and in June 2012, Mohamed Morsi, the FJP candidate, won the first free presidential elections. Even the end of the Morsi regime on July 3, 2013, does not mean the end of political Islam, as discussed in this book.

In light of the Arab Spring, this book addresses the role of state policies as an unexamined dimension of the politicization of Islam. It adopts an institutional approach to introduce state actions into the analysis of political influence of religious changes at both the domestic and international levels. Institutionalization refers to the way new sociopolitical situations are translated into the creation or adaptation of formal institutions such as constitutions, laws, administrative bodies, and agencies. The adoption of the nation-state model by Muslim majority countries after the collapse of the Ottoman Empire has been the decisive political change that led to the reshaping of values and institutions. These changes have translated into the hegemonic status of Islam.

First, it is important to note the difference between a dominant religion, an established religion, and a hegemonic religion. A religion is dominant when it is the religion of the majority of a given country. In such cases, the dominant religion continues to impart historical and cultural references considered "natural" and "legitimate." Religious symbols and rituals become embedded in the public culture of the country. Examples of such dominant religions include Protestantism in the United States or Catholicism in France and Poland. An established religion is a church recognized by law as the religion of the country or the state and sometimes financially supported by the state, as with the Church of Denmark. Usually, the existence of an established church is not incompatible with the legal protection of religious minorities and freedom of speech. A religion becomes hegemonic, however, when the state grants a certain religious group exclusive legal, economic, or

---

[22] Olivier Roy, *Globalized Islam: The Search for a New Ummah* (New York: Columbia University Press, 2004), 5. Asef Bayat, *Making Islam Democratic: Social Movements and the Post-Islamist Turn* (Palo Alto: Stanford University Press, 2007), 10.

political rights denied to other religions. In other words, religious hegemony refers to legal and political privileges granted to a specific religious group, which in most but not all cases is the dominant religion.

Second, hegemonic religion and state regulation of religion are not the same. The latter may assume several forms, with legal neutrality on one end of the spectrum, legal privilege on the other end, and many nuances between the two. Legal neutrality, as understood and codified in most secular democracies, entails recognition and legal protection of all religions. Separation of religion and state is not a necessary prerequisite for legal neutrality, which can be implemented even when there is state cooperation with religions (e.g., most European democracies). It is worth noting that legal neutrality does not mean the practice of law is always neutral. Frequently, the dominant religious group serves as an implicit standard for the legal work concerning other religious groups.[23] Most importantly, legal neutrality has been continuously challenged throughout history by discriminatory political practices. One of the most recent examples is the increase of restrictions on Muslim minorities in Western European democracies.[24]

Preexisting research has measured state involvement in religion[25] by using the following criteria:

a) The constitution of the country officially recognizes one religion.
b) The state finances places of worship and clerics.
c) The legal system includes some provisions of religious law.
d) State schools teach religious doctrines.

There are several issues with such a list. First, it does not account for the political ponderation of each feature. For example, inscription of religion in the constitution can be merely symbolic, as in the United Kingdom, or the existence of blasphemy law can be obsolete, as in Denmark. Second, each of these features can be implemented in various ways, some granting equality to all religions and others being discriminatory. For example, does the state provide funding for all religions, as in Belgium, or to one religion only, as in Greece? Are all religions taught in public schools or is only one taught? The responses to these questions allow us to identify different degrees of involvement, from legal neutrality on one end of the spectrum to legal privileges on the other end. In these conditions,

[23] Lori G. Beaman, "The Myth of Pluralism, Diversity, and Vigor: The Constitutional Privilege of Protestantism in the United States and Canada," *Journal for the Scientific Study of Religion* 42.3 (2003): 311–25.

[24] Jonathan Fox and Yasemin Akbaba, "Securitization of Islam and Religious Discrimination: Religious Minorities in Western Democracies, 1990 to 2008," *Comparative European Politics*, May 13, 2013, doi: 10.1057/cep.2013.8.

[25] Jonathan Fox and Shmuel Sandler, "Separation of Religion and State in the Twenty-First Century: Comparing the Middle East and Western Democracies," *Comparative Politics* 37.3 (2005): 317–35. Brian J. Grim and Roger Finke, *The Price of Freedom Denied: Religious Persecution and Conflict in the 21st Century* (New York: Cambridge University Press, 2011). Mark Chaves, Peter J. Schraeder, and Mario Sprindys, "State Regulation of Religion and Muslim Religious Vitality in the Industrialized West," *The Journal of Politics* 56.4 (1994): 1087.

legal privilege occurs not only when one religion is implicitly or explicitly defined as the religion of the state or the nation but also when it is granted financial resources and/or legal rights denied to all other religious groups.

The unexpected and often unseen consequences of legal privilege are state restrictions and controls over the activities of the official religion, usually involving the following:

- A ministry of religious affairs and ad hoc administration to manage the official religion
- Government regulation of the use of religious symbols or activities
- Limitations by state laws and policies on freedom of expression (apostasy law)
- Penalties for the defamation of the official religion (blasphemy law)
- Government interference with worship

The other side of legal privileges is the tacit or explicit discrimination toward religious groups not recognized as the official religion. For example:

- Minority groups do not receive government funds or resources for education, religious programs, or maintenance of property or organizations.
- Domestic or foreign religious groups are forbidden to proselytize.
- Conversion from the official religious group to another is severely restricted if not fully forbidden.
- The government is hostile toward religious minorities or may adhere to a policy of nonintervention in the case of harassment or persecution of these groups.[26]

To sum up, the hegemonic status of a religion is a combination of two or more of the following characteristics:

1. Nationalization of institutions, clerics, and places of worship of one religion
2. Insertion of the doctrine of that religion in the public school curriculum (beyond the religious instruction, i.e., in history, civic education, etc.)
3a. Legal discrimination of other religions in education, public funding, public expression, and so forth
3b. Legal restrictions of freedom of speech and expression as well as restrictions of women's rights (marriage/divorce/abortion) based on the prescriptions of that religion

As shown in Table 1.1 out of the forty-one Muslim-majority countries, twenty-three scored the maximum of three on a three-point scale measuring hegemonic Islam according to the three rubrics outlined previously.

These characteristics are not specific to Muslim countries and can be found, for example, in Sri Lanka where Buddhism is granted a hegemonic status;

---

[26] Grim and Finke, *The Price of Freedom Denied*, 208–209.

The Making of Islam

TABLE 1.1. *Scores of Hegemonic Islam*

	Nationalization	Law	Education
SCORE OF 3	✓	✓	✓
Egypt			
Saudi Arabia			
Pakistan			
Algeria			
Morocco			
Malaysia			
Bangladesh			
Jordan			
Kuwait			
Somalia			
Qatar			
UAE			
Sudan			
Yemen			
Iran			
Afghanistan			
Libya (under Qadaffi)			
Bahrain			
Comoros			
Brunei			
Mauritania			
Tunisia			
Iraq			
SCORE OF 2	✓	–	✓
Syria			
Oman			
Turkey			
Uzbekistan			
SCORE OF 1	–	–	✓
Tajikistan			
Nigeria			
Mali			
Niger			
Chad			
Kyrgyzstan			
Turkmenistan			
Indonesia	–	✓	–
SCORE OF 0	–	–	–
Albania			
Kosovo			
Guinea			
Kazakhstan			
Azerbaijan			
Burkina Faso			
Sierra Leone			

Note: This table groups countries in an unusual way (Saudi Arabia/Egypt for example) because it scores only institutional arrangements as they stand today. It does not reflect or contextualize the political and social forces at work in each country that are obviously very different and diverse.

Another caveat is that some countries are not present in the chart. For example, Lebanon provides an example of confessionalism, which proportionally allocates political power and represents the demographic distribution of the recognized religions. Gambia, and Senegal recognize all religions and legally provide education and resources for all religious institutions. As a result, these countries do not fit into the brackets provided here. I decided to add Indonesia even though, like Senegal, it recognizes all religions. However, because of the absence of civil marriage and the tensions between religious groups around family issues and conversion, I chose to give a score of one to Indonesia.

this status also applies to the Orthodox Church in Greece.[27] Nevertheless, legal privileges characterize the majority of Muslim countries, where legal and political rights have generally been granted to the dominant orientation of Islam but not to other religious groups, Islamic or otherwise.[28] More infrequently, privilege is accorded to a religious minority, such as the Sunni in Bahrain or in Iraq (before 2003). Indonesia, Senegal, and Lebanon are the only exceptions in the Muslim world in their attempts to create regimes of legal neutrality (although discriminatory practices do exist). Interestingly, they are also the only countries that qualify as democratic, according to the Freedom House index. For that reason, while democracy can accommodate some forms of state involvement in religion, the hegemonic status granted to one religion can be an issue for democratic, life or for the transition to democracy, as we shall discuss in Part III.

The next section analyzes the correlation between institutionalization and politicization of Islam.

INSTITUTIONALIZATION OF ISLAM AND ITS CORRELATION TO POLITICIZATION

An institutional approach to religion has the advantage of highlighting the correlation between state actions and the creation of political forms of Islam. Political Islam in this context is broader than Islamism and means nationalization of Islamic institutions and personnel; usage of Islamic references in political competition by state actors and opponents (Islamism); religiously motivated social unrest or violence; and internationalization of Islam-orientated political movements or conflicts.

By shedding light on state actions, this book avoids the current dilemma of international relations theories, which frame religion as either the independent or the dependent variable.

The clash of civilizations has been the most discussed theory in which cultures in general and Islam in particular are apprehended as the independent variable. Samuel Huntington states that social conflicts are the result of clashes across civilizations and religions. However, as abundantly proven by social sciences,[29] civilizations are not homogenous, monolithic players in world politics with an inclination to "clash"; rather, they consist of pluralistic, divergent, and convergent actors and practices that are constantly

---

[27] Stanley Jeyaraja Tambiah, *Buddhism Betrayed?: Religion, Politics, and Violence in Sri Lanka* (A Monograph of the World Institute for Development Economics Research) (Chicago, IL: University of Chicago Press, 1992).

[28] Our approach is consistent with the data produced by Jonathan Fox in "World Separation of Religion and State Into the 21st Century," *Comparative Political Studies* 39.5 (2006): 537–69, and Jonathan Fox and Shmuel Sandler, *Religion in World Conflict* (London: Routledge, 2006), on government involvement in religion, where Muslim-majority countries score the highest.

[29] Grim and Finke, *The Price of Freedom Denied.*

evolving.[30] Thus, the clash of civilizations view fails to address not only conflict between civilizations but also conflict and differences within civilizations. In particular, evidence does not substantiate Huntington's stance that countries with similar cultures are coming together, while countries with different cultures are coming apart. In fact, as the data presented in this book demonstrate, religious homogeneity increases conflicts and the probability of politicization of religion. In the same vein, according to the Pew data, 33 percent of countries dominated by one religion have a high level of religious-based violence, compared to 20 percent of countries where no religion dominates.[31]

The institutionalized approach to religion also differs from explanations of social or political behaviors based on religious traditions. Terrorist or security studies that assume the origin of political violence in some decontextualized cultural or religious specificities fall into this trap. More specifically, the large body of literature on jihad, al-Qaʿida, and terrorism, usually, with a few exceptions,[32] considers religion a cause, if not the primary cause, of terrorist activities worldwide. The same essentialist approach characterizes research that focuses on the ideological content of political Islamic movements without systematically linking it to specific social and political contexts. This is a tendency noted throughout the whole approach to religion, particularly Islam, in the international relations discipline.[33] To a certain extent, the same critique can be made for some constructivist work when it is limited to the discursive approach, which views cultures as rhetorical practices and narratives.[34] That is why, as argued in the next section, our approach will broaden some of the fundamental tenets of constructivism by including institutions and legal practices.

An institutional approach to Islam further differs from the dominant body of research that analyzes political Islam as the dependent variable. This literature is dominated by the social movement theory, which rightly points out that ideology is only one aspect of political mobilization.[35] More distinctly, politicization of Islam is attributed to the combination of a strong

---

[30] Peter J. Katzenstein, *Civilizations in World Politics: Plural and Pluralist Perspectives* (London: Routledge, 2010).

[31] Grim and Finke, *The Price of Freedom Denied*, 67.

[32] Robert Anthony Pape, *Dying to Win: The Strategic Logic of Suicide Terrorism* (New York: Random House, 2005).

[33] Frédéric Volpi, *Political Islam Observed: Disciplinary Perspectives* (New York: Columbia University Press, 2010).

[34] Katzenstein, *Civilizations in World Politics*.

[35] Doug McAdam and David A. Snow, *Readings on Social Movements: Origins, Dynamics and Outcomes* (New York: Oxford University Press, 2010). Sidney G. Tarrow, *Power in Movement: Social Movements and Contentious Politics* (Cambridge: Cambridge University Press, 1998).

ideology[36] with some "opportunity structures." The most significant structures are the political failure of secular national projects,[37] the deepening of economic crises, and the demographic bulge.[38] This literature is relevant for understanding the multiple mechanisms of politicization, but it does not explain why Islamism prevails over other forms of political mobilization.

As already mentioned, most of these approaches operate on the implicit dichotomy between a secular state and political groups that use Islam as an oppositional tool at both the national and international levels. An institutional approach shifts the perspective from a polarized state-religion focus to complex sets of interactions between the two entities, such as adaptation, cooperation, and competition. It considers state-Islam relations, particularly the construction of Islam as the hegemonic religion, as a condition for its politicization. In other words, Islam is not antidemocratic per se, but certain forms of state-religion interaction are, such as regulating, restricting, or privileging religious activities.

 In the scholarly literature, existence of Islamic-based political parties and/or religious-based political violence is usually considered a strong indicator of political Islam. These two indicators are not automatically linked. In some situations, there are Islamic-based political parties without political violence, or vice versa, and sometimes both Islamic political parties and political violence exist. My analysis of political Islam throughout this book does not rely on these two indicators for several reasons. First, as already mentioned, these indicators provide a limited approach to political Islam by reducing it to political opposition. For example, in almost all Muslim countries, between one and ten Islamic-based political parties exist. This does not include countries that ban all political parties, including Saudi Arabia and Qatar, or that severely restrict them, such as Syria and Uzbekistan – both situations leading to a limited influence of this particular factor. In the seventeen countries with Islamic parties, the influence of these organizations varies by state, ranging from Iran, where only Islamic parties that do not oppose the Islamic Republic can participate in elections, to Malaysia, where the Islamic parties are small opposition parties with

[36] Quintan Wiktorowicz, "Anatomy of the Salafi Movement," *Studies in Conflict and Terrorism* 29.3 (2006): 207–39. Ian Shapiro, Rogers M. Smith, and Tarek E. Masoud, *Problems and Methods in the Study of Politics* (Cambridge: Cambridge University Press, 2004). Amaney A. Jamal, *Barriers to Democracy: The Other Side of Social Capital in Palestine and the Arab World* (Princeton, NJ: Princeton University Press, 2007).

[37] Gilles Kepel, *Jihad: The Trail of Political Islam* (London: I. B. Tauris, 2004). Kai Hafez, *Radicalism and Political Reform in the Islamic and Western Worlds* (Cambridge: Cambridge University Press, 2010).

[38] Sami Zubaida, *Islam, the People and the State: Political Ideas and Movements in the Middle East, Third Edition* (London: I. B. Tauris, 2009). Bruce B. Lawrence, *Defenders of God: The Fundamentalist Revolt against the Modern Age* (San Francisco. CA: Harper & Row, 1989).

minimal support. Usually, in the case of authoritarian regimes, Islamic parties tend to dominate the political scene, as in Egypt or Turkey. However,
when political systems are more open, the preeminence of Islamic political
parties tend to decline, as we shall discuss in Parts II and III. In the case
of the former Soviet countries, which do not score at all on the three factors of hegemonic Islam, one can argue there are Islamic parties. However,
unlike the countries with a score of three, they do not dominate political
life. Another serious limit of the political parties indicator is that the main
influence of political Islam is not reflected solely in political parties but in
the strength of Islam in society and social movements that develop social,
professional, and cultural networks, granting Islam legitimacy outside the
narrow scope of professional politics.[39] It is similar to the role played by the
Catholic Church in Poland[40] or the Orthodox Church in Greece,[41] where
in both countries, there are no religious parties but religion nevertheless
influences social and political matters. In all Muslim majority countries,
these Islamic social movements exist either officially or unofficially and are
particularly strong in countries with scores ranging from three to two.

The methodological challenge is even greater when it comes to religious-
based political violence. In order to prove this particular point, I attempted
to correlate the political violence of Muslim countries with their respective
level of institutionalization of Islam or hegemonic score. For this purpose,
Figure 1.1 was built to illustrate religious-based political violence conducted
by state and nonstate actors in each Muslim-majority country between
2006 and 2011.[42] Incidents include terrorist attacks, state-led (e.g., military, police) assaults against minority religious groups, and incarceration or
police abuse based on religious beliefs. Sixty-three percent of the countries
with a high level of institutionalized Islam (score three to two) experienced
more than 200 incidents. The obvious problem with such statistics is that
they flatten out the social importance of different acts of discrimination. For
example, one sectarian riot in one country can lead to several hundred killings but will count as only one incident. On the opposite side, several incidents of police or legal abuses of religion can be listed in another country,

[39] Richard P. Mitchell, *The Society of the Muslim Brotherhood* (London: Oxford University
Press, 1993); Laura Deeb and Mona Harb, "Politics, Culture, Religion: How Hizbullah Is
Constructing an Islamic Milieu in Lebanon," *Review of Middle East Studies* 43.2 (2010):
198–206.
[40] Tim Bale and Aleks Szczerbiak, "Why Is There No Christian Democracy in Poland – and Why
Should We Care?" *Party Politics*, May 30, 2008, http://ppq.sagepub.com/content/14/4/479.
[41] Constantine P. Danopoulos, "Religion, Civil Society, and Democracy in Orthodox Greece,"
Journal of Southern Europe and the Balkans 6.1 (April 2004): 41–55.
[42] U.S. State Department International Religious Freedom Reports; National Consortium for
the Study of Terrorism and Responses to Terrorism Global Terrorism Database; Human
Rights Watch World Reports.

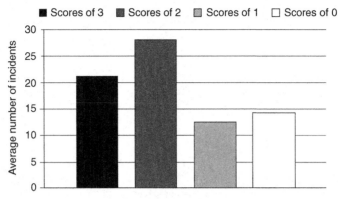

FIGURE 1.1. Hegemonic Islam and political violence.

thereby increasing its total on the index. However, because our main goal was to identify frequency or pattern of discrimination *between* countries, we counted state or institution abuses *and* incidents by citizens that were not punished by law. In this regard, the significant variation is between countries with scores of two to three on the institutionalization scale of Islam and the rest of the fifteen countries with scores of one to zero. The latter do not experience the same level of religiously motivated political violence. It is important to note that the countries with a score of zero are primarily former communist countries that have maintained a high level of repression on all religions, including Islam, which explains their higher level of incidents than score one countries (Figure 1.1).

As a final objection to these two indicators of politicization of Islam – existence of political parties based on Islam and religiously motivated political violence – it is worth emphasizing their extreme volatility under the influence of social and political events like external intervention, civil war, ethnic conflicts, or economic crises.

In sum, this exercise shows that it would be misleading to limit the political role of Islam to either Islamic parties or political violence. At a deeper level, citizens of Muslim-majority countries share the idea that national and Islamic identity are two sides of the same coin even if they do not favor Islamic parties or engage in sectarian violence. This deep conviction translates into the opinion that Islam should play a role in public life, which is systematically expressed in recurrent pollings across Muslim-majority countries. At the same time, the respondents favor democracy and do not see any incompatibility between democracy and Islam (Table 1.2).[43]

---

[43] Source details for table 1.2 are available at http://www.pewglobal.org/files/2012/05/Pew-Global-Attitudes-2012-Egypt-Report-Topline.pdf p. 27, accessed June 6, 2013; http://www.pewglobal.org/files/2012/07/Pew-Global-Attitudes-Project-Arab-Spring-TOPLINE-Tuesday-July-10-2012.pdf p.56, accessed June 6, 2013.

The Making of Islam

TABLE 1.2. *Muslims' Opinions on Democracy and Islam*

			2010	2012
Islam plays a **large** role in political life	Egypt	This is **good**	95%	61%
		This is **bad**	2%	30%
	Turkey	This is **good**	44%	57%
		This is **bad**	49%	33%
	Tunisia	This is **good**		82%
		This is **bad**		11%
	Indonesia	This is **good**	91%	
		This is **bad**	7%	
Islam plays a **small** role in political life	Egypt	This is **good**	3%	14%
		This is **bad**	27%	69%
	Turkey	This is **good**	26%	35%
		This is **bad**	33%	39%
	Tunisia	This is **good**		27%
		This is **bad**		56%
	Indonesia	This is **good**	25%	
		This is **bad**	69%	

		2013
Islamic law (Shariʿa) should be the official law in your country	Egypt	74%
	Turkey	12%
	Tunisia	56%
	Indonesia	72%

		2010	2011	2012
Democracy is preferable to any other form of government	Egypt	60%	71%	67%
	Turkey	76%	66%	71%
	Tunisia			63%
	Indonesia	64%	58%	

Source: Pew 2010, 2012, taken from a Polling the Nations Search (role of Islam). Pew 2013, Shariʿa.

The foundational role of Islam in almost all Muslim states can explain that apparent contradiction. Consequently, the next chapters analyze how the hegemonic status of Islam is at the core of nation building and how Islam's politicization is a component of nationalization. For this reason, we focus on countries defined as secular according to Western standards, meaning countries generally perceived to have a secular ruling elite educated or otherwise openly influenced by the West, such as Egypt before and after the January 25 revolution, Iraq under Saddam Hussein, Turkey, Tunisia, and Pakistan.

2

Nation-State Building and the Inclusion of Muslim Polities within the Westphalian Order

This book combines institutional and norm diffusion approaches to analyze the political modernization that occurred after the collapse of the Ottoman Empire, during the colonial period, and in the nation-building phase. The institutional approach focuses on the gradual social and cultural changes that can either generate novel institutions over long periods of time or produce unexpected breakdowns in existing institutions at critical thresholds. The norm diffusion perspective sheds light on the influence of international factors in the shaping of institutions.

In ways similar to constructivist analysis, our inquiry questions the premise of anarchy and equality of state actors as the given in international relations. In this vein, several studies have shown that far from being anarchic, international politics is continuously redefined by relations of power that shape institutions and rules. For example, Shmuel Eisenstadt, as well as Dominic Sachsenmaier, Jens Riedel, Nissim Otmazgin, and Eyal Ben-Ari, have demonstrated how the European society of states provided the standard for international politics and measures of civilization.[1] Additionally, Vali Nasr and Bobby Said[2] have shown that the adoption of the nation-state concept in Muslim-majority countries was the consequence not only of war or colonial power but also of the inclusion of Muslim polities in the international system. The major thesis of this book is that politicization of Islam has been a major outcome of this inclusion, an idea that has not yet been fully explored.

[1] Shmuel Eisenstadt, *The Great Revolutions and the Civilizations of Modernity* (Boston, MA: Brill, 2006). Dominic Sachsenmaier, Jens Riedel, and Shmuel Eisenstadt, *Reflections on Multiple Modernities: European, Chinese, and Other Interpretations* (Leiden: Koninklijke Brill, 2001); Nissim Otmazgin and Eyal Ben-Ari, *Popular Culture and the State in East and Southeast Asia* (New York: Routledge, 2012).

[2] See Bobby S. Said, *A Fundamental Fear: Eurocentrism and the Emergence of Islamism*, second edition (New York: Palgrave, 2003). Nasr, Seyyed Vali Reza, *Islamic Leviathan: Islam and the Making of State Power* (New York, Oxford University Press, 2001).

At the core of Islam's politicization lie the structural changes unleashed by the transition from premodern empire to modern nation-state. This transition led to the rise of authoritarian "Promethean" regimes where state actors imposed very invasive social and cultural transformations upon their societies. This chapter focuses on the mechanisms of diffusion of the nation-state in Muslim countries, followed by an analysis in Chapter 3 of its embodiments in institutions and political practices.

In the past, norm diffusion has been researched in two major ways. A first wave of literature on norm diffusion, from the 1980s through the late 1990s, primarily addressed the conversion of old norms to new ones, such as the conversion of human rights principles into international norms.[3] A second wave of scholarship (starting in the late 1990s) emphasizes local actors and their agency, thus capturing the resistance that often occurs with the introduction of new norms into a given society or culture. This book follows the second wave of literature on diffusion by adopting an insider perspective, which entails examining the role of domestic political structures and agents in normative changes. In this regard, the localization framework presented by Amitav Acharya is particularly relevant to show how politicization of Islam was the outcome of the continuous integration of Muslim polities into the international system after the downfall of the Ottoman Empire.

Acharya highlights four stages of diffusion: prelocalization, localization, adaptation, and amplification. *Prelocalization* refers to the initial response to extrinsic norms, usually a response of resistance. *Localization* encompasses the active reframing and reconstruction of foreign ideas by local actors, including (but not limited to) state actors. *Adaptation* (through grafting novel ideas and pruning established ones) refers to the creation of institutions and norms through syncretization of external influence and local practices. Finally, *amplification* occurs when new instruments and practices are developed from these syncretized new norms. As adaptation is often difficult to separate from localization, this book combines the two into a single term – *localization*. Islam was incorporated into the nation-building enterprise and constructed as a political hegemon through this dual process of local framing and adaptation.[4] The amplification stage will be addressed in Part II of this book by analyzing the rise and influence of

[3] See Ethan A. Nadelmann, "Global Prohibition Regimes: The Evolution of Norms in International Society," *International Organization* 44 (1990): 483. Thomas Risse, Stephen C. Ropp, and Kathryn Sikkink (eds.), *The Power of Human Rights: International Norms and Domestic Change* (New York: Cambridge University Press, 1999). Kathryn Sikkink and Margaret Keck, *Activists beyond Borders: Advocacy Networks in International Politics* (Ithaca, NY: Cornell University Press, 1998).

[4] Amitav Acharya, "How Ideas Spread: Whose Norms Matter? Norm Localization and Institutional Change in Asian Regionalism," *International Organization* 58 (2004): 248.

Islamist movements as outcomes of new political norms brought by the nation-state.

PAN-ISLAMISM AND PAN-ARABISM AS RESISTANCE TO IMPOSITION OF WESTERN NORMS

In Muslim countries, the prelocalization stage occurred prior to the formation of states during the Ottoman Empire's reign and amidst the rise of Western imperialism. The symbolic moment of the prelocalization was the inclusion of the Ottoman Empire within the Westphalian order under the Treaty of Paris in 1856. The treaty itself ended the Crimean War and was the first time the Ottoman Empire participated as a political actor in the international order. Hence, it opened the possibility for non-European polities to be part of the international community and to form alliances with the West.[5] In the aftermath of this symbolic inclusion, three disparate factors led to the diffusion of the Westphalian state system in the Middle East: the decline and collapse of the Ottoman Empire; the rise of local nationalist movements in urban centers such as Cairo, Tunis, Baghdad, and Damascus; and the emergence of Western colonies with demarcated territorial boundaries that pursued their own interests and experienced territorial disputes with each other. It is in this environment that pan-Islamism and pan-Arabism emerged as major resistance movements.[6] They were both reactions to the rise of Western liberalization rhetoric and imperialist threats in the Ottoman Empire. Pan-Islamism was an intellectual and political movement that viewed the universal Islamic community (*umma*) as the ideal basis and source for modern political unity, in which the life and works of the Prophet Muhammad and his first four "well guided" (*Rāshidūn*) successors, or caliphs, served as a model. Toward the end of the Ottoman Empire, the Western threat became more acute, with European incursions into Egypt and Tunisia in 1798 and 1881, respectively. These imperialist exploits greatly impacted nineteenth-century reformers, such as Jamal al-Din al-Afghani (1838–97) and his disciple, Mohammad Abduh (1849–1905), who, in their journal *al-Urwa al-Wuthqa* (The Firmest Bond), urged all Muslims to bond under *al-Wahda al-Islamiyya* (Muslim unity) in the face of Western imperialism.[7] The popularity of the Ottoman caliphate also increased, and the caliph was recognized as the head of the Muslim state on a diplomatic par with

---

[5] Michelle Burgis, "Faith in the State? Traditions of Territoriality and the Emergence of Modern Arab Statehood," *Journal of the History of International Law* 11 (2009): 40.
[6] Cemil Aydin, *The Politics of Anti-Westernism in Asia: Visions of World Order in Pan-Islamic and Pan-Asian Thought* (New York: Columbia University Press, 2007), 32.
[7] Ibid., 61.

Western rulers.[8] Accordingly, pan-Islamism refashioned the concept of the caliph, emphasizing his status as the Prophet Muhammad's vice-regent in order to buttress the empire's legitimacy in the international state system.

Thus, in direct resistance to the international norm of the nation-state, pan-Islamism attempted to redefine the political community in Ottoman lands by giving precedence to the transnational dimension of the Islamic solidarity, thereby turning it into an ideological tool.[9] For example, at the onset of World War I, the Ottoman Empire increased efforts by initiating propaganda that utilized pan-Islamic ideas and fomented Muslim disobedience against the Western colonizers.[10] It is important to note, however, that, even after World War I, pan-Islamism was not an ideology of indiscriminate hatred or rejection of the West. The reformulation of pan-Islamism as a categorically anti-Western ideology happened after World War II and formed the basis for the antimodernist and reactionary positions of contemporary radical groups like al-Qaʿida. With the creation of nation-states after World War II, the political goal of a unitary Islamic community was defeated and progressively replaced by the aspiration of implementing Islamic policies within each nation-state.[11] At the same time, political leaders, intellectuals, and ideologues continued to appeal to Islamic transnational solidarity to recreate the umma.

Emerging at the same time as pan-Islamism, pan-Arabism reached its height in the 1960s and centered on the idea that all Arab peoples, as a linguistic and cultural community, should unite under one banner. It originated in the *al-Nahḍa* (renaissance) movement that took place during the late nineteenth and early twentieth centuries with the revival of Arabic poetry and literature and the rise of print media.[12] This cultural awakening, as a rejection of Western cultural norms, was partially a response to the Western influence described earlier. Politically, pan-Arabism was first endorsed by *Sharīf* Hussein bin ʿAli (1908–17), the *sharīf* of Mecca, who sought independence from the Ottoman Empire. In espousing an Arabist political vision, he inspired the Arab Revolts of 1916. As the ideology of Arab nationalism gained popularity across the Middle East and the British allied with the Arabs, the Ottoman Empire began to slowly crumble.[13] When pan-Arabism inevitably competed with pan-Islamist ideals, political projects separated

---

[8] Ibid., 33.

[9] Ibid., 60.

[10] Ibid., 109–10.

[11] Jacob M. Landau, *The Politics of Pan-Islam: Ideology and Organization* (Oxford: Clarendon Press, 1990), 249.

[12] Rashid Khalidi, *The Origins of Arab Nationalism* (New York: Columbia University Press, 1991).

[13] Mary C. Wilson, "The Hashemites, the Arab Revolt, and Arab Nationalism," in Rashid Khalidi (ed.), *The Origins of Arab Nationalism* (New York: Columbia University Press, 1991), 204–31.

into those based on the umma and those based on cultural and territorial nationalism.[14]

As Acharya's localization framework suggests, local actors in Muslim-majority countries resisted external (Western) norms because of fears that these new norms could undermine existing beliefs and practices. As a result, both the pan-Islamic and pan-Arab movements shaped resistance to foreign domination in all Muslim-majority countries after the collapse of the Ottoman Empire. Hence, all forms of resistance against the West framed and depicted European modernization, along with its nation-building and secularization components, through a local lens and relied on an Islamic or Arab terminology.

A brief review of the resistance movements in Egypt, Iraq, Pakistan, Turkey, and Tunisia illustrates this point. Egypt became the core location of the *Salafiyya* intellectual and political movement, the goal of which was to revive the Islamic ethos in order to counter Western imperialism. Mohammad Abduh, a disciple of Jamal al-Afghani, reinterpreted the basic principles of Islam in light of modern reason.[15] While arguing that Islamic principles were consistent with modern Western rules of logic, Abduh simultaneously promoted an intellectual and cultural program, rather than a physical war, to fight Western imperialism. In 1905, one of Abduh's followers, Shaykh Rashid Rida (1865–1935), founder of the journal *al-Manar* (The Lighthouse), continued Abduh's legacy but added a more activist element.[16] Reflecting on the golden age of Islam when the caliphate was the sole spiritual and political authority for the entire Islamic community[17] and acknowledging that resurrecting such a caliphate would be impossible given contemporary realities, Rida called instead for the unity of all Muslims under the leadership of a renewed caliph.

These ideas strongly influenced the activism of Hassan al-Banna (1906–49), founder of the Muslim Brotherhood. From its inception in 1928, the Brotherhood's objective was to provide an Islamic alternative to the influence of Western culture and politics. Al-Banna borrowed from Abduh and Rida the idea that Islam could be a tool of intellectual resistance to Western culture and imperialism.[18] At the time of its creation, the Brotherhood's objectives competed with more secular nationalist agendas. This was especially true when, as a sign of King Farouk's (1936–52) pan-Islamist ideals,

---

[14] John Willis, "Debating the Caliphate: Islam and Nation in the Work of Rashid Rida and Abul Kalam Azad," *The International History Review* 32 (2010): 711.

[15] Christina Phelps Harris, *Nationalism and Revolution in Egypt* (Stanford, CA: Houton & Co., 1964), 116.

[16] Ibid., 130.

[17] Dale Eickelman and James Piscatori, *Muslim Politics* (Princeton, NJ: Princeton University Press, 1996), 31.

[18] See Chapter 8 for the development of the Muslim Brotherhood in the Egyptian context.

an alliance between the Egyptian monarchy and the Muslim Brotherhood took place in the 1940s to counter the nationalist and secular Wafd party.[19]

However, the Muslim Brotherhood went through several phases of conflict with leaders of the nation-state over the course of the following decades. During and after World War II, it created a private military apparatus to support the Arab revolts against the British colonial presence and also allied with Germany, which led King Farouk to accuse the Brotherhood of disloyalty. The conflicts with the state increasingly intensified under Gamal Abdel Nasser (1956–70) and his successors, as we shall discuss in Part II.[20]

In Syria and Iraq, the creation of the Ba'th Party in 1956 was the direct outcome of the political influence of pan-Arabism. At this time, this was the "creed of all political activists" in the region, and the founders of the Ba'th Party, Michel Aflaq (1910–89) and Salah Bitar (1912–80), came to embody this broad-based, territorial, nationalist movement and reiterated the threat of cultural and political Westernization to the pan-Arab ideal. This political project led to tentative unifications such as the United Arab Republic (1958–61) between Egypt and Syria. The positions of the early Ba'athist leaders regarding Islam were ambiguous. On one hand, Aflaq was a secular Christian, but on the other hand, he considered Islam an integral component of the Arab nation.[21] As Aflaq envisioned it, Arabism was an ideology "whose spirit is Islam."[22] Despite this inclusion of Islam in pan-Arabist ideals, however, the party's political and governing structures were secular. Similarly, in Iraq, the Ba'th Party gained power because of the widespread belief in pan-Arab nationalism, in addition to popular resistance to foreign influences on the government and the strong desire to get rid of the oppressive ruling elite.[23] Such circumstances eventually led to the rise of Saddam Hussein in 1979 as the head of state and to the construction of Iraq as a unified Arab nation (see Chapter 3). As biographer Felicia Okeke-Ibezim explains, "Saddam [saw] himself as a proud Arab nationalist ... the defender of Holy Islam ... [and] a valiant knight leading the Arabs into a battle against the infidel."[24] Thus, Saddam implemented policies that emphasized Arab unity, such as his Arab National Charter in 1980, to increase cooperation toward

[19] Richard Mitchell, *The Society of the Muslim Brotherhood* (New York: Oxford University Press, 1993), 16.

[20] See Part II for the relationship between the Muslim Brotherhood and Nasser, Sadat, and Mubarak.

[21] Liam Anderson and Gareth Stansfield, *The Future of Iraq?: Dictatorship, Democracy, or Division* (New York: Palgrave Macmillan, 2004), 66.

[22] Ibid., 66.

[23] John F. Devlin, "The Baath Party: Rise and Metamorphosis," *The American Historical Review* 96 (1991): 1404.

[24] Felicia Okeke-Ibezim, *Saddam Hussein: The Legendary Dictator* (New York: Ekwike, 2006), 9.

common goals in the Arab world. Further, with the change of governance in nearby Iran in 1979 and the subsequent Iran-Iraq War (1980–8), the Ba'th Party faced competition from the pan-Islamist agenda of the Iranian Islamic Republic. As a result, Saddam increasingly emphasized the specificities of an Arab Iraq distinct from its neighboring Islamic republic in Iran.

In contrast, the creation of Pakistan was based on the idea of a political refuge for Muslims, but pan-Islamism was not the main source of inspiration for the partitioning of the Indian subcontinent. Nevertheless, prior to the movement for independence from British-ruled India led by poet-philosopher Mohammad Iqbal (1877–1938) and Muhammad Ali Jinnah (1876–1948), several pan-Islamist movements had gained significant support. First, Sayyid Ahmad Raza Khan Barelvi (1856–1921) created a populist Islamic revivalist movement in the late 1800s. Formally termed the *Ahl e Sunnat wa Jama'at* (People of the Sunna and Community), this movement had both Sunni and Sufi origins and was known for its more liberal perspective on Islam in the sense that it upheld the concept of intercession between the Divine and humans against the more puritan Wahhabi and Deobandi groups, which deny such intercession.[25] This revivalist trend was followed by the pro-Ottoman Khilafat movement, led by Maulana Mohammad Ali (1878–1931) and Maulana Shaukat Ali (1873–1938), who declared the allegiance of Indian Muslims to the Ottomans during a conference held in Karachi in July 1921.[26] However, when Kamal Ataturk abolished the caliphate in 1924, the Khilafat movement quickly lost momentum in India.

These pan-Islamist movements set the stage for Iqbal and Jinnah to encourage and promote the existence of a Muslim nation set apart from the hegemony of India's Hindu majority. Iqbal proposed a separate Muslim state in 1930 as the highest ideal and course of action.[27] Later, Jinnah adopted and promoted this idea with the creation of the Muslim League. Correspondence between Iqbal and Jinnah reveals that they thought only a two-state system could liberate Muslims from the non-Muslim majority.[28] In a speech to the Punjab Muslim Students Association in March 1944, Jinnah strongly promoted the creation of Pakistan as an implementation of Muslim ideals.

[25] Kemal Karpat, *The Politicization of Islam: Reconstructing Identity, State, Faith, and Community in the Late Ottoman State* (Oxford: Oxford University Press, 2002), 46. Maulana Qasim Nanautwi (b. 1833–d. 1880) and Maulana Rasheed Ahmad Gangohi (b. 1829–d. 1905) formed the Deobandi Islamic movement in Deoband, India, in 1866 as a way to preserve Islamic values against the corrupting influence of the West. Nanautwi believed Islam could fulfill the educational and political aspirations of Muslims in the Indian subcontinent and therefore opposed the British influence. The Deobandi interpretation of Islam is rigorous and puritanical.

[26] Akbar Ahmed, *Jinnah, Pakistan, and Islamic Identity: The Search for Saladin* (London: Routledge, 1997), 70.

[27] Anwar Hussein Syed, *Pakistan: Islam, Politics, and National Solidarity* (New York: Praeger, 1982), 42.

[28] Ibid., 50.

Turkey offers a different case of norm diffusion because its nation-building project was the direct outcome of tensions and conflicts within the Ottoman Empire between pan-Islamic and nationalist trends. The last Ottoman sultans, such as Abdulhamid II (1876–1909), used pan-Islamic ideas to promote imperial unity and maintain their control over different parts of the empire penetrated by Western political ideas.[29] As Kemal Karpat suggests, "religious" activities were used to nationalize the *millets*[30] of the Ottoman dynasty.[31] Abdulhamid repaired holy sites in Mecca, Medina, and Karbala; renovated mosques and schools throughout the empire; and gave priority to printing and widely distributing the Qur'an.[32] These activities reinforced his position as the caliph in the eyes of subjects for whom Islam was a significant marker of identity.

In the final years of the Ottoman Empire, however, the Young Turk movement (beginning in 1908) emerged as an alternative political project to the reinforcement of the caliphate. Young Turk Ahmet Riza (1859–1930) was known for his attempts to reconcile Islam with Western ideas. According to Umat Azak, Riza's project was an "anti-clerical struggle to refashion Islam as a private matter and as a rational belief compatible with modernization."[33] In other words, the Young Turk movement was not necessarily anti-Islam but stood against the caliphate's Islamically oriented version of the political community. Confronted with independence movements (Armenian, Greek, etc.) sprouting throughout the empire, the Young Turks emphasized their own Turkishness, spread the idea of a Turkish nation, and promoted a local form of Islam in which prayers and sermons would be performed in the Turkish language.[34] With the collapse of the Ottoman Empire at the end of World War I, the nationalist movement took complete ascendancy in the Turkish-speaking provinces of the empire and led to the creation of modern Turkey.

In Tunisia, allegiance to the umma was manifested in a pervasive loyalty to the caliphate as a way to resist reforms initiated by the modernist elite under French influence, such as Muhammad al-Sadiq Bey (1859–81). From 1864 until 1881, after France became the official protector of the country under the Treaty of Bardo,[35] pan-Islamist ideals induced continuous unrest against the urban Westernized elites who at the time asserted their supremacy over the country with the support of the French. Subsequently, in the wake of World War I, the sense of transnational Islamic belonging, stemming from

[29] Karpat, *The Politicization of Islam*, 125.
[30] *Millets* were religious communities regulated by their own civil rules. They were the corner-stone of the Ottoman social order and political system.
[31] Ibid., 229.
[32] Ibid., 231.
[33] Umat Azak, *Islam and Secularism in Turkey: Kemalism, Religion and the Nation State* (London: I. B. Tauris, 2010), 5–6.
[34] Karpat, *The Politicization of Islam*, 305.
[35] Signed on May 12, 1881, between France and Tunisia (Muhammad al-Sadiq Bey), by which Tunisia became a French protectorate.

solidarity with the Ottomans, persisted with the formation of the Destour Party in 1920. The leader of the party, Shaykh Abdelaziz Taalbi (1920–34), spoke little French and was a student of the *Salafiyya* movement.[36] The party's membership drew from the educated elite fluent in Islamic and Arabic cultures (in contrast to the elite that was influenced by French culture). Although it ultimately accepted the existence of the French protectorate, the party elite viewed European influences as obstacles to a Muslim renaissance.

Interestingly, Destour was the predecessor to the Neo-Destour Party that arose in 1934 and spearheaded the nationalist movement under Habib Bourguiba (1957–87). With the formation of the Neo-Destour Party, many of the Islamic connections to nationalism were minimized and thus began to fade. However, although Bourguiba would later be known for his secular orientation and his dismantling of Islamic institutions and political neutralization of the ulama (Muslim scholars) during the anticolonial movement, he was often referred to as *al-Mujahid al-Akbar* (the greatest warrior).[37] In the same vein, Bourguiba relied on Islamic institutions and symbols to mobilize the masses in his anticolonial "jihad." For instance, his party held meetings in mosques and *zawāyā* (Sufi meeting places) and urged the public to pray five times a day for the national martyrs.[38] This treatment of Islam stands in stark contrast to his policy after Tunisian independence in 1956, as the Personal Status Law of 1957 abolished Shariʿa courts, banned the hijab, and restricted polygamy. This brought into focus Tunisia's French influences and a secular nationalist identity over an Arab-Islamic identity (see Chapter 5 on Islam in the legal system).[39] In other words, during the fight for Tunisian independence, Islam was part of the rhetoric against colonial powers, but after independence, it was typically presented as a symbol of the past. As occurred in Turkey, Westernization understood as modernization was deemed representative of the newly formed country's future.

NATION BUILDING AND FRAMING OF NEW NORMS

The second stage of Acharya's framework, localization, involves two processes: (1) local initiatives such as framing, and (2) adaptation, including grafting and pruning. In the first process, local actors borrow and frame external norms in ways that establish their value to the local audience. These actors must efficiently incorporate new norms into existing ones to avoid these new

---

[36] Clement Henry Moore, *Tunisia since Independence: The Dynamics of One-party Government* (Berkeley: University of California Press, 1956), 27.

[37] Interestingly, he was also known as *Combattant Suprême*, which reveals the French connotations of Bourguiba's anticolonial character, while *al-Mujahid al-Akbar* reflects "the Islamic associations of the other of these ostensibly synonymous terms." Michael Brett, "Review of Norma Salem, *Habib Bourguiba, Islam and the Creation of Tunisia*," in *African Affairs* 87.346 (1998): 126–8, accessed April 26, 2011, http://www.jstor.org/stable/722820.

[38] Marion Boulby, "The Islamic Challenge," *Third World Quarterly* 10.2 (1988): 592.

[39] John Esposito, *Islamic Threat: Myth or Reality?* (New York: Oxford University Press, 1999).

norms being seen as stooges of outside forces. Through the framing process described later in this chapter, political and cultural agents use the language familiar to their local community to better adapt these new norms to the local ones.[40] Framing and adapting often occur simultaneously and cannot be entirely separated. That is, framing may lead to adaptation of a new norm, and adaptation of a new norm may in turn lead to more framing.

In this regard, the nation-building process in Muslim countries resulted in a decisive reorganization of the society-state-religion nexus in ways unknown in the premodern era. Under the caliphate, Islamic institutions and clerics had not been subordinated to political power. Most historians[41] argue that divisions of labor and hierarchies of power between temporal and spiritual authorities were fairly well-established by the tenth century. In the medieval period, there were certainly official ulama working on behalf of political rulers and providing religious justification for their policies, in ways comparable to those of the modern period. However, the major distinction from modern times is that religious authorities and institutions were financially and organizationally independent from the political power.

The caliphs also acknowledged the cultural and religious diversity of society, although this acknowledgment did not translate into an egalitarian legal and political status for all religions and ethnicities. The umma was defined as the sum of the territories and populations under caliphate rule, encompassing an extensive distribution of ethnic, cultural, and linguistic groups, including Muslims, Christians, Jews, Zoroastrians, Baha'is,[42] and Druze. Even though the caliphate represented the example of the original community that followed the message of the Prophet Muhammad, in reality its power was defined by geography and comparable to that of any secular dynasty ruling multiple ethnic and religious groups.[43] This tension between the ideal (of a community following the model of the Prophet) and the political reality was apparent in the distinction between Shari'a and *siyār* forged by the jurisconsults. Shari'a referred to the laws that applied to Muslims, while *siyār* designated the laws that applied to non-Muslims living under caliphate rule, or to the relations between the caliphate and non-Muslims at the international level.[44] Strikingly, the modern perception of the umma

---

[40] Acharya, "How Ideas Spread," 243.

[41] See Hamid Enayat, *Modern Islamic Political Thought* (New York: I. B. Tauris & Co Ltd., 2005); Ira M. Lapidus, *A History of Islamic Societies*, second edition (Cambridge: Cambridge University Press, 2002).

[42] Mirza Husayn-Ali Nuri, also known as Baha-ullah ("the Glory of God") founded Baha'ism in the mid-nineteenth century in Iran. Baha'is are monotheists and believe in a number of prophets, including Jesus and Mohammad. The core tenets of the religion comprise the unity of religion and the equality of humanity.

[43] Albert Habib Hourani, *Arabic Thought in the Liberal Age, 1798–1939* (Cambridge: Cambridge University Press, 1988), 12.

[44] The concept of siyār was developed in the early centuries of Islam by al-Shaybani (748–805) and later codified by al-Sarakhsi (d. 1101): "The siyār ... describes the conduct of the

has been stripped from this imperial definition. Today, the consensus among Muslim scholars is that the umma refers to a spiritual, nonterritorial community distinguished by the shared beliefs of its members. The umma is therefore often seen as a type of citizenship that all Muslims share independently of territory.[45] Contemporary theologian Yusuf al-Qaradawi,[46] discussing the split between Sunni and Shi'i Muslims, illustrates this modern and predominant vision of the umma as a transnational alliance of Muslims that excludes non-Muslims: "I believe in the unity of the Muslim Nation with all its groups, sects and doctrines, since the entire umma believes in one Book and one Messenger, and faces one *qibla* (direction)."[47]

As the Ottoman Empire collapsed, the emergence of the state as the central political institution went hand in hand with the homogenization of the different national communities. That is, nation building systematically omitted and sometimes eradicated particular ethnic, religious, and linguistic groups to create one nation defined by one religion and one language. This homogenization process also led to a politicized narrative of religion, which I call political Islam. In this regard, Muslim countries are not exceptional; with the advent of the modern nation-state, the rules of engagement between religion and politics have been redefined everywhere. This means that, contrary to the dominant liberal narrative, religion has not become politically irrelevant (see the Conclusion of Part I).[48]

Generally speaking, the architects of all nation-states outside of the Western world had to determine to what degree the core collective identity of the country

believers in their relations with the unbelievers of enemy territory as well as with the people with whom the believers had made treaties, who may have been temporarily (*musta'mins*) or permanently (*dhimmīs*) in Islamic lands; with apostates, who were the worst of the unbelievers ... and with rebels." Burgis, "Faith in the State?" 40.

45 Riaz Hassan, *Faithlines: Muslim Conceptions of Islam and Society* (Oxford: Oxford University Press, 2002), 94.

46 Al-Qaradawi is an influential Sunni jurist and television figure who hosts Al-Jazeera's *Al-Shari'a wal-Hayat* (Shari'a and Life). He is a graduate of Al-Azhar University but was exiled from Egypt under Mubarak. A reformist who maintains strong ties to the Muslim Brotherhood, he opposed the military overthrow of the Morsi regime.

47 "Al-Qaradawi's Statement on Shi'ites," *Islamopedia Online*, April 22, 2010, accessed June 13, 2013, http://www.islamopediaonline.org/fatwa/al-qaradawis-statement-shiites. Qibla refers to the direction of Mecca that should be faced by Muslims when praying. It is often indicated in mosques by the mihrab (niche).

48 This dominant political narrative does not necessarily reflect cultural and political evolution, even in the West. For example, in France, which is typically presented as the paradigm of political modernization associated with the disappearance of religion, the Jacobin phase of the French Revolution and its accompanying "Cult of Reason" went beyond the notion of civil religion that Rousseau had defined earlier. In other words, modern secularism, as it is generally understood, has introduced substitutes for theistic religion. These substitutes have taken a bewildering variety of forms; for example, dedication to charismatic leaders, such as Mao and Stalin, resemble behavior exhibited by religious movements. As Mircea Eliade said, "The great majority of the irreligious are not liberated from religious behavior, from theologies and mythologies." Mircea Eliade, *Myths, Dreams and Mysteries: The Encounter between Contemporary Faiths and Archaic Realities* (New York: Harper & Row, 1961), 205–6.

should be sacrificed in exchange for the Western institutions and technologies necessary to strengthen the state both militarily and economically.[49] Each state has responded differently to this dilemma. In the case of the nations built on the collapse of the Ottoman Empire, the diffusion of international norms of statehood was decisive in the fabrication of Islam as a political religion. The emergence of new political norms tied to nationalism generally resulted in state narratives that either referenced Islamic terminology or were diversely articulated within an Islamic framework. Localization of these norms occurred as state actors actively reframed them using local vocabulary.[50] As noted previously, both pan-Islamism and pan-Arabism contributed to the broad appeal of independence from Western imperialism.[51] That is why Islamic references were ultimately used to localize the nation-building process and legitimize state actors and policies. The outcome of such localization was the inclusion of Islam within the new state institutions.

As already mentioned, the adaptation of outside norms into local contexts involves grafting and pruning, which in Muslim countries has primarily taken place through the nationalization of Islamic institutions and the incorporation of Islam in the legal and education systems. In sum, the localization phase has entailed the marshaling of these domains to appropriate Islam as a tool for the elaboration of the nation-state.

For each country, the data presented in the following chapters address the role of Islam in nation building and the constitution, the legal system, and the education system. Chapters 3 through 6 cover the period from the creation of each nation-state to the present and explore these issues:

1. The constitutional inscription of Islam (Chapter 3)
2. The nationalization of Islamic institutions and clerics (Chapter 4)
3. Islam in the legal system (Chapter 5)
4. The integration of Islam in public education (Chapter 6)

A fifth domain, the use of Islamic terms such as umma, jihad, and Shari'a in public discourse by secular state leaders, will not be discussed in this book for two reasons. First, the use of Islamic rhetoric by national leaders has been amply studied.[52] Second, this book prioritizes the concrete (and much less known) embodiment of these cultural references in diverse institutions and laws.

---

[49] Prasenjit Duara, *Rescuing History from the Nation: Questioning Narratives of Modern China* (Chicago, IL: University of Chicago Press, 1995). The adjective *core* refers to an essentialized vision of culture and identity, but most of the time, such essentializations drove political reforms at the time.

[50] Acharya, "How Ideas Spread," 239–75.

[51] Malik Mufti, *Sovereign Creations: Pan-Arabism and Political Order in Syria and Iraq* (Ithaca, NY: Cornell University Press, 1996).

[52] See, for example, Jamal Al-Shalabi, "Democratic Principles in Naseri Discourse," *Journal of the Social Sciences* 31 (2003); Ofra Bengio, *Saddam's Word: The Political Discourse in Iraq* (New York: Oxford University Press, 1998).

3

Islam in the Constitution

The phrasings that define Islam at the constitutional level can differ slightly from one country to another: "Islam is the religion of the state" or "Islam is the religion of the country." They all lead, however, to the same outcome: the creation of Islam as a foundational element of the modern nation. As already mentioned, this is also the case for a country like Turkey that does not mention Islam in the constitution but has nevertheless included Islam in the homogenization process of nation building.

"ISLAM IS THE RELIGION OF THE STATE"

References to Islam in a state's constitution often reinforce the negation or minimization of religious and/or ethnic diversity, as has occurred in modern Egypt. After the Free Officers' coup turned into a revolution in 1952, the monarchy and the 1923 constitution were abolished under the new president, Gamal Abdel Nasser. Despite the secular Arab nationalist orientation of the new regime, Article 3 of the 1956 constitution declared that "Islam is the religion of the State, and the Arabic language is its official language." In the 1971 constitution introduced by Anwar al-Sadat (1970–81), Article 2 reiterated that Islam was the religion of the state and added, "The principles of Islamic Shari'a are *a* main source of legislation."[1] This article was amended on May 22, 1980, to state: "The principles of Islamic

---

[1] When Sadat came to power, he had to deal with Nasser's continued popularity and with the appeal of his ideas, which persisted despite the 1967 defeat. To counterbalance the influence of Nasserist and leftist groups, Sadat moved toward encouraging Islamist groups that turned against him after the Camp David Accords. Sadat managed to secure a tacit pledge from the religious leaders that they would limit the scope of their political activities. In the bargain, Sadat had to accommodate the Brotherhood through the highly publicized amendment to the constitution.

Shariʿa are *the* main source of legislation." As a result, sources outside of Shariʿa supposedly no longer influenced legislation.

Article 2 and its 1980 amendment caused much controversy among political actors. On one hand, Islamists argued that Egypt was not an Islamic state and was in fact an enemy to Islam and Islamization.[2] The Islamists also resented that the ulama were merely a vehicle for the perpetuation of state power. On the other hand, the ulama maintained their defense of Egypt as an Islamic state. Beyond the Islamist-ulama dispute, the more secular components of Egyptian leadership were also divided over whether Egypt was indeed an Islamic state with Shariʿa as the main source of law, or if the Islamic marker was just one more way for the state to legitimize its power. To resolve this issue, the Supreme Constitutional Court (SCC) made two landmark rulings on the implications of Article 2. The first one stated in 1985 that Shariʿa could not operate as a binding law in its own right, and that its provisions had to be incorporated into positive state law. Moreover, this ruling asserted that the amended Article 2 did not undermine other preexisting aspects of the constitution because it had no retroactive effect. In 1993, the second ruling essentially legalized the use of more liberal forms of *ijtihād*, adhering to the principle of public interest (*maslaha*), so that Egyptian lawmakers could create and interpret laws based on Islamic principles without being too limited by traditional jurisprudence.[3] Article 2 was upheld under Mubarak's 2005 and 2007 constitutional amendments.

After the January 25, 2011, revolution and Hosni Mubarak's departure from power on February 11, 2011, the issue of Article 2 arose once again. Specifically, on February 16, 2011, a group of intellectuals from different religious and political affiliations signed a statement calling for the removal of Article 2 while emphasizing the necessity of democratic principles and national unity. The main opponents of the article included Coptic groups and the Qurʾanists, as well as minor segments of the younger generation of the Muslim Brotherhood.[4] The Copts argued that it discriminates against religious minorities and "institutionalizes sectarianism."[5] Pope Shenouda III (1923–2012), at the time the patriarch of Egypt's Coptic community,

---

[2] Jakob Skovgaard-Petersen, *Defining Islam for the State* (Leiden: Brill, 1997), 218.

[3] For more on the two rulings, see Chapter 5 on Islam in legislation, specifically the section on Islam as a source of law in constitutions.

[4] *Ahl Al-Qurʾan*, or the Quʾranists, is a branch of Islam that focuses solely on the Qurʾan as the authority for religious interpretation. It calls for a secular democratic state based on an interpretation of the Qurʾan as the primary and sole source of religious guidance. The Qurʾanists have faced direct criticisms and rejection from mainstream Sunni Muslim scholars in addition to outright harassment and persecution by security services.

[5] Quoted by Naguib Sawiris, a prominent Egyptian Copt, in "Post-Mubarak Era Public Debates over Shariʿa in the Constitution," *Islamopedia Online*, accessed December 28, 2011, http://islamopediaonline.org/country-profile/egypt/islam-and-constitution/post-mubarak-era-public-debates-over-sharia-constitution.

also suggested that "every minority has the right to maintain their own religious law," and as such, the article should be removed or expanded to consider non-Muslims. Additionally, for the Qur'anists, Article 2 goes against Qur'anic principles. Overall, opposition to this article was based on civic or liberal grounds and focused on its discriminatory nature, arguing that it neglects the presence and rights of the 10–15 percent of Egyptians who are Christians by creating judicial discrimination.[6]

On the other hand, those supporting the article, ranging from moderate Islamist intellectuals like Mohamed Selim El-Awa (head of the Egyptian Association for Culture and Dialogue) to Salafi activists such as shaykh Muhammad Hassan,[7] argued that the Islamic identity of Egypt is uncontested, and Shari'a does not compel non-Muslims to follow it. Grand shaykh of Al-Azhar Dr. Ahmad Al-Tayyeb also rejected the calls for amending Article 2, affirming that it should remain untouched because Egypt is an Islamic country.[8] His official position is that Article 2 is one of the pillars of the state and the nation, and any talk about changing it is an invitation to sectarian tensions and a threat to freedom and democracy.

Many other intellectual and secular voices also supported maintaining Article 2 without change. As might be expected, these voices included members of the Muslim Brotherhood, although they have not been unified on this question, as well as Nobel prize winner Mohamed El-Baradei.[9] The strongest opponents to the article's removal were the Salafis, who conducted an extensive campaign collecting signatures and organizing a large demonstration to retain Article 2 in the constitution because "Islam is the state

---

[6] Samir Grees, trans. Aingeal Flanagan, "Religion is for God, the Homeland is for All: The Debate over Article 2 of the Egyptian Constitution," *Islamopedia Online* (March 14, 2011), accessed November 13, 2011, http://www.islamopediaonline.org/editorials-and-analysis/religion-god-homeland-all-debate-over-article-2-egyptian-constitution.

[7] Muhammad Hassan is a Salafi cleric born in Dikernis, Egypt, in 1962. Hassan is the author of several articles and books and maintains a regular presence in online video media with lectures on Islamic lifestyle and practice. He received a bachelor's degree in media from Cairo University and completed his doctorate at Al-Azhar University with a thesis titled, "The Prophet's Approach to Calling Others," *Al-Yom Al-Saabi'*, April 4, 2012, accessed June 13, 2013; http://www3.youm7.com/News.asp?NewsID=645925; and *Islam Way*, accessed June 13, 2013, http://ar.islamway.net/scholar/28.

[8] Shiren Ding, "Players in the Debate over Amending Article 2 of the Egyptian Constitution," *Islamopedia Online* (March 25, 2011), accessed November 13, 2011, http://www.islamopediaonline.org/blog/players-debate-over-amending-article-2-egyptian-constitution.

[9] El-Baradei (b.1942) is a lawyer and diplomat who served as the Director General of the International Atomic Energy Agency (IAEA) from 1997 to 2009. He was a joint winner (with the IAEA) of the Nobel Peace Prize in 2005. With the end of the Mubarak era, he became leader of the liberal opposition and on April 28, 2012, launched the Constitution Party. After the fall of President Morsi in July 2013, he was appointed vice president of the interim government but resigned on August 14, 2013, in protest of the military crackdown on pro-Morsi demonstrators. See Part II.

religion."[10] Interestingly, some in the Christian community did not believe amending the article is necessary because it affirms the right of Christianity as a minor source of Egyptian law, while Islam remains the major one.[11]

In early 2011, the committee appointed by the Supreme Council of the Armed Forces (SCAF) to draw up a new constitution did not plan on amending Article 2, thus reaffirming the country's status as an Islamic state.[12] Similarly, in July 2012, the Constituent Assembly's subsidiary committee, tasked with drafting the first chapter of the constitution, agreed unanimously to maintain the phrasing of Article 2 from previous constitutions, which states: "the principles of Islamic Shari'a are the primary source of legislation." This decision reflected the Salafi clout in the Constituent Assembly, and it came as a sort of compromise only after the Salafis in the assembly tried to modify the phrase by removing "principles" from the article,[13] which would have made possible the implementation of Islamic law in legal domains such as penal or criminal law (*hudood*).[14] Yasser Borhamy, a member of the Constituent Assembly and vice-president of the Salafi movement al-Da'wa (Call), said, "We are against a theocratic state but insist that the second article state that Shari'a, not its principles, is the main source of legislation to separate the state from radical secularism."[15] In the end, this phrasing was not adopted in the constitution ratified in December 2012.

Nevertheless, the Salafis in a sense won one battle during the drafting of the new constitution, with the addition of the term *consultative* in Article 1, which reads, "The Arab Republic of Egypt is democratic, consultative, constitutional and modernized...." The term *consultative* is a literal translation of *shūra*, which comes from the Qur'an. Most significantly, the Salafis were the main force behind Article 219 of the 2012 constitution that stated: "The principles of Islamic Shari'a include its commonly accepted interpretations, its fundamental and jurisprudential rules and its widely considered sources,

---

[10] *Reuters*, accessed November 13, 2011, http://ara.reuters.com/article/topNews/idARACAE 71O0GF20110225.

[11] Shiren Ding, "Players," *Islamopedia*, accessed November 13, 2011, http://www.islamopedia-online.org/blog/players-debate-over-amending-article-2-egyptian-constitution.

[12] "Islam Likely to Stay Egypt's State Religion: Sources," *Al Arabiya*, February 17, 2011, accessed November 13, 2011, http://www.alarabiya.net/articles/2011/02/17/138073.html.

[13] Noha El-Hennawy, "In battle over Shari'a, Salafis lay groundwork for the future," *Egypt Independent*, July 11, 2012, accessed July 14, 2012, http://www.egyptindependent.com/news/battle-over-sharia-salafis-lay-groundwork-future-0.

[14] *Hudood* Ordinances entail harsh punishments usually connected with apostasy laws, discussed further in Chapter 5 on Islam in the legal system. Gamal Essam El-Din, "Salafists battle for a religious state in Egypt," *Ahram Online*, July 12, 2012, accessed July 14, 2012, http://english.ahram.org.eg/NewsContent/1/64/47554/Egypt/Politics-/Salafists-battle-for-a-religious-state-in-Egypt.aspx.

[15] "Update: Agreement reached over Article 2 of new constitution," *Al-Masry Al-Youm*, July 10, 2012, accessed July 14, 2012, http://www.egyptindependent.com/news/update-agreement-reached-over-article-2-new-constitution.

as stated by the schools of Sunna and Gamaa" (see the English translation of the 2012 constitution in Appendix II). [16] The Salafis also tried to modify the phrasing of Article 3 to read "Sovereignty is for God and it is the source of authority" instead of "Sovereignty is for the people alone and they are the source of authority." However, Article 3 has been upheld as it was under Mubarak. [17] The Salafis' aggressive push to implement a stronger reference to Islam in the constitution alarmed secular and Copt representatives in the assembly, contributing to the growing distrust of the Morsi regime that eventually led to its demise in 2013 (see Chapters 8 and 9).

Ultimately, Article 2 of the constitution adopted in 2012 did not change from the 1971 version. It reads: "Islam is the religion of the state and Arabic its official language. Principles of Islamic Shari'a are the principal source of legislation."

At the same time, Article 5 states that "[s]overeignty is for the people alone and they are the source of authority. The people shall exercise and protect this sovereignty, and safeguard national unity in the manner specified in the Constitution." [18] Since the demise of Morsi in July 2013, opponents to the 2012 constitution have vehemently criticized Article 219, which in their view could lead to the Islamicization of the legislative work. The ten-member committee of experts, who on September 1, 2013, handed suggestions for amendments to the 50-member-committee, recommended the removal of Article 219. [19] The Salafist Nour Party, which has one representative on the 50-member committee, warned against eliminating 219, arguing that it "would strip Egypt of its Islamic identity". Nour said it could agree to the removal of 219 if the wording of "principle" were eliminated from Article 2. However, in a spectacular shift of position, Al-Nour head, Younis Makhioun, announced on September 15, 2013, that the party would accept any decision Al-Azhar makes regarding constitutional amendments that refer to Egypt's Islamic identity. [20] It means that Article 219 has been removed from the new draft of the constitution released in November 2013 and that principles of Shari'a, not Shari'a in itself, are mentioned in Article 2.

Another major point of contention regarding the Egyptian constitution is the provision for freedom of religion. Article 46 of the constitution under Mubarak read: "The state shall guarantee the freedom of belief and the

---

[16] Gamal Essam El-Din, "Salafists battle for a religious state in Egypt," *Ahram Online*, July 12, 2012, accessed July 14, 2012, http://english.ahram.org.eg/NewsContent/1/64/47554/Egypt/Politics-/Salafists-battle-for-a-religious-state-in-Egypt.aspx.

[17] Ibid.

[18] *Egypt's Draft Constitution Translated 2012*, accessed January 21, 2013, http://www.egypt-independent.com/news/egypt-s-draft-constitution-translated.

[19] http://english.ahram.org.eg/NewsContent/1/64/81649/Egypt/Politics-/Islam-to-remain-state-religion-in-Egypts-new-const.aspx

[20] See http://www.dailynewsegypt.com/2013/09/16/al-nour-party-changes-position-on-article-219/ Accessed September 18 2013.

freedom of practicing religious rights."²¹ Freedom of belief is absolute, and
the state protects the right to worship in accordance with the customs prevailing in Egypt on the condition that public order is not prejudiced and
public morals are not offended.²² Additionally, under the 2012 constitution,
Article 43 addressed freedom of belief in these terms: "[F]reedom of belief is
an inviolable right" and "[t]he state shall guarantee the freedom to practice
religious rites and to establish places of worship for the divine religions, as
regulated by law."²³ But Article 44 introduced for the first time the prohibition of insult to all prophets: "Insult or abuse of all religious messengers and
prophets shall be prohibited."²⁴

In the same vein, Article 81 limited freedom of press by referring to
respect of the principles of the constitution, meaning principles of Shariʿa
as mentioned in Article 2. Article 81 read: "Rights and freedoms pertaining
to the individual citizen shall not be subject to disruption or detraction. No
law that regulates the practice of the rights and freedoms shall include what
would constrain their essence. Such rights and freedoms shall be practiced in
a manner not conflicting with the principles pertaining to State and society
included in Part I of this Constitution."

The post-Mubarak constitution was suspended on July 3, 2013. A transitional constitution was adopted five days later.²⁵ The document includes provisions for Islam as the official religion of the state and Shariʿa as its main source of
legislation.²⁶ Therefore it is not surprising that the wording of Article 2 has not
been altered in the draft of the new constitution finalized in November 2013.²⁷

In the same vein, the requirement to declare one's religious status on government identification document has been a recurring issue before and after
the 2011 Revolution, sometimes leading to apostasy charges. One example
that attracted considerable attention is that of Mohamed Hijazy, who in 2008

²¹ *Egyptian Constitutional Declaration 2011*, accessed November 13, 2011, http://www.egypt.
gov.eg/english/laws/constitution/default.aspx.
²² Curtis F. Jones, "The New Egyptian Constitution," *The Middle East Journal* 10 (1956): 301.
²³ *Egypt's Draft Constitution Translated 2012*, accessed January 21, 2013, http://www.egypt-
independent.com/news/egypt-s-draft-constitution-translated.
²⁴ Ibid.
²⁵ "Egypt's interim constitutional declaration draws criticisms," Ahram Online, July 9, 2013,
accessed August 4, 2013, http://english.ahram.org.eg/NewsContent/1/64/76110/Egypt/
Politics-/Egypts-interim-constitutional-declaration-draws-cr.aspx
²⁶ "Islam to remain state religion in Egypt new constitution," http://english.ahram.org.eg/
NewsContent/1/64/81649/Egypt/Politics-/Islam-to-remain-state-religion-in-Egypts-new-
const.aspx, accessed on September 15, 2013.
²⁷ Almost all political forces protested this temporary document, from Tamarod, Al-Gamaʿa
Al-Islamiya, the National Salvation Front (whose criticism was later withdrawn), the 6
April Movement, the Coptic Church (which objected to the removal of an article allowing non-Muslims to use their personal religious rules in private matters), and the Al-Nour
Party. "Interim constitution rejected by Church, NSF and Salafis," Egypt Independent,
July 10, 2013, accessed August 4, 2013, http://www.egyptindependent.com/news/interim-
constitution-rejected-church-nsf-and-salafis.

converted from Islam to Christianity, but a court ruling denied him the right to change his religion on his national ID. Another problem has intensified with the introduction of electronic IDs, which, unlike paper IDs, do not provide the option of choosing "Other" for religion. As a result, minority religious groups, particularly Baha'is, have experienced issues regarding their religious identity. A March 2009 ruling by the Supreme Administrative Court denied the Baha'i identity because the state does not recognize the religion; Egyptian authorities consequently began issuing IDs to Baha'is with a dash (-) beside "Religion."[28] Overall, protection of freedom of religion and freedom of speech is more than ever under debate since the end of the Morsi regime (see Chapters 8 and 10).

ISLAM AS THE RELIGION OF THE STATE AND THE NATION AS ARAB

Even in nation-states with a strong secular tradition, such as Iraq under Saddam Hussein's Ba'thist regime, references to Islam were made in all constitutions from 1958 to 1991, declaring Islam the religion of the state.[29] At the same time, the Iraqi state promoted an Arab-Sunni identity by downplaying or ignoring the contributions and rights of the Shi'a and the Kurds as well as oppressing or repressing them at different periods.[30] As a result, the secular ideology of the state served as a vehicle to forge the Iraqi national identity as Sunni and Arab.

After the United States invaded Iraq in 2003 and ousted Saddam Hussein, Iraqis voted in their first postwar election in early 2005, assigning the members of the National Assembly to begin work on a new Iraqi constitution, which was approved in October of the same year.[31] The resulting constitution states in Article 2.1(a): "Islam is the official religion of the State and a basic source of legislation. No law can be passed that contradicts the undisputed rules of Islam." This seems to be tempered by Article 2.1(b), which states, "No law can be passed that contradicts the rights and basic freedoms outlined in this constitution." Furthermore, according to Article 2.2 "This constitution guarantees the Islamic identity of the majority of the Iraqi people and the full religious rights for all individuals and

---

[28] "Egypt Officially Changes Rules for ID Cards," *Bahai World News Service* (April 17, 2009), accessed December 27, 2011, http://news.bahai.org/story/707.

[29] "Iraqi Constitutions," *Global Justice Project: Iraq*, accessed April 19, 2011, http://www.gjpi.org/library/primary/iraqi-constitution/.

[30] The Republic of Iraq was established by a coup d'état in 1958 by a group of Arab Nationalists. Saddam Hussein took over the presidency of the republic in 1979, although he was widely recognized as the power behind President al-Bakr after the 1968 Ba'ath military coup.

[31] For the complete text of the Iraqi Constitution in English: "Full Text of Iraqi Constitution," *Washington Post*, accessed November 13, 2011, http://www.washingtonpost.com/wp-dyn/content/article/2005/10/12/AR2005101201450.html; full text of the constitution in Arabic, accessed November 13, 2011, http://www.iraqnaa.com/dastor.htm.

the freedom of creed and religious practices." Thus, religious freedom is a constitutionally protected right, and the government progressively modified the legal system to address many of the legal issues around religious minorities.[32]

A contentious issue with the constitution included a prohibition on *takfir* – accusing Muslims of disbelief. The proscription ostensibly was proposed to protect Shiʿa because the term has been used against them; however, references that deemed Shiʿa religious sites and authorities as sacred or holy were considered too sensitive and deleted from the final version of the constitution. A ban on Baʿthism was also contested by Sunni groups because many of them were former members of the now outcast and outlawed party. The dispute was ultimately resolved by changing the wording of the ban to make it applicable solely to "*Saddamist* Baʿthism," which would technically allow for the establishment of a Baʿathist Party along the lines of Syria or pre-Saddam Iraq.[33]

The contradictory nature of these constitutional articles may cause issues in the future, and it remains to be seen whether the rights of religious minorities will be protected or if Iraq's officially sanctioned forms of Islam will prevail. This is especially pressing considering the reported instances of stigmatization, discrimination, and acts of violence against members of religious minority groups, such as Christians, Mandaeans, Yazidis, and Jews (see Part III). These include abuses by militiamen and members of the security forces, employment discrimination, and lack of representation in public office. Multiple churches have also been attacked in major Iraqi cities, and Christians have been subjected to violence since the implementation of the 2005 constitution.[34] Specifically, "Christian and Yazidi businesses viewed as 'un-Islamic,' such as liquor stores, were vandalized in Baghdad and the area under the Kurdistan Regional Government (KRG) during 2011."[35] Additionally, in 2011, three attacks on Christian churches left several persons wounded but none dead.[36] There was further violence against Yazidi and Mandaean populations according to the Mandaean Human Rights Group, which reported kidnapping and deaths in 2011.[37]

---

[32] "Final Draft of the Iraqi Constitution, Analysis and Commentary," *Carnegie Endowment* (August 2008), accessed November 13, 2011, http://www.carnegieendowment.org/files/FinalDraftSept16.pdf.

[33] Ibid.

[34] Richard Seymour, "New Constitution Threatens Iraq's Ethnic Groups," *The Middle East* 364 (2006): 60–1.

[35] United States Commission on International Religious Freedom, USCIRF Annual Report 2012 – Countries of Particular Concern: Iraq, March 20, 2012, accessed January 22, 2013, http://www.unhcr.org/refworld/docid/4f71a67526.html.

[36] Ibid.

[37] Ibid.

PAKISTAN: FROM A MUSLIM TO AN ISLAMIC STATE

The constitutional evolution of Pakistan reflects the ambiguities of a foundational political project that oscillated from a state for Muslims to an Islamic state. Although Pakistan was conceived as a separate homeland for the Muslims of India, Muhammad Ali Jinnah did not envision a political role for Islam in the new nation. In a speech to the Constituent Assembly three days before Pakistan's creation on August 14, 1947, he stated: "You will find that in the course of time Hindus will cease to be Hindus and Muslims will cease to be Muslims, not in the religious sense, because that is the personal faith of each individual, but in the political sense as citizens of the State."[38] Thus, Jinnah's vision of the role of Islam in the new polity was fundamentally different from that of pan-Islam and Islamic actors such as Abul Ala Mawdudi[39] (1903–79) and the Deobandi ulama, who initially opposed the movement for a separate state for Muslims because it would not be an Islamic state.[40]

Although the 1956 constitution proclaimed in Article 1, "Pakistan shall be a Federal Republic to be known as the Islamic Republic of Pakistan," this invocation remained largely symbolic, which was in line with Iqbal's conceptions of Islam and Jinnah's vision for Pakistan.[41] The second constitution of 1962 even omitted "Islamic" from the state appellation, renaming the country simply the "Republic of Pakistan." It also articulated subtle but significant changes in the Islamic provisions of the constitution. For example, the omnipotent sovereignty of Allah was acknowledged, although it was not given explicit authority over the public sphere as it had in the 1956

---

[38] Jinnah was the leader of the political movement for an India independent from British colonialism and later the leader in creating a separate homeland, Pakistan, for the Muslims of India. Jinnah was also the president of the Muslim League, a political party with a generally secular outlook. Farhat Haq, "Pakistan: A State for the Muslims or an Islamic State?" *Religion and Politics in South Asia* (New York: Routledge, 2010), 122.

[39] Mawdudi (1903–79) was a journalist and a religious scholar and eventually founded the Jamaat-e-Islami in the early 1940s as a way to advocate his "back to roots" approach, which opposed the West.

[40] However, once the state became a reality, the Islamists and the ulama vigorously joined the debate on whether Pakistan should be an Islamic state or a Muslim state. The ulama organized themselves into political parties and have played an active role in politics; they have also made alliances with the Islamists (particularly Jamaat-e-Islami). Islam assumed a political role in Pakistan, which created an Islamic state, and more recently, with the steady Islamization of Pakistani politics, it has evolved into an Islamist state.

[41] "Pakistan Constitution 1956," *Pakistan Space*, accessed November 13, 2011, http://pakistanspace.tripod.com/archives/56_00.htm. In March 1949, the first Constituent Assembly passed the aims and objectives of the constitution (i.e., the basis and principles as the framework for the future constitution) known as the Objectives Resolution. Later, the Objectives Resolution was included in the 1956 constitution as the preamble. The full resolution can be found in Javaid Saeed, *Islam and Modernization: A Comparative Analysis of Pakistan, Egypt, and Turkey* (Westport, CT: Praeger Publishers, 1994), 76.

constitution. Additionally, Article 5 omitted references to the Qur'an and *Sunnah* as the authentic sources of Islamic guidance.[42] With the adoption of the third constitution in 1973, however, the official state name reverted to the "Islamic Republic" as a result of demands from newly elected Islamic leaders who claimed: "Islam shall be the state religion of Pakistan."[43]

It is important to point out that all three constitutions (1956, 1962, and 1973) delineated the symbolic status of state identity by asserting the Islamic character of civil law (see Chapter 4). In addition, the 1973 constitution stipulated that the state would "bring the existing laws into conformity with the injunctions of Islam as set out in the Qur'an and Sunnah, and that no law contradictory to such injunctions was to be enacted."[44] Under pressure from Islamist groups, the 1973 constitution was revised the following year to include an amendment to Article 260, which henceforth defined Ahmadis[45] as non-Muslims.[46] With the introduction of martial law under Mohammad Zia-ul-Haq (1977–88), the state underwent a complex process of Islamicization, especially in the legal sphere, and with the passage of the 1979 *Hudood*[47] Ordinances, the state moved further away from the secular and pluralist vision of its founders.

While Article 20 of the current constitution mandates freedom of religion and Article 25 establishes equality of all citizens, in practice, discrimination against religious minorities, including Christians, Baha'is, Hindus, and

---

[42] Moreover, Articles 6, 7, and 8 left the implementation of norms (e.g., the elimination of usury and the discouragement of alcohol and drug use, gambling, and prostitution) to the concerned officials and the organs of the state, effectively excluding judicial intervention. Haq, "Pakistan: A State for the Muslims or an Islamic State?" 133.

[43] "The Role of Islam in the State," *Islamopedia*, accessed November 20, 2011, http://www.islamopediaonline.org/country-profile/pakistan/role-islam-State. For more information see "Islam Shall be the State Religion of Pakistan," *Pakistani Constitution*, accessed November 20, 2011, http://www.pakistaniorg/pakistan/constitution/.

[44] Saeed, *Islam and Modernization*, 82.

[45] Ahmadiyya, the adherents of which are called Ahmadis, is an Islamic reform movement founded by Mirza Ghulam Ahmad in India at the end of the 1800s. The core difference between Ahmadis and other Muslims relates to the possibility of other prophets after the Prophet Muhammad. One Ahmadi faction, the Qadiyani, holds that Ghulam Ahmad was a prophet. The other faction, the Lahori, holds that Ghulam Ahmad was a *mujaddid* who was to renew Islam. The Qadiyani branch of the Ahmadiyya is regarded as heretical by most Sunni and Shi'i Muslims. See "Aḥmadīyah," *The Oxford Encyclopedia of the Islamic World*.

[46] The amended Article 260 states, "A person who does not believe in the absolute and unqualified finality of the Prophethood of Muhammad (peace be upon Him), the last of the Prophets or claims to be a prophet, in any sense of the word or of any description whatsoever, after Muhammad (peace be upon Him), or recognizes such a claimant as a prophet or a religious reformer, is not a Muslim for the purposes of the Constitution or Law." Martin Lau, "Shari'a and National Law in Pakistan," in Jan Michiel Otto (ed.), *Shari'a Incorporated* (Amsterdam: Leiden University Press, 2010), 396.

[47] *Hudood* refers to the specific punishments for crimes as defined by traditional Islamic jurisprudence. For more information on *hudood* crimes, see Chapter 5.

Ahmadis, does exist and is not legally reprimanded.[48] For example, in direct contradiction to Article 20, district-level authorities consistently refuse to grant permission for the construction of non-Muslim (i.e., Ahmadiyya and Baha'i) places of worship.[49] Local and international monitors, such as the 2009–10 International Freedom Report for Pakistan, document that Christians, Sikhs, and Hindus all face societal discrimination and are subject to religious violence. However, the Ahmadi are the only minority specifically addressed in discriminatory legislation. Created under Zia-ul-Haq, the Ahmadi-specific criminal laws of 1984 reiterate the discriminatory nature of the 1974 law, prohibiting Ahmadis from referring to themselves as Muslims.[50] Under Articles 298b and 298c, Ahmadis can be sentenced to up to three years in prison if they refer to themselves as Muslims.[51] As a result, the Pakistani state retains the authority to constitutionally define who is and who is not a Muslim and can legally sanction Ahmadis as *wajib ul-qatl* or "worthy of death."[52]

Additionally, similar to the discrimination issues created by national identity card regulations in Egypt, the Pakistani state designates religious affiliation on passports and requests religious information on national identity card applications. Although Ahmadis cannot legally register as Muslims, they generally choose not to identify themselves as non-Muslims.[53] As a result, the true number of Ahmadis in the state is difficult to assess, and Ahmadis continue to boycott elections because they cannot vote without a national identity card. Moreover, when applying for a passport, every Pakistani Muslim must sign a statement deriding Ahmad and denouncing his followers as non-Muslims.[54] Thus, the constitutional rights and protections for religious minorities are undermined by a legal system that discriminates against certain citizens and leaves them socially and politically vulnerable to abuses by state and local authorities as well as by fellow

---

[48] Part II, Article 20: "Freedom to profess religion and to manage religious institutions. Subject to law, public order and morality: (a) every citizen shall have the right to profess, practice and propagate his religion; and (b) every religious denomination and every sect thereof shall have the right to establish, maintain and manage its religious institutions." Part II, Article 25: "Equality of all citizens. (1) All citizens are equal before law and are entitled to equal protection of law," Pakistani Constitution, accessed November 13, 2011, http://www.pakistaniorg/pakistan/constitution/.

[49] "Pakistan," *International Freedom Report 2009*, accessed November 13, 2011, http://www.State.gov/g/drl/rls/irf/2009/127370.htm.

[50] Articles 298b and 298s, a.k.a. Ordinance XX.

[51] Lau, "Shari'a and National Law in Pakistan," 420.

[52] Mira Sethi, "Pakistan's Medieval Constitution," *The Wall Street Journal* 255.143 (June 22, 2010): A21. Ahmadis are often targets of accusations of blasphemy. Please refer to Chapter 5 "Shari'a and Apostasy," on Islam in the legal system.

[53] "Pakistan," *International Freedom Report* (2009), accessed November 13, 2011, http://www.State.gov/g/drl/rls/irf/2009/127370.htm.

[54] Ahmad refers to Mirza Ghulam Ahmad, who was a nineteenth-century Punjabi reformer and the founder of the Ahmadi movement. Sethi, "Pakistan's Medieval Constitution," A21.

civilians. In 2005, eight Ahmadis were killed at a mosque in the province of Punjab, and in the same region the following year, a mob burned down homes and shops belonging to Ahmadis, forcing them to flee.[55] More than eighty Ahmadis were killed on May 29, 2010, in coordinated assaults on two mosques in Lahore.[56] After the attack, Pakistani Minister for Minorities Shahbaz Bhatti pledged to protect the Ahmadi community, and President Zardari was prompt to condemn the killings as Pakistani officials blamed the attack on the Pakistani Taliban. However, many Ahmadis denounced the government's continuous failure to ensure their protection and cited previous instances of discrimination by the state.[57]

In the same vein, the situation of the Shi'i population has steadily deteriorated, especially in the Baluchistan province, an area home to historically marginalized ethnic minorities that stretches beyond Pakistan to the southern regions of its neighbors to the west, Afghanistan and Iran.[58] In 2013, this region has witnessed an increase of kidnappings, and in February of the same year, a bomb in Quetta killed almost 100 civilians, which led to accusations by Shi'a groups of state inability at both the local and national levels to stem sectarian attacks.[59]

THE RELIGION OF THE COUNTRY IS ISLAM

The political treatment of Islam in Tunisia strikes a balance between the inclusion of Islam in the constitution and the secular policies mandated by Habib Bourguiba and, later, by Ben Ali (1987–2011). Adopted on June 1, 1959, and amended on July 12, 1988, Article 1 of the Tunisian constitution states: "Tunisia is a free, independent and sovereign state. Its religion is Islam, its language is Arabic and its type of government is the Republic."[60]

[55] Sethi, "Pakistan's Medieval Constitution," A21.
[56] "Deaths in Pakistan Mosque Raids," *Al-Jazeera English*, May 29, 2010, accessed October 23, 2011, http://english.aljazeera.net/news/asia/2010/05/20105294369226840.html. Ali Sethi, "One Myth, Many Pakistans," *New York Times*, June 12, 2010, accessed October 23, 2011, http://www.nytimes.com/2010/06/13/opinion/13sethi.html?scp=1&sq=%22one%20myth,%20many%20pakistans%22&st=cse#.
[57] The Associated Press, "Pakistan: An Official Promise to Protect the Ahmadi Sect," *New York Times*, June 2, 2010, accessed October 23, 2011, http://www.nytimes.com/2010/06/02/world/asia/02briefs-AHMADIS.html.
[58] "Balochistan: Pakistan's Forgotten War," *Al Jazeera*, accessed June 14, 2013, http://www.aljazeera.com/photo_galleries/programmes/20121512424995 4716.html.
[59] "The Failure of Governance in Quetta," *Islamopedia Online*, March 3, 2013, accessed June 14, 2013, http://islamopediaonline.org/video/failure-governance-quetta.
[60] It invokes a symbolic reference to God in the preamble: "In the name of God, the Merciful, the Compassionate." The preamble also states that the will of the Tunisian people is "to remain faithful to the teachings of Islam, to the unity of the Greater Maghreb, to its membership of the Arab community, and to cooperation with the peoples who struggle to achieve justice and liberty." Article 38 states that the religion of the president must be Islam. At the same time, the 1956 constitution guarantees the freedom of religion in Article 5: "The

However, Bourguiba's regime emphasized a Western, secular orientation over Islamic identity and excluded religion from public life, banning parties with a religious or Islamic platform.[61] In an interesting parallel to Turkey, Bourguiba's regime worked to purge Islam from public and political spaces. One of the key differences with Turkey lies in Tunisia's constitutional declaration that Islam is the religion of the state, thus identifying Tunisia as a Muslim state. In contrast, Turkey's constitution valorizes "laicism."[62] Following a bloodless coup in November 1987, Zine El-Abidine Ben Ali seized power from Bourguiba and promised democratization. However, Ben Ali continued his predecessor's vision by refusing to recognize religious parties and criminalizing any party that combined religion and politics.

In both Bourguiba's and Ben Ali's eras, the Tunisian state maintained strict surveillance over Islamists. The government denied Islamist activists passports and revoked their identity cards. It prevented them from gaining employment, acquiring legal counsel, and even using public telephones.[63] The government also restricted the wearing of "sectarian dress," which included the hijab, beards, and *qamīs* (long garb for men), despite the constitution providing for Islam as the official state religion. Additionally, while no laws against conversion existed, proselytizing to Muslims was illegal (as it was deemed to disturb the public order), and government officials discriminated against converts from Islam to another religion through bureaucratic proceedings (e.g., denying institutional promotions that could encourage conversion).[64] As a result, the reference to Islam in the constitution was regulated by the state's promotion of a particular version of Islam suiting its interests, which restricted freedom of religious expression while advocating a homogenous Muslim identity that contributed to state legitimization.

Republic of Tunisia shall guarantee the inviolability of the human person and freedom of conscience, and defends the free practice of religious beliefs provided this does not disturb public order" accessed October 23, 2011, http://confinder.richmond.edu/admin/docs/Tunisiaconstitution.pdf.

[61] For more information on Islamic parties in Tunisia and the Islamic Tendency Movement (Mouvement de Tendance Islamique – MTI), subsequently known as Hizb al-Nahda, see Esposito and Piscatori, "Democratization and Islam," 431, accessed April 20, 2011, http://www.jstor.org/stable/4328314; L. B. Ware, "Ben Ali's Constitutional Coup in Tunisia," *Middle East Journal* 42.4 (1988): 588, accessed April 26, 2011, http://www.jstor.org/stable/4327834.

[62] Marion Boulby asserts that Bourguiba did not present himself as a secularizing reformer like Ataturk but as a modernist reformer of Islam. Marion Boulby, "The Islamic Challenge: Tunisia since Independence," *Third World Quarterly* 10.2 (1988): 590–614, accessed May 10, 2011, http://www.jstor.org/stable/3992658.

[63] "Tunisia," *International Freedom Report* (2001), accessed November 13, 2011, http://www.State.gov/g/drl/rls/irf/2001/5740.htm.

[64] "Tunisia," *International Freedom Report* (2010), accessed November 13, 2011, http://www.State.gov/g/drl/rls/irf/2010/148847.htm.

With the Jasmine Revolution and the ousting of President Ben Ali on January 14, 2011, interim president Fouad Mebazaa (January 15, 2011, through December 13, 2011) called for the election of a council to write a new constitution. On October 23, 2011, Tunisia held its first elections since the revolution, and the Islamist party Ennahda (the Renaissance Party) won a solid plurality with 42 percent of the vote in the Constituent Assembly.[65] The Constituent Assembly began debating the first article of the constitution in February 2012, and it ultimately decided that the new constitution will not amend the nature of Islam in the old constitution and that Islam will remain the religion of the state.[66] However, some political parties such as the Congress for the Republic (CPR), Ennahda's ally, expressed the desire for no state religion, and the Progressive Democratic Party (PDP) proposed that references to religion and language be removed from the constitution's preamble and statement of general principles, and instead be left as part of the body of the constitution.[67] In contrast Ennahda, with the majority in the Tunisian Constituent Assembly, suggested only a minimal rewording of Article 1 while maintaining the phrase "[Tunisia's] religion is Islam."[68]

The final draft of the constitution was still under review when the NCA suspended its activities indefinitely in August 2013 (see Part II). The polarizing question of religion in the constitution emphasizes the opposite visions of the post Ben Ali state: with, on one hand, the Ennahda assertive Islamic identity of the new regime and, on the other hand, the fear of what representative Samia Abbou called an "ikhwan constitution," an allusion to the Muslim Brotherhood (al Ikhwan al Muslimun).[69]

There are many references to Islam in the draft constitution. The second paragraph of the preamble establishes that it is "based on the teachings of

---

[65] The election for the National Council was to take place on July 24, 2011, but it was pushed back to October 2011 because of insufficient time to prepare for voting; almost four hundred thousand Tunisians in the country did not have voting cards. Eileen Byrne, "Tunisia Opts to Reform Constitution," *Financial Times*, March 3, 2011, accessed June 20, 2011, http://www.ft.com/cms/s/0/36fbocfa-4671-11e0-aebf-00144feab49a.html#axzz1KeKzpafT. Tarek Amara, "Tunisia Opposition Slam October Election Date," *Reuters*, May 26, 2011, accessed June 20, 2011, http://www.reuters.com/article/2011/05/26/us-tunisia-election-idUSTRE74P3R020110526.

[66] Kareem Fahim, "Tunisia Says Constitution Will Not Cite Islamic Law," *New York Times*, March 26, 2012, accessed July 2, 2012, http://www.nytimes.com/2012/03/27/world/africa/tunisia-says-constitution-will-not-cite-islamic-law.html.

[67] Wafa Ben Hassine, "Constituent Assembly Debates Arab-Muslim Identity in Tunisian Constitution," *Tunisia Live*, February 21, 2112, accessed June 30, 2012, http://www.tunisia-live.net/2012/02/21/constituent-assembly-debates-arab-muslim-identity-in-tunisian-constitution/.

[68] Found in Ennahda's platform published: http://www.businessnews.com.tn/pdf/programme-ennahdha0911.pdf, September 2011, accessed July 1, 2012, [Translated from: *"Tunisie est un État libre et indépendant: Sa religion est l'islam, sa langue l'arabe, son régime la république et sa priorité la concrétisation des objectifs de la révolution."*]

[69] "Consensus urged on Tunisia constitution," *Maghrebia*, July 25, 2013, accessed August 4, 2013, http://magharebia.com/en_GB/articles/awi/features/2013/07/25/feature-01.

Islam and its objectives." The first article establishes that Tunisia's "religion is Islam." Article 6 calls for state "sponsoring religion; ensuring freedom of belief, conscience, and religious practice, and the protection of holy sites; ensuring the neutrality of mosques and houses of worship from partisan recruitment."

Article 73, approved by the Constituent Assembly, reads: "Running for Presidency of the Republic shall be a right entitled to every male and female elector who bear the Tunisian nationality by birth, and whose religion is Islam."[70] This provision maintains the Islamic identity of the president (a carryover from previous constitutions) but removes the gender limitation. Article 141 states: "No amendment to the Constitution may be prejudice to Islam, being the religion of the state."[71] However, the ultimate format of the Tunisian Constitution is indeterminate because these issues – and their official wording – remain contentious.

Interestingly, the draft maintains the reference to Palestine from the previous constitution with a sentence in the preamble "recognising all rightful movements for liberation, with special emphasis on the Palestinian Liberation Movement."[72]

TURKEY AS THE EXCEPTION

Turkey is one of the rare states that does not refer to Islam in its constitution and yet has not seen a decline in the role of Islam in society and politics. As such, Turkey appears as the exception to the rule because Islam has been used by state elites as a tool for national homogenization. The creation of Turkey as a nation-state after the collapse of the Ottoman Empire opened a phase of political and social Westernization under the aegis of Kemal Ataturk (1923–38). However, Ataturk's attempt at radical secularization ultimately led to state control over Islam that forcefully suppressed its public presence, but not to the separation of religion and state as one might find in the United States or France.[73] In this sense, Turkey's constitutional approach has provided a unique laicism in which religion is not part of public life but is still controlled and reshaped by state policies.

Although Article 2 of the original 1924 constitution stated that "the religion of the Turkish state is Islam; the official language is Turkish; the

---

[70] Draft Constitution of the Republic of Tunisia, June 1, 2013, accessed June 13, 2013, http://www.marsad.tn/uploads/documents/projet_constitution_01_06_2013.pdf.

[71] Ibid.

[72] Ibid.

[73] Ataturk's secularization measures did not have a large effect on the countryside, and upon his death in 1938, resistance to secularization grew. With the economic downturn during and after World War II, "financial hardship led to a feeling of discontent which changed people's indifference to the nonreligious outlook of the Republic People's Party (RPP) to resentment against the party, which was considered antireligious." Saeed, *Islam and Modernization*, 48.

seat of government is Ankara," Turkey eliminated the clause designating Islam the state religion in 1928, thus officially declaring the state secular, or in official terms, "laic."[74] A later constitution in 1982 identified the Turkish Republic as a secular state in Article 2, "whilst simultaneously creating an agency to manage religious affairs within the general administration by way of Article 136," which ensured continuity of the Office of Religious Affairs.[75] As mentioned earlier, such principles of laicism did not lead to a separation of Islamic institutions from the state. Instead, the state has secured firm control over all religious activities while excluding Islam from the political sphere and the social space. This exclusion of Islam has extended to the banning of all forms of head and body covering in public places, including universities and civil service buildings.[76] Although in February 2008, the Turkish parliament amended the constitution allowing women to wear a headscarf in universities,[77] this ban was reinstated and the amendment annulled by the Constitutional Court only a few months later in June 2008.[78]

In sum, the state has built a social artifact of a homogenous nation of Muslims by not only suppressing religious expression but also ignoring and repressing expressions of religious and ethnic diversity.

For example, included within that 99.8 percent Muslim majority is a sizable and repressed Alevi minority, which is in fact the second-largest religious community in Turkey.[79] One of the various forms of discrimination against the Alevis is manifested in the identification cards policy; Alevis cannot register themselves as Alevis because the faith is not officially recognized.[80] According to government classification, Alevism is considered a subdivision of Sunni Islam; thus, on their identity cards, Alevis are categorized as Sunni Muslims even though Alevis do not identify themselves

---

[74] The principle of laicism was officially introduced into the Turkish constitution in 1937.

[75] Mustafa Kocak, "Islam and National Law in Turkey," in Jan Michiel Otto (ed.), *Shari'a Incorporated* (Amsterdam: Leiden University Press, 2010), 249.

[76] The headscarf ban in public institutions was instated after the 1997 military soft coup. Hakan Yavuz, *Islamic Political Identity in Turkey* (Oxford: Oxford University Press, 2003), 99.

[77] Yigal Schleifer, "Turkey Votes to Lift Head-Scarf Ban, but Battle Continues," *Christian Science Monitor*, February 11, 2008, accessed July 8, 2012, http://www.csmonitor.com/World/Middle-East/2008/0211/p07s02-wome.html.

[78] "Turkey: Situation of women who wear head-scarves," *Immigration and Refugee Board of Canada*, May 20, 2008, accessed July 8, 2012, http://www.unhcr.org/ref-world/docid/4885a91a8.html.

[79] According to Radio Free Europe-Radio Liberty in 2002, the Alevi population ranged from 15 percent to 30 percent of the Turkish population. The Turkish Alevi community claims the numbers are closer to 30 to 40 percent of the population. "Turkey: Court Ruling Shows Authorities' Refusal to See Alevism as a Religious Community," *Religioscope*, February 18, 2002, accessed May 20, 2011, http://www.religioscope.com/info/notes/2002_023_alevis.htm.

[80] Kocak, "Islam and National Law in Turkey," 263.

with the wider Sunni population.[81] As a result, many Alevis reject Islam as their religious identity because in Turkey, Islam is largely synonymous with Sunni Islam. Most Alevis would prefer to leave the entry for religion blank, but this option has not been accepted by the state because such a statement is considered separatist. The imposition of Sunni identity is also apparent in the education system, based on Article 24 of the 1982 constitution, which mandates religious education for all students in primary and secondary school.[82] Not surprisingly, which mandatory religious lessons are taught according to the doctrine of majority Sunni population, while the Alevi minority students are legally bound to participate in these classes.[83]

Under the ongoing negotiations for European Union (EU) admission, Turkey has met the Copenhagen Criteria, and since February 2011, it has entered the final stage of negotiations for EU admission.[84] However, as of late 2010, many civil and human rights NGOs deemed the reform process incomplete because of the state's deficient human rights record, specifically regarding the torture of political dissidents and the lack of religious (and ethnic) freedoms.[85] Moreover, the 2010 Conclusions on Turkey showed that respect for and protection of minorities (including protection of languages and religions), as well as fundamental cultural rights, did not meet EU standards.[86]

---

[81] Alevis believe in "Alevism as true Islam, a separate religion, a belief system, a humanistic philosophy, a culture, an ethnic community, a way of life or political position." Joost Jongerden, "Violation of Human Rights and the Alevis in Turkey," in Paul J. White and Joost Jongerden (eds.), *Turkey's Alevi Enigma: A Comprehensive Overview* (Leiden: Koninklijke Brill NV, 2003), 80. Moreover, Alevis are often classified under the branch of Shi'i Islam, but it is more accurately a syncretic religion that incorporates aspects of Shi'i Islam along with heterodox, monotheistic traditions and pantheistic beliefs. Additionally, Alevis do not identify themselves with the Twelver Shi'is of Iraq and Iran.

[82] Jongerden, "Violation of Human Rights and the Alevis in Turkey," 80.

[83] While initially the religious and moral education classes were taught in accordance to Sunni principles, the syllabus has changed to currently incorporate ethics studies and the philosophy of all religions in a move toward emphasizing tolerance.

[84] Turkey officially applied for EU membership in 1987. The Copenhagen Criteria are the criteria defined by the 1992 Treaty of Maastricht for a nation to apply for EU membership. "Council Conclusions on EU-Turkey Readmission Agreement and Related Issues," *Council of the European Union*, February 24–5, 2011, accessed April 23, 2011, http://www.consilium.europa.eu/uedocs/cms_data/docs/pressdata/en/jha/119501.pdf.

[85] Kristy Hughes, "Turkey and the European Union: Just Another Enlargement," *A Friends of Europe Working Paper*, (2004), accessed March 15, 2011, http://www.cdu.de/ed/doc/Friends_of_Europe_Turkey.pdf. "Conclusions on Turkey," *Extract from the Communication from the Commission to the Council and the European Parliament "Enlargement Strategy and Main Challenges 2010–2011," COM(2010)660 Final*, (2010), accessed March 20, 2011, http://ec.europa.eu/enlargement/pdf/key_documents/2010/package/conclusions_turkey_en.pdf.

[86] "Conclusions on Turkey," 2010.

As part of President Ergodan's agenda to bring Turkey more in line with the standards of the EU, a referendum was held in 2010 to make changes to the Turkish constitution, and Article 10 on Equality before the Law (minorities and cultural rights) was amended. While the 1982 constitution protects against discrimination on the basis of "language, race, colour, sex, political opinion, philosophical belief, religion and sect, or any such considerations," the amended version ensures that "measures taken for this purpose shall not be interpreted as contrary to the principle of equality."[87] Other rights in the new constitution include an increase in children's rights (Article 41), the right to collective bargaining for civil and public servants (Article 53 and Article 128), and a number of judicial reforms. As a result, the 2011 Conclusions on Turkey report has been more favorable, stating that the European Parliament "supports the government's ongoing dialogue with religious communities, including the Alevis, as well as the Greek, Armenian, Aramean and other Christian communities."[88] In 2012, very limited progress was made regarding freedom of thought, conscience, and religion, specifically in the protection of minority religious groups or those of no faith. At the time of this writing, the framework of the European Council on Human Rights (ECHR) that could protect Alevis and other religious minorities has not yet been adopted.[89]

---

[87] "Law No 5982 Amending Certain Provisions of the Constitution," translated by Secretariat General for European Union Affairs, *Government of Turkey, Prime Ministry*, August 19, 2010, accessed March 18, 2011, http://www.abgs.gov.tr/files/Bas%C4%B1nMusavirlik/haberler/constituional_amendments.pdf.

[88] Even so, the European Parliament says that it "is disappointed, however, that only limited progress has been made on the legal framework for the functioning of these communities, notably as regards their ability to obtain legal personality, to open and operate houses of worship, to train clergy and to resolve property problems not addressed by the law on Foundations … the Government to pay special attention to educational materials in schools, which should reflect the religious plurality of Turkish society, and to the need for unbiased learning materials." "European Parliament Resolution on Turkey's 2010 Progress Report," *European Parliament*, March 9, 2011, accessed May 19, 2011, http://www.europarl.europa.eu/sides/getDoc.do?pubRef=-//EP//TEXT+TA+P7-TA-2011-0090+0+DOC+XML+V0//EN.

[89] European Commission "Commission Staff Working Document: Turkey 2012 Progress Report," *Communication from the Commission to the European Parliament and the Council: Enlargement Strategy and Main Challenges 2012–2013*, 2012, accessed January 21, 2013, http://ec.europa.eu/enlargement/pdf/key_documents/2012/package/tr_rapport_2012_en.pdf.

4

Nationalization of Islamic Institutions and Clerics

The modern nation-state supplies public services previously offered by religious institutions, such as court systems, education, and social welfare. As a result, the state came to effectively control and reform Islamic institutions and to harness their social influence as a political instrument to legitimize and/or promote its vision and interests through nationalization. During these consolidation efforts, the independent institutions of waqf and madrasa (religious foundations and Islamic schools) were the first to come under state control.[1]

To explain how the state came to control religious institutions as part of the nation-building project, Ali Dessouki offers "four methods of subordination": the elimination of religious institutions' independent sources of income; administrative reorganization of the institutions and structural changes; the abolishment or integration of the Shari'a courts into a national court system; and the integration and absorption of religious education into the national educational system.[2] Importantly, in all cases, the state nationalized previously independent Islamic institutions and absorbed their leaders under state ministries, often transforming clerics into civil servants.[3] This chapter addresses the nationalization of Islamic institutions, and the following two chapters address the state-run legal and educational systems.

[1] Wael B. Hallaq, *An Introduction to Islamic Law* (New York: Cambridge University Press, 2009), 116.

[2] Ali Dessouki, "Official Islam and Political Legitimation in the Arab Countries," in Barbara Freyer Stowasser (ed.), *Islamic Impulse* (London: Croom Helm, 1987), 135–6.

[3] "In Islam, which does not recognize any priestly class, such a class in the form of Ulema or religious leaders in recent centuries has existed and continues to exert its influence. The separation of religion and state, in the Islamic context, therefore, actually means to neutralize the power and influence of a class which has no legitimate reason, on the basis of the Qur'an, to exist in the first place." Javaid Saeed, *Islam and Modernization: A Comparative Analysis of Pakistan, Egypt, and Turkey* (Westport, CT: Praeger Publishers, 1994), 49.

NATIONALIZATION OF RELIGIOUS ENDOWMENTS AND
APPROPRIATION OF RELIGIOUS LEGITIMACY

In Pakistan, starting in the 1960s under Ayub Khan (1958–69), the state brought religious foundations and major shrines under the administration and centralized control of the Department of Religious Endowments and the Advisory Council for Islamic Ideology.[4] In 1959, the West Pakistan Waqf Properties Ordinance enabled the government to take control of and manage shrines, mosques, and all waqf properties, including agricultural lands, shops, houses, and temporary lodging sites.[5] To extend the authority of the Department of Religious Endowments, similar acts were passed in 1961 and in 1976. These Auqaf acts were "intended to undercut the political power of both the hereditary *pir* families (the *sajjada-nishins*, or hereditary administrators) and the ulama."[6] This also included changing the significance of the shrines and of the saints affiliated with them.[7] Ayub redefined these Islamic institutions[8] not only by integrating their functions into the state administration but also by establishing state involvement in their management. To fully nationalize the shrines, the state had to first demonstrate that the Auqaf Department could maintain them better than the sajjada-nishins and then discredit the traditional religious functions of the sajjada-nishin as superfluous.[9] In other words, this was a direct attack on the traditional role of the Sufi leaders as well as a maneuver to replace[10] the sajjada-nishin and to redefine the shrines as "multifunctional religious and social welfare centers

---

[4] Farhat Haq, "Pakistan: A State for the Muslims or an Islamic State?" in Ali Riaz (ed.), *Religion and Politics in South Asia* (New York: Routledge, 2010), 125.

[5] S. Jamal Malik, "Waqf in Pakistan: Change in Traditional Institutions," *Die Welt des Islams,* New Series, 1990, Bd. 30, Nr. 1/4, 63–97, accessed May 20, 2011, http://www.jstor.org/stable/1571046, p. 72

[6] A pir is the title for a Sufi master, often translated *saint*. *Sajjada-nishin* signifies a holder of a shrine. Katherine Ewing, "The Politics of Sufism: Redefining the Saints of Pakistan," *The Journal of Asian Studies* 42.2 (1983): 251–68, accessed March 20, 2011, http://www.jstor.org/stable/2055113, p. 258. Ayub was highly influenced by the work of Javed Iqbal, the son of Mohammad Iqbal. Javed Iqbal emphasized in his book *Ideology of Pakistan* the imperative for abolishing the shrines and crippling the power of the sajjada-nishin; Mohammad Iqbal also criticized the shrine cults and the lower ranks of Islamic scholars. Malik, "Waqf in Pakistan," 74.

[7] Ewing, "The Politics of Sufism," 251.

[8] The Sufi shrines were the loci of folk piety, as they functioned to bring Islam to the masses, and were a powerful tool for unifying the people.

[9] Ewing, "The Politics of Sufism," 260.

[10] "The absolute authority of the saint or the holder was thus replaced by the more or less omnipotent but nevertheless anonymous governmental position of *Administrator Auqaf....* The difference, of course, was that his power was not theologically or religiously legitimized but only secularly and ideologically." Malik argues that this transformation was possible through the "de-mystification" of these traditional roles by the state. Malik, "Waqf in Pakistan," 75.

administered by the Auqaf Department."[11] In this way, Ayub (and the subsequent Bhutto government) chose to link his secular government to the religious authority of the Sufi establishment.[12] Sufism thus offered legitimacy to secular leaders defined as representatives of a Muslim democracy.

At the same time, Ayub consistently attempted to marginalize the Islamist opposition by propagating a modernist interpretation of Islam with a limited role in public life.[13] The transformation of clergy into civil servants was a determinant element of such a strategy. As religious institutions were nationalized under the growing power of the Auqaf Department, the clergy of the religious institutions was incorporated into the bureaucracy of the state as employees. The income, which the Auqaf Department accrued through nationalization, was returned to the foundations as salaries, but by holding the purse strings, the state protected its official ideological interests.[14] Moreover, the state controlled the content of the Friday sermons by regulating funds to the *khutaba* (preachers, who deliver the Friday sermon to the congregation) and the *a'imma* (prayer leaders) through the Auqaf Department. In other words, because the state controlled the disbursal of salary, the Friday sermons were guaranteed to conform to the state's agenda in the mosques, which were nationalized and tied to the Auqaf Department. In the same vein, Ayub established an Islamic research center in 1960 to propagate a state-sponsored modernist interpretation of Islam, thus appropriating Islamic legitimacy from the ulama.[15]

Although Ayub's reforms were an attempt to weaken the political influence of Islam by promoting a privatized modernist interpretation of the religion, the outcome was the opposite. Bhutto (1971–3), in office between Ayub (1958–65) and Zia-ul-Haq (1978–88), continued the policies of his predecessor and increased the nationalization by widening the Auqaf Department's sphere of influence.[16] It is then not surprising that Zia-ul-Haq's regime,

---

[11] Ewing, "The Politics of Sufism," 264. —— ✗

[12] "In the Sufi tradition, political leadership is clearly separated from spiritual authority." Ibid., 253.

[13] Haq, "Pakistan: A State for the Muslims or an Islamic State?" 133.

[14] Malik, "Waqf in Pakistan," 75.

[15] The Central Institute of Islamic Research was established in 1960; after the promulgation of the 1962 constitution, it was renamed the Islamic Research Institute. Haq, "Pakistan: A State for the Muslims or an Islamic State?" 134. The objectives of the Islamic Research Institute were "(1) to define the fundamentals of Islam 'in a rational and liberal manner and to emphasize, among others, the basic Islamic ideals of universal brotherhood, tolerance and social justice'; (2) to interpret Islam 'in such a way as to bring out its dynamic character in the context of the intellectual and scientific progress of the modern world.'" Saeed, *Islam and Modernization*, 95–6.

[16] Until Bhutto's term, nationalized endowments were organized at the provincial level, but they became more directly centralized under the administrator general of Auqaf for Pakistan. However, under Zia, the endowments were once again put under the control of the provincial government's administrator Auqaf. Malik, "Waqf in Pakistan," 77.

often presented as the turning point in the Islamization of the Pakistani state, actually maintained Ayub's nationalization of Islamic institutions and his policy toward the shrines. Zia, however, placed greater emphasis on the role of the Islamists and ulama by characterizing them (rather than the Sufis) as the traditional saints of the shrines.[17]

In the same vein, the nationalization of the *zakat* (almsgiving) system during the Zia era enabled the state's control over the funding of madrasas. Although such a measure did not allow the state to provide decent education (and did not really stop the private funding of madrasas), the Awqāf Department granted itself the right to change the curricula of religious schools with endowments.[18] Likewise, under Zia, the state began to appoint *imams* in rural mosques, thus bringing the rural clergy deeper under the civil servant structure of the Awqāf Department.[19]

Similarly, the Egyptian state appropriated religious legitimacy by nationalizing Islamic foundations and institutions of learning with the hope of weakening the social and political influence of the Muslim Brotherhood. Nasser's first steps to undermine the independence of Islamic institutions were the 1952 land reform laws. These laws put all waqf lands, which had grown since the time of Muhammad Ali (1805–48) to represent some 12 percent of all arable lands in Egypt, under the control of the new Ministry of Endowments (*Wizarat al-Awqāf*).[20] Because the revenues from the *awqāf* were used to fund religious institutions, the Ministry of Endowment also gained control over mosques, a practice continued from Nasser's time until the present.[21]

---

[17] The symbolic change brought by Zia was the reconstitution of the Islamic Ideological Council, comprising eminent personalities and scholars of Islamic jurisprudence. Saeed, *Islam and Modernization*, 100. The council serves as an advisory body to parliament on how to bring existing laws into conformity with Islamic injunctions and to ensure that parliament makes no law contrary to the injunctions of Islam. According to Article 30 (1) of the 1973 constitution, its function is "to make recommendations to Parliament and the Provincial Assemblies as to the ways and means of enabling and encouraging the Muslims of Pakistan to order their lives individually and collectively in all respects in accordance with the principles and concepts of Islam as enunciated in the Holy Qu'ran and Sunnah; (b) to advise ... on any question referred to the Council as to whether a proposed law is or is not repugnant to the Injunctions of Islam; (c) to make recommendations as to the measures for bringing existing laws into conformity with the Injunctions of Islam and the stages by which such measures should be brought into effect; and (d) to compile in a suitable form for the guidance of Parliament ..., such injunctions of Islam as can be given Legislative effect." http://www.pakistani.org/pakistan/constitution/part1.html, accessed January 2, 2014.
[18] Malik, "Waqf in Pakistan," 78.
[19] Ewing, "The Politics of Sufism," 252.
[20] Tamir Moustafa, "The Islamist Trend in Egyptian Law," Simons Papers in Security and Development, No. 2, School for International Studies, Simon Fraser University, Vancouver, May 2010.
[21] Saeed, *Islam and Modernization*, 120. Similarly, this occurred in Algeria in 1971, in Libya in 1973, and in the United Arab Emirates as late as 1980. Wael B. Hallaq, *An Introduction to Islamic Law* (Cambridge UK: Cambridge University Press, 2009), 138.

State control over mosques includes mosque officials, preachers, imams, muezzins (the ones who call believers to daily prayers), religious schools, religious foundations, and voluntary benevolent societies.[22] Additionally, the High Council for Islamic Preaching also decides the topics covered in the Friday sermons (khutbas) of state-controlled mosques.

State control over Al-Azhar was perhaps the most important symbol of the nationalization of Islam. Al-Azhar is one of the largest Islamic universities in the Sunni world, and it has played a key role in Islamic learning since the eighth century. Law 103 of 1961 reorganized the institution of Al-Azhar and placed it under the jurisdiction of the Ministry of Endowments. According to this law, the president of the republic controlled important appointments in the institution, including the appointment of the grand shaykh of Al-Azhar. Prior to the reforms, the shaykh was the highest authority over the ulama, that is, the graduates from the university (with students nominated by mosques all over Egypt). After the nationalization of Al-Azhar, the shaykh's role was reduced to a symbolic position and did not retain any actual authority over the ulama.[23] It is also important to note that despite the change in the grand shaykh of Al-Azhar's position, the role of the grand mufti of Egypt grew as part of the Ministry of Justice. The grand mufti heads the Egyptian Fatwa Office (*Dar al-Ifta' al-Miṣriyya*) and offers nonbinding legal opinions, but, most importantly, the grand mufti retains complete autonomy to issue fatwas.[24] Additionally, the High Council of Al-Azhar that oversees the university curriculum[25] was reorganized to include three government-appointed experts in university education and representatives from the ministries of Endowments, Education, Justice, and Treasury.

✕ As a symbol of this absorption of Islamic institutions into the state apparatus, Nasser chose the Al-Azhar pulpit to address Egyptians during the Tripartite Invasion of Egypt by Britain, France, and Israel in 1956.[26] In the

---

[22] Saeed, *Islam and Modernization*, 120.

[23] The mufti of the republic holds a symbolic role more than an active one. "The mufti is employed by the Ministry of Justice but is only vaguely related to the court system, primarily through the task of scrutinizing death sentences that have to be in conformity with the rules of *fiqh*. With the abolishment of the Shari'a courts in 1955, some minor tasks, previously the preserve of the chief *qadi*, were transferred to the State mufti, the most important of which today is the announcement of the beginning of the Islamic lunar months based on the observation of the new moon." Jakob Skovgaard-Petersen, *Defining Islam for the Egyptian State* (Leiden: Brill, 1997), 92.

[24] "Ali Gomaa Grand Mufti of Egypt," accessed March 10, 2011, http://www.aligomaa.net/faq.html.

[25] The curriculum of Al-Azhar was also reformed with the addition of three new departments: medicine, agriculture, and commerce. It is important to note the lack of any disciplines in the social sciences. Saeed, *Islam and Modernization*, 122.

[26] This particular performance became a staple of Nasser's political style: the use of both the Arab and Islamic elements of Egypt's heritage to mobilize support for his policies and bid for leadership domestically and regionally.

same vein, Nasser solicited the ulama for legal opinions (fatwas) on the entire range of his activities, in order to capitalize on the emotional appeal of Islam to the masses as well as to legitimize socialist ideology on the basis of Islam.[27] Like Nasser, Sadat made use of Al-Azhar to legitimize his politics. Through fatwas, Sadat justified multiple political acts, from overturning his predecessor's land reform policies to the *infitah* (economic liberalization) and the peace treaty with Israel. Although the religious establishment enjoyed greater freedom of expression under Sadat,[28] a network of district offices was established to select imams by granting preaching licenses for state mosques and monitoring their activities. Preachers of all private mosques were similarly required by the Ministry of Endowments to gain a license.[29]

Thus, Nasser and Sadat marginalized Islamists from the political arena through centralization and appropriation of religious legitimacy, and at the same time, they used Islam to legitimize foreign and domestic programs by calling on Islamic leaders to provide cultural, moral, and spiritual support.[30]

Unsurprisingly, the January 25, 2011, revolution opened a debate on the relationship between state and Islamic institutions. Al-Azhar has emerged as the major benefactor of the tensions between Muslim Brothers, Salafists, and the army (see Part III for more details). In less than a year after the ousting of Mubarak, the Islamic university was granted greater internal autonomy and its role in legislative work was officially inscribed in Article 4 of the short-lived 2012 constitution. This particular article is in discussion to be removed from the working draft of the new constitution, which is under way at the time of this writing. But it does not mean that Al Azhar will lose its role of mediator between Islamist and secular forces (see Chapters 10 and 11).[31]

In Tunisia, as part of the overall social and economic modernization, Bourguiba began to target Islamic institutions in the name of progress. This meant legal, educational, and land reforms brought the structures of national religious life under state control, which politically neutralized the ulama. Interestingly, the state also nationalized Jewish and Christian institutions, although they receive fewer subsidies than Islam.

The state appropriated public *hubus* (land holdings of Islamic foundations) in 1956 and abolished private hubus a year later.[32] As a result, one hundred fifty thousand acres of land, which was the main source of income

---

[27] Saeed, *Islam and Modernization*, 134.

[28] Consequentially, "The Shakyh al-Azhar, for instance, from time to time took positions in opposition to government policies, although, on the whole, he remained at the moderate modernist center of religious politics." Ibid., 125.

[29] Tamir Moustafa, "Conflict and Cooperation between the State and Religious Institutions in Contemporary Egypt," *International Journal of Middle East Studies* 32.1 (2000): 3–22.

[30] Saeed, *Islam and Modernization*, 135.

[31] See Nathan J. Brown, *Islam and Politics in the New Egypt* (Washington, DC: Carnegie Endowment for International Peace, April 2013).

[32] Phillip C. Naylor, *North Africa: A History from Antiquity to the Present* (Austin: University of Texas Press, 2009), 212.

for the ulama, became state property.[33] Educational reform was also a central component of the state's modernizing effort. This was done by eliminating private Islamic schools and depriving the ulama of their traditional educating role.

Throughout the 1980s, Ben Ali established the Faculty of Theology as the new center of Islamic learning, directed and supervised by the state[34] to replace Zaytuna University, which was the Tunisian equivalent to Al-Azhar.[35] As a result of the Jasmine Revolution and the political victory of the Islamists, Zaytuna officially reopened as an Islamic university in May 2012. Classes began slowly, given a dearth of books and other materials, but are expected to form an important front in the government's struggle against religious extremism. Minister of Religious Affairs Noureddine Khadami expressed his hope that "if we succeed in establishing sound Shari'a sciences, we will ensure that the country will be fine, with citizenship realized and human rights respected."[36]

It is important to note that Islam is not the only religion under state control. Since Bourguiba, the government has also placed and paid clerics of Jewish and Christian faith. This status has not changed since the Jasmine Revolution. The government is responsible for security in synagogues and has subsidized maintenance for some. It pays the grand rabbi's salary, and government employees maintain Jewish cemeteries. All Christian religious organizations established prior to independence in 1956 were officially recognized by the government, and fourteen churches were recognized to serve all sects in the country.

Interestingly, this state acknowledgment of other faiths appears to be a breach in the hegemonic status of Islam. However, the small size of the religious minorities has not challenged the supremacy of Islam under either Bourguiba or Ben Ali, or after the Jasmine Revolution (see Chapter 11).

Bourguiba also established a Ministry of Religious Affairs to oversee religious buildings that became state properties and clerics who became state employees. Additionally, one of the tasks of the Ministry of Religious Affairs has been to organize the training of imams and preachers at the post-1989 Zaytuna University under the Institute of Shari'a.[37] Ben Ali also

[33] Marion Boulby, "The Islamic Challenge: Tunisia since Independence," *Third World Quarterly* 10.2 (1988): 590–614, accessed May 10, 2011, from the Jstor database, available at the Jstor website: http://www.jstor.org/stable/3992658, p. 592.

[34] Susan Waltz, "Islamist Appeal In Tunisia," *Middle East Journal* 40.4 (1986): 651–70, accessed May 10, 2011, from the Jstor database, available at the Jstor website: http://www.jstor.org/stable/4327425, p. 660.

[35] Zaytuna University was reinstated as an educational university in 1989.

[36] "Zitouna Mosque to resume Religious Teaching," Magharebia, April 18, 2012, http://magharebia.com/en_GB/articles/awi/features/2012/04/18/feature-02, accessed September 17 2013.

[37] Malika Zeghal, "Religious Education in Egypt and Tunisia," in Osama Abi-Mershed (ed.), *Trajectories of Education in the Arab World: Legacies and Challenges* (New York: Routledge, 2007), 117.

appointed several well-known laymen to the Higher Islamic Council and made provisions for the council to deal with matters of student and faculty curricula.[38] According to the Council's website, it is "obligatorily consulted on the programs of the Zaytuna University and religious teaching in the schools."[39] However, the National Constituent Assembly's Commission on Constitutional Bodies voted against enshrining the Council in the draft Tunisian constitution in April 2013.[40]

BA'ATHIST PURGE OF ISLAMIC INSTITUTIONS

Although in the earlier stages of the Iraqi Ba'th regime the Shi'i endowments remained independent, the state increasingly controlled and repressed Shi'i clerics and institutions, especially after 1968, in order to quell any possibility of uprising.[41]

Part of this repression included shutting down the Kufa University in Najaf along with seizing all of the school's funds.[42] Starting in 1969, the state confiscated religious endowments and in 1978 took control over Shi'i revenues.[43] Similarly, the widespread nationalization of private companies profoundly affected the status of Shi'i clerics because most of these businesses provided funds to religious establishments.[44] By the time Saddam Hussein stepped into the presidency in 1979, the state controlled the Shi'i waqf and madrasa.[45]

The Ba'thist government shut down Twelver Shi'i[46] institutions, restricted religious publications through strict censorship, authorized alcohol sales in Shi'i shrine cities, repressed activist ayatollahs, and put down demonstrations by force.[47] However, the Western political culture of Saddam's Ba'th party largely ignored the Shi'i seminars (*ḥawzas*[48]), and Saddam established a compromise with the Shi'i clergy by allowing the observance of rituals and

---

[38] L. B. Ware, "Ben Ali's Constitutional Coup in Tunisia," *Middle East Journal* 42.4 (1988): 598–9, accessed May 10, 2011, from the Jstor database, available at the Jstor website: http://www.jstor.org/stable/4327834.

[39] "The Higher Islamic Council of the Republic of Tunisia," *Presidency of the Government,* accessed June 13, 2013, http://www.pm.gov.tn/pm/article/article.php?id=212&lang=en.

[40] "Tunisia opposition thwarts Ennahda efforts to constitutionalise Islamic Council," *Middle East Online,* April 3, 2013, accessed June 13, 2013, http://www.middle-east-online.com/english/?id=57891.

[41] Lawrence E. Cline, "The Prospects of the Shi'a Insurgency Movement in Iraq," *Journal of Conflict Studies* 20.2 (2000).

[42] Ibid.

[43] Efraim Karsh, *Saddam Hussein: A Political Biography* (New York: Grove Press, 2002), 142.

[44] Cline, "The Prospects of the Shi'a Insurgency Movement in Iraq," 2000.

[45] Yitzhak Nakash, *The Shi'is of Iraq* (Princeton, NJ: Princeton University Press, 2003), 271.

[46] Twelver Shi'as believe that there have been twelve imams since the death of Ali and his two sons, and that the redeemer (the Mahdi) will be the twelfth imam returned to save mankind. Approximately 85 percent of Shi'is believe in Twelver Shi'a.

[47] Juan Cole, *Sacred Space and Holy War: The Politics, Culture, and History of Shiite Islam* (London: I. B. Taurus 2002), 179.

[48] A *ḥawza* is a religious seminar, a traditional Islamic institution of higher learning.

festivals.[49] At the same time, Saddam made it clear he would not tolerate the use of religion in politics, especially political dissidence against the Ba'thist regime. In practice, Saddam used the dual tactics of *tarḥīb and targhīb*, as Iraqis would say, which meant that, "he terrorized with one hand and offered rewards with the other."[50] In other words, while harshly repressing Shi'i opposition, Saddam offered political and economic concessions such as funding for refurbishing shrines and mosques.[51] Moreover, he showed greater deference to the ayatollahs and tried to win them over.[52] However, he did not succeed in acquiring the support of the Marja Ayatollah al-'Uzma Abu al-Qasim al-Khu'i (1899–1992) or that of Sayyid Muhammad Baqir al-Sadr (1935–80), the two highest religious authorities who viewed relations with the regime as *haram* (forbidden)[53]; as a result, Saddam condemned Sadr to execution in 1980.

Yet, this accommodating policy changed with the advent of the Islamic Revolution in Iran and the Iran-Iraq War (1980–8).[54] Thus, with the onset of the Iran-Iraq War, the compromise between the state and the Shi'a clergy ended.[55] Additionally, in 1994, following the First Gulf War (1990–1), Saddam started a "faith campaign" to promote Islam in the hopes of capitalizing on the growing anti-Western sentiment in the Middle East. This faith campaign entailed the inclusion of mandatory Islamic education in school curricula, with the goal of unifying the Iraqi nation (see Chapter 6).

After the fall of Saddam in 2003, the Shi'i religious institutions engaged in intense political activity, especially in the intellectual hubs of Najaaf and Karbala. Shi'a clergy quickly moved to establish governance in these two cities, blocking the ability of American troops to influence Iraqi politics there. In 2003, members of the Shi'i clergy organized neighborhood security, garbage collection, firefighting, jobs, health care, and financial assistance to the needy, among other government-style projects.[56] The relative independence of the hawza under the Ba'thist rule was mainly

---

[49] Hanna Batatu, "Iraq's Underground Shi'a Movements: Characteristics, Causes and Prospects," *Middle East Journal* 35.4 (1981): 578–94, accessed June 23, 2011, from the Jstor database, available at the Jstor website: http://www.jstor.org/stable/4326306, p. 591.

[50] Ibid.

[51] Lawrence E. Cline, "The Prospects of the Shi'a Insurgency Movement in Iraq," *Journal of Conflict Studies* 20.2 (Fall 2000), accessed January 4, 2014, http://journals.hil.unb.ca/index. php/jcs/article/view/4311/4924.

[52] Anna Batatu, "Iraq's Underground Shi'a Movements," *Middle East Journal* 35.4 (Autumn 1981): 578–594.

[53] Ibid., 592.

[54] Søren Schmidt, *Shi'a-Islamist Political Actors in Iraq: Who are They and What do They Want?* (Copenhagen: Danish Institute for International Studies, DIIS 3, 2008), 11.

[55] Ibid., 12.

[56] Terrill, "Nationalism, Sectarianism, and the Future of the US Presence in Post-Saddam Iraq," 20.

due to independent financial support from *khums*[57] and from pilgrims from outside Iraq. This independence ultimately allowed the Shiʻi clerical organizations to regulate the social and public order in the holy cities and to reestablish themselves as completely independent religious organizations.

SUPPRESSION OF RELIGIOUS ENDOWMENTS $-legacy)$

Islamic institutions were also nationalized in Turkey, not only by integrating the clerical establishment into the administrative structure of the state but also by appointing laymen into positions that were once the distinctive functions of the clergy. In other words, the state melded religious authorities and laymen into the state institutions in charge of Islam. The Turkish government nationalized religious property under the Ministry of Religious Affairs and Pious Foundations (*Şeriye ve Evkaf Vekaleti*), which came under the direct authority of the prime minister. Thus, in a seemingly contradictory move, Ataturk eradicated Islamic references from social and public life and strongly embedded Islam within state institutions. On one hand, the office of the Şeyhülislam (the mufti at the head of the Ottoman religious hierarchy) was closed; the Sheikh ul-Islam, chief expounder of the holy law was dismissed from the cabinet[58]; the Latin alphabet replaced Arabic; Arabic and Persian influences were removed from the Turkish language[59]; and all religious sects and titles such as sheikh, dervish, or mausoleum guard were abolished. In 1925, religious orders and societies were suppressed and members of the clergy were forced to wear a uniform dress mandated by the state, thus physically minimizing their social presence and excluding Islam from the public sphere.[60] On the other hand, the state took strong control over all Islamic institutions and personnel.

Such a policy separated the official bastions of Islam from the Ottoman polity, and it was intended not so much to separate religion and state but to minimize religious influence in politics and bring religious legitimacy under state control.[61] Following the same logic, the madrasas were shut down (until 1949) while religious schools were incorporated into the unified

---

[57] Khums literally means one-fifth and is likened to a tithe. It represents the amount of money out of one's total income a Shiʻi believer owes on a yearly basis to his marjaʻ (the cleric to whom he makes spiritual allegiance, hence obeying his rulings and decisions).

[58] Edward Mead Earle, "The New Constitution of Turkey," *Political Science Quarterly*, 40.1 (1925): 86.

[59] Mustafa Kocak, "Islam and National Law in Turkey," in Jan Michiel Otto (ed.), *Shariʻa Incorporated* (Amsterdam: Leiden University Press, 2010), 244.

[60] Saeed, *Islam and Modernization*, 160.

[61] Carter Vaughn Findley, *Turkey, Islam, Nationalism, and Modernity: A History, 1789–2007* (New Haven, CT: Yale University Press, 2010), 252. Kocak, "Islam and National Law in Turkey," 242.

system of national education, and religious instruction was removed from the curriculum in 1930.[62] Additionally, in contrast with the 1961 constitution, the 1982 constitution placed education, instruction of religion, and ethics under state supervision and control.[63] In this way, the state deprived Islam of the role it once occupied in the public space and retained control over religion and religious institutions. For example, in 1997, with the military coup pushing out the Islamist-led coalition, religious schools (*imam hatip*) were closed to middle school students and religious education became optional for high school students.[64] Interestingly, the March 2012 education law introduced by the AKP party undid the 1997 reform by reopening the option of religious education for middle school students.[65]

[62] Ibid., 244.
[63] Ibid., 248.
[64] Andrew Finkel, "What's 4+4+4?" *International Herald Tribune*, March 23, 2012, accessed July 14, 2012, http://latitude.blogs.nytimes.com/2012/03/23/turkeys-education-reform-bill-is-about-playing-politics-with-pedagogy/.
[65] It also extended the compulsory years of education from eight to twelve. Wendy Zeldin, "Turkey: Controversial Education Reform Legislation Passed," *The Law Library of Congress*, April 17, 2012, accessed July 14, 2012, http://www.loc.gov/lawweb/servlet/lloc_news?disp3_l205403094_text.

5

Islam in the Legal System

The integration of the waqf and maddrasa into the new state system irremediably changed the status of religious authorities. Additionally, the content and methods of legal-religious work were deeply transformed by the building of new institutions. In other words,[1] a radical transformation of Shari'a occurred through its codification as well as its reduction to mostly family law. The consequence has been the hybridization of secular and religious references in civil legislation and the shaping of public virtues by Islamic references, which has contributed to the resurgence of apostasy and blasphemy cases in the past three decades.

CODIFICATION AND REDUCTION OF SHARI'A

With the collapse of the Ottoman Empire, Shari'a courts in the new nation-states were eliminated and replaced by secular legislation in almost all aspects of social, economic, and penal domains.

In Turkey, Shari'a courts were dismantled upon independence in conjunction with the abolition of the caliphate, and all religious courts were subordinated to the Ministry of Justice.[2] In 1926, a legal codification based on different European models replaced traditional Islamic jurisprudence.[3] In the Maghreb, Morocco, Tunisia, and Algeria adopted the French legal model, which helped maximize state control over the legal system upon independence.[4]

---

[1] "State sovereignty without a State-manufactured law is no sovereignty at all." Wael B. Hallaq, *An Introduction to Islamic Law* (Cambridge, UK: Cambridge University Press, 2009), 169.
[2] Edward Mead Earle, "The New Constitution of Turkey," *Political Science Quarterly* 40.1 (1925): 85.
[3] Javaid Saeed, *Islam and Modernization: A Comparative Analysis of Pakistan, Egypt, and Turkey* (Westport, CT: Praeger Publishers, 1994), 160.
[4] Ann Elizabeth Mayer, "Reform of Personal Status Laws in North Africa," *Middle East Journal* 49.3 (1995): 432–46, accessed June 23, 2011, from the Jstor database, available at the Jstor website: http://www.jstor.org/stable/4328833, p. 433.

In Egypt, soon after Nasser's revolution, under Law 462 of 1955, Shari'a courts along with all *milliya* (Christian ecclesiastical and Jewish rabbinical communal courts) were abolished. In Iraq, in 1970, Saddam Hussein stripped the Shari'a courts of their power and incorporated the personal status courts into the regular court system while maintaining the 1959 Iraqi Law of Personal Status, which is based on Islamic law and continues in post-Saddam Iraq. The legal system in Pakistan is a hybrid of English common law and Islamic law. While Islamic law was largely restricted to the sphere of personal status, with Zia's Islamicization program in 1978, a parallel Shari'a court system was created and significant amendments to the penal code as well as anti-blasphemy laws were introduced.

Generally speaking, the transformation of the legal system was the culmination of a process that started during the colonial period, when most of the Shari'a courts underwent restructuring as their jurisdiction was increasingly limited.[5] As a result, the only domain remaining under the influence of Islam was family law. Under colonial rule, Islamic personal status legislation was preserved for the simple reason that it was not perceived as a threat to the colonial powers.[6] This reduction of the Shari'a domain went hand in hand with its codification. In the Islamic tradition, Shari'a refers to principles from which the Islamic jurisconsultus provides concrete rules or laws (*fiqh*). This meant that, for centuries, legal work was not codified but was in continuous flux through the work of various muftis (legal scholars) and qadis (judges). This nonwritten aspect of Shari'a also granted social influence and political independence to the ulama, who were the only ones who could issue concrete rulings based on Shari'a.[7] The colonial powers drastically changed Shari'a by demanding that religious authorities put it in writing, to include it as civil law in the legal system. As a result, *talaq* (divorce); *khul* (marital dissolution); *ila* and *zihar* (child custody and family maintenance); but also estates, bequests, and succession became inscribed in codes. In this regard, the postcolonial rulers inherited the situation created in the colonial period. It is important to note that the family codes reforms do not obey the traditional procedures of Islamic jurisprudence. Instead, these changes are based within the Shari'a framework, mostly referring to the principles of *ijtihād* (interpretation), and *talfiq* (amalgamation), employed by the judges to justify reforms for the sake of public welfare.

Parallel to the reduction and codification of Shari'a, the new state rulers secularized most of the legal system by changing the court system, penal code, commercial code, and so forth. For example, the Turkish Penal Code

[5] Hallaq, *An Introduction to Islamic Law*, 101.
[6] Ibid., 115.
[7] Ibid., 120.

(1929) was based on the German Penal Code, and the Code of Bankruptcy was adopted from the Swiss Federal Code.[8] However, despite this secularization, or rather because of it, as shown in Chapter 3, most states retained Islam in the constitution as a symbolic reference within the new legal and political order. As a result, two provisions that were only implicit in the Ottoman constitution of 1876 became explicit.[9] The first provision was the proclamation of Islam as the religion of the state. The second one was that the head of state should be a Muslim. As a general rule, in countries where Islam is constitutionally declared the official religion, Shari'a is also implied or explicitly stated as "a" source or "the" source of the laws. As the case of Egypt illustrates (at least until the January 25, 2011, revolution), these Islamic provisions had little effect on constitutional and political practice in the sense that they did not restrict or confine legislation within a strictly Islamic framework.

SHARI'A AS "A" OR "THE" SOURCE OF LEGISLATION

As already presented in Chapter 3, Article 2 in Egypt's constitution has been a source of conflict with regard to Islamic principles in the constitution. In 1985, the Supreme Constitutional Court (SCC) ruled that Islamic provisions must be incorporated into positive state law for judges to apply them, and judges cannot refuse to enforce legal provisions, even if they consider that they violate principles of Islamic law.[10] In the same decision, the SCC decided that the amendment of Article 2 had no retroactive effect; that is, only laws adopted after 1980 have to be consistent with Shari'a although eventually preexisting legislation would have to become concordant with Shari'a.

In a second ruling in 1993 on Article 2, the SCC made a distinction between two kinds of sources for Shari'a principles: definite[11] and indefinite. Indefinite sources make their corresponding principles relative, flexible, and dynamic, thus allowing for *ijtihād*. Because the space occupied by the definite norms of Shari'a is limited, the "majority of Shari'a rules would

[8] Mustafa Kocak, "Islam and National Law in Turkey," in Jan Michiel Otto (ed.), *Shari'a Incorporated* (Amsterdam: Leiden University Press, 2010), 244.

[9] The Ottoman constitution of 1876 was the model for constitutional development in the new Middle Eastern and North African states.

[10] "Personal Status Laws in Egypt: FAQ," *Promotion of Women's Rights Project*, accessed June 11, 2011, http://www2.gtz.de/dokumente//gtz2010–0139en-faq-personal-status-law-egypt.pdf.

[11] These are the only ones for which interpretative reasoning (*ijtihād*) is not authorized because they possess an unshaken chain of precedents that are not debatable. Since they embody the foundations of Islamic Shari'a, they admit no interpretation and no modification.

be derived from its indefinite norms."[12] Thus, almost all principles of Shari'a identified by the Supreme Constitutional Court so far have been considered relative, meaning the People's Assembly is entitled to codify and adapt their content in accordance with the current needs of Egyptian society.[13] Moreover, the SCC clearly ruled that other sources may be employed and consulted in the legislative process.[14] As a result, the constitutional provision of Shari'a in Article 2 did not have any real consequences for the legislation, which remained secular in content and in spirit. Case in point: Egyptian civil and penal codes are ultimately derived from French codes, and Egypt has been moving toward the Anglo-American code with regard to commercial and corporate laws.

Since the January 25, 2011, revolution, however, the status of Article 2 has been reopened for discussion in the Constituent Assembly's debates. As already described in Chapter 3, despite the ongoing dispute over the wording of Article 2, it has remained the same since the 1971 constitution. In the short-lived 2012 constitution, a clause was added stipulating that the opinions of the Al-Azhar ulama would be solicited in matters relating to Shari'a, although some Salafi groups had pushed for Al-Azhar to work in a binding legislative capacity.[15] The final wording of Article 4 in the 2012 constitution states:

Al-Azhar is an encompassing independent Islamic institution, with exclusive autonomy over its own affairs, responsible for preaching Islam, theology and the Arabic language in Egypt and the world. Al-Azhar Senior Scholars are to be consulted in matters pertaining to Islamic law. The post of Al-Azhar Grand Sheikh is independent and cannot be dismissed. The method of appointing the Grand Sheikh from among members of the Senior Scholars is to be determined by law. The State shall ensure sufficient funds for Al-Azhar to achieve its objectives. All of the above is subject to law regulations.[16]

This new constitutional provision opened the possibility of a greater influence of Islamic Law on secular politics. Due to the constitution's suspension, Al Azhar did not have time to use its new power, as it was pulled in different directions by "a multiplicity of voices and streams both

---

[12] Brown et al., "Inscribing the Islamic Shari'a in Arab Constitutional Law," 74.
[13] "Personal Status Laws in Egypt: FAQ."
[14] Brown et al., "Inscribing the Islamic Shari'a in Arab Constitutional Law," 74.
[15] On the other hand, at least in the short term, granting jurisdiction to Al-Azhar may not benefit the Salafi goal because Grand Sheikh Ahmed al-Tayyeb has made moves to ensure the independence of the institution from the state as well as from any Salafi or Muslim Brotherhood influence. Noha El-Hennawy, "In battle over Shari'a, Salafis lay groundwork for the future," *Egypt Independent*, July 11, 2012, accessed July 14, 2012, http://www.egypt-independent.com/news/battle-over-sharia-salafis-lay-groundwork-future-0.
[16] *Egypt's Draft Constitution Translated 2012*, accessed January 21, 2013, http://www.egypt-independent.com/news/egypt-s-draft-constitution-translated.

within and outside the institution."[17] One example of the new political role of Al Azhar was illustrated in 2013 by the discussion of the law on Islamic bonds (*sukuk*). Al Azhar exercised its new power by expressing its concern that the law was un-Islamic.[18] The Shura Council heeded these reservations before the sukuk bill was approved. Mention of Al Azhar's role in legislation has disappeared from the revised draft of the constitution released in November 2013.

Although the constitution in Pakistan does not directly reference Islam as the official source of legislation, it is often understood that the constitution "endorses [an] Islamic principle of justice."[19] At the same time, Part 9 of the 1973 constitution states, "All existing laws shall be brought in conformity with the Injunctions of Islam as laid down in the Holy Qur'an and Sunnah."[20] This article suggests that even though Islamic law may not be official Pakistani law, no law can contradict Islamic law either. Furthermore, one important Pakistani document, the Objectives Resolution of 1949,[21] states that "Muslims shall be enabled to order their lives in the individual and collective spheres in accordance with the teachings and requirements of Islam as set out in the Holy Qur'an and Sunnah."[22] In other words, the Islamic principles and the legal system, which does not endorse Islam directly, are constantly held in tension.

The consequence has been the increasing influence of Islamic laws on social life. For example, according to Article 31 – chapter 2 of the constitution, the state must enable Muslims to carry out their religious duties, including through direct promotion of Qur'anic studies and the study of the Arabic language.[23] Additionally, Article 37 prohibits the drinking of alcohol for Muslims. Article 40 requires the preservation of "fraternal relations" with other Muslim countries.[24]

---

[17] Nathan J. Brown, "Post-Revolutionary Al-Azhar," *The Carnegie Papers* (Washington, DC: Carnegie Endowment for International Peace, 2011), 11.

[18] "Sukuk Law in State of Flux until Al-Azhar Review," *Egypt Independent*, April 4, 2013, accessed June 17, 2013, http://www.egyptindependent.com/news/sukuk-law-state-flux-until-al-azhar-review.

[19] Martin Lau, *The Role of Islam in the Legal System of Pakistan* (Leiden: Brill, 2006), 95–119.

[20] Martin Lau, "Shari'a and national law in Pakistan," in Jan Michiel Otto (ed.), *Shari'a Incorporated* (Amsterdam: Leiden University Press, 2010), 411.

[21] The Objectives Resolution of 1949 was adopted by the Constituent Assembly of Pakistan and stated that while Pakistan would be influenced by Western models, the state would also fit within the parameters of Islam.

[22] Lau, "Shari'a and national law in Pakistan," 411.

[23] Ibid., 393.

[24] Ibid.

These Islamic bases of the constitution have influenced the content of the criminal codes and family law (see next section on civil law). Article 228 establishes the Council of Islamic Ideology (CII), which acts as an advisory board for Islamic legal issues[25] and drafts Islamic alternatives to laws declared by the federal Shari'a courts to be in contradiction with Islamic principles. One of these redraftings included the Criminal Law Act of 1997 that implemented Islamic provisions for murder and assault.[26] However, a more progressive CII under Mohammad Khalid Masud (2004–10) hardly used the law, which is at the time of this writing very much dormant. In the same logic that elevates the Islamic principles of the state above the rule of secular law, the Enforcement of Shari'a Act of 1991 protects the government from review by a judicial body.

In post-Saddam Iraq, one of the crucial points of contention is Islam's role in the legal system and its subsequent influence on social life. During the preparation of the 2005 constitution, the main Shi'i Islamic group, the Supreme Council for the Islamic Revolution in Iraq (SCIRI), pushed for Islam to be a basic or fundamental source of legislation, while Kurdish proposals attempted to change the language so that Islam would be considered a source of legislation. Many secularists, women's and human rights groups also argued that Shari'a does not address all aspects of modern civil law. Thus, there was a question of how dependent on Islamic principles Iraqi laws would be, and to what extent modern civil law would be incorporated into the new constitution.

The first public draft of the constitution, published in the Iraqi newspaper *Al Mada*,[27] did not state that Islam would be a source of legislation. However, subsequent pressure by Shi'a Islamist parties led by the SCIRI resulted in a text representing far greater commitment to Islam. A 2005 draft from the Constitutional Committee included passages that would be the foundation of the final Article 2, specifying that Islam was the official religion of Iraq, and that "it is the basic source of legislation. No law may be enacted that contradicts [Islam's] tenets and provisions." However, the U.S. government expressed strong concern over the definition of Islam as "the" basic source of legislation rather than "a" source of legislation because of the fear that it could lead to an Islamic state with no room for secular law. Proposals by Kurdish groups went as far as removing the term *basic* in the text so that Islam would be defined as "a source of legislation," and new suggestions also included "the first source," "a main source," and "a source among sources." The version

---

[25] Ibid., 411.
[26] Ibid., 412.
[27] *Al Mada Newspaper*, June 30, 2005, http://www.almadapaper.com/sub/06-426/6.pdf.

ultimately agreed upon was that of the Kurds, defining Shariʿa as "a" source of legislation, only after Grand Ayatollah Sistani approved of the wording.[28]

SHARIʿA AND CIVIL LAW

The evolution of the Egyptian family code encapsulates the hybrid and contradictory nature of civil law under most of modern states. First, it reveals the lack of nonconfessional or civil marriage and the use of selective *ijtihād*; but at the same time it shows successive procedural reforms to improve women's equality with men.

Egyptian personal status law originates from the dominant Hanafi School of jurisprudence,[29] which was the official school during the Ottoman Empire.[30] Although the law for personal status is deemed civil, it refers to Shariʿa as a legal basis for Muslims, and to the comparable religious principles as the civil law for each of the non-Muslim communities, which had been formerly applied by *milliya* tribunals. In other words, the fact that matters of personal status have been transferred to civil courts and removed from the Islamic authorities does not mean that a secular civil status exists in Egypt.[31] Therefore, no legitimate civil act is possible if two persons of different religions or of no declared religion want to marry. If the two spouses do not belong to the same denomination or religious tradition, the general law in Egypt, which is the Muslim personal status law, is *de facto* applied. It is, therefore, not surprising that interreligious marriages are very rare.

In the case of marriage between two persons of the same faith who are not Muslims, such as Copts or other Christians, according to the old *milliya* system their marriage is registered as a religious act within the court of their religious institutions (which are subject to administrative

---

[28] A. S. Deeks and M. D. Burton, "Iraq's Constitution: A Drafting History," *Cornell International Law Journal* 40 (2007): 1–88. N. Feldman and R. Martinez, "Constitutional Politics and Text in the New Iraq: An Experiment in Islamic Democracy," *Fordham Law Review* 75.2 Article 20, 2006.

[29] The Hanafi School, currently in use in Egypt, Pakistan, India, China, Turkey, Balkans, and the Caucus, is one of four schools of Sunni Islamic jurisprudence. The other three are the Shafiʿi School – Indonesia, Malaysia, Brunei, Dar as Salam, Yemen; the Hanbali School – Saudi Arabia; and the Maliki School – dominant in North Africa (Morocco, Algeria, Tunisia, Libya), West Africa (including Mauritania), the United Arab Emirates, and Kuwait. The Jaʿfari School is used by Shiʿa-dominated Iran.

[30] "Personal Status Laws in Egypt: FAQ."

[31] George N. Sfeir, "The Abolition of Confessional Jurisdiction in Egypt: The Non-Muslim Courts," *Middle East Journal* 10:3 (1956): 248–56.

regulations and are under the review of the State Council and of the Supreme Constitutional Court).[32]

Civil laws have been repeatedly amended through state initiatives, mostly to improve women's status.[33] In 1920 and 1929, two laws were adopted to enlarge the grounds upon which a woman could initiate divorce. These included personal harm, failure to provide maintenance, absence of the husband, condemnation of the husband to jail, and serious or incurable defect or disease – all reasons already recognized in the Islamic tradition. In practice, however, divorce by a woman remained very difficult under the personal status laws, which were biased in favor of the man. In 2000, a major modification was made with the introduction of the Khul Law, after an intense campaign of women's rights organizations.[34] Under this Khul Law, a woman can now obtain a divorce without her husband's consent and without having to prove harm, if she returns the dowry.[35] Although the Khul Law is allowed according to traditional Islamic jurisprudence, Salafi and other conservative Muslim groups have found ways to criticize and challenge it on religious and legal grounds. As a result, in 2002, Article 20 of the amended Personal Status Law (*El-Khole'* Article) was brought before the Supreme Constitutional Court, but the court ruled the article constitutional on December 26, 2002.

Thus, while the 1929 reforms were based on the doctrine of *talfiq* (selection),[36] the adoption of the Khul Law as late as 2000 reflects the malleability of the Islamic framework, which is often readjusted in the name of the public interest or under specific political pressures.

Similarly, in Iraq, the personal status code is not constitutionally mandated to accord with Shariʿa, but the Iraqi Personal Status Law of 1959 maintained the Islamic framework and is largely based on religious sources. The first monarchical constitution of Iraq in 1925 stated in Article 76, "The Shara [Shariʿa] courts alone shall be competent to deal with actions relating to the personal status of Moslems and actions relating to the administration of Waqf foundations."[37] However, the interim

---

[32] "Personal Status Laws in Egypt: FAQ."

[33] Ibid.

[34] Amira Mashhour, "Islamic law and gender equality: Could there be a common ground?; A study of divorce and polygamy in Shariʿa law and contemporary legislation in Tunisia and Egypt," *Human Rights Quarterly* 27.2 (2005): 562–96.

[35] Ibid., 584 and 595. As much as the Khul Law has been praised as innovative, it is worth pointing out that the rights offered to women in the new law were already granted in classical Islamic jurisprudence.

[36] These reforms allowed an individual to go outside of his own personal school of law and select a resolution to his specific issue from the other three schools of law.

[37] "Constitution of the Kingdom of Iraq," *Global Justice Project: Iraq*, accessed March 19, 2011, http://www.gjpi.org/wp-content/uploads/iraqiconst19250321.htm.

constitution of 1970 in use during Saddam Hussein's regime dropped the stipulation that personal status must be governed in accordance with Islamic law; it refers to Islam only once to declare in Article 4, "Islam is the religion of the State."[38] At the same time, Saddam Hussein maintained the Iraqi Law of Personal Status of 1959, which applies to all Iraqis (Shi'a and Sunni Muslims alike) except Christian and Jewish minorities. As a result, it unified the personal status law for Sunnis and Shi'a, while the Christian and Jewish minorities were allowed to keep their own separate systems, once again in concordance with the historical *milliya* system. Additionally, despite its basis in Shari'a, the 1959 law removed authority from the Sunni and Shi'a religious authorities and stripped them of their oversight of personal status courts,[39] which were then integrated into the regular court system.

The main benefactors of the Iraqi Personal Status Law since its instatement have been women. The marriage age was raised to eighteen, polygamy was abolished, and marriage without the woman's consent was forbidden.[40] Women were also granted additional rights in divorce cases. Although the law is not entirely gender-neutral (there are no female judges, for example), the shift of power from Shari'a courts to personal status courts greatly improved the lives of women in Iraq, especially women subject to stricter interpretations of Islamic law under religious authorities, and these legal provisions have been maintained in post-Saddam Iraq. *De facto* compliance, however, is complicated by several issues. First, the Revolutionary Command Council (RCC) makes "conservative interpretations of Islamic norms, patriarchal traditions, economic factors and tribal customs which place the most severe constraints on women's rights and autonomy."[41] In the same vein, Muslim women are forbidden to marry outside their faith. The civil code does not address *mut'a,* or temporary marriages,[42] a Shi'i practice

---

[38] "Iraqi Constitution," *Global Justice Project: Iraq*, accessed March 19, 2011, http://www. gjpi.org/library/primary/iraqi-constitution/.

[39] Nathan J. Brown, "Debating Islam in Post-Baathist Iraq," *Policy Outlook: Democracy and Rule of Law Project,* Carnegie Endowment for International Peace, accessed March 21, 2011, http://www.carnegieendowment.org/files/PO13.Brown.FINAL2.pdf#search='Iraqi% 2C%20personal%20status%20law, p. 5.

[40] Layla Al-Zubaidi, "The Struggle over Women's Rights and the Personal Status Law: A Test Case for Iraqi Citizenship?" *Orient* 52.2 (2011): 39–51

[41] Iraq Legal Development Project, "The Status of Women in Iraq: Update to the Assessment of Iraq's *De jure* and *De facto* Compliance with International Legal Standards," 2006, accessed January 23, 2013, http://apps.americanbar.org/rol/publications/iraq_status_of_women_ update_2006.pdf, p. 106.

[42] Mut'a marriage (also transliterated as *mutah*) is a form of temporary marriage sanctioned under Shi'i law. Mut'a marriage must have a specified time period (*mudda*) and there must be a payment made to the woman (a dowry). The woman must be eligible to marry. If these conditions are met, the man and woman are permitted to have sexual relations for the period of the mut'a. See Satyoki Koundinya, "The Concept of Mutah Marriage: Is it a Social Evil?"

reinstated after Saddam's downfall.[43] Troublesome reports emerged in 2006 of the murders (by their families) of two women after being involved in a mut'a.[44]

Although the Madjala, the 1956 Tunisian code, does not constitutionally state that laws are to be interpreted according to Islamic jurisprudence, it symbolically made reference to Islamic principles.[45] It was at the time revolutionary as it introduced dramatic reforms,[46] including prohibiting of polygyny (unprecedented except in Turkey),[47] banning extrajudicial divorce,[48] and allowing either spouse to divorce without proof of fault.[49] Despite this equality in terms of divorce, some disparities between genders remained in the 1956 code that will be amended later on. For example, a 1993 law provided more rights and autonomy to women by abolishing the requirement of obedience to husbands and introduced the possibility for wives to share with their husband's part of the financial burden of the family.[50]

Under Ben Ali, the liberalization of the family code continued, notably with the 1993 amendment that gave women the right to pass on Tunisian nationality to their children even if the husband is not Tunisian (or Muslim). However, the nationality transfer can occur only with the children's father's permission. Another amendment in 2002 allowed for the mother to give permission in cases where the father has died or is incapacitated.

The 1956 code was promoted by Tunisian rulers as the most modern and progressive set of civil laws in Muslim-majority countries at the time. Nevertheless, it came into being only with the agreement and support of eminent jurists and scholars such as the shaykh of the Zaytuna University.[51]

Social Science Research Network, August 27, 2010, accessed June 6, 2013, http://ssrn.com/abstract=1666848.

[43] "Abuse of Temporary Marriages Flourishes in Iraq," National Public Radio, October 19, 2013, accessed June 18, 2013, http://www.npr.org/templates/story/story.php?storyId=130350678. The practice of temporary marriage has seen a dramatic increase in recent years – not just in Iraq, but in several nearby countries as well – and has been met with a heavy online commentary, largely by human rights activists citing the mut'a's tendency toward prostitution and forced sex, and by Islamic groups arguing both for and against the validity of the practice within the religion.

[44] Ibid., 107.

[45] Mayer, "Reform of Personal Status Laws in North Africa," 434.

[46] Ibid. According to traditional Islamic law, the financial maintenance of the family is the husband's responsibility. Asserting the same responsibility for women in the marriage was another step toward greater equality of status.

[47] Article 18.

[48] Article 30.

[49] Article 32.

[50] Mashhour, "Islamic Law and Gender Equality: Could There Be a Common Ground?" 587.

[51] J. N. D. Anderson, "The Tunisian Law of Personal Status," *The International and Comparative Law Quarterly* 7.2 (1958): 262–79.

For this reason, it was firmly based on Shari'a principles (unlike the Turkish code).[52] This meant that Bourguiba justified these reforms as a liberal interpretation of Islamic texts, invoking the principles of interpretation or *ijtihād* and of public welfare (maṣlaḥa) and their application to traditional Maliki jurisprudence. In a speech given on August 3, 1956, ten days before the new code was promulgated, he underlined the role of *ijtihād* in the following terms:

Just as our ancestors made the effort to reflect upon the means to reach those ends fixed by Islam, we must in turn furnish the same effort to adapt the life of the community to the imperatives of our time, in the framework of the general principles of Islam. The human mind [*esprit*], in its evolution, gives the notion of right a content varying according to the era: that which was admissible fourteen centuries ago is no longer so in our time. Reason would be failing in its role if it closed itself to conceptions that, different in their contingency from traditional conceptions, respond in their essence to the imperatives of justice, of equity, and respect of the human character [*personnalité*].[53]

According to Kenneth Perkins, Bourguiba believed his own *ijtihād* or interpretation of Islam to be more legitimate even than that of religious scholars.[54] Despite these continuous changes toward greater equality between genders, it is worth mentioning that some controversial issues remain at the time of this writing, mainly relating to interreligious marriage, rape, and inheritance, which have not been addressed since the 2011 Jasmine Revolution.[55]

For Pakistan, family and civil laws are codified in the 1961 Muslim Family Law Ordinance (MFLO). It restricts men's privileges in areas such as divorce and polygamy. For example, in the case of divorce, the wife must be notified within ninety days for a divorce to be valid, and failure to comply results in a one-year prison sentence for the husband and a fine of five thousand rupees.[56] Moreover, men can seek a polygamous marriage only in certain cases, including sterility and/or physical or mental illness.[57] However,

---

[52] Ibid., 264. For instance, Section 23 (later amended in 1993 to reaffirm women's autonomy) provides that the wife must share financial responsibilities of the family if she has private means.

[53] Michel Camau and Vincent Geisser, *Le Syndrome autoritaire: la politique en Tunisie de Bourguiba a Ben Ali [The Authoritarian Syndrome: Politics in Tunisia from Bourguiba to Ben Ali]* (Paris: Presses de Sciences-po, 2004), 71.

[54] Kenneth Perkins, *A History of Modern Tunisia* (New York: Cambridge University Press, 2004), 136, 141. See also Mounira Charrad, *States and Women's Rights: The Making of Postcolonial Tunisia, Algeria and Morocco* (Berkeley: University of California Press, 2001).

[55] See Chapter 10.

[56] Lau, "Shari'a and national law in Pakistan," 416.

[57] Ibid., 415.

the Zina Ordinance (which is one of five criminal laws instituted with the Hudood Ordinances of 1979 added onto the penal code)[58] criminalized adultery and fornication and contributed to the deterioration of women's condition. The Zina Ordinance has been particularly abused in the case of rape because an allegation of rape is regarded as a confession of sex outside of marriage. This ordinance prescribes severe punishments for individuals convicted of the crime, including *rajm*, or stoning to death, as well as public lashings. According to a 2003 Report of the National Commission on the Status of Women (NCSW), 80 percent of female prisoners in Pakistani jails were incarcerated on charges under the Zina Ordinance. The report also highlighted abuses in the law: Zina charges are frequently brought (by family members) against women who choose to marry of their own free will or without their parents' consent, or by husbands against their divorced wives if they choose to remarry. Additionally, many Pakistani women are deprived of inheritance rights.[59]

In stark contrast, Turkey has eliminated Islamic provisions in its family law because there was no influence of Shari'a on the Turkish national law. The disappearance of Shari'a jurisprudence has actually been attributed to the dualistic law of the Ottoman Empire, which facilitated the adoption of European legal codes even before the Republic was created. In 1917, a new family code based on European principles was promulgated and "established unity in the court structure as competences in the field of family law were removed from the Religious Courts."[60] However, unity of the court system was not achieved until the 1926 Civil Code. This civil code replaced the *Mecelle*, (based on Shari'a) and was modeled after the 1912 Swiss civil code. The new law banned polygamy and gave equal divorce rights to the husband and wife.[61] The Civil Code of 2001 is an update to the 1926 version with an addition stating that the family forms the basis for society and functions on equality between spouses. While Islam does not directly influence the legal system, it has maintained its influence indirectly on society; this is apparent in the way Islam has become the main political force (see Chapter 8).

---

[58] The five criminal laws that make up the 1979 Hudood Ordinances are Prohibition Order IV, which prohibits the sale and consumption of alcohol and drugs; the Offences against Property Ordinance, which relates to theft and armed robbery; the Offence of Zina Ordinance, which deals with rape, abduction, adultery, and fornication; the Offence of Qazf Ordinance, which prohibits false accusation of *zina*; and the Execution of the Punishment of Whipping Ordinance, which prescribes whipping for those convicted under the Hudood Ordinances.

[59] Lau, "Shari'a and National Law in Pakistan," 417.

[60] Kocak, "Islam and National Law in Turkey," 240.

[61] Ibid., 243.

SHARI'A AND APOSTASY

The redefinition of Islamic legal provisions in the nation-building phase has led to an unprecedented situation in which the state defines civil laws through an Islamic lens and acts as the guardian of religious truth. The recent increase of blasphemy and apostasy cases is the direct consequence of this moral nature of the state. In pre-modern Muslim polities, apostasy and blasphemy as public acts were crimes, meaning that a public declaration or act of apostasy was a disruption of the social order and was therefore punishable by death. However, religious scholars clearly stated at the time that the political punishment did not entail a moral judgment on the person guilty of such an act.[62] In the modern period, the opposite is true: a moral judgment performed by public actors on a person's behavior leads to public condemnation.

With regard to apostasy, two situations can be found. First, a handful of countries such as Iran, Yemen, Sudan, Pakistan, and Saudi Arabia have explicitly introduced or reintroduced Islamic provisions concerning penal laws or hudood punishments of apostasy as a crime.[63] Second, in the vast majority of Muslim countries, where public rules of apostasy have been formally removed from the legal system, the personal aspects of apostasy are often connected to the implementation of civil laws.[64] As Kamran Hashemi notes:

Despite their partial insertion in legislation, public rules of Muslim traditions of apostasy are not applicable anymore and therefore have been gradually abandoned in case law. Yet, the remnants of personal aspects of these traditions, notably the family law consequences of apostasy, such as dissolving the marriage of the convert, though they might not be incorporated in legislation, can be found in domestic case law.[65]

In Islamic tradition, *apostasy* is the overarching term for three different phenomena: conversion, blasphemy, and heresy.[66] However, these nuances

---

[62] See Baber Johansen, "Apostasy as Objectified and Depersonalized Fact: Two Recent Egyptian Court Judgements," *Social Research* 70.3 (Fall 2003): 687–710.

[63] Abdullah Saeed and Hassan Saeed, *Freedom of Religion, Apostasy and Islam* (Aldershot, Hants, England: Ashgate, 2004), 1.

[64] Kamran Hashemi, "Religious Legal Traditions, International Human Rights Law and Muslim States," *Studies in Religion, Secular Beliefs and Human Rights* vol. 7 (Boston, MA: Martinus Nijhoff Publishers, 2008), 23.

[65] Hashemi, "Religious Legal Traditions, International Human Rights Law and Muslim States," 23.

[66] Otto, "Towards Comparative Conclusions on the Role of Shari'a in National Law," 633.

are sometimes lost in the wording of state legislation, as explained in the following section.

Conversion and Proselytization

The Qur'an establishes the principle of free choice in religion or belief: "Duress is not permissible in religion, as the path has become clear from falsehood" (The Qur'an, 2:256).[67] However, during the classical period of Islamic history, conversion from Islam to another religion was considered not only a matter of personal faith but also, and more importantly, a political act because it threatened the fabric of the community, especially in cases where it publicly attacked the Islamic principles of the society through acts of proselytization or public disclaimers of Islamic faith.[68] Following the same logic, it was part of the *Dhimmī*[69] condition that non Muslims refrain from propagating their religion among Muslims.[70] In other words, conversion was punishable as a crime because it was defined as an act of political rebellion endangering the whole community, but it was not a moral judgment on the personal search for truth (this aspect was part of the person interiority or soul). It is worth noting that the legal conditions for a condemnation for apostasy were very difficult to meet, hence making punishment an exceptional practice throughout the premodern phase of Islamic history.[71]

According to Muslim legal tradition, the consequences of an act of apostasy affect civil and penal laws. It is in the domain of family law (related to issues of marriage, divorce, inheritance, and child custody) that the recent cases of apostasy have resurfaced. For example, in Egypt, when two persons of different religions want to marry, the Muslim personal status code is *de facto* applied.[72] Besides the obvious discrimination against other religions (or no religion at all), this provision has consequences for the person who converts from Islam to another religion by affecting his or her family status.[73] It means that the convert may lose custody of his or her children,

---

[67] Ibid., 27.
[68] Ibid., 28.
[69] *Dhimmī* refers to a non-Muslim subject or "protected person" under Shari'a law as defined under the Muslim empire's rulings. It included Ahl Al Kitab (People of the Book, i.e., Jews and Christians) and sometimes other religious minorities.
[70] Hashemi, "Religious Legal Traditions, International Human Rights Law and Muslim States," 51.
[71] Ibid., 28.
[72] Maurits S. Berger, "Apostasy and Public Policy in Contemporary Egypt: An Evaluation of Recent Cases from Egypt's Highest Courts," *Human Rights Quarterly* 25.3 (2003): 720–40.
[73] Hashemi, "Religious Legal Traditions, International Human Rights Law and Muslim States," 60.

be deprived of inheritance, or be divorced by the judge.[74] For instance, the Court of Cassation in Egypt declares that an apostate will lose child custody, will be denied inheritance, and may not enter a new marriage. Furthermore, an apostate's marriage is considered void (*batil*) because separation (*tafriq*) is legally mandated. The case of scholar Nasr Hamed Abu Zayd (1943–2010) is very telling regarding the civil consequences of modern apostasy. In 1996, the Court of Cassation ruled that his writings on Islam represented an act of apostasy.[75] Abu Zayd was a doctoral student in the department of literature at Cairo University working on historicized interpretation of the Qur'an.[76] Upon reviewing his scholarly work for his professorship application in 1995, Abdul Sabbour Shahin, the head of Islamic Studies at Cairo University, condemned his work as "blasphemous" and said his ideas meant he was an infidel. With this declaration, a court case started against him,[77] and Shahin led the crusade against Abu Zayd, who was ultimately condemned as a *zandiq* (heretic).

As detailed in the next section, heresy and apostasy are usually differentiated in Islamic tradition. Nevertheless, in this case, condemnation as a heretic entailed the same legal consequences as condemnation as an apostate. As a result, Abu Zayd's marriage was declared void because Shari'a forbids the marriage of a Muslim woman to a non-Muslim man, and the ruling raised widespread objections from human rights groups in Egypt and beyond.

It is important to note that there is no penalty in the criminal law for declaring someone an apostate in Egypt since the penal system is secular. The case against Abu Zayd could be made through the *ḥisba* procedure. Legally, a case of *ḥisba* allows any Muslim (with no direct personal interest in the litigation) to file a case or testify against a fellow Muslim suspected of violating the essential tenets of the Islamic faith. In January 1994, a lawyer filed a lawsuit demanding that Abu Zayd and his wife divorce, saying that Abu Zayd's alleged apostasy was a basis for separating him from his wife.[78] The court rejected the claim based on the absence of direct personal interest. However, the Cairo Court of Appeals accepted the argument. The marriage between Abu Zayd and his wife, Ibtihal Younis,

---

[74] In contrast, in Pakistan, the discriminatory rules of religious legal traditions on inheritance have been abandoned, and Muslims and non-Muslims can inherit from each other. Ibid., 83.

[75] There is no penalty under the law for declaring someone an apostate in Egypt.

[76] Hashemi, "Religious Legal Traditions, International Human Rights Law and Muslim States," 114.

[77] Mostafa Mohie, *Nasr Hamed Abu Zaid: The End of a Controversial Scholarly Legacy*, Al-Masry Al-Youm English Edition, May 7, 2010, accessed June 10, 2011, http://www.almasryalyoum.com/en/node/54206.

[78] Berger, "Apostasy and Public Policy in Contemporary Egypt," 720–40.

professor of French literature at Cairo University, was nullified in 1995. It is worth pointing out that Abu Zayd's alleged apostasy was not related to any declaration that he made but based strictly on the interpretation of his work.[79]

Other intellectuals have also been taken to court in apostasy cases, including film-maker Youssef Chahine (1926–2008) and novelist Nawal El Saadawi (b. 1931) as well as her husband, novelist Sherif Hetata (b. 1964). In 1996, however, the Egyptian government prohibited the filing of apostasy cases by introducing a law that made it impossible for citizens to file a *ḥisba* lawsuit, restricting its use to the prosecutor only. This change was attributed to the state's battle with Islamists, who were abusing the charges of apostasy and engaging in "intellectual terrorism," as it was phrased by the rulers at the time.[80]

Other significant cases of apostasy relate to conversion to Islam, notably when Coptic women are concerned. For example in December 2004, Wafaa Constantine, the wife of a Coptic priest, allegedly converted to Islam and disappeared, resulting in allegations of her subsequent imprisonment by the Coptic Church. A similar case occurred in July 2010, when Camilia Shehata Zakher, the wife of a Coptic bishop, disappeared from her home for a few days. Coptic activists speculated that she had been kidnapped and forced to convert to Islam or had run away and converted of her own free will. Protestors staged large-scale demonstrations demanding to know what had become of her. In the case of Camilia, the Egyptian authorities claimed she had left home following a quarrel with her husband, and the heads of the Coptic Church ultimately stated that she had never converted to Islam at all and that she was safe and sound.

The Camilia affair raised fury in Islamist and jihadi circles, as reflected in a series of reactions and incidents: one of those activists, calling himself "Asim al-Jaddawi," on the jihadi forum *Shumūkh al-Islam* urged Bedouins in Sinai to kidnap and kill Christian tourists in retaliation for the alleged kidnapping and incarceration of the Coptic women who converted to Islam. On September 1, 2010, Mauritanian cleric Abu

---

[79] This raises another set of questions on what constitutes a public act of apostasy because in the classical jurisprudence, the condemnation for apostasy implied public declaration but did not mention writings. After the separation ruling, the Abu Zayds settled in the Netherlands, where he became a professor of humanism and Islamic studies at Utrecht University; he died in Cairo in July 2010. Adel Darwish, "Professor Nasr Hamed Abu Zayd: Modernist Islamic philosopher who was forced into exile by fundamentalists," *The Independent*, July 14, 2010, accessed March 21, 2011, http://www.independent.co.uk/news/obituaries/professor-nasr-hamed-abu-zaid-modernist-islamic-philosopher-who-was-forced-into-exile-by-fundamentalists-2025754.html.

[80] Johansen, "Apostasy as Objectified and Depersonalized Fact."

Al-Mundhir Al-Shinqiti[81] issued a fatwa permitting the killing of Egyptian Copts. Similarly, in its claim of responsibility for the October 31, 2010, attack on a church in Baghdad, al-Qa'ida in Iraq stated that the attack was a response to Camilia's abduction and that the Coptic Church had forty-eight hours to free "the Muslim women incarcerated in Egyptian convents"; otherwise al-Qa'ida would target Christians in Egypt and elsewhere. The Egyptian Endowments Minister at the time, Muhammad Hamdi Zaqzouq, even hinted that demonstrations over the Camilia affair had triggered the deadly attack on the Baghdad church and al-Qa'ida's threats against Egyptian Christians.

While Camilia has since appeared on video affirming her faith in Christianity, suspicions of forced disappearances attributed to Coptic Christians in Egypt have not subsided. Protests against alleged kidnappings of Muslim women occurred simultaneously in early 2013 in Kom Ombo and Al-Wasta, prompting assaults on Christians and requiring security forces to protect churches from angry crowds throwing rocks and Molotov cocktails.[82] As with the Camilia case, no evidence was produced of actual conversion.

In addition to the consequences of conversion on family status, there is legislation against proselytizing activities. In Tunisia the government[83] prohibits proselytization by non-Muslims and has asked groups to leave or refused to renew visas if they are suspected of propagating their faith.[84] In Egypt there is no legal ban on proselytizing, but the government restricts efforts to proselytize to Muslims and often prosecutes alleged acts under blasphemy laws.[85] In the case of Pakistan, the blasphemy law, which functions like an

---

[81] Abu al-Mundhir al-Shinqiti is known as an internal critic of jihadist movements. "Jihadism's Widening Internal Divide: Intellectual Infighting Heats Up," *Jihadica*, January 29, 2013, accessed June 27, 2013, http://www.jihadica.com/jihadism%E2%80%99s-widening-internal-divide-intellectual-infighting-heats-up. Although not much is public about al-Shinqiti's background, he publishes essays and books on the website *Minbar al-Tawhid wal-Jihad* (tawhed.ws) http://www.alarabiya.net/articles/2011/02/06/136507.html.

[82] "Clashes Break Out at Egyptian Church over Kidnapping Rumours," *Ahram Online*, February 28, 2013, accessed June 18, 2013, http://english.ahram.org.eg/NewsContent/1/64/65830/Egypt/Politics-/Clashes-break-out-at-Egyptian-church-over-kidnappi.aspx.

[83] Human Rights Watch, "Tunisia: 20 Human Rights Questions for Political Parties Presenting Candidates in the October 23 Constituent Assembly Election," 2011, accessed January 23, 2013, http://www.hrw.org/news/2011/08/09/tunisia-20-human-rights-questions-political-parties-presenting-candidates-october-23.

[84] State Department, "Tunisia: Country Specific Information," accessed January 23, 2013, http://travel.state.gov/travel/cis_pa_tw/cis/cis_1045".html.

[85] American Center for Law and Justice, "Religious Freedom and Persecution in Egypt," 2009, accessed January 23, 2013, http://media.aclj.org/pdf/egypt_memo.pdf.

apostasy law,[86] provides the only example of legislation in a Muslim state that prohibits and punishes proselytization by a specific religious group, that is, the Ahmadis.[87] Specifically, Article 298-C of the blasphemy law states that an Ahmadi who proselytizes will be punished with imprisonment and a fine.[88]

Blasphemy

Sabb means "insulting," especially against God and the Prophet Muhammad as well as religious figures (for example, the twelve Shi'i imams for the Shi'i jurists). It is important to clarify that "according to Muslim jurists, insult is a matter of relativism and the customs (*urf*) of each society are the criterion for recognizing the offence."[89] Initially, the early *sabb* cases were against non-Muslims, but they later came to apply to Muslim offenders as well.[90] Any individual Muslim can make an accusation of *sabb* and is also obliged, according to some jurists, to implement punishment on the offender.[91]

In Pakistan, blasphemy is defined by several articles of the constitution. Article 295A forbids outraging religious feelings. Article 295B contends that defiling a printed copy of the Holy Qur'an is punishable with life imprisonment.[92] Article 295C was amended in 1991 as a result of the 1991 Shari'a Act. It defines *sabb* as the (in)direct use of derogatory remarks and so forth in respect of the Holy Prophet.[93] It also defines the legal consequences of *sabb* as death, imprisonment, and/or a fine.[94] Article 298A states that insulting holy persons other than the Prophet Muhammad will be punishable by imprisonment and/or a fine.[95]

---

[86] Saeed and Saeed, *Freedom of Religion, Apostasy and Islam*, 1.

[87] For a definition of Ahamadiyaa, see Chapter 3, footnote 45.

[88] Hashemi, "Religious Legal Traditions, International Human Rights Law and Muslim States," 60.

[89] Ibid., 53.

[90] Ibid., 32.

[91] Ibid., 32.

[92] "The Text of Pakistan's Blasphemy Laws," *Muhammadanism*, accessed May 10, 2011, http://www.muhammadanism.org/Government/Government_Pakistan_Blasphemy.htm.

[93] Hashemi, "Religious Legal Traditions, International Human Rights Law and Muslim States," 86.

[94] "Whoever by words, either spoken or written or by visible representation, or by any imputation, innuendo, or insinuation, directly or indirectly, defiles the sacred name of the Holy Prophet Mohammed shall be punished with death, or imprisonment for life, and shall also be liable to fine." "The Text of Pakistan's Blasphemy Laws."

[95] "The Text of Pakistan's Blasphemy Laws."

As previously mentioned, the Ahmadi have been specifically targeted by Articles 298B[96] and 298C,[97] better known as Ordinance XX. They reiterate the 1974 law, which declares that Ahmadis are non-Muslims. They forbid Ahmadis from engaging in certain religious practices associated with Islam, especially public manifestations of these acts, such as "declaring their faith publicly, using the traditional Islamic greeting, and referring to their places of worship as mosques."[98]

According to the 2012 International Religious Freedom Report from the U.S. Department of State, thirty cases were registered under blasphemy laws between January and November. Of these, eleven were identified as Christians, five as Ahmadis, and fourteen as Muslims. At least seventeen people are on death row for blasphemy charges, and twenty have received life sentences.[99] Therefore, these blasphemy laws not only affect Muslims in Pakistan but also extend to the Christian population. For example, after the religiously motivated murder of eight Christians in July 2009, the Pakistani minister of minorities called for a review of the blasphemy laws, declaring:

---

[96] Article 298B states:

Misuse of epithet, descriptions and titles, etc. Reserved for certain holy personages or places.

1. Any person of the Qadiani group or the Lahori group (who call themselves Ahmadis or by any other name) who by words, either spoken or written or by visible representation:
   a. Refers to or addresses, any person, other than a Caliph or companion of the Holy Prophet Mohammad (PBUH), as "Ameerul Momneen", "Khalifat-ul-Momneen", "Khalifat-ul-Muslimeen", "Sahaabi" or "Razi Allah Anho";
   b. Refers to or addresses, any person, other than a wife of the Holy Prophet Mohammed (PBUH), as Ummul-Mumineen;
   c. Refers to, or addresses, any person, other than a member of the family (Ahle-Bait) of the Holy Prophet Mohammed (PBUH), as Ahle-Bait; or
   d. Refers to, or names, or calls, his place of worship as Masjid;
      shall be punished with imprisonment or either description for a term which may extend to three years, and shall also be liable to fine.

2. Any person of the Qadiani group or Lahori group, (who call themselves Ahmadis or by any other names), who by words, either spoken or written, or by visible representations, refers to the mode or form of call to prayers followed by his faith as "Azan" or redites Azan as used by the Muslims, shall be punished with imprisonment of either description for a term which may extend to three years and shall also be liable to fine.

[97] Article 298C states, "Persons of Qadiani group, etc, calling himself a Muslim or preaching or propagating his faith. Any person of the Qadiani group or the Lahori group (who call themselves Ahmadis or any other name), who directly or indirectly, poses himself as a Muslim, or calls, or refers to, his faith as Islam, or preaches or propagates his faith, or invites others to accept his faith, by words, either spoken or written, or by visible representation or in any manner whatsoever outrages the religious feelings of Muslims, shall be punished with imprisonment of either description for a term which may extend to three years and shall also be liable to fine."

[98] Mira Sethi, "Pakistan's Medieval Constitution," *Wall Street Journal* 255.143 (2010): A21.

[99] From 1987 to 2012, a total of 1,170 people have been charged under the blasphemy laws. "Pakistan," *International Freedom Report*, 2012, accessed June 18, 2013, http://www.state.gov/documents/organization/208650.pdf.

"This law is being misused. People have been extra-judicially kill[ed] and falsely implicated and are now behind bars."[100] On January 4, 2011, Salman Taseer, Governor of Punjab, was assassinated by his bodyguard from an elite force of the Punjab police for speaking in support of Aasia Bibi, a Christian woman sentenced to death by the Lahore High Court for blaspheming the Prophet. The assassination sent shock waves through the country and around the world.[101] In particular, it has been a huge blow to the country's progressive forces, which are now under extreme personal threat in their efforts to develop a more tolerant Pakistan. Governor Taseer was the most prominent politician who spoke out against the misuse of the country's blasphemy laws against minorities. Since the law's promulgation in Pakistan, hundreds of people have been accused of *sabb*.[102] These cases mainly concern instances in which the accused was expressing an opinion rather than *sabb*.[103]

In the same vein, people react promptly to any attack on the figure of the Prophet Muhammad. For example, there was unrest throughout Pakistan when the film *The Innocence of Muslims* was released with Arabic dubbing in early September 2012.[104] Protestors clashed with police and security in Islamabad near the American diplomatic enclave, and deaths were recorded in Karachi and Peshawar. Furthermore, railways minister Ghulam Ahmad Bilour made a bounty offer of $100,000 for the death of the filmmaker responsible for the movie.[105]

In Egypt, blasphemy is a crime under Article 98(f) of the Penal Code, as amended by Law 147/2006):

Whoever exploits religion in order to promote extremist ideologies by word of mouth, in writing or in any other manner, with a view to stirring up sedition, disparaging or contempt of any divine religion or its adherents, or prejudicing national unity shall be punished with imprisonment between six months and five years or paying a fine of at least 500 Egyptian pounds.[106]

[100] Lau, "Shari'a and National Law in Pakistan," 420.
[101] "Salmaan Taseer Murder Throws Pakistan into Fresh Crisis," *The Guardian*, January 4, 2011, accessed June 9, 2011, http://www.guardian.co.uk/world/2011/jan/04/punjab-governor-murder-pakistan.
[102] Saeed and Saeed, *Freedom of Religion, Apostasy and Islam*, 1.
[103] Hashemi, "Religious Legal Traditions, International Human Rights Law and Muslim States," 88.
[104] The American-made film raised indignation across Muslim countries for representing the Prophet Mohammed and for doing so in an insulting fashion. BBC, "Pakistan Film Protests: 19 Die in Karachi and Peshawar," 2012, accessed January 23, 2013, http://www.bbc.co.uk/news/world-asia-19678412.
[105] BBC, "Anti-Islam film: US condemns Pakistan minister's bounty," 2012, accessed January 23, 2013, http://www.bbc.co.uk/news/world-asia-19692971.
[106] "Criminalizing Incitement to Religious Hatred – Egypt Case Study," Office of the High Commissioner on Human Rights, accessed June 18, 2013, http://www2.ohchr.org/english/issues/opinion/articles1920_iccpr/docs/Hossam_Nairobi.pdf.

"Divine religion" in this context refers to the Abrahamic religions – Islam, Christianity, and Judaism.[107]

After the 2011 Egyptian revolution, insulting prophets was defined as an unconstitutional act for the first time. Article 44 of the Egyptian constitution adopted in 2012 reads: "It is forbidden to insult any messengers or prophets." A number of cases have been brought in 2012 and 2013 against citizens for insulting Islam or the Prophet Muhammad, including Coptic lawyer Romani Mourad; Shi'i teacher Muhammad Asfour; and, most famously, Sunni satirist Bassem Youssef.[108] This article has been removed from the revised draft of the constitution finalized November 2013 and is to be submitted to a vote in January 2014.[109]

Similarly, as a consequence of the protests against *The Innocence of Muslims* in September 2012, the Tunisian constituent assembly debated inscribing a blasphemy law in the constitution, as we shall discuss in Part III. Turkey has no specific law against blasphemy, although provisions in the penal code against "religious insult" are used to punish those who do speak ill of sacred acts or people[110] (see Part III). In 2013, the renowned pianist Faizal Say was punished through such a law for "mocking Islam" in a tweet.[111]

Heresy

While *apostasy* refers to a Muslim who has formally renounced Islam and blasphemy refers to insult by both Muslims and non-Muslims, heresy refers

---

[107] For example, the chair of the U.S. Commission on International Religious Freedom (USCIRF), Katrina Lantos Swett, stated, "These kinds of charges have increased significantly over the past two years and have chilled the dissenting views of not only Egyptian Muslims, but Christians and other minorities. In fact, during the democratic transition in Egypt, there has been a notable increase in 'contempt of religion' cases that disproportionately affect Coptic Orthodox Christians." "EGYPT: Use of Blasphemy-like Charges Must End," USCIRF, April 5, 2013, accessed June 18, 2013, http://www.uscirf.gov/news-room/press-releases/3967.html.

[108] Youssef is a cardiologist who became famous making satirical videos after the Egyptian Revolution, originally posting them to YouTube. The success of these videos earned Youssef a television program called *Al-Barnameg* (The Program), which has enjoyed widespread success among Egypt's liberal opposition. He was arrested and questioned in 2013 after allegedly insulting Islam and President Mohammad Morsi. See http://www.theguardian.com/world/2013/mar/31/egypt-orders-arrest-tv-satirist.

[109] Mariam Rizk and Osman Al Shamoubi, "Egypt Constitution 2013 vs. 2012: A Comparison," *Al-Ahram Online*, December 9, 2013, accessed December 10, 2013, http://english.ahram.org.eg/NewsContent/1/64/88644/Egypt/Politics-/Egypts-constitution–vs–A-comparison.aspx.

[110] Matthew Vella, "Blasphemy? It's not criminal – Council of Europe," *maltatoday*, 2009, accessed January 24, 2013, http://www.maltatoday.com.mt/2009/03/08/t13.html.

[111] See "Turkish composer and pianist convicted of blasphemy on Twitter," *The Guardian*, April 15, 2013, accessed June 25, 2013, http://www.guardian.co.uk/world/2013/apr/15/turkish-composer-fazil-say-convicted-blasphemy.

to a Muslim's "unbelief on grounds of his opinion being different from that of the majority or orthodoxy."[112] Those accused of heresy then, are Muslim believers who might offer a heterodox interpretation of Islam not sanctioned by the orthodoxy or who might advocate internal reform.

The act of declaring other Muslims heretics or unbelievers is called *takfīr*. *Takfīr* has had a destructive impact on freedom of religion, opinion, and expression, and arbitrary *takfīr* has been the main source of intrareligious violence, especially in Pakistan.[113] This is the case of the Ahmadis specifically targeted in sections 298B and 298C of the Penal Code, as already mentioned earlier. There is a similar campaign against the Zikris,[114] which would give them the same non-Muslim status as Ahmadis. Along the same line, Alevis in Turkey are discriminated against because the government considers Alevism[115] a heterodox Muslim sect. Additionally, Shiʿa are the most frequently targeted group of anti-heresy policies across Sunni-majority countries. In addition to Muslim minority sects, Sufi orders have also been banned as heretical in many countries. For instance, in Turkey, the Sufi religious-social orders (*tariqats*) were officially banned during Ataturk's rule.

Takfīr also allows for abuses by governmental authorities targeting peaceful religious groups that may oppose the government agenda. In Egypt, there have always been tensions between the Islamists and the state; with the increase of radicalized forms of political Islam, security laws were added to the Penal Code in 1992, which directly target those who promote or advocate "extremist" ideology and can lead to ambiguous interpretations.[116] For example, in 2003, the State Security Intelligence Service, under the pretense of these security laws, arrested Mohamed El-Derini, a Shiʿi Muslim. He was arrested again in 2004, apparently because of his religious beliefs, and was released from administrative detention fifteen months later. In the wake of the 2011 Revolution, Egyptian Shiʿis have attempted to establish some measure of political presence. These efforts have prompted negative responses from Salafi leaders such

---

[112] Hashemi, "Religious Legal Traditions, International Human Rights Law and Muslim States," 33.
[113] Ibid., 54.
[114] The Zikris, whose name derives from the Arabic word *dhikr* ("remembrance" of God) follow the teachings of Nur Pak (c. 1400), who claimed to be the Messiah and who is seen by Zikris as a prophet. Zikris are concentrated in the Pakistani province of Baluchistan, the homeland of Nur Pak. The center of Zikri belief lies in recitation of *dhikr* (recitation of the names of God). See "Zikris," *Religious Minorities in the Muslim World*, accessed June 25, 2013, http://iml.jou.ufl.edu/projects/spring05/shullick/others.htm.
[115] Alevism is a movement of mystical Islam, largely located in Turkey. Alevis believe that God lies within all humans and that ethical conduct is paramount. Although they do not consider themselves to be Shiʿa, they do believe in the twelve imams. Alevis embrace religious diversity and lack a defined hierarchy. See David Shankland, "Alevis", *The Oxford Encyclopedia of the Islamic World*, accessed January 2, 2014, http://www.oxfordislamicstudies.com.ezp-prod1.hul.harvard.edu/article/opr/t236/e0985?_hi=0&_pos=2.
[116] Ibid., 106.

as Muhammad El-Marakby, a member of the board of *Anṣār al-Sunna* (the followers of the Sunna) who vehemently opposed the creation of a Shi'i party on the basis that it was a threat to Egyptian interests (by facilitating Iranian influence). Similarly, in June of 2013, during a conference of Sunni clerics including Safwat Hegazi[117] and Yusuf al-Qaradawi,[118] a statement was released calling for jihad against Shi'a in Syria, amalgamating Shi'a believers with the Iranian regime and Hezbollah, further emphasizing the "other" nature of Egyptian Shi'a.[119]

Since January of 2011, Salafi groups have been very vocal and aggressive against all minorities as well as Sufis. For example, the High Council for the Protection of Ahl Al-Bayt, the umbrella organization for Shi'is in Egypt, appealed to the Grand Shaykh of Al-Azhar, Ahmed Al-Tayyeb, to stop Salafi calls for the excommunication of Sufis and for the destruction of shrines.[120] Shi'a and Sufis have also accused Salafi preachers of inciting violence, burning churches and shrines, and disparaging religious figures. The implications of this hatred were clear in the June 2013 beating death of four Shi'is in the town of Zawyat Abu Musallam, near Giza. One resident of the village stated, "We're happy about what happened. It should have happened long ago."[121]

Baha'is are also considered heretics in Egypt, and Al-Azhar holds that Baha'ism is not recognized by Muslims. The U.S. Department of State estimates that there are approximately 1,500 to 2,000 Baha'is in Egypt, although exact figures are difficult to obtain because the government does not recognize the faith.[122] After the 2011 Revolution, Baha'is continue to face widespread and institutionalized discrimination. For example, when asked whether Baha'is and secular individuals could join the Freedom and

---

[117] Hegazi is an Islamic preacher and a member of the National Council for Human Rights who is close to former President Mohammad Morsi. When he was interviewed in 2009, he declared that Buddhism, Zoroastrianism, and Baha'ism were not religions but were manmade.

[118] In the past, he has characterized Shi'is as "heretics." See "The politics of sects," Al-Ahram Online, October 5, 2008, accessed July 11, 2013, http://weekly.ahram.org.eg/2008/916/eg5.htm, and Peter Mandaville, "Yusuf al-Qaradawi," *Oxford Encyclopedia of the Islamic World*, accessed June 15, 2013, http://www.oxfordislamicstudies.com.ezp-prod1.hul.harvard.edu/article/opr/t236/e1230?_hi=1&_pos=1.

[119] "Clerics In Egypt Call For Global Jihad Against Regime's Shiite Allies," *Eurasia Review*, June 18, 2013, accessed June 18, 2013, www.eurasiareview.com/18062013-clerics-in-egypt-call-for-global-jihad-against-regimes-shiite-allies-oped/.

[120] "'Ahl Al-Bayt' yaslam risala ila Shaykh Al-Azhar wal-Mufti wal-Baba Shenouda," Al-Yawm Al-Sabe', April 29, 2011, accessed June 18, 2013, www.youm7.com/News.asp?NewsID=392970.

[121] "Egypt villagers 'proud' of killing Shiites," *Global Post*, June 24, 2013, accessed June 25, 2013, http://www.globalpost.com/dispatch/news/afp/130624/egypt-villagers-proud-killing-shiites.

[122] "Egypt," *International Freedom Report*, 2012, accessed June 18, 2013, http://www.state.gov/documents/organization/208598.pdf.

Justice Party, Ahmed Diab, head of the Brotherhood political section, replied in a press release on April 4, 2011, that the party has set conditions for membership based on an Islamic frame of reference and that anyone who agreed with these conditions would be welcome.[123] In the same vein, the Minister of Education, Ibrahim Ghoneim, reaffirmed in 2013 that Baha'is do not have the right to enroll in public schools.[124] Baha'i ceremonies remain banned in public and Baha'is have difficulty marrying because Egypt does not recognize Baha'i personal law.[125]

SYNTHESIS OF CHAPTERS 3, 4, AND 5: MAKING MODERN ISLAM THROUGH THE STATE

In the interests of shoring up their legitimacy among populations accustomed to centuries of imperial modes of governance, as well as to counter threats by pan-Islamists, the architects of nascent postcolonial states co-opted Islamic educational and charitable institutions and clerical authorities. This occurred through nationalizing endowments, creating ministries of religious affairs, and shaping the Islamic character of the nation by including Islam in the constitution as a key source of the state's law and social role. Thus, Islam is defined as the religion of the state in the constitutions of countries such as Egypt, and even if it is not defined the way it is in Iraq or Turkey, other institutional mechanisms (education, family law) have ensured its social legitimacy. Al-Azhar, the world's preeminent Sunni theological religious institution, has been co-opted by the state in efforts to bolster its legitimacy, reducing the Shaykh's authority and bringing religious schools and mosques under the state's control. Different authoritarian regimes have exercised similar measures to control religious institutions and to suppress Islamic authorities who might compete with the state. The inclusion of Islam within state institutions has nationalized Islamic discourses, authorities, and teachings, giving rise to multiple versions of hegemonic Islam. While most legal codes were based on European models, the primacy of Shari'a in the sphere of family law was retained, and dominant forms of Islam received legal privilege, which affected the status of minorities. For example, adherents of distinct Islamic sects, such as the Baha'i in Egypt and the Alevis in Turkey, were either amalgamated to the Muslim majority or rejected as heretics.

---

[123] Mohamed Alaa, "Egypt," http://www.islamopediaonline.org/country-profile/egypt/religious-minorities-and-freedom-religion/baha%E2%80%99, accessed June 29 2013.

[124] "Bahais cannot enroll in public schools, education minister says," *Egypt Independent*, January 6, 2013, accessed June 18, 2013, http://www.egyptindependent.com/news/bahais-cannot-enroll-public-schools-education-minister-says.

[125] "Egypt," *International Freedom Report*, 2012.

This nationalization of Islam has irremediably affected the religious tradition that was reconstructed in order to fit within diverse state policies. In this regard, it is important to emphasize the decisive role of the state in the modernization of Islam in particular, and the building of the national identities in general. From a Western point of view, this political development is quite counterintuitive because there was a greater dialectic at play between state and nation across Europe, and in some cases such as the United States, the nation even preceded the state. Because postcolonial Muslim states preceded and created the national community, sometimes from *tabula rasa*, as in Turkey or Pakistan, they have acted as Promethean actors, creating new institutions and opportunities as well as new political allegiances and Islamic identities. In this regard, the public education system of these Promethean states has been critical in the building of modern Islam as hegemonic Islam.

6

Teaching Islam in Public Schools

With the creation of state education systems, curricula and textbooks have socialized new generations to the idea that national identity and Islamic identity are two sides of the same coin. By inscribing Islam within the public education system, the state posits itself as the protector of Islamic heritage and assumes "the responsibility to provide children and youths with trustworthy religious guidance."[1]

This use of Islam in the nationalization process goes hand in hand with the exclusion or marginalization of all other religious groups. Despite attempts to focus on tolerance in religious instruction, religious minorities are neglected and discriminated against in most of the public education curricula. Additionally, because the concept of tolerance is promoted only in the context of religious instruction, other parts of the curricula (history/social studies) remain infused with Islamic terms such as jihad and continue to instill ideas of Islamic supremacy and unity against the so-called infidels.

In this regard, it is important to note that Islamic references are not limited to religious education but are incorporated throughout the entire public school curriculum. They permeate history, social studies, and civics textbooks, and even appear in mathematics.[2] Such a "functionalization of

---

[1] "Groups claiming independent authority to interpret Islamic scriptures and transmit Islamic culture undermine one of the basic foundations of the state's moral legitimacy: its protection of the Islamic heritage.... Islam, the official religion of the Egyptian state, is a matter of vital government interest." Gregory Starrett, *Putting Islam to Work: Education, Politics, and Religious Transformation in Egypt* (Berkeley: University of California Press, 1998), 5.

[2] Pittman and Chishtie examine how Islam has penetrated the mathematics curriculum in Pakistan, apparent in the provided examples and explanations based on Islamic law and traditions. For example, a typical mathematics exercise deals with the issue of inheritance and distribution of an estate. In these problems, the widow is given an eighth of the estate and the sons and daughters receive the rest of the estate with the sons receiving twice the shares of the daughters. The final piece of information becomes learned and assumed knowledge for other exercises thereafter. Holger Daun and Geoffrey Walford (eds.), "Education Strategies among

religion," as Gregory Starrett terms it,[3] illustrates the socialization process at work, where the state exerts social control and assumes moral authority by promoting a "proper Islamic identity" and, by extension, the cultivation of "good social behavior" (ādāb ijtimaʿiya) in the citizenry. For example, in Egyptian primary school textbooks, the school is portrayed as the source of the child's moral leanings, which the child will then share with his/her family.[4] Thus, while Egyptian textbooks focus on responsibility and duty as main Muslim values,[5] these are virtues taught in schools and therefore primarily associated with state and public behaviors, as opposed to private virtues. Similarly in Turkey, the main objective of the Directorate of Religious Affairs is "to create 'good citizens' with civic responsibility toward the state."[6]

For this chapter, I collected and analyzed primary and secondary school textbooks from Iraq, Egypt, and Tunisia that were in use at the time of this writing, most of them published in the 2000s. I also utilized similar scholarly analysis done on Pakistani and Turkish textbooks.[7] The focus of this analysis was Islamic education textbooks (reflected in a variety of names: "Islamic Insight," "Religious Studies," "Islamic Culture and Religious Studies," etc.) and national and civic education textbooks. The content analysis of these materials shed light on the association between Islamic religious terms (jihad, umma) and political terms (nation, state, citizen).

UMMA VERSUS NATION

References to the umma in textbooks are used to legitimize the national community. As a result, however, such a reference complicates issues of citizenship and national identity because while religious identity bolsters national unity, it also undermines national distinctiveness in favor of the larger Islamic community."[8] The idea of Islam as central to one's identity

Muslims in the Context of Globalization: Some National Case Studies," *Muslim Minorities* 3 (2004): 113.

[3] Starrett, *Putting Islam to Work*, 10.

[4] Ibid., 143.

[5] Johana Pink, "Nationalism, Religion and the Muslim-Christian Relationship: Teaching Ethics and Values in Egyptian Schools," *Center for Studies on New Religions*, 2004, accessed April 11, 2011, http://www.cesnur.org/2003/vil2003_pink.htm.

[6] M. Hakan Yavuz, *Islamic Political Identity in Turkey* (Oxford: Oxford University Press, 2003), 49.

[7] The results for Egypt and Iraq are accessible on *Islamopedia Online*: http://www.islamopediaonline.org/country-profile/egypt/islam-and-education-system/survey-textbook-and-curricular-content and http://www.islamopediaonline.org/country-profile/iraq/islam-and-education-system, accessed September 17 2013.

[8] Naureen Durrani and Mairead Dunne, "Curriculum and National Identity: Exploring the Links between Religion and Nation in Pakistan," *Journal of Curriculum Studies* 42.2 (2010): 229. "The fourth aspect of national identity is that it connects a group of people to a particular geographical place ... ethnic or religious identities often have sacred sites or places of origin,

places priority on the umma over the nation, and as a result, the state grants symbolic supremacy to the umma in terms of religious solidarity. In Pakistani textbooks, for example, identification with the umma and Pakistan are used interchangeably, creating the conditions for a strong social and cultural influence of Islam (see Part II).

Identification with other transnational projects such as pan-Arabism can also challenge the national identity. In the case of Egypt, religious educational texts have gone through two phases: the pan-Arabist focus under Nasser and Sadat, and the nationalist/Egypt-first emphasis under Mubarak. The first phase illustrates the political instrumentalization of the umma under nation-state regimes while also asserting the primacy of the Egyptian identity. As Olivier Carré showed, 72 percent of the content of religious education was devoted to political and social matters.[9] In the textbooks, the umma is superior to the Arab nation and to the country of Egypt; however, the Arab nation and culture should work for the good of the Muslim umma because Arab unity is regarded as an essential article of the Islamic faith. One text quoted by Carré provides the following invocation: "O God! Bring to us unity! O God! Re-unite the Arabs in one nation. When that happens ... they will form the most powerful, the richest, the most knowledgeable and the most important of nations!"[10] In a perfect example of grafting and pruning, the umma and the Arab nation intermesh and reinforce each other. Carré concludes, "The texts call young Egyptians to feel and think of themselves as Arabs above all and to apply their Arabism and their sense of identity with the Muslim Umma."[11] Moreover, Javaid Saeed points out that although the textbooks of the Nasser period were marked by a façade of secularism, they were in fact very much influenced by fundamentalist Islamic beliefs.[12]

In the second phase, national identity takes precedence. Even religious textbooks focus on allegiance to Egypt as the *waṭan* or homeland, and in the 2002/2003 textbooks, there is almost no reference to Arabism or the Islamic umma. For instance, the first-year primary textbook tells how Allah saved Meccans' homeland from the "*Sha'b al-Fīl*" (the People of the Elephant) and

but it is not an essential part of having the identity that you should permanently occupy that place.... A nation, in contrast, must have a homeland." David Miller, *On Nationality* (Oxford: Oxford University Press, 1995), 24.

[9] Olivier Carré. "L'Ideologie politico-religieuse nasserienne a la lumiere des manuels scolaires," *Politique Etrangere* 37 (1972): 536. See excerpts from *Islamic Socialism*, by Mustafa al-Sibai, in Sami A. Hanna and George H. Gardner (eds.), *Arab Socialism* (Leiden: Brill, 1969), 66–79. Translated by the author. For the complete text, see *Middle East Journal* 26 (Winter 1972): 55–68. See also Joseph P. O'Kane, "Islam in the New Egyptian Constitution: Some Discussions in al-Ahram," *Middle East Journal* 26 (Spring 1972): 137–48.

[10] Carre, "L'Ideologie politico-religieuse nasserienne a la lumiere des manuels scolaires," 537.

[11] Ibid.

[12] Javaid Saeed, *Islam and Modernization: A Comparative Analysis of Pakistan, Egypt, and Turkey* (Westport, CT: Praeger Publishers, 1994), 138.

concludes with a poem that goes: "And you, Muslim students, have to love your homeland [watan] / And defend it if it is attacked by any aggressor / Because you live in it and eat from its food / And drink from the water of its blessed Nile."[13] The focus on the iconic Nile River clearly promotes national identity, which is in direct contrast to the first phase, in which education revolved around the idea of Arab nationalism in order to emphasize Arab identity over Egyptian identity. It is not clear at the time of this writing what the emphasis of the new educational policies post-January 25, 2011 will be.

In all our case studies, the supremacy of the umma is tempered by the textbooks' promotion of allegiance to the state and the state's version of Islam. In other words, even when the textbooks depict the umma as the point of reference, they notably also propagate each particular state's version of Islam as the true Islam of the umma.

Thus, each state promulgates a unique representation of Muslim identity to strengthen national unity and to cement state authority. Furthermore, each country's curriculum reflects local histories, as well as the degree of the Islamist clout in educational policy and the policy interests of the state. Despite this diversity, textbook representations of Muslim identity do share four features, which further promote unity and reinforce state authority: (a) the blurring of sectarian divisions to promote a singular and unified Islam; (b) the fostering of national uniqueness through a master narrative of victimization to inculcate a sense of unity against oppressors; (c) the grounding of this uniqueness in the implicitly or explicitly proclaimed superiority of Islam; and relatedly, (d) the misrepresentation or omission of Christians and Jews from religious instruction.

ISLAM IS SINGULAR AND MONOLITHIC

In all the countries surveyed, the textbooks avoid sectarian distinctions by simultaneously promoting a singular representation of Islam and scrupulously not mentioning any Islamic sect by name. Consequentially, religious education is compulsory, and for adherents of all Islamic sects, the Sunni tradition of the dominant group is taught as the sole version of Islam, while Christian students are exempted from Islamic education or are sometimes offered alternative Christian education. As a result, Islamic references forge a fictitious and homogenous community within the state and the umma.

The most relevant example in this regard comes from Turkey, which as a secular state promotes Islam as primarily Turkish, "existing in a vacuum apart from its Middle Eastern context, oblivious to existing sectarian or minority differences, and serving as a locus of identity for feelings

---

[13] "Survey of Textbook and Curricular Content," *Islamopedia Online*, accessed August 4, 2013, http://www.islamopediaonline.org/country-profile/egypt/islam-and-education-system/survey-textbook-and-curricular-content.

of Turkish nationalism."[14] Hakan Yavuz terms this Turkification of Islam "internal secularization" because the state imagines and promotes its vision of Islam in terms of modern concepts like nationalism.[15] Thus, the contradiction of a secular state and compulsory religious education is reconciled by the fact that "Islamic knowledge is reformulated and presented in a way that functionalizes Islam, equating religious study with any other subject."[16] Religious instruction is advertised as necessary and obligatory because Islamic values are practical and useful to society. Moreover, religion acts as divine legitimization "for the pillars of the official ideology of the 'secular' State."[17]

According to Article 24 of the Turkish constitution, "Education and instruction in religion and ethics shall be conducted under state supervision and control. Instruction in religious culture and moral education shall be compulsory in the curricula of primary and secondary schools. Other religious education and instruction shall be subject to the individual's own desire, and in the case of minors, to the request of their legal representatives."[18] While the last part of Article 24 is an important caveat, it is clear that it is not upheld, especially in the case of Alevi students, who are required to attend lessons in religious culture and ethics promoting Sunni Islam.[19] Thus, the teaching of religion allows the state to further its vision of a Turkish-Sunni society by using compulsory religious education classes to teach Islam as a Turkish religion reflecting the Sunni Islamic interpretation. As a result, the textbooks emphasize the conflation of Turkishness and Islam by including pictures of mosques and holy shrines in Turkey and presenting all Muslim scholars as Turkish, while cutting off Islamic history after the Turks accepted Islam.[20] In addition to inculcating the idea of Turkish Islam, textbooks do not mention sectarian divisions within Islam or religious minorities of Turkey, implying that there is no alternative to the Turkish-Sunni identity.

---

[14] Ozlem Altan, "Turkey: Sanctifying a Secular State," in Eleanor Abdella Doumato and Gregory Starrett (eds.), *Teaching Islam: Textbooks and Religion in the Middle East*, 197–214 (Boulder, CO: Lynne Rienner Publishers, 2007), 212.

[15] Yavuz, *Islamic Political Identity in Turkey*, 5.

[16] Ibid., 202.

[17] Ibid., 212.

[18] "The Constitution of the Republic of Turkey," accessed June 28, 2011, http://www.anayasa.gov.tr/images/loaded/pdf_dosyalari/THE_CONSTITUTION_OF_THE_REPUBLIC_OF_TURKEY.pdf. Religious education was actually reintroduced into the curriculum in 1949 and "consisted of two hours of instruction on Saturday afternoons, but was restricted to those children whose parents had explicitly requested such education." Mustafa Kocak, "Islam and National Law in Turkey," in Jan Michiel Otto (ed.) *Sharia Incorporated* (Amsterdam: Leiden University Press, 2010), 245.

[19] "Compulsory Religious Education an Abuse of Human Rights, Says European Court," *National Secular Society*, October 12, 2007, accessed November 10, 2011, http://www.secularism.org.uk/compulsoryreligiouseducationanab.html.

[20] Altan, "Turkey: Sanctifying a Secular State," 203.

As described in Chapter 3, Pakistan, Egypt, Tunisia, and Iraq all constitutionally declare Islam the state religion, but the teaching of Islam in each country
varies according to the social and religious features of the society and the political orientation of the regime. As detailed later in this chapter, in Pakistan, a "ritualistic" approach of Islam is propagated using "religious symbolism to counter
economic discontent, political dissent, and ethnic nationalism."[21] In Tunisia and
Egypt, under authoritarian rulers, compulsory religious education aimed to discredit the political and social influence of Islamist opposition groups. During
Saddam's regime in Iraq, textbooks emphasized homogeneity and denied the
Sunni-Shi'i sectarian divide in order to impose unity on Iraqi society.

The official curriculum of the Pakistani state schools equates Islam with
national identity by teaching that Muslim identity and Pakistani identity are
synonymous, thus ignoring religious, ethnic, linguistic, and regional diversity.[22]
Therefore, students defined being Pakistani as being Muslim, which meant
complete adherence to Islamic rituals, as a result of their education emphasizing religious symbols and rituals such as *namaz*, (recitation of the Qur'an), and
so forth.[23] In this way, the state is able to promote national unity through the
concept of Islamic unity despite the multiethnic and linguistic nature of the society.[24] Especially after the secession and creation of Bangladesh in 1971, ethnic
diversity was perceived as the biggest threat to national unity and sovereignty.
In these conditions, the "ritualistic" version of Islam served as a unifying ideology to downplay and domesticate sectarian, ethnic, and provincial sentiments,
which in turn promoted homogeneity, solidarity, and unity through Islam.

While Pakistani education does not favor the Sunni or Shi'i tradition, the
curriculum teaches that there is a distinction between "good" and "bad"
Muslims, and by extension "good" and "bad" Pakistanis.[25] The "good"
Muslims are those who are pious or who follow Islamic rituals and customs, while the "bad" Muslims are those who follow "un-Islamic customs."
As a result, no acknowledgment or recognition of multiple ways of practicing Islam is possible. For example, Muslim students must declare in writing
that they believe that the Prophet Muhammad is the final prophet, with no
exemption for Ahmadis, who do not share such a belief.[26]

---

[21] Durrani and Dunne, "Curriculum and national identity," 216.
[22] Ibid., 222. Although non-Muslims are not required to participate in the Islamic studies
classes, they are generally not offered religious teaching of their own beliefs. Some schools
do offer ethics classes for non-Muslim students, but they are not widespread. "Pakistan,"
International Freedom Report, 2010, accessed November 13, 2011, http://www.State.gov/g/
drl/rls/irf/2010/148800.htm.
[23] Durrani and Dunne, "Curriculum and national identity," 223, 231.
[24] Pakistan is divided into four provinces: the North West Frontier Province (NWFP), Punjab,
Sindh, and Baluchistan, and each province roughly represents a different major ethnic group
within the state. Ibid., 219.
[25] Ibid., 231.
[26] This educational treatment of the Ahmadi contradicts Article 22 of the constitution, which
states in Part II on safeguards as to educational institutions in respect of religion: "No person attending any educational institution shall be required to receive religious instruction,

In Tunisia, Bourguiba introduced compulsory Islamic education into the Tunisian public education system. Although the initial teaching was defined as liberal or progressive, it became more "Islamicized" when the state sought an alliance with Islamists to counter its leftist opponents. Bourguiba's intention at the time was to maintain political control over the main institutions while allowing a more conservative culture in the hands of the Islamists.[27] As a result, between 1970 and 1975, the education system went through several reforms that emphasized a greater connection of modern Tunisia with its Islamic heritage. This was apparent when the later period of Tunisia's contemporary history was integrated into that of the Islamic empire.[28] Islamic references were also utilized to justify secular forms of government. At the same time, the tension between Bourguiba's secular orientation and the Islamist influence on education was apparent, as is seen for example in the chapter, "الخلافة مؤسسة مدنية, Succession is a Civil Institution," for the third year of Islamic teaching, in which the author argues that through a succession of dynasties and caliphates, Muslims realized that any government should be a civil one and therefore Muslim history from the Ummayad to the Abbassid was a testimony to the separation of politics and religion.[29]

Mohamed Charfi, who was in 1991 the minister of national education and a strong opponent of the Islamicization of Tunisian education, issued a law to foster in the new generations a greater sense of equality among individuals and especially between genders. The new textbooks paid greater attention to discrimination and segregation based on religious belief; parity between disciplines was promoted, meaning that students would be equally educated in the sciences, history, and language as well as in religious matters; and a focus on political and human rights was added to the duties of citizenship. Religious education was also reshaped to promote women's rights and equality with men.[30]

---

or take part in any religious ceremony, or attend religious worship, if such instruction, ceremony or worship relates to a religion other than his own." "The Constitution of the Islamic Republic of Pakistan," accessed May 8, 2011, http://www.pakistani.org/pakistan/constitution/; "Pakistan," *International Freedom Report*, 2009, accessed November 13, 2011, http:// www.State.gov/g/drl/rls/irf/2009/127370.htm.

[27] Mohamed Charfi and Hamadi Redissi, Trans. Susan Emanuel, "Teaching Tolerance and Open-Minded Approaches to Sacred Texts," 2003, accessed June 9, 2011, http://www. amacad.org/pdfs/routledge12.pdf, p. 167.

[28] Ibid., 168.

[29] This is a succinct English outline of the Arabic original text: "لقد ادراك المسلمون من قبل الحقيقة ووعوها، نعني دنوية الحكم ومدينته. وعلى هذا النحو مارسوا السلطة. ولذلك، لا نجد دولة من الدول التي تعاقبت على الحكم في الاسلام وبالاستناد الى شريعته قد سميت دولة اسلامية بل نسبت تلك الدول الى اصحابها والقائمين بها، مثل الخلافة الاموية، العباسية، الحمدانية...وهذا دليل على التمييز بين السياسي والديني، او بين الدنيوي والديني." in Ali Harb, "*al-Khilafa Mu'assasa Madaniya* الخلافة مؤسسة مدنية" or "Succession is a Civil Institution." *Book in the Muslim Thinking: For the Third Year Students in Secondary Education. Ministry of Education*, Tunisia (Tunis: National Pedagogic Center, n.d.), pp. 50–1.

[30] In this chapter, "المرأة بين الشريعة والفقهاء, Women between the Shari'a and Scholars," the author argues that many Muslim scholars and thinkers misinterpret the verses in the Qur'an and

This emphasis on tolerance has continued after the Jasmine Revolution of 2011. While Islam remains the only religion taught in public schools, the emphasis of the teaching is on the aspects of Islamic tradition that foster equality, unity, and acceptance. At the same time, the Ennahda Party is trying to reform the educational system to establish a more Islamic culture and to provide greater awareness of the benefits of Islamic morality. For example, the Ennahda youth movement offers Islamic lessons in its party offices.[31] However, radical changes seem unlikely given the country's history of secular education. Moreover, the Ministry of Education (at the time of writing) is led by Abdellatif Abid of the secularist Ettakatol Party, making any substantial shifts toward stricter Islamic education unlikely.[32]

While both Islam and Christianity are taught in Egyptian public schools, parents cannot choose the religion their children are taught. According to Article 19 of Egypt's constitution: "Religious education shall be a principal subject in the courses of general education." If one of the parents is Muslim, the child is considered Muslim and will be placed accordingly. The tradition of Islam taught at schools is Sunni Islam, without distinction among

the saying of the Prophet that talk about women's rights in the society. For example, the Quranic verse 49:13, that reads,"يا أيها الناس إنا خلقناكم من ذكر وأنثى وجعلناكم شعباً وقبائل لتعارفوا إن أكرمكم عند الله أتقاكم." (الحجرات) ("O mankind, indeed We have created you from male and female and made you peoples and tribes that you may know one another. Indeed, the most noble of you in the sight of Allah is the most righteous of you") (Sahih International Translation, http://www.islamicity.com/mosque/arabicscript/Ayat/49/49_13.htm) is used to justify his argument that Islam calls for equality between men and women. He explains that instead of integrating women in the society and having them practice the rights that Islam gives them, those scholars issue fatwas to constrain women in houses, which make them an example of ignorance. This is a summary of the original Arabic, which reads, "إنه بدل أن يسعى المسلمون لتأهيل المرأة من الوجهة الإجتماعية حتى تستثمر بحق ما يعطيها الإسلام من الحقوق فإن الإصلاح الذي عولجت به هو زجها في أعماق البيوت محجوبة عن العالم أجمع بما يجعلها مثال للجهل والبله والغبن وسوء التربية." See Al-Tahir al-Haddad. *"al-Mara' Bayn al-Shari'a wa-l-Fuqaha'* should be al-Mara' Bayn al-Shari'a wa-l-Fuqaha'* "المرأة بين الشريعة والفقهاء" or "Women between the Shari'a and Scholars." Book in the Muslim Thinking: For the Seventh Year Students in Secondary Education. Ministry of Education and Training (Tunis: National Pedagogic Center, n.d.), pp. 66–7.

[31] "The Salafist Temptation: The Radicalization of Tunisia's Post-Revolution Youth," *Combating Terrorism Center at West Point*, April 23, 2013, accessed June 18, 2013, http://www.ctc.usma.edu/posts/the-salafist-temptation-the-radicalization-of-tunisias-post-revolution-youth.

[32] Information in this paragraph from Muhammad Faour, "Religious Education and Pluralism in Egypt and Tunisia," *The Carnegie Papers* (2012). Responding to a report published in August 2013 stating that 100,000 students had withdrawn from school the previous year, Secretary General of the General Union of Secondary Education (part of the influential UGTT) Lassaad Yacoubi accused religious "pseudo-charities" of convincing poor families to pull their daughters from school. Likewise, former Education Minister Abdellatif Abid saw in this figure a sign of the urgency of curricular and administrative reform. In light of these setbacks, the council of ministers approved in September 2013 a series of newly funded projects, including ten relating to education. Most of these will increase funding to teachers and administrators over the following year.

the different schools therein or any mention of Shi'a.[33] According to James Toronto and Muhammad Eissa's study on Islamic education in Egypt, "the curriculum, from beginning to end, leaves Muslim students with the impression that Sunni Islam is the only and correct version of Islam in existence."[34] Such a teaching contradicts the reality Egyptian students live in, where several mosque-shrines dedicated to Shi'i figures exist and are visited and celebrated by Sunni and Shi'a alike. Additionally, the lack of information on Sufism in public religious education stands in stark contrast to the Sufi influence at all levels of Egyptian society.[35] Nowhere are sectarian identities discussed, lest they induce fragmentation and subsequent instability in the national identity; instead, the majority Sunni Islamic tradition is offered as "the" Egyptian norm.

In a way comparable to the situation described for Tunisia under Bourguiba and Ben Ali, the educational system was one of the main arenas of tension and competition between the state and the Islamists.[36] Thus, while the Egyptian state's education prioritizes Egyptian identity, for the Islamists as political opponents, the goal of Islamic education should not be to reinforce national identity but rather to uphold the nation-transcending Muslim community (umma).[37] After the 2011 revolution, the Muslim Brotherhood has advocated a greater presence of Islamic concepts in education, seeing Islam as "the most important component of their national character."[38] As a sign of this new orientation, a picture of feminist activist Doriya Shafiq was deleted from Egyptian textbooks because she was not wearing the hijab. However, Muhammad Sherif, advisor to the Egyptian Ministry of Education, responded that the removal had "nothing to do with the alleged 'Brotherhoodization' of the curriculum and education."[39]

According to an anonymous governmental source, since the military coup of 2013, Egypt's education authorities have recalled and destroyed thousands of textbooks because they were glorifying the ousted Islamist president Muhammad Morsi and his Muslim Brotherhood group in the conduct of the 2011 Revolution.[40]

[33] Sami Aldeeb, "Religious Teaching in Egypt and Switzerland," *Text sent to the symposium organized by The Movement for Human Rights*, Beyrouth, 2000.

[34] James A. Toronto and Muhammad S. Eissa, "Egypt: Promoting Tolerance, Defending against Islamism," in Eleanor Abdella Doumato and Gregory Starrett (eds.), *Teaching Islam: Textbooks and Religion in the Middle East* (Boulder, CO: Lynne Rienner Publishers, 2007), 44.

[35] Ibid., 45.

[36] Ibid., 30.

[37] Saeed, *Islam and Modernization*, 224.

[38] Faour, "Religious Education and Pluralism in Egypt and Tunisia," 11.

[39] "Education Ministry faces heat after deleting unveiled feminist from textbooks," *Egypt Independent*, January 1, 2013, accessed June 18, 2013, http://www.egyptindependent.com/news/education-ministry-faces-heat-after-deleting-unveiled-feminist-textbooks.

[40] See "Egypt destroys textbooks praising Mursi, Brotherhood, Gulf News, September 16 2013, accessed September 21, 2013, http://gulfnews.com/news/region/egypt/egypt-destroys-textbooks-praising-mursi-brotherhood-1.1232182.

Interestingly, textbooks reinforce the state's religious legitimacy because they utilize religious methods and materials of education: memorization and oral recitation, Qur'an, Hadith, and biographies of prominent Muslims. Additionally, the objectives of the curricula include teaching the proper recitation of the Qur'an, rituals, and correct Islamic dress and behavior.

The main purpose of the curricula, however, is not to teach Islamic tradition but to provide religious legitimacy to state policies. [41] For example, textbooks stress the importance of "loving the homeland which God bestowed on us.... Our noble religion commands us to develop it, to work for its glory and to defend its land and people."[42] In a lesson to first graders about the topic of love, the textbook offers a series of illustrations about recommended objects of love; the first being "the flag of my country," followed by the teacher, family, and friends.[43]

The Islamic instruction in Iraq under Saddam Hussein is a case in point of the use of Islam for national purpose. A Sunni version of Islam was promoted in Iraqi textbooks, even though the majority of the population was Shi'i. It included Sunni prayer stances and a certain bias toward the Sunni version of Islamic history. Further, most books contained Saddam's image, and all social studies, civics, and history books – as well as Islamic history – included substantial content on the history and ideology of the Ba'th Party. Students learned the importance of "loyalty to the (Arab) people and to the leadership of 'the Party' and the revolution."[44] Islam was used consistently to support such indoctrination: the party's history was presented in the context of early Islamic history (lessons on the first Muslims were taught alongside the history of modern-day Iraq),[45] while the party's ideology was presented within that of Islamic teachings, with Saddam depicted as their champion. The Iran-Iraq war of 1980–8, for instance, was presented in Arab and Islamic history textbooks as a modern version of the seventh-century Arab-Islamic victory over the Persians in the battle of Qaddisiyya:

The battle of Qaddissiya of our ancestors was repeated by the champion of Arabism and Islam, our leader Saddam Hussein (may Allah protect and guide him) against the Persian enemy.[46]

---

[41] Toronto and Eissa, "Egypt: Promoting Tolerance, Defending against Islamism."
[42] *Seventh year, second semester Islamic education textbook*, 2002–3 school year, 30.
[43] Pink, "Nationalism, Religion and the Muslim-Christian Relationship," 44.
[44] *Tarbiya Wataniya Saf Khamis Ibtida'iya* (National Education, level 5 elementary School), Iraqi Ministry of Education, 2001, p. 29, as analyzed and translated by Tova Reznik for *Islamopedia Online*, see http://www.islamopediaonline.org/country-profile/iraq/islam-and-education-system/rebuilding-iraq%E2%80%99s-education-system-and-addressing-fo. Accessed August 2, 2013.
[45] *al-Tarikh al-'Arabi al-Islami li-l-Saf al-Khamis al- Ibtida'i*, 1988, 33.
[46] *al-Tarikh al-'Arabi al-Islami li-l-Saf al-Thani al-Mutawasat*, Islamic Studies for level 2 of middle school, Iraqi Ministry of Education, 1999, 58. As analyzed and translated by Tova Reznik for *Islamopedia Online*: http://www.islamopediaonline.org/country-profile/iraq/

The Saddam curriculum also aimed to indoctrinate students with the belief in a homogeneous Iraqi society. Ethnic and cultural diversity was downplayed and little mention was made of any distinct groups. On the other hand, proclamations of coexistence and cooperation were frequent. Students were told that "Iraqis feel unified; they cooperate and are proud of their deep connection to one another." This so-called camaraderie, a common theme especially at the primary level, was taught by way of discounting distinct characteristics and maintaining an appearance of a homogenous Iraq. The theme in this excerpt, taken from a seventh grade social studies book, echoes throughout the curriculum:

The people of Iraq are a single firm unit – from the north to the south ... Living together for thousands of years generated unity between (the Iraqi) people. Iraqi blood was fused in its defense.[47]

Despite the proclaimed secularism of Baʿthist ideology, Islamic references were often used and quotes from the Qur'an were interspersed throughout lessons highlighting Baʿthist principles. A lesson instructing students to limit their materialistic consumption for the sake of their country and nation (Umma) is accompanied by a quote from the Qur'an: "Those who squander are the brothers of demons" (17:27). By conserving and avoiding materialism, students were taught, they would "triumph against the greed of the American, British, and Zionist enemies."[48]

After the United States invaded Iraq and ended the Saddam regime in 2003, the new Ministry of Education's general curriculum directorate, in partnership with UNESCO and USAID, established a committee for curriculum development to drastically change the nature and content of religious teaching. The committee consisted of Iraqi educators and education experts chosen by the United States, who consulted with other local leaders in education, particularly Islamic education.[49] The massive endeavor to provide Iraq's sixteen thousand schools with revised study materials began with the removal of all images of Saddam Hussein and Baʿth content from textbooks. A subsequent step involved the introduction of new materials that would promote tolerance, respect, and appreciation for a pluralistic Iraqi society by recognizing its religious and ethnic components rather than discounting them.

In a broad sense, the prevalence of abstract concepts of tolerance in the Saddam-era curriculum was likely a factor in the decision to continue the use

islam-and-education-system/rebuilding-iraq%E2%80%99s-education-system-and-addressing-fo, accessed August 2, 2013.

[47] *al-Tarbiya al-Wataniya li-l-Saf al-Khamis al-Ibtida'i*, 2001, 12.

[48] Ibid., 37.

[49] A. Hadithi, "Shaikh Dr. Hamid Abd El Aziz, the Director of the Department of Islamic education, in an interview with Al-Raed," *Al-Raed Magazine*, Iraq (2010): 58; "A New History of Iraq," *The Guardian*, November 24, 2003, accessed June 19, 2011, http://www.guardian.co.uk/education/2003/nov/25/schools.schoolsworldwide.

of some old textbooks with revisions in the new curriculum (this is especially the case with regard to Islamic studies). A significant shift, however, is evident in the new curriculum with regard to specific Iraqi social groups, which were conspicuously ignored in the Saddam era. This shift includes revisions in civics, social studies, and history textbooks to teach students about Iraq's "ethnic and religious diversity,"[50] mentioning different Iraqi ethnic and religious groups, such as Kurds, Turkmen, Yazidis, Sabians, and Christians, by name.[51] While Saddam-era textbooks mentioned Christians, they did so only in the context of ancient Islamic history, and Jesus was presented as a Muslim prophet. Jews, despite having been a significant component of Iraqi society for centuries, are mentioned in a limited sense in both old and new curricula, in the context of relations with the Prophet Muhammad in ancient Islamic history and with regard to the Zionist movement and Palestine.

One of the major revisions in Iraqi textbooks has been the recognition of Shiʻi groups, as opposed to the original textbooks that contained a Sunni bias. This recognition of religious and sectarian diversity, while a goal in and of itself, is also the basis for a unified, stable Iraq. Within this context, the role of the individual citizen is to support the nation. Religious and sectarian distinctions often serve in civic and social studies lessons to teach the importance of solidarity among different groups. Each citizen, along with each distinct ethnic or religious component of Iraqi society, is responsible for protecting the nation and fostering harmony within it. These excerpts come from the new curriculum's seventh grade civics textbook:

Despite the fact that different (Iraqi) factions were subjected to injustice and abuse, they held fast to their love for their country and its cohesion.[52]

National unity means the adherence of individuals to their society's shared goals in order to protect such cohesion, by such means as defending the homeland ... regardless of ethnic or religious diversity, or differing opinions.[53]

However, the revised content was instantly criticized for sectarian bias against Sunnis, and subsequently retracted. Since 2003, the curriculum has undergone continuous change, and several revised versions have been printed only to be retracted because of public opposition. One of the most contentious topics has concerned the way prayer is taught at the primary level. Though prayers under Saddam followed Sunni doctrine, the instructional images that accompanied them were ambiguous and could not be identified with either the Sunni or Shiʻi sects.[54] Elements that would distinguish

[50] *Sixth grade Social Studies*, 14, accessed April 11, 2011, http://www.iraqicurricula.org/.
[51] *Seventh grade Civics*, 8, accessed April 11, 2011, http://www.iraqicurricula.org/.
[52] Ibid., 18.
[53] Ibid., 19.
[54] *al-Tarbiya al-Islamiya li-l-Saf al-Awwal al-Ibtida'i*, First grade Islamic Studies, Iraqi Ministry of Education, 2001, see also *al-Tarbiya al-islamiya*, Islamic Studies Grade 2–6, Iraqi Ministry of Education, 2000–2.

the prayer as belonging to either of the two were conspicuously missing – a decision that was perhaps made with the regime's authoritarian aims in mind.[55]

The new curriculum has addressed the imbalance in a number of ways. A revised Islamic studies textbook in circulation in 2008 depicted both ways of praying. Yet another textbook depicted two brothers, Muhammad and Ahmad, praying according to Sunni and Shi'i guidelines alongside one another.[56] While a more inclusive approach to Islamic studies was the stated reason for the change, the move backfired and triggered a wave of accusations that the changes were politically motivated and that the Shi'i-led government was deliberately "fostering injustice and sectarianism" by differentiating between Sunnis and Shi'is.[57] According to a report by *al-Sharq al-Awsat* in 2009, parents and teachers accustomed to instruction under the Saddam regime, especially Sunnis, expressed concern that "teaching more than one way of praying might confuse children" and "lead to discrimination and sectarianism."[58] They said they hoped children would be taught about Islam in a more general way that "did not differentiate between sects" because Muslims are "one people with one religion and one God."[59]

Politicians and religious authorities immediately joined the dispute, further fueling suspicions that changes to the curriculum were politically motivated. Sunni politicians accused the Shi'a-led Ministry of Education of fomenting sectarianism, and Shi'i leaders responded in kind. Ayatollah Ali al-Sistani stated publicly that he supported changes and that a single curriculum should reflect "all the beautiful colors of Iraqi society" rather than being separate for Shi'i or Sunnis.[60] Statements by Internet commentators accused Sistani of "colluding with the (U.S.) occupiers" to develop the curriculum because they "sought sectarian strife" in Iraq.[61] And though most complaints were lodged by Sunnis who felt they were discriminated against by Shi'a, one of Iraq's leading Shi'i clerics, Grand Ayatollah Bashir al-Najafi,

---

[55] "Young Iraqis Are Losing Their Faith in Religion," *New York Times*, 2008, accessed July 15, 2011, http://www.nytimes.com/2008/03/03/world/africa/03iht-youth.4.10662930.html.

[56] "Sectarian change programs influence Iraqi curricula," *Al-Raeed*, 2010, accessed July 15, 2011, http://www.al-raeed.net/raeedmag/preview.php?id=1807.

[57] In Arabic (translated citation): "The Changing of the Islamic Studies curriculum in Iraq to teach prayer based on Shi'a practice ... with pictures," *Hanin Network*, accessed November 16, 2010, http://www.hanein.info/vb/showthread.php?t=106760&page=1.

[58] "Widespread Criticism from Parents and Teachers over Iraqi Curriculum," *Al-Sharq Al-Awsat*, 2009, accessed July 15, 2011, http://www.aawsat.com/details.asp?section=4&art icle=548076&issueno=11336.

[59] Ibid.

[60] "Shi'a Authorities Demand Changes to Iraqi Curricula," *Al-Sharq Al-Awsat*, 2008, accessed July 15, 2011, http://aawsat.com/details.asp?section=4&article=494568&issueno=10942.

[61] "Sistani and What I Learned from Him," *Al 3 Nabi*, accessed July 15, 2011, http://www.al3nabi.com/vb/f2/t45544.html.

also denounced the new books, arguing that they fostered sectarianism by imposing one sect's control over another.

A Sunni member of parliament and chairman of the Committee on Education, Alaa Makki, agreed that the new curriculum could worsen sectarian relations and stated it should focus instead on "the shared aspects [of Islam]."[62] Makki accused the Education Ministry of distributing the books without his knowledge. The charge was vehemently denied by Iraq's minister of education, Islamic Daʿwa Party member Khudayr al-Khuzai. Al-Khuzai (who has been since 2010 third vice president under Prime Minister al-Maliki) was later accused by Internet commentators of facilitating undue Iranian influence in the revision process by having the new textbooks published in Iran rather than Iraq. Some secular leaders have since criticized the involvement of religious figures. For example, Mithal al-Alusi, a former independent Sunni legislator, argued against what he claimed was undue Shiʿi influence, contending that education experts, not clerics and politicians, should decide the curriculum.[63]

The lessons were eventually retracted. Ironically, they were replaced by images nearly identical to those used during the Saddam regime that could not be identified with either sect. In addition, parents were instructed to teach their children how to pray. In some revised lessons, however, both Shiʿi and Sunni prayers accompanied the ambiguous images. Still other books included Shiʿi, rather than Sunni versions, with notes to students that only "some Muslims" follow the specific tradition depicted.[64] The impasse clearly remains unresolved.

Another addition to the new textbooks is the recognition of certain ethnic minorities. In particular, the Kurdish population has been included as part of the Iraqi population.[65] The following excerpts from the new curriculum's primary and secondary civics and social studies textbooks highlight efforts

---

[62] "Iraqi Schoolbooks Criticized for Sectarian Bias," *Institute for War and Peace Reporting*, February 2010, accessed July 16, 2011, from http://iwpr.net/report-news/iraqi-school-books-criticised-sectarian-bias.

[63] Ibid.

[64] "Islamic Studies," *Accelerated Learning Track*, Level 3, 81, accessed April 11, 2011, http://www.iraqicurricula.org/.

[65] At the same time, another problematic issue that arose immediately after 2003 was the manner in which potentially controversial historical events were addressed. Most history relating to Israel, the Kurds, the United States, the Iran-Iraq War, and the First Gulf War, for example, was deleted rather than rewritten in the haste to redistribute books after the invasion. "Turning the Pages on Iraq's History," *Christian Science Monitor*, November 2003, accessed July 17, 2011, http://www.csmonitor.com/2003/1104/p11s01-legn.html. A satisfactory solution was never reached, and many modern historical events and issues simply remained out of the curriculum, a situation described by a U.S. advisor to Iraq as going from "one-sided to no-sided" ("A New History of Iraq"). Currently, history textbooks (printed in 2009–10) still exclude these topics for the most part, with the exception of Israel, whose relation to Palestinian history is prominent.

to teach students about the country's Kurdish population. The lessons stress Kurdish loyalty to the larger Iraqi community:

The Kurds are the second largest group in Iraq.... They have lived in harmony with Arabs since ancient times.... They have defended Iraq and live as brothers united by love for it.[66]

The majority of Iraq's residents have an Arab identity both in terms of their history and civilization ... in addition to the presence of different national (identities), such as the Kurds, whose virtuous Iraqi citizenship unifies them.[67]

Updated maps in the new curriculum show a pluralistic Iraq by detailing the ethnic diversity of the different provinces. This is a clear break with the maps used under Saddam Hussein's regime, which, being Ba'thist and pan-Arab in character, did not take into account ethnic or religious diversity.[68] Since the fall of Saddam's regime, a significant number of politicians, along with religious authorities, have been at the center of this now high-profile debate.[69] And while most opponents claim that the new texts promote Shi'i interpretations of Islam at the expense of Sunni Islam, complaints fall on all sides of the political and religious spectrum.[70] Many also feel that the United States overstepped its boundaries with regard to Iraq's internal affairs, especially in 2003, following reports that USAID had demanded that religious references be limited or banned from certain texts.[71] Islamic religious authorities, already wary of U.S. interference, saw the curriculum project as an American plan to Westernize Iraqi schools. Shaykh Abdul Settar Jabber, who headed a leading Sunni group, called the curriculum project a U.S. attempt to "break Iraqi identity."[72]

ISLAM IS THE RELIGION OF THE OPPRESSED

In addition to the elimination of sectarian diversity within Islam, an underlying master narrative permeates history textbooks especially, portraying

---

[66] *Seventh grade Civics*, 15.
[67] *Sixth grade Social Studies*, 12.
[68] "A New Iraqi Curricula," *Islamopedia Online*, accessed November 1, 2011, http://www.islamopediaonline.org/country-profile/iraq/islam-and-education-system/new-iraqi-curricula.
[69] "Throwing Old Textbooks Out," *Niqash*, 2010, accessed May 11, 2011, http://www.niqash.org/content.php?contentTypeID=74&id=2688&lang=0.
[70] In Arabic (translated citation): "What are Iraqi students learning in regards to Islamic classes and history?" accessed November 3, 2010, http://ejabat.google.com/ejabat/thread?tid=43b24a057f3f8293&hl=ar&table=/ejabat/label?lid%3D0b1f3766f29foa9a%26hl%3Dar&pli=1.
[71] "Rewriting the Textbooks: Education Policy in Post-Hussein Iraq," *Harvard International Review*, 2006, accessed July 17, 2011, http://hir.harvard.edu/energy/rewriting-the-textbooks?page=0,0/ (refers to *London Financial Times* source).
[72] "A New History of Iraq," *The Guardian*, 2003, accessed July 17, 2011, http://www.guardian.co.uk/education/2003/nov/25/schools.schoolsworldwide.

Islam and Muslims as eternal victims of real and potential enemies.[73] This victim narrative provides a foundational story that unites the umma and bolsters a sense of nationalism through a common historical memory of constant assault upon the Muslim community by various named and unnamed foes. The characterization of Islam as the religion of the oppressed both serves as the lens through which the nationalist mytho-history is constructed and influences how non-Muslim religions are portrayed through discourses of inclusion and exclusion.

While religious education textbooks highlight national identity through the state's specific interpretation of Islam, the teaching of history often focuses on the general Islamic history of the umma instead of only national history within state borders. Like all history textbooks, the historiography engages in selective tradition, through which the states are able to "magnify and exaggerate their evaluation of historical events in order to highlight the glory and greatness of Muslims.... This method aims at reviving religious and national feelings in the hearts of Muslim children in order to make them feel proud of their glorious past and to sow hope in their souls that one day they will be able to restore this glory and take their revenge on the West."[74] In particular, history textbooks focus on the renaissance of Islamic thought during the golden age of Islam in contrast to the darkness in which Westerners lived during the Middle Ages.

At the same time, another common thread throughout history textbooks is the consistent victim narrative. Both history and religious textbooks emphasize the hardships of the Prophet Muhammad and the tribal wars fought against nonbelievers. As a result, from the nascent stages of the historical narrative, Islam is portrayed as always on the defensive. Continuity is created between the threats of the past against the original Muslim community and the current threats against the national community. In this way, textbooks not only create and emphasize a shared past with the umma but also promote national cohesion and unification against this threat through discussions of *al-Walā' wa al-Barā'* (loyalty and enmity) and jihad. The threats come from past, present, or possible future enemies: the "West"; imperialistic ambitions of specific countries such as the United States; modern-day Jews; Israel and Zionists; and an unnamed, faceless, and perpetual threat to Islam and the nation.

For instance, in the case of the Pakistani history curriculum, the textbooks construct "a myth of an ever-looming enemy ready to harm Pakistan."[75] As a result the military is upheld as the "chief pillar of Pakistani

[73] Eleanor Abdella Doumato and Gregory Starrett (eds.), *Teaching Islam: Textbooks and Religion in the Middle East* (Boulder, CO: Lynne Rienner Publishers, 2007), 5.

[74] Recep Kaymakcan and Leirvik Oddbjørn (eds.), *Teaching for Tolerance in Muslim Majority Societies* (Istanbul: Center for Values Education (DEM) Press, 2007), 123.

[75] Durrani and Dunne, "Curriculum and national identity," 226.

identity,"[76] because it protects and defends Pakistan and Islam from "the others." In this regard, India is the national enemy par excellence.[77] In addition to the textbook portrayals of the external Hindu threat, Durrani and Dunne find that the teachers also construct the Pakistani identity by emphasizing its opposition to Hindu India. Moreover, the Hindu/Indian threat surfaces in the presentation of historical events such as the "different wars that took place between Hindus and Muslims at various points in history before and after the partition of India."[78] In these discussions of conflict, religious imagery is employed "to naturalize religious nationalism and jihad."[79] Additionally, the selective use of historical events emphasizes military heroism and consequently the willingness to fight as an essential feature of being a Muslim.[80] Hindus or Indians are not the only "others" in these textbooks; the United States is also perceived as the "other." As a consequence, students are taught to justify the buildup of arms and uphold the army as protection.[81]

Similarly, Turkish social studies and history textbooks employ a discourse that assumes that all the states around Turkey and even some groups within the society itself are hostile toward Turks.[82] The result is an implicit message of the need for constant vigilance against "external and internal threats" or the "others." These "others" are categorized as either "others among us" under which religious minorities are included, or "others among them" such as Christians. By perceiving religious minority groups within Turkey and Christians outside of Turkey as "others" and "internal and external threats," these textbooks clearly imply that the "us" is the state's Turkish-Sunni identity.

The notable exception to this victimization discourse and perception of the West as the enemy is found in Tunisian textbooks. For example in one of these textbooks, the author argues that among the factors that contributed to the collapse of the Arab-Islamic civilization, the most important was the abandonment of traditions. In these conditions, the most crucial way to ensure progress and modernization is openness and interaction with other civilizations.[83] The author of the textbook offers Europe as a paradigm of modernity because of the separation of religion from the state.[84] Moreover, in the same textbook, the author argues that

---

[76] Ibid.
[77] Ibid., 224.
[78] Ibid., 225.
[79] Ibid.
[80] Ibid., 232.
[81] Ibid., 228.
[82] Kaymakcan and Oddbjørn, *Teaching for Tolerance in Muslim Majority Societies*, 37.
[83] *Book in the Muslim Thinking: For the Second Year Students in Secondary Education*, Ministry of Education, Tunisia (Tunis: Pedagogical National Center, n.d.).
[84] Succinct English outline of the Arabic original text: "لا نختلف اذا قلنا انه من بين عوامل انهيار الحضارة": العربية الاسلامية هو تخليها عن اهم تقاليدها وهي الانفتاح على الحضارات الاخرى والتفاعل مع تراث الآخرين بما يضمن

the Arab Renaissance of the nineteenth century came about only because of the influence of the developed, secular West on the backward East (before Western colonization).[85] This is significant because in no other Muslim-majority country's textbook is the West depicted in such a positive fashion or given such an influential role through colonization. Such a praise of the West is not really surprising in light of Bourguiba's efforts toward modernization, which he equated with Westernization. While this extreme of touting colonization as enlightened modernization is not continued in the new textbooks, they do promote modernization conflated with secularization. In the chapter, "Qur'an and the Liberation of Human Beings,"[86] of a 2006 textbook, the author forcefully argues that God sent the Qur'an to liberate people's minds by replacing religious authority with a civic, democratic state (*al-dawla al-madaniya al-demoqratiya*).[87] Interestingly, this argument has been central in the discourse and strategies of the Ennahda party since the Jasmine Revolution (see Part III).

Similarly, the Egyptian curriculum does not manifest an attitude of confrontation or rivalry with the West, which as a term is rarely even used.[88] Instead, the textbooks teach an overarching principle that Muslims should gain benefits and enjoyment from any source, including from the West, but should beware of violating Islamic principles.[89] Instead, it can be inferred that Egyptian education stresses unity against extremist elements of society and Islamists, thus discrediting the opposition and simultaneously further legitimizing the state.

As a consequence, the combined forces of the victim narrative, the propagation of a defensive attitude against enemies, and inclusive/exclusive language promotes resistance. However, it is worth noting that there is no explicit content in the textbooks encouraging or inciting violence for the sole cause of religion. Instead, jihad is invoked as a defensive mechanism of the

التقدم والتمدن. إن أهل اوروبا وصلوا الى ما وصلوا اليه بمزيد خصب او اعتدال في اقاليمهم...إن الديانة النصرانية لا تتداخل
في التصرفات السياسية. وإنما بلغوا تلك الغاية والتقدم بالتنظيمات المؤسسة على العدل السياسي وتسهيل طرق الثروة." Khair al-Deen al-Tunisi, "Achievement of Goals through Organizations," *Book in the Muslim Thinking: For the Second Year Students in Secondary Education*, pp. 61–62.

[85] Succinct English outline of the Arabic original text: "ان النهضة العربية تولدت جزئيا من ذلك اللقاء الحضاري." "بين غرب متقدم وافد وشرق متخلف." Dr. Muhammad 'Aziz al-Hbabi, "Islam Today: New Awareness." *Book in the Muslim Thinking: For the Second Year Students in Secondary Education*, p. 76.

[86] Ahmad Khalaf Allah. "Al-Qur'an wa Tahrir al-Insan القران وتحرير الانسان," or "Qur'an and the Liberation of Man," *Book in the Muslim Thinking: For the Third Year Students in High School*. Ministry of Education, Tunisia (Tunis: The Pedagogical National Center, 2006), 36.

[87] Succinct English outline of the Arabic original text: "القرآن الكريم: هو عند الناس جميعاً كتاب دين...وعندي أنه الكتاب الذي نزل من السماء ليحرر العقل البشري من تلك القيود التي كان يرسف فيها بإسم الدين، والتي قيدته بها السلطات الدينية التقليدية." Ibid.

[88] The primary enemy of Egyptian Muslims presented in the textbooks seems to be religious fanaticism and the rival Islamist agenda within society. Another enemy is the Zionist expansionist threat, despite the peace treaty between Israel and Egypt.

[89] Toronto and Eissa, "Egypt: Promoting Tolerance, Defending against Islamism," 36.

national identity. The basic meaning of jihad is "to be striving or struggling with one's own self, or for social justice, or any righteous cause, or under certain conditions, such as an armed struggle or just war."[90] Specifically, when jihad as a military struggle is mentioned, it is rarely in the context of aggression. Instead, it is portrayed as a defensive response.[91] The usage of the term jihad in textbooks varies from country to country, and it ranges from blunt advocacy of violence in the name of jihad to rejection of jihad as an expression of unbridled fanaticism.

For example, in Egyptian textbooks, "terrorism is strongly condemned and tolerance is continually advocated."[92] The textbooks emphasize that "violence only begets violence; God therefore ordered Muhammad to use patience and forgiveness."[93] Furthermore, because of the importance of Islamist political violence in Egypt, the textbooks stress:

Extremism has been seen even among some Muslims.... So you must not permit yourself to engage in extremism in any situation. Avoid it through deep understanding, calm thinking, and ease and tolerance, and there is no harshness or oppression or extremism in it.... Islam forbids terrorism.[94]

As a result, acts of terrorism are strongly condemned as divisive and detrimental to Egyptian society as a whole, and jihad is explained as follows: "The Muslim, before he embarks on jihad (military struggle) should undertake the battle of the 'greater jihad' [*al-jihād al-akbar*] with his own nature and passions, his desires, and his personal and family interests."[95]

ISLAM IS THE SUPERIOR RELIGION

Recently, there has been a strong emphasis on religious tolerance in most countries' textbooks, including those of Turkey and Egypt, in a shift away from divisive extremist elements. Despite this nominal emphasis on tolerance, there is much confusion because of inherent contradictions "in promoting tolerance and respect for other religions and at the same time including material that instills an exclusivist, triumphalist attitude by emphasizing the pre-eminence of the Muslim community."[96] Thus, Muslim students learn to respect non-Muslims in a religious context while at the same time facing encouragement to unite against "infidels," that is, the political enemies of

---

[90] Kaymakcan and Oddbjørn, *Teaching for Tolerance in Muslim Majority Societies*, 227.
[91] Ibid.
[92] Doumato and Starrett, *Teaching Islam*, 46.
[93] Mohamed Alaa, "Survey of Textbooks And Curricular Content, Egypt Profile, *Islamopediaonline*, accessed July 2, 2013.
[94] Ibid.
[95] Ibid.
[96] Toronto and Eissa, "Egypt: Promoting Tolerance, Defending against Islamism," 49.

the umma.[97] Such contradictory statements reveal the different meanings of Islamic references according to the religious or political contexts in which they appear. At the end, the political meaning takes precedence because of the central role of the state in defining Islam as a modern religion.

Similarly, the ideas of tolerance and equality of all religions promoted in some parts of the curriculum are in contradiction with the superiority of Muslims implicitly conveyed in other parts. Although the pupil is never taught explicitly that being Muslim makes him/her better, it is clearly implied that being Muslim definitely puts him/her in a superior position; that Islam is "the best and most complete religion"; that Muhammad is superior to other prophets; and that whoever does not accept Islam and chooses another religion will "lose" and have a difficult time in the afterlife.[98] Specifically, Egyptian textbooks emphasize the topics of tolerance and peace for national unity, yet "the implicit (and sometimes explicit) message is that Islam and Muslims are superior in God's sight and that other religious communities have an inferior spiritual status."[99] In the same vein, in Tunisian textbooks, Islam is described as the last, true, and complete version of the monotheistic Revelation.[100] This idea is not emphasized in 2001 textbooks, however; instead, there is more injunction for religious freedom and freedom of thought in Islam.[101]

As Pakistani education defines membership to the nation on the basis of religious identity, the curriculum thus excludes non-Muslim Pakistanis from national identity. Furthermore, the curriculum even alienates them by portraying non-Muslim Pakistanis as evil, anti-Muslim, and "the enemy."[102]

[97] Golnar Mehran, "Iran: A Shi'ite Curriculum to Serve the Islamic State," in Eleanor Abdella Doumato and Gregory Starrett (eds.), *Teaching Islam: Textbooks and Religion in the Middle East* (Boulder, CO: Lynne Rienner Publishers, 2007), 53–70.

[98] "Religious Studies," Grade 3, p. 22, in Eleanor Abdella Doumato and Gregory Starrett (eds.), *Teaching Islam: Textbooks and Religion in the Middle East* (Boulder, CO: Lynne Rienner Publishers, 2007), 38.

[99] Toronto and Eissa, "Egypt: Promoting Tolerance, Defending against Islamism," 38.

[100] Islam brings a complete and unique era for humankind: "الرسالات السماوية هي في واقع الامر دين واحد، وإن جاء على فترات ومراحل مختلفة آخرها و أكملها الاسلام." In Kamaal 'Abd-Allah al-Mahdi, Kamaal 'Abd-Allah al-Mahdi. "آثار الإيمان في المجتمع التوحيد بين الرسالات السماوية" or "Effect of Faith in the Society, Uniformity Among the Three Heavenly Messages," *Book of Islamic Education for the First Year Students, in Secondary Education*, Ministry of Education, n.d., Tunisia. pp. 37–8.

[101] *Book in the Muslim Thinking: For the First Year Students in Secondary Education*, Ministry of Education, Tunisia, 2001. Kamaal Abd-Allah al-Mahdi, "al-Hurriya Qa'idat al-Hukm الحرية قاعدة الحكم" or "Freedom is the Foundation for Ruling," *Book in the Muslim Thinking: For the Third Year Students in High School*, Ministry of Education, Tunisia, The Pedagogical National Center, 2006, 38–9. Moreover, the 2006 textbooks assert that Islam is a religion for everyone and not just for Muslims.
See Ali Hasab Allah. "Qur'an is a General Miracle," in *Book in the Muslim Thinking: For the Third Year Students in High School*. Ministry of Education, Tunisia. The Pedagogical National Center. 2006. p. 92.

[102] Durrani and Dunne, "Curriculum and national identity," 230.

Thus, students often perceive non-Muslim Pakistanis not as Pakistanis but as internal enemies. Moreover, in Pakistani textbooks, discussions of "the other" are marked by a sense of good versus evil and Islamic superiority. "The other" is depicted as non-Muslim and evil, thus conflating the concept of being non-Muslim with being evil. According to Durrani and Dunne, "the representations of non-Muslims in negative ways impacted on students to the extent that some questioned universal human values,"[103] implying that non-Muslims may not even be considered human or be accorded the same human rights that Muslims have. Misrepresentations or omissions of the other monotheistic religions are closely related to this idea of the superiority of Islam.

Similarly, textbooks in Tunisia still use language that places Islam above other religions. Islam is described as not only newer but preferable to those religions that preceded it: "a new view of the universe and mankind as individual and in society." These books, however, do not necessarily denigrate other Abrahamic religions. According to the *Book of Islamic Education*, God sent down the Torah to Moses; Jesus later corrected the mistakes of the Jews; and once people were ready, God sent an all-encompassing final message through the Prophet Muhammad.[104] This stands in contrast with the textbooks of most of the other countries discussed in this chapter.

MISREPRESENTATION OR OMISSION OF JEWS AND CHRISTIANS

In contemporary Egyptian history textbooks, the Christian Coptic culture and history, which have played integral roles in Egyptian history, are either extremely underrepresented or not represented at all.[105] When Coptic culture and history are provided, there seems to be a taboo on informing about Christian dogma. This exclusion is partly due to the denial of the existence of religious conflict, which, given the recent history of violent attacks carried out by Islamist groups in Egypt, is also a way of disassociating Egyptians from divisive, extremist elements. An acknowledgment of religious conflict in Egyptian history would bring attention to discrimination against religious minorities, which would then undermine national unity.[106] Additionally, Western Christianity is portrayed as an inferior, "essentially non-religious culture, which is primarily a military and economic rival, which Oriental Christians and Muslims have had to defend against by way of 'national unity' since the dawn of civilization."[107]

[103] Ibid., 228.
[104] Shaykh 'Uthmaan Muhammad Hablli, "The Effect of Faith in the Society, Uniformity Among the Three Heavenly Messages," in the *Book of Islamic Education for the First Year Students, in Secondary Education* (Ministry of Education, Tunisia).
[105] Kaymakcan and Oddbjørn, *Teaching for Tolerance in Muslim Majority Societies*, 126.
[106] Pink, "Nationalism, Religion and the Muslim-Christian Relationship."
[107] Kaymakcan and Oddbjørn, *Teaching for Tolerance in Muslim Majority Societies*, 135.

While there is no monolithic, typical Islamic approach to presenting non-Islamic religions, there is an underlying emphasis on the correctness of the Islamic view and the constant approach of interpreting other religions based on an Islam-centric perspective. These presentations vary temporally and geographically, and they range from very negative and biased to more objective portrayals. However, in general, "the corruptions of Christianity and Judaism are used as a means to extol the superiority of Islam as a whole."[108]

In the case of Egypt, there is a continuity of anti-Jewish sentiment from the old to the new curriculum. In a discussion about Jews and Muslims in Medina, Jews are described as "known for certain characteristics that are typical of them throughout their generations.... Their wiliness and wars against Islam, however different in style and form, have had the same objectives."[109] Furthermore, Jews are portrayed as "religiously and humanly racist and their racism and animosity go beyond Islam and Muslims to all other people and religions. They have no loyalty to whatever nation they live in and have no respect to its covenants and laws. Jews of yesterday are the Jews of today and tomorrow."[110]

Examining the material on Christianity in the 2000 and 2005 secondary and primary school textbooks in Turkey gives a clear picture of the significant change in approach and presentation of Christianity in the new and inclusive model. Notably, no presentation of Judaism is available. A plausible explanation may be that Judaism was not extensively or even particularly taught. It seems that information on Judaism as a religion was not provided, but linkages were inexplicitly constructed between the negative portrayal of the Jews of Jesus' time and Judaism, thus indirectly portraying Judaism negatively. Furthermore, in history textbooks, the religious connection of Jews with Palestine is neglected and Jews are never referred to as inhabitants of the land, either in the past or the present. Instead, only Muslims and Christians (and their holy places) are mentioned.[111]

In Turkey, three topics frequently presented in textbooks focus on Christianity from a historical point of view: Jesus, the role of St. Paul in Christianity, and the Scriptures. When discussing Jesus, the textbooks always use respectful language, and they recognize and portray him as a great prophet.[112] The first year of secondary school textbooks provides a

---

[108] Betty Anderson, "Jordan: Prescription for Obedience and Conformity," in Eleanor Abdella Doumato and Gregory Starrett (eds.), *Teaching Islam: Textbooks and Religion in the Middle East* (Boulder, CO: Lynne Reinner Publishers, 2007), 71–88, 72.

[109] *Tenth year, first semester Islamic education textbook*, 39.

[110] *Tenth year, second semester Islamic education textbook*, 74–7.

[111] Kaymakcan and Oddbjørn, *Teaching for Tolerance in Muslim Majority Societies*, 127.

[112] Recep Kaymakcan, "Curriculum and Textbook Revisions Regarding the Image of the 'Religious Other' in Turkish Religious Education," in Recep Kaymakcan and Oddbjørn Leirvik (eds.), *Teaching for Tolerance in Muslim Majority Societies* (Istanbul: Center for Values Education (DEM) Press, 2007), 18.

narration of the different life stages of Jesus (birth and crucifixion) in terms of Christian sources. On the other hand, primary school textbooks "mainly follow an Islamic confessional method to portray the life of Jesus without referring to Christian sources."[113]

The main themes covered include his unique birth, childhood, baptism and mission, healing of the sick, relation to the Jewish community, and crucifixion. In particular, the issue of the negative response by the Jewish community to Jesus's mission is strongly criticized by the textbooks. Some controversial points concerning Jesus's birth and crucifixion are emphasized, and the Islamic view, often supported by Qur'anic verses, is represented as the correct and moderate view between the more extreme views of Christianity and Judaism. On the issue of Jesus's unique birth, the textbooks reject the accusation of a non-virginal birth, which is an explanation offered by the Jewish community, and even go so far as to condemn the Jews' unfaithful attitude with a reference from the Qur'an. In response to the Christian claim of Jesus's divinity, the textbooks state that this explanation is a corruption of the Christian faith and firmly oppose any claim that Jesus was the son of God.

On the issue of Jesus's crucifixion, the Turkish textbooks recognize the importance of this event to Christianity and portray the Jews in a negative, culpable light. The textbooks state that Islam rejects the death of Jesus on the cross, and argue using a Qur'anic quote that a person resembling Jesus was actually executed in his place. With regards to the role of St. Paul in Christianity, the textbooks emphasize his key position in the formation of Christianity, but the textbooks do not aim to describe the important role he occupies as far as Christianity understands it.[114] They do offer, however, an Islamic interpretation of St. Paul's role, which portrays him as a scapegoat by focusing on his role in corrupting Jesus' original message and ultimately Christianity. Notably, the textbooks provide further information on St. Paul's background as the son of a Jew and draw attention to his dramatic conversion experience. The textbooks imply that St. Paul's views strongly influenced the agenda of the Christian councils and ultimately caused the divisive rupture creating the Orthodox Church and the Catholic Church.

Similarly, the Turkish textbooks offer an Islamic interpretation of the Scriptures. Primarily and inaccurately, the textbooks present the Gospels as a book revealed by God to Jesus. According to this interpretation, after Jesus' death this "holy book was corrupted by religious scholars as happened to the Torah."[115] Thus, the main focus lies on the four Gospels, the issue of originality, and when and how these Gospels were canonized by Christians in history. The textbooks argue that the Gospels have been corrupted by

---

[113] Ibid.
[114] Ibid., 21.
[115] Ibid., 22.

emphasizing contradictory points, errors, and the description of events that occurred after the death of Jesus.

A new curriculum for secondary religious education was introduced in 2005, which provided a more modern, pluralistic model. For both primary and secondary school, it emphasizes the importance of teaching other religions to create a culture of peace and tolerance in the face of globalization. While religious education is compulsory, there is an exception: a non-Muslim student has the right to withdraw from taking a course on religious education. However, there is no provision made for an alternative class, such as an ethics course, for those who have withdrawn from religious education.[116] Furthermore, the previous method of presenting the basic notions of each religion separately has been replaced by a thematic approach in which the different religions' perspectives are offered and analyzed together on a topic. That is, "academics within faculties of theology and teachers of Religious Education pay much attention to the accurate presentation of non-Islamic religions in order to overcome obstacles in traditional approaches."[117]

Concretely, old textbooks for religious education classified religions as "divinely originated" or "non-divine." Two subdivisions fell under "divinely originated": "distorted religion" and "undistorted religion." In this manner of classification, the old textbooks placed Christianity under the category of a "distorted divinely originated religion," thereby implying an underlying prejudice against Christianity. No such classification appears in the new textbooks, indicating a significant step in the approach toward understanding other religions. Instead, a different, neutral organization of religions in the curriculum is offered: Abrahamic or divine religions (Islam, Christianity, and Judaism), Chinese and Japanese religions, Hindu religions, and traditional religions. As one would expect, the priority in the curriculum is given to Islam, Christianity, and Judaism. However, there is still a bias toward Muslim understandings of Christianity and Judaism. For example, Qur'anic verses dominate the section on sacred books while only very brief information is provided about the Torah and the Gospels without offering any direct references from either. Furthermore, the textbooks explicitly state that, according to Islamic belief, these other books have not been preserved in their original form, implying that the Qur'an is the only uncorrupted and truly sacred text.[118]

---

[116] Ibid., 17.

[117] However, it is important to note that while theoretically this approach is ideal, because the majority of the students in the classroom environment are Muslim, the thematic approach could lead to distortions and inaccurate understandings of non-Islamic religions. Kaymakcan and Oddbjørn, *Teaching for Tolerance in Muslim Majority Societies*, 30.

[118] Ibid., 99.

Additionally, more space and importance have been given to non-Islamic religions in the new Turkish curriculum. For example, in the previous curriculum, Christianity was covered only in the textbook of the sixth year of primary school; in the new curriculum, Christianity is presented throughout the sixth, seventh, and eighth years of primary school. Moreover, in the discussion of ethics and values, the new textbooks offer quotes from the Qur'an as well as from other sacred scriptures, especially the Bible. In this manner, the textbooks emphasize the points of agreement on ethical values instead of the conflicts of religious controversies.[119] At the same time, in March 2012, the Grand National Assembly of Turkey steamrolled an educational reform bill, which increased the influence of Islamic schools by allowing students to enroll in religious imam hatip schools in middle school, whereas before only high school students could attend these religious schools.[120] As a result, accusations against the AK party under Prime Minister Recep Tayyip Erdogan of "promoting religious conservatism by stealth" have increased.[121]

Thus, while significant reforms are being made to public education curricula and textbooks through a focus on tolerance, as long as the state continues to conflate religious identity with national identity, true tolerance will not be achieved. Even very secular leaders such as Gamal Abdel Nasser, Habib Bourguiba, and Saddam Hussein have employed Islamic terms in their political discourse, further amalgamating national and religious identity. In this way, umma, jihad, and Shari'a have gained a central place in modern Muslim political projects to become mainstays not only as religio-political terms in the state repertoire for the last fifty years but also as core elements of the education system in Muslim states.

---

[119] While the new curriculum emphasizes religious plurality and tolerance, it is interesting to note that even the broader view of Christianity in textbooks is simplified to a singular description: "They not only disregard the diversity within Christianity but also ignore the existence of diversity within the Islamic tradition." Kaymakcan and Oddbjørn Leirvik, *Teaching for Tolerance in Muslim Majority Societies*, 26.

[120] Associated Press, "Turkey passes hotly contested school reform bill," *Fox News*, March 30, 2012, accessed July 14, 2012, http://www.foxnews.com/world/2012/03/30/turkey-passes-hotly-contested-school-reform-bill/.

[121] Simon Cameron-Moore, "Turkey passes school reform law viewed by critics as Islamic," *Al Arabiya News*, March 30, 2012, accessed July 14, 2012, http://www.alarabiya.net/articles/2012/03/30/204265.html.

Conclusion of Part I

The Principle of the Secular
Self–Secularism and Religion Revisited

As highlighted in the previous chapters, the invention of Islam as a modern religion is closely associated with the building of the nation-state. The efforts by so-called secular states to limit the social influence of religion actually led to nationalization of religious identities and, therefore, to their politicization, defying the expectations of earlier modernization theories.[1]

As a result, the political development of Muslim nation-states leads to a more complex approach to secularity than does the separation of church and state principle.

In this regard, political and social modernization in Muslim countries stands in stark opposition to the dominant Western narrative according to which the religious identity of the individual departs from national identity and becomes increasingly privatized with the expansion of political and civic rights (even though this story does not reflect the diversity and nuances of the historical experiences of the European and American nations, as I argued in Chapter 1).

Charles Taylor has superbly demonstrated[2] that Western secularity is the culmination of an historical progression of ideas, leading to the "authentic" religiosity being associated with personal commitment and with the conception of the world as immanent. The separation of the "worldly" from the "transcendent" led to the private versus public disjunction. This separation was accelerated through the Reformation and laid the groundwork for the ascendance of a neutral, self-sufficient secular order, leading to the contemporary situation where belief in God is

---

[1] Michelle Burgis, "Faith in the State? Traditions of Territoriality, International Law and the Emergence of Modern Arab Statehood," *Journal of the History of International Law* 11.1 (2009): 76–7.

[2] Charles Taylor, *A Secular Age* (Cambridge, MA: Harvard University Press, 2007).

considered one among many viable spiritual options. An environment in which the private and public are separated in this way does not necessarily prevent believers from enjoying the right to fully express their religious identity, although they can occasionally face challenges that nonbelievers do not. For instance, the controversy over Salman Rushdie's *The Satanic Verses* or the Danish cartoon crisis are signs that Muslims who live in Western secular democracies are struggling with this framework of the immanent being limited to the personal level of religious commitment.[3]

In contrast, modern religion in Muslim countries is positioned on the platform of the state with the consequence that the latter has defined modern Islam as a code of public morality. In other words, there is often a correlation of national and religious identities in present-day Muslim countries. As a result of this fusion, a moral hierarchy is established in which the national government intervenes in the personal lives of its citizens on topics that range from dress to social relations and culture.

More specifically, one of the consequences of the building of hegemonic Islam has been the moralization of the public order as the state has increasingly used Islamic principles to assert its legitimacy. For example, the state is authorized to distinguish between the civil and religious dimensions of citizens' acts and, on that basis, decide whether the acts are enforceable, punishable, or otherwise deserving protection or exemption under the law. Included in that process are the often unarticulated understandings about what Islam is or what it should be. Hence, the state is always drawing a line between the religious and the secular, and retaining sole authority to do so. Hussein Agrama describes secularism in most Muslim countries as primarily a state action, or what he calls "active secularism."[4] One way to think about the principle of active secularism is to see the state as promoting a modern Islam, defining the spaces it should inhabit, authorizing the sensibilities that are appropriate for it, and then working to discipline the religious tradition so that it conforms to this abstract notion, fits into those spaces, and expresses those sensibilities.[5]

In sum, most Muslim states, to some degree, have utilized Islamic references to forge a public morality of what is good and what is wrong in politics and who is a good and who is a bad citizen. It is worth emphasizing that this analysis concerns the norms of the dominant political culture but does

---

[3] Jytte Klausen, *The Cartoons That Shook the World* (New Haven, CT: Yale University Press, 2009).
[4] Hussein Ali Agrama, "Secularism, Sovereignty and Indeterminacy: Is Egypt a Secular or a Religious State? *Comparative Studies in Society and History* 52.3 (2010): 495–523.
[5] Ibid.

not represent the behaviors and ethics of many citizens of Muslim-majority countries who do not systematically conform their personal life to these expectations. But the norm of the good citizen tells another story.

In other words, the role of Islamic practices in the definition of public morality has been central to the civic and national identities of postcolonial Muslim societies. It is therefore misleading to think that Muslim societies did not undergo a process of modernization. In fact, from the eighteenth century onward, their modernization process has created renewed tensions between modern and religious individuals. The monitoring of the female body and of freedom of expression have become the major site of these tensions – triggering persistent discussion among religious authorities, politicians, and women's groups on alternative and sometimes conflicting models of rightness of what is modern and what is Islamic. This attentiveness to the body has translated into state prescriptions that range from sexual rules to *mores* of modesty, while freedom of expression is continuously redefined and disputed for the sake of the national community's interests as opposed to the rights of the individuals. To capture the complexity of these non-Western forms of modernization, it is therefore necessary to broaden our understanding of religion and secularism beyond beliefs, on one hand, and separation of religion and politics, on the other hand.

ISLAM AS A CODE OF PUBLIC MORALITY: WOMEN'S BODIES AS A CONTESTED POLITICAL SITE

Over the past fifty years, the state has become a central, if not the most important, agent of redefining Islamic law and religious orthodoxy, leading to a reshaping of Islamic norms. Such a reconstruction of religious norms is at odds with the dominant perception of secularism as a disassociation between public behavior and religious norms. In other words, secularism for Muslim countries may not mean the removal of religion from either the public or political sphere.

The woman's body has become the main site of this politicization of Islam, by state and nonstate actors alike. The politicization of the female body is a general feature of Muslim societies, from the colonial to postcolonial periods. A consistent theme throughout these different phases is that women are the symbolic embodiment of morality, and therefore are the key to securing familial, national, and religious values in an uncertain maelstrom of social change.

This political discipline imposed on the female body has taken opposite directions. As we have seen at the political foundations of Turkey and Tunisia, state intrusion led to the unveiling of women as citizens of the modern nation. More recently, however, Islamic dress code has been imposed on women as part of a redefinition of citizenship. Iran is a case in point; after the Islamic revolution in 1979, morality police enforced strict

Islamic dress codes including the hijab and the chador. In some ways, the chador was actually a symbol of the success of Khomeini and the Islamic Revolution, and women wore or were forced to wear Islamic dress as a sign of support. At the same time, when women wanted to express their individuality, through Western clothing or otherwise, it was interpreted as a political act and was therefore repressed. Nowadays, the ways Iranian women wear their headscarves reflect political positions ranging from liberal to conservative. Instead of wearing the black scarf as initially mandated, women have begun to wear brightly colored scarves that reveal more of their hair, especially in urban areas such as Tehran. As a result, there have also been a growing number of arrests and citations for women wearing "bad hijab."[6]

The same trend emerged in Afghanistan under the Taliban and in Chechnya, where women have been harassed and abused by individuals and law enforcement agents, and some have even been shot at by paintball guns if they were seen without the hijab.[7] In the aftermath of the overthrow of former president Alu Alkhanov and the rise of Ramzan Kadyrov as head of the Chechen republic in 2007, an Islamic "virtue campaign" became a priority for the Chechen state. Kadyrov has been known to support *de facto* "modesty laws" and "headscarf rules" that prohibit women from working, going to school, and appearing in public if they do not wear headscarves.[8] Furthermore, he has openly acknowledged polygamy and honor killings as parts of Chechen society.[9]

This political discipline of the body is far from being an idiosyncrasy of Muslim-majority countries. Legislation against the hijab and niqab in European countries proceeds from the same logic. The distinction in Muslim countries lies in conflating the moral hierarchy of gender roles with the legitimacy of the political community. We have seen how in Egypt and Pakistan, Islamic prescriptions can be used to redefine the good citizen, particularly during periods of political instability. As greater social mobility for both men and women threatens the existing governmental structure and its power, principles of family are evoked to mitigate social change. These principles feed into the dominant status of gender hierarchies, thus politicizing what in premodern Muslim societies had been strictly part of the social sphere. As conceptions of family are entangled with political consciousness and

---

[6] "Crackdown in Iran over Dress Codes," *BBC News*, April 27, 2007, accessed September 3, 2013, http://news.bbc.co.uk/2/hi/6596933.stm.

[7] "You Dress According to Their Rules," *Human Rights Watch*, March 10, 2011, http://www.hrw.org/en/node/97046/section/6.

[8] Ibid..

[9] It should be noted that these so-called laws are not actual legislation; rather, they are social and political codes instated in 2007 by a public television announcement by Kadyrov. However, Kadyrov has made enforcing these dress codes a matter of national duty and part of a new form of citizenship, commending men who harass women for not wearing modest Islamic dress.

the formation of national identity, Islam becomes construed in a way that permits gender inequality as a means of maintaining social harmony. The control of women and maintenance of gendered moral hierarchies render a sense of national security and authority over conditions of social change that cannot be easily controlled. Through this process, Islam becomes incorporated as a political ideology in service of the state.

PREEMINENCE OF THE COMMUNITY
OVER THE RELIGIOUS SELF

Similarly, we have seen in the previous chapters that the religious self is often defined by ritual action and public behavior. In all of the countries surveyed, a combination of culturally constructed values (*adāb*) and Islamic law creates social customs, which emphasize the social over the individual being. In other words, daily interactions reinforce the idea that the self is subordinated to social obligations. This standard extends to the very definition of equality. Whereas in the West equality is defined by uniform sets of individual rights, in the countries studied, equality is the equal obligation of individuals to promote communal welfare. We have analyzed in Chapters 3 and 4 the consequences of this definition on freedom of speech. In a similar fashion, the moral obligation of the family allows no room for the promotion of self above the interests of the community. Therefore, any conceptions of female emancipation are regarded as dissonant with the cultural values of the nation, often defined in religious terms. A case in point is the controversy created by Turkish Prime Minister Recep Tayyip Erdogan in May 2012, when he told a gathering of the women's branches of his Justice and Development Party that "each abortion is one Uludere" – a reference to air strikes on a village on the Iraqi border that killed thirty-four civilians in December. Abortions, said the prime minister, are "a sneaky plan to wipe the country off the world stage."[10] It is worth noting that the same rhetoric is also present in Western democracies as shown by the political agenda of Christian fundamentalist groups in the United States. But these claims do not operate (at present) within the same legal and political environment.

Generally speaking, gendered roles in the family reflect a hierarchy of social positions that directly affect women's lives in both the private and public spheres. For example, at the core of the nationalist ideology of

---

[10] Justin Vela, "'Abortions are like air strikes on civilians': Turkish PM Recep Tayyip Erdogan's rant sparks women's rage," *The Independent*, May 30, 2012, accessed July 14, 2012, http://www.independent.co.uk/life-style/health-and-families/health-news/abortions-are-like-air-strikes-on-civilians-turkish-pm-recep-tayyip-erdogans-rant-sparks-womens-rage-7800939.html. It should be noted that abortions are currently legal in Turkey.

the countries surveyed, there is an element of self-preservation in order to secure moral capital in a rapidly Westernizing world. Globalization and consumerism both pose threats to the social composition of these regions of the Muslim world, which, in their instability, regard this trend as one of moral depravity. Within this globalizing cultural setting, in which the terms and values of social relations are mutating, the reflex in most Muslim countries is to subordinate the rights of individuals, frequently women, in favor of social cohesion and political welfare. Government officials, therefore, have relied on the preestablished moral capital of religion and the familial structure to control the social upheaval stirred by Western influences. Consequentially, women's behavior and sexuality often become restricted.

Presently, control of women's bodies and sexuality has guaranteed both continuity and stability in the public sphere. Religious and political leaders alike reinforce this presumption of women's role in family and society. The result is continuous tensions over the legitimate definition of women's rights, setting advocates of self-empowerment against protectors of the political community as defined in Islamic terms.

It is important to note that the body is a topic through which many Islamic religious authorities and institutions have critiqued postmodern society.[11] In this light, Islam serves as a countercultural voice that simultaneously rebukes Western cultural hegemony and serves political interests. In other words, Islam is conveniently used by both politicians and religious authorities in Middle Eastern countries to critique Western and secular values regarding the woman's body as the major site of this cultural and political tension between the West and Islam, past and present, and individual versus collective rights.

However, religious norms and references cannot be completely controlled by the state, especially at a time of global communication and expedited circulation of ideas that increase debate over Islamic orthodoxy. This means that the circulation by flow of ideas and transnational cultural agents who influence Islamic religiosity increasingly challenge state policies.

Then how can we make sense of these modernized forms of Islamic religiosity? Although there is no clear answer to such a question, I contend that one possibility is to shift away from the dominant definitions of religion and secularism in order to disentangle these concepts from Western politics and history.

---

[11] See, for example, the religious positions of Salafi groups that define moral positions through control of the body. See Roel Meijers (ed.), *Global Salafism: Islam New Religious Movement* (New York, Columbia University Press, 2009).

THREE DIMENSIONS OF RELIGION AND
THREE LEVELS OF SECULARITY

There is no doubt that the work of Talal Asad and Michael Connolly has strongly questioned the universal definition of religion as a set of beliefs.[12] In fact, our exploration of Muslim territories shows that belonging and believing more than beliefs and religious doctrines are at stake in the politicization of Islam, at least from the citizens' point of view.[13] The distinction between believing, belonging, and behaving comes from sociologists working on modern forms of religiosity. They refer respectively to beliefs, religious practices, and collective identity. These three dimensions have historically been systematically linked or associated in the definition of a person's religiosity. However, recent sociological analyses have shed light on their increasing disjunction as well as on their multiple interactions.[14] For example a person can believe without behaving or belonging; can belong without believing or behaving; or can behave without believing.

In Muslim countries, the transformation brought by the nation-state has primarily affected citizens' belonging to Islam by linking religious and national identifications. I have described how from national historiography to civil law, political socialization has introduced belonging to the hegemonic form of Islam as synonymous with belonging to the nation. For this reason, what was in the Islamic tradition considered part of the social or private sphere has increasingly become political (conversion/blasphemy/sexuality).

These public and collective assertions of Islam are different from personal religious practices or beliefs. Actually, an analysis of the disjunctions between belonging and behaving can explain the intriguing and apparently contradictory political changes in Turkey, Tunisia, Pakistan, and even Iraq. All started as secular national projects grounded in Islamic references. This meant that Islam and the nation were combined in one collective belonging to counter Islamic transnational projects (pan-Islamism). At the same time, the first national phase

---

[12] In *Genealogies of Religion*, Talal Asad describes the status of religion in medieval society as very different from the place religion holds in the modern age. He argues that Christianity during this period functioned as a "great cloak" that defined an adherent's entire experience of the world. It possessed an "all-embracing capacity" – a distinctive practice and belief system – that disciplined the religious subject and nurtured certain virtues. Religion was not some essentially distinct form of culture, process of reasoning, or experiential state that existed apart from other cultural experiences. It encompassed the cultural horizon of the subject's practices and assumptions about the world. Talal Asad, *Genealogies of Religion: Discipline and Reasons of Power in Christianity and Islam* (Baltimore, MD: Johns Hopkins University Press, 1993).

[13] From the theological point of view, religious interpretation has been drastically changed by this nationalization of Islam; see General Conclusion.

[14] G. Davie, *Religion in Britain since 1945: Believing without Belonging* (Oxford: Blackwell, 1994). D. Hervieu-Léger, "Religion und sozialer Zusammenhalt in Europa," *Transit* 26 (2003): 101–19.

occurred in all of these countries in secularization of citizens' religious practices in terms of dress code, gender relations, and lifestyle. In the past three decades, however, partially through the pressure of Islamist movements, these societies have gone through an Islamization of social life as reflected in increased wearing of the hijab, as well as in Islamically correct behaviors and speech. Consequentially, political tensions are not concerning belonging anymore, in the sense that Islamists have come to term with the national framework (as discussed in Part II) and the vast majority do not advocate an Islamic state or a caliphate. In these conditions, citizens' Islamically correct behaviors and speech are now the major object of contention between political and religious actors.

In sum, the politicization of Islam has not for the most part affected beliefs (except in the case of the Islamic Republic of Iran with the introduction of the *veleyat-e faqih* concept).[15] But it has changed the belonging to the Islamic tradition by mingling it with national belonging. It has also modified religious praxis by transforming personal practices into public behaviors. We will see in Part III that now that most Islamists have renounced the Islamic state and that the largest political challenges and contestations concern the expansion of Islamic behaving into the public space, or more precisely, the regulation of public behaviors through Islamic norms. Although outside the scope of this book, it is worth mentioning that politicization of Islam has also dramatically modified theological work by reducing and instrumentalizing religious interpretations and norms (see General Conclusion).

In these circumstances, scholarly investigation cannot limit itself to beliefs or theological discussions because this can be a dead end, as reflected in the deceptive perception of a return of religion, or return of God. Instead, looking at belonging and behaving and the ways they are interconnected helps us solve the puzzle of apparently very secular projects leading to political battles over Islamically correct social behaviors. In other words, the increased social and political visibility of Islam is not caused by an increase in beliefs. People are not stronger believers than they used to be, but their identification to belonging and behaving has certainly shifted. Then, the role of religion in politics can be apprehended through the ways religious and political belongings overlap or intersect. It means that collective identifications and public norms are reshaped by Islamic values or principles and vice-versa, even in the case of secular regimes such as Turkey, Tunisia, or Pakistan.

As a consequence, the use of the term *secularism* to describe any of these social and religious evolutions just adds to the confusion. That is why I prefer the term *secularity* and reserve the term *secularism* for the multiple ideological and cultural narratives that Western countries have built

---

[15] This concept means Guardianship of the Jurist. It was forged by Ayatollah Khomeini (1902–89) in 1970 to justify the political guidance of religious figures. See *Islam and Revolution: Writings and Declarations of Imam Khomeini*, translated and annotated by Hamid Algar (Berkeley, CA: Mizan Press, 1981).

to justify separation of religion and politics. Secularity, by contrast, is best defined by two major principles – equality of all religions in public spaces and political neutrality of the state vis-à-vis all religions.[16] This can be legally implemented in multiple ways, according to the specific political culture and history of each country, as, for example, the differences between European countries and the United States attest. Ultimately, these specific cultures frame social expectations about the status of religion in the public sphere. In the West, the disjunction between private and public behaviors is one of the major expectations. The cultural and political expectations about religion and politics are different in Muslim countries.

In an attempt to efficiently identify the different regimes of secularity in these countries and elsewhere, it is useful to distinguish three levels of secularization: institutional, social, and individual. The first is the most commonly surveyed and entails the legal status of religions and their relationship with state institutions. The second refers to the social legitimacy of religious practices and actors. This is the level that fascinated Tocqueville in his observation of American democracy three centuries ago because the social and civic value granted to religious groups and actions contrasted with the methods of France, where religious motivations or behaviors in social life were (and remain) uncivil at best, or at worst, a threat to the whole social fabric. The individual level refers to the personal ethics of citizens committed to living together without religious or theological justifications. Holyoake's 1896 publication *English Secularism* offers an iconic definition of secular ethics as:

a code of duty pertaining to this life, founded on considerations purely human, and intended mainly for those who find theology indefinite or inadequate, unreliable or unbelievable. Its essential principles are three: (1) The improvement of this life by material means. (2) That science is the available Providence of man. (3) That it is good to do good. Whether there be other good or not, the good of the present life is good, and it is good to seek that good.[17]

No country is at the same point on each of these levels, making it impossible to get a "one size fits all" model of secularity. For example, it can be said that France and the United States share institutional secularity but differ greatly on the status of religion in society or at the level of individuals. The same is true for the regimes of secularity specific to Muslim countries. Thus, France and Turkey share a certain illegitimacy of religion in social life but do not provide the same legal and institutional status to religions. More generally, it is

---

[16] Usually scholars apprehend secularity as the social and political conditions that influence the ways citizens adhere to religion (see Taylor, *A Secular Age*). My definition emphasizes equality before the law (of all religions) and neutrality of the state (vis-à-vis all religions) as major principles that can be implemented in different legal and political ways.

[17] George Jacob Holyoake, *English Secularism: A Confession of Belief* (Chicago, IL: The Open Court Publishing Company, 1896), 35.

possible to distinguish several types of arrangements between the three levels. For example, American secularity is a "benevolent" secularism defined by a separation of state and religion, combined with social acceptance of religion and toleration of multiple individual creeds and lifestyles. European democracies, on the other hand, are characterized by more "invasive" forms of secularism, exemplified in multiple forms of cooperation between state and religion at the institutional level, different degrees of social illegitimacy of religion, and restricted forms of religious expression at the individual level.

On the opposite side of the spectrum, lack of institutional separation, exclusive social role of one religion, and limited recognition of religious pluralism at the individual level are the characteristics of hegemonic Islam but are by no means limited to Muslim countries. In fact, Buddhism in Sri Lanka, the Orthodox Church in Greece, and Judaism in Israel can also be defined as hegemonic.[18]

More generally, the combination of these three levels in each of the countries discussed in this volume shows that the social and individual levels of secularity are at the core of the dominant political challenges posed by political Islam. It is not to say that the institutional level is not an issue in the sense that political and legal discrimination of religious minorities and control of the state over religions are major impediments to secularization. At the same time, the institutional level is not the site of intense contestations as it was in the 1970s or 1990s. If there is one thing we can learn from the Arab awakening, it is that Islamists are now at ease with the secular state system (as we shall argue in Chapters 8 and 9).

By contrast, how to belong as a believer or a nonbeliever to the nation and how to act politically and religiously in the public sphere have become crucial to the evolution of both secularity and religiosity across Muslim countries. Introducing these three levels (institution/social/individual) and how they relate to each other could lead to a different taxinomy of secular regimes. But our goal in this book is more modest: simply to shed light on the evolving meanings ascribed to religion, ethics, politics, citizenship, and how these meanings reshape the identification of social groups or individual actors to the national community, the state, or Islam. In these conditions, by distinguishing institutional, social, and individual levels of secularity as well as believing, belonging, and behaving aspects of religiosity, we can identify which of these three levels are at stake and mutually influence each other when actors talk or legislate about Islam, democracy, human rights, or secularism.

To sum up, Islamic norms have become part and parcel of the political project of the nation-state. Forged on Islamic references, the public morality

---

[18] In the case of Israel, Judaism is the main feature of the national identity, but it is not officially the religion of the state, and even more interestingly, freedom of expression is not completely limited by religious norms.

shaped by the nation-state has also modified Islamic ethics, leading to the unexpected preeminence of Islamic public values over the virtues of the self. For example, while most of the rules of classical Islam gave priority to the protection of the religious person, state intervention in modern times has transformed these rules into public values where gender relations and dress code, as well as Muslim and non-Muslim relations are evaluated according to the public interest.

This intertwined fabric of the state and Islam explains why Islamism became the major political force in most Muslim countries, as analyzed in Part II. It also sheds new light on the democratization process under way in the wake of the Arab Spring (analyzed in Part III).

PART II

ISLAMISM AS THE PREEMINENT POLITICAL FORCE PRE– AND POST–ARAB SPRING

OVERVIEW

The electoral success of Ennahda in Tunisia, the Freedom and Justice Party (FJP) in Egypt, the Justice and Development Party (PJD) in Morocco, and the Justice and Development Party (AKP) in Turkey highlights the centrality of Islamism in political transitions from authoritarianism.

However, this is not to say that secular political forces are nonexistent. In fact, they have played a significant role in the Arab Spring revolutions, and they have been decisive in the postauthoritarianism phase as shown by the fall of President Morsi in July 2013.

Most interestingly, as we shall discuss in Chapter 9, secular influences do not come primarily from professional political parties but from civil society itself: youth groups, women's organizations, artists, and entrepreneurs: in other words, all the forces that were decisive in the uprisings against the authoritarian regimes. It is, however, important to keep in mind that "secular" in this context does not mean privatization or rejection of the social influence of Islam; instead, it refers to a dismissal of what Bassam Tibi calls Shari'atization[1] of politics, meaning the implementation of a fixed medieval code of penal and civil laws as some Salafi groups advocate.

In other words, Islamism is only one facet of political Islam, broadly defined as a national political culture. For this reason, it will remain relevant to future political developments.

More specifically, Islamism can be interpreted as an amplification of the framing and pruning of Islam by the authoritarian state described in Part I. Amplification occurs when new ideas and practices emerge through a never-ending dialectic between grafting of new ideas and influence of the local context. While the state has appropriated Islam through means of institutionalization and nationalization, Islamist opposition groups have, in turn,

---

[1] Bassam Tibi, *The Sharia State: Arab Spring and Democratization* (Abingdon: Routledge, 2013).

used Islam's staying power in society as a source of opposition to the state. Even if their popularity has declined in the postauthoritarian phase in Egypt and to a certain extent in Tunisia, they will remain a significant political force.

As a result, the Islamist oppositions fit the description of a "Strategic and Conflict Capable Group" (SCCG).[2] According to this theory, four conditions are required for a capable political group to emerge: (1) a certain degree of formal institutions; (2) ideological coherence; (3) legitimacy and credibility; and (4) potential for social mobilization. An evaluation of the Islamist movement through each of these categories reveals that Islam has been a central component politics in Muslim countries since their independence because it operates within the political framework created by the nation-state. While the SCCG primarily intended to measure a group's capacity for political opposition, I have used it as a way to assess the political strength of Islamist movements in opposition or in power. To do so, I have documented each of the four categories by compiling preexisting research on Islamism, adding original documents from political parties and declarations from political leaders related to the Arab Spring revolutions. Therefore, the next chapters will address the role of Islamic institutions in the rise of Islamism (Chapter 7), the ideological strength of Islamist opposition (Chapter 8), and the reasons for the political credibility of Islamists and their political mobilization skills (Chapter 9).

---

[2] Kai Hafez, *Radicalism and Political Reform in the Islamic and Western Worlds* (New York: Cambridge University Press, 2010), 103.

7

Political Opposition through Islamic Institutions

Precisely because they weren't political parties, Islamic institutions were able to survive under authoritarian regimes. While political opponents often fled into exile or were jailed or killed, Islamic institutions became an underground rallying point for political opposition.

In almost all of the countries examined in this volume, rulers repressed political parties, but did not – and could not – completely eradicate religious institutions or activities. This fact is a key difference between Muslim authoritarian regimes and communist countries, where religious institutions were often systematically dismantled or outlawed. The maintenance of Islamic institutions has indirectly provided venues for political opposition. As Kai Hafez suggests, especially in "hard authoritarian states such as Iraq (under Saddam Hussein), Syria, Libya or Tunisia, it was and is impossible for an opposition to take shape in the first place, unless it moves abroad.... The only groups who make their presence felt as opposition forces in these states are Islamic fundamentalist organizations."[1]

Several types of religious institutions shaped political mobilization. First, mosques became spaces for political organization, and religious festivals turned into platforms for oppositional political discourse. Thus, a difference emerged between official Islam or state-run Islamic institutions (such as universities, mosques, and the Ministry of Religious Endowments) and unofficial Islamic institutions, which became vehicles for political opposition. As a result, religious authorities also became important actors in this underground resistance. In these circumstances, it should come as no surprise that, when allowed, political parties with an Islamic component emerged as the most influential political force.

[1] Kai Hafez, *Radicalism and Political Reform in the Islamic and Western Worlds* (Cambridge: Cambridge University Press, 2010), 107.

RELIGIOUS PLACES, SPACES, AND ACTIVITIES

In Egypt, the mosque emerged quickly as the only open political space, especially when the Muslim Brotherhood was prohibited from operating as a political group under Nasser and Mubarak. As discussed in Chapter 2, the 1952 land reform laws undermined the independence of Al-Azhar and brought the waqf lands under the control of the new Ministry of Endowments (*Wizārat al-Awqāf*).[2] As a result, mosques fell under state control and unofficial places of worship,[3] which were not registered by the Ministry of Endowments, sprang up as venues of free speech. Members of these mosques congregated in houses and vacant buildings or under the guise of official social clubs.

In the mid-1970s, the Sadat regime authorized the building of private mosques (*ahlī*) as well as private charities and endowments funded by zakat collection at a local level,[4] which led to the development of social services often linked to private mosques. As a consequence, in the first decade of Hosni Mubarak regime, there was dramatic increase in the number of informal mosques, from forty thousand in 1981 to seventy thousand in 1989.[5] This meant religious gatherings could not be prevented, despite the arrest and imprisonment of thousands of Islamists.[6] In the mid-1990s, some of these private mosques were renationalized and brought under state control. Still, unofficial mosques allowed opposition movements to organize outside of state control. The Muslim Brotherhood was able to organize and to mobilize its followers within these spaces of uncensored political discourse.

Shiʿa in Iraq

In the same vein, Iraqi Shiʿa resisted political oppression through religious activities that became *de facto* acts of resistance. As described in Chapter 3,

[2] Tamir Moustafa, "The Islamist Trend in Egyptian Law," Simons Papers in Security and Development, School for International Studies, Simon Fraser University, No. 2, May 2010.

[3] Interestingly, these unofficial mosques have the same status as Coptic churches. A license from the Ministry of Endowments is required to build a church, but many have been shut down and many more operate without an official license. In October 2011, an attempt of the transitory government to unify all places of worship under the same law failed. "Religious committee rejects unified law on places of worship," *Egypt Independent*, October 16, 2011, accessed November 30, 2011, http://www.almasryalyoum.com/en/node/505701.

[4] Daniela Pioppi, "Is there an Islamist Alternative in Egypt?" Istitute Affari Internazionali (IAI), February 3, 2011, accessed March 8, 2013, http://www.iai.it/pdf/DocIAI/iaiwp1103.pdf.

[5] Asef Bayat, "Revolution without Movement, Movement without Revolution: Comparing Islamic Activism in Iran and Egypt," *Comparative Studies in Society and History* 40.1 (1998): 136–69.

[6] Hafez, *Radicalism and Political Reform in the Islamic and Western Worlds*, 108.

in 1968, the Ba'th regime began to shut down universities and to confiscate Shi'i religious endowments. However, under Saddam's regime, there was a compromise with members of the Shi'i clergy to maintain independent education institutions (*hawza*), as long as they did not mix religion and politics. Still, the *hawza* in Najaf and Karbala were significantly restricted; the number of scholars was fewer than before Saddam assumed power in 1968, and only Iraqis were allowed to study there. Moreover, many scholars were jailed and killed during the 1980s. Clerics and students could not publish any of their research findings.[7] Nonetheless, *hawza* maintained financial independence from Saddam's regime by keeping the right to collect *khums*,[8] which can amount to many millions of dollars.

Moreover, Shi'is used religious festivals, rituals, and processions, such as Muharram,[9] to express political resistance to the regime.[10] For example, the Shi'i organization al-Da'wa (the Call)[11] encouraged participation in the annual ceremonial processions commemorating the martyrdom of Husayn[12] as a form of protest to connect the religious fervor of the ritual

---

[7] Augustus Richard Norton, *Middle East Policy* 18.1 (Spring 2011): 140.

[8] As already mentioned, *Khums* (one-fifth in Arabic) is a tax or donation given to a cleric (*marja'iyya*) that the donor deems a religious authority. For clerics such as Grand Ayatollah Ali al-Sistani (see p. 130 on his leadership), the total amount of the *khums* has been estimated to be millions of U.S. dollars. It has been reported that the Sistani network distributes over $5 million per month as stipends to students and teachers in Damascus, Karbala, and Mashahad toward education and research. Babak Rahimi, "Ayatollah Sistani and the Democratization of Post-Ba'athist Iraq," United States Institute of Peace Special Report, June 2007, accessed August 23, 2011, from http://www.usip.org/files/resources/sr187.pdf.

[9] Muharram is the first month of the Islamic calendar and a sacred month for Shi'is who mourn in remembrance of Husayn (626–680), the second son of Prophet Mohammed, who was killed in the Battle of Karbala on the tenth of Muharram.

[10] "Shi'a in Iraq," *Global Security.org*, accessed August 2, 2011, http://www.globalsecurity.org/military/world/iraq/religion-Shi'a1.htm.

[11] A group of Shi'i leaders, including Grand Ayatollah Mohammad Baqir al-Sadr (1935–1980), formed al-Da'wa in 1957. It drew mainly from the ayatollahs and youth in Najaf and promoted Islamic values and ethics as part of political activism (http://www.islamicdawaparty.com/?module=home&fname=history.php&active=7, accessed on August 17, 2013). To counter the growing threat of secular Arab nationalism and leftist ideology, its goals included: "indoctrinate revolutionaries, fight the corrupt regime, and establish an Islamic State; then it would go on to implement Islamic laws and export the Islamic revolution to the rest of the world." Rodger Shanahan, "Shi'a political development in Iraq: The case of the Islamic Dawa Party," *Third World Quarterly* 25.5 (2004), accessed July 24, 2011, 943–54. T. M. Aziz, "The Role of Muhammad Baqir al-Sadr in Shi'i Political Activism in Iraq from 1958–1980," *International Journal of Middle East Studies* 25.2 (May 1993): pp, accessed August 11, 2011, http://www.jstor.org/stable/164663, 207–22, 209. Although at first al-Da'wa operated primarily inside Iraq, its influence spread to the Gulf countries such as Kuwait, where it is said to have contributed to the U.S. Embassy bombings in 1983.

[12] Husayn (626–80) was the grandson of the Prophet Muhammad. His father, Ali, was the fourth caliph, and the first imam by Shi'i Muslims. Husayn was killed at the Battle of Karbala

with al-Daʿwa's ideology.[13] In 1977, when police attempted to interfere with the Muharram processions, crowds stormed a police station while shouting, "Saddam, remove your hand! The people of Iraq do not want you!"[14] This incident was especially potent given that in 1975 the state cancelled the annual Muharram procession as a response to riots that had occurred during the festival the previous year. Despite the ban, al-Daʿwa organized the procession two years later in 1977, and the state responded with large-scale arrests of Shiʿa and clerics.[15] Protestors shouted verses from the Qurʾan such as "The power of God is above theirs" and "Victory shall come from God."[16]

Religious Activism in Turkey

Similarly, in Turkey, the state's religious apparatus played a key role in the expansion of the social basis of the Islamist movement[17] by operating as crucial vehicles for the recruitment, dissemination, and legitimization of the Islamist opposition's ideas.

However, in contrast to the Islamist opposition in Egypt and Iraq, the major forums for Islamic opposition groups were Sufi orders, rather than mosques or religious festivals. Under Ataturk's secular-oriented regime, Law 677 formally abolished Sufi orders in November 1925, including banning Sufi titles such as *hoca, shaykh, baba,* and *dede* (teacher, elder, saint/wise man, and religious leader) and prohibiting turbans and robes in public except in instances of official state duties.[18]

Despite being outlawed, Sufi orders maintained strong social networks that spread Islamism throughout Turkey after 1925. In fact, some Sufi groups later had a hand in political parties such as the National Order Party and National Salvation Party (although not all Sufi groups had an interest in politics). When the more religiously conservative Democratic Party took power after Ataturk's death in 1938, state policies on Islam

---

after refusing to swear allegiance to the Umayyad caliph Yazid I. Shiʿis consider Husayn the third imam, and revere him for his martyrdom. See "Husayn ibn Ali," *Oxford Encyclopedia of the Islamic World,* ed. John L. Esposito (New York: Oxford University Press, 2009).

[13] Hanna Batatu, "Iraq's Underground Shiʿa Movements: Characteristics, Causes and Prospects," *Middle East Journal* 35.4 (1981): pp, accessed, July 30, 2011, http://www.jstor.org/stable/4326306 578–94, 589.

[14] Ibid., 590.

[15] Rodger Shanahan, "Shiʿa political development in Iraq," 946.

[16] Aziz, "The Role of Muhammad Baqir al-Sadr in Shiʿi Political Activism in Iraq from 1958–1980," 214.

[17] Mustafa Sen, "Transformation of Turkish Islamism and the Rise of the Justice and Development Party," *Turkish Studies* 11.1 (March 2010): 59–84.

[18] Ibid.

relaxed slightly, and as a result, Sufi orders such as the Nakshabandi or the Qadiri regained some of their original activity and saw a resurgence in their popularity.[19] As Şerif Mardin argues, the political importance of Sufi brotherhoods in Turkey lies in personal relationships of patronage, friendships, and associations rather than institutional influence.[20] These networks of patronage and friendship ultimately contributed to the agendas of political parties such as the National View Movement and the Justice and Welfare Party (AKP), as well as those of influential political figures such as Abdullah Gul, the president of Turkey (2007 to the present), or former Speaker of Parliament and Vice Prime Minister Bülent Arinç (2009–present), known for their unofficial connection with the Naqshbandi Order.

Tunisia: University Helps Breed Political Opponents

In the beginning of Bourguiba's presidential rule, leftists and pan-Arabists were stronger than the Islamist opposition. For this reason, Bourguiba, like other authoritarian leaders in the region, allowed Islamic organizations to form in order to counterbalance these secular forces.[21] As a result, Rached Ghannouchi founded the Movement of the Islamic Tendency (*Mouvement de la Tendence Islamique* [MTI], also known as *al-Ittijāh al-Islāmī*) in 1981.[22] Initially, MTI followers were mostly

[19] The Naqshbandi Order traces its lineage to the Prophet Muhammad through Abu Bakr, the first Caliph, and is known for its political involvement in Turkey and elsewhere. The order draws inspiration from Muhammad Baha ad-din an-Naqshabandi (1318–89) and emphasizes mental strength as an essential component of its teachings, which include rejecting music, saying *dhikr* (repetition of the names of God), and strict adherence to shari'a. The Kadiri order originated from two Sufi saints: Abdul Qadir al Geylani and Ahmed ar Rifai. It was founded in the early 1900s in Instanbul. Its members claim nonpolitical affiliation, www.qadiri-rifai.org/english. See also Rabasa and Larrabee, "The Rise of Political Islam in Turkey" (Santa Monica, Rand Corporation, 2008), 14.

[20] Şerif Mardin, *Religion and Social Change in Modern Turkey: The Case of Bediuzzaman Said Nursi* (Albany: State University of New York Press, 1989).

[21] "Islamic Movements in Northern Africa: Islamic Fundamentalism in Africa and Implications for US Policy," US House of Representatives Committee on Foreign Affairs, May 20, 1992, accessed July 17, 2011, http://www.danielpipes.org/218/islamic-movements-in-northern-africa. Susan Waltz, "Islamist Appeal in Tunisia," *Middle East Journal* 40.4 (1986): 651–70.

[22] Rached al-Ghannouchi was born in 1941 and graduated from the University of Zaytuna. After founding the MTI in 1981, Ghannouchi and his followers were arrested several times by the Bourguiba regime. After his second period in prison, Ghannouchi went into exile in London for twenty-two years. The founder of Ennahda, Ghannouchi, returned to Tunisia from exile in January 2011. "Tunisia: The advent of liberal Islamism," *Religioscope*, January 30, 2011, accessed July 6, 2011, http://religion.info/english/interviews/article_516.shtml. Ennahda later became a power in the Tunisian legislature. "Tunisia's al-Nahda to Form

concerned with Islamic education and had two distinct levels of activity: (1) promoting conferences and gatherings in secondary schools, and (2) organizing lessons on Islam for mosques and small groups in homes or sometimes in the streets.[23] As a result, this Daʿwa, or missionary activity, helped the movement gain support, especially among students. This effort would later pay off in terms of political clout. They also allied with the state-sponsored Association for the Safeguarding of the Holy Qur'an[24] that became a cover for Islamists to disseminate their ideology and gain supporters, despite their general disagreement with state policies.

As Bourguiba's policies became more secular (see Part I), Zaytuna University, which was also known to have many MTI sympathizers, became a refuge for scholars and political dissenters. It is important to note that many opposition figures, including MTI founder Rached Ghannouchi, emerged from the Zaytuna educational system and maintained connections with faculty members, thus creating an underground network of political, religious, and educational dissent.

Additionally, the mobilization of students on campuses helped the MTI to gain momentum in the late 1960s and early 1970s and to compete with Marxist activists. They opened small mosques in student centers or dormitories that became places for studying and debating the works of the Egyptian Muslim Brotherhood, such as the writings of Sayyid Qutb. At times, confrontations between Islamists and Marxist groups on campuses turned violent. For example at the University of Tunis on December 26, 1977, several leftist students attacked a general meeting organized by Islamists with knives, injuring several.[25] Similarly, in March 1982, a group of Islamist students was attacked in Manouba in the suburbs of Tunis. These clashes (and other nonviolent ones) helped to garner support for the Islamists' cause and to strengthen their position against the leftist political views. Furthermore, the universities were crucial for organizing demonstrations and spreading the ideology even after the movement was officially banned. For example, students organized political meetings and defended the MTI leaders jailed by the Bourguiba regime by publishing political statements in MTI newspapers.[26]

Party," *Al-Jazeera English*, March 1, 2011, accessed July 6, 2011, from http://english.al-jazeera.net/news/middleeast/2011/03/20113113281226638.html.
[23] Ghannouchi's interview with Mohamed Elhachmi Hamdi in Mohamed Elhachmi Hamdi, *The Politicization of Islam: A Case Study of Tunisia* (Boulder, CO: Westview Press, 1998), 19.
[24] The Association was formed in 1970 by a group of traditional scholars, and was recognized and supervised by the Department of Religious Affairs.
[25] Elhachmi Hamdi, *The Politicization of Islam: A Case Study of Tunisia* (Boulder: Westview Press, 1998), 26.
[26] Ibid., 46.

In sum, throughout the Middle East, Islamists used religious spaces and festivals to promote their political and religious platforms. In many of these countries, the state had a monopoly on the regulation of religious places and events – and yet that monopoly inadvertently benefited the Islamists by providing the only open space for political dissent.

RELIGIOUS FIGURES AND AUTHORITIES

Islamist opposition was also facilitated by certain religious authorities and scholars. In this regard, it is sometimes difficult to distinguish between Islamic and Islamist forms of opposition. The former refers to religious figures who adopt an explicit political agenda (in terms of promoting an Islamic state, defining an electoral strategy, etc.), while the latter is carried by more secular actors (intellectuals, members of the middle class), acting within political parties or movements. The role of Iraqi Shiʻi clerics under Saddam is an example of an Islamic resistance. At that time, the primary goal of the ayatollahs organized under the Daʻwa movement was not to establish an Islamic state but to protect Shiʻi institutions from being subdued under Saddam's regime.

Since the fall of Saddam, religious institutions, including the intellectual hubs of Najaf and Karbala, have reopened. Clerics of the marjaʻiyya,[27] the Shiʻi religious establishment, have become increasingly important in Iraqi politics. In fact, their approval is decisive for the endorsement of political candidates as well as voting patterns.

The major clerical authority in Iraq is Grand Ayatollah al-Sistani,[28] who is also the religious reference of the majority of Twelver Shiʻis elsewhere in the world, and holds significant sway over political matters. Sistani's mosque, which was shut down by Saddam in 1994, reopened in 2003 and quickly became an important religious and political center for the global Shiʻi community. Although the exact number of Sistani's followers is unknown, according to some estimates, he is the marjaʻ (religious authority) of at least 40 percent of the world's Shiʻi population.

Sistani manifests his involvement in politics by issuing fatwas on certain critical issues. For example, in a 2003 fatwa he criticized the coalition in

---

[27] A *marjaʻ* is an authority who provides religious guidance to lay Shiʻis. The rulings of the *marjaʻ* are binding to the ones who recognize him as their tutelary authority. The marjaʻiyya is the Shiʻi religious establishment composed of all the marjaʻs.

[28] Grand Ayatollah Ali al-Sistani (b.1930), originally from Iran, is a student of Grand Ayatollah Abu al-Qasim al-Khoei (1899–1992), who was also an Iranian cleric and a vocal opponent of Ayatollah Khomeini's idea of wilayat al-faqih. When Khoei died in 1992, Sistani inherited al-Khoei's network, which made him one of the most powerful religious figures in the Middle East.

charge of organizing the elections for the Constituent Assembly, stating that the interim governing council working with the occupation authority lacked legitimacy and that the election plan for the transitional legislature did not guarantee it would "truly represent" the Iraqi people.[29] Sistani sought a parliament that he said would represent the "will" of Iraqis in "a just manner and would prevent any diminution of Islamic law."

Because of Sistani's comments, the elections were postponed until May 2004. However, Sistani said he was not satisfied because the elections for the constitution's draft still would not be "one person, one vote" elections; instead the coalition leaders would draft the text. Thus, Sistani encouraged thousands of protesters to take to the streets in January 2004, months ahead of the scheduled elections.[30] The same month that Sistani's followers marched in the streets, the *Asia Times* online edition ran an article headlined, "When Sistani speaks, Bush listens." The article's author, Ehsan Ahrari, described Sistani as "the most powerful man in Iraq today ... He communicates with his followers through written edicts (fatwas), and everyone, including the US president, listens."

As a result, the election process was reassessed, and direct elections for the transitional national assembly were rescheduled for January 2005. Sistani encouraged all Iraqis to vote, not just members of the Shi'i community, an act he would repeat in another fatwa five years later.[31]

Sistani also made a pivotal statement in 2005 on the controversy over Islam as a source of legislation in the constitution. As discussed in Part I, the dispute concerned Article 2, which originally stated that Shari'a "is the basic source of legislation ... [and] No law may be enacted that contradicts [Islam's] tenets." The Supreme Council of the Islamic Revolution in Iraq (SCIRI)[32] was the main advocate for Islam to be the fundamental source of legislation, while Kurdish proposals suggested that Islam be considered simply *a* source of legislation. When Sistani agreed with the latter wording: Islam as "*a* source of legislation," it was adopted in the constitution.[33]

Since the withdrawal of U.S. troops in 2011, Sistani has encouraged Iraqis to take initiative in building an autonomous, independent process

---

[29] Juan Cole, trans., "Sistani Position on New Elections," *Informed Comment*, 2003, accessed July 14, 2011, http://www.juancole.com/2003/11/sistani-position-on-new-elections.html.

[30] Juan Cole, "The Iraq Election: First Impressions," *CommonDreams.org*, January 31, 2005, accessed July 115, 2011, http://www.commondreams.org/views05/0131-25.htm.

[31] "Ayatollah Sistani encourages participation in upcoming parliamentary elections in Iraq," *Islamopedia Online*, April 22, 2010, accessed July 10, 2011, http://www.islamopediaonline.com/fatwa/ayatollah-sistanis-encourages-participation-upcoming-parliamentary-elections-iraq.

[32] See Chapter 5: Islam in the Legal System.

[33] "Islam as a Source of Legislation," *Islamopedia Online*, August 30, 2011, accessed September 10, 2011, http://islamopediaonline.org/country-profile/iraq/islam-and-nation-State-building/islam-source-legislation.

of political transition and governance. While Sistani has indeed recognized that the transitional government in Iraq will not immediately have full legitimacy, he has also made it clear that the United States should not interfere in Iraqi elections. That is to say that Iraq must lean on international organizations like the United Nations, rather than on the United States.[34] The latter has recognized that overt interference would undermine the unstable Iraqi government's attempts at solidifying its authority and legitimacy. As a result, reports have indicated that Obama wrote a secret letter to Sistani, urging him to exert his influence over the squabbling political factions in Iraq.[35] This information further corroborates the fact that (1) Sistani has been both influential and effective in promoting democracy in Iraq and (2) he has maintained his distance from building relations with the United States, though in his own fashion he promotes a similar end goal in Iraq as does the United States.

He explicitly called for a "civil state" and not a "religious state" in response to the December 2012 Sunni demonstrations.[36] He issued several fatwas such as the prohibition on fighting the Kurds, on July 11, 2012, and the call on Ashura, on December 7, 2012, for moderate and restrained celebrations that would not hurt the sensitivities of other religious groups.[37]

In early January 2013, Sistani proposed a national reconciliation plan that was welcomed by several Iraqi political parties. The plan called for a timely implementation of the demands of the Sunni protestors and comprehensive reforms in the political and security arenas, clearing prisons and freeing prisoners not found guilty. Sistani also pushed for the participation of all political groups in the political decision-making process until the 2014 elections. Speaking of the increase in sectarian violence, he has stressed that he would support Sunni Muslims until their legitimate objectives materialize. This plan has been referred to as a "roadmap" for exit from the ongoing crisis in Iraq. On January 13, 2013, in Najaf, Sistani met with Martin Kobler, the special representative of the UN Secretary General

---

[34] "June 30 and Beyond: What Happens after the U.S. Transfers Power to Iraq?" The Brookings Institute, May 24, 2004, accessed January 28, 2013, http://www.brookings.edu/~/media/events/2004/5/24iraq/20040524.pdf.

[35] Barbara Slavin, "Obama Sent a Secret Letter to Iraq's Top Shi'a Cleric," *Foreign Policy*, August 5, 2010, accessed January 28, 2013, http://www.foreignpolicy.com/articles/2010/08/05/obama_sent_a_secret_letter_to_iraqs_top_Shi'a_cleric?page=0,1.

[36] Mustafa al-Kadhimi, "Sistani Calls for 'Civil State' in Iraq," *Al-Monitor Iraq Pulse*, January 16, 2013, accessed January 28, 2013, http://www.al-monitor.com/pulse/originals/2013/01/iraq-sistani-calls-civil-state.html.

[37] "Iraq's Senior Shi'a Clerics Prohibit Arab-Kurdish War," *Rudaw*, July 12, 2012, accessed January 28, 2013, http://www.rudaw.net/english/kurds/5513.html; "Zanjeer or Qama Zani on Ashura During Muharram," *Mazloom Hussain*, December 7, 2012, accessed January 28, 2013, http://www.ezsoftech.com/mazloom/zanjeer.asp.

for Iraq. In a press conference after the meeting, Kobler announced that "the UN's vision is consistent with that of Sistani on resolving the crisis."[38]

However, efforts for sectarian reconciliation came under threat as a wave of violence swept Iraq in May and June 2013. The crisis began when bombings on two consecutive days in locations across the country killed more than 450 persons.[39] The attacks have sparked fear of another civil war similar to the sectarian violence of 2006 and 2007, with Prime Minister Nouri al-Maliki demanding that the country leaders "prevent civil war from taking place" and urging the Sunnis and Shi'a to pray together.[40] In response to rising violence against minorities, an Iraqi Council for Interfaith Dialogue was established in March of 2013 as a platform to highlight and address inter-religious and ethnic divisions.[41] In the same vein, Sunni and Shi'i parties announced that they would form a cross-sectarian voting bloc for the next Iraqi elections in an attempt to demonstrate cooperation and solidarity.[42] Sunni demonstrators in Anbar, however, rejected the reconciliation, stating that "Sunnis have no other recourse in Iraq except armed confrontation and the formation of independent provinces."[43]

In a similar effort to temper possible sectarian confrontation, the ayatollahs do not hesitate to directly oppose some laws. For example, Maliki's State of Law coalition suffered a blow in July 2013 when Shi'i leaders in Najaf announced their opposition to the Maliki-backed "closed list" electoral system for the 2014 parliamentary elections. Shaykh Ahmed Al-Safi said in a Friday sermon that "*al-Marja'iyya al-Islāmiyya* [or the 'Religious Establishment'] supports the open ballot system, as the closed ballot system has dealt us parliamentarians unaccustomed to parliamentary work who are out of touch with the citizens."[44]

---

[38] Hatem Oday, "Sistani Warns against Sectarianism in Iraq," Naria Tanoukhi, trans., *Al-Monitor*, January 14, 2013, accessed January 28, 2013, http://www.al-monitor.com/pulse/politics/2013/01/iraqi-dialogue-sectarianism.html.

[39] "Sectarian Violence Erupts Again across Iraq," *Al-Monitor*, May 21, 2013, accessed June 20, 2013, http://www.al-monitor.com/pulse/originals/2013/05/iraq-violence-truce-efforts-saadi.html.

[40] "Maliki Scrambles to Address Deteriorating Iraqi Security," *Al-Monitor*, May 23, 2013, accessed June 20, 2013, http://www.al-monitor.com/pulse/originals/2013/05/iraq-security-breakdown-crisis-baghdad.html.

[41] "Iraqi Interfaith Council Tries to Protect Minorities," Al-Monitor, June 11, 2013, accessed June 13, 2013, http://www.al-monitor.com/pulse/originals/2013/06/iraq-interfaith-dialogue-council-minorities.html?utm_source=&utm_medium=email&utm_campaign=7500.

[42] "Ahzab sunniya wa shi'iya 'iraqiya tabdhal juhudan li-tashkil jabha jadida yataz'amuha al-Maliki wa-l-Mutlaq" (Sunni and Shi'i parties: Iraqi efforts to form a new front led by al-Maliki and al-Mutlaq), *Al-Hayat*, June 6, 2013, accessed June 20, 2013, http://alhayat.com/Details/521175.

[43] "Iraq More Divided Than Ever," *Al-Monitor*, May 20, 2013, accessed June 18, 2013, http://www.al-monitor.com/pulse/politics/2013/05/iraq-protests-saadi-initiative-divided.html.

[44] The federal court rejected the closed-list system in 2010 as unconstitutional on the basis that it did discriminate against groups in society. In a closed-list system, voters can only vote for

Muqtada al-Sadr (b. 1973)[45] is another influential cleric in Iraqi political life. His rise in popularity is partially related to his family ties, both to his father-in-law, Mohammad Baqir al-Sadr (1935–80),[46] and his father, popular cleric Grand Ayatollah Mohammed Sadiq al-Sadr (1943–99).[47] Before he died, Grand Ayatollah Sadiq al-Sadr left instructions for his followers to emulate Kazim al-Husayni al-Ha'iri, a lesser cleric in the Shi'i hierarchy, until one of Sadiq's students reached a higher level of religious authority. In 2003, Al-Ha'iri issued a fatwa that instructed Shi'i Muslims in Baghdad to support Muqtada al-Sadr and to fight against the American occupation.[48] It was through this endorsement that the youthful al-Sadr rose to power as a religious and military figure. Although he is not recognized as a fully legitimate ayatollah by Shi'i clerics, he has nonetheless gathered a significant following.[49]

political parties as a whole and have no influence on the order in which party candidates are elected. Since 2010, elections have taken place under the "Saint Lego" system in which losing political lists are allowed to contribute their votes to the winning list of their choice. Maliki and State of Law are not expected to do well under this system and have been trying to revoke it.

45 Muqtada al-Sadr is the son of Grand Ayatollah Mohammed Sadiq al-Sadr and son-in-law of the prominent Mohammad Baqir al-Sadr. The al-Sadr family traces its lineage directly to the prophet through Jafar al-Sadiq, which has contributed to its significant religious standing in Shi'i clerical circles. He has been an outspoken critic of the U.S. presence in Iraq since 2003, and developed the Mahdi militia as a formidable force fighting the U.S.-Iraqi alliance in Najaf. His support comes mostly from the lower classes in Sadr City, a district in Baghdad.

46 Baqir al-Sadr was an Iraqi Shi'i cleric, a grand ayatollah, and the founder of the Islamic Da'wa Party in Iraq in 1957.

47 Grand Ayatollah Sadiq al-Sadr was a revered Iraqi Shi'i cleric known for inspiring Shi'is to revolt against Saddam Hussein in southern Iraq during the end of the 1990–1 Gulf War.

48 Pierre-Jean Luizard, "The Sadrists in Iraq: Challenging the United States, the Marja'iyya and Iran," in *The Shi'a Worlds and Iran*, ed. Sabrina Mervin (New York: SAQI Books, 2010), 258.

49 Muqtada al-Sadr is perhaps Sistani's biggest rival in Iraq. For example, he criticized Sistani for remaining quiet about the U.S. offensive in Najaf (particularly in Sadr City) in 2008. (Greg Bruno, "Muqtada al-Sadr," May 16, 2008, accessed August 18, 2011, http://www.cfr.org/iraq/muqtada-al-sadr/p7637. al-Sadr has also criticized the SCIRI support-base, which is partially backed by Sistani. The difference between Sistani and Muqtada al-Sadr is also sociological. Sistani's followers belong to the merchant upper class, in contrast to al-Sadr's supporters, who tend to come from dispossessed urban areas like Sadr City in Baghdad. ("Will the Bloodstained Shi'a Resist the Urge to Hit Back?" *The Economist*, March 2004, accessed August 21, 2011, http://www.economist.com/node/2482093). Moreover, while Sistani encouraged voting in the 2005 elections, al-Sadr opposed the elections as illegitimate because they were taking place under the U.S. occupation. al-Sadr continued his public outspokenness about the presence of U.S. troops, stating that if U.S. troops did not leave by December 31, 2011, "the military operations will be resumed in a new and tougher way" (http://www.alsadronline.net/en/). However, in September 2011, al-Sadr suggested he would call off the violence of the Mahdi army to give U.S. troops a chance to leave Iraq. Sameer N. Yacoub and Lara Jakes, "Muqtada al-Sadr, Iraqi Cleric, Tells Followers to Stop Attacking U.S. Troops," September 11, 2011, accessed October 17, 2011, http://www.huffingtonpost.com/2011/09/11/iraqi-cleric-stop-attacking_n_957733.html. Additionally, al-Da'wa leaders echoed al-Sadr's call for U.S. troops to leave Iraq. Yochi J. Dreazan, "U.S. Troop Withdrawal Motivated by Iraqi Insistence, Not U.S. Choice,"

Al- Sadr went into self-imposed exile in 2007 (coordinated with the 2007 U.S. troop surge) to study in Qom, Iran. Upon his return, he rallied a significant following. He negotiated a deal in 2010 to support Prime Minister Nouri al-Maliki's second term, despite tensions that arose after al-Maliki launched an offensive attack on the Mahdi Army in 2008 during al-Sadr's exile.

Al-Sadr has reinvented himself politically after the withdrawal of American forces from Iraq, advocating a "civil and democratic Iraq, the rule of law, social justice, and fair governance" while creating alliances with the Kurds and supporting term limits for the prime minister.[50] This new role as a political intermediary emerged during protests in 2012, when al-Sadr used his political clout to promote compromise and consensus. An example of this continued moderate position can be seen in al-Sadr's response to the increasing violence in 2013, when he called on Iraqis to "eliminate hatred from [their] hearts, defuse sectarian rancor, and return to God."

al-Sadr has also been an outspoken and vigorous critic of Prime Minister al-Maliki.[51] In 2013, he issued a final warning to the government to "assume its duty of protecting the people," adding that the government must "expel incompetent and disloyal members of the security corps who are only after power and recognition."[52] Many of the Sunni demonstrators also backed an ultimatum from al-Sadr to Maliki to withdraw government support from the group Asa'ib Ahl Haq, a Shi'i militant group led by Qais al-Khazali[53] that has deployed into greater Baghdad following the series of May 2013 bombings.

National Journal, October 21, 2011, accessed October 17, 2011, http://www.nationaljournal.com/u-s-troop-withdrawal-motivated-by-iraqi-insistence-not-u-s-choice-20111021.

[50] "The New Muqtada al-Sadr Seeks Moderate Image," *Iraq Business News*, March 13, 2013, accessed June 20, 2013, http://www.iraq-businessnews.com/2013/03/13/the-new-muqtada-al-sadr-seeks-moderate-image/.

[51] Sadr–Maliki Political Crisis Heats Up," *Asharq Al-Awsat*, April 11, 2013, accessed June 20, 2013, http://www.aawsat.net/2013/04/article55298421.

[52] سماحة السيد القائد يوجه نداء الى الشعب والحكومة بعد موجة التفجيرات المستمرة

or "The Leader's appeal to the people and the government after a continued wave of attacks," *The Office of Muqtada al-Sadr*, May 27, 2013, accessed June 21, 2013, http://jawabna.com/index.php/permalink/6505.html.

[53] Qais al-Khazali founded Asa'ib Ahl Haq in 2004 after he was expelled from the Mahdi Army. He was captured by U.S. forces in March 2007 and transferred to Iraqi custody in December 2009 in exchange for British computer consultant Peter Moore, held captive by Asa'ib Ahl Haq since May 2007. "Qais al-Khazali: from kidnapper and prisoner to potential leader," *The Guardian*, December 31, 2009, accessed June 25, 2013, http://www.guardian.co.uk/world/2009/dec/31/iran-hostages-qais-al-khazali. Freed in January 2010, Qais has expressed support for the Maliki government while strengthening ties to Muqtada al-Sadr's camp. Sam Wyer, *The Resurgence of Asa'ib Ahl al-Haq*, a report for Institute for the Study of War, December 2012. Asa'ib Ahl Haq (the "Righteous League") is one of several categorized by the United States as "Special Groups," primarily Shi'i resistance organizations with alleged Iranian funding. Asa'ib Ahl Haq claims to have engaged U.S. forces in more than six

This political role of Shi'i figures will probably persist as long as sectarian disputes are at the center of the Iraq political scene (as we shall discuss in Chapters 10 and 11).[54]

Pakistan: From Nominal Muslim Identity to Politicized Forms of Islam

Pakistan is also a relevant case of fusion between Islamic figures and political opposition as well as Islamist opposition. At the same time, Pakistan is unique because it was explicitly built as a nation-state for Muslims, although diverse groups interpreted such a project differently. While the Westernized urban elite represented by Muhammad Ali Jinnah and Mohammed Iqbal led the way for the formation of Pakistan as a state for Muslims, the religious authorities were divided; some supported Pakistan as a nation of Muslims while others favored a pan-Islamist ideal.

For example, the Barelvi[55] ulama supported the formation of the state of Pakistan and thought that any alliance with Hindus (such as that between the Indian National Congress and the Jamiat ulama-I-Hind [JUH]) was counterproductive.[56] In 1925, a group of Barelvi ulama worked toward independence from India, specifically assisting Jinnah's Muslim League.[57] After the creation of Pakistan, the All-India Sunni Conference (AISC) reorganized itself as the Jamaat-e-ulama-i-Pakistan (JUP) in March 1948 with significant support from Muslims in the Sindh and Punjab regions.

Barelvi support for a state for Muslims has been continuous in Pakistani political life. However, not all religious authorities agreed with the idea of a Muslim nation. For the most part, the ulama rejected the idea of Muslim nationalism on the grounds that the emotional and political allegiances to

thousand instances and in recent years is speculated to have formed a special relationship with Prime Minister Nouri al-Maliki's government.

مقابلة | قيس الخزعلي: حزب الله أبرز حركة مقاومة في المنطقة والعالم

or "Qais al-Khazali: 'Hizballah is the most prominent resistance movement in the region and the world.'" Al-Akhbar, June 20, 2012, accessed June 24, 2013, http://www.al-akhbar.com/node/32660.

54　"كتلة المطلك تحتج على الحكومة وتتخوف من "تهديدات عصائب أهل الحق

or "Al-Matalak group protests the government, concerned over 'Asa'ib Ahl Haq threats,'" *Shafaaq News*, May 8, 2013, accessed June 21, 2013, http://www.shafaaq.com/sh2/index.php/news/iraq-news/57302--qq.html

55　The Barelvi is a revivalist Islamic movement created by Imam Ahmed Raza Khan (1856–1921) that played a decisive role in the renewal of Islam in modern India.

56　Ashok K. Behuria, "Sects within Sect: The Case of Deoband-Barelvi Encounter in Pakistan," *Strategic Analysis* 32.1 (2008): 63.

57　The dominance of the Barelvi ulama in the Pakistan movement can be gauged from the fact that out of the thirty-five ulama members of the Masaikh Committee appointed by the league to utilize the support of [Sufi] pirs for the Pakistan movement. As many as thirty were of Barelvi persuasion. See Behuria, "Sects within Sect," 65.

the state created by a national identity undermined the solidarity of the umma.[58] Two major revivalist movements advocated for an Islamic political community rather than a Muslim nation: the Deobandi and the Islamists. The Deobandi embraced the pan-Islamist vision and were a central force in the movement for independence from the British colonial power.[59] Jamaat-e-Islami, created in 1941 by Sayyid Abul Ala Mawdudi, was the other major religio-political movement against the idea of a nation-state for Muslims. In Mawdudi's view, political sovereignty belongs to God; therefore, Islamic law should be the supreme law of the land, not just one source of law. This tension between different political projects continues to be central to the role of Islam in Pakistani politics today.

THE EVOLVING STATUS OF ISLAMIC PARTIES

Islamists became the major political opposition against authoritarian regimes, even where they were not allowed to create political parties. That is why they organized rapidly after the demise of Ben Ali in Tunisia and Mubarak in Egypt, and were able to mobilize more efficiently than the secular parties.[60]

---

[58] Saadia Toor, *The State of Islam: Culture and Cold War Politics in Pakistan* (London: Pluto, 2011), 9.

[59] See Chapter 1. The Khilafat movement was a pan-Islamic political movement against the British colonists in India from 1919–24. It became part of a wider Indian independence movement through its alliance with Gandhi, despite being a movement for Muslims. For more information, see Behuria, "Sects within Sect," 62.

[60] For a brief description of secular parties in Tunisia, see footnote 167 p. 157. In Egypt, the Wafd is the oldest secular party. It was formed under the monarchy and led the 1919 Revolution against British rule. It was disbanded after the 1952 revolution under Egypt's new military rulers, but was reconstituted in 1978 under Sadat. Today, al-Wafd has one of the largest networks in the political arena with presence in twenty-four to twenty-six governorates (Egypt is divided into twenty-seven governorates overall). It has a tense relationship with the Muslim Brotherhood dating back to the 1930s and 1940s when the king used Islamists to counterbalance the growing leftist opposition in Egypt. Al-Wafd calls for democracy, freedom of speech, and the freedom of the judiciary. Although it was at first part of the Democratic Alliance with the FJP, al-Wafd withdrew its membership from the coalition and became independent from any official alliance. The party joined the National Salvation Front (NSF) in 2012 when the group formed, although it suggested that it might withdraw from the NSF if it decided to participate in 2013 parliamentary elections, which the al-Wafd Party did not recognize as legitimate. (Mohamed Hossan Eddin, "Wafd Party considers pulling out of NSF," *Egypt Independent*, April 19, 2013, accessed August 15, 2013, http://www.egyptindependent.com/news/wafd-party-considers-pulling-out-nsf.) After the fall of President Morsi, al-Wafd condemned the actions of the Muslim Brotherhood, stating "[they aim] to drag the Egyptian people into a civil war and to create a state of chaos so as to hijack the legitimacy of people." (Mohamed Hossan Eddin, "Wafd Party says Brotherhood wants civil war," *Egypt Independent*, July 16, 2013, accessed August 15, 2013, http://www. egyptindependent.com/news/wafd-party-says-brotherhood-wants-civil-war.).

The Freedom and Justice Party, created in February 2011 in Egypt, is not officially an Islamic party. Although it operates mainly with Muslim Brotherhood members, it is financially independent from the movement. Its secular nature is reflected by the fact that its membership is open to Copts, even with the appointment of a Copt as a vice president. One of the party's slogans: "Freedom is the solution and justice is the application" is at least symbolically a clear departure from the previous "Islam is the solution" slogan of the Muslim Brotherhood.[61]

At its foundation, the Freedom and Justice Party had 8,821 members residing across Egypt's twenty-seven governorates, including 900 women and 93 Copts.[62] According to a 2011 survey by Al-Ahram Centre for Political and Strategic Studies,[63] the party has steadily gained supporters. Moreover, the FJP won 47 percent of the vote in elections for the People's Assembly. According to opinion polls conducted in May 2012, when Egyptians were asked whether they believed women had more, fewer, or about the same rights under the FJP-led government, 40 percent responded that women had *more* rights than before. In contrast, when asked a similar question regarding the rights of religious minorities, only 22 percent responded that minorities had more rights while 35 percent responded that minorities had about the same rights.[64] According to a 2013 Pew poll, 52 percent of the public viewed the FJP favorably. The secular National Salvation Front had a 45 percent favorability rating, and the Salafi Nour Party was viewed favorably by 40 percent of the population.[65]

In addition, the constitutional referendum of December 2012 won a 63.8 percent vote of approval, but studies by Global Research, a center for research on globalization, have indicated that the election was skewed. Only 32.9 percent of all eligible voters actually cast their ballot. This translates to 17.1 million voters (out of the 52 million eligible voters)

[61] "The Muslim Brotherhood's Freedom and Progress Party," *Islamopedia Online*, August 1, 2011, accessed December 12, 2011, http://www.islamopediaonline.com/country-profile/egypt/islam-and-electoral-parties/muslim-brotherhood%E2%80%99s-freedom-and-progress-party.

[62] Ibid.

[63] "Support to Freedom and Justice Party Increases," *Danish Institute for Parties and Democracy*, October 14, 2011, accessed October 16, 2011, http://dipd.dk/2011/10/support-to-freedom-and-justice-party-increases/.

[64] "Polling the Nations," *ORS Publishing*, May 8, 2012, accessed January 28, 2013, http://poll.orspub.com/document.php?id=quest12.out_3161&type=hitlist&num=1&action=addf av&%3C?php%20echo%20;%20?%3E.

[65] At the same time, the majority of the respondents were less hopeful for the future than they were in 2011. "Egyptians Increasingly Glum," *Pew Research Center*, May 16, 2013, accessed June 20, 2013, http://www.pewglobal.org/files/2013/05/Pew-Global-Attitudes-Egypt-Report-FINAL-May-16-2013.pdf.

actually casting their ballot to vote in the referendum. Further analysis pointed out that 10.9 million Egyptians favored the draft of the constitution, meaning that only 13.3 percent of the overall population was actually in favor of the constitution. These figures indicate that had there been more participation, the turnout for the constitutional referendum might have been different.[66]

In the 2011 parliamentary elections in Egypt, secular parties such as the Egyptian Bloc coalition[67] and the New Wafd (or al-Wafd) Party were only able to garner 6.8 percent and 7.6 percent of the seats, respectively. In contrast, the Democratic Alliance bloc, including the FJP, won 44.9 percent of the seats, and the Salafi parties under the Islamist Bloc won 25 percent of the seats. Nevertheless, secular opposition has been growing and organizing itself since Morsi rose to power in 2012 (see Chapter 8). One of the peaks of this secular opposition was the massive protests against the Islamist regime on June 30, 2013, in which millions of demonstrators across the country took to the streets. They led to the creation of the 30 June Front, a coordinating political body consisting of opposition political and revolutionary forces and led by the Tamarud campaign to organize protests and their political demands.[68] It had a decisive influence on the military's intervention to end Morsi's presidency on July 3, 2013, and opened a new transition phase with the suspension of the 2012 constitution and the preparation of new presidential and parliamentary elections. Following the military crackdown on the FJP members and the Muslim Brotherhood, their political future is in jeopardy; Article 74 of the 2013 draft of the constitution explicitly forbids political parties on the basis of religion.

The al-Wasat Party is another example of a political party influenced by Islamist ideology. Al-Wasat was formed in 1996 but was only officially recognized in February 2011 after the fall of Mubarak. It is an offshoot group from the Muslim Brotherhood having separated due to generational and ideological disagreements within the movement. This younger group of activists objected to the centralized nature of the Brotherhood decision making and to its lack of internal democracy. They also distanced themselves

[66] Mahdi Darius Nazemroaya, "Egypt's Constitutional Referendum: Did President Morsi Hijack Democracy?" Strategic Culture Foundation, January 22, 2012, accessed January 28, 2013, http://www.globalresearch.ca/statistically-examining-cairos-constitutional-referendum-did-morsi-hijack-democracy/5320067.

[67] The coalition's members include the Free Egyptians Party, the Egyptian Social Democratic Party, and Al-Tagammu Party.

[68] "Hundreds Protest Egypt's Constitution in Alexandria in Absence of Islamists," *Ahram Online*, December 28, 2012, accessed June 20, 2013, http://english.ahram.org.eg/NewsContent/1/64/61428/Egypt/Politics-/Hundreds-protest-Egypts-constitution-in-Alexandria.aspx.

from the *da'wa* (missionary) dimension of the Muslim Brotherhood[69] and focused instead on political strategy with a liberal ideological background.

The al-Wasat Party emphasizes a more liberal interpretation of Islam based on *wasaṭiyya* (or the "Middle Path"), which stresses minority and women's rights and democracy.[70] Al-Wasat identifies primarily with Islam, but its members include Christians. Their leader and founder, Abul-Ila Mady, described the party as

more developed, more moderate and more open-minded than those other Islamist groups. Most of us are young; we use modern language to express our thoughts and we are open to cooperation with the West. We have taken elements from many different perspectives.[71]

The party has often been compared to the Welfare Party in Turkey, especially in the mid-1990s when both the Welfare Party and al-Wasat had just taken off as influential groups in their respective countries. In 2012, the al-Wasat Party showed support for the Muslim Brotherhood-led constitution. In return, it secured nine appointed seats on the Shura Council in December 2012, where it previously had not gained any major political victories.[72] This has been a contentious issue because al-Wasat's outright support for the constitution reflects a dissonance within the party's own political ideals.[73] Approving the constitution was part of al-Wasat's overall strategy for the parliamentary elections initially planned for April 2013. By showing support for the constitution, the party ensured political representation on the Shura Council, but it could then revert to representing the moderate middle of the Egyptian political spectrum. Additionally, al-Wasat held talks in January 2013 with a number of moderate Islamist parties to discuss the possibility of a centrist-Islamist alliance in the April 2013 elections (before the parties were suspended). In April 2013, al-Wasat made an appeal for

---

[69] The origins of the al-Wasat party in the Muslim Brotherhood prompted the governmental Political Parties Committee (PPC) to refuse it a license upon its creation in 1996, fearing it would be a back door for Brotherhood participation. However, in February 19, 2011, al-Wasat gained a court ruling legitimizing its presence.

[70] "Al-Wasat Party," *Islamopedia Online*, August 2011, accessed December 15, 2011, http://www.islamopediaonline.com/country-profile/egypt/islam-and-electoral-parties/al-wasat-party.

[71] Karim al-Gawhary, "'We are a Civil Party with an Islamic Identity': An Interview with Abu 'Ila Madi Abu 'Ila and Rafiq Habib," *Middle East Research and Information Project*, April–June 1996, 31.

[72] Ahmed Aboul Enein, "Morsy appoints 90 members to Shura Council," *Daily News Egypt*, December 23, 2012, accessed January 28, 2013, from http://www.dailynewsegypt.com/2012/12/23/morsy-appoints-90-members-to-shura-council/.

[73] Nicholas Gjorvand, "The Future of al-Wasat Party," *Daily News Egypt*, January 16, 2013, accessed January 28, 2013, http://dailynewsegypt.com/2013/01/16/the-future-of-al-wasat-party/.

a new national dialogue, urging reconciliation and unity around the goals of the revolution, instead of political division.[74] Al-Wasat's moderate role was reaffirmed by its call for "national reconciliation" in anticipation of the massive protests of June 30, 2013.[75]

In June 2013, a number of al-Wasat members (including representatives to the party's general assembly) resigned because the party's policies hewed too close to those of the Muslim Brotherhood.[76] After the military coup of July 2013, leading members of the al-Wasat party expressed their desire for a middle path, including early elections and opposition parties participating in the democratic process.[77] However, on July 29, Aboul-Ela Madi and Essam Sultan, pro-Morsi leaders of al-Wasat, were arrested.[78] The party released several statements in July and August 2013 criticizing the military for its use of violence against the pro-Morsi protesters.[79] It also joined with ten other Islamist-leaning parties the National Alliance to Support Legitimacy (NASL, in Arabic *al-Taḥāluf al-Waṭanī li-Daʿm al-Sharʿiyya*), a group that took a major role in organizing pro-Morsi demonstrations and sit-ins, including those at the Raba'a al-Adawiyya mosque. The mission of the NASL is to "protect the choices of the Egyptian people … denounce violence, resist thuggery and continue the people's revolution … using peaceful and legal means."[80]

End of Mubarak Regime Opens Politics to Salafis

The Islamist trend, however, is not the only political movement referring to Islam. Since the end of the Mubarak regime, Salafis, former Jihadi groups, and even Sufis have created political parties.

---

[74] "Wasat Party to Suggest New National Dialogue," *Egypt Independent*, April 17, 2013, accessed June 20, 2013, http://www.egyptindependent.com/news/wasat-party-suggest-new-national-dialogue.

[75] "Al-Wasat Party Calls for Urgent 'National Reconciliation' Meeting," *Al-Ahram*, June 15, 2013, accessed June 20, 2013, http://english.ahram.org.eg/NewsContent/1/64/74054/Egypt/Politics-/AlWasat-Party-calls-for-urgent-national-reconcilia.aspx.

[76] "Mass resignations at al-Wasat party," *Daily News Egypt*, June 29, 2013, accessed August 5, 2013, http://www.dailynewsegypt.com/2013/06/29/mass-resignations-at-al-wasat-party/.

[77] "Islamist Nour, Wasat parties cautiously positive about Egypt military statement," *Ahram Online*, July 1, 2013, accessed August 5, 2013, http://english.ahram.org.eg/NewsContent/1/64/75435/Egypt/Politics-/Islamist-Nour,-Wasat-parties-cautiously-positive-a.aspx.

[78] "Pro-Morsi Wasat Party leaders arrested," *Ahram Online*, July 29, 2013, accessed August 5, 2013, http://english.ahram.org.eg/NewsContent/1/64/77678/Egypt/Politics-/ProMorsi-Wasat-Party-leaders-arrested.aspx.

[79] Hend Kortam, "Blame and condemnation after Rabaa violence," *Daily News Egypt*, July 28, 2013, accessed August 5, 2013, http://www.dailynewsegypt.com/2013/07/28/blame-and-condemnation-after-rabaa-violence/.

[80] "11 Islamist parties launch 'Legitimacy Support' alliance," *Ahram Online*, June 28, 2013, accessed August 11, 2013, http://english.ahram.org.eg/NewsContent/1/64/75145/Egypt/Politics-/-Islamist-parties-launch-Legitimacy-Support-allian.aspx.

Although Salafis[81] have been present in Egypt for centuries, only since the revolution have they organized themselves into political parties. Alexandria-based Salafis were the main agents in the creation of the al-Nour Party in 2011, which had roughly five thousand founding members. The popular al-Nour Party stems from the Salafi Daʿwa, which was established by students at Alexandria University in the 1970s and remains one of the best-organized Salafi movements in Egypt, although Salafism in itself is not a hierarchical organization.[82] Yasser Metwalli, a founding leader of the party, stressed that it consists of Salafi youth and had no connection to Salafi clerics.[83] At the same time, Metwalli has said that the party has "a religious frame of reference" – a distinction used in recent Egyptian politics – and that it "will oppose anything that contradicts Islamic Shariʿa, even if it is accepted by the majority."[84]

The al-Nour Party had to convince the Political Parties Committee that it was not formed on a religious, gender, class or sectarian basis. Thus, the president of al-Nour at the time, Emad Eddine Abdel-Ghaffour, "called on Christians to join the party, stressing that the party is for all Egyptians and is not restricted to any one group."[85] Unlike the Muslim Brotherhood's FJP

[81] Salafism is a multifaceted Sunni Islamic movement that advocates returning to the practices of early Muslims. The term salaf *as-salah*, or the worthy ancestors, refers to the first generation of Muslims whose pious conduct is considered worthy of emulation. While the term *salafi* has been used in Islamic writing for centuries, the movement coalesced around the same time as Wahhabism in the eighteenth century, and the two terms are closely related (although the similarities and differences are disputed). In Egypt, Salafism has been an important societal trend since the twentieth century, although it remains divided into a number of distinct groups. Perhaps the most important of these groups is the Al-Sunna Al-Muhammediyya Society (also known as *Ansar Al-Sunna*), which was founded in 1926 by Shaykh Mohamed Hamed El-Fiqi. Like other Salafi groups, the Society opposes Sufism and innovation in religion, but it prefers to avoid involvement in politics. A more political group is *al-Daʿwa al-Salafiyya*, the Salafi Call, which was founded in the 1970s and which emerged on its own in the 1980s after its members refused to join the Muslim Brotherhood. The group founded the al-Nour Party after the Revolution and is more strongly influenced by Wahhabism than the other Egyptian Salafi movements. *Al-Madkhaliyya* is another Salafi group that advocates for obeying political rule even if it does not follow shariʿa. Finally, activist Salafism is a trend that rejects political participation as raising human law above divine law. Its members are supportive of political violence, including the 9/11 attacks. For more, see "Salafi Groups in Egypt," *Islamopedia Online*, http://www.islamopediaonline.org/country-profile/egypt/salafists/salafi-groups-egypt.

[82] Noha El-Hennawy, "With Nour Party, Salafis attempt to tap into party politics," *Al-Masry Al-Youm*, May 19, 2011, accessed July 20, 2011, http://www.almasryalyoum.com/en/node/442772.

[83] "Egypt: Salafis Attempt to Form Political Party, POMED, May 19, 2011, accessed July 19, 2011, http://pomed.org/blog/2011/05/egypt-salafis-attempt-to-form-political-party.html/.

[84] "With Nour Party, Salafis Attempt to Tap into Party Politics," *Egypt Independent*, May 19, 2011, accessed June 18, 2013, http://www.egyptindependent.com/news/nour-party-salafis-attempt-tap-party-politics.

[85] "Al-Nour Party Calls on Copts to Join," *Al-Ahram* through *Islamopedia Online*, June 18, 2011, accessed June 20, 2011, http://www.islamopediaonline.org/news/al-nour-party-calls-copts-join.

or the al-Wasat Party, the discourse of the al-Nour Party was less accepting of democracy,[86] at least until the 2011 parliamentary elections. In the first round of these elections, it emerged as the second party after the FJP in terms of seats in the People's Assembly.[87] Later it solidified that position in the final election, earning 25 percent of the seats.[88] It won the same percentage of votes in elections for the Shura Council.[89] Since then, al-Nour has, at least in public, had a spectacular change of position on democracy and the Islamic state. Tellingly, Abdel Ghaffour declared, "We reject the idea of a religious state. It is unacceptable."[90]

Despite his calls for an alliance of all Islamist strands, in December 2012 Abdel Ghaffour announced his departure from the al-Nour Party and the creation of a new party, al-Watan. The reason for this split was the conflict between Abdel Ghaffour's followers and those of Shaykh Yassir al-Burhami,[91] the spiritual leader of al-Nour. Although the al-Nour Party spokesman Nader Bakkar claimed that the split was for administrative reasons, ideological and political differences came into play. Officially, the al-Nour Party declared that the division occurred because Abdel Ghaffour accepted a position on President Morsi's team as a special advisor while president of the al-Nour Party, and this presented a conflict of interest.[92]

However, the more determinant cause for Abdel Ghaffour's resignation was Shaykh Yassir El-Burhami's clerical oversight of the al-Nour Party. Abdel

---

[86] According to Metwalli, "We talk about democracy as long as it does not contradict Islamic shari'a." See El-Hennawy, "With Nour Party, Salafis attempt to tap into party politics," June 14, 2011, accessed July 20, 2011, http://www.almasryalyoum.com/en/node/468155.

[87] "Egypt Elections: Preliminary Results [Updated]," *Jadaliyya*, accessed December 5, 2011, http://www.jadaliyya.com/pages/index/3331/egyptian-elections_preliminary-results_updated-#Stage__1_new.

[88] "Egyptian Elections," *Jadaliyya*, January 9, 2012, accessed June 20, 2013, http://www.jadaliyya.com/pages/index/3331/egyptian-elections_preliminary-results_updated-.

[89] "Results of Shura Council elections," *Carnegie Endowment for International Peace*, February 29, 2012, accessed June 20, 2013, http://egyptelections.carnegieendowment.org/2012/02/29/results-of-shura-council-elections.

[90] 'Alaa' Bayoumi, "Egypt's al-Nour Party: We Have to Respect Egypt's Treaties," *Al Jazeera* through *Islamopedia Online*, December 20, 2011, accessed January 1, 2012, http://www.islamopediaonline.org/news/egypts-al-nour-party-leader-we-have-respect-egypt%E2%80%99s-treaties.

[91] Salafi preacher Yasser El-Borhami is one of the founders of the Salafi Call, one of the groups that led to the creation of the Nour Party in 2011. In 2013 he stated that he would call for President Morsi's resignation if massive protests on June 30 came to fruition. See "Salafi leader: Morsy Should Step Down if Millions Protest," *Egypt Independent*, June 6, 2013, accessed June 20, 2013, http://www.egyptindependent.com/news/salafi-leader-morsy-should-step-down-if-millions-protest.

[92] Bel Trew, "The Brotherhood needs us more than we need them: Salafi Nour Party spokesman," *Ahram Online*, October 15, 2012, accessed January 28, 2013, http://english.ahram.org.eg/NewsContent/1/64/55616/Egypt/Politics-/The-Brotherhood-needs-us-more-than-we-need-them-Sa.aspx.

Ghaffour repeatedly complained about the lack of internal democracy in the party because of the shaykh's close monitoring of all matters. Members of the party who resigned with Abdel Ghaffour reported disappointment in the political management of the party, which they saw as departing from the foundational ideology of the Salafi Call.[93] In sum, al-Watan differs from al-Nour in the fact that it claims to be a political party first and foremost with reference to the Qur'an and Sunnah. Abdel Ghaffour has declared that there will be no group of shaykhs controlling the al-Watan Party.[94] However, the party's legitimacy was severely compromised in June 2013 when 130 of its members, including leaders of its specialized committees, resigned because of conflict with the leadership and unclear party goals.[95]

In addition to al-Nour, there are three other Salafi parties: the al-Fadila Party (the Virtue Party), the al-Asala Party (the Authenticity Party), and the al-Sh'ab Party (the People's Party). They have agreed to form a coalition under Hazem Abu Ismail's[96] Raya Party, which has stated its disagreement with both the Muslim Brotherhood and al-Nour.[97] Although al-Nour, al-Fadila, al-Asala, and al-Sha'b all seem to adopt democratic rules, the emergence of the Salafis as a political power has threatened the liberal camp, which also includes women's groups and Coptic Christians. This is very much due to their previous anti-secular stance, fervent comments, and menacing actions during the 2011 revolutionary protests in Tahrir Square. In the same vein, they changed their revolutionary anthem from "The people want to topple the regime" to "The people want to apply God's law."[98]

[93] "Egypt's Salafi Parties Split, Weakening Influence," Sami-Joe Abboud, trans., *Al-Khaleej* by *Al-Monitor*, January 2, 2013, accessed January 28, 2013, http://www.al-monitor.com/pulse/politics/2013/01/salafist-schism-nour-watan-egypt.html.

[94] Zeinab el Gundy, "Salafi split brings new choices, complications for voters," *Ahram Online*, January 23, 2013, accessed January 28, 2013, http://english.ahram.org.eg/NewsContent/1/64/62908/Egypt/Politics-/Salafist-splits-bring-new-choices,-complications-f.aspx.

[95] "Mass Resignations in Egypt's Salafi al-Watan Party," *Ahram Online*, June 15, 2013, accessed June 20, 2013, http://english.ahram.org.eg/NewsContent/1/64/74006/Egypt/Politics-/Mass-resignations-in-Egypts-Salafist-AlWatan-Party.aspx.

[96] Hazem Abu Ismail is a Salafi politician and lawyer. In 2012 he ran for president but was disqualified after revelations that his mother held U.S. citizenship. In 2013, Abu Ismail launched the Raya ("Flag") party, intended to unite Salafis and Islamists. See "Abu Ismail Builds on Support by Launching a New Party in a Turbulent Political Scene," *Egypt Independent*, March 14, 2013, accessed June 20, 2013, http://www.egyptindependent.com/news/abu-ismail-builds-support-launching-new-party-turbulent-political-scene.

[97] "Egypt's Salafis Split Ahead of Elections," *Al-Jazeera*, January 14, 2013, accessed June 18, 2013, http://www.aljazeera.com/indepth/features/2013/01/2013114105047960749.html.

[98] The Salafis' increasing political influence was seen in their numerical presence at the July 29, 2011, demonstration, which was dubbed "Friday of Unity" after an agreement was reached between Islamists and the January 25th activist coalition, calling for "united demands, shared chants and slogans, and avoidance of controversial issues." Mohamed Fadel Fahmy, "Islamists hold massive protest in Egyptian square," *CNN*, July 29, 2011, accessed August 1, 2011, http://www.cnn.com/2011/WORLD/meast/07/29/egypt.islamic.protesters/index.html?iref=allsearch. However, in response to the majority presence and Islamic tone of the protest, "the few secular

"None of these parties espouses violence as a political tactic," Khalil al-Anani wrote in 2011.[99] As evidenced in the split within the al-Nour Party, the Salafis are indeed more open-minded to some democratic principles, but shari'a remains their principal ideology. The most spectacular shift happened when the al-Nour Party stressed that it wanted a democratic and civil state with Islamic authority.[100] At the same time, the Salafi understanding of the civil state and democracy remains open to question. For example, Muhammad Hassan[101] averred in a news report that Islam does not contradict the idea of a civil state, but the important question is whether this state complies with shari'a and the Sunnah of the Prophet.[102]

Since 2011, they have increasingly drifted away from the FJP. In early January 2013, the FJP passed a parliamentary election law requiring at least one female candidate for any party with four or more candidates on the party list. Ahmed Ali, the Salafi Da'wa's Shura Council member, claimed that the Brotherhood had passed an unconstitutional law that was simply a political maneuver to acquire favor from anti-Islamist political forces. During the previous elections, the al-Nour Party listed its female candidates at the bottom of the ballots and did not place pictures of female candidates on its posters or billboards.[103]

The divergence between the Salafis and the FJP is also related to the dominant presence of the Brotherhood in Egyptian politics. One of the al-Nour

activists who attended contended that they were silenced; some said they were escorted from the square. Most of them decided to boycott the event … ceding the square to the more religious." Anthony Shadid, "Islamists Flood Square in Cairo in Show of Strength," *New York Times*, July 29, 2011, accessed July 29, 2011, http://www.nytimes.com/2011/07/30/world/middleeast/30egypt. html?pagewanted=1&_r=1. At the demonstration, Islamic slogans dominated Tahrir Square with chants saying, "Islamic, Islamic, neither secular nor liberal." Other chants that once rang, such as "Hold your head up high; you're Egyptian," were substituted with "Hold your head up high; you're Muslim" in addition to banners that read "Islamic law is above the Constitution." Shadid, "Islamists Flood Square in Cairo in Show of Strength." Reza Arslan, however, emphasizes that the Salafi "muscle," "many of them associated with the Muslim Brotherhood," at the July 29 demonstration was "a reflection of their superior organizational skills and their ability to mobilize their members." Reza Arslan, "The Islam debate Egypt needs," *The Washington Post*, August 4, 2011, accessed August 19, 2013, http://www.washingtonpost.com/blogs/on-faith/post/the-islam-debate-egypt-needs/2011/08/04/gIQAw47HuI_blog.html.

99   Khalil al-Anani, "Salafobia," *Al-Masry Al-Youm*, August 5, 2011, accessed August 6, 2011, http://www.almasryalyoum.com/en/node/483504.

100 Waleed Abdul Rahman, "Al-Nour: Egypt's Salafis go mainstream," *Asharq Alawsat*, June 20, 2011, accessed July 22, 2012, http://www.asharq-e.com/news.asp?section=3&id=25602.

101 Shaykh Mohamed Hassan is a popular Salafi preacher known for advocating death punishments for apostasy, while asserting that there is no compulsion in religion – that is, that no one can be forced into being a Muslim.

102 "Salafi Political Participation," *Islamopedia Online*, August 2, 2011, accessed July 16, 2012, http://www.islamopediaonline.org/country-profile/egypt/salafists/salafi-trends-political-participation.

103 Aly al-Malky, "Salafist slam FJP over female candidate requirements in draft elections law," *Al-Masry al-Youm*, January 19, 2013, accessed January 28, 2013, http://www.egyptinde-pendent.com/news/salafis-slam-fjp-over-female-candidate-requirements-draft-elections-law.

Party's leaders, Khaled Alam Eddin, stated in January 2013, "The Salafi current is diverse ... and cannot be ignored, dismissed or excluded from politics and governance, as it represents a wide range of people."[104] Eddin further voiced his conviction that the Brotherhood will eventually lose its preeminence within the parliament and the political arena because it is not truly representative of the diversity within Egypt. The Salafis have steadily reared their heads to exert political influence, gathering momentum as they attempt to unify their front against the Brotherhood. As the opposition to the Morsi regime grew, the Salafis refrained from taking part in either pro- or anti-Morsi demonstrations on June 30, 2013, condemning the Muslim Brotherhood for feeding political polarization.[105] In a similar attempt to remain neutral, on the last day of President Morsi's tenure, the Salafi Call's political arm, the al-Nour Party, called on him to set up early elections to avoid "civil war." After Morsi's fall, they endorsed the secular opposition's main demands: early presidential elections, creation of an interim government of technocrats, and a committee for constitutional amendments.

In the same vein, the Salafi Call abstained from pro-Morsi protests in July 2013, citing a desire to prevent violence.[106]

However, al-Nour's support to the transitional process has been both partial and controversial. It criticized the transitional government's cabinet, stating that it was overly homogenous and simply replaced one dominant group – that of Morsi and the Muslim Brotherhood – with another.[107] The party also faced internal opposition due to its cooperation with the Egyptian military after the removal of President Morsi.[108] When the confrontation between pro-Morsi protesters and the army came to a standstill, Salafi leaders attempted to mediate between the two. Preacher Ahmad al-Hassan declared in his televised sermon on August 3, 2013 that he conveyed

---

[104] Virginie Nguyen, "Salafi leader criticizes Brotherhood for excluding other groups," *Al-Masry Al-Youm*, January 24, 2013, accessed January 28, 2013, http://www.egyptindependent.com/news/salafi-leader-criticizes-brotherhood-excluding-other-groups.

[105] "Islamist Nour and Wasat Parties, Cautiously Positive on Military Statement," *Ahram Online*. Accessed July 1, 2013. http://english.ahram.org.eg/NewsContent/1/64/75435/Egypt/Politics-/Islamist-Nour,-Wasat-parties-cautiously-positive-a.aspx.

[106] "Salafi Da'wa calls on Egyptians to unite," *Daily News Egypt*, July 7, 2013, accessed August 5, 2013, http://www.dailynewsegypt.com/2013/07/07/salafi-dawa-calls-on-egyptians-to-unite/.

[107] "Nour Party criticises proposed Egypt cabinet," *Ahram Online*, July 16, 2013, accessed August 5, 2013, http://english.ahram.org.eg/NewsContent/1/64/76599/Egypt/Politics-/Nour-Party-criticises-proposed-Egypt-cabinet.aspx.

[108] "Egypt's Salafi divide over Mursi ouster," *Asharq Al-Awsat*, July 5, 2013, accessed August 5, 2013, http://m.asharq-e.com/content/1373128265623311800/Top%20Stories. Although al-Nour agreed to participate in the shaping of a new Egyptian Constitution, it added "[t]he party objects to the principle of the constitutional amendments taking place under an appointed president and through a committee whose work is reigned over by individuals appointed by that same president." Shaimaa Fayed, "Islamist al-Nour Party to help shape new Egyptian constitution," Reuters, August 12, 2013, accessed August 15, 2013, http://www.theglobeandmail.com/news/world/islamist-al-nour-party-to-help-shape-new-egyptian-constitution/article13712995/.

the demands of the National Alliance to Support Legitimacy to Abdel Fattah al-Sisi: to stop the bloodshed and to not forcibly disperse the sit-ins.[109] It did not, however, prevent the army crackdown on the two major pro-Morsi sit-ins on August 14.

Two other Islamist parties connected to previous jihadi groups have formed in the post–Mubarak era: the Building and Development Party (affiliated with the Islamic Group) and the Safety and Development Party (affiliated with al-Jihad).

Al-Gamaʿa al-Islamiyya (the "Islamic Group"), which began its activities during the 1970s, was Egypt's largest radical group. Significant violence associated with this Islamist group includes the deaths of fifty-eight foreign tourists in Luxor in November 1997 and the 1995 attempted assassination of President Hosni Mubarak in Addis Ababa. The group was formerly under the spiritual leadership of Shaykh Umar Abd al-Rahman (b. 1938), currently serving time in the Unites States for his role in the 1993 World Trade Center bombings. However, in the last decade, the group renounced violence and has instead turned its efforts to social programs. Al-Gamaʿa al-Islamiyya attempted to form a political party, the Building and Development Party, to run in the 2011 elections. The Committee for Political Parties' Affairs rejected the party's formation because of a violation of the Political Parties Law, which prohibits the formation of political parties based solely on religion. The group submitted an appeal on the ruling and asked for public support, claiming that the 1977 law was outdated.

Prior to his resignation as leader of al-Gamaʿa al-Islamiyya, Assem Abdel Maged repeatedly emphasized the allegedly revised ideology of the party. In an attempt to exemplify the party's change, he outwardly reassured Copts and urged all Egyptian political forces to include them in dialogue. Al-Gamaʿa al-Islamiyya was a strong supporter of the new constitution drafted by the Morsi administration. However, Morsi's exclusion of Al-Gamaʿa al-Islamiyya from the president's Human Rights Council, as well as from regional governorship positions, left party leaders bitter until they were granted their first governor appointments in 2013.

As a consequence, the party drifted away from the Morsi regime and resolved to create a major Muslim coalition to the exclusion of the FJP. For this purpose, in January 2013, the Gamaʿa al-Islamiyya leader met with the Nour Party, the Watan Party, the Wasat Party, the Asala Party, and a number of revolutionary youth coalitions that support the "Islamic project."

Some of this opposition to Morsi was mellowed by the appointment of Adel el-Khayat, an al-Gamaʿa al-Islamiyya member, as governor of Luxor on June 19, 2013. On the same day, the party had a dramatic volte-face

---

[109] "Egypt Islamist figures set three demands in meeting with El-Sisi," *Ahram Online*, August 4, 2013, accessed August 16, 2013, http://english.ahram.org.eg/NewsContent/1/64/78256/Egypt/Politics-/Egypt-Islamist-figures-set-demands-in-meeting-wit.aspx.

and denied culpability in the 1997 terrorist attacks.[110] This did not prevent a swift and severe reaction to this appointment: Tourism Minister Hisham Zaazou resigned over the nomination, and opposition figures called for protests against both the nominee and President Morsi.[111] As a consequence, the newly appointed Luxor governor resigned on June 25, 2013, only a few days after his nomination. At the same time, the leadership of al-Gama'a al-Islamiyya reached out to other Salafi parties and started a movement called *Tagarrud* ("impartiality") to support the Morsi regime and counter the anti-Morsi demonstrations of June 30, 2013.[112]

After Morsi's fall, al-Gama'a al-Islamiyya was harshly critical of the army and the transitional government, accusing them of illegitimately removing Morsi from power and calling for the resignation of interim president Adly Mansour.[113] The group also stated that the transitional constitution was illegitimate because it was the result of an appointed president rather than an elected one.[114] Al-Gama'a Al-Islamiyaa leader and former member of the Shura Council, Safwat Abdelghany, equated Abdel Fattah al-Sisi, the head of the army, with Syria's Bashar Al-Assad.[115] After the deaths of at least thirty-eight people near the Raba'a al-Adawiyya mosque in late July 2013, al-Gama'a al-Islamiyya issued a statement describing the military's actions as a "hideous massacre."[116] However, Aboud El-Zomor, a leading figure of the movement, declared in August 2013 "I gave my orders to al-Gama'a al-Islamiya and the Building and Development Party [the group's political wing] that anyone who does not follow the peaceful way of protest, or participates in any attack on a government building or organisation, or army, or police, or church and so on, will be dismissed from al-Gama'a al-Islamiya and the party."[117]

[110] "Egypt's Al-Gamaa Al-Islamiya Denies Involvement in 1997 Luxor Massacre," *Ahram Online*, June 19, 2013, accessed June 20, 2013, http://english.ahram.org.eg/NewsContent/1/64/74458/Egypt/Politics-/Egypts-AlGamaa-AlIslamiya-denies-involvement-in–L.aspx.

[111] Ibid.

[112] "Gama'a al-Islamiya Organises Pro-Morsi Protests to Counter 'Rebellion' Campaign," *Al-Bawaba*, June 6, 2013, accessed June 20, 2013, http://www.albawaba.com/news/gamaa-al-islamiya-organises-pro-morsi-protests-counter-rebellion-campaign-497409.

[113] "Egypt: Al-Gamaa Al-Islamiya Demands Interim President Resignation," *Aswat Masriya*, July 7, 2013, accessed August 5, 2013, http://allafrica.com/stories/201307070139.html.

[114] "Al-Gamaa Al-Islamiya rejects Egypt's interim constitution," *Ahram Online*, July 9, 2013, accessed August 5, 2013, http://english.ahram.org.eg/NewsContentP/1/76081/Egypt/AlGamaa-AlIslamiya-rejects-Egypts-interim-constitu.aspx.

[115] "Pro-Morsi group compares El-Sisi to Syria's Assad," *Ahram Online*, July 25, 2013, accessed August 5, 2013, http://english.ahram.org.eg/NewsContent/1/64/77344/Egypt/Politics-/ProMorsi-group-compares-ElSisi-to-Syrias-Assad.aspx.

[116] "Egypt's Al-Gamaa Al-Islamiya calls for end to turmoil after 'massacre'," *Ahram Online*, July 27, 2013, accessed August 5, 2013, http://english.ahram.org.eg/NewsContent/1/64/77548/Egypt/Politics-/Egypts-AlGamaa-AlIslamiya-calls-for-end-to-turmoil.aspx.

[117] "Al-Gamaa Al-Islamiya won't return to violence," *Al Ahram*, http://english.ahram.org.eg/NewsContent/1/64/79765/Egypt/Politics-/AlGamaa-AlIslamiya-won%E2%80%99t-return-to-violence-Leader.aspx, August 23, 2013, accessed September 22, 2013.

After the fall of Mubarak in 2011, another radical group, al-Jihad, formed a political party called al-Salāma wa al-Tanmiyya, (The Safety and Development Party). Its main ideological points include freedom of expression for preachers in mosques, the abolishment of secular faculty at Al-Azhar, the creation of media policy in accordance with shari'a, the segregation of boys and girls after primary school, the reintroduction of Muslim schooling, and the importance of women's political and social participation within the limits of family needs.[118] Defining themselves as "the Independent Islamic Trend," the founders stated that their party is based on peaceful political participation and respect for pluralism, the constitution, and the law.[119]

The rise of other Islamic political parties is caused by fear of the political influence of Salafis. For example, two Sufi trends have formed political parties: the Tarīqa Rifāʿiya, the largest Sufi order in Egypt, announced the creation of Sawt al-Hurīyya (the Voice of Freedom Party), and the ʿAzmeyya Tarika declared the establishment of Tahrir Masr (the Egyptian Liberation Party). Despite internal criticism that Sufi orders should remain religious groups and not engage in politics, Shaykh Alaa Abul Azayem, leader of Tahrir Masr, argued that the parties were formed to protect Sufism, especially against the threat of Salafi parties that could potentially dissolve Sufi orders if they gained power. Although the parties primarily exist to protect Sufi interests, they claim to be open to all Egyptians, including Copts.[120]

However, Abdel Hady el-Kassaby,[121] the grand Shaykh of the Sufi orders, expressed disagreement with the Sufi political engagement. He claimed in an October 2012 interview that Sufis should not form political parties because of illegality and because of the duty of Sufis to promote religious thought, not politics. He did not object to Sufi members running for office, but he disagreed with Sufism being a political platform for a party. The differences between Shaykh el-Kassaby and Shaykh Alaa Abu Azayem[122] resulted in a battle over the spiritual

---

[118] "Al-Jama'a Al-Islamiyya and the Safety and Development Party," August 1, 2011, accessed August 5, 2011, http://www.islamopediaonline.com/country-profile/egypt/islam-and-electoral-parties/al-jama%E2%80%99-al-islamiyya-and-safety-and-development-p.

[119] Ibid.

[120] "Contested Sufi Electoral Parties: The Voice of Freedom Party and the Liberation of Egypt Party," August 1, 2011, accessed August 5, 2011, http://www.islamopediaonline.org/country-profile/egypt/islam-and-electoral-parties/contested-sufi-electoral-parties-voice-freedom-par. "Given their commitment to non interference in politics, Sufi orders enjoyed freedom during the Mubarak regime and regularly express support of Mubarak, his son, and the National Democratic Party," according to the *Islamopedia* entry. "After the departure of Mubarak, Sufists have complained of conspiracies, intimidation, and violence by Salafi groups."

[121] Abdel Hady el-Kasaby is, as of the time of writing, the leader of the Supreme Sufi Council and a member of the Shura Council, representing the Gharbia governorate. See "Al Kasaby: 'Any reformation starts with morals and ethics; no reformation without righteousness,'" *Twenty.7 Magazine*, May 11, 2013, accessed June 20, 2013, http://twentysevenmag.com/13/?p=690.

[122] Alaa Abu Azayem is a Sufi shaykh of the al-Azmeyya order. He has been a member of the Supreme Sufi Council since 2002. See "Alaa Abul Azayem," *Islamopedia Online*, accessed June 20, 2013, http://www.islamopediaonline.org/profile/alaa-abul-azayem.

leadership of the Sufi order. Shaykh Azayem's supporters criticized el-Kassaby's appointment, stating that it was part of a conspiracy led by the state security apparatus and Mubarak's former National Democratic Party (NDP, disbanded in April 2011) of which el-Kassaby was a member.[123]

The end of the Morsi regime again raised the possibility of political violence in the name of Islam. For example, the Sinai became a locus of terroristic activity where extremists killed at least forty people, most of them members of the military, in July and August 2013, causing the Egyptian army to intensify its counterterrorism efforts and kill at least sixty militants while arresting another hundred.[124]

More critically, the risk of violence by different Islamist groups, from Muslim Brothers to Salafis, cannot be ruled out in response to the bloody crackdown against pro-Morsi protestors that led to more than five hundred deaths on August 14, 2013.

Islamic Groups and Sectarian Politics

In Iraq, unofficial political organizations were primarily formed by Shi'i groups opposing the Ba'thist regime under Saddam. For these organizations, the networks and authority of the clerics were essential for recruiting and mobilization. Hizb al-Da'wa al-Islamiyya, the Islamic Call Party, and the Supreme Council for the Islamic Revolution in Iraq (SCIRI) were the major political groups with a Shi'i orientation.

After the fall of Saddam, these political groups became official, with significant changes to their political agendas. For example, al-Da'wa has embraced a nationalist (rather than religious) platform that emphasizes basic public services and security. The coalition campaign manager put it succinctly: "Right now we have priorities. People have no houses, no food, no security. There are essential needs for people."[125]

Al-Da'wa drew its authority from two sources: the leadership of the party itself, which was founded by a council of prominent religious and intellectual figures,[126] and the authority of the marja', Muhammad Baqir al-Sadr.[127]

---

[123] "Contested Sufi Electoral Parties: The Voice of Freedom Party and the Liberation of Egypt Party," *Islamopedia Online*, accessed January 28, 2013, http://www.islamopediaonline.org/country-profile/egypt/islam-and-electoral-parties/contested-sufi-electoral-parties-voice-freedom-par.

[124] "Egypt says Sinai patrols kill 60 militants since Morsi ouster," *The Jerusalem Post*, August 7, 2013, accessed August 9, 2013, http://www.jpost.com/Middle-East/Egypt-says-Sinai-patrols-kill-60-militants-since-Morsi-ouster-322352.

[125] Amit R. Paley, "In Iraq's Provincial Elections, Main Issue Is Maliki Himself," *The Washington Post*, January 17, 2009, accessed August 16, 2013, http://articles.washington-post.com/2009-01-17/world/36921869_1_maliki-state-of-law-coalition-kurdish-bloc.

[126] These members included Mohammed Salih al-Adeeb, Sayid Murtadha Alaskary, Abdul Sahib Dukheil, Sayid Mohammed Mahdi al-Hakim, Sayid Mohammed Baqir al-Hakim, Mohammed Sadiq al-Qamoosee, and Sayid Talib al-Rafa'ee.

[127] Laurence Louer, *Transnational Shi'a Politics: Religious and Political Networks in the Gulf* (New York: Columbia University Press, 2008), 84.

Al-Daʿwa's major political vision came from Baqir al-Sadr's concept of *wilāyat al-umma* (governance of the people), promoting core values of liberty, equality, and justice as essential tenants of Islam.[128] According to the party's principles, "In Iraq there can be no place for movements which promote suicide bombings against innocents, which try to spread enmity between different branches in Islam, and which deny women the most basic of human rights." Since the fall of Saddam Hussein, it has become one of the main parties in the United Iraqi Alliance, which won the December 2005 elections. Nouri al-Maliki became secretary general of the party in 2007.

Because of its dual principle of authority, al-Daʿwa was at odds with other Shiʿi groups such as the Message Movement, also known as the Shiraziyyun, whose authority derived solely from Ayatollah Sayyid Muhammad al-Shirazi (1928–2001).[129] It was created by Sayyid Taqi al-Mudarrisi[130] (b. 1945) in the 1960s, although the exact founding date is unknown.[131] It changed its name to the Islamic Organization Action in 1979. Much of the Message Movement's legitimacy came from outside Iraq. Shirazi's connections with Ayatollah Khomeini prior to the Iranian Revolution and his considerable support from the Shiʿi populations near Karbala threatened the authority of the Baʿth Party, and he was exiled from Iraq in 1971. He died in Iran in 2001. His brother, Grand Ayatollah Sayid Sadiq al-Shirazi (b. 1942) is part of the Najaf clerics who since 2003 have been characterized by a low political profile.

Despite Shirazi's exile, the Islamic Action organization remained politically effective for two reasons: its connections to religious authorities and its ability to provide social services. It was debilitated, however, by the assassination of one of its top members in 2003, right after the fall of Saddam. In 2005, it joined the United Iraqi Alliance, which won most of the seats in the December 2005 National Assembly election, but it continues to play a marginal role in Iraqi politics.[132]

---

[128] However, in the 1980s, al-Sadr forbade his students from joining the al-Daʿwa party. For this reason, al-Daʿwa switched allegiance to Abu al-Qassim al-Khoei, another leading scholar in Najaf. http://www.islamicdawaparty.com/?module=home&fname=values.php&active=5.

[129] Muhammad al-Shirazi was a Najafi scholar who came from a family line of scholars such as Grand Ayatollah Mirza Hassan Shirazi, famous for his fatwa on tobacco during the Tobacco Movement in Iran, and Grand Ayatollah Muhammad Taqi Shirazi, an important leader in the 1920 revolution in Iraq. Muhammad al-Shirazi was a known opponent of the Baʿthist regime in Iraq and was exiled to Lebanon (and later Kuwait) in 1971.

[130] Sayyid Taqi al-Mudarrisi is an Iraqi *marjaʿ* and one of the highest Shiʿi clerics in Iraq. See "Biography," *Office of Sayed Mahdi Almodarresi*, accessed June 20, 2013, http://www.modarresi.org/english/biography.htm.

[131] See Louer, *Transnational Shiʿa Politics*, 96–8.

[132] National Consortium for the Study of Terrorism and Responses to Terrorism, http://www.start.umd.edu/start/data_collections/tops/terrorist_organization_profile.asp?id=40, accessed August 14, 2013.

The third opposition group, the Supreme Council for the Islamic Revolution in Iraq (SCIRI), was formed by Sayyid Hadi al-Mudarassi (b. 1946) in 1982 during the Iran-Iraq War. SCIRI was based in Tehran under the leadership of Mohammad Baqir al-Hakim (1939–2003).[133] Its offices spread to areas of Kurdistan in northern Iraq, London, Syria, Vienna, and Geneva.[134] It promoted the idea of an Islamic state and agreed with Khomeini's concept of *vilayat e-faqih*.[135] SCIRI was organized under a general assembly of seventy members that represented various scholars and movements as well as Kurdish and Sunni Islamists.[136]

SCIRI was originally designed as an umbrella movement to unite Iraqi Shi'a under one political organization, but it failed to do so, especially given the ideological differences between SCIRI and al-Da'wa.[137] Several units implemented SCIRI ideas and actions under its general assembly: the foreign relations unit, the publicity unit, the information and investigation unit, the social services unit, the administration and finance unit, and finally, the military unit (the Badr Brigade).[138] These units constituted an unofficial institution that attracted followers throughout Iraq and created a network to undermine the Ba'thist regime.

Like al-Da'wa, SCIRI made several significant organizational changes after 2003. First, it transitioned the Badr Brigade to the Badr Organization, which focused on security rather than military opposition. Second, while its main purpose was to resist the remains of the Ba'thist regime, SCIRI also wanted to promote the concept of an institutional state in Iraq. It participated in the 2005 elections, winning 30 of the 128 seats designated to the United Iraqi Alliance.[139] However, it also continued to resist Sunni parties through the Badr Corps.

---

[133] Mohammad Baqir al-Hakim (1939–2003) was another important Najafi cleric who was arrested in 1972 for promoting *mut'a* marriage (temporary marriage), and was partially responsible for uprisings in Najaf in 1977. In 1983, 125 members of his family were arrested and 18 executed in response to the formation of SCIRI. He was soon exiled but returned in 2003 to Iraq. His initial response to the downfall of the Hussein regime was critical of the U.S. invasion but supportive of the overthrow of Saddam. Shortly after his return, he was killed in August 2003 by a car bomb next to the Imam Ali Mosque, the holiest site in Najaf.

[134] "Islamic Supreme Council of Iraq (ISCI)," *GlobalSecurity.org*, accessed August 7, 2011, http://www.globalsecurity.org/military/world/para/sciri.htm.

[135] Accessed August 7, 2011, http://www.almejlis.org/more.php?thisid=3559&thiscat=43.

[136] Dai Yamao, "Iraqi Islamist Parties: Reconstruction of their Activities and Ideologies based on Primary Sources," *IraqiStudies.org*, July 16–17, 2008, accessed August 7, 2011, http://www.iraqistudies.org/English/conferences/2008/papers/yamao.pdf, 6.

[137] "Islamic Supreme Council of Iraq (ISCI)," *GlobalSecurity.org*, accessed August 7, 2011, http://www.globalsecurity.org/military/world/para/sciri.htm.

[138] Ibid.

[139] Reidar Visser, "SCIRI, Daawa, and Sadrists in the Certified Iraq Elections Results," *Historiae. org*, February 11, 2006, accessed September 13, 2011, from http://www.historiae.org/sciri.asp.

In 2007, as SCIRI changed its name to the Islamic Supreme Council of Iraq (ISCI) to disassociate itself from militancy, the Badr Organization officially separated from ISCI to become an autonomous political party led by Hadi al-Amiri.[140] As a result, ISCI has become more involved in politics, although the Badr members are still seen as representing the ISCI.[141] Despite an outward ban on using religious symbols in Iraqi campaigns, ISCI continues to project a predominantly Shiʻi platform, using Shiʻi religious chants and prayers for its campaign posters and evoking the image of Imam Husayn,[142] alienating the more secular and nationalist factions of Iraqi society.

After becoming leader of the ISCI in 2009, Sayid Ammar al-Hakim stressed the importance of recognizing and embracing Iraqi diversity as a strategy to draw attention away from its alienation of secular and nationalist factions. The party, nonetheless, maintains a commitment to creating an autonomous Shiʻi government in southern Iraq.[143]

As a result of this push for diversity, many Turkmen and Kurds, also largely Shiʻi, have taken up alliances with ISCI. For example, in early 2013 al-Hakim welcomed a delegation headed by Turkman politician Shaykh Muhammad Taqi al-Mawla to underscore ISCI's recognition of Iraq's diversity and the struggle of Turkmen amidst adversity.[144] Reaching out to minority groups is one strategy for the party to regain voters lost in the 2009–10 elections.

Provincial elections in 2013 seem to suggest that these efforts were in part successful, as the ISCI gained eight seats (out of a total of sixty-one).

---

[140] Hadi al-Amiri is, at the time of writing, the minister of transportation (2009–) and a member of the Iraqi parliament. He is still the head of the Badr Organization, which is no longer the military organization it was during post-invasion Iraq.

[141] David C. Gompert, Terrence Kelly, and Jessica Watkins, "Security in Iraq: A Framework for Analyzing Emerging Threats as US Forces Leave," RAND Report, 2010, accessed September 29, 2011, http://www.ndu.edu/inss/docUploaded/RAND_Gompert1.pdf.

[142] Matthew Duss and Peter Juul, "The Fractured Shiʻa of Iraq: Understanding the tensions within Iraq's majority," *Americanprogress.org*, January 2009, accessed October 11, 2011, http://www.americanprogress.org/issues/2009/01/pdf/Shiʻa_elections.pdf.

[143] "في استقباله السامرائي.. السيد عمار الحكيم يدعو الى عدم تهميش اي مكون في تشكيل الحكومات المحلية" or "In his meeting with al-Samirani, Sayyid Ammar al-Hakim petitions against marginalization in the formation of local governments," *President of the Islamic Supreme Council of Iraq*, June 20, 2013, accessed June 22, 2013, http://bit.ly/1aE32PH.

[144] "Stressing that Iraq's value and wealth lie in its diversity, Sayyid Ammar al-Hakim receives a delegation from the Alliance of Turkmen Political Forces headed by Shaykh al-Mawla," *President of the Islamic Supreme Council of Iraq*, January 22, 2013, accessed January 28, 2013, http://www.almejlis.org/eng/more/4181-1/Stressing-that-Iraqs-value-and-wealth-lie-in-its-diversity,-Sayyid-Ammar-al-Hakim-receives-a-delegation-from-the-Alliance-of-Turkmen-Political-Forces-headed-by-Shaykh-al-Mawla.

The party also grew closer to the Muqtada al-Sadr's Movement in a mutually beneficial alliance at the expense of Prime Minister Nouri al-Maliki's State of Law Alliance.[145] Following bombings on July 28, 2013, which killed hundreds and the escape of five hundred al-Qaʻida affiliated prisoners from Iraqi prisons in late July, ISCI leader Ammar al-Hakim joined Muqtada al-Sadr in a statement calling on al-Maliki to resign.[146]

Several Sunni Islamist parties have also emerged in Iraq, although their influence has been significantly less than that of the Shiʻi organizations. For example, although its platform is officially nonsectarian, the Iraqi Islamic Party (IIP) promotes Islamic values of justice and peace.[147] Formed in 1960, the IIP is intellectually linked to the Muslim Brotherhood but appears to have no official political affiliations with the Egyptian group. However, the IIP did refer to the Muslim Brotherhood as "our brothers in Egypt" in congratulating Morsi on winning the presidency in 2012. Some of the IIP's principles include "Muslims and non-Muslims must enjoy the same 'political, public, and individual rights'; a democratic order is required in which non-Muslims have the right to elect their own representatives and to vote for a (Muslim) president; the legal system should be neither Islamic nor positivist, but society should be ruled according to shariʻa law; national resources belong to the people; national unity must be upheld on the basis of common citizenship."[148] Furthermore, the leadership of the party called for joint Sunni-Shiʻi membership within the Iraqi Islamic Party. But Sayyid Muhsin al-Hakim, the ranking Shiʻa cleric, declined and forbade Shiʻi cooperation with the party.[149]

The IIP has played the largest Sunni role in the Iraqi legislature since 2013. Yet the party continues to have limited legitimacy and uncertain popular support; it did not show that it could win large-scale Sunni vote in the provincial elections.[150] As a result, key leaders of the movement, such as Vice

[145] Ahmed Ali, "The Revival of the Islamic Supreme Council of Iraq: 2013 Iraq Update #28," *Institute for the Study of War*, July 2013, accessed August 6, 2013, http://iswiraq.blogspot.com/2013/07/the-revival-of-islamic-supreme-council.html.

[146] Hamza Mustafa, "Iraq: Sadr and Hakim demand Maliki resignation," *Asharq Al-Awsat*, July 31, 2013, accessed August 6, 2013, http://www.aawsat.net/2013/07/article55311805.

[147] "The Iraqi Islamic Party (IIP)," *Islamopedia Online*, accessed September 13, 2011, http://www.islamopediaonline.com/websites-institutions/iraqi-islamic-party-iip.

[148] Graham E. Fuller, "Islamist Politics in Iraq after Saddam Hussein," USIP Special Report, No. 108, accessed August 9, 2003, http://www.usip.org/sites/default/files/sr108.pdf.

[149] Ibid.

[150] Anthony H. Cordesman, Adam Mausner, and Elena Derby, "Iraq and the United States: Creating a Strategic Partnership," *CSIS: Center for Strategic and International Studies*, June 2010, accessed August 3, 2010, http://csis.org/files/publication/100622_Cordesman_IraqUSStrategicPartner_WEB.pdf, 80.

President Tariq al-Hashimi, split from the party to join nationalist coalitions for the 2010 elections.[151] Sunni support and alliances with nationalist parties led to success at the polls for Ayad Allawi's Iraqiyya coalition in 2010.

The IIP makes up the largest Sunni group in the Tawafuq Front (Iraqi Accord Front), a coalition of Sunni parties formed for the 2010 elections on a secular platform. The Tawafuq Front developed after the Sunni boycott of the elections in January 2005, when it became clear that Sunni participation in the political process was crucial. Islamic scholar Adnan Dulaimi[152] called for discussions that eventually led to its establishment. The three primary components of the Front are Ahl al-Iraq (People of Iraq), the National Dialogue Council, and IIP.

Despite the violence and marginalization facing the Sunni minority in Iraq, Tawafuq and the IIP have, for some time, remained opposed to the creation of a federalist state that in their view would only generate more violence and discord amongst the Iraqi people.[153] Although Sunnis' views of federalism have changed since 2010, the IIP maintains that a federalist system aids "foreign powers'" plan for the separation of Iraq through the exploitation of Kurdish and Arab nationalist sentiment.[154]

In 2013, a new Sunni force emerged: the Mutahidoun (United) Coalition, led by Usama al-Nujeifi, secretary of the Parliament. This new bloc won 35 seats with 518,968 votes in the 2013 Iraqi governorate elections, with especially strong performances in the governorates of Anbar and Ninawa. The bloc traces its roots to the Arab nationalist al-Hadba party, known for opposing Kurdish militarism in the Mosul area. For the first time in post-Saddam Iraq, Mutahidoun entered a partnership with the al-Ahrar bloc of Muqtada al-Sadr, taking away from Maliki's State of Law Coalition, the ruling of the Bagdad Governorate.[155]

---

[151] Ibid.

[152] Sunni leader Adnan al-Dulaimi has focused on two major issues: ending U.S. occupation of Iraq, and strengthening and protecting interests of the Sunni group against the ascendency of the Shi'a. Shortly after the fall of Saddam Hussein, he became the head of the Sunni Endowment, or Waqf, but the government removed him from that post in August 2005, raising protests from several Sunni groups, among them the Association of Muslim Scholars.

[153] "Discrimination against Sunnis and the question of federalism revived," *Islamopedia Online*, accessed January 28, 2013, http://www.islamopediaonline.org/country-profile/iraq/islam-and-major-political-movements/discrimination-against-sunnis-and-question-.

[154] "المشروع السياسي للحزب الإسلامي العراقي" or "The Iraqi Islamic Party Political Platform," The Iraqi Islamic Party, accessed June 22, 2013, http://www.iraqiparty.com/page/our-project/.

[155] Mustafa al Kadhimi, "Political Alliances Shift in Bagdad," *Al-Monitor*, accessed August 14, 2013, http://www.al-monitor.com/pulse/originals/2013/06/new-iraqi-government-formation.html

In sum, Shi'i involvement in politics, which can be traced back to the resistance to Saddam, came to dominate Iraqi politics since 2003 and has influenced the emergence of parallel Sunni political groups. The end result is sectarian politics in which secular forces have not yet gained legitimacy.

An Islamic Opposition Grows in Turkey

The Islamist opposition in Turkey began as a peripheral movement but grew into a series of political parties that came to dominate the political scene. The starting point for such an evolution was the establishment of a multi-party system in 1946. Subsequently, as early as 1950, the Democratic Party, which was much more lenient toward Islamic values, started to relegitimize Islam in the public and political spheres.[156] The more liberal policies of the Democratic Party throughout the 1950s and 1960s ultimately set the stage for the rise of Islamist parties. In the 1970s, Necmettin Erbakan (1926–2011),[157] who would later become prime minister, merged several Islamist factions to create the Milli (National Vision or National View) movement.[158] This movement led to the creation of the Order Party (MNP) in 1970, later replaced by the National Salvation Party (MSP) in 1972. After its banning by the 1980 military coup, the MSP reemerged as the Welfare Party in 1983. These three parties ultimately gave rise to the current Islamist organization in Turkey, the Justice and Development Party (AKP). The leaders of these former parties promoted a new economic and social order based on "national/Islamic" principles, and their main goal was to restore a national Islamic order as an end to the Westernization process, which they saw as corrupt.[159]

After Turkey's economic crisis, Prime Minister Recep Tayyip Erdogan of the AKP formed a single-party government, taking over as prime minister in 2003 after his party won the 2002 elections. Before the ascent of this mildly Islamist party into power, secular parties such as the Republican People's Party and the Democratic Left Party dominated the Turkish government.[160] For the past decade, however, the AKP has been the dominant party, and

---

[156] Rabasa and Larrabee, "The Rise of Political Islam in Turkey," 36.
[157] Erbakan was a Turkish engineer and politician who presented the ideology of the National View Movement in a 1969 manifesto titled *Milli Görüş*. He was also the first Islamist prime minister of Turkey in 1996 before the military soft coup deposed him in 1997.
[158] Rabasa and Larrabee, "The Rise of Political Islam in Turkey," 31.
[159] Ibid., 40.
[160] The Republican People's Party is the official Kemalist Party in Turkey, and since Ataturk's rule, the party has mostly consisted of secular elite and pro-Western members. The Democratic Left Party (DLP) was formed in 1985 by Rahsan Ecevit, who was the wife of Bulent Ecevit, a former prime minister banned after the 1980 coup. Bulent Ecevit later won the election in 1999 under the DLP and became Turkey's prime minister once again. The party was officially declared a social democratic party, and was also affiliated with Kemalist ideology.

Erdogan enjoyed great popularity in Turkey until 2012.[161] It has described itself as a conservative democratic party rather than an Islamist one, representing a clear break from previous parties, which openly declared their affiliation with Islam. Furthermore, the AKP works within the framework of Turkish national identity and utilizes secularism in a way that enhances its legitimacy as a democratic party while simultaneously maintaining a culturally Islamic façade. Instead of opposing Western political values as other Islamic parties did previously in Turkey, the AKP embraces Western ideas and has even promoted more liberal market policies that have helped turn the country's economy around.[162]

Additionally, the AKP has embarked on a strategic plan to remain entrenched in Turkish politics by reorganizing municipalities. It has devolved some powers to local administrators, giving governors extra freedom and financial means within their respective municipalities. Such an initiative has been very well received throughout the country, garnering support from the pro-Kurdish Peace and Democracy Party.[163] However, some issues stymied enthusiasm for the AKP in 2012, such as the Turkish economy's slowing pace, Prime Minister Erdogan's method of managing the troubles in Syria, and peace talks that have unfolded between the militant Kurdistan Workers' Party and the AKP.

Prime Minister Erdogan has also faced criticism for the repeated crackdown on media and journalists since 2011. An October 22, 2012, report by the Committee to Protect Journalists (CPJ) stated that seventy-six journalists had been imprisoned in the previous year. Sixty-one of these were imprisoned as a result of publishing work or reporting on Kurdish issues.[164] In December 2012, the CPJ updated these figures, revealing slight progress on press freedom in Turkey: the number of imprisoned journalists dropped to forty-nine.[165]

In May 2013, the Turkish government faced increased discontent in the wake of protests in Istanbul's Taksim Square, where the police attacked

---

[161] Fatih Ozatay and Guven Sak, "The 2000–2001 Financial Crisis in Turkey," 2002, accessed August 8, 2011, http://www.brookings.edu/es/commentary/journals/trade/papers/200208 ozatay.pdf.

[162] Rabasa and Larrabee, "The Rise of Political Islam in Turkey," 48.

[163] "Turkey's AKP Plans to Consolidate Power in Local Administrations Ahead of 2014 Presidential Election," *World Markets Research Limited*, January 24, 2013, accessed January 28, 2013, http://www.cospp.com/news/2013/01/24/turkey-s-akp-plans-to-consolidate-power-in-local-administrations-ahead-of-2014-presidential-election.html.

[164] Michael Koplow, "Turkey's War on Journalists," *The Atlantic*, October 24, 2012, accessed January 28, 2013, http://www.theatlantic.com/international/archive/2012/10/turkeys-war-on-journalists/264049/#.

[165] "For Turkey, World's Leading Jailer, a Path Forward," *Committee to Protect Journalists*, December 11, 2012, accessed June 20, 2013, http://www.cpj.org/blog/2012/12/for-turkey-worlds-leading-jailer-of-the-press-a-pa.php.

journalists, leaving at least fourteen injured.[166] This repression raised the question of a possible return to authoritarianism that will be further discussed in Chapter 8.

In Tunisia, Islamists Emerge as a Major Force

Islamist organizations in Tunisia have not been as widespread as in countries like Pakistan, especially given the secular structure of the government with its Francophone influence. Still, Islamists have emerged as the major political force since the demise of Ben Ali, although new secular parties have emerged as serious contenders in 2013.[167]

[166] "Press Freedom Groups Condemn Turkish Police Violence against Journalists," *The Guardian*, June 6, 2013, accessed June 20, 2013, http://www.guardian.co.uk/media/greenslade/2013/jun/06/journalist-safety-turkey.

[167] The Interior Ministry announced in late July 2011 that the total number of official parties has reached 100, compared to a prerevolution total of eight parties that were heavily influenced by the state. (Soufiane Ben Farhat, "Cent partis politique sur la place: Et moi, et moi et moi," *La Presse*, July 22, 2011.) As a result of alliances, the total number of parties is constantly in flux. Also important to note is that a total of 145 groups have petitioned for party status but were refused. For example, the al-Tahrir Party has been mentioned in the press yet has not been given legal status because it is considered an extremist party. There are also many independent parties that are able to present themselves and their candidates on the *Afkar Mostakella* (*Independent Ideas*) website. (http://afkar.tn/faq.php.) The majority of the parties are "centrist parties," including those on "center right" and "center left." Additionally, there are four liberal parties, eleven socialist parties, nine communist parties, two "green"/environmentalist parties, and five Islamist parties. The most significant secular parties are the Democratic Modernist Pole (PDM), Ettakatol (the Democratic Forum for Work and Liberties), the Democratic Progressive Party (PDP), and the Congress for the Republic (CPR). The nine major secular parties garnered about 30 percent of the vote in the October 2011 parliamentary elections, and the two leading parties, CPR with 8.7 percent of the vote and Ettakatol with 7 percent of the vote, entered into an alliance with Ennahda, which won a plurality with 37 percent of the vote. The main opposition bloc is the largely left-wing, anti-Islamist Popular Front, whose members include the Democratic Patriot's Movement (the party of the assassinated Chokri Belaid), the Worker's Party, the Tunisian Ba'th Movement, and ten other parties. The most popular opposition party, Nidaa Tounes ("The Call for Tunisia" party) was created in 2013 by Beiji Caid Essebsi, who held political positions under Bourguiba and Ben Ali and was the interim prime minister from February to December 2011. In March 2013, a Sigma poll estimated Nidaa would take 90 National Constituent Assembly (NCA) seats compared to just 68 by Ennahda should an election take place. "Tunisia Poll Shows Nidaa Tunis More Popular Than Ennahda," *Al-Monitor*, May 15, 2013, accessed August, 15, 2013, http://www.al-monitor.com/pulse/politics/2013/05/tunisian-poll-ennahda-popularity-declines-nidaa-tunis.html. It lists among its founding values freedom of thought, belief, and creation, justice and equality between those of differing social classes, viewpoints, and sexes; and openness to the world. In addition to welcoming members of the former party of Ben Ali (RCD) who had been barred from other parties, Nidaa Tounes formed a political union with the Republican Party and three others, and in its first year netted nine NCA members who defected from their respective parties to represent Nidaa.

Of the parties legalized in 2011, Ennahda was the most notable.[168] Despite Bourguiba's promises to cooperate with Islamists, when the MTI applied for legal recognition as a political party in 1984, some of its members, including its founder, Ghannouchi, and its secretary-general, 'Abd al-Fattah Muru, were arrested and sentenced to more than ten years in prison.[169] In response, the MTI organized mass demonstrations and protests at Tunisian universities. Following these clashes, the MTI was allowed to form a "cultural society" in 1985, but it never gained political recognition under Bourguiba.[170]

Ben Ali's rise to power in 1987 revived hope of gaining political recognition for the MTI. In fact, Islamists played a large role in the opposition movement against Bourguiba in his last days, and Ben Ali utilized Islamic language and rhetoric in speeches to legitimize his rise to power. However, Islamists soon realized Ben Ali would be no more supportive than Bourguiba was of creating a state with more Islamic values, which significantly impacted their strategy in the wake of the 1989 elections.

In 1989, the name of the MTI was changed to Hizb Ennahda (the Renaissance Party) to comply with a law that prohibited political parties with religious references.[171] However, the party was still banned, and Ennahda was not allowed to participate in the elections. As a result, its members ran as independents – mobilizing the masses to the point that the authorities became concerned by its rising influence. Their fears proved to be legitimate when Ennahda candidates gained a significant level of support (15 percent of the vote) in the 1989 elections. Seeing a threat to his power, Ben Ali initiated a crackdown on Ennahda by jailing its leaders. The group was officially banned, meaning much of its inner workings had to take place in secret[172] until the party's revival in March 2011.

The current political leadership of Ennahda claims to be a "moderate" party that "seek[s] to participate in a democratic system, support[s] the separation of mosque and state, and would not scale back women's rights."[173] However, rivals, such as the Populist Party, have accused Ennahda of promoting a moderate policy in order to gain significant influence over the governing structure and of planning to gradually introduce more conservative laws. The party has been compared to the AKP in Turkey in terms of its moderate approach, although Ennahda's leader, Rached Ghannouchi,

---

[168] Tunisia's interim government legalized Ennahda in March 2011. "Tunisia legalizes Islamist group Ennahda," *BBC News*, March 1, 2011, accessed July 17, 2011, http://www.bbc.co.uk/news/world-africa-12611609.

[169] Henry Munson Jr., "Islamic Revivalism in Morocco and Tunisia," *Muslim World* 76.3–4 (1986).

[170] Alexis Arieff, "Political Transition in Tunisia," Congressional Research Service, February 2, 2011, accessed September 19, 2011, http://fpc.State.gov/documents/organization/156511.pdf.

[171] Ibid.

[172] For more information on the inner workings of the secret organization, see the section on social mobilization in Chapter 3.

[173] Arieff, "Political Transition in Tunisia."

used more of a radical-style rhetoric in the past against the Bourguiba and Ben Ali regimes. In the October 2011 elections, Ennahda won 42 percent of the vote and took ninety-one seats in the Constituent Assembly. To assuage concerns regarding an Islamist party in power, Ennahda has continuously asserted its ability to respect all religions and emphasized its compatibility with a democratic society. Importantly, all other Islamic trends in Tunisia, either Jihadi or Salafi, remained marginal in the elections.[174]

However, since 2012, Salafis have resorted to street violence to oppose Ennahda's government. In December 2012, brawls broke out between alcohol vendors and Salafis, and in once instance, a hotel was raided and vandalized as Salafis declared hotel guests infidels. As a result of an increase of similar violent acts, the Ennahda party engaged in dialogues with the nonviolent Salafi groups in late December 2012, while Ghannouchi took a stricter stance with the violent Salafi groups by arresting them and refusing

---

[174] In addition to the Ennahda movement beginning in the late 1970s, several other radical factions broke away from the MTI and formed their own groups. Notably, a second group that was dissatisfied by the relative moderation of the MTI is the Hizb al-Tahrir al-Islami, or the Party of Islamic Liberation (PLI), which was especially active in the early 1980s. This party was successful at recruiting Tunisian armed forces, in particular students from the Air Force Academy. (Munson, "Islamic Revivalism in Morocco and Tunisia," 212.) The PLI was led by Shaykh Abd Qadim Zalloum. The group was originally formed in 1952 in Jordan by Shaykh Taqi Eddine Nabhani, but did not move to Tunisia until 1977 under Zalloum. According to a 1985 document, the party wanted "to show the failure of all politics today that are founded on rules other than those revealed by God." Furthermore, it "call[ed] on the sons of the grand Islamic umma to rise with [it] and to work to reestablish the Caliphate which the impious colonizers have suppressed and to reestablish Islam in the Islamic territories." ("Two Tracts from the Tunisian Branch of the Party of Islamic Liberation," March 8, 1985, in Francois Burgat and William Dowell, *The Islamic Movement in North Africa* (Austin: Center for Middle Eastern Studies, University of Texas at Austin, 203–4). Similarly, another more radical movement that won over several former members of the MTI was Islamic Jihad. This group was formed in 1984 and included a lieutenant in the Tunisian army, Kilami Ouchachi; a preacher from the region of Sfax, Habib Dhaoui; and an activist and editor for *Al Maarifa*, A. Lazreq.

See Michael Collins Dunn, "The Al Nahda Movement in Tunisia: From Renaissance to Revolution," in John Ruedy (ed.) *Islamism and Secularism in North Africa* (New York: St. Martin's, 1994), 155. Islamic Jihad claimed responsibility for the bombings of four hotels in Sousse and Monastir in 1987. Seven men from the group were condemned to death in late 1987 in connection with these bombings. Although little is known about the leadership or structure of this group, its presence was recognized by the press as late as 1991, and its former members may have contributed to some of the more radical factions that have emerged since the fall of Ben Ali in 2011. In particular, Ansar al-Shari'a in Tunisia (AST) is a Salafi group that has risen since the Jasmine Revolution. It has been known for its jihadist ideology although it has publicly refrained from calls to violence. The group has increased its publicity and public activities, such as holding rallies and creating Facebook pages – gaining attention from online Arabic-language jihadist forums such as Ansal al-Mujahidin. (Aaron Y. Zelin, CTC Sentinel, "The Rise of Salafis in Tunisia After the Fall of Ben Ali," August 1, 2011.) The AST also held a conference on May 25, 2011, that about one hundred supporters attended. However, gleaning information from the Facebook page, there are possibly a few hundred total supporters. In response, in late June 2011, the Tunisian transitional government started cracking down on jihadists, including arresting prominent members of AST. Thus, one of AST's main goal has become the release of its prisoners from Tunisian jails.

to talk with them.[175] In May 2013, Ennahda heightened its rhetoric, when Prime Minister Ali Larayedh declared that the Salafi group Ansar al-Sharia was not "a legal organisation, and must either follow the law or 'end its existence.'"[176]

The efforts to combat radical Salafis intensified in 2013, with an operation targeting terrorists around Mount Chaambi in western Tunisia, a hotbed of jihadist activity.[177] The government banned Ansar al-Shariʻa on May 19, 2013, after the group clashed with the police forces and was suspected of increased political violence, including the July 25 assassination of opposition leader and member of the National Constituent Assembly Mohamed Brahmi. Additionally, Ansar al-Shariʻa leader, Abu Iyadh, is wanted in connection to the 2012 attack on the American embassy in Tunis.[178]

Islamic Political Groups Multiply in Pakistan

In Pakistan, Islamic parties and factions are more numerous than in any other country studied in this volume. These political organizations can be divided into four main categories: the Muslim League parties that try to maintain the original message of founder Dr. Jinnah; the Barelvi parties; mostly aligned with the Muslim League; the Deobandi parties; and the Islamist parties such as the Jamaat-i-Islami that advocate for an Islamic state. Interestingly, none of these parties have experienced a political success comparable to that of the Muslim Brothers in Egypt or Ennahda in Tunisia. The relationship of Ansar al-Sharia to foreign jihads and domestic unrest is disputed. However, in August 2013, Prime Minister Ali Larayedh declared the group terrorists, criminalizing their activities and asserting a tie between them and Al Qaeda in the Islamic Maghreb.

Muslim League Parties

The Muslim League reemerged as a significant political force when several Muslim League parties re-formed under the government of General

[175] "Two years on since revolution, Tunisia struggles with new political realities," *Al Ahram Online*, January 14, 2013, accessed January 28, 2013, http://english.ahram.org.eg/NewsContent/2/8/62468/World/Region/Two-years-on-since-revolution,-Tunisia-struggles-w.aspx.

[176] "Tunisia has Finally Turned Up the Heat on the Salafis," *The Financial Times*, May 20, 2013, accessed June 20, 2013, http://www.ft.com/cms/s/0/6b4e8ab2-c14f-11e2-9767-00144feab7de.html#axzz2WpIujkmF.

[177] Nissaf Slama, "Ongoing Operations Around Chaambi Mountain Target Armed Fighters," *Tunisia Live*, August 5, 2013, accessed August 6, 2013, http://www.tunisia-live.net/2013/08/05/ongoing-operations-around-chaambi-mountain-target-armed-fighters/

[178] Roua Khlifi, "Despite Ban and Alleged Role in Assassination, Ansar al-Sharia Continues Activities," *Tunisia Live*, August 1, 2013, accessed August 6, 2013, http://www.tunisia-live.net/2013/08/01/ansar-al-sharia-continues-activities-despite-ban-and-alleged-role-in-assassination/.005D

Pervez Musharraf, who took power in a bloodless military coup and headed the country from 1999 to 2008. These parties are the Pakistan Muslim League– Quaid-e-Azam (PML-Q) and the Pakistan Muslim League – Nawaz (PML-N). The PML-N believes in a "peaceful world for a humane and socially just society with equal opportunities of all in light of the principles of Islam."[179] It is led by former Pakistani Prime Minister Nawaz Sharif. Conversely, the PML-Q was formed as a centrist party and was a known supporter of more secular-oriented President Musharraf. The PML-Q claims to be the continuation of the All-India Muslim League formed in 1906, and like Jinnah in 1948, argues that Pakistan shouldn't be a theocratic state and that all citizens should enjoy the same rights and privileges.[180] The group, led by Chaudry Shujaat Hussain, is one of the largest coalitions supporting President Asif Ali Zardari's Pakistan People's Party (PPP)-led regime. However, in October 2011, eight PML-Q members of parliament submitted resignations and announced they were withdrawing from the coalition because they felt the government had not addressed the concerns of the masses. Additionally, members have been moving away from the PML-Q and joining the rival PML-N as well as the Pakistan Tehreek-e-Insaf (PTI).[181] After a landslide loss in 2013 election primaries, PML-Q moved to cut its ties with the PPP and forged an alliance with Pakistan Tehreek-e-Insaf (PTI) in a bid to remain electorally viable.[182]

Despite their claims of "moderation," leaders of the PML-Q staunchly support blasphemy laws. The PML-Q has also contested the U.S. drone strikes in the NWFP and tribal regions and has opposed the restoration of NATO supply routes to Afghanistan in response to a U.S./NATO attack on Sala in 2011.[183]

At the 2012 "Istehkam-i-Pakistan" Conference, PML-Q Vice President Ajmal Khan Wazir called for immediate cessation of drone strikes, claiming that they targeted innocent people and caused mental distress to Pakistan's

[179] PML-N Manifesto, "What do we want," accessed September 19, 2011, http://www.pmln.org/party/op_36_what-do-we-stand.pmln.

[180] "Manifesto of Pakistan Muslim League: The Quaid-i-Azam's Vision," accessed September 19, 2011, http://www.pml.org.pk/pml-manifesto.php.

[181] "PML-Q gives gov a jolt" *Daily Times*, October 5, 2011, accessed October 7, 2011, http://www.dailytimes.com.pk/default.asp?page=2011%5C10%5C05%5Cstory_5-10-2011_pg1_5. "More PML-Q Members join PML-N," *The Express Tribune*, October 25, 2011, accessed November 1, 2011, http://tribune.com.pk/story/281803/more-pml-q-members-join-pml-n/.

[182] "Alliance between PPP, PML-Q Unofficially Over," *The Nation*, June 6, 2013, accessed June 20, 2013, http://www.nation.com.pk/pakistan-news-newspaper-daily-english-online/national/06-Jun-2013/alliance-between-ppp-pml-q-unofficially-over.

[183] "Pakistan Muslim League- Quaid-e-Azam (PML-Q)," *Islamopedia*, accessed January 28, 2013, http://www.islamopediaonline.org/country-profile/pakistan/islam-and-politics/pakistan-muslim-league-quaid-e-azam-pml-q.

citizens. He also claimed that chemical weapons had been used in drone strikes. The party's 2013 budget also calls for the creation of a fund for victims of drone strikes and decries the dual policy of "condemning publicly but condoning privately."

Barelvi Organizations

As discussed in Part I, the Barelvi ulama were the major actors in the Jamiat-Ulema-i Pakistan that supported the creation of the state. After 1948, however, the relationship between the Pakistani state and the Barelvi has varied. Like the Deobandi JUI, in 2002 the Barelvi JUP aligned itself with the Muttahida Majlis e-Amal (MMA), a coalition of Islamist parties that believed Pakistani President Musharraf had become a tool of U.S. foreign policy. The MMA campaigned on promises to enforce shari'a law and to support the withdrawal of U.S. forces operating in Pakistan in the campaign against international terrorism.[184] The JUP has also joined other Islamist parties such as the Jamaat-e-Islami (JI) in October 2011 in protesting the ongoing U.S. influence on Pakistani domestic politics.[185]

While the party has spoken out against religious extremism, it has also maintained its opposition to the West. Its subsequent actions reflect this complex stance in Pakistani politics. In 2009, the JUP opposed the peace deal made with the pro-Taliban organization Tehrik-e-Nifaz-e-Shariat-e-Mohammadi (TNSM). And yet, at the same time, in 2009, JUP allied with Sunni Tehreek, a militant organization, to form a coalition called Sunni Ittehad Council (SIC). This coalition vehemently opposes the removal of blasphemy laws. JUP members announced that these laws would stand because Pakistan will not cave to the impulses and coercion of the West.[186] The party reaffirmed this commitment in 2012, vowing to protect blasphemy laws "at all cost."[187]

---

[184] "Jamiaat-e-Ulamma-Pakistan (JUP), Jamiat Ulema-e-Pakistan (JUP), Assembly of Pakistani Clergy, Jamiat Ulema-i-Pakistan, Niazi faction (JUP/NI), Jamiat Ulema-i-Pakistan, Noorani faction (JUP/NO)," *GlobalSecurity.org*, accessed October 9, 2011, http://www.globalsecurity.org/military/world/pakistan/jup.htm.

[185] "Religious, Political Parties Rally Against US," *Dawn*, October 1, 2011, accessed October 12, 2011, http://www.dawn.com/2011/10/01/religious-political-parties-rally-against-us.html.

[186] "Jamiat Ulema-e-Pakistan (JUP)," *Islamopedia Online*, accessed January 28, 2013, http://www.globalsecurity.org/military/world/pakistan/jup.htm.

[187] "JUP Vows to Guard Blasphemy Law," *The Nation*, October 15, 2012, accessed June 20, 2013, http://www.nation.com.pk/pakistan-news-newspaper-daily-english-online/national/15-Oct-2012/jup-vows-to-guard-blasphemy-law.

Deobandi Organizations

With the call for a Pakistani state, several Deobandi scholars, most notably Maulana Ali Ahmad Thanqi (1863–1943) and Maulana Shabbir Ahmad Usmani (1885–1949), defected from the dominant Deobandi vision represented by the Jamiat-ul-Ulama-i-Hind (JUH) and realigned themselves with the Muslim League. Their separation resulted in the creation of the All India Jamiat-ul-Ulema-i-Islam (JUI), or All India Assembly of Islamic Clergy (headed by Usmani),[188] which promoted the formation of an all-Muslim state as defined by Jinnah and Iqbal, despite the secular nature of their nationalism.

After party leader Maulana Fazlur Rehman[189] (b. 1953) attempted to align the JUI with the pro-democracy movement against General Zia's Islamization campaign, the JUI split into different factions. Two of these splinter groups are especially important in the current political landscape of Pakistan: the Jamiat Ulema-e-Islam (of Fazlur Rehman), or JUI-F, which is the main JUI group, and the Jamiat Ulema-e-Islam, or JUI-S, led by Sami ul Haq.[190] The JUI-S gained attention when in May 2011 Muslim clerics affiliated with the party appealed to the Supreme Court of Pakistan to ban the Bible.[191]

The JUI-F is often linked to the Taliban. When the latter came to power in Afghanistan in 1996, both the JUI-F and the Taliban gained popular support from Pashtuns living in NWFP, Baluchistan, and the Federally Administered Tribal Areas (FATA).[192] Fazlur Rehman has even admitted his attempts to bring about an Islamic revolution in Pakistan, describing the Taliban as an "ideal Islamic system." Cleric and politician Maulena Abdul Ghani was a prominent leader of the JUI-F, who headed a madrassa in Chaman called Al Jamia Islamia that was believed to serve as a recruitment ground for Taliban rebels.[193]

---

[188] Behuria, "Sects within Sect," 63.

[189] Rehman is a Pakistani politician and the secretary general of the MMA. He is also a National Assembly member and a known opponent of the Muslim League.

[190] Haq is the director of the Darul Uloom Haqqania and is known for his ties to the Taliban. He has also served as a member of the Senate of Pakistan.

[191] "Pakistan: Muslim Clerics from JUI-S demand Bible ban," *Ahmadiyya Times*, May 21, 2011, accessed October 19, 2011, http://ahmadiyyatimes.blogspot.com/2011/05/pakistan-muslim-clerics-from-jui-s.html.

[192] Magnus Norell, "The Taliban and the Muttahida Majlis-e-Amal (MMA)," *China and Eurasia Forum Quarterly* 5.3 (2007): 72.

[193] Owais Tohid, "Pakistan's Frontier Passes Islamic Law, Ranking Islamabad," *The Christian Science Monitor*, June 10, 2003, accessed October 12, 2011, http://www.csmonitor.com/2003/0610/p07s02-wosc.html. In fact, upon his death on October 26, 2011, the Taliban released a statement expressing its "unprecedented condolence" for the death of the Pakistani politician and JUI-F deputy, saying Ghani showed great courage in supporting the Taliban movement after the U.S.-led invasion of Afghanistan in 2001.

JUI-F has brokered deals between the Pakistan military and tribal militants in the Waziristan region, in the southern part in 2004 and then in the northern part in 2006. The JUI-F and JUI-S have come together, upholding a common platform on the issue of U.S. drone strikes in these Pakistani tribal regions. Domestically, however, the JUI-F's political positions have taken various turns. While it opposes the blasphemy laws in Pakistan and calls for change, the JUI-F has opposed bills condemning domestic violence against women. Leaders of this movement claim that no issue for women's rights existed until women rose up and created the issue. Their political presence within the government is mainly a result of support for the PPP. Consequently, in 2010, Maulana Sherani of the JUI-F party was appointed as the chairman of the Council of Islamic Ideology.[194] The JUI-F party leaders also forged ties with the PML-N, which led to the JUI-F being given a ministerial post in June 2013.[195]

Islamist Parties

Similar to other Islamic groups, Jamaat-e-Islami (JI) has had an ambiguous relationship with the Pakistani state. At times, the state has used the JI as a tool to combat opposition groups, for example when Ayub Khan wanted in the 1950s and 1960s to counter the growing leftist force in the country. However, the JI's support of Khan was short-lived because the JI was less concerned with fighting the leftist opposition and more with fighting Khan's modernization policies on issues such as divorce and polygamy that contradicted the JI's vision of an Islamic society.

The state again co-opted the JI under General Zia-ul-Haq's regime, which sought to increase the role of Islam in Pakistani public life. The JI initially endorsed Zia's Islamization measures with the goal of dominating the state-sponsored process.[196] The JI founder, Mawdudi, even came out in full support of Zia's policy, describing it as a "renewal of the covenant" between Islam and the government.[197] However, in the long term, the JI felt the Zia reforms were not sufficient, especially with regard to implementing

---

[194] "Jamiat Ulema-e-Islam (JUI)," *Islamopedia Online*, accessed January 28, 2013, http://www.islamopediaonline.org/country-profile/pakistan/islam-and-politics/jamiat-ulama-e-islam-jui.

[195] "JUI-F May Get Ministerial Slot Next Week," *The Nation*, June 20, 2013, accessed June 20, 2013, http://www.nation.com.pk/pakistan-news-newspaper-daily-english-online/editors-picks/20-Jun-2013/jui-f-may-get-ministerial-slot-next-week.

[196] Seyyed Vali Reza Nasr, *The Vanguard of the Islamic Revolution: The Jama'at-i Islami of Pakistan (Comparative Studies on Muslim Societies)* (London; L. B. Taurus & Co. Ltd., 1994), 266.

[197] Lieutenant General Faiz Ali Chisti, *Betrayals of Another Kind: Islam, Democracy, and the Army in Pakistan* (Cincinnati, OH: Stosius, 1990), 16.

shariʿa. The JI continues to advocate for the implementation of Islamic rule, which remains its major claim.[198] Additionally, there have been strong ties between JI and al-Qaʿida. Various terrorists were discovered in the homes of JI officials and leaders over the past ten years. JI, similar to many other Pakistani political parties, has taken an anti-Western approach in politics. It has opposed reforms of the blasphemy laws because it claims that modifications are a reflection of bowing to the power of the West. It has also advocated stopping U.S. drone strikes,[199] and in 2013 it joined the PTI and other coalition partners to issue a resolution condemning the use of drones.[200]

Overall, it is important to note that until the most recent decade, these Muslim and Islamic parties had not had a significant impact on Pakistani elections (Table 7.1). Out of the 226 elected seats (others are reserved for

TABLE 7.1. *Number of National Assembly Seats for Islamist Parties in Elections 1988–2013*

		1988	1990	1993	1997	2002	2008	2013
Muslim	PLM-N	54	206	73	137	19	91	125
League	PLM-Q	–	–	–	–	126	59	2
Parties	PLM-F	–	–	–	–	–	5	5
Deobandi Parties	JUI	7	6	4 (with IJMª)	–	(MMA-63)	–	–
	JUI-F	–	–	–	2	(MMA-63)	7	10
JI		56 (with IJIᵇ)	106 (with IJI)	3	Boycott	(MMA-63)	Boycott	3
MMA alliance		–	–	–	–	63	–	–
Pakistan Tehreek-e-Insaaf (PTI)		–	–	–	–	–	–	28

ª IJM – Islami Jamhoori Mahaz
ᵇ IJI – Islami Jamhoori Ittehad

Notes: The 2008 election results came from http://pakelectionsonline.org/web/

Sources:
1. http://tribune.com.pk/story/552368/pakistan-elections-2013-total-voter-turnout-55/
2. http://election2013.geo.tv/
Number of National Assembly Seats for Islamist Parties in Elections 1988–2008

[198] "Prospects for Pakistan," *Legatum Institute* January 2010, accessed June 20, 2013, http://www.li.com/docs/publications/2010-publications-prospects-for-pakistan.pdf.

[199] "Jamaat-i-Islami (JI)," *Islamopedia*, accessed January 28, 2013, http://www.islamopediaon-line.org/country-profile/pakistan/islam-and-politics/jamaat-i-islami-ji.

[200] "Taking a Stand: Joint Resolution against Drone Strikes Submitted," *The Express Tribune*, June 5, 2013, accessed June 20, 2013, http://tribune.com.pk/story/559362/taking-a-stand-joint-resolution-against-drone-strikes-submitted/.

women and minorities), the only Islamic parties with significant influence in the National Assembly have been the various factions of the Muslim League – unless the other parties were part of a larger coalition such as the Islami Jamhoori Ittehad or the MMA. This can most likely be explained by the fact that the Pakistan Muslim League parties tend to have more secular orientation concerning Islam in politics and the status of minorities, which is more in tune with mainstream Pakistani positions on these topics.

However, as we have seen especially through the example of the JI, the Islamic-oriented parties have disproportionately influenced the national discourse about Islamic values in politics when compared to the number of Islamic party members elected to the National Assembly.

8

Ideological Strength of Islamist Opposition

Contemporary Islamist ideology is the offspring of the pan-Islamist and revivalist movements analyzed in Part I of this book. However, after several decades under authoritarian rule, the strategy and doctrine of Islamists have adjusted to the national framework, which has entailed compromising with the state and reorienting their political discourse toward social justice and the fight against corruption.

ISLAMISM AS A NATIONAL OR COUNTER-NATIONAL PROJECT

As shown in Part I, Islamism was, at the end of the Ottoman Empire, opposed to nationalism, perceived as a Western imported concept. However, after the decolonization process, the nation ceased to be a foreign and Western concept and became the framework in which politics took place. Thus, Islamist opposition movements gradually used Islam more as an alternative to the secular nationalism promoted by state elites and less as a way to promote a pan-Islamic caliphate. In this sense, they have increasingly operated within the context of the newly defined national political community. In this regard, the evolution of the Muslim Brotherhood from a transnational movement to diverse national ideologies is paradigmatic of this change.

In Egypt, the Muslim Brotherhood believed it held the key to true Islam, and therefore to rightful authority, whereas the state policies were impure. Hassan al-Banna argued that the purest period of Islam was during its golden age, when Muhammad and his successors, the Four Rightly-Guided Caliphs, ruled the umma. Thus, the Muslim Brotherhood's ultimate political goal was to create an Islamic order or *niẓām islāmī*, which emphasized a foundation in shari'a. While al-Banna advocated the implementation of shari'a, the Brotherhood's program also recognized the nonlegal aspects of its vision and worked to improve the social, economic, and political aspirations of the Egyptian people.

That is why "Egypt was the logical and historically right place for Islam to base itself.... Egypt had a unique role to play in Islam's resurgence."[1] al-Banna illustrates this point in the following argument:

The Muslim Brothers, true to the faith, plead that the nation be restored to Islam. Egypt's role is unique, for just as Egyptian reform begins with Islam, so the regeneration of Islam must begin in Egypt, for the rebirth of "international Islam," in both its ideal and historical sense, requires first a strong "Muslim state" (*dawla muslima*).[2]

It appears that al-Banna's pan-Islamic vision was strongly grounded in Egyptian society, where in his view, the reform of international Islam should start.

As a result, domestic politics had strong effects in shaping Muslim Brotherhood's ideology over time. After the death of al-Banna in 1949 and the Free Officers' coup in 1952 that removed the monarchy from power, the relationship between the Brotherhood and the state changed from one of cooperation to mistrust. At first, the Muslim Brotherhood was allowed to continue as an organization under Gamal Abdel Nasser despite the abolishment of existing political parties in 1953. However, the Muslim Brotherhood's refusal to grant legitimacy to a regime that did not implement shari'a soon led to organized demonstrations and protests. In October 1954, a young member of the Muslim Brotherhood allegedly attempted to assassinate President Nasser, and the Brotherhood was subsequently outlawed. Members were arrested, jailed, and received death sentences. Such a political change modified the Muslim Brotherhood's strategy to directly oppose the state. This event also accounted for the divisions within the movement on how to deal with the state.

In the same vein, the turn toward radicalization, largely caused by the increased repression of the state, reinforced the nationalization of the Islamist strategy by focusing on the fight against the ruler. Sayyid Qutb's (1906–66) redefinition of jihad as the fight against the unjust ruler was instrumental in such an evolution. In *Milestones* (1964), Qutb argued that Egyptian society was steeped in *jahiliyya*, or ignorance.[3] Therefore, Egypt was living under a *takfīr* regime, or a regime that had renounced Islam.[4] Qutb called for jihad to battle the *jahiliyya* of the Nasser regime because

[1] Richard P. Mitchell, *The Society of the Muslim Brotherhood* (New York: Oxford University Press, 1993), 217.

[2] Ibid., 232.

[3] *Jahiliyya* in the Islamic tradition refers to the pre-Islamic stage, which ended with the Prophet Muhammad. Qutb gives the term a very different meaning: because Egyptians do not live under shari'a law, they experience, in his view, a situation comparable to the pre-Islamic period and live in *jahiliyya*, hence justifying the fight against the ruler, even if this ruler is a Muslim. Sayyid Qutb, *Milestones*, 1964, trans. CreateSpace (2005), 23.

[4] Barbara H. E. Zollner, *The Muslim Brotherhood: Hasan al-Hudaybi and Ideology* (New York: Routledge, 2009), 86.

to him, the Egyptian state stood in direct opposition to the ideal Islamic political community. However, Qutb's vision led to several schisms within the Muslim Brotherhood because several groups such as Islamic Jihad and al-Takfir wa al-Hijra[5] adopted the jihad against the unjust ruler as their priority.[6]

Muhammad abd al-Salaam Faraj (1954–82), the founder of Islamic Jihad – the group involved in President Anwar Sadat assassination in 1981 – went even further in his national jihad approach. In his text, *The Absent Obligation*, Faraj argued that the Egyptian rulers had been "brought up over colonial tables be they Christian, Communist or Zionist. What they carry of Islam is nothing but names, even if they pray, fast and claim to be Muslims."[7] Furthermore, Faraj argued that the time to restore the caliphate of Islam was immediate, and it was "obligatory upon every Muslim to do his utmost to implement [it]."[8] Faraj promoted jihad as a sixth pillar of Islam, meaning that every Muslim was obligated to immediately undermine the state and replace it with a caliphate. This conception of jihad became global when some of these radical opponents, including al-Zawahiri (b.1951), left Egypt to join the jihad in Afghanistan, which led to the formation of al-Qaʻida in 1998.[9]

---

[5] Of the violent groups that adopted Qutb's conception of jihad, the offshoot group Takfir wa al-Hijra is of particular importance because it still has a presence in Egypt today, as well as roots in Syria and Lebanon. It was formed in the 1960s by Shukri Mustafa, who in prison became part of a Muslim Brotherhood splinter group called Jamʻat al-Muslimin (Society of Muslims), and was inspired by Sayyid Qutb's text *Milestones*. Like many radical groups, Takfir wa al-Hijra aspired to the golden age of Islam under the first Four Rightly Guided Caliphs, and its main goal was to establish a renewed universal Islamic umma under a true caliph. Takfir believed that the present condition of the world is *jahiliyya* (ignorance), and that all four schools of Islamic jurisprudence were puppets of corrupt rulers that were using Qur'anic interpretations to their own advantage. Following the *takfīrī* ideology of Qutb and expanding on it, Takfir wa al-Hijra declared the Egyptian state itself infidel and denounced all symbols of legitimacy, including government services, laws, conscription to the army, and the legal and educational systems. As a result, Takfir wa al-Hijra members were dedicated to living a life apart from Egyptian society. Further, this state of *jahiliyya* justified their interpretation of jihad as a physical and violent resistance against the state, but one that was delayed. This delay was mostly due to the Takfir members' beliefs that their leader, Mustafa, was the Mahdi, and would lead the new Muslim community as caliph as part of God's final reign on earth. However, other groups such as Islamic Jihad did not embrace a delayed conception of jihad. See David Zeidan, "Radical Islam in Egypt: A Comparison of Two Groups," *Middle East Review of International Affairs* 3.3 (September 1999): 1–10, accessed October 10, 2011, http://meria.idc.ac.il/journal/1999/issue3/zeidan.pdf.

[6] Barry Rubin, *Islamic Fundamentalism in Egyptian Politics* (Basingstoke: Palgrave MacMillan, 2002), 56.

[7] Muhammad ʻAbdus Salam Faraj, *Jihad: The Absent Obligation* (Birmingham: Maktabah al Ansaar, 2000), 25.

[8] Ibid., 17.

[9] See Fawaz Gerges, *The Far Enemy: Why the Jihad Became Global* (New York: Cambridge University Press, 2005).

In contrast, the mainstream Muslim Brotherhood operated under the guidance of Hasan al-Hudaybi (1891–1973),[10] who in his book *Du'at la Qudat* (*Preachers, Not Judges*), published after his death, explicitly criticized the *takfīrī* ideology of Qutb.[11] al-Hudaybi directly questioned Qutb's idea of jihad and instead preached faith, patience, and perseverance. He argued that the duty of all Muslims was "to enact all of God's orders and statutes and to pave the way for the establishment of His religion."[12] More specifically, under al-Hudaybi, the Muslim Brothers began to discuss (1) their involvement in Egyptian political life, (2) their compromise with the Egyptian state, and (3) the acceptance of democratic rules.

Political Party versus Social Movement

Since its conception, the Muslim Brotherhood was envisioned as a social movement encompassing all aspects of social and religious life.[13] After the death of al-Banna in 1950, the leadership of the Muslim Brotherhood went to al-Hudaybi, who was chosen by the Society's Guidance Council because of his reputation as a judge, which would help combat the society's affiliation with violence and reinforce its image as a social organization. As both Richard Mitchell and David Johnston argue, al-Hudaybi wanted the society's secret apparatus dismantled and the group to be only a "religious society."[14]

In the 1950s, al-Hudaybi argued that only God, not man, could judge if a society is in a state of *jahiliyya*. The implications of this argument were that al-Hudaybi supported the Egyptian state, asserting "God has delegated to the Muslim nation many aspects of their political, economic and social life.... He has revealed to us that this delegation is for the application and realization of purposes he has determined."[15] Despite this compromising strategy, Nasser in the mid-1960s and Mubarak decades later continued to crack down on the Muslim Brotherhood and all affiliated Islamist groups that posed a threat to the regime, making no distinction between violent and nonviolent opposition.

Under the leadership of Umar al-Tilmisany (1904–86, in office 1972–86), the Muslim Brotherhood became further involved in activities of

---

[10] Al-Hudaybi was the second "General Guide" for the Society of Muslim Brotherhood. He was trained as a lawyer and was known for his careful scholarship. In 1965, he was imprisoned in a crackdown against the Brotherhood by Nasser, and released in 1971 by Sadat.

[11] Zollner, *The Muslim Brotherhood*, 63.

[12] David L. Johnston, "Hassan al-Hudaybi and the Muslim Brotherhood: Can Islamic Fundamentalism Eschew the Islamic State?" *Comparative Islamic Studies* 3.1 (2007): 43.

[13] For a description and organization of these activities, see section on state oppression.

[14] Johnston, "Hassan al-Hudaybi and the Muslim Brotherhood," 40; Mitchell, *The Society of the Muslim Brotherhood*, 204.

[15] Johnston, "Hassan al-Hudaybi and the Muslim Brotherhood," 47.

national interest. Under President Sadat (in power 1970–81), the movement was further integrated within the Egyptian political sphere. For example, in 1976 Sadat permitted opposition parties to function (although he did not overturn the long-standing ban on the Brotherhood). In the same vein, the Mubarak regime in the 1980s brought a new level of tolerance without lifting the ban, which gave the organization a significant level of legitimacy to participate, with some success, in the 1984 elections through an alliance with the al-Wafd Party, gaining fifty-eight seats in parliament.[16]

Al-Hudaybi's ideology resulted in the creation of Muslim Brotherhood's programs in multiple aspects of Egyptian society, such as social services and education. The emphasis on social activism over professional politics explains the debate and divisions within the Muslim Brotherhood on creating a political party after the demise of the Mubarak regime. In particular, the younger generation of the movement raised objections about the creation of the Freedom and Justice Party (FJP), which, in their eyes, should not divert all the resources of the group away from its main mission that remains social and broad in scope and cannot be reduced to partisan activities.[17] This position was in some ways a premonition of the political failure that ended with the deposition of Morsi in July 2013.

On September, 23, 2013, as a consequence of the military coup, the Cairo administrative court outlawed the Muslim Brotherhood, which was registered as an NGO in March 2013. It also announced that it would have its funds, buildings, and assets confiscated by the interim government. The following day, however, the interim government issued a declaration that it would not dissolve the Muslim Brotherhood until all litigation steps were exhausted.[18] Therefore, at the time of this writing, it seems that the movement is back to its status before the January 2011 revolution: outlawed and repressed.

Right after the demise of Mubarak, when the Muslim Brothers emerged as the only organized political group, nobody could have predicted such a reverse of fortune. Because they had a strong grounding in multiple levels of the Egyptian society, their opponents at the time worried about their political advantage of turning their followers into voters.[19] As a response to the criticism, the FJP repeatedly asserted its intention to participate in a broad-based parliament. Moreover, the Muslim Brotherhood pledged not

---

[16] Ibid., 49.

[17] "The Muslim Brotherhood's Freedom and Progress Party," *Islamopedia Online*, August 1, 2011, accessed December 12, 2011, http://www.islamopediaonline.com/country-profile/egypt/islam-and-electoral-parties/muslim-brotherhood%E2%80%99s-freedom-and-progress-party.

[18] "Government postpones dissolution of Brotherhhood," September 24, 2013, accessed September 24, 2013, http://english.ahram.org.eg/NewsContent/1/64/82409/Egypt/Politics-/Egypt-government-postpones-dissolution-of-Brotherh.aspx.

[19] The elections were postponed from September 2011 until the end of November 2011 to give parties other than the FJP more time to organize.

to, directly at least, nominate a candidate for president, so as not to create a monopoly over the government. However, going against the mainstream Muslim Brotherhood's declaration, former member of the movement's Guidance Bureau, Abdel Moneim Aboul Fotouh,[20] nominated himself as an independent presidential candidate in June 2011. As a result, the Muslim Brotherhood's Shura Council decided to dismiss him as a member on the grounds that the Muslim Brotherhood itself was not attempting to control state institutions or political parties.[21] It appears that during this initial phase of the transition, the Muslim Brotherhood made an effort to appease the West and secularists by downplaying its potential influence over Egyptian politics. Ultimately, however, the group went back on both promises, as it contested all seats in parliament, winning just under half of them, and fielded a candidate, Mohamed Morsi, for the country's highest office, which raised questions about the group's integrity and honesty.[22] This volte-face contributed to the loss of popularity of the party, which, from this moment onward, lost credibility steadily until Morsi's ousting in July 2013 (see Chapter 9).

Compromise with the State

One of the most significant signs of the shift toward accommodation with the state came under authoritarian rule during the 2005 parliamentary elections when the Mubarak regime allowed the Muslim Brotherhood more space and freedom to conduct its electoral campaign, in compliance with the Bush Freedom Agenda.[23] As a result, the Brotherhood won 20 percent of the vote despite blatant election rigging and proved itself a contending opposition group to the incumbent regime. Further political professionalization continued in 2007 as it issued its platform without actually forming a party. This platform brought to the fore front important controversies about its position on citizenship rights, the role of the official religious establishment, and the interpretation of shariʿa, as will be discussed in the section below.[24]

---

[20] Fotouh (b.1952) is a physician and the secretary general of the Arab Medical Union.

[21] Noha el-Hennawy, "Brotherhood youth blast decision to expel Abouel Fotouh," *Almasry Al Youm*, June 19, 2011, accessed September 12, 2011, http://www.almasryalyoum.com/en/node/469394.

[22] Youssef Hamza, "Islamists campaigning hard for Egyptian presidency," *The National*, May 20, 2012, accessed July 22, 2012, http://www.thenational.ae/news/world/islamists-campaigning-hard-for-egyptian-presidency.

[23] At the time, the U.S. president said Egypt should show the way toward democracy.

[24] Nathan J. Brown and Amr Hamzawy, *The Draft Party Platform of the Egyptian Muslim Brotherhood: Foray into Political Integration or Retreat into Old Positions?* (Washington, DC: Carnegie Endowment for International Peace, 2008).

The attitude of compromise has been amplified since the ousting of Mubarak. When the protests against the ruling Supreme Council of the Armed Forces (SCAF) turned violent in late November 2011, the Brotherhood refused to continue its participation because the protestors demanded postponed elections, and the potential for the rise of instability could compromise the first round of elections that the FJP was clearly poised to win.[25] However, after its victory in the parliamentary elections, the FJP multiplied its appeasing gestures toward the SCAF. In December 2012, it announced that it would not participate in antimilitary rallies because the handover of power to civilians must occur in a stable environment.[26] Implicitly, this move meant that the FJP was following the SCAF's timetable of presidential elections that were finalized after a run-off between two candidates in June 2012. Instead of participating in actions opposing the SCAF, the Brotherhood moved to a "more subtle form of protest,"[27] which included boycotting the Advisory Council.[28]

Mohamed Morsi, head of the FJP before his election as Egyptian president, called this council "an attempt to sidestep the will of the people ... They [the SCAF] are trying to handcuff the new parliament."[29] Then, in his first symbolic moves as president, Morsi tried to both assuage and challenge the Egyptian military. For instance, he acknowledged the powerful SCAF by attending a military parade when he was inaugurated. He also made what was seen as a conciliatory gesture, thanking the military for its role in keeping the nation together after Mubarak's fall.[30] Yet, on July 8, about a week after he was sworn in, in one of his first acts as president, he issued a decree to reinstate the People's Assembly. The move was seen worldwide as an act of defiance against the SCAF, which had ordered the People's Assembly

---

[25] Daniel Nisman, "Egypt Elections: The SCAF's Window of Opportunity?" *Middle East Online*, December 11, 2011, accessed December 23, 2011, http://www.middle-east-online. com/english/?id=49449.

[26] Jailan Zayan, "Egypt brotherhood rallies behind military to save political gains," *Middle East Online*, December 4, 2011, accessed December 27, 2011, http://www.middle-east-on-line.com/english/?id=49636.

[27] Nisman, "Egypt Elections: The SCAF's Window of Opportunity?"

[28] The Advisory Council was a SCAF-appointed body created in mid-December 2011 to over-see the appointment of the 100-member constituent assembly designated to draft a new constitution before an Islamist-dominated parliament comes into power. See Nada Huseein Rashwan, "Two Leading Politicians Condemn Military Attack on Tahrir, Scold SCAF," *Jadaliyya*, December 17, 2011, accessed January 8, 2012, http://www.jadaliyya.com/pages/ index/3580/two-leading-politicians-condemn-military-attack-on.

[29] Hatem Maher, *Jadaliyya*, December 11, 2011, accessed January 4, 2012, http://www.jadali-yya.com/pages/index/3479/brotherhood_scafs-advisory-council-handcuffs-parli.

[30] "Morsi's Praise of Army Generals Leaves Some Revolutionaries Cold," *Ahram Online*, July 1, 2012, accessed July 13, 2012, http://english.ahram.org.eg/NewsContent/36/122/46585/ Presidential-elections-/Presidential-elections-news/Morsis-praise-of-army-generals-leaves-some-revolut.aspx.

dissolved over a court ruling that found the parliamentary election law unconstitutional.[31] But then, four days later, Morsi indicated he would abide by a rapid Supreme Court ruling that overturned his presidential decree to reinstate the People's Assembly.[32] In August 2012, Morsi tried to gain political independence from the SCAF by removing the leader of the Supreme Council of Armed Forces (SCAF), Mohammed Tantawi,[33] and nominating Abdel Fattah al-Sisi,[34] an officer who seemed more in line with the ideology of the Muslim Brotherhood. While the dismissal was framed as a retirement, crowds celebrating the announcement in Tahrir Square chanted, "Marshal, tell the truth, did Morsi fire you?"[35] In November 2012, Morsi went one step further by adopting a constitutional decree that granted him the right to draw up a new legislative assembly.[36]

This initiative stirred up such levels of protest and resistance that Morsi was forced to annul this expansion of powers in December 2012. This act was another fatal blow to the legitimacy of Morsi's government. It irremediably annihilated any ability for the regime to build trust with the different political protagonists and paved the way for the continuous social unrest that would lead to the military intervention of July 2013.

[31] Steve Hendrix and Ernesto Londono, "Egypt's Morsy makes Bid to Reinstate Islamist Parliament, *Washington Post*, July 8, 2012, accessed July 22, 2012, http://www.washingtonpost.com/world/egypts-morsi-makes-bid-to-reinstate-islamist-parliament/2012/07/08/gJQAQTnDWW_story.html.

[32] "Morsy Says He Will Respect Court's Ruling on People's Assembly," *Egypt Independent*, July 11, 2012, accessed July 22, 2012, http://www.egyptindependent.com/news/morsy-says-he-will-respect-court-s-ruling-people-s-assembly.

[33] Mohammed Hussein Tantawi (b. 1935) served in a number of conflicts under the Mubarak regime, including the Six Days War, the Yom Kippur War, and the first Gulf War. He was appointed Minister of Defense and commander of the Egyptian military in 1991, serving through the overthrow of Mubarak. Tantawi headed the Supreme Council of the Armed Forces (SCAF) from its instatement on February 11, 2011, to June 30, 2012.

[34] Abdel Fattah al-Sisi (b. 1954) became Minister of Defense and Commander in Chief of the Egyptian military in August 2012. He was, at least initially, perceived as being friendly toward the Muslim Brotherhood. For example, in his thesis for the U.S. Army War College he defended the interdependence of Islam and politics as necessary for the success of democracy in the Middle East. In the same vein, Gamal Hishmat, spokesman for the FJP, declared him "100 percent patriotic" when he was appointed (Robert Springborg, "Sisi's Islamist Agenda for Egypt: The General's Radical Political Vision," Foreign Policy, July 28, 2013, accessed August 13, 2013, http://www.foreignaffairs.com/articles/139605/robert-springborg/sisis-islamist-agenda-for-egypt). Ironically, he was instrumental in the overthrow of President Morsi in July 2013. As part of the turnover of power, Al-Sisi was appointed Deputy Prime Minister on July 16, 2013.

[35] "Crowds in Cairo Praise Morsi's Army Overhaul," *Al Jazeera*, August 13, 2012, accessed January 28, 2013, http://www.aljazeera.com/news/middleeast/2012/08/201281215511142445.html.

[36] "Egypt's Constitutional Decree Crisis," *Al Jazeera Center for Studies*, December 6, 2012, accessed January 28, 2013, http://studies.aljazeera.net/en/positionpapers/2012/12/2012126742876179.htm.

Between Democracy and Authoritarian Temptation

The first real political platform of the Muslim Brothers was issued in 2007. It stirred a public debate on Islam and democracy that in some ways has contributed to the greater inclusion of liberal values into the movement's program and in the Freedom and Justice Party (FJP) agenda. Back in 2007, however, the positions expressed in the platform on women and Copts as well as the proposal to create an ulama council raised a lot of questions about their commitment to democracy. The controversy was caused primarily by the proposal to create an ulama council.

The Ulama Council (or Council of Religious Scholars) represented a divergence from the Muslim Brotherhood's previous interpretation of Islam as a frame of reference toward a stricter implementation of Shari'a principles. This council would have been elected by the full body of all religious scholars in the country and would have advised the legislative and executive branches on matters of religious interpretation. Importantly, the council would have had more than a consultative role, as its decisions would have been binding in matters where Islamic jurisprudence cannot be subject to interpretation. This proposal was at the time interpreted as an attempt to put all politics under the tutelary authority of the clerics in a way comparable to Iran's system. Interestingly, the 2012 Egyptian constitution contained a remnant of this idea of clerical guidance by granting Al-Azhar the right to review legislation (see Chapter 9).

Another reason for concern was that the 2007 platform asserted that neither women nor Copts could become president in a Muslim state.[37] Moreover, the platform included no clear reference to opening the movement to all Egyptians regardless of their religion.[38] In reaction to the apparent conservative influences in this document, several prominent Brotherhood members, including Abdel Moneim Aboul Fotouh, Gamal Hishmat, and Issam El-Erian (who became vice chair of the Freedom and Justice Party after 2011), rapidly formed a modernist group. This camp denied that this platform represented the movement's objectives as a whole and decried it as the strategy of a small radical group within the Brotherhood.

Hence, after the ousting of Mubarak, the platform of the Freedom and Justice Party illustrated a greater sense of compromise than the 2007 version: there was no more mention of an ulama council that would supersede the elected institutions, and Copts and women were acknowledged as full citizens.[39]

---

[37] This discussion is based on Brown and Hamzawy, *The Draft Party Platform of the Egyptian Muslim Brotherhood.*

[38] Ibid.

[39] See http://www.fjponline.com/articles.php?pid=80 for specifics.

To reach out to a wider range of voters, the Freedom and Justice Party was officially declared a secular party and opened its membership to Copts and women. The FJP's secretary-general and cofounder Dr. Sa'd Katatny claimed the party had 8,821 founding members – which grew to an FJP-estimated one million by 2012[40] – across Egypt's twenty-seven governorates. He stressed that this number included more than 900 women and 93 Copts.[41] In the same vein, right after the presidential election, one of Morsi's political councilors declared that the new president was considering picking a woman and a Copt as vice president.[42] However, the likely pick, Munir Fakhry Abdel Nour, turned down the position (which was eliminated in the 2012 constitution).[43]

Right after the revolution, there was some willingness on all parts to communicate. For example, Coptic bishops and clerics held a well-publicized meeting with FJP leaders, even though their initiative reportedly did not have the formal approval of the Coptic Church.[44] After Morsi's election as president, acting pope Anba Pachomius and a senior Coptic delegation visited the presidential palace to congratulate him on his victory. Pachomius told Morsi that his election was "a comfort to all Egyptians."[45] In return, Morsi assured the Coptic delegation he would maintain close contacts and not allow anyone to "condescend" to them, although months later he did not attend Pachomius's enthronement ceremony but instead chose to send one of his representatives.[46]

This mutual engagement was short-lived, and the relations between the Morsi administration and the Copts (as well as all Egyptian Christians)

[40] Jeffrey Martini et al., *The Muslim Brotherhood, Its Youth, and Implications for U.S. Engagement*, RAND National Defense Research Institute: 2012, quoting "Rub' A'da' Hizb al-Hurriya wa-l-'Adala Laysu Ikhwan اخوان ليسوا والعدالة الحرية حزب اعضاء ربع" or "25% of Freedom and Justice Party members are not Muslim Brothers," *Al-Youm Al-Sabi'*, May 17, 2011, http://bit.ly/18jx2kB.

[41] "The Muslim Brotherhood's Freedom and Progress Party," *Islamopedia Online*, August 1, 2011, accessed July 16, 2012, http://islamopediaonline.org/country-profile/egypt/islam-and-electoral-parties/muslim-brotherhood%E2%80%99s-freedom-and-progress-party.

[42] Dina Ezzat, "Mursi's First Messages," *Al-Ahram*, July 5, 2012, accessed July 22, 2012, http://weekly.ahram.org.eg/2012/1105/eg1.htm.

[43] "Coptic Tourism Minister Denies Offer of Egypt Vice-presidency," *Ahram Online*, July 8, 2012, accessed June 21, 2013, http://english.ahram.org.eg/NewsContent/3/12/47134/Business/Economy/Coptic-tourism-minister-denies-offer-of-Egypt-vice.aspx.

[44] "The Coptic Church," *Islamopedia Online*, August 1, 2011, accessed July 12, 2012, http://www.islamopediaonline.org/country-profile/egypt/religious-minorities-and-freedom-religion/coptic-church.

[45] "President-elect Morsi Receives Acting Pope of Egypt's Coptic Church," *Islamopedia Online*, June 27, 2012, accessed July 12, 2012, http://www.islamopediaonline.com/news/president-elect-morsi-receives-acting-pope-egypts-coptic-church.

[46] "Egypt's Morsi 'will not attend' Coptic pope ceremony," *AFP*, November 12 2012, accessed October 1 2013 http://www.google.com/hostednews/afp/article/ALeqM5hpUR4Y2wpRHcyuplpEh9ZBpiCsMg?docId%3DCNG.cddd441c7c4ca34f51e4e1f72f107e16.1e1.

deteriorated. All churches withdrew from the ongoing national dialogues initiated by Morsi in December 2012. To respond to concern about the protection of civil rights in the new constitution, Father Rafik Gerish, a Catholic representative in the dialogues, claimed that the discussions were in fact "unproductive" and did not "yield the desired results."[47] In April 2013, two mourners were killed and ninety others injured when assailants attacked a funeral for victims of anti-Copt violence in Cairo. After the attack, at Cairo's Saint Mark Cathedral, the headquarters of the Coptic Orthodox Church, Pope Tawadros II, criticized Morsi's failure to protect Copts, stating, "This comes under dereliction of duty ... which is the responsibility of the security apparatus."[48] The church also issued a list of demands to President Morsi for equal application of the law to all Egyptian citizens, including Shi'is, and protection of minorities.[49] Pope Tawadros described Coptic life under Morsi as characterized by "a sense of marginalisation and rejection, which we can call social isolation."[50]

President Morsi's advisor for democratic transition, and Coptic intellectual, Samir Morcos added to the voices of dissent when he resigned in late 2012 after Morsi issued the controversial decree giving himself legislative power. He explained that Morsi ignored his advisement and seized constitutional power without consulting him.[51] Morcos's resignation echoed the liberal boycott of the constitutional committee as a protest of the lack of inclusion of leftist groups, Copts, and women.[52]

Even though these political openings toward copts were timid and not very successful, they were also criticized by the Salafis.[53]

---

[47] "Egypt churches withdraw from Morsi's national dialogue," *Al Ahram Online*, January 24, 2013, accessed January 28, 2013, http://english.ahram.org.eg/NewsContent/1/64/63180/Egypt/Politics-/Egypt-churches-withdraw-from-Morsis-national-dialo.aspx.

[48] "Egypt's Coptic Pope Criticises Morsi over Cathedral Attacks," *Ahram Online*, April 9, 2013, accessed June 21, 2013, http://english.ahram.org.eg/NewsContent/1/64/68830/Egypt/Politics-/Egypts-Coptic-pope-criticises-Morsi-over-cathedral.aspx.

[49] "Coptic Church Submits Demands to Morsy," *Egypt Independent*, April 10, 2013, accessed June 21, 2013, http://www.egyptindependent.com/news/coptic-church-submits-demands-morsy.

[50] "Egypt's Pope Says Islamist Rulers Neglect Copts," *Ahram Online*, April 26, 2013, accessed June 21, 2013, http://english.ahram.org.eg/NewsContent/1/64/70168/Egypt/Politics-/Egypts-Pope-says-Islamist-rulers-neglect-Copts.aspx.

[51] "Morcos: Morsy's Constitutional Declaration Hinders Democratic Transition," *Egypt Independent*, October 24, 2012, accessed June 21, 2013, http://www.egyptindependent.com/news/morcos-morsy-s-constitutional-declaration-hinders-democratic-transition.

[52] "Liberals and Leftists Resign from Constitution-writing Panel in Egypt," *The Washington Post*, March 25, 2012, accessed June 21, 2013, http://articles.washingtonpost.com/2012-03-25/world/35448298_1_islamist-parties-free-egyptians-ghar.

[53] Generally speaking, Salafis have been very adamant to present the Brothers as overly liberal. For example, after the Muslim Brotherhood established its own soccer team as a form of public outreach, Salafi cleric Abu Ishaaq Al-Huweini suggested in response that soccer is a

After their political victory in the 2011 parliamentary elections, some Salafi leaders acknowledged publicly the Coptic community. For example, Mohamed Hassan[54] cited from the Sunna on how Islam stresses the protection of the lives of Copts, and non-Muslims generally, in the Muslim state.[55] Another Salafi scholar asserted that Muslims love Christians in Egypt, although they reject their beliefs, and insisted that Islam urges the protection of Copts.

Nonetheless, most Salafi remain hostile toward freedom of religion for religious minorities. For instance, Abu Ishaq al-Heweny[56] suggested imposing a *jizya* or tax on non-Muslims as a way to alleviate the state's financial problems.[57] Another symbolic example of hostility toward religious minorities was the fatwa issued in January 2013 by the Committee for the Legitimate Rights and Reform declaring it haram, or forbidden, to wish Copts a Merry Christmas.[58]

Overall, as under the Sadat and Mubarak regimes, violence and harassment against Copts has continued. In March 2011 in Qena, a number of Salafis, including an off-duty policeman, accused a Copt of renting an apartment to a prostitute. They cut off one of his ears and mutilated the other.[59] As was the case under Mubarak, the police did not interfere to implement the law but rather called for reconciliation among the religious communities.[60] Acts of violence in 2013 included the aforementioned incident at Saint Mark's Cathedral and a preceding incident at al-Khosous where sectarian violence erupted after

---

form of fun banned by Islam. James M. Dorsey, "Muslim Brotherhood takes to the soccer pitch," *Al-Arabiya*, May 6, 2011, accessed January 3, 2012, http://english.alarabiya.net/articles/2011/05/06/148085.html.

54   Sheikh Mohamed Hassan is a popular Salafi preacher known for advocating death punishments for apostasy while asserting that there is no compulsion in religion – that is, that no one can be forced into being a Muslim.

55   http://www.youtube.com/watch?v=CQ5QJxET8q4&feature=related.

56   Shaykh Abu Ishaq al-Heweny is a Salafi imam specializing in interpretation of hadith. He was born in Hewen, a village in the Nile delta, and attended primary and secondary school in Kafr al-Sheikh prior to advanced studies in Spanish at Cairo's University of Ain Shams. "Mawqaʿ Fadilat al-Shaykh Abi Ishaq al-Hiweny موقع فضيلة الشيخ ابي اسحاق الحويني " or "Sheikh Abi Ishaq Al-Heweny Website," accessed June 25, 2013, http://www.alheweny.org/aws/play.php?catsmktba=661.

57   http://www.youtube.com/watch?v=6ZfbWtbYG9k.

58   Haitham El-Tabei, "First Christmas for Egypt Copts under Islamist rule," *AFP*, January 6, 2013, accessed January 28, 2013, http://www.google.com/hostednews/afp/article/ALeqM5h5wpgVO5Tre2UgXUF1SoV8sYrzYw?docId=CNG.be14a436685537a4e41bae07031bf8f4.5e1.

59   Paul Marshall, "Egypt's Other Extremists," *Hudson Institute*, May 16, 2011, accessed July 22, 2012, http://www.hudson.org/index.cfm?fuseaction=publication_details&id=7987.

60   "Salafi Violence against Copts," *Islamopedia Online*, August 2, 2011, accessed July 16, 2012, http://islamopediaonline.org/country-profile/egypt/salafists/salafi-violence-against-copts.

Coptic youths and women were accused of leaving graffiti on an Islamic institution.[61]

The sectarian violence has increased further since the military coup of July 2013. According to a report released on September 24, 2013, by the Egyptian Centre for Public Policy Studies (ECPPS), the attacks against Copts in Upper Egypt in the wake of president Morsi's ouster were the most extensive in Egypt's modern history. The most comprehensive wave of attacks was triggered by the dispersal of the two main pro-Morsi sit-ins in Cairo and Giza on August 14, which left hundreds dead and thousands injured.[62]

Women's rights have also been very much discussed since the Islamists' rise to power. While women were an active component of the Tahrir protests, their rights and status were marginalized in the transition phase. For example, Nehad Abdul Komsan, from the Egyptian Center for Women's Rights, raised concerns in January 2013 about the representation of women's interests during the drafting of the constitution, since it was primarily Egyptian male representatives who oversaw the constitution process. Women also feared that the writing of the constitution was intentionally ambiguous about the specific rights of women. Case in point: when Article 36 of the 2012 constitution mentioned equality between men and women, the wording pointedly limited this equality by referring to the rules of Islamic jurisprudence: "The state is committed to taking all constitutional and executive measures to ensure equality of women with men in all walks of political, cultural, economic and social life.... [w]ithout violation of the rule of Islamic jurisprudence."[63] By contrast, Article 11 of the 1972 constitution did not introduce such a limitation.[64] In the draft of the revised constitution to be submitted to referendum in January 2014, references to Islamic jurisprudence have been removed from Article 10 that dealt with gender equality: "The state will ensure equality between men and women in all aspects of political, economic, social, and cultural life. The state will take extensive initiatives to ensure that females are not discriminated against in employment

---

[61] "Family accused of sparking al-Khosous religious violence turn themselves in," *Al-Ahram Online*, April 15, 2013, accessed June 22, 2013, http://english.ahram.org.eg/NewsContent/1/64/69273/Egypt/Politics-/Family-accused-of-sparking-AlKhosous-religious-vio.aspx.

[62] See "August sectarian attacks largest in Egypt history," September 24, 2013, accessed September 24, 2013, http://english.ahram.org.eg/NewsContent/1/64/82403/Egypt/Politics-/August-sectarian-attacks-largest-in-Egypt-history-.aspx.

[63] Mona Alami, "Egypt Constitution Will Be Bad News For Women, Activists Say," *USA Today*, January 13, 2013, accessed January 28, 2013, http://www.usatoday.com/story/news/world/2013/01/11/egypt-constitution-women-rights/1784135/.

[64] The 1972 constitution read, "The state shall guarantee the proper balance between the duties of women towards the family and their work in society, considering their equal status with men in the fields of political, social, cultural and economic life without violation of the rules of Islamic jurisprudence."

and that they are represented in the parliament. The state will also protect women against all elements of violence."

In addition to intolerance toward Copts and women, doubts about the acceptance of democracy by the new regime increased rapidly in the first year of Morsi's tenure because of what became known as the "Brotherization" of Egyptian politics. This term refers to the nomination of Brotherhood members to key governmental positions. Of Morsi's ninety appointments to the Shura Council in December 2012, twenty-seven were members of Islamist parties, and several were senior members of the Muslim Brotherhood, including Essam al-Erian and Sobhi Saleh.[65] In an August 2012 reshuffling of the presidential cabinet, Morsi appointed four members of the Muslim Brotherhood to posts, while three members were nominated shortly thereafter to governorships.[66] Another cabinet reorganization in early 2013 expanded the Muslim Brotherhood's influence on the government, as it took control of the ministries of transportation, local development, and interior trade.[67] Simultaneously, the Muslim Brotherhood represented half of the president's advisory team (after walkouts by members of other parties)[68] and pushed for appointments to key diplomatic posts, including in Qatar and Turkey.[69] The party also controlled the governorships in eleven out of twenty-seven districts after Morsi announced the appointment of seven new Muslim Brotherhood governors in June 2013.[70] This announcement sparked protests across the country, especially in Luxor and Gharbiya.[71] In Luxor, the protests were particularly vehement as the new governor, Adel el-Khayat, was a founding member of al-Gama'a al-Islamiyya, the Islamist group implicated in the 1997 Luxor massacre that killed ninety-seven foreigners and four Egyptians. Although al-Gama'a al-Islamiyya denied its involvement in

[65] "Islamists and old regime men in Morsy's Shura Council appointments," *Islamopedia*, accessed January 28, 2013, http://www.islamopediaonline.org/news/islamists-and-old-regime-men-morsys-shura-council-appointments.

[66] "Brotherhood puts forward three members for governerships," *Al-Masry Al-Youm*, January 13, 2013, accessed January 28, 2013, http://www.egyptindependent.com/news/brotherhood-puts-forward-three-members-governorships.

[67] "Skepticism over new Egypt Cabinet reshuffle," *Ahram Online*, January 6, 2013, accessed June 21, 2013, http://english.ahram.org.eg/NewsContent/1/64/61906/Egypt/Politics-/Skepticism-over-new-Egypt-Cabinet-reshuffle.aspx.

[68] "Morsi's advisory team less diverse after months of walkouts," *Ahram Online*, February 19, 2013, accessed June 21, 2013, http://english.ahram.org.eg/NewsContent/1/64/65135/Egypt/Politics-/Morsis-advisory-team-less-diverse-after-months-of-.aspx.

[69] "Muslim Brotherhood figures seek Egypt diplomatic posts," *Ahram Online*, January 19, 2013, accessed June 21, 2013, http://english.ahram.org.eg/NewsContent/1/64/62823/Egypt/Politics-/Muslim-Brotherhood-figures-seek-Egypt-diplomatic-p.aspx.

[70] "Seven of 17 new regional governors from Egypt's Muslim Brotherhood," *Ahram Online*, June 16, 2013, accessed June 21, 2013, http://english.ahram.org.eg/NewsContent/1/64/74184/Egypt/Politics-/Seven-of--new-regional-governors-from-Egypts-Musli.aspx.

[71] "Brotherhood's FJP condemns violent protests over new Islamist governors," *Ahram Online*, June 19, 2013, accessed June 21, 2013, http://english.ahram.org.eg/NewsContent/1/64/74430/Egypt/Politics-/Brotherhoods-FJP-condemns-violent-protests-over-ne.aspx.

the massacre, popular anger at the group and at el-Khayat did not abate.[72] As a consequence, the newly appointed Luxor governor resigned on June 25, 2013, only a few days after his nomination.[73] However, while Brotherization affected the most visible positions, it did not change the true condition.

During Morsi's leadership, concerns also grew about the question of freedom of speech and freedom of press. For example, there was a noticeable increase of law suits for insults to the president (although one could argue that this was the outcome of a "liberalization" of some sort, as opposed to the jail terms or censure that characterized the Sadat and Mubarak era). The trial that received the broadest media coverage concerned satirical talk show host Bassem Youssef, who in January 2013 was accused of insulting President Morsi for his "temporary adoption of extensive powers." Youssef, known fondly as the "Egyptian Jon Stewart," asked in one of his episodes whether Egyptians had removed one dictator only to replace him with another. While the suit against him was brought by a private attorney not connected with the government, his prosecution was considered part of a larger trend of media repression that worried many activists.[74] Suspicions were aroused surrounding the forced retirement of *Al-Ahram* chief editor Hani Shukrallah, who blamed an administration run by the Muslim Brotherhood for the loss of his position.[75] Many traced the event to the appointment of Brotherhood sympathizer Mamdouh al-Wali[76] as chairperson of *Al-Ahram*, which they claimed was a move to craft the newspaper into an outlet for the Brotherhood-led administration, a role it purportedly played for the Mubarak regime in past decades.[77]

[72] "Luxor protests against al-Gama'a al-Islamiya govenor continue," *Ahram Online*, June 20, 2013, accessed June 21, 2013, http://english.ahram.org.eg/NewsContent/1/64/74515/Egypt/Politics-/Luxor-protests-against-AlGamaa-AlIslamiya-govenor-.aspx.

[73] "Islamist Egyptian governor of Luxor resigns," *Al-Arabiyya*, June 23, 2013, accessed June 24, 2013, http://english.alarabiya.net/en/News/middle-east/2013/06/23/Egypt-s-hardline-Islamist-to-resign-as-Luxor-governor.html.

[74] "Satirical show host Youssef under investigation for alleged Morsi insult," *Al-Ahram Online*, January 1, 2013, accessed January 28, 2013, http://english.ahram.org.eg/NewsContent/1/64/61620/Egypt/Politics-/Satirical-show-host-Youssef-under-investigation-ov.aspx. Olga Khazan, "Meet Egypt's Jon Stewart, who is now under investigation for satire," *Washington Post*, January 2, 2013, accessed January 28, 2013, http://www.washingtonpost.com/blogs/worldviews/wp/2013/01/02/egypt-bassem-youssef-jon-stewart-investigation/.

[75] "Al Ahram sends editor into early retirement; Brotherhood to blame?" *Egypt Independent*, January 18, 2013, accessed January 28, 2013, http://www.egyptindependent.com/news/al-ahram-sends-editor-early-retirement-brotherhood-blame.

[76] Mamdouh al-Wali, appointed chairperson of *Al-Ahram* in 2012, is head of the Journalists Syndicate (نقابة الصحفيين) and a Morsi-appointed member of the Shura Council. "Mamdouh al-Wali: Rajul al-Sulṭa Yas'I li-Akhwinat al-Saḥafa
ممدوح الولي.. رجل السلطة يسعى لأخونة الصحافة" or "Mamdouh al-Wali: Man in charge seeks to Brother-ize the press" *Al-Badeel*, December 26, 2012, accessed June 25, 2013, http://elbadil.com/hot-issues-cases/2012/12/26/89368.

[77] "Ahram Online Editor Says Brotherhood Drove Him Out of Institution," *Jadaliyya*, February 17, 2013, accessed June 25, 2013, http://www.jadaliyya.com/pages/index/10236/ahram-online-editor-says-brotherhood-drove-him-out.

In sum, the Islamists' access to power after the end of the Mubarak era did not result in the imposition of a caliphate or pan-Islamist project. It actually confirmed their acceptation of the state system, as the result of a long process that started as early as the 1970s. Most ironically, it illustrated the "presidentialist" temptation to which Morsi succumbed, as did the former authoritarian presidents before him. Ultimately, his unwillingness or inability to change the system, as we will discuss in the subsequent chapters, resulted in his fall from power.

Islamic Turkishness versus Secular Turkishness

As early as the 1940s, the Islamist discourse was geared toward the creation of a Turkish Islamic state to counter the secular national project. In other words, an "Islamic Turkishness" was proposed as a distinct counter idea to the Kemalist "secular Turkishness." First, writers Necib Fazil Kisacurek (1904–83) and Osman Yuksel (1917–83) embraced the idea of Turkish nationalism, unlike earlier Islamists of the 1920s, who considered nationalism antithetical to the Islamic principle of universal Muslim brotherhood.[78] Their publications in the *Buyuk Dogu* (*The Great Orient*) and *Serdengecti* (*Forlorn Hope*) magazines propagated the synthesis of Islam and Turkish nationalism instead of viewing them as divergent ideologies.

In the same vein, Said Nursi (1876–1960) helped promote the compatibility of religion and modernity in his major Qur'anic exegesis, *Risale-i Nur* (*Epistle of Light*), which was read by many grassroots religious groups in Turkey.[79] Mehmed Zahid Kotku (1897–1980), as cheikh of the Naqshabendi order, also played an influential role in nationalizing Islamism. He established study circles around the country and promoted a strategy that combined religious activism with nationalist identity, advocating for a more direct role of religion in the public sphere.[80] Finally, Fethullah Gulen[81] has emphasized the Islamic ethic of education and used Mustafa Kemal to endorse the creation of Turkish Islam.[82] Gulen combines the idea of Turkish nationalism with Islamic religiosity and education to assert the compatibility

---

[78] Anwar Alam, "Islam and Post-Modernism: Locating the Rise of Islamism in Turkey," *Journal of Islamic Studies* 20.3 (2009): 360.

[79] Ibid., 361.

[80] Ibid.

[81] Fethullah Gulen (b. 1941) is an Islamic thinker and activist whose teachings have their roots in the Sufi order of Said Nursi. He leads the Gulen Movement, which emphasizes education, interfaith dialog, and Islam's role in the modern world that has become a transnational organization with several millions of followers all over the world. Gulen emigrated to the United States in 1999 following a Turkish campaign against his ideology. His website is http://www.fgulen.com/en/.

[82] Ibid., 362.

of Muslim and Turkish identities, although the Gulen movement is now truly transnational, with organizations and followers throughout Europe, North America, and Asia.

These previous movements have influenced the ideology of the Islamic parties that preceded the Justice and Development Party (AKP). It is worth pointing out that at its inception in 1969, the pioneer of all these parties, Milli Gorus,[83] or National View Movement, envisioned a unified Islamic umma under Turkey's leadership, believing Turkey was best qualified to govern the Muslim world because of its geographic location, large size and population, and historical legacy of the Ottoman Caliphate.[84]

The rise of the AKP brought a change in ideology from that of its predecessors. From the beginning, the AKP rejected "old school Islamism"[85] and claimed to be a "conservative democratic" party. This meant that its platform promoted universal values such as democracy, human rights, rule of law, pluralism, respect for diversity, and limited government.[86] William Hale and Ergun Ozbudun argue that for the AKP, secularism is actually a basic condition for social peace and therefore an essential ideology.[87] Mustafa Sen describes the transformation of Turkish Islamism in the following terms:

Indeed the AKP has been one of the most dynamic sociopolitical forces in Turkey and presented itself as the main agent of transformation that would bring economic development and greater democracy. From the outset, the AKP has willingly adopted the political agenda, set by a series of economic and political crises in the 1990s, about economic and political stability, democratization, and EU accession.[88]

To explain the ideological changes that have taken place in Turkey's major Islamist party (AKP), Gamze Cavdar defines three pillars of its "new Islamist

---

[83] Millî Görüş was a religio-political movement initiated in 1969 by Islamist activist Necmetin Erbakan (1926–2011) that became the matrix for a series of Islamist parties that were outlawed one after this other for violation of Turkish secularism: The National Salvation Party (MSP), which replaced the National Order Party (MNP), established itself as a party of the urban poor and the provincial middle class. The MSP party leader, Necmettin Erbakan, regarded the Kemalist attempt to replace the Islamic-Ottoman state and culture with a Western model as a historic mistake. Instead, the MSP's goal was to build a "national (Islamic) order." The Welfare Party (RP) and its ideology differed slightly from that of the liberal MSP. While it expressed the same hostility to Westernization, the Welfare Party's proposed economic program, called the "Just Order," stressed the need for greater social justice and equality as a way to end Western influence.
William Hale and Ergun Ozbudun, *Islamism, Democracy, and Liberalism in Turkey: The Case of the AKP* (New York: Routledge, 2009), 6; Angel Rabasa and F. Stephen Larrabee, The Rise of Political Islam in Turkey (RAND National Defense Research Institute, 2008), 41–2.
[84] Haleand Ergun, *Islamism, Democracy*, 6.
[85] Alam, "Locating the Rise of Islamism in Turkey," 372.
[86] Hale and Ozbudun, *Islamism, Democracy, and Liberalism in Turkey*, 20.
[87] Ibid.
[88] Mustafa Sen, "Transformation of Turkish Islamism and the Rise of the Justice and Development Party," *Turkish Studies* 11.1 (March 2010): 59–84.

thinking" that distinguish it from previous Islamist parties. First, the goal of the party is not explicitly defined in Islamic terms; instead, the AKP leaders seek greater religious freedoms within the parameters of a secular and democratic political system.[89]

Second, the influence of the surrounding intellectual arena has been a significant factor in this change of orientation. For example, a group of intellectuals led by Ali Bulac[90] argued in a new magazine released just before the November 2002 elections that the new Islamist trend was a response to domestic and international developments through the lens of Islamic values. Advisor to the AKP government Yalcin Akdogan speaks to this intellectualism when he argues that the "'conservative democracy' combines international norms with local values and cultures."[91]

Third, the rise of conservative capitalists in Anatolia has also been a major element in the new vision of the Islamist party. This group is described as "culturally conservative, politically nationalist ... and on the side of free enterprise."[92] Its emergence was the outcome of the Özal Reforms, the namesake of Prime Minister Turgut Özal, who endorsed them in the mid-1980s. The Özal Reforms were primarily implemented to stabilize and stimulate the lagging economy by encouraging export growth instead of continued importation of goods. Ultimately, they weakened the state's control over the economy. This economic strategy created a new class of entrepreneurs and capitalists known as the "Anatolian bourgeoisie" in the provincial parts of the country, which historically maintained a more traditional and Islamic outlook.

The rise of the Anatolian "tigers" put an end to the enduring class conflict and ideological polarization between the laicist elite and the more conservative and religious lower classes. This new "bourgeoisie" had strong roots in Islamic culture and became the core constituency of the AKP, thereby making Islamism a more mainstream ideology. These ideological and sociological changes explain why the AKP has grown from an opposition movement to a governing party.

Because of its nonviolent move away from military rule to democracy, the AKP has emerged as a model for Egypt and Tunisia transitions. Additionally, its support for the Palestinian cause (which increased after the 2010 flotilla

---

[89] Gamze Cavdar, "Islamist New Thinking in Turkey: A Model for Political Learning?" *Political Science Quarterly* 121.3 (2006): 481.

[90] Ali Bulac (b. 1951) is a Turkish and Islamist intellectual known for his positions on the contemporary Islamic world, problems in Muslim thought, social change, and critiques of modernization. He writes for *Zaman*, a major, high-circulation newspaper in Turkey founded in 1986. Seven Erdogan, "Muslim Response to the 'Western Question': Ali Bulac's Contribution," (August 2010): 24–5, http://etd.lib.metu.edu.tr/upload/12612269/index.pdf.

[91] Gamze Cavdar, "Islamist New Thinking in Turkey: A Model for Political Learning?" *Political Science Quarterly* 121.3 (2006): 483.

[92] Ibid.

incident)[93] increased its popularity domestically and internationally across the Middle East.[94]

However, the influence of the Turkish model of democracy declined dramatically both domestically and internationally in 2013. Increased media repression and suppression of freedom of speech brought international condemnation, including from Amnesty International, which reported: "Criminal prosecutions frequently targeted non-violent dissenting opinions, particularly on controversial political issues."[95] As mentioned in the previous chapter, journalists have faced persecution, with forty-nine jailed – the highest number anywhere in the world – and at least fourteen were injured in the Taksim Square crisis.[96]

The administration of Prime Minister Erdogan also faced criticism from women's rights groups over the government's actions and Erdogan's personal views, when in 2010 he stated: "I don't believe in equality between men and women."[97] In the same vein, his government proposal to limit abortion rights triggered so much controversy that it was ultimately abandoned, although caesarian rights were limited.[98] Further, 42 percent of Turkish women report being subjected to physical or sexual violence without any legal recourse.[99]

Conservative social values also underlie the 2013 legislation limiting the presence of alcohol in public space by banning advertising, forbidding new alcohol licenses for institutions within 100 meters of religious or educational spaces, removing images of drinking from television, and outlawing

---

[93] The flotilla incident occurred on May 31, 2010, when Israeli forces boarded a Turkish aid ship bound for the Gaza Strip and opened fire, killing nine Turkish activists and injuring dozens more. The ship was attempting to cross Israel's Gaza blockade. In response, the Turkish government withdrew its ambassador from Israel and expelled Israel's ambassador from Ankara. They were both reinstated in March 2013. See "Q&A: Israeli deadly raid on aid flotilla," *BBC News Middle East*, March 22, 2013, accessed June 21, 2013, http://www.bbc.co.uk/news/10203726.

[94] Robert Tait, "Egypt: Doubts cast on Turkish claims for model democracy," *The Guardian*, February 13, 2011, accessed January 28, 2013, http://www.guardian.co.uk/world/2011/feb/13/egypt-doubt-turkish-model-democracy.

[95] "Turkey," *Amnesty International Annual Report 2013*, 2013, accessed June 21, 2013, http://www.amnesty.org/en/region/turkey/report-2013.

[96] "Press freedom groups condemn Turkish police violence against journalists," *The Guardian*, June 6, 2013, accessed June 20, 2013, http://www.guardian.co.uk/media/greenslade/2013/jun/06/journalist-safety-turkey.

[97] Daniel Steinvorth, "Erdogan the Misogynist: Turkish Prime Minister Assaults Women's Rights," *Spiegel Online*, June 19, 2012, accessed June 21, 2013, http://www.spiegel.de/international/europe/turkish-prime-minister-erdogan-targets-women-s-rights-a-839568.html.

[98] "Rape, abortion and the fight for women's rights in Turkey," *The Guardian*, September 9, 2012, accessed June 21, 2013, http://www.guardian.co.uk/commentisfree/2012/sep/09/reape-abortion-fight-womens-rights-turkey.

[99] "USAK Report: Violence against Women in Turkey," *The Journal of Turkish Weekly*, March 8, 2012, accessed June 21, 2013, http://www.turkishweekly.net/news/132146/.

the display of bottles of alcohol in shop windows. Erdogan depicted the law as "ordered by faith."[100] Even more significant, in November 2012, Erdogan announced a constitutional reform to create a "Turkified version of the U.S. executive system."[101] If the reform is adopted, the president will be able to dissolve the parliament and to appoint and dismiss ministers, ambassadors, and senior officials without parliamentary approval.[102] Consequently, suspicions have arisen that Erdogan wants to run for president and that the proposed measures will give him too much power. For example, Suyehl Batum, a member of the opposition Republic People's Party (CHP), has stated "Erdogan wants a dictatorship. He wants a presidential system in which he retains power over his party and chooses his prime minister at will."[103] At the time of this writing, the process of drafting the constitution has been sidelined by the aftermath of the Teksim protests.[104]

Authorities' actions regarding the May 2013 protests – including the detention of hundreds of protestors, restrictions on social media, and a bill to increase domestic monitoring of citizens – were internationally criticized as repressive.[105] The European Parliament issued a nonbinding resolution characterizing the actions of Turkish security forces as "heavy-handed" and condemning "the disproportionate and excessive use of force by the Turkish

---

[100] "Alcohol laws spark renewed religious debate in Turkey," *The Financial Times*, May 29, 2013, accessed June 21, 2013, http://www.ft.com/intl/cms/s/0/161dddae-c870-11e2-8cb7-00144feab7de.html#axzz2WpIujkmF.

[101] Göksel Bozkurt, "AKP proposes its version of presidential system," *Hurriyet Daily News*, November 22, 2012, http://www.hurriyetdailynews.com/akp-proposes-its-version-of-presidential-system.aspx?pageID=238&nid=35188.

[102] See http://digest.electionguide.org/2013/06/21/constitutional-reform-in-turkey-and-the-recent-protests/#sthash.zdfOJLJ1.dpuf.

[103] "Erdogan's ambition weighs on hopes for new Turkish constitution," *Reuters*, February 18, 2013, accessed June 21, 2013, http://www.reuters.com/article/2013/02/18/us-turkey-constitution-idUSBRE91H0C220130218.

[104] Although the AKP dominates the Legislative Assembly, it needs the support of other political parties to get the reform approved. It came closer to finding an ally by reaching out to the pro-Kurdish Peace and Democracy Party (BDP), which indicated it might accept the AKP proposal in exchange for more comprehensive protections Kurdish rights: "[s]pecifically, the BDP requests a reduction in the prohibitively high 10% electoral threshold, increased local autonomy, better protected linguistic rights, and the rephrasing of a constitutional article that refers to all citizens of Turkey as 'Turkish.'" See Katherine Krueger and Ayesha Shug, "Constitutional Reform in Turkey," *Muftah*, July 8, 2013, accessed August 5, 2013, http://muftah.org/constitutional-reform-in-turkey-and-the-recent-protests/. But the BDP remains divided in its willingness to cooperate with the prime minister, and so talks have continued to stall. "Turkey's Kurtulmus Sets July Deadline for New Constitution," *Bloomberg*, May 10, 2013, accessed June 21, 2013, http://www.bloomberg.com/news/2013-05-10/turkey-s-kurtulmus-sets-july-deadline-for-new-constitution.html.

[105] "Erdogan cracks down," *The Economist*, June 21, 2013, accessed June 21, 2013, http://www.economist.com/news/europe/21579873-vicious-police-tactics-have-reclaimed-taksim-square-and-other-places-protest-high.

police" along with "the deterioration of freedom of the press."[106] To regain national and international credibility, the Erdogan government promised to suspend the demolition of the Gezi Park and organized a series of workshops to analyze the protests. It has also launched initiatives like the "Alevi opening" to improve the democratic rights of the Alevi community, as well as to open peace talks with Kurds.[107]

The most decisive initiative directly related to the aftermath of the Taksim protests (and probably to the ousting of the Morsi regime in Egypt as well) has been the July 2013 governmental proposal to change Article 35 of the Turkish military's internal laws in order to remove the possibility of the military getting involved in domestic affairs. According to Lami Bertan Tokuzlu, "There have been cases where military officials helped the demonstrators by, for example, handing out gas masks on the streets" when "the government is really taking a hard line against the demonstrators. This situation would be ripe for a military intervention."[108]

Additionally, Erdogan announced on September 30, 2013, his long-awaited democratic package. It includes political reform to improve Kurdish political representation and legislation to punish hate crime but no significant recognition of the Alevi and Greek Orthodox minorities.[109]

Overall, the protests have undeniably altered the domestic popularity and international image of Erdogan. But that does not mean his regime is over, as we will discuss in the subsequent chapters. Nevertheless, it appears even more clearly than in the Egyptian case that the loss of popularity of the AKP is caused by the slowdown of the democratization process and the move away from nationalist to Islamist discourse.

Tunisia: Islamic Ideology and the Secular State

In Tunisia, Islamic ideology was also a counter-national project to the secular policies of the state, seen as antireligious. As described in Part I, Bourguiba's actions against Islam included, for example, prohibiting the use of the hijab in public in 1957 and suggesting in 1960 that fasting during Ramadan was not religiously obligatory. Thus, the Islamic ideology of the MTI and of

---

[106] "European Parliament resolution on the situation in Turkey," *European Parliament*, June 12, 2013, accessed June 21, 2013, http://www.europarl.europa.eu/sides/getDoc.do?pubRef=-// EP//NONSGML+MOTION+P7-RC-2013-0305+0+DOC+PDF+V0//EN.

[107] Veda Ozer, "Will the Gezi effect rehabilitate Turkish democracy?" *Daily News*, July 2, 2013, http://www.hurriyetdailynews.com/will-the-gezi-effect-rehabilitate-turkish-democracy.aspx ?pageID=449&nID=49827&NewsCatID=466, accessed July 2, 2013.

[108] "Turkey plans legal reform to prevent coup," *Deutsch Welle*, accessed August 5, 2013, http://www.dw.de/turkey-plans-legal-reform-to-prevent-coups/a-16927618.

[109] "Erdogan Democracy Package: What does it offer minorities?" *Al Monitor*, October 1, 2013, accessed October 1, 2013, http://www.al-monitor.com/pulse/originals/2013/09/ democratization-package-kurds-turkey-minorities.html?utm_source=&utm_medium= email&utm_campaign=8280.

Rached Ghannouchi was largely a response to Bourguiba's seemingly anti-Islamic attitude. In particular, Ghannouchi thought that both secularism and Arabism were contradictory to Islamic values:

I realized Arab nationalism was in opposition to Islam, while Arab sentiments and identity ... and Islam were one and the same thing. At that time, I was a member of the Nasserite Nationalist party of Syria, but once I learned its true meaning I chose to abandon it and adopted Islam in its totality.[110]

Consequently, according to the MTI's ideology, the state was the enemy of Islam. The Islamic movement did not recognize the government as legitimate and claimed to be the true guardian of Islam and thus the only representatives of the truth.

A second influential factor concerning Ghannouchi's ideology was the inability of citizens to receive adequate religious education in Tunisia. Reflecting on his earlier struggles while attending the Zaytuna mosque in high school, Ghannouchi remarked, "I remember we used to feel like strangers in our own country. We had been educated as Muslims and as Arabs, while we could see the country totally molded in the French cultural identity. For us, the doors to any further education were closed since the university was completely 'westernised.'"[111] Building on the concept of *jahiliyya* as defined by Sayyid Qutb in Egypt, Ghannouchi reinterpreted the idea of *jahili* societies in a specifically Tunisian context as those "which are not founded on the basis and values of Islam and which do not comply with its laws and teachings."[112] For Ghannouchi, Qutb had made it clear that Muslims had to choose between Islam and *jahiliyya*, or ignorance. These ideas polarized the dichotomy between the Islamists (representatives of the truth) and the Tunisian government (representative of *jahiliyya*). Although Ghannouchi later did not refer to *jahiliyya* on a regular basis, this idea was evident in the MTI's criticism of the Tunisian government.

Jahiliyya directly referred to the secularist policies of Bourguiba and later to those of Ben Ali as well. Ghannouchi especially related to Qutb and Mawdudi's idea of secularism as the opposite of religion. Mohammed Elhachmi Hamdi wrote, "For the Tunisian Islamists, as well as for the vast majority of Islamists in the Arab world, Mawdudi's argument is representative of their stand against secularism."[113] Moreover, this concept of *jahiliyya* also influenced the requirements for membership in the MTI. The eligible members were considered first-class Muslims who were fully aware of the issues (concerning the lack of education in Islam) in modern Tunisia and

---

[110] Rached Ghannouchi, interview, *Arabia*, April 1985, found in Mohamed Elhachmi Hamdi, *The Politicization of Islam: A Case Study of Tunisia* (Boulder, CO: Westview Press, 1998).

[111] Abdul Hasib Castineira, "Nobody's Man – but a Man of Islam," *Arabia* 4.4 (April 1985): 18.

[112] Rached Ghannouchi, *Maqalat* (Paris: Dar al-Karawan, 1984), 132. Hamdi, *Politicization of Islam*, 78.

[113] Hamdi, *Politicization of Islam*, 93.

were part of the Islamic movement. In contrast, the "second-class" Muslims were considered to not fully understand the political implications of Islam.[114]

As the Tunisian state increasingly repressed the MTI movement, Ghannouchi became more involved in politics, rather than just education. In particular, he addressed the idea of "Islamic democracy" as a specific solution to Tunisia's problems. In his words, "It was an intellectual necessity for the Islamic movement to offer clear answers to the challenges facing Islamic thought in a country such as Tunisia, which had become extremely Westernized. There was no other alternative."[115]

However, exile in London from 1989 to 2011 changed his positions on Islam and democracy, and he started to write on how democracy embodies Islamic principles.[116] He argued about the Islamic meaning of elections and people sovereignty. His thinking evolved from the conception of an Islamic state and how it relates to a civil state, in which free elections, redistribution of power, and respect for human rights are embedded in the true meaning of Islam. These views manifested themselves in Ennahda's strategy after the demise of Ben Ali in 2011. The Ennahda platform addressed the role of Islam by stating, "Islam constitutes a fundamental and moderate reference [point] that is in interaction, through the effort of interpretation and application (ijtihad), with every human experience whose usefulness is established."[117] Ennahda's campaign program, a fifty-page document, aimed to address concerns from anti-Islamist circles by promising "to safeguard religious freedom, the rights of minorities and the status of women" by protecting their right "against any imposed dress code."[118]

In March 2, 2012, during a speech at the Center for the Study of Islam and Democracy in Washington, DC, Ghannouchi discussed the role of Islam and the state in these terms:

Islam since its inception and throughout its history has not known this separation between state and religion in the sense of excluding religion from public life. And Muslims, to this day, have been influenced by Islam and inspired by its teachings and guidance in their civic life, with the distinction remaining clear. This distinction between the religious and the political is also clear in the thought of Islamic scholars/jurists.[119]

---

[114] Qusayy Salih Al-Darwish, "Yahduthu fi Tunis," pp. 16–17, found in Hamdi, *Politicization of Islam*, 82.

[115] Rached al-Ghannouchi, "al-Harakat al-Itijah al-Islami fi Tunis," vol. 3. pp. 12–123, found in Hamdi, *Politicization of Islam*, 102.

[116] Rached Ghannouchi, "Participation in non-Islamic Government," in Charles Kurzman (ed.), *Liberal Islam: A Source Book* (New York: Oxford University Press, 1998), 89–95.

[117] "Le Programme Du Mouvement Ennahdha," accessed July 13, 2012, http://www.slideshare.net/Ennahdha/programme-du-parti-ennahdha.

[118] "Tunisia poll favorite vows democracy based on Islamic values," *Al Arabiya News*, September 14, 2011, accessed December 4, 2011, http://www.alarabiya.net/articles/2011/09/14/166883.html.

[119] Rached Ghannouchi, translated and transcribed by Brahim Rouabah, *CSID*, appearance in March 2, 2012, sponsored by the Center for the Study of Islam and Democracy

In the same speech, he also asserted the commitment of the Islamist government to freedom of religion:

The primary orbit for religion is not the state's apparatuses, but rather personal/individual convictions. The state's duty, however, is to provide services to people before anything else, to create job opportunities, and to provide good health and education not to control people's hearts and minds. For this reason, I have opposed the coercion of people in all its forms and manifestation and have dealt with such controversial topics such as al-Riddah (apostasy) and have defended the freedom of people to either adhere to or defect from a religious creed.[120]

In May 2013 during another visit to Washington, DC, he reaffirmed strongly the compatibility between Islam and democracy:

There is no contradiction between Democracy and Islam. Democracy does not mean that governance should be particularly granted to secularists who consider the Islamists as enemies of the state who therefore should be either imprisoned or exiled. It does not mean either excluding secularists from power and marginalizing their role in the drafting of the Constitution simply because they did not get a majority in the elections ... the alliance between Islamists and secularists is important for the establishment of a democratic and free society able to handle its differences, through a deep and sincere dialogue.[121]

Nevertheless, women's groups expressed concerns about the risk that Ennahda would reinstate strict Islamic provisions in family law. One of these activists, Zouhair Mahlouf, explained at a lunch rally, "We want the rights of women to be protected, we don't want Tunisia to go back to the Middle Ages, and we want respect for the role of women in society.... We don't want a theocracy in Tunisia, we want democracy."[122] In response, Ennahda leaders have multiplied reassuring declarations to assuage these fears,[123] saying, for example, "The code of personal status [established by Bourguiba] and women's rights cannot be touched."[124] Moreover, during the Constituent Assembly debate in 2011 and 2012, the final decision was not to inscribe Shari'a in the constitution, as

in Washington DC. See entire transcript here: http://blog.sami-aldeeb.com/2012/03/09/full-transcript-of-rached-ghannouchis-lecture-on-secularism-march-2-2012/.

[120] Ibid.

[121] Speech of Rached Ghannouchi at the CSID annual conference, May 29 2013, Washington, DC; see http://www.youtube.com/watch?v=By04Rc2Bf80&feature=youtu.be&noredirect=1, accessed July 1, 2013.

[122] Alexander Gobel, "Political Islam in Tunisia: Who's Afraid of Rached Ghannouchi?" *Qantara*, March 14, 2011, accessed November 16, 2011, http://www.islamopediaonline.com/news/political-islam-tunisia-whos-afraid-rachid-ghanouchi.

[123] Andrew Hammond, "Tunisia's Ghannouchi too liberal for some Islamists," *Reuters*, October 25, 2011, accessed July 22, 2012, http://www.reuters.com/article/2011/10/25/us-tunisia-ennahda-ghannouchi-idUSTRE79O76020111025.

[124] "Tunisia's Islamist frontrunner urges clean election," *Radio Netherlands Worldwide: Africa*, September 13, 2011, accessed December 4, 2011, http://www.rnw.nl/africa/bulletin/tunisias-islamist-frontrunner-urges-clean-election.

we will discuss further in Chapter 10. In an interview with the French magazine *Express*, Ghannouchi explained, "What is important is to avoid imposing
religious or political behaviors or beliefs on people."[125]

Regardless, discrimination against women remains a concern, especially
in light of existing indecency laws. For example, in September 2012, three
Tunisian police officers harassed a couple. Two officers raped the woman
while the other took her fiancé to an ATM to extort cash from him.[126] When
the couple filed a complaint, the officers accused the woman of indecent
behavior, saying the couple was in an "immoral position." This accusation
could have resulted in the couple being incarcerated for up to six months.
This case created major international backlash. The Tunisian minister of justice claimed that nothing had been proven and that the couple was simply
attempting to taint Tunisia's international image.[127]

Another liberal component of Ghannouchi's vision of Islamic democracy is
the status of non-Muslims in Tunisian society. Although Jews and Christians are
still quite wary of the Islamist party gaining significant influence over political
decisions, Ghannouchi has tried to reassure them. For example, he declared,
"Until now, Tunisian society has not been a society of minorities; it is a Muslim
society whose religious minorities are respected.... Religious freedom is guaranteed by the Constitution and the values of Arabic Islamic culture."[128] In early
January 2012, a group of ultraconservatives staged an anti-Semitic rally upon
the arrival of Hamas's Ismail Haniya to Tunisia, chanting, "Kill the Jews" and
"Crush the Jews." Ghannouchi released a statement on behalf of Ennahda
in the aftermath of the incident to distance himself and his party from such
behavior, stating that the anti-Semitic slogans "do not represent Islam's spirit
or teachings."[129] In addition, when the offices of the Tunisian Association for
the Defense of Minorities were attacked in January 2013, Interior Minister Ali
Larayedh, an Ennahda member, promised to look into the matter and to handle
it personally.[130]

[125] "Rached Ghannouchi: Le salafisme tel qu'on le voit en Tunisie est un projet de guerre
civile," *Business News*, March 28, 2012, accessed July 22, 2012, http://www.businessnews.
com.tn/Rached-Ghannouchi-Le-salafisme-tel-qu%C3%82'on-le-voit-en-Tunisie-est-un-
projet-de-guerre-civile,520,30181,3.

[126] http://www.cnn.com/2012/10/02/world/africa/tunisia-rape-protest/index.html

[127] "In Tunisia, a rape victim is prosecuted for 'public indecency,'" *Kapitalis* via *Islamopedia*,
October 4, 2012, accessed January 28, 2013, http://www.islamopediaonline.org/news/
tunisia-rape-victim-prosecuted-public-indecency.

[128] Emily Parker, "Tunisia's Election Results and the Question of Minorities," *Jadaliyya*,
November 28, 2011, accessed December 2, 2011, http://www.jadaliyya.com/pages/
index/3310/tunisias-election-results-and-the-question-of-mino.

[129] Bouazza Ben Bouazza and Paul Schemm, "Tunisia's Islamist Party Slams Anti-Semitic
Chants," *Associated Press*, January 9, 2012, accessed July 22, 2012, http://www.huffington-
post.com/2012/01/09/tunisias-islamist-party-anti-semitic_n_1194085.html.

[130] "Tunisia NGO accuses pro-Islamist group of attack," *AFP*, January 9, 2013, accessed January
28, 2013, http://www.moroccoworldnews.com/2013/01/73295/tunisia-ngo-accuses-pro-
islamist-group-of-attack/.

However, intolerance is visible both in society and on the right of the political spectrum. In fact the moderation expressed by Ghannouchi has disturbed many Salafis and some Muslim Brothers who consider him too liberal and go as far as describing him as an apostate.[131]

In 2013, tensions between Salafis and Tunisian authorities increased as Ennahda strengthened its criticism of intolerance and rejection of political violence. The governmental reaction against Salafi was a response to the assassination of opposition leader Chokri Belaid in February 2013, attributed to jihadi elements as well as to incidents on the border area of Jebel ech Chambi.[132]

The Ennahda government has also taken concrete action, including the removal of Salafis setting up tents near Tunis to preach[133] and the suspension of an Ansar al-Shariʿa[134] conference called "a threat to public order." Ansar al-Shariʿa spokesman Seifeddine Rais was detained in June 2013 by authorities after stating that blood would be spilled in response to the banning of the conference.[135] Another Salafist, Abu Zaid Al-Tounsi, was arrested after defending jihad on television and stating he was ready for jihad in Tunisia.[136]

Despite its rejection of political intolerance, Ennahda continues to face opposition from a number of groups, five of whom (al-Massar, Nidaa Tunis, al-Joumhouri, the Socialist Party, and the Patriotic Democratic Labor Party) joined forces to create the coalition "Unity for Tunisia" in April 2013.[137] The opposition gained strength after the aforementioned assassination of Chokri Belaid, which led to the resignation of Prime Minister Hamadi Jebali, who was replaced by Ali Larayedh. The secular Ettakatol party, which is partnered with Ennahda in Tunisia's ruling coalition, convinced Larayedh to allow the appointment of four independent ministers as a way of securing parliamentary approval for the new government. A popular movement modeled around the Egyptian Tamarud campaign claimed in July 2013 to

---

[131] Hammond, "Tunisia's Ghannouchi too liberal for some Islamists."

[132] Mischa Benoit-Lavelle, "New Tunisian Government Faces Old Challenges," *Al-Monitor*, March 10, 2013, accessed June 22, 2013, http://www.al-monitor.com/pulse/originals/2013/03/tunisia-new-government-technocrat-challenges.html.

[133] Mohammad Yassine al-Jalassi, "Is the End Coming for Ennahda's Salafist Ties?" *Al-Monitor*, January 14, 2013, accessed June 22, 2013, http://www.al-monitor.com/pulse/contents/articles/politics/2013/05/tunisia-salafist-ennahda-relations.html.

[134] For a description of Ansar al Shar'ia, see Chapter 7.

[135] "Tunisia security blocks salafi conference," *Salon*, May 19, 2013, accessed June 22, 2013, http://www.salon.com/2013/05/19/tunisia_security_blocks_salafi_conference_3/.

[136] "al-Qabd ʿala al-Salafi Abu Zayd al-Tunsi," *BBC News Arabic*, April 3, 2013, accessed June 22, 2013, http://www.bbc.co.uk/arabic/middleeast/2013/04/130403_tunisian_salafist_abou_zeid.shtml.

[137] "Tunisian Opposition Unites Against Islamist Government," *Al-Monitor*, April 9, 2013, accessed June 22, 2013, http://www.al-monitor.com/pulse/politics/2013/04/tunisia-opposition-unites-against-islamist-government.html.

have gathered one hundred and eighty thousand signatures to support the dissolution of the government.[138] In the summer of 2013, protests were growing and the political crisis was characterized as the worst since the fall of Zine El-Abidine Ben Ali. However, these events remain fluid and the eventual outcome is unclear.

Adding to the depth of political turmoil in Tunisia is the never-ending drafting of the constitution that has been ongoing since 2011. Although a draft was finalized in June 2013, Mustapha Ben Jafaar suspended the National Constituent Assembly (NCA) indefinitely on August 6, 2013, in response to the volatile political atmosphere created by the assassination of opposition leader Mohammed al-Brahmi. Further, there was anger among members of the National Constituent Assembly (NCA) over changes made during the National Dialogue conference. The conference, which was initially intended to discuss only the most controversial articles,[139] made changes to several other articles, according to NCA member Mabrouka Mbarek.[140]

In brief, Ennahda has handled the transition from authoritarian regime in a more efficient way than the Egyptian FJP did, reaching out to all political forces and attempting a more inclusive approach to governance. Nevertheless, building trust is a fragile process that has been weakened by two major blows: the assassination of two secular political opponents successively in February and July of 2013. The very slow drafting of the constitution has also raised doubts from all sides of the political spectrum over the Ennahda's willingness to move forward with the transition.[141] Finally, the increasing activism and intolerance of Salafi elements on the right of Ennahda casts a shadow on their "authentic" commitment to democracy by stalling the reform process to symbolic and identity politics.

Competing Religious Visions in Post-Saddam Iraq

Under Saddam Hussein's regime, especially after the Iranian Revolution in 1979, much of Shi'i ideology was directly or indirectly influenced by

---

[138] "Tunisia's Tamarod gathers steam: Another domino effect?" *Middle East Online*, July 4, 2013, accessed August 6, 2013, http://www.middle-east-online.com/english/?id=59892

[139] They concern three years' exemption from constitutional control, for laws adopted under the ruling Islamist party Ennahda as well as extension of the legislative powers of the Constituent Assembly until the election of a new parliament. See "Tunisia begins landmark discussion on draft constitution," *Global Post*, July 1, 2013, http://www.globalpost.com/dispatch/news/afp/130701/tunisia-begins-landmark-debate-draft-constitution-0, accessed July 1, 2013.

[140] "Final Draft of Constitution Announced, but Approval Remains Questionable," *Tunisia Live*, June 3, 2013, accessed June 21, 2013, http://www.tunisia-live.net/2013/06/03/final-draft-of-constitution-announced-but-approval-remains-questionable/.

[141] On September 3, 2013, the ruling coalition leaders set a one-month timeline for completion of the constitution and arrangement of elections despite the withdrawal of more than sixty members of the National Constituent Assembly in protest of lack of real progress.

Ayatollah Khomeini's concept of *vilayat e-faqih*. Some groups, such as the Society for the Islamic Revolution in Iraq (SCIRI), which was formed in 1982, subscribed to this concept. Others, like Sayyid Muhammad Shirazi, proposed an alternative concept of *shura al-fuqaha*, which would establish a college (Shura Council) of grand ulama rather than one single ayatollah as a ruler. And others like Sistani rejected political guidance by clerics altogether.

However, despite their different Islamic vision of politics, various Shi'i groups explicitly or implicitly recognized and worked within the national Iraqi framework. For instance, Mohammed Baqir al-Sadr[142] provided principles of Islamic governance[143] and stressed the importance of Shari'a as the foundation of the state. He explained that Islam not only should provide the economic framework for social development and justice but also is a national political project that offers the solution for all realms of governance and for people's welfare. Another significant religious figure, Mohammad Mohammad Sadiq al-Sadr, father of Muqtada al-Sadr,[144] believed in the principle of *vilayat e-faqih*, but reinterpreted the Khomeini term *wilaya 'amma*, which means "applying to all believers." His alternative, *wilaya khaṣa*, means "applying to a given territory," thus emphasizing authority over a particular nation-state.[145] As a result, he proclaimed his own vilayat e-faqih over Iraq, defying both the political authority of Saddam Hussein and the spiritual authority of Ayatollah Khomeini and his successor, Khameini.[146] In sum, while these leaders stressed an Islamist political vision,

---

[142] Muhammad Baqir al-Sadr (1935–80) is not to be confused with Mohammad Mohammad Sadiq al-Sadr (1943–1999), a grand ayatollah who inspired Iraqis in the 1990s, or Muqtada al-Sadr, who led the post-2003 Shi'i opposition surge in Iraq.

[143] In his 1975 work *Islamic Political System*, al-Sadr provides four mandatory principles of Islamic governance: (1) Absolute sovereignty belongs to God; (2) Islamic injunctions are the basis of legislation. The legislative authority may enact any law not repugnant to Islam; (3) The people, as vice-regents of Allah, are entrusted with legislative and executive powers; (4) The jurist holding religious authority represents Islam. By confirming legislative and executive actions, he gives them legality. Rodger Shanahan, "Shi'a Political Development in Iraq: The Case of the Islamic Dawa Party," *Third World Quarterly* 25.5 (2004): 946–7.

[144] Students of Sadiq al-Sadr were mainly young, underprivileged, urbanized Shi'is from grass-roots areas of Saddam City (al-Thawra), a neighborhood in Baghdad, and the tribal areas in the southeastern marshes of Iraq called al-'Amara. As such, Sadiq al-Sadr provided the ideological tools for opposing the injustice of the poor, urban population under Hussein. Although Sadiq al-Sadr did not have any formal ideological or organizational structures associated with his name, his ideology partially inspired uprisings in Iraq in 1991 (known as the Iraqi *intifada*), and later influenced Muqtada al-Sadr's political project.

[145] Peter Harling and Hamid Yassin Nasser, "The Sadrist Trend: Class Struggle, Millenarianism and Fitna," in *The Shi'a Worlds and Iran* (New York: SAQI Books, 2010), 286.

[146] Ibid., 286. Although at times Sadiq al-Sadr was considered Baghdad's marja'iyya and endorsed some Ba'thist Party policies prior to the 1991 invasion of Kuwait, Sadiq al-Sadr was best known for openly denouncing Saddam's government after the intifada, and was executed by the regime in 1999.

they also worked within the parameters of the Iraqi nation-state as opposed to creating a pan-Islamic state.

Since the fall of Saddam in 2003, the ideology of most Islamic groups has materialized into political parties. While Shi'i clerics have had a decisive influence in shaping the political terms of the new Iraq, multiple Sunni parties have also emerged. With the collapse of the Arab and Sunni Iraq forged by Saddam, the greatest challenge is for all religious groups to partake in the rebuilding of a pluralist nation.

In this regard, a key issue is the debate on federalism and sectarianism.[147] Most significantly, the US-led postwar civil administration, or Coalition Provisional Authority (CPA), launched an extensive de-Ba'thification program, simultaneously vilifying and comprehensively removing all Sunnis from their posts. It created the foundation for the Sunni distrust of the new Shi'i political elite that has since undermined the democratization process.[148] Tellingly, after the CPA transferred power to the Iraqi interim government in June 2004, Iraq's most prominent Sunni party, the Iraqi Islamic Party (IIP), withdrew from the interim government in November of the same year.[149] Additionally, there was widespread Sunni rejection of the constitution. Even after the IIP evolved in 2005 into the Iraqi Accordance Front (Tawafuq),[150] it withdrew in 2007 from al-Maliki's cabinet following a dispute over power sharing. In 2009, Tawafuq boycotted parliament, alleging that holding sessions was unconstitutional because the parliament speaker had not been elected.

In response to the mounting sectarian threat, Ayatollah Sistani repeatedly discouraged violence. For example, during the incessant attacks of Sunni on Shi'is at the time of the U.S. occupation, he issued a fatwa stating, "the Islamic nation is passing through difficult conditions and facing tremendous challenges that threaten its future. Everybody knows the necessity for us to stand together and reject the sectarian tension to avoid stirring sectarian differences."[151]

Although decentralization has often been associated in political discourse with increased sectarian rift, it gained significant momentum on June 23,

---

[147] Iraq's population of 30 million is approximately 97 percent Muslim – 60 percent Shi'a and 40 percent Sunni. Throughout reconstruction, the Sunni religious elite has attempted to undermine the Shi'a-dominated coalitions in power.

[148] The de-Ba'thification program included barring Ba'th Party members from "future employment in the public sector" and prevented the reintegration of significant numbers of Sunni politicians and their followers into the new system. See Chapter 11 for a discussion of the political consequences of de-Baathification on the democratic prospects of Iraq.

[149] Robert H. Reid, "A fine balance," *The Guardian*, November 10, 2004, accessed October 13, 2011, http://www.guardian.co.uk/world/2004/nov/10/iraq3.

[150] Its platform for the December 2005 parliamentary elections included revision of the new Iraqi constitution, repealing of the de-Ba'thification laws and restoration of the Iraqi army, which had been a Sunni-dominated officer corps.

[151] Mussab al-Khairalla, "Baghdad Truck Bomb Kills at Least 95," *Reuters*, February 3, 2007, accessed October 9, 2011, http://www.reuters.com/article/2007/02/03/idUSIBO352532.

2013, when a diverse coalition of forces – among them Shi'i leader al-Sadr's al-Ahrar Movement, the Sunni Mutahidoun Coalition, the Democratic Alliance of Kurdistan (DPAK), and the ISCI – successfully passed amendments to the Provincial Powers Law, granting powers to local governments. The amendments, which had been opposed by several groups including Prime Minister Nouri al-Maliki's State of Law coalition, signaled a dramatic shift toward decentralization, bestowing upon local governments – through the Federation Council – precedence in areas of mutual administration with the central government; an increase in powers to provincial governors and their appointees; and a fivefold increase in petrodollar shares for the provinces from which oil is exported.[152]

Increased autonomy for the provinces, however, does not preclude political conflict at the provincial level. Officials elected in the June 2013 governorate vote in al-Anbar province, for example, have endured a prolonged and stalled effort to establish alliances that would form a government and nominate a governor. Many of the smaller blocs remained undecided on the larger blocs with which they would enter a coalition to form a majority. The two lists vying to lead a majority include the Aberoun bloc (close to al-Maliki), which won five seats, and the Mutahidoun bloc, which won eight seats. Ali Abel Sadah writes for *Al-Monitor* that "liberals in Anbar province felt that the local government was stolen from them through electoral fraud, to be controlled by Islamists."[153]

The position of Islamic parties on the legitimacy and mechanisms of elections has been diverse and variable. For example, Sistani has been instrumental in encouraging Iraqis to vote in both the 2005 and 2010 elections.[154] On the other hand, Muqtada al-Sadr opposed the 2005 elections because he considered them to have taken place while still under occupation, making them illegitimate. On the Sunni side, the IIP pulled out of the January 2005 elections citing their unheeded calls to postpone elections until safeguards were instituted to protect them against violence on election day.[155] The IIP argued that violence plaguing the north and west of Baghdad made a free and fair vote impossible.

The departure of American troops at the end of 2011 once more raised the fear of sectarian tensions. The Shi'a-dominated government issued an arrest warrant against Tariq al-Hashimi, the Sunni vice president and one

---

[152] The law also sets the groundwork for a parliamentary committee to gradually transfer the powers of several national ministries to provincial administrations, which decentralists consider a key step in realizing Article 116 of the Iraqi constitution, which reads, "The Federal System in the Republic of Iraq will be composed of a capital city, regions, decentralized provinces and local administrations."

[153] Ali Abel Sadah, "Iraq's Anbar Province Struggles To Form Government."

[154] "Sistani Position on New Elections," *Informed Comment*, trans. Juan Cole, http://www.juancole.com/2003/11/sistani-position-on-new-elections.html.

[155] Election day was marred by more than 100 armed attacks on polling stations.

of the most prominent Sunni leaders in the country. Hashimi denied the charges accusing him of running a personal death squad that assassinated security officials and government bureaucrats. He accused Maliki's government of using the country's security forces to persecute political opponents, specifically Sunnis. He has been living in exile in Turkey and has been sentenced to death in absentia.

On December 26, 2011, the Sadr bloc led by cleric Muqtada al-Sadr called for parliament to be dissolved and early elections to be held, the first open challenge to Maliki from within his Shi'i coalition. While this move was not enough to immediately bring down the Maliki government, it increased the political instability that had grown in the country.

Adding to the growing distrust between Sunni and Shi'i, Maliki's government welcomed Asa'ib Ahl Haq, an Iranian-backed militia, into Iraq's political system. The entrance of this new player into Iraqi politics has exacerbated sectarian fault lines while potentially empowering Iran at a moment of rising military and economic tensions between Tehran and Washington. It could also tilt the nation's center of gravity closer to Iran. The American military holds that the group has financial and training support from Iran's elite Quds Force, an allegation Iranian officials deny. Critics within the Sunni and Shi'i groups in Iraq say Maliki may use the group's credentials as Shi'i resistance fighters to divide challengers in his own Shi'i coalition and weaken Sadr's powerful bloc, which draws its political lifeblood from the Shi'i underclass.[156]

At the same time, the resurgence of al-Qa'ida attacks since 2012 has generated a unity of sorts among political parties in Iraq. For example, Muqtada al-Sadr realized the possibility of bloody retaliation from Shi'a citizens. Consequently, he systematically condemned all al-Qa'ida attacks, including the string of assaults in October 2012. He emphasized that these attacks are not led by the Sunni people as a whole but by a particular radical fraction of the population. Sadr visited a Baghdad church in early January 2013 that had been the site of a bloody attack in 2010, and then visited one of Baghdad's most prominent Sunni mosques, an overture to other religious groups in the context of a growing competition with Maliki.[157] In the same vein, Sadr joined Sunnis and Kurds in calling for the ouster of Prime Minister Nouri al-Maliki in 2013, stating that participation in Maliki's government was a "sin." After Maliki postponed elections in Sunni-dominated Anbar and Mosul in 2013, Sadr stated that "marginalizing Iraq's Sunnis

[156] Michael Kamber, "Iraq," *New York Times*, December 4, 2012, accessed January 28, 2013, http://topics.nytimes.com/top/news/international/countriesandterritories/iraq/index.html.

[157] Tova Rznik, "Al-Qa'ida and the faltering Sahwa movement," *Islamopedia Online*, accessed January 28, 2013, http://www.islamopediaonline.org/country-profile/iraq/transnational-influence/al-qaeda-and-faltering-sahwa-movement.

is an unforgivable disaster. The postponement of provincial elections ... is not permissible."[158] He also tested other cross-sectarian alliances by inviting Sunni and Christian candidates to run in the 2013 provincial elections under the Sadrist banner. After these elections, which ran over several months because of security concerns, the alliance of Sadr's al-Ahrar bloc and other minority parties was able to form a majority coalition in Baghdad that outnumbered al-Maliki's State of Law Coalition.[159] While it is unclear if this state of affairs will last, it is obvious that Sadr is willing to work across sectarian lines. Al-Sadr's strategy of coalition building continued through July 2013, when he announced the formation of a partnership with Ammar al-Hakim's Islamic Supreme Council of Iraq (ISCI) in a move he characterized as "strengthen[ing] the Iraqi, national, Islamic Shi'a alliance." Al-Ahrar MP Mohammed Ridha al-Khafaji also added that the coalition would be open to Kurds and Sunnis.[160] Taken together, these moves could position him as a nationalist and help him shed the baggage of the past, when his militias were linked to some of the worst sectarian violence in Iraq.

Street protests against Prime Minister al-Maliki, largely carried out by Sunnis in Fallujah in January 2013, took a bloody turn as clashes broke out between stone-throwing civilians and armed police forces. Shortly after the bloodshed, the parliament passed a law seeking to limit al-Maliki's reign by preventing him from assuming a third term. Al-Maliki's coalition boycotted the vote, while other parties called the law unconstitutional.[161] The measure was adopted, but al-Maliki's supporters continued to contest its legality.[162] Iraq's Federal Supreme Court ruled in March 2013 that the parliamentary session when the third term law was passed was legal, but it has delayed ruling on the legality of the law itself. Supporters of the measure worry that the court will delay ruling until after the 2014 elections in an attempt to avoid controversy.[163]

---

[158] "Muqtada al-Sadr: Staying In Iraqi Government a 'Sin,'" *Al-Monitor*, March 22, 2013, accessed June 22, 2013, http://www.al-monitor.com/pulse/originals/2013/03/sadr-letter-against-maliki.html.

[159] "Setback for Al-Maliki," *Al-Ahram Weekly*, June 19, 2013, accessed June 25, 2013, http://weekly.ahram.org.eg/News/3073/19/Setback-for-Al-Maliki.aspx.

[160] Hamza Mustafa, "Iraq: Sadr and Hakim form new "strategic" alliance," *Asharq Al-Awsat*, July 11, 2013, accessed August 8, 2013, http://www.aawsat.net/2013/07/article55309198.

[161] Yasir Ghazi and Tim Arango, "Iraq Parliament votes to keep Maliki from seeking new term," *New York Times*, January 26, 2013, accessed January 28, 2013, http://www.nytimes.com/2013/01/27/world/middleeast/iraq-parliament-votes-to-keep-maliki-fromseeking-new-term.html.

[162] "Iraq MPs to bar Maliki from third term," *The News*, January 27, 2013, accessed January 28, 2013, http://www.thenews.com.pk/Todays-News-1-156593-Iraq-MPs-to-bar-Maliki-from-third-term.

[163] Mushreq Abbas, "Iraqi Federal Court Delays Ruling on Term-Limit Law," *Al-Monitor*, July 3, 2013, accessed August 8, 2013, http://www.al-monitor.com/pulse/originals/2013/07/iraq-federal-court-ruling-delay-term-limit-law.html.

The Syrian crisis has affected the Iraqi sectarian dynamic as well. Fearing an alliance between Sunni insurgents in Iraq and Sunnis fleeing Syria, President al-Maliki controversially ordered border guards to turn away people seeking to cross from Syria.[164] In June 2013, the Iraqi government moved eight thousand troops in a bid to stop border crossings by those looking to fight in Syria. However, a limited number of Sunnis and Shi'is have gone to Syria, the former to join the rebels and the latter to join Assad's forces.[165] In addition, Iraqi Kurds have become increasingly bold in opposing the government, hopeful of a Kurdish region in unstable Syria.[166]

From a State for Muslims to an Islamic State

In Pakistan, being a Muslim was a distinctive feature of becoming a citizen. Even the Islamist trend, represented by the Jamaat-e-Islami (JI), decided to operate within the state framework and made the Islamization of political institutions and society its major goal – despite its initial opposition to the nation-state. However, what the concept of a nation-state means to Muslims in Pakistan is split between two different political interpretations. First, represented by the Muslim League and founding fathers such as Jinnah and Iqbal, is the idea of a state for Muslims. Second, represented by the JI and beginning with the state policies of Zia-ul-Haq, is the idea of an Islamic state.

Jinnah and Iqbal argued for the ideal of Muslim nationalism, but not the formation of an Islamic state. For Jinnah, Muslims in India comprised a separate nation from the Hindus, and therefore he advocated for a special state in which Muslims would be not just a minority but a nation.[167] However, Jinnah also acknowledged that Pakistan would not just be for Muslims but that there would be Pakistani nationals of other religious faiths.[168] Thus,

---

[164] Tim Arango, "Syrian war's spillover threatens a fragile Iraq," *New York Times*, September 24, 2012, accessed January 28, 2013, http://www.nytimes.com/2012/09/25/world/middleeast/iraq-faces-new-perils-from-syrias-civil-war.html?pagewanted=all&_r=0.

[165] "Iraq Moves Troops To Syrian Border," *Al-Monitor*, June 18, 2013, accessed June 22, 2013, http://www.al-monitor.com/pulse/originals/2013/06/iraq-moves-troops-syria-border.html.

[166] Mohammed A. Salih, "Syrian conflict threatens to fracture Iraq," *Christian Science Monitor*, December 27, 2012, accessed January 28, 2013, http://www.csmonitor.com/World/Middle-East/2012/1227/Syrian-conflict-threatens-to-fracture-Iraq.

[167] He argued that "the only solution for the Muslims of India, which will stand the test of trial and time, is that India should be partitioned so that both the communities can develop freely and fully according to their own genius economically, socially, culturally and politically." Speech at the Muslim University Union, Aligarh on March 10, 1941, in Mohammad Ali Jinnah and Jamil-ud-din Ahmad (eds.), *Speeches and Writings of Mr Jinnah* (Lahore, Pakistan: Muhammad Ashraf, 1947), 236–7.

[168] In his speech to the Constituent Assembly of Pakistan in 1947, Jinnah stated, "Now I think we should keep that in front of us as our ideal, and you will find that in course of time Hindus would cease to be Hindus and Muslims would cease to be Muslims, not in the religious

unlike the pan-Islamist groups, neither Jinnah nor Iqbal favored a world-wide Muslim state, and national identity, while heavily influenced by Islam, was also considered secular. This secular notion of the Pakistani state was seemingly contradicted by the ideology of Iqbal, who differentiated between the secularism of Europe, which separates church and state, and Muslim nationalism, which integrates religious ideals in the national identity of the state (in this case, Pakistan).[169] However, Iqbal too proposed a separate state. At the same time, it is important to note that Iqbal's proposal suggests not an Islamic state but a state where Muslims can have a shared culture, ethics, and identity. Islam thus emerged as an element of cohesion for the Pakistani nation, but this was not translated into Islamic politics. Inspired by and supported by Jinnah and Iqbal, the Muslim League was formed in 1906 as the primary promoter of a state for Muslims. Following Jinnah's lead, the Muslim League argued for the two-nation theory,[170] which eventually led to the formation of Pakistan in 1947. The vision of Pakistan as a state for Muslims was dramatically transformed by the Islamization that took place under General Zia.

Pakistan as an Islamic State

The turning point in the ideology of the Pakistani state came with General Zia-ul-Haq and his Islamization campaign (1977–88). Well known for turning Pakistan into a "global center for political Islam,"[171] Zia wanted Pakistan to be an ideological state guided by the military and intelligence services. He declared, "Pakistan, which was created in the name of Islam, will continue to survive only if it sticks to Islam.... I consider the introduction of the Islamic system as an essential prerequisite for the country."[172]

---

sense, because that is the personal faith of each individual, but in the political sense as citizens of the State." *Dawn*, Independence Day Supplement, August 14, 1999. Transcribed from printed copy by Shehzaad Nakhoda, http://www.pakistani.org/pakistan/legislation/constituent_address_11aug1947.html.

[169] In a speech to the All-Indian Muslim League, Iqbal argued: "The conclusion to which Europe is consequently driven is that religion is a private affair of the individual and has nothing to do with what is called man's temporal life.... In Islam, God and the universe, spirit and matter, church and State, are organic to each other." From December 29, 1930, presidential address at All-India Muslim League, Sir Mohammad Iqbal, *Speeches and Statements of Iqbal* (Lahore: Al-Manâar Academy, 1948), 6–7.

[170] The two-nation theory was based on the idea that "two different civilizations which are based mainly on conflicting ideas and conceptions," namely Hindus and Muslims, should adopt a two-state system where each civilization could live without being predominated by the other.

[171] Husain Haqqani, *Pakistan: Between Mosque and Military* (Washington, DC: Carnegie Endowment for International Peace, 2005), 131.

[172] *Pakistan Times*, July 6, 1977. Zia is also quoted as saying: "The basis of Pakistan was that the Muslims of the sub-continent are a separate culture ... in the last seven years there

Some of Zia's Islamization reforms included a ban on alcohol consumption, harsher criminal and penal codes, greater observation of Islamic holidays and fasts, taxation according to religious law (zakat), the restructuration of the Shari'a court system, and finally, the banning of elections on the basis that they were "not permissible" in Islam.[173]

Such an evolution met the expectations of the JI and its ideologue, Mawdudi, who, unlike Jinnah and Iqbal, was a strong proponent of an Islamic state. In his book *The Islamic Law and Constitution* (1941), he gives two central reasons for the advancement of an Islamic state in Pakistan: first, that the intellectual and religious background of Islam is different from the West, and second, that the younger and more educated generations of Muslims have become estranged from their religion.[174] Under Zia, the JI and the Pakistani state enjoyed a close relationship, as the JI joined Zia's cabinet and controlled ministries that expanded its influence through education and youth services.[175] In this way, Islam became a central component of state structure and policies.[176]

Controversy in the Current Political Context

The regional context and especially the Afghan-Soviet War (1979–89) hardened the ideological differences between the various political actors. Further, the emergence of the Taliban in Afghanistan in the mid-1990s led to divisions among previously united Islamist groups. For example, during her second term (1993–6), on one hand, Bhutto was coerced into supporting the emerging Taliban and especially the Jamiat Ulema-e-Islam (JUI), which had ties to the Bhutto coalition government as well as to the Taliban in the Pashtun provinces bordering Afghanistan.[177] On the other hand, the JI started a campaign to demand Bhutto's resignation, eventually leading to

---

has been a complete erosion of the moral values of our society.... Therefore, to my mind the most fundamental and important basis for the whole reformation of society is ... the moral rejuvenation which is required first and that will have to be done on the basis of Islam, because it was on this basis that Pakistan was formed." Interview with Ian Stephens, January 6, 1979, *President of Pakistan General Mohammad Zia ul-Haq: Interviews to Foreign Media* vol. II (Islamabad: Government of Pakistan, undated), 2–5.

[173] Graham E. Fuller, *Islamic Fundamentalism in Pakistan: Its Character and Prospects* (RAND, National Defense Research Institute, 1991).

[174] Mawdudi, *Islamic Law and Constitution*, http://www.teachislam.com/dmdocuments/ Maulana_Maududi_The_Islamic_Law_&_Constitution.pdf.

[175] Haqqani, *Pakistan: Between Mosque and Military*, 138.

[176] Later, after the 1990 election, the relationship between the Islamists, including the JI, and the state was similar to that of Zia-ul-Haq, especially with the prime minister being PML-N member Nawaz Sharif. Sharif appeased the Islamists by ordering women to cover their heads in public and prohibiting women's swimming on television during the 1992 Olympics, citing immodesty.

[177] Haqqani, *Pakistan: Between Mosque and Military*, 240.

the killing of three Pakistan People's Party (PPP) activists in June 1996 and a massive strike in Karachi, citing government corruption.[178] As discussed in previous chapters, the confrontation of two different visions of the Pakistani nation is also reflected in completely opposite stances on human rights that divide the country between an individually centered approach of rights promoted by the secular elite and an Islamic conception of the national community centered on collective rights.

The divide between Pakistani political forces is exacerbated by the influence of the Afghan conflict at its borders. The United States is preparing to largely withdraw its forces from Afghanistan between 2013 and 2014 and hand over its mission to the newly created and (so far) ill-prepared Afghan army. Before doing so, it wants to make sure that all security concerns in the region are addressed. Therefore, it has been publicly increasing its pressure on Pakistan to crack down on militant activities on its soil that may destabilize or destroy whatever order the United States has put in place in the region during its almost decade-long presence.[179] The U.S. military and security establishments are convinced that elements in the Pakistani military are providing support for different militant groups, notably the al-Haqqani network based in North Waziristan, to maintain their influence in Afghanistan as the United States departs from the country.[180] Relations between the two countries in dealing with militants remain very tense. For example, since the attack against Bin Laden in May 2011, the American administration has been expressing growing frustration about cooperating with Pakistan in the fight against terrorism. As late as June 2012, the United States publicly accused the Pakistani Inter-Services Intelligence (ISI) of providing safe haven and support for al-Qaʿida linked militants who were crossing the border to Afghanistan and conducting attacks on U.S. forces. On the Pakistan side, irritation against the Obama administration has increased with the escalated drone strikes that have occasionally killed Pakistani civilians and soldiers. Pakistan's prime minister, Nawaz Sharif,[181] who took office in early June 2013, issued a typical

[178] Ibid., 245.

[179] Deb Riechmann and Heidi Vogt, "Panetta: Patience with Pakistan 'reaching limits,'" *Associated Press*, accessed June 7, 2012, http://news.yahoo.com/panetta-patience-pakistan-reaching-limits-085857670.html.

[180] Juan Cole, "The Panetta/Pakistan War of Words," *Informed Comment*, accessed June 8, 2012, http://www.juancole.com/2012/06/the-panetta-pakistan-war-of-words.html.

[181] Nawaz Sharif served two terms as prime minister (1990–3 and 1997–9) before being elected in June 2013. He led the Pakistan Muslim League (the Pakistan Muslim League-Nawaz, PML-N after 1993), and after clashing with army commander General Pervez Musharraf, he was overthrown and exiled to Saudi Arabia. He returned to Pakistan in 2007 with continued popular support, and currently heads the PML-N. See Nawaz Sharif, *Encyclopædia Britannica*, September 16, 2013, accessed November 13, 2013, http://www.britannica.com/EBchecked/topic/538837/Nawaz-Sharif.

rebuke of U.S. drone policy in his inaugural remarks, stating: "The chapter of daily drone attacks should stop."[182] Earlier during Sharif's previous term, U.S. drones killed a leader of the Pakistani Taliban, leading them to reject negotiation with Sharif and exacerbating tensions in American-Pakistani relations.[183]

Almost unanimously, a basic tenet of Pakistani political parties is opposition to the West. Most of them are strongly opposed to the drone warfare and do not take well the pressures to revise Pakistani politics and laws according to Western principles. They dislike America's interference and wish to uphold certain elements of Pakistan's Islamic state, such as the blasphemy laws. Notably, Mufti Kifayatullah, a member of the provincial legislature in the Khyber Pakhtoon Khwa assembly, launched a fiery diatribe against the U.S. involvement in Pakistan and the murder of Bin Laden on May 2, 2011. He threatened the United States in these terms: "However, those willing to fight and die in the name of Islam will be still around, God willing. My sacrifices in the past finished off the British Empire. My sacrifices brought down the Soviet Union. And God willing; my sacrifices will destroy America."[184]

Overall, it appears that Islamists became influential political actors when they operated within the national framework under authoritarian rule. As soon as they are in power and attempt to implement some form of Islamic politics, their popularity tends to decline. That is why the focus on social justice during their time as political opponents was so appealing. In other words, the political evolution of Egypt and Tunisia since 2011 illustrates what happens when Islamists stray away from the nationalist framework.

THE ISLAMIST UTOPIA OF SOCIAL JUSTICE

The concept of social justice as the cornerstone of Islamic society is conceived by Islamic actors as the antidote to oppressive, corrupted regimes and has been instrumental in Islamist rhetoric and influence. However, it is much more difficult to implement once Islamists are in power. Somewhat

---

[182] "Pakistan demands end to U.S. drone strikes – for the ninth time," *Foreign Policy*, June 5, 2013, accessed June 22, 2013, http://blog.foreignpolicy.com/posts/2013/06/05/pakistan_calls_for_end_to_us_drone_strikes_again.

[183] "U.S.-Pakistan Relationship and the Future of Afghanistan," *Brookings Institute*, June 5, 2013, accessed June 22, 2013, http://www.brookings.edu/blogs/up-front/posts/2013/06/05-us-pakistan-relationship-future-afghanistan-riedel.

[184] Wajahat Masood, "Pakistani cleric legislator threatens the destruction of the US," *Islamopedia*, June 22, 2011, accessed January 28, 2013, http://www.islamopediaonline.org/news/pakistani-cleric-legislator-threatens-destruction-us.

contradictory to the overarching goal of social justice, Islamist rulers have usually pursued the same neoliberal policies as the secular regimes before them, sometimes with great success, as in Turkey under the AKP's rule. Interestingly, these politics are at odds with the initial Islamist conception of social justice.

For example, Hasan al Banna developed a program emphasizing the revival of true Islam in order to bring about effective and responsible reforms for the people. He viewed political parties, political leaders, and partyism as manifestations of greed and personal interest rather than the public good. Moreover, the secular orientation of the state was a façade for capitalist exploitation, as its leaders were "tools of British and Western ideologies – the leaders of cultural 'domestic imperialism.'"[185] The capitalism propagated by the state led to social injustice because it not only "paralyzes the strength of the nation in work and production" and "destroys human dignity and rights," but it also "violates the spirit of religion."[186] Under these circumstances, the revival of Islam was the only way to Egypt's social and political regeneration. In the same vein, al-Banna criticized the hybrid legal system with the introduction of Western legal codes as corruption of the "nation's thought, mind, and logic."[187] As a result of the implementation of foreign laws, "the law of Egypt has no relation to its citizens … [and] the inharmonious relation of revealed and man-made law has served to shatter the 'unity' of the nation."[188]

Thus, the Muslim Brotherhood's ultimate goal was to create an Islamic order, or *nizām islāmī*, that emphasized the religious foundation of the legal order. At the same time, the Brotherhood's program recognized the importance of reason for understanding Shari'a and reflected an understanding of the social, economic, and political aspirations of the Egyptian people. Hence, al-Banna advocated a number of economic reforms that included land redistribution, the introduction of social-welfare programs, and the replacement of foreign capital by local investment. Despite this initial economic and social vision, the economic policies of Islamists in recent history have conformed to the neoliberal orientation of the previous secular regimes while simultaneously attempting social redistribution.

For example, since their access to power in Egypt, the Islamists' concern for social justice has been channeled into shaping economic policies to boost the country's development by increasing public spending, which includes an allowance raise to the basic salary of public sector workers and pensioners,

[185] Mitchell, *The Society of the Muslim Brotherhood*, 218.
[186] Ibid., 221.
[187] Ibid., 223.
[188] Ibid., 223–4.

and a rise in payments provided to the poor.[189] Importantly, while this policy might in the short term improve the economy, in the long term the high budget deficit, possible inflation, and lack of clear political reforms raise doubts that the country could secure the loan from the International Monetary Fund (IMF) it so desperately needs to sustain such economic policies for social justice. Nevertheless, an agreement in principle for a $4.8 billion loan was reached in November 2012 to ameliorate the budget gap of 200 billion Egyptian pounds.[190] Political turmoil in Egypt has delayed the finalization of the agreement, as the IMF made it clear that a strong commitment to reform was required.[191] After Morsi's overthrow, plans for the IMF loan to Egypt were delayed at least until the interim government gained international approval.

The urgency of the IMF loan process is heightened by the severity of the deterioration of Egypt's economic crisis, which was portrayed by former finance minister Samir Radwan as the worst since the Great Depression. Key drivers of the crisis include rising food prices, lost tourism revenue, lack of a social safety net, rising inflation, and falling foreign reserves, as well as the lack of a long-term vision for the economy.[192] President Morsi did little to address these concerns and focused instead on the defense of the country's Islamic identity.[193] For example, in early January 2013, the cabinet approved a draft law on Islamic bonds (sukuk) that permit foreigners to own Islamic bonds and shares in local factories and businesses.[194] The hope behind such a law is that it might increase opportunity for investors from the Gulf and hence alleviate the Egyptian economy's dependence on international loans.[195]

[189] Nadine Marroushi, "Living on borrowed time: Morsy's political economics," *Egypt Independent*, July 16, 2012, accessed July 22, 2012, http://www.egyptindependent.com/news/living-borrowed-time-morsy-s-political-economics.

[190] However, the process has been delayed because of the growing political unrest in 2013.

[191] "IMF Points to 'Progress' in Aid Talks with Egypt," *Ahram Online*, June 20, 2013, accessed June 22, 2013, http://english.ahram.org.eg/NewsContent/3/12/74556/Business/Economy/IMF-points-to-progress-in-aid-talks-with-Egypt.aspx.

[192] Patrick Kingsley, "Egypt 'Suffering Worst Economic Crisis since 1930s,'" *The Guardian*, May 16, 2013, accessed June 22, 2013, http://www.guardian.co.uk/world/2013/may/16/egypt-worst-economic-crisis-1930s.

[193] "Going to the Dogs," *The Economist*, March 30, 2013, accessed June 22, 2013, http://www.economist.com/news/middle-east-and-africa/21574533-unless-president-muhammad-morsi-broadens-his-government-egypts-economy-looks.

[194] http://www.egyptindependent.com/news/cabinet-approves-islamic-bonds-draft-law.

[195] The World Bank and African Development Bank have also offered their aid to help finance the Egyptian economy. Mohamed Abdel Atty, "International institutions offered to finance Egypt economy, says minister," *Al-Masry Al-Youm*, February 16, 2011, accessed January 28, 2013, http://www.egyptindependent.com/news/international-institutions-offered-finance-egypt-economy-says-minister.

As occurred in Egypt, Tunisian Islamists have since the beginning of their mandate, prioritized religious and moral issues as well as themes of foreign domination, rather than focusing on economic policy making. For example, Ghannouchi criticized the Tunisian education system in these terms:

What idea will our pupils get of the teachings of Islamic thought when they cannot find – in the whole text book – even a single quotation from one of the contemporary Muslim thinkers.... Will the pupils not think that Islam has ceased to exist, that ... [it] has nothing to do with solving our social, economic, and political problems?[196]

He also criticized Tunisian society for a number of fundamental problems with regards to Islamic morals, which included, in his view, "the problem of self-confidence, the problems of sex, individualism and the lack of readiness to offer help and sacrifice for others, cultural imitation, the problem of economic development and its relationship with morality, etc."[197]

At the same time, Ghannouchi has repeatedly emphasized that the priorities of Ennahda are tackling unemployment and putting an end to the corruption so rampant during the Ben Ali regime.

In his May 2013 talk in Washington, DC, Rached Ghannouchi discussed the economic and social issues remaining after the overthrow of Ben Ali in these terms:

The first challenge [we face] is the economic/ social one. We all know that this factor was one of the main elements behind the revolution ... people's expectations are very high and their patience is very low. Also the economic situation in our main trading partners in Europe is affecting our exports and affecting tourism. Despite these problems the government has managed to reduce unemployment by 2% from 18 to 16%. Also growth went up from -2% when we took over to 3.5%. For 2012 the number of tourists had also gone up and we received 6 million tourists last year. However the young people who made the revolution in Sidi Bouzid and Kasserine have not seen any improvement in their lives and this is a challenge that will need many years to tackle.[198]

Similar to the FJP in Egypt, Ennahda has addressed economic issues by increasing public spending over two phases: a recovery stage (2011–12) and the start-up stage, which was slated for 2013. The recovery stage has included increasing expenditures, supporting regional growth, and creating public job opportunities. Specifically, the state has raised direct support for basic materials, including fuel, electricity, and transportation, especially

---

[196] Ghannouchi, *Maqalat*, 132.
[197] Ibid., 30.
[198] Ibid.

for middle- and low-income groups.[199] After the recovery stage, in early 2013, Tunisia began to confront its aging banking system, with audits of the country's three largest banks and likely consolidation of numerous smaller banks.[200] Tunisia also signed a $1.75 billion loan agreement with the IMF, approved in June 2013.[201] However, the country remains plagued by inflation and unemployment. These problems were graphically illustrated by the March 2013 immolation death of Adel Khadri, an unemployed cigarette vendor in Tunis. A spokesman for the Tunisian Ministry of the Interior attributed the death of Khadri to the economic situation, stating, "[h]e is unemployed and came to Tunis a few months ago. He was very fragile, psychologically broken, and that is why he set himself on fire."[202]

Economic policy in Tunisia is rooted in the alleviation of poverty through multiple means, such as promoting the overall buying power of the Tunisian population, but also fostering international cooperation and, in particular, the integration of Maghrebi nation markets. This could potentially include Egypt. Some of the Ennahda economic goals include decreasing inflation from 6 percent to 3 percent and almost doubling the overall revenue. Finally, the administration's 2012–16 overarching ambition is to increase jobs and reduce unemployment to 8.5 percent.[203]

In Turkey, social justice was also a key ideological component of the Islamist movement. Islamist organizations have continued to provide the social services once maintained by foundations (*vakiflar*) during the Ottoman Empire. These organizations were "legal corporations founded on the basis of continual use of proceeds from a reserved form of property, such as a house, land, or shop."[204] They often provided public services such as road construction or the distribution of food. From these Ottoman foundations, "the appeal of political Islam as a viable alternative to secular social democracy arises not only from the strength of its moral argument in favor of equity but also from specific and concrete anti-poverty projects

---

[199] Lahcen Achy, "Ennahda Proposes Big Spending to Stimulate Tunisia's Economy," *Al-Monitor*, May 28, 2012, accessed July 22, 2012, http://www.al-monitor.com/pulse/business/2012/04/tunisian-economy-weak-performanc.html.

[200] "Tunisia: Economic revival depends on banking reconstruction," *Financial Times*, May 28, 2013, accessed June 22, 2013, http://www.ft.com/intl/cms/s/0/7a8978c4-c196-11e2-9767-00144feab7de.html#axzz2X0BFyg4T.

[201] "IMF Loan Aims to Help Tunisia Boost Growth, Protect Poor," *IMF*, June 17, 2013, accessed June 22, 2013, http://www.imf.org/external/pubs/ft/survey/so/2013/CAR061713A.htm.

[202] "Tunisia vendor dies after self-immolation," *Al-Jazeera*, March 13, 2013, accessed June 26, 2013, http://www.aljazeera.com/news/middleeast/2013/03/201331385433367799.html.

[203] Khaled ben Rajab, "Economic Profile of Ennahda: Diversification of banking system and 'open sky' membership," *Tunisia Live*, November 5, 2011, accessed January 28, 2013, http://www.tunisia-live.net/2011/11/05/economic-profile-of-ennahda-diversification-of-banking-system-and-open-sky-membership/.

[204] Jenny Barbara White, *Islamist Mobilization in Turkey: A Study in Vernacular Politics* (Seattle: University of Washington, 2002), 200.

designed to improve the material conditions of the disadvantaged."[205] As a consequence, "people's expectations of what the state ought to deliver is increasing while the state's capacity to provide these much needed services is rapidly in decline. This phenomenon creates a crisis of governance and a loss of authority on the part of the state."[206]

Later on, these foundations were utilized by Islamist parties to provide welfare for their people.[207] The Welfare Party entered the government in 1995 and promoted an economic program, the Just Order, which stressed the need for greater social justice and equality against negative Western influence.[208] It was at the time the "best organized of all the political parties, with a legion of devout Muslims, especially women, who did volunteer work for the party and provided a network of social-welfare help to the poor."[209] And finally, the AKP has "presented itself as the main agent of transformation that would bring economic development and greater democracy" especially through its efforts toward EU accession.[210]

This meant delinking economic reforms from politics and ensuring the steady growth of the Turkish economy. "The party made health care and housing credits more accessible, distributed food, increased grants for students, improved the infrastructure of poorer urban districts, and made minority rights for Kurds and non-Muslims a priority."[211] As a result, the Turkish economy grew at an average rate of 7.5 percent annually between 2002 and 2011. Furthermore, per capita income skyrocketed in just nine years from $2,800 in 2002 to $10,000 in 2011. Though economic development has slowed down in 2012, the AKP still focuses immense resources and attention to further economic growth.[212] While the economy remains strong, falling foreign investor confidence is a concern in a country that relies on external capital.[213]

---

[205] Öniş, "The political economy of Islamic resurgence in Turkey," 748.
[206] Ibid., 745.
[207] One example of a Turkish foundation (vakiflar) with Islamic roots is the Insan Hak ve Hurriyetleri ve Insani Yardum Vakfi, the IHH Humanitarian Relief Foundation. First registered in 1995, the IHH supplies humanitarian relief for war, earthquakes, hunger, and conflict both inside and outside Turkey. One of its main projects in Turkey is to provide support to orphans, including holding an annual international orphan meeting in Turkey. Its Sponsor Family Project has offices in all provinces across Turkey, as well as offices in 130 foreign countries (Insani Vardim Yakfi, accessed October 9, 2012, www.ihh.org.tr.).
[208] Ibid., 41–2.
[209] Sen, "Transformation of Turkish Islamism," 76.
[210] Ibid.
[211] Ibid.
[212] In 2013, the stock market fell more than 20 percent in less than a month after the Taksim protests. Omer Taspinar, "Turkey: the new model?" Brookings Institution, April 2012, accessed January 28, 2013, http://www.brookings.edu/research/papers/2012/04/24-turkey-new-model-taspinar.
[213] "The Turkish economy: Strong but vulnerable," *The Economist*, June 15, 2013, accessed June 22, 2013, http://www.economist.com/news/europe/21579491-turkey-remains-highly-exposed-loss-confidence-foreign-investors-strong-vulnerable.

In Iraq, Saddam's repression fostered an ideology of social justice among the Shi'i opposition. For example, Shirazi argued that education was a sign of social justice and that it was "imperative that Muslims gain sufficient knowledge regarding all and every aspects of their personal and social lives in the fields of science, medicine, technology etc."[214] Similarly, al-Da'wa promoted Islamic values and ethics in Iraqi society and believed that an Islamic state would bring true social justice to Iraq.

Economic inequality between the majority Shi'i population and the Sunni population, which had been once allied with the Ba'thist state, is still prevalent in Iraq, although there have been significant changes since 2003. For example, several regions in the nation's south or in the predominantly Shi'i slums in the center of the country surrounding Baghdad are the poorest of the economic groups. In these Shi'i areas, such as Babil, Wassit, Qadisiyya, and Muthanna, 35 percent of the residents fall into the poorest economic group, which is very high in comparison to 22 percent for the country overall and only 15 percent in majority Sunni regions.[215]

Shi'i clerics have suggested that social justice will come with the establishment of a successful Iraqi democracy. For this reason, they support thousands of Iraqis annually through their khums donations, which are distributed to various religious schools, hospitals, and other social services.[216]

Reviewing the ideological components of Islamist opposition in Turkey, Egypt, Iraq and Pakistan highlights a few significant common points, despite very different national situations. First, everywhere the pan-Islamist project was retailored and adjusted to the nation-state framework. This adjustment translated into participation in elections, acceptance of the state system, and ultimately acceptance of democracy as the only viable alternative to authoritarianism. This strategy can partially explain the popularity of Islamic parties under authoritarian rule. Once in power, the Turkish example shows that the consolidation of this popularity depends on Islamists' ability to provide democratic and economic reforms, very much in line with the promises that the authoritarian Promethean state never fulfilled. Thus, when the Islamists do not display the capacity or willingness to implement democratic reform or to improve the economy, or if they resort primarily to some form of "identity" politics, they quickly lose legitimacy. In other words, the ideological strength of Islamist opposition is linked to their adaptation

---

[214] Imam Shirazi, *The Islamic System of Government*, trans. Z. Olyabek (London: Fountain Books, 2001), 21.

[215] "Iraq: Economic Recovery Assessment," *USAID*, February 2009, accessed August 16, 2011, http://www.countrycompass.com/_docs/assessments/Iraq_Economic_Recovery_Assessment. pdf.

[216] See Chapter 9 section on "Mobilization Skills."

and the grafting of their own references onto the concepts of nation and state.

This ideological strength of the Islamists is increased by their status as pure, authentic opponents, as well as their organizational and mobilization skills that proved critical in their electoral success in the post–Ben Ali and post-Mubarak regimes.

9

From Martyrs to Rulers

The credibility of Islamists across different social groups has been strong because they use the vocabulary and values of Islam to combat the corruption and nepotism of the state. In this sense, they reach out not only to the disenfranchised segments of Muslim countries but also to a large coalition of middle and sometimes upper classes who wish to curb the prevailing influence of the state. Two main factors bolstered the popularity of the Islamists: unfulfilled promises of education and social progress made by the Promethean authoritarian state.[1] For this reason, Islamist opposition has gained legitimacy and credibility in three distinct ways: by being the oppressed group *par excellence*; by taking state prerogatives in providing social services to the whole society; and by skillfully employing different means to mobilize support for its platform.

The social services dimension has been abundantly surveyed;[2] therefore this chapter focuses on the oppressed status of Islamists and their techniques

[1] Ayub, 1991 – quoted from Kai Hafez, *Radicalism and Political Reform in the Islamic and Western Worlds* (Cambridge: Cambridge University Press, 2010), 101.

[2] For example, see: Saad Eddin Ibrahim, "Egypt's Islamic Activism in the 1980s," *Third World Quarterly* 10.2 (April 1988): 632–57, October 15, 2011, http://www.jstor.org/stable/3992660. "Egypt: Social Programmes Bolster Appeal of Muslim Brotherhood," IRIN, February 22, 2006, accessed October 15, 2011, http://www.irinnews.org/report.aspx?reportid=26150. Asef Bayat, "Revolution without Movement, Movement without Revolution: Comparing Islamic Activism in Iran and Egypt," *Comparative Studies in Society and History* 40.1 (1998). Denis J. Sullivan and Sana Abed-Kotob, *Islam in Contemporary Egypt: Civil Society vs. the State* (Boulder, CO: Lynne Rienner Publishers Inc., 1999). Pakistan: Karachi's Madrasas and Violent Extremism, *International Crisis Group Asia Report*, No. 130, 2007. Joshua T. White, Pakistan's Islamic Frontier, 2009, accessed September 13, 2011, https://www.globalengage.org/attachments/837_jwhite_pakistan.pdf. Masooda Bano, "Marker of Identity: Religious Political Parties and Welfare Work – The Case of Jama'at i Islami in Pakistan and Bangladesh," Religions and Development Research Programme, University of Oxford, Working Paper 34, 2009, http://www.eldis.org/gohome&id=45210&type=Document#.UsZVdvaE6G. Earthquake jihad: the role of jihadis and Islamist groups after the 2005 earthquake, by Jawad Hussain Quereshi, ICG, July 2006, *Humanitarian Exchange Magazine* 34, accessed September 19, 2011,

of social mobilization. It also discusses the erosion of their popularity since the Arab Awakening.

STATE OPPRESSION OF ISLAMIST MOVEMENTS

Being the "oppressed" meant that Islamists did not benefit from the nepotistic practices of the regimes and therefore gained an aura of purity and honesty, not to mention martyrdom, that no other political actors could claim, at least until the Arab Spring.[3]

In this regard, the rise to power in 2011 of political actors who spent many years in jail under Mubarak or Ben Ali was a spectacular reversal of fortune. For example, FJP vice chairman Essam al-Erian spent eight years in jail between 1981 and 2010. In Tunisia, the former prime minister, Hamadi Jebali (served December 2011–March 2013), spent a total of sixteen years in jail, ten of them in solitary confinement. Ali Larayedh, who was prime minister in 2013, spent fifteen years in prison under the Ben Ali regime. His wife was also imprisoned and sexually abused.[4] Ennahda Chairman Rached Ghannouchi was imprisoned in 1981 and again in 1987 for a total of four years, spending another twenty-two years in exile.

The Muslim Brotherhood gained legitimacy and credibility for being the "oppressed" group, from Nasser to Mubarak. The arrest, imprisonment, and torture of Brotherhood members legitimized them in the eyes of the population, and the group gained more and more supporters. As early as 1954, after an alleged attempt to assassinate Nasser by a Muslim Brotherhood member, the movement was outlawed and thousands of members were arrested, tortured, and put on trial. Some were even sentenced to death, including General Guide Hasan Al-Hudaybi (although his death sentence was later changed to life imprisonment). Even under Sadat, whose policies were more lenient, the movement remained banned. After the Muslim Brotherhood responded to the Darshour Earthquake in 1992 by providing large-scale social and

http://www.odihpn.org/report.asp?id=2815. "Qazi seeks nation's help for Islamic Revolution," *The Nation*, October 21, 2011, accessed November 12, 2011, http://nation.com.pk/pakistan-news-newspaper-daily-english-online/Regional/Lahore/21-Oct-2011/Qazi-seeks-nations-help-for-Islamic-revolution. WORDE White Paper, Traditional Muslim Networks: Pakistan's Untapped Resource in the Fight against Terrorism, 2010, 6. "Disaster & Emergency Relief," *Al-Mustafa Welfare Trust*, accessed October 8, 2011, http://www.almustafatrust.org/content/Our-Work/What-We-Do/Disaster-Emergency-Relief/index.htm. "Our Health Projects," *Al-Mustafa Welfare Trust*, accessed October 8, 2011, http://www.almustafatrust.org/content/Our-Work/What-We-Do/Our-Health-Projects/index.htm. Al-Akhtar Trust, SATP.org, accessed October 9, 2011, http://www.satp.org/satporgtp/countries/pakistan/terroristoutfits/Al-Akhtar_Trust.htm. Laurence Louer, *Transnational Shia Politics: Religious and Political Networks in the Gulf* (New York: Columbia University Press, 2008).
[3] The exercise of power has started to alter this status, although, at the time of this writing, it is too early to draw any definitive conclusion regarding the political future of these movements.
[4] "Ali Laarayedh," *Tunisia Live*, December 17, 2011, accessed June 24, 2013, http://www.tunisia-live.net/whoswho/ali-laarayedh/.

medical assistance, the government cracked down on them again, conducting office raids, interfering with student union elections to keep their members from running, and making hundreds of arrests. Over the course of Egypt's history, Brotherhood members were often imprisoned prior to elections to curb their influence. This occurred as late as 2010, when the movement claimed more than one thousand of its members were arrested, including eight parliamentary candidates running independently.[5]

Similarly, state repression increased Ennahda's credibility, especially in the eyes of other "secular" opponents. The bread riots of 1983 and 1984[6] constituted a crucial moment in bringing together leftist and Islamist opponents to the Bourguiba regime. It consequentially contributed to the insertion of Ennhada into mainstream political opposition.[7] In February 1987, Bourguiba cracked down on the General Union of Tunisian Students (UGTE), the Islamist university group, and in March, he arrested thirty-eight leaders of MTI, including Rached Ghannouchi.[8]

At first, under Ben Ali the Islamists seemed to gain leverage; more than 600 members of the MTI imprisoned since 1983 were freed in 1987, and in May 1990, Ben Ali pardoned Rached Ghannouchi as well as 233 other prisoners.[9] However, later in 1990, Ben Ali instated a law that prohibited political parties from questioning personal status issues such as women and family, which essentially precluded the MTI platform from engaging legally on the political scene and merely reaffirmed the ban on the Ennahda movement. The result was another round of protests, arrests, and imprisonments. In the same vein, in 1991, the government discovered chemical products in the offices and dormitories of students in the University of Tunisia, intended to fabricate Molotov cocktails. Three students were killed by gunfire during confrontations with the police.[10]

Rached Ghannouchi's exile following his release from prison in 1989 also contributed to the party's aura. He did not return to Tunisia until January 2011 when Ben Ali was ousted.[11] His return reignited the Ennahda movement in Tunisia; some members even suggested he should run as a presidential candidate in the upcoming elections, although he declined. Since

[5] "Egypt Muslim Brotherhood Says More Than 1000 Arrested," *BBC News*, November 10, 2010, accessed November 12, 2011, www.bbc.co.uk/news/world-middle-east-11807640.

[6] A series of protests where the population's anger was directed against the sharp increase of bread prices.

[7] Fifty people were killed that day. Mohamed Elhachmi Hamdi, *The Politicization of Islam: A Case Study of Tunisia* (Boulder, CO: Westview Press, 1998), 47.

[8] Michael Collins Dunn, "The al-Nahda Movement in Tunisia: From Renaissance to Revolution," in John Ruedy (ed.), *Islamism and Secularism in North Africa* (New York: St. Martin's, 1994), 150–64.

[9] Burgat and Dowell, *The Islamic Movement in North Africa*, 232.

[10] Ibid., 244.

[11] Tunisian Islamist Leader Rached Ghannouchi Returns Home, January 30, 2011, *BBC News*, accessed July 17, 2011, http://www.bbc.co.uk/news/world-africa-12318824.

2011, Ghannouchi has become, not only a spokesperson for the Ennahda movement, but also a symbol of the New Tunisia. More than ten thousand people congregated to meet him upon his arrival at the airport.[12] When he heard that Ennahda candidates won a 42 percent plurality of the vote in the October 2011 elections, Ghannouchi claimed, "We will continue this revolution to realize its aims of a free Tunisia, independent, developing, and prosperous in which the rights of God, the Prophet, women, men, the religious, and the non-religious are assured because Tunisia is for everyone."[13]

In Iraq, being a member of the "oppressed" group was true for the whole Shi'i population. As discussed in Part I, the dominant form of institutionalized Islam under the Ba'thist state was Sunni, even though the majority of the population is Shi'a. The promotion of a Sunni Iraqi identity led to mass discrimination against Shi'a in government positions, jobs, and education.[14] Therefore, many of the more prominent Islamist opposition groups and social movements established under the Ba'thist regime were Shi'a in nature.

The promotion of a secular Arab identity was Saddam's primary strategy to achieve national unity. As a result, any surge of Shi'i political activism was met with swift suppression. The threat of militant Islam spreading from the 1979 Iranian revolution increased the regime's suspicions toward Shi'a. At this time Saddam began to use a method known as "the carrot and the stick," or *tawhib* and *targhib*,[15] in his relationship with the Iraqi Shi'i community. With the Iran-Iraq War (1980–8), sectarian tensions were heightened, and more than fifteen thousand Shi'is were expelled from Iraq. This increased repression was further indication, if needed, of the regime's conflation of Sunni with Iraq and Shi'a with Iran.[16]

For this reason, Shi'i clerics gained significant authority as symbolic figures of the oppressed group under the Ba'thist regime. The 1970s and early 1980s marked the rise of Shi'i opposition through al-Da'wa al-Islāmiya (the Islamic Call) and al-Mujahidin (The Muslim Warriors, as described in Chapter 7).[17]

[12] Lin Noueihed and Tom Perry, "Tunisian Islamists show strength at chief's return," *Reuters*, January 30, 2011, accessed July 17, 2011, http://www.reuters.com/article/2011/01/30/us-tunisia-idUSTRE70J0IG20110130.

[13] Philip Seib, "Islamists Facing Tests," *Huffington Post*, November 8, 2011, accessed July 17, 2011, http://www.huffingtonpost.com/philip-seib/islamists-facing-tests_b_1077794.html.

[14] Significantly, by the late 1970s, Shi'is formed a majority in the Ba'ath Party, but with the "Sunnization" and dominance of the Tikriti clan in positions of power, they were proportionately excluded from the party.

[15] See Chapter 7.

[16] This is also when security forces imprisoned, tortured, and killed Shi'i leader Muhammad Baqir al-Sadr, "the unwilling symbol of Shi'i resistance," and his sister Amina Bint al-Huda, "the daughter of righteousness."

[17] Al-Mujahidin emerged in 1979 following the Iranian revolution. Al-Da'wah al-Islamiyah is an older movement dating to the late 1950s/early 1960s. Hanna Batatu, "Shi'i Organizations

Since Saddam's fall, the strength of the clerical hierarchy and its long experience of underground resistance, as well as the lifting of restrictions on the religious establishment, have allowed Shi'i religious figures to gain significant political power. The reversal of fortune is such that today the Sunni complain that they have become the oppressed group and the victims of retaliation from the Shi'i groups. Discrimination against Sunnis is waged through job loss under the de-Ba'athification measures, which were carried out indiscriminately, specifically in the new security apparatus. Additionally, more than 400 candidates – 60 percent of whom were Sunni – were banned from participating in the 2010 elections. In the worst cases, Sunni communities have faced large-scale detentions and targeted killings by Shi'i death squads, many times in retaliation for violence committed by al-Qa'ida against the Shi'i population. One of the bloodiest waves of reprisal killings of Sunnis (with more than one thousand dead within a few days) occurred in 2006 after the bombing of the Shi'i al-Askari Mosque by al-Qa'ida.[18] In 2012, Sunni politicians from the Iraqiyya party boycotted the parliament after Vice President Tariq al-Hashimi[19] was sentenced to death and other Sunni politicians were arrested. Prime Minister al-Maliki dismissed Sunni Finance Minister Rafie al-Issawi in December 2012. In 2013, three Sunni ministers – Education Minister Mohammed Ali Tamim, Science and Technology Minister Abdulkarim al-Samarraie, and Agriculture Minister Ezzedine al-Dawleh – resigned after violence between Sunni protestors and the Iraqi military.[20]

The cycle of violence between Sunnis and Shi'is seems endless, with each group claiming to be the victim. In this regard, 2013 was particularly bloody. According to the United Nations, in the first seven months of the year at least 4,137 Iraqis were killed, 1,057 of those in July alone, representing the highest levels of violence in the country since 2006.[21]

---

in Iraq: al-Da'wa al-Islamiyah and al-Mujahidin," in Juan Cole and Nikki Keddie (eds.), *Shi'ism and Social Protest* (New Haven, CT: Yale University Press, 1986), 179.

[18] "Discrimination against Sunnis and the Question of Federalism Revived," *Islamopedia*, November 9, 2011, accessed January 1, 2011, http://www.islamopediaonline.org/country-profile/iraq/islam-and-major-political-movements/discrimination-against-sunnis-and-question-.

[19] Tariq al-Hashimi (b.1942) served as the secretary general of the Iraq Islamic Party until 2009 and as vice-president of Iraq in the government formed after the 2005 elections. In December 19, 2011, Iraq's Judicial Council issued an arrest warrant for Hashimi, accused of orchestrating bombing attacks. He fled to Iraqi Kurdistan to avoid arrest. The Central Criminal Court of Iraq convicted him and sentenced him in absentia to death on September 9, 2012.

[20] "Two Iraq Sunni ministers quit after deadly clashes," *Ahram Online*, April 23, 2013, accessed August 9, 2013, http://english.ahram.org.eg/NewsContent/2/8/69990/World/Region/Two-Iraq-Sunni-ministers-quit-after-deadly-clashes.aspx.

[21] "Iraq: July deadliest month in years as violence kills over 1,000 people, UN reports," *UN News Service*, August 1, 2013, accessed August 9, 2013, http://www.un.org/apps/news/story.asp?NewsID=45546#.UgULEGTwLIw.

In contrast to the other countries where Islamic groups were persecuted and oppressed, state policy in Turkey actually helped legitimize the Islamist movement. As mentioned before, the Özal Reforms, which brought economic power to the more religiously conservative Anatolian bourgeoisie, provided Islamists with funds to organize politically. More importantly, "Under Özal's more tolerant approach to religion, Muslim groups and brotherhoods were given greater freedoms and were allowed to finance the construction of private schools and universities."[22] The Özal Reforms opened up economic and social space for Islamists as a political group. Furthermore, the 1961 constitution, while reaffirming the ideology of laicism, granted freedom of the press and expression as well as associational freedom. In this new context, a number of Islamic-oriented parties emerged, the most important being the MNP (National Order Party – 1970),[23] the progenitor of the AKP. According to Ziya Onis, "The religious symbolism associated with political Islam provided the unifying bond that helps to engineer a cross-class alliance, bringing together individuals with markedly different status in society."[24]

In the same vein, after the 1980 coup, the military imposed an agenda of Islamization to consolidate the new regime and constitution of 1982.[25] Under the military's tutelage, religious education was made a compulsory subject in all schools, and state-controlled moral and religious education became part of the curriculum.[26] Consequentially, social norms were based on the new "Turkish-Islamic synthesis" of "the family, the mosque, and the barracks."[27] These Islamization policies helped expand the political space of the Welfare Party (RP), which came to fill the vacuum left by the traditional social democratic parties. The Justice and Development Party's (AKP) moderate, nonconfrontational rhetoric therefore became attractive to a diverse array of voters ranging from Islamists to rural nationalists and moderate urban voters.[28] Additionally, the AKP appealed to middle- and working-class voters unsatisfied with the economic plans of the outgoing government.[29] From 1997 to 2001, economic crisis and social discontent extended the

---

[22] Angel Rabasa and F. Stephen Larrabee, *The Rise of Political Islam in Turkey* (RAND National Defense Research Institute, 2008,) 39.

[23] The MNP would later be banned in 1971 during the military coup and reemerge as the National Salvation Party (MSP) in 1972.

[24] Ziya Öniş. "The political economy of Islamic resurgence in Turkey: The rise of the Welfare Party in perspective," *Third World Quarterly* 18.4 (1997): 743–66, http://www.jstor.org/stable/3993215, p. 748.

[25] Ibid., 750.

[26] Rabasa and Larrabee, *The Rise of Political Islam in Turkey*, 37.

[27] Ibid.

[28] Soner Cagaptay. "The November 2002 Elections and Turkey's New Political Era," *Middle East Review of International Affairs* 6.4 (December 2002): 42–8, http://meria.idc.ac.il/JOURNAL/2002/issue4/cagaptay.pdf, p. 42.

[29] Ibid.

political support of diverse segments of Turkish society for the AKP, which has since become the dominant party.[30] In other words, whereas in countries such as Egypt and Tunisia, the Islamists were oppressed, in Turkey, state policies allowed the rise of an independent economic elite that was Islamically oriented, and which later became the social basis of the AKP party.

Since 2012, however, the popularity of the AKP has started to decline due to conjunction of economic stagnation, presidentialization of the regime, and consequences of the Syrian crisis on Turkey's international role. It is worth keeping in mind, however, that this alteration of popularity does not mean the end of Erdogan regime in particular or the AKP as a whole. While a Pew poll found a 62 percent approval rating for the prime minister in June 2013, MetroPOLL data indicate that the AKP's popularity dropped to a two-year low of 35 percent in June 2013 before rebounding to 42 percent in July.[31] Additionally, a 2012 Gallup polling indicates that dissatisfaction with the AKP goes back further than the Taksim protests; 48 percent of respondents approved of the job done by the leadership of the country, compared to 57 percent the year before.[32] As mentioned in Chapter 7, the Taksim Square protests undeniably affected Erdogan's popularity and will probably lead to changes in the AKP's strategy, most notably the Kurdish peace process and the plans for a presidential system.[33]

MOBILIZATION SKILLS PRE– AND POST–ARAB SPRING

Social mobilization skills have with no doubts, facilitated Islamists' appeal to a large sector of society. As stated by Kai Hafez, "Islamic fundamentalism's greatest attribute is probably its social multifunctionality."[34]

---

[30] After the "February 28 process" ousting the Welfare Party from power in 1997, a schism occurred within the once-unified Milli Görüş – Islamist opposition; one side was supported the old guard or "the traditionalists" (*Gelenekçiler*) under Erbakan, while the other side was constituted by the young guard or "the modernists"/ "the reformists" (*Yenilikçiler*) led by Recep Tayyip Erdoğan, who was at the time the mayor of Istanbul. However, before the Islamist movement officially split, the Virtue Party (FP) succeeded Welfare until again, the Constitutional Court dissolved it in 2001. The traditionalists created the Felicity Party (SP) while the modernists founded the Justice and Development party (AKP).

[31] "Erdogan's Popularity Topline," Pew Research Service, June 5, 2013, accessed August 9, 2013, http://www.pewglobal.org/2013/06/05/erdogan-favorability-topline/. Onur Ant, "Erdogan Facing Elections Can't Count on Basci Aid: Turkey Credit," Bloomberg, July 17, 2013, accessed August 9, 2013, http://www.bloomberg.com/news/2013-07-16/erdogan-facing-elections-can-t-count-on-basci-aid-turkey-credit.html.

[32] Nathan Wendt, "Turks Grew Discontent With Leaders, Freedom Before Unrest," Gallup, June 14, 2013, accessed August 9, 2013, http://www.gallup.com/poll/163061/turks-grew-discontent-leaders-freedom-unrest.aspx.

[33] See Ayesha Chugh and Katherine Krueger, "Constitutional Reform in Turkey."

[34] Kai Hafez, *Radicalism and Political Reform in the Islamic and Western Worlds* (New York: Cambridge University Press, 2010), 112.

Social mobilization translates in the capacity for a group to rally members or sympathizers through different means including communication, personal and group connections, and various forms of social actions. Therefore, the ramifications of multiple social networks facilitate political mobilization. In these conditions, the influence of Islamists came primarily from their capacity to operate as a social movement at the grassroots level, providing social services of all sorts.[35] In this regard, its perspective has always been larger and more inclusive than partisan politics. It also explains why the estimates of the Brotherhood membership varied between 600 and 100,000, prior to the January 2011 revolution.[36] Unlike secular or liberal political groups, the Muslim Brothers (and most Islamists in general) have privileged grounded interactions in neighborhoods, cities, and villages and usually have not discriminated in their services to the population on ideological or even religious grounds.[37] This amorphous and diffuse network was a decisive element in the political success of Islamists after the 2011 revolutions. During the 2011 parliamentary elections in Egypt, the Brotherhood demonstrated that it could channel its social capital into partisan politics, with its Freedom and Justice Party garnering 49 percent of the vote. Similarly, the Brotherhood made use of its networks in the presidential campaign, and its candidate Mohamed Morsi won the elections even though he was expected to come fourth or fifth in the race according to various Egyptian opinion polls.[38] Mosques that were an instrument for political resistance under authoritarian regimes became another asset for political mobilization after the Arab Spring. In both Egypt and Tunisia, a major complaint was raised during the 2011 and 2012 elections by the other political actors against the use of mosques by Islamists for political ends. For example, Salafis complained that Ennahda attempted to advertise in the mosques for their party during the 2011 parliamentary elections.[39] In Egypt, the FJP's rival in the presidential race, Ahmad Shafiq, accused the Brothers of waging a "black campaign," using mosques to endorse Mohamed Morsi and tarnish the image of the other candidates. He claimed that on one Friday, 80 percent of the mosques in Egypt attacked him and

[35] Richard P. Mitchell, *The Society of the Muslim Brothers* (London: Oxford University Press, 1969), 163–80.

[36] Scott Atran, Egypt's bumbling Brothers, *New York Times*, February 2, 2011, http://www.nytimes.com/2011/02/03/opinion/03atran.html?_r=0.

[37] For a study of the Islamist movement in Turkey see Jenny B. White, *Islamist Mobilization in Turkey: A Study in Vernacular Politics* (Seattle: University of Washington Press, 2001). For Egypt see Mohamed Fahmy Menza, *Patronage politics in Egypt: the National Democratic Party and Muslim Brotherhood in Cairo* (London, Routledge Press, 2013).

[38] Sabri Hasanain, "Ishti'al harb istitla'at al-ra'i fi intikhabat ar-ri'asa al-masriyya," *Elaph. com*, accessed May 16, 2012, http://www.elaph.com/Web/news/2012/5/736077.html.

[39] Wiam Melki, "Salafists Take Over Kram Mosque," *Tunisia Live*, October 16, 2011, accessed July 22, 2012, http://www.tunisia-live.net/2011/10/16/salafist-taking-over-the-area-of-kram/.

urged their congregations to vote for Morsi.[40] Another prominent feature of Islamist movement in Egypt and Tunisia has been its skillful mobilization of voters in rural areas, while more secular parties limited their action to urban zones. In Egypt, the areas of Upper Egypt and governorates like Wadi al-Gedid, Assiut, and Hamdeen Fayoum went to the Brotherhood, while Ahmed Shafiq won the Delta region and Sabbahi[41] won the Mediterranean. It is worth noting that Salafi parties have become the major rivals of the Muslim Brothers in rural areas, as attested by their electoral results during the 2011 parliamentary elections.

In the 2011 parliamentary elections, the Ennahda party won a plurality with 90 of 217 elected seats in the National Assembly – 40 percent of the overall vote – and emerged as the only professional post–Ben Ali political party.[42] Like the FJP, Ennahda won the majority of seats in the least-populated governorates, including Tataouine, Tozeur, and Zaghouan, in addition to winning in Tunisia's three largest cities: Tunis, Sfax, and Sousse.[43] Its strong performance at the polls was in large measure a result of the popularity of its message and its outreach methods. Specifically, while other parties disseminated dense information explaining their platforms, Ennahda's campaign literature gave clear instructions to voters on where to find Ennahda's logo and how to correctly mark their choices on the ballot. This was especially important information for voters with limited literacy, as familiarity with the logo for them would be decisive. Other political parties focused on advertising their campaign, but the myriad of political parties and sudden flow of information and platforms overwhelmed many voters, who could not distinguish among the parties. In comparison, Ennahda realized that advertising would not increase its visibility or effect on voters. Its grassroots, boots-on-the ground method of campaigning by focusing on direct interaction with voters was ultimately more effective.[44]

The Arab Spring uprisings, however, brought new major challenges to the political preeminence of the Islamists. First, they no longer have a monopoly on political mobilization. Neither the Muslim Brotherhood nor Ennahda played a central role in the Tunisian and Tahririan protests that eventually brought down Ben Ali and Hosni Mubarak. Even more significantly, they can

[40] "Muslim Brotherhood Statement 2 in Response to General Shafiq's Allegations, Black Propaganda," *Ikhwan Web*, June 11, 2012, accessed July 22, 2012, http://www.ikhwanweb. com/article.php?id=30084.

[41] Hamdeen Sabahi (b.1954) was an opposition figure to Sadat and Mubarak regimes. He gained his political credibility by being jailed 17 times during their presidencies. He is the leader of the Egyptian Popular Current and co-leader of the National Salvation Front.

[42] See Part II, Chapter 7.

[43] Allan Bradley, "Tunisian Election Results Tables," *Tunisia Live*, October 24, 2011, accessed July 22, 2012, http://www.tunisia-live.net/2011/10/24/tunisian-election-results-tables/.

[44] Erik Churchill, "Tunisia's Electoral Lesson: The Importance of Campaign Strategy," *Carnegie Endowment*, October 27, 2011, accessed July 22, 2012, http://carnegieendowment.org/2011/10/27/tunisia-s-electoral-lesson-importance-of-campaign-strategy/6b7g.

also be the target of mass mobilizations, as evidenced in the June 30, 2013, protests in Egypt or the Taksim demonstrations in Istanbul. Additionally, mobilization for collective action through social media has aged their mobilization style, as we shall discuss in the next section.

More generally, since the Arab Spring, the priority given to professional politics through the creation of political parties and the exercise of power is affecting the social legitimacy of Islamism as a social movement. Case in point: In the student union elections of March 2013, the Brotherhood received 34 percent of the vote, just half of what it received the previous year.[45] Likewise, the Brotherhood's influence within professional unions has declined in the post-Mubarak era, as attested by several conflicts between some unions and the short-lived Morsi government.[46] In brief, it seems that the end of authoritarian regimes has eroded Islamists' political credibility by opening opportunities for new contenders with different styles and strategies of mobilization. Most significantly, their rise to power is altering their previous aura of martyrs and "pure" political actors.

FROM OPPRESSED TO RULERS

Since the 2012 electoral victory of Islamist parties in Egypt and Tunisia, many observers have raised the question of whether this newly acquired political influence will erode their legitimacy in the near future. For example, in Egypt, between the 2011 parliamentary elections and the May 2012 presidential elections, there was a sort of consensus emerging from media coverage and pollings that the first months of power of the Freedom and Justice Party had eroded its popular basis.

The main reason invoked for this loss of popularity was the disappointment created by the FJP in not keeping its promises. In the weeks that followed the removal of President Hosni Mubarak, the FJP said it would contest only about 30 percent of all seats in parliament and that it had no plans to field its own candidate for president. But, as described in Chapter 8, the group went back on both promises.[47] That is when pollings started also to express Morsi's loss of popularity among Egyptians.

---

[45] "Elections from 21 universities: 34% to the Muslim Brothers, 66% to the Independent Union, والمستقلين المدنية للتيارات 66% و» الإخوان»لـ 34% :جامعة 21 في الانتخابات,ا" *Al-Masry Al-Yawm,* March 21, 2013, accessed June 24, 2013, http://www.almasryalyoum.com/node/1583896.

[46] The Center for Trade Union and Workers' Services, for example, blamed the Freedom and Justice Party in May 2012 for the delay of a key law that would determine how trade unions would be formed. "Labor organization accuses FJP of hindering trade union freedoms law," *Al-Masry Al-Youm,* May 30, 2012, accessed June 26, 2013, http://www.egyptindependent. com/news/labor-organization-accuses-fjp-hindering-trade-unions%E2%80%99-freedom-law-nehal-news-1.

[47] Youssef Hamza, "Islamists campaigning hard for Egyptian presidency," *The National,* May 20, 2012, accessed July 22, 2012, http://www.thenational.ae/news/world/ islamists-campaigning-hard-for-egyptian-presidency.

Because these polls are probably not reliable because of problems of sampling and methodology, we present them not as a reliable source of information on the legitimacy of Islamists but only to show that these numbers were actually influential and carried some political weight in justifying the ousting of Mohammed Morsi.

For example, May 2012 Gallup polling indicated a significant decline of favorable opinions toward the FJP and to a certain extent toward the Salafis.[48] At the same period, the findings from the University of Maryland polling on May 4–10 indicated that while the FJP won the largest block in the parliamentary elections, Morsi trailed in last place, garnering only 8 percent support.[49] It is also noteworthy that the majority of respondents, 71 percent, said that the Muslim Brotherhood's decision to field its own presidential candidates was a mistake. Ultimately, these polls were contradicted by the results of the presidential election that gave Morsi the majority of the vote with 51.7 percent (although Shafiq's polling was almost at the same level as Morsi's percent of intended voters, and the latter ended up garnering 48 percent of the suffrage).

Another Gallup polling indicates that the popularity of President Morsi and the FJP plummeted before the governmental overthrow of July 2013. Confidence in the national government dropped from fifty-seven percent in November 2012 (right before Morsi issued his constitutional decree) to 29 percent in June 2013, while the approval rating inverted over the same time period, going from 63 percent approval to 69 percent disapproval. The popularity of the FJP in particular declined from 67 percent to 19 percent over the same time period.[50] Similarly, polling by the Egyptian Center for Public Opinion Research before the June 30 protests indicated widespread dissatisfaction with Morsi's leadership: 64 percent of the Egyptian population believed his performance was worse than expected, while only 8 percent believed it was better than expected.[51] These low approval rates will be instrumental in the justification by opposition figures of the overthrow of Morsi government. Finally, according to a telephone poll conducted by Baseera for Al-Hayat TV network on July 1, 2013, 73 percent of respondents believed President Morsi did not make a single good decision during

---

[48] "Popular support for Egypt's Islamist parties on wane: Gallup poll," *Ahram Online*, May 18, 2012, accessed July 22, 2012, http://english.ahram.org.eg/News/41988.aspx.

[49] Shibley Telhami, "What Do Egyptians Want? Key Findings from the Egyptian Public Opinion Poll," Brookings Institute, May 21, 2012, http://www.brookings.edu/research/reports/2012/05/21-egyptian-election-poll-telhami.

[50] Mohamed Younis, "Egyptians' Views of Government Crashed Before Overthrow," Gallup, August 2, 2013, accessed August 9, 2013, http://www.gallup.com/poll/163796/egyptian-views-government-crashed-overthrow.aspx.

[51] "Egypt opinion polls reveal dissatisfaction with Morsi," *Ahram Online*, July 2, 2013, accessed August 18, 2013, http://english.ahram.org.eg/NewsContent/1/64/75491/Egypt/Politics-/Egypt-opinion-polls-reveal-dissatisfaction-with-Mo.aspx.

his first year in office, while 63 percent believed their standard of living had worsened.[52] It is worth noting that the drop of opinion in favor of the Muslim Brotherhood has not, however, been accompanied by a significant transfer of support to secular forces. In the same poll, no party or political movement engendered more than 29 percent confidence except the Nour Party. Moreover, only 60 percent of Egyptians could name interim President Adly Mansour, and only 30 percent could name interim Prime Minister Hassem el-Beblawy.[53]

Besides the reliability of polling, there is no doubt that Morsi lost credibility and popularity, as attested by the massive protests of June 2013 in Cairo. The loss of credibility was related to the lack of governance skills, while the decline of popularity was caused by Morsi's inadequate responses to the population's demands.

The FJP's methods of governing in 2012 and 2013 alienated and frustrated all other political groups from "secular" to Salafis. First, the drafting and adoption of the constitution by an assembly dominated by Islamists was a major reason for the growing suspicion of political protagonists. For example, as early as October 2012, a coalition of opposition groups demanded a new Constituent Assembly to fulfill the revolution in terms of economic opportunity and national unity.[54] The constitution was under question for its Islamist leaning, especially concerning women's rights and freedom of expression. The government was further criticized for its attempts to silence secularist-driven protests against the new constitution in October 2012.[55] In the same vein, the FJP and Morsi faced a number of protests and disapproval from the diverse opposition groups because of what was called the "Brotherization" of Egyptian politics (see Chapter 8).

At the same time, popular opposition to Morsi has grown steadily throughout 2012 and 2013. At the time of the commemoration of the second anniversary of the January 2011 revolution, political instability and turmoil erupted in the streets against the Morsi government, showing the frustration of many segments of the Egyptian population. At an October 19, 2012, march, thousands of Egyptians protested in Tahrir Square against Morsi for "recreating Mubarak's old regime" through an unrepresentative constitution. Smaller pro-government rallies took place at the same time,

---

[52] Ibid.

[53] "Poll: 40% do not know interim president, 70% do not know PM," *Egypt Independent*, July 23, 2013, accessed August 5, 2013, http://www.egyptindependent.com/news/poll-40-do-not-know-interim-president-70-do-not-know-pm.

[54] "Opposition groups launch initiative demanding new Constituent Assembly," *Ahram Online*, October 24, 2012, accessed October 24, 2012, http://english.ahram.org.eg/NewsContent/1/64/56400/Egypt/Politics-/Opposition-groups-launch-initiative-demanding-new-.aspx.

[55] Issandr el Amrani, "When protest serves power," *International Herald Tribune*, October 23, 2012, accessed January 28, 2013, http://latitude.blogs.nytimes.com/2012/10/23/a-first-protest-against-the-muslim-brotherhood-consecrates-its-hold-on-power/.

leading to street fights and leaving 100 injured.[56] On January 25 and 26, 2013, riots erupted in several cities. More than forty people were killed and hundreds were injured throughout Cairo, Alexandria, Beheira, Luxor, Kafr el-Sheikh, Gharbia, Sharqia, Ismailia, and Suez, leading President Morsi to declare a state of emergency on January 28, 2013, and to call the opposition to a national dialogue.[57]

In April 2013, a movement called Tamarod ("rebellion") began gathering signatures for a petition condemning President Morsi and calling for early presidential elections. In June 2013, Tamarod released a statement claiming it had obtained 22 million signatures. A countermovement, Tagarod ("impartiality"), claimed to have collected 13 million signatures in favor of President Morsi.[58] Morsi's appointment of Adel el-Khayat, a controversial founding member of al-Gamaʿa al-Islamiyya, to the governorship of Luxor added to tensions, and violent protests against el-Khayat forced him to resign in June 2013.[59] The culmination of the protests was reached on June 30, 2013, when several millions took to the streets to express their discontent with the regime.[60] That is when, to counter the political chaos, the Egyptian armed forces issued a televised statement on July 1, 2013, announcing that Egyptian political forces had forty-eight hours to "fulfil the people's demands"; otherwise the army would take action to include all political currents.[61] At the end of the political ultimatum, the army announced the removal of President Morsi and the nomination of the head of the High Constitutional Court, Adly Mansour, as the interim president until new parliamentary and presidential

[56] Salma Shukrallah, "Thousands in Tahrir on Friday demand an 'Egypt for all Egyptians,'" *Ahram Online*, Oct. 19, 2012, accessed October 24, 2012, http://english.ahram.org.eg/NewsContent/1/64/56030/Egypt/Politics-/Thousands-in-Tahrir-demand-an-Egypt-for-all-Egypti.aspx.

[57] Ironically, a few days before the riot, a poll released January 13, 2013, by an independent Egyptian polling agency, Baseera, revealed that Morsi's popularity might be salvageable. It indicated that Morsi's approval rating in the sixth month of his term went up to 63 percent from 57 percent in the prior month. However, his overall rating was still well below his 78 percent approval rating during his first few months of presidency. "Two days of protests and violence leave Egypt on the edge," *Al Ahram Online*, January 26, 2013, accessed January 28, 2013, http://english.ahram.org.eg/NewsContent/1/64/63378/Egypt/Politics-/Two-days-of-protests-and-violence-leave-Egypt-on-e.aspx.

[58] "Further competition between Tamarod and Tagarod," *Daily News Egypt*, June 22, 2013, accessed June 24, 2013, http://www.dailynewsegypt.com/2013/06/22/further-competition-between-tamarod-and-tagarod/.

[59] "Islamist Egyptian governor of Luxor resigns," *Al-Arabiyya*, June 23, 2013, accessed June 24, 2013, http://english.alarabiya.net/en/News/middle-east/2013/06/23/Egypt-s-hardline-Islamist-to-resign-as-Luxor-governor.html.

[60] "Will Egypt Have Its Second Revolution on June 30?" *Al-Monitor*, June 9, 2013, accessed June 24, 2013, http://www.al-monitor.com/pulse/originals/2013/06/egypt-second-revolution-morsi-anniversary.html.

[61] "Egypt military gives political forces 48 hours to resolve crisis," *Al Ahram*, accessed July 1, 2013, http://english.ahram.org.eg/NewsContent/1/64/75415/Egypt/Politics-/Egypt-military-gives-political-forces--hours-to-re.aspx.

elections.[62] After the government turnover of July 2013, the army initiated a crackdown on Islamist leaders and Muslim Brotherhood officials, including former President Mohamed Morsi. Among those arrested were Brotherhood leader Mohammed Badie (along with eight other senior Brotherhood members) and al-Wasat Party leaders Abul-Ela Madi and Essam Soltan. Egyptian prosecutors decided in August 2013 to investigate charges of espionage and murder against Morsi. The dispersal on August 14, 2013, of the Muslim Brotherhood's sit-in by the army led to more than 500 deaths and several thousand injured, and raised international outcry.[63]

Similarly, Ennahda's popularity has declined since the Tunisian Jasmine Revolution as well. Polling in May 2013 (before the political crisis of July and August of 2013) indicated that it would lose an election to its secular opponent, Nidaa Tunis. The same poll showed that more than 70 percent of Tunisians were dissatisfied with the ruling coalition, led by Ennahda.[64] According to another poll, conducted in August by Zogby Research Services, among 3,031 Tunisians, only 26 percent of the interviewees expressed support to Ennahda while two-thirds of Tunisians believe their country is moving in the wrong direction.[65] The lengthy process of drafting a constitution, the perceived neglect of secular interests, and the killing of opposition leaders Mohammed Brahmi and Chokri Belaid fueled popular anger that reached a high point in early August, with tens of thousands of protestors taking to the streets and calling for the government's resignation. As a consequence, the National Constituent Assembly was suspended in July 2013. At the same time, Ettakatol threatened to withdraw from the government if Ennahda did not dialogue with opposition parties and create a more technocratic government. In an attempt to solve the crisis, the ruling party agreed to resign on September 28, 2013.[66] After protracted negotiations and protests, a technocratic government was formed on December 14, 2013, with

[62] "Egypt New Interim President: Judge Adly Mansour," http://english.ahram.org.eg/ NewsContent/1/64/75638/Egypt/Politics-/Egypts-new-interim-president-Judge-Adly-Mansour.aspx, accessed July 3, 2013.

[63] For example, U.S. President Barack Obama cancelled a joint military exercise between the two countries. The United Nations called for the violence to end, although its rebuke was not official and reflected divisions among the Security Council over how to respond to the crisis. Among Islamic countries, Turkey termed the events a "massacre." "Reactions to Egyptian Crackdown on Pro-Morsi Camps," *Associated Press*, August 15, 2013, accessed August 15, 2013, http://abcnews.go.com/International/wireStory/ reactions-egyptian-crackdown-pro-morsi-camps-19966083.

[64] "Tunisia Poll Shows Nidaa Tunis More Popular Than Ennahda," *Al-Monitor*, May 15, 2013, http://www.al-monitor.com/pulse/politics/2013/05/tunisian-poll-ennahda-popularity-declines-nidaa-tunis.html.

[65] "Tunisians lose faith in Ennahda, Revolution, *Al-Monitor*, October 1 2013, accessed October 1 2013, http://www.al-monitor.com/pulse/originals/2013/09/ennahda-tunisia-resign-missteps-revolution.html?utm_source=&utm_medium=email&utm_campaign=8280# ixzz2gUBt7rMP.

[66] "Tunisia crisis: Tens of thousands join protest," *BBC News*, August 6, 2013, accessed August 9, 2013, http://www.bbc.co.uk/news/world-africa-23597308. "Tunisians ruling islamists

the controversial appointment of Mehdi Jomaa (minister of industry under the Layaradeh government) as prime minister.

Ultimately, the question can be raised of the competency of political actors who have never been in charge before. In this regard, several elements have contributed to the FJP's political failure.

WHY DID MORSI FAIL?

First, there is the difficulty of addressing new forms of protest and political communication through social media, which has become the privileged channel of politics for urbanized youths. The April 6 Youth Movement clearly illustrates this new trend, as it has gained real political weight since the revolution and has played a central role in protesting against the SCAF. Politically unaffiliated youths also play a role in enforcing government accountability, maintaining an online "Morsi Meter" (http://www.morsimeter.com/) that tracked Morsi's fulfillment of promises made to the Egyptian people. They have been decisive actors in the coordination of the massive protests of June 30, 2013, and the subsequent ousting of President Morsi. Generally speaking, the Arab Spring revolts have been sparked by a new category of activists: "citizen journalists" who utilize social media to share their political experience as a powerful mobilization tool.[67] Wael Ghonim, the Google executive who started a Facebook page calling attention to the death of businessman Khalid Said (who would be later used in strategizing and planning the January demonstrations), dubbed the happenings "Revolution 2.0." Additionally, twenty-five-year-old blogger Asmaa Mahfouz posted a video of her impassioned call to Egyptians to join protests at Tahrir Square on January 25 (National Police Day) that went viral and thus attracted significant attention to the cause. More recent protests in Egypt have been at least partially organized online by "netizens," who used Facebook pages to coordinate marches.[68] There is no reason to think this form of political mobilization will disappear anytime soon. In Tunisia, Facebook is the number one source of news. Fifty-two percent of the population lists Facebook among their top three news sources, more than any other outlet. The largest users of Facebook for news purposes are younger people, who use it for information on current events.[69]

agree to stand down," *BBC News*, September 28, 2013, accessed October 1, 2013, http://www.bbc.co.uk/news/world-asia-2431519228 September 2013.

[67] See Nadia Idle and Alex Nunns, eds., *Tweets from Tahrir: Egypt's Revolution as It Unfolds, in the Words of the People Who Made It* (New York: OR Books, 2011).

[68] Jeffrey Fleishman, "Egypt protestors put their wills on Twitter, Facebook," *Los Angeles Times*, October 18, 2011, accessed October 19, 2011, http://articles.latimes.com/2011/oct/18/world/la-fg-egypt-twitter-wills-20111019.

[69] Media Use in the Middle East: an Eight-Nation Survey," *Northwestern University in Qatar*, June 2013, accessed June 26, 2013, http://qatar-news.northwestern.edu/wp-content/uploads/6 -18 -13-MenaMediaUse_Regional-AR.pdf.

It provides a critical voice regarding more traditional media forms including television and newspapers; as a Tunisian pollster noted, "Social media is very aware ... Pressure comes from social media when there is something [untrue expressed on the radio or television]."[70]

This is not to say, however, that this new kind of activism reflects the views of the whole country. Actually rural areas remain in the pre-digital age and are therefore still very much influenced by the grass-root activism of Islamists (as attested by the election results of 2011 and 2012). But this urbanized style of protest has more political impact both nationally and internationally. In this regard, Morsi's governance has dramatically highlighted the growing gap between the senior leaders of the Muslim Brotherhood and the cultural style of the vast majority of the young urbanized population. Not only he did not address the Tahrir protesters' calls for social justice and equality, he did not even speak their language. The FJP maintained the hierarchical and secretive culture that suited an underground movement but was deemed undemocratic in the post-2011 revolutionary context. For this reason, the FJP's failure will require a rethinking of the Muslim Brotherhood's strategy, leadership, and communication if they want to keep in touch with the "Facebook" generation.

In other words, new modes of social protest and political communication are emerging that are rapidly making the Muslim Brothers' methods "dépassé." The April 6 movement and the Tamarud campaign are exemplary of a new political genre of mass mobilization through the mediation of social media. To a certain extent, they appear as the Facebook version of the *sans-culottes*, the urban movement made of disparate components of the Parisian working class that initiated mass protests in different phases of the French Revolution.[71] Because they could not offer any clear political vision or visible leader, more professional political actors ultimately instrumentalized their revolts and aspirations in a strikingly similar way to what happened to the Tahririans, both in January 2011 and in June 30, 2013.

The second reason for the FJP's failure is its inability to improve the economic situation of the country. In this regard, the incompetence of the new rulers was reflected in Egypt's economic woes: it has experienced at least sixteen credit downgrades between the revolution and May 2013.[72] The country's foreign reserves are only large enough to cover around three months of

[70] Tunisians Find Facebook Number One Source of News, Says New Study," *Tunisia Live*, June 20, 2013, accessed June 24, 2013, http://www.tunisia-live.net/2013/06/20/tunisians-find-facebook-number-one-source-of-news-says-new-stud/.

[71] Eric Hobsbawm, *The Age of Revolution* (London: Weidenfeld & Nicolson, 1962).

[72] "Only Politics Can Save Egypt's Economy," *Al-Monitor*, June 13, 2013, accessed June 24, 2013, http://www.al-monitor.com/pulse/originals/2013/06/egypt-economy-political-crisis-stagnant.html.

borrowing.[73] Egypt's forecasted growth rate is just 2 percent, and the country faces power outages, rising prices, fuel shortages, and inflation.[74] The Morsi government showed little evidence of a functional plan to solve these problems – the Muslim Brotherhood spearheaded the so-called Renaissance Project (*al-Naḥḍa*), which aimed to cut unemployment and create opportunities for greater production, but it led to very few true reforms.[75] The IMF loan sought by the Morsi government remained unrealized.

Adding to the unpopularity of the Morsi regime was the rise of criminality and the return to political violence (see Chapter 8). According to the Interior Ministry, homicide rates tripled and reported armed robberies grew by a factor of ten between 211 and 2013.[76]

In sum, Morsi lost his popularity because of his inability to provide economic and social solutions that would have assuaged the demands that led to the ousting of Hosni Mubarak in the first place. The popular protests against Morsi in June 2013 were an attack not on his Islamic politics but on his failure to efficiently provide better social and economic conditions. Even worse, during his short reign, conditions deteriorated dramatically.

Morsi's major mistake was to focus on identity politics – his rush to adopt a new constitution, his insistence on the Islamic character of Egyptian society, his repression of freedom of speech in the name of Islam – while these identity politics were not the population's major expectation or desire. As a consequence, this strategy provided leverage and justification to the military and state elites for removing him from power, taking advantage of the popular protests to phrase the discontent as a reaction to the Islamicization of the Egyptian state. Such an argument was of course very "reasonable" in the eyes of the Western powers.[77]

---

[73] "Foreign currency reserves rise to US$16 billion in May," *Egypt Independent*, June 7, 2013, accessed June 24, 2013, http://www.egyptindependent.com/news/foreign-currency-reserves-rise-us16-billion-may.

[74] Bessem Sabry, "Only Politics Can Save Egypt's Economy," *Al Monitor*, June 13, 2013, http://www.al-monitor.com/pulse/originals/2013/06/egypt-economy-political-crisis-stagnant.html#.

[75] "Egypt's Long-Term Economic Recovery Plan Stalls," *New York Times*, May 2, 2013, accessed June 26, 2013, http://www.nytimes.com/2013/05/02/world/middleeast/02iht-m02-egypt-renaissance.html.

[76] "Crime rates in post-revolutionary Egypt soar amid security woes," *Al-Arabiya*, May 4, 2013, accessed August 9, 2013, http://english.alarabiya.net/en/News/middle-east/2013/05/04/Crime-rate-soars-in-post-revolutionary-Egypt-amid-security-woes.html.

[77] This acceptance of the military coup started to falter when the army cracked down on Islamists and multiplied arrests. European Union foreign policy chief Catherine Ashton released a statement that she was "following with concern the latest developments in Egypt and deeply deplores the loss of life during [the] demonstrations ... [she] calls on all actors to refrain from violence and to respect the principles of peaceful protest and non-violence." "EU's Ashton 'deeply deplores' deaths in Egypt protests," *Deutsche Welle*, July 27, 2013, accessed August 9, 2013, http://www.dw.de/eus-ashton-deeply-deplores-deaths-in-egypt-protests/a-16979554.

To conclude, although it is too early to draw any definitive conclusion on the future of the Muslim Brothers in Egypt, it is also premature to assume its death in the current Egyptian context. Doing so would be limiting Islamism to the Freedom and Justice Party, which was not even created until after the 2011 revolution. As described in Chapter 8, Islamism is first and foremost a social movement. In the past four decades, Egyptian society has been the Muslim Brothers' major field of action, as they built networks, civil society, and social programs. In this regard, their perspective has always been larger and more inclusive than factional politics. This is likely why, when the FJP was created, some members of the movement were adamant about not putting all their resources in one basket. As they rightly assumed, a social movement often loses its holistic approach once it enters electoral competition.

Germany's Foreign Minister Guido Westerwelle called for restraint and a "fresh democratic start in the country," while French Foreign Minister Laurent Fabius called for Morsi to be released. "German foreign minister Westerwelle calls for restraint in Egypt as protests continue," *Deutsche Welle*, August 1, 2013, accessed August 9, 2013, http://www.dw.de/german-foreign-minister-westerwelle-calls-for-restraint-in-egypt-as-protests-continue/a-16991415. "French foreign minister calls on Egypt to release Morsi," *France 24*, July 30, 2013, accessed August 9, 2013, http://www.france24.com/en/20130730-eus-ashton-meets-morsi-amid-renewed-cairo-protests.

Conclusion of Part II

How Can Islamism Remain a Significant Political Force after the Arab Spring?

Our overview of the political influence of Islamism seems to indicate that its political centrality was closely related to the authoritarian nature of the state. First, religious places were the only free spaces, facilitating the politicization of religious settings, functions, and discourses. Second, the framework of the nation-state obliged most Islamists to "nationalize" their political agenda. Third, repression by state rulers provided Islamists with an aura of authenticity that no other opponents could claim.

Interestingly, our case studies show that when political systems become more open, the success or failure of Islamists is not directly related to their Islamic politics. The comparison between Tunisia, Egypt, and Turkey shed light on two intertwined reasons for the role of political Islam in the democratization phase: on one hand, the marginalization or subversion of the authoritarian state system and on the other hand, the grounding of Islamism across different social groups.

In order to understand why these factors come into play, it is necessary to underline that there are three major ways to finish a revolution: destroy the previous regime and rebuild from scratch, marginalize the major actors of the ancien régime, or subvert the ancien régime from within. Given the specifics of our case studies, only the first two ways will be discussed.[1]

---

[1] The third way characterizes the Indonesian transition to democracy that began in 1998 with the fall of authoritarian president Suharto. The democratizing push after the fall of Suharto has not been accompanied by a bureaucratic turnover. Rather, the philosophy of the reform has been gradualism, a series of smaller democratic changes instead of the wholesale removal of bureaucrats. See Vedi R. Hadiz, "Reorganizing Political Power in Indonesia: A Reconsideration of So-Called 'Democratic Transitions'," *The Pacific Review* 16:4 (2003), 591–611 and Ross H. Mcleod, "The Struggle to Regain Effective Government under Democracy in Indonesia," *Bulletin of Indonesian Economic Studies* 41:3 (2005).

For this reason, civic turnover has been slow and the bureaucracy retains administrators left over (or left in power) from before the 1998 transition. The result is "interdepartmental rivalries, overlapping sectoral authorities, and high bureaucratic fragmentation" that impede Indonesia's continued democratic progress. Christian von Luebke, "Post-Suharto Indonesia,"

As in the French revolution, the *tabula rasa* method was used during the Islamic revolution in Iran. This meant removing the old hierarchies in the administration, repressing or executing the top leaders of the bureaucracy and army, and replacing the old rules with new ones influenced by Islamic principles. The end of the Saddam regime also opened a *tabula rasa* of some sort. But unlike Iran, the destruction of the old system, or rather its collapse, was not followed by a systematic replacement of old authorities by new personnel and new rules, resulting instead in a continuous cycle of retaliation between

Stanford Program on International and Cross-Cultural Education, Fall 2009, accessed July 26, 2013, http://iis-db.stanford.edu/docs/381/Post-Suharto.pdf.

Indeed, "only the top layer of the bureaucracy has been replaced [and] many state officials have not embraced the new procedures and standards that accompany decentralisation and democratic reform." Hans Antlöv, Derick W. Brinkerhoff, and Elke Rapp, "Civil Society Organizations and Democratic Reform: Progress, Capacities, and Challenges in Indonesia," *37th Annual Conference, Association for Research on Nonprofit Organizations and Voluntary Action,* November 2008, http://www.rti.org/pubs/antlov_csos_in_indo_arnova. pdf. Indonesia's transition process is therefore interesting because structural democratization has not been accompanied by a personnel turnover, leaving much of the *ancien régime* in place, only governed by different rules. The result is that the officials of the old bureaucracy accepted reform not on altruistic bases but for strategic reasons: as Hadiz notes, "old interests and such uncivil forces as local bosses and political gangsters may reinvent themselves and appropriate the democratization process, and thereby exercise predatory power through money politics and political thuggery" Hadiz, 2003.

The impact of the democratic transition on the military has been complicated and somewhat controversial. On the one hand, the military has been completely removed from the formal political process and its power over civilian forms of government has diminished. On the other, the military remains a key player in local politics (due to its territorial structuring) and it continues to finance itself. See Marcus Mietzner, "The Politics of Military Reform in Post-Suharto Indonesia: Elite Conflict, Nationalism, and Institutional Resistance," *East–West Center Policy Studies* 23 (2006), accessed May 13, 2013, http://scholarspace.manoa.hawaii. edu/bitstream/handle/10125/3497/PS023.pdf?. The transition has largely left untouched the military's day-to-day functioning, with Ross Mcleod arguing that "in practical terms the army remains as strong as ever – indeed, it is arguably even stronger, now that Soeharto is not there to keep it under control" Mcleod, 2005. This strength may explain why the army has accepted democratization – although it stood to lose formal influence, it was also able to parlay its new role into consolidated local powers.

Siddharth Chandra and Douglas Kammen hypothesize another possible reason that the military went along with reform; specifically, that due to the internal dynamics of the military, there was a differential incentive for younger officers to support reform, as it would aid their career prospects. Siddharth Chandra and Douglas Kammen, "Generating Reforms and Reforming Generations: Military Politics in Indonesia's Democratic Transition and Consolidation," *World Politics* 55.1 (October 2002), 96–136. Divisions within the military have thus benefited the processes of democratization. However, as with the bureaucracy, there is a lingering Suharto-influenced culture in the military, exemplified by "the military doctrines, which are premised on the assumption that the armed forces are not an instrument of the state but the guardian of the regime, [and which] are still in use ... and cannot be expected to be amenable to the principles of civilian supremacy." Baladas Ghoshal, "Democratic Transition and Political Development in Post-Soeharto Indonesia," *Contemporary Southeast Asia* 26.3 (December 2004), 506–29.

the members of the old and the new regime, who happened to be from different religious sects, as we discussed in Chapters 8 and 9.

The second way, building alliances against the *ancien régime* and marginalizing it, was successfully implemented in Turkey. The bureaucracy and the military have traditionally possessed a tremendous amount of political power. However, the rise of the Justice and Development Party (AKP) led to alliances between historically marginalized forces in Turkey (including devout Muslims, liberals, and socialists), alliances that changed the balance of power at the expense of the Kemalist bureaucracy. Among the reforms implemented by the AKP were increased state control over independent regulatory agencies[2] and constitutional amendments such as the overhaul of the system of judicial appointments. These changes have attracted broad-based support, to the extent that "virtually all of the actors in Turkish politics [approve] of the reconfiguration of domestic power away from the bureaucracy."[3] An important part of the marginalization of the *ancien régime* in Turkey was thus the creation of a coalition around reform that undermines the bureaucracy's ingrained power. Additionally, these changes have been facilitated by Turkey's efforts to join the EU, which translated into "reforms that made the bureaucratic control of politics more and more difficult."[4]

As part of the extensive Turkish bureaucracy, the military has been similarly marginalized, losing some of its traditional power over Turkish political life. Military suspicions of the AKP's rule, ingrained in the Kemalist distrust of Islamic forces, came to a head in 2007 after Prime Minister Recep Tayyip Erdogan nominated Abdullah Gül to the presidency. Concern over growing Islamization led the military to declare, "If necessary, the Turkish Armed Forces will not hesitate to make their position and stance abundantly clear as the absolute defenders of secularism."[5] It then seemed that the military was poised to remove the country's rulers, as it had in the past. However, no coup materialized. The government built upon this inaction by prosecuting top military officials in the Ergenekon cases, bringing military spending under the aegis of the High Council of Auditors and centralizing military power under the control of Ministry of Defense. The result was the rapid decline of the military's political influence. Necati Polat states that for "all practical purposes, the army seems to have been forced out of the equation in Turkish politics."[6]

---

[2] Isik Ozel, "The Politics of De-Delegation: Regulatory (In)dependence in Turkey," *Regulation and Governance* 6.1 (March 2012), 119–129.

[3] Necati Polat, "Regime Change in Turkey," *International Politics*, 50 (2013): 440.

[4] Polat, "Regime Change in Turkey," 447.

[5] Ömer Taşpınar, "Turkey: The New Model?," *Brookings Institution*, April 2012, accessed August 19, 2013, http://www.brookings.edu/research/papers/2012/04/24-turkey-new-model-taspinar.

[6] Polat, "Regime Change in Turkey," 443.

In sum, the rise of the AKP combined with Europeanization and a coalition supporting reform – including liberals, intellectuals, and the AKP's core demographic of devout Muslims – has resulted in the demise of the traditional bureaucratic hegemony.

If we turn to Tunisia and Egypt, neither Ennahda nor the FJP attempted a *tabula rasa* strategy like in Iran. They also have been unable to marginalize the *ancien régime* like the AKP did. As discussed in Chapters 8 and 9, the FJP's inability to build alliances with diverse political forces is undeniably part of its failure. Although Ennahda had more success in building coalition, it has not translated into a significant level of political trust. The reason lies in the fact that this coalition is not grounded in a large social basis. In other words, a broad socio-economic basis is not supporting the Ennahada regime and did not support the Morsi regime either. This means that not only the state elite but also important segments of the middle class have resisted Islamist policies. Here again, the contrast with Turkey is striking. As described in Chapters 7 and 8, Ozul's neoliberal reforms created opportunities for the economic development of provinces, resulting in the commercial prosperity of Anatolian entrepreneurs, also known as the "Anatolian Tigers." When they moved to urban centers, they provided a stable funding base for the AKP and established a new business elite that is pious religiously, conservative socially, and financially strong in the heart of urban Turkey.

In contrast, the exodus of the rural population to major urban centers in Egypt did not translate into economic improvement, but actually resulted in a greater deterioration of the material conditions of the population. The economic development of the Tunisian society was different: Ben Ali's policies contributed to the growth of a significant urban middle class but unlike the Turkish one, it was financially dependent on the state and therefore "loyal" to it. This means that in the post–Ben Ali transition, this middle class has not been a major supporter of the Ennahda regime, and it has expressed mounting discontent about the rapid deterioration of its material condition since the Jasmine Revolution. In sum, "the supporters of the Brotherhood are the poor who stand to lose a great deal; supporters of the Turkish Islamists are the entrepreneurs who believe that their time has come."[7]

The third crucial difference between the Turkish experience and the Egyptian and Tunisian ones concerns the influence of the army on the national economy. The army's power in Turkey began to shrink as the economy grew on the backs of new industries, practices, and entrepreneurs. This deprived the Turkish armed forces of a key lever. The Egyptian military, on the other hand, took the lead in liberalization and economic change and succeeded in building strong and thriving business interests. They retain both economic

[7] Bernard Siman, "The Islamist Government Experiments in Egypt and Turkey," *World Review*, July 30, 2013, accessed August 7, 2013, http://www.worldreview.info/content/islamist-government-experiments-turkey-and-egypt.

and political powers that give them the ability to intervene decisively and effectively when Egypt's stability – or their interests – are threatened.

In these conditions, the real reason for Morsi's ousting is that the army has been in charge all along, playing the role of tutelary authority over the political experiment that was the FJP government. It is helpful to recall that the 2011 protests in Tahrir Square did not, on their own, bring down Mubarak. It is only because the army abandoned the president that the Mubarak regime could collapse. Additionally, the army only accepted the FJP government once it was assured that the FJP would not interfere with the security and foreign policy of the country, which remain army prerogatives. It has even been argued that the military entered a phase of passive resistance against the Morsi regime, contributing to the paralysis of the major state institutions. As Freedom House's Nancy Okail wrote earlier this year, "Although Mubarak was toppled, the institutional structure of his regime is still very much in place, with the same mentality, organizational culture, and approach to silencing dissent, including through crackdowns on civil society."[8] Intriguingly, the frequent power blackouts that plagued Egyptians' life in the last months of the Morsi regime "miraculously" stopped after June 30th.

What pushed the military back into the forefront of politics was the rise of social and political frustrations and the subsequent increase in social unrest. As with 2011, the army is calling the shots. The claim of the June 30 protesters that they were in charge is naïve. The reality is that the military leaders have used the protests against Morsi to their benefit, as they did in 2011 with the protests against Mubarak. This does not mean that they want to be in the political spotlight, however. Like any praetorian regime, the army's preference is to lead from the backseat, but to lead nevertheless.

In sum, the different trajectories of Islamism in Egypt, Tunisia, and Turkey show that the major obstacles do not lie in the Islamic agendas per se. They are rather connected to the marginalization of the major forces of the previous system backed up by a broad socio-economic basis. Additionally, as discussed in Part I, the decline of Islamism or even more specifically of Islamic parties will not end political Islam. As long as Islam remains hegemonic, political Islam will persist. In these conditions, is it possible to talk about the emergence of Muslim democracies? And what will this mean? This is the question addressed in Part III.

---

[8] Nancy Okail, "Two Years after Mubarak's Fall, Torture and Denial Continue Unabated in Morsi's Egypt," Freedom House, February 11, 2013, accessed August 18, 2013, http://www.freedomhouse.org/blog/two-years-after-mubarak%E2%80%99s-fall-torture-and-denial-continue-unabated-morsi%E2%80%99s-egypt.

THE DISJUNCTION OF DEMOCRACY AND SECULARISM – LESSONS LEARNED FROM THE ARAB SPRING

10

The Rise of Unsecular Democracies: The Conundrum of Religious Freedom in Muslim Democracies

As scholars have rightly argued, the Arab Spring revolutions were not initiated by Islamists or caused by political Islam. Additionally, a legitimate argument can be made that the institutionalization of Islam within the state apparatus and its public presence is not in itself an obstacle to successful democratization. After all, the Tunisian transition since the demise of Ben Ali fulfilled the four major requirements for democratization. First, different protagonists reached a sufficient agreement about political procedures to produce an elected government. Second, a free and popular vote elected the transition government. Third, this government now has the *de facto* authority to generate new policies. Fourth, the executive, legislative, and judicial branches do not *de jure* share power with other bodies (e.g., the military or a religious power).[1] However, the assassination of Chokri Belaid in February 2013 was a fatal blow to the building of political trust and strained the different protagonists' agreement to work together toward new institutions. The assassination of Mohamed al-Brahmi, another secular opponent, in July 2013, deepened the political crisis, leading in September 2013 to the agreement of the Islamist-led coalition to consider a resignation.[2]

In the case of Egypt, the transition to democracy is even more compromised for the reasons raised in Chapters 8 and 9. In 2013 the army took the political lead with the asserted goal to move the transition forward after the political paralysis brought to the country by two years of FJP governance. After the crackdown on pro-Morsi protestors on August 14, 2013, and the multiplication of arrests of Islamists, this goal seems in jeopardy. At the same time, the transitory government released in November 2013 a revised constitution that could be submitted to vote in January 2014.

---

[1] See Alfred C. Stepan, Juan J. Linz, and Yogendra Yadav, *Crafting State-Nations: India and Other Multinational Democracies* (Baltimore, MD: Johns Hopkins University Press, 2011).

[2] Ennhada agreed to enter negotiations with all other political forces though the mediation of the powerful Union of the Tunisian Workers. The resignation of the Islamist-led government, included in the road map as an outcome of the negotiations, occurred on December 14, 2013, with the nomination of a more technocratic government.

In the same vein, Erdogan's political initiatives in 2012 and 2013 raised concerns about a possible return to authoritarianism in Turkey. Finally, in Iraq, the challenge for the different political protagonists is to reach a consensus on a type of regime that would allow a fair distribution of power between religious and ethnic groups.

In a way comparable to the evolution of post-communist eastern European countries, it appears that the end of authoritarian regimes does not lead to democracy. To better define these hybrid regimes political scientists have created new typologies. One that distinguishes between praetorian regimes and competitive authoritarianism is relevant to our argument.[3] In competitive authoritarianism, the four domains of democratic governance are acknowledged: (1) open, free, and fair elections; (2) all adults possess the right to vote; (3) political rights and civil liberties, including freedom of the press, freedom of association, and freedom to criticize the government without reprisal, are broadly protected; and (4) elected authorities possess real authority to govern, in that they are not subject to the tutelary control of military or clerical leaders. Unlike democracies, however, competitive authoritarian regimes are characterized by frequent violations in one or several of these domains, especially when it comes to independence of the judiciary, independence of executive and legislative power, and/or freedom of the press and political opposition. Iraq and Turkey are examples of such regimes. At the same time, competitive authoritarianism differs from other hybrid forms that mix authoritarian and democratic rules, such as praetorian regimes in which military rulers overturn the legal and political rule of elected institutions through the application of emergency laws. Pakistan and Egypt since the 2011 revolution can be defined as praetorian regimes.

As already mentioned earlier, Tunisia seems to be on the path for democracy since it has fulfilled the major conditions for transition. Even in this case, however, the possible Tunisian democracy will retain some Islamic features. I call this kind of democracy unsecular.

UNSECULAR DEMOCRACY VERSUS COMPETITIVE
AUTHORITARIANISM

In addition to these obstacles directly related to the implementation of democracy, state-Islam regulations will be crucial to further political development. In this regard, surveys[4] show that some forms of government

---

[3] Steven Levitsky and Lucan A. Way, "Elections without Democracy: The Rise of Competitive Authoritarianism," *Journal of Democracy*, 13 (2) April 2002: 51–65.

[4] See Jonathan Fox and Shmuel Sandler, *Religion in World Conflict* (London: Routledge, 2006).

involvement in religion (like recognition of religious holidays) are more compatible with democracy than others (legal privilege to one religion over others). In this sense, the compatibility between Islam and democracy is indirectly related to the nondemocratic forms of state regulations of Islam and other religions described in Part I. That is why religious freedom will be critical to democratization. But such a change cannot be implemented without the dismantling of Islam as a hegemonic religion. This does not mean separation of state and Islam but refers to some equidistance between the state and all religions, as we will discuss in the next chapter.

The protection of religious freedom is the conundrum of Muslim-majority countries. For example, Charles Rowley and Nathaniel Smith found in their study based on the World Values Survey that in Muslim-majority countries public opinion tends to be more favorable toward democratic values than it is in non-Muslim countries.[5] Yet those Muslim-majority countries themselves are not democratic. While authors like Michael Ross have argued that the presence of oil in the economy is a factor in impeding democracy,[6] Rowley and Smith advance that in the case of Muslim countries there is a direct correlation between the lack of democracy and the lack of religious freedom (as opposed to other civil liberties). The variables they used to assess religious freedom in their study were (1) the level of general respect of religious freedom by the state; (2) the ability of foreign missionaries to operate; (3) the limits on proselytizing, preaching, or conversion; (4) social attitudes toward other religions; and (5) attitudes toward nontraditional religions. In particular, the study found that restrictions on conversion or proselytizing were the biggest inhibitors to religious freedom in Muslim-majority countries.

Such studies confirm my main argument that the modern political culture of Muslim countries, defined by an association of citizenship, Islam, and national identity, is the major impediment for liberal politics.

In other words, accepting democracy does not mean automatic acceptance of all civil liberties listed by Levistky and Way in their third level of democratic governance. It can instead lead to a selective implementation of women's rights, religious minorities' rights, and freedom of speech. This selection poses a challenge to the "inclusion-moderation paradigm that serves to evaluate the acceptation of democracy by political groups that are usually anti system and/or violent."[7] This paradigm asserts that greater

---

[5] Charles Rowley and Nathanael Smith, "Islam's democracy paradox: Muslims claim to like democracy, so why do they have so little?" *Public Choice* 3.4 (2009): 273–99.

[6] Michael Ross, *The Oil Curse: How Petroleum Wealth Shapes the Development of Nations* (Princeton, NJ: Princeton University Press, 2012).

[7] See Jillian Schwedler, "Can Islamists Become Moderates?: Rethinking the Inclusion-Moderation Hypothesis," *World Politics* 63.2 (April 2011): 347–76.

inclusion of religious parties in the political system happens under several possible circumstances: incentives from the state (as discussed in Part II); or the influence of external factors (such as external intervention in Iraq or Libya). It is indeed proven that greater inclusion of religious parties in the political system leads to greater moderation. The evolution of the Egyptian Salafis and Jihadis since January 2011 is a case in point: once anti-system, they seem to have accepted the principles of election and the state framework (see Part II). But such moderation does not concern all aspects of freedom of expression or gender equality. In these conditions, the alternative for religious parties is not only between being anti-system or pro-system. The acceptance of the system can be combined with a persistence of what Stathis Kalyvas calls *unsecular politics*. He means "a political context in which religious ideas, symbols, and rituals are used as the primary (though not exclusive) instrument of mobilization by at least one major political party (i.e., a credible contender of power)."[8] I would add that unsecular politics is not limited to political parties, but can also be inscribed in the constitution and in the law when religious principles are utilized as sources of legislation or define the boundaries of public space. In such circumstances, *unsecular* defines the whole political system.

Unsecular politics can happen anywhere, as with, for example, the rise of religious claims to prohibit abortion or same-sex marriage in American democracy. By contrast, when the rule of law and the allocation of public resources differentiate on religious grounds, we can talk of unsecular democracies, not simply of unsecular politics. One can object that unsecular democracy is an oxymoron in the sense that there is no real democracy without protection of civil liberties by law. I argue that the defining feature of an unsecular democracy is not the rejection of all civil liberties but of some that are seen as a threat to the national community. For example, our case studies show that free and fair elections, the right to political opposition and organization, the right to express political opinions, and freedom of the press (to a certain extent) are now accepted not only by political leaders but, most importantly, by the majority of the citizens of these countries. Less clear is the acceptance of the rights granted to the person, from sexual freedom to the right to exit or criticize Islam. In these conditions, unsecular democracy refers to regimes in which individual freedoms are limited on religious grounds. This limitation does not concern all individual freedoms but more specifically what I call the rights of the self (see Conclusion of Part I). In other words, economic and political rights

---

[8] Stathis Kalyvas, "Unsecular Politics and Religious Mobilization," in *European Christian Democracy*, ed. T. Kselman and J. A. Buttigieg (Notre Dame: University of Notre Dame Press, 2003), 293–320.

are usually granted, but rights directly related to sexuality (homosexuality/ contraception/abortion/indecency) or spirituality (conversion/blasphemy) are not. Even if citizens do not belong to the majority religion, they have to conform to its limits in public space. To sum up, unsecular democracies are regimes that limit rights of the self on religious grounds for all citizens. These limitations concern the third level of secularity (that of the individual), but do not necessarily affect the institutional or social level of secularity. A historical example of unsecular democracy is the United States prior to the second wave of secularization in the nineteenth century. At that time, all religious groups had reached an equal status vis-à-vis the state, but individuals' freedom of speech was limited by religious norms. It took several critical lawsuits by atheists, free thinkers, and deists to establish the right for the individual to think outside of his or her church and to be able to freely express opinions that do not conform to any religious doctrine.[9] Based on this historical example, it is important to distinguish discriminatory practices that happen everywhere, even in the oldest democracy, from institutional discrimination inscribed in the law. Contemporary examples of unsecular democracies include Poland, Mexico, or Argentina, where limitations of freedom of the self are based on religious grounds (abortion/contraception).

In the case of discrimination against minority groups inscribed in the law, regimes cannot qualify as unsecular democracies. They instead illustrate different forms of competitive authoritarianism and hybrid regimes with hegemonic forms of Islam. For example, Pakistan is an example of a praetorian regime.[10] Even in the case of recurrent respect for elections, Pakistan would still not qualify as an unsecular democracy because of the second-class status of entire groups of the population (Shi'a, Ahmadiyya) and the lack of respect for the rule of law in general.

With the persistent respect for suffrage since the 2000s and the 2012 constitutional change (which bars the military from intrusion in politics),

---

[9] Christopher Grasso, "The Boundaries of Toleration and Tolerance: Religious Infidelity in the Early American Republic," in Chris Beneke and Christopher S. Grenda (eds.), *The First Prejudice: Religious Tolerance and Intolerance in Early America* (Philadelphia: University of Pennsylvania Press, 2011), 286–302.

[10] During the 2013 elections, for the first time in Pakistan's history, one democratically elected government peacefully turned power over to another. The election was not free of controversy, however, as there were allegations of vote tampering on the part of the winning PML-N party. There was also a disturbing trend of candidates being assassinated, mostly by the Pakistani Taliban. Among those killed were MQM candidate Sajid Qureshi (and his three-year-old son), Awami National Party (ANP) candidate Sadiq Zaman Khattak, MQM candidate Fakhr-ul-Islam, and independent (MQM-backed) candidate Shakeel Ahmed. JUI candidate Mufti Syed Janan was targeted by a bomb on May 7, 2013, but survived the attack. ("11 dead in blast at JUI-F election rally," *The Express Tribune*, May 7, 2013, accessed August 15, 2013, http://tribune.com.pk/story/545518/ blast-at-jui-f-rally-in-hangu-leaves-several-injured/.)

Turkey has evolved from a praetorian regime to what Levitsky and Conway call competitive authoritarianism in the sense that all protagonists recognize the legitimacy of the four domains of democracy, but tensions and challenges have arisen about their implementation.[11] It can also be described as a Jacobinist republic (a reference to the cultural homogenization undertaken by French revolutionaries) to highlight the "Sunnification" of the Turkish nation that we described in Chapters 3, 4, 5 and 6.[12]

While both proselytizing and conversion are legal, some minorities (including Alevis, Christians, and Baha'is) face popular persecution and harassment for undertaking these activities. Individuals' freedom of expression is also limited because laws forbid the defamation of religion. More importantly, Erdogan's temptation to authoritarianism since 2012 and 2013 (discussed in Chapters 8 and 9) questions altogether the probability of further democratization because of the increased repression of journalists and popular protests. In 2012, the country passed reforms as part of the "Third Judicial Package," which amended some laws limiting freedom of expression but did not remove most of these limitations. Similarly, the democratic package announced by Erdogan on September 2013 did not remove most of these limitations,[13] nor did it contain significant improvement in religious freedom.[14]

So where does this leave Egypt, Tunisia, and Iraq? It is too early to tell if these countries are on the path of democratization. In the best possible scenario, they may function under a strong electoral system (at least for Tunisia) and at the same time not accommodate cultural and religious expression of certain categories of citizens, such as religious or ethnic minorities. Egypt's politics are unlikely to move away from hegemonic Islam because of the political weakness of the Coptic minority. In fact, since the January 25 revolution, the impetus to remain religiously exclusivist is only one of the challenges of the new regime. The other even more immediate risk concerns the tutelary authority of the military overseeing the functioning of new political institutions. In other words, Egypt may not only remain hegemonic in the management of religion but also become a praetorian regime. The military coup against the Morsi government in July 2013, the nomination of military officials to governorate positions in the interim government, and the bloodshed against pro-Morsi protestors on August 14, 2013, are signs of the solidification of a praetorian regime in the years to come. On the other hand, even if it lacks the pressure to acknowledge pluralism

---

[11] Steven Levitsky and Lucan A. Way, *Competitive Authoritarianism: Hybrid Regimes after the Cold War* (New York: Cambridge University Press, 2005).
[12] It is worth mentioning that Jacobinist republics can be full-fledged democracies, like France.
[13] "Turkey," *Amnesty International Annual Report 2013*.
[14] See Chapter 8, p. 187

that diversity engenders, Tunisia displays some indicators of an unsecular democracy. Finally, when it comes to Iraq, although religious (and ethnic) diversity is now inscribed at the foundation of the post-Saddam regime, the challenge is to move away from sectarian divides toward religious and ethnic pluralism.

TUNISIA: BETWEEN JACOBINIST REPUBLIC AND UNSECULAR DEMOCRACY

Leading up to the October 2011 elections, a multiparty system began to take shape. The Interior Ministry announced in late July 2011 that the total number of official parties had reached 100 from a prerevolution total of 8.[15]

At the October 2011 elections, more than 90 percent of registered voters showed up at the polls, and the election was considered fair and, to a large extent, free of corruption. Being the victorious party, Ennahda entered a ruling coalition with the two secular parties that had won more seats: the Congress for the Republic (CPR) and Ettakatol.

Yet all current indicators show that, despite this secular coalition in power, it is highly improbable that Islam will be dislodged from its hegemonic status. More precisely, a consensus has emerged to keep the legacy of the previous state-Islam arrangement, which means maintaining Islam in the constitution and keeping state control over religious institutions. At the same time, all religious groups will be regulated by the same law, even if limitation of individual freedom of expression will be maintained, if not reinforced.

Debate on Article 1 of the Future Constitution

Article 1 of the former regime's constitution, which has been preserved in the 2013 draft of the new constitution, reads: "Tunisia is a free, independent and sovereign State. Its religion is Islam, its language is Arabic and its type of government is the Republic." Additionally, the president is legally stipulated to be Muslim. The extent to which Islam will be incorporated into the future constitution has generated heated discussions among the political protagonists in the Constituent Assembly.

The different stances on inscribing Islam in the constitution emerged during a February 2012 assembly session, when Ennahda assumed there was a consensus regarding Islam as the religion of the state – a point that virtually all parties addressed while campaigning for office in the 2011

---

[15] The total number of parties is constantly in flux as a result of alliances between parties.

National Constituent Assembly (NCA) elections. However once in power, the CPR was among those to voice disagreement and proposed that no official religion be written into the constitution.[16] CPR members argued that the preamble should focus on affirming the state's civic character, thereby giving explicit protection to minorities' rights. In that same session, Issam Chebbi from the Party for Democracy and Progress (PDP) proposed that references to religion and language be removed from the constitution's preamble and retained in the body of the constitution. Ultimately, Ennahda announced on March 25, 2012, on national television, that the new constitution would keep Article 1 intact. In a move that follows the middle ground, Zoubair Chhoudi, spokesperson of Ennahda, stated, "We felt it incumbent upon us to undertake an action that will unite Tunisians – not further divide them. The recognition of Tunisia as an Arab-Muslim state is more than enough to reinforce the country's identity."[17] Additionally, the clause stating that the president of Tunisia must be Muslim has been upheld. However, the gender condition – that is, the president must be male[18] – has been removed.

In the same vein, on March 26, 2012, Ennahda declared its opposition to including Shari'a in the constitution, effectively putting an end to the intense debate that emerged, on this point in the previous months.[19] As such, the drafting committee has decided to maintain the status quo by refusing to inscribe Shari'a as a source of legislation in the new constitution, thus signaling the move away from the Salafi influence[20] and by going back, once more, to the legacy of the Bourguiba regime.

---

[16] Wafa Ben Hassine, "Constituent Assembly Debates Muslim Identity in Tunisian Constitution," *Tunisia Live*, February 21, 2012, accessed July 14, 2012, http://www.tunisia-live.net/2012/02/21/constituent-assembly-debates-arab-muslim-identity-in-tunisian-constitution/.

[17] Carolyn Lamboley, "Tunisia's Leading Party Reaffirms Commitment to Arab-Muslim Identity," *Tunisia Live*, March 26, 2012, accessed July 18, 2012, http://www.tunisia-live.net/2012/03/26/tunisias-leading-party-reaffirms-commitment-to-arab-muslim-identity/.

[18] Article 38, Head of State: "The President of the Republic is the Head of the State. His religion is Islam." *United Nations Public Administration Network*, accessed July 19, 2012, http://unpan1.un.org/intradoc/groups/public/documents/cafrad/unpan004842.pdf.

[19] In response to Ennahda's refusal to inscribe Shari'a into the constitution, al-Qa'ida leader Ayman al-Zawahiri called for Tunisian Muslims to rise up against Ennahda because it is following a version of Islam meant to please the West. Khawla Ammar, "Audio Recording of al-Qa'ida Leader Ayman al-Zawahiri Released Denouncing Ennahdha," *Tunisia Live*, June 11, 2012, accessed July 19, 2012, http://www.tunisia-live.net/2012/06/11/audio-recording-of-al-Qa'ida-leader-ayman-al-zawahiri-released-denouncing-ennahdha/.

[20] Kareem Fahim, "Tunisia Says Constitution Will Not Cite Islamic Law," *New York Times*, March 26, 2012, accessed July 17, 2012, http://www.nytimes.com/2012/03/27/world/africa/tunisia-says-constitution-will-not-cite-islamic-law.html.

But the situation remained complicated by the ambiguity of Ennahda's position. While the party's official platform was that Ennahda would not instate Shari'a in the new constitution, after the elections, other Ennahda leaders voiced different stances on the issue. For instance, during a demonstration on March 16 2012, the president of the Ennahda parliamentary group, Sahbi Atig, declared that Shari'a would be the main source of legislation.[21] In contrast, in an interview with *La Presse* in late March 2012, Ettakatol member and president of the Constituent Assembly Mustapha Ben Jaafar affirmed that the party opposed the inclusion of Shari'a in the constitution: "We think that the term 'shari'a' adds nothing. On the contrary, it can complicate the situation."[22] That is why when other Ennahda leaders expressed their support to the inclusion of Shari'a in the constitution, Ben Jafaar threatened to withdraw Ettakatol from the coalition.[23] In an attempt to deny this internal dissonance, Rached Ghannouchi explained in a radio interview with *FM Express* in early April 2012 that the decision by Ennahda to keep Shari'a law out of the constitution was unanimous, stating, "What is important is to avoid imposing religious or political behaviors or beliefs on people."[24] In June 2013, Ghannouchi stated that the draft constitution did not enshrine Shari'a but that it included Islamic values.[25] In sum, the discussion of Shari'a revealed that Ennahda is not a homogenous bloc but is composed of diverse and sometimes contradictory subgroups. Most interestingly however, its leaders continuously adjust their strategy to the broader political landscape and take into account political voices (including the seculars voices).

These debates illustrate the shift of Tunisia from a Jacobinist republic toward a more symbolic approach to the status of Islam in the political system. Significantly, the new regime has not contested the status of Jewish and Christian groups that are also supported by the state (see Chapter 4). At the same time, political initiatives to improve the legal protection of minorities have been very marginal, if not nonexistent. This is largely due to

---

[21] Duncan Pickard, "The Current Status of Constitution Making in Tunisia," *Carnegie Endowment for International Peace*, April 19, 2012, accessed July 17, 2012, http://carnegieendowment.org/2012/04/19/current-status-of-constitution-making-in-tunisia.

[22] "Mustapha Ben Jafaar: Rien au monde ne pourra arrêter le processus démocratique en Tunisie," *La Presse*, March 30, 2012, accessed July 18, 2012, http://www.ettakatol.org/fr/328-mustapha-ben-jaafar-rien-au-monde-ne-pourra-arr%C3%AAter-le-processus-d%C3%A9mocratique-en-tunisie.html.

[23] Duncan Pickard, "The Current Status of Constitution Making in Tunisia."

[24] "Tunisian Islamist Rached Ghannouchi: I'm a Salafist of sorts & Why No shari'a?" *Islamopedia Online*, April 2, 2012, accessed July 18, 2012, http://islamopediaonline.org/news/tunisian-islamist-rached-ghannouchi-im-salafist-sorts-why-no-shariah.

[25] "Tunisia draft constitution not based on shari'a," *Middle East Online*, June 6, 2013, accessed June 23, 2013, http://www.middle-east-online.com/english/?id=59160.

the fact that Tunisia has a very homogenous population of Muslim Arabs, although minority voices have attempted to speak up.

For example, a demonstration on March 25, 2012, sparked concerns when a Salafi preacher called for Tunisian youth to wage war against the country's Jews.[26] In response, Roger Bismuth, the president of the Tunisian Jewish Community, has brought a case against this preacher for incitation to hatred. Additionally, this incident affected Tunisia's minority Amazigh[27] population because it reflected a growing trend of promoting an Islamist Tunisian identity, excluding minority identities, both non-Arab and non-Muslim.[28] Since then, President Moncef Marzouki, head of the Constituent Assembly Mustapha Ben Jaafar, and leader of Ennahda Rached Ghannouchi, have all declared their support for the Jewish community and promised to defend the rights of all citizens and minorities.[29]

As Alfred Stepan demonstrated,[30] the probability of a secular form of state-religion relationships is higher when a sufficient level of religious and/or ethnic diversity is present. However, in Tunisia, the proportion of non-Muslims is almost insignificant; 98 percent of the population is Arab and Muslim, while the remaining population is split mostly between Christians and Jews.[31] As a result, religious minorities are too small to put pressure on political groups to change the current status of Islam. Therefore, the question of legal neutrality of the state for all religions has not been brought into public discussion.

Consequently, there has been no debate on removing the prohibition on proselytization that was established under Ben Ali. There has also been no discussion on the existence of a Habus Ministry (Ministry of Religious Affairs). For example, Ennahda has not questioned the status of civil servants granted to clerics under authoritarian rule. So while all clergy in charge during the Ben Ali regime have been stripped of their positions, the Ministry of Religious Affairs, headed by an Ennahda member, remains responsible for filling those vacant positions. It also holds authority over mosque activity as well as the right to hire and dismiss mosque personnel as the ministry

---

[26] Emily Parker, "Tunisia's Preamble: Space for Minorities within an 'Arab-Islamic Identity,'" *Tunisia Live*, July 14, 2012, accessed July 18, 2012, http://www.tunisia-live.net/2012/07/14/tunisias-new-preamble-and-the-question-of-minorities/.

[27] Amazigh (plural Imazighen) refers to the Berbers, an ethnic Muslim group present in North Africa, characterized by a different language and culture than the Arabs.

[28] Ibid.

[29] Kouichi Shirayanagi, "President of the Tunisian Jewish Community to Take Salafist Preacher to Court," *Tunisia Live*, March 27, 2012, accessed July 18, 2012, http://www.tunisia-live.net/2012/03/27/president-of-the-tunisian-jewish-community-to-take-salafist-preacher-to-court/.

[30] Alfred Stepan, Juan J. Linz, and Yogendra Yadav, *Crafting State-Nations: India and Other Multinational Democracies* (2011).

[31] "The World Factbook: Tunisia," *Central Intelligence Agency*, accessed December 20, 2011, https://www.cia.gov/library/publications/the-world-factbook/geos/ts.html.

sees fit. Nevertheless, rights granted to individuals are the most challenging aspect of the current transition, as is illustrated by the continuous controversies about women's rights and blasphemy.

Women's Rights and Reform of the Family Code

Ennahda has very adamantly reassured women that the Family Code will not be changed. At the same time, issues remain in the existing code that have not been debated. For example, according to the U.S. State Department's Report on Religious Freedom, the Tunisian government forbids and sometimes does not recognize (if performed abroad)[32] marriage between a Muslim woman and a non-Muslim man. Moreover, a non-Muslim woman married to a Muslim Tunisian man suffers legal disadvantages such as the inability to inherit from her Muslim husband (nor can he inherit from her) and the inability for her children to inherit from her. Similarly, in case of rape, the Tunisian Penal Code provides various punishments, including death and life imprisonment. Yet it doesn't actually protect victims of rape because there are ways for perpetrators to evade punishment, for instance by marrying the victim.[33] Moreover, spousal rape brings no punishment. This ambiguity in the legal treatment of women's rights came to the forefront of political debates when hundreds of Tunisians protested in October 2012 in support of a woman who was raped by the police but faced accusations of violating modesty laws.[34]

Despite these abuses, secularists and Islamists seem to have reached a consensus on the protection of women's rights. But this consensus does not include Salafists. For example, in February 2012, several Tunisian Islamic organizations hosted Egyptian cleric Wagdi Ghoneim,[35] infamous for his

---

[32] Regarding marriages between a Muslim woman and a non-Muslim man performed abroad, the report notes, "On occasion, the government did not recognize the legality of such marriages, forcing the couple to seek a court ruling to legitimize the marriage. Cases are decided arbitrarily, particularly when the family in Tunisia contests the foreign marriage." Bureau of Democracy, Human Rights, and Labor, "July–December, 2010 International Religious Freedom Report: Tunisia," U.S. Department of State, September 13, 2011, accessed July 16, 2012, http://www.state.gov/j/drl/rls/irf/2010_5/168277.htm.

[33] "Tunisie – Comment la loi protege les violeurs," *Slate Afrique*, April 12, 2012, accessed July 22, 2012, http://www.slateafrique.com/85497/tunisie-vices-cachees-legislation-droits-femmes-viol.

[34] "The woman says that three police officers stopped her in a car last month, and that one of them held her fiancé back while the other two raped her. The police officers deny wrongdoing, saying she was engaged in immoral behavior with her fiancé when they stopped her" (*New York Times*, October 2, 2012, http://www.nytimes.com/2012/10/03/world/africa/tunisia-protesters-support-woman-in-rape-case.html, accessed October 25, 2012).

[35] Dr. Wagdi Abd El Hamied Mohamed Ghoneim is an Egyptian-Qatari Islamic preacher. A businessman by trade, he serves as secretary-general of both the Traders' Union of Alexandria and the Division of Accounting and Auditing within the Traders' Union of Greater Cairo. "الشيخ وجدي غنيم Asheikh Wagdi Ghoneim," طريق الاسلام *Islam Way*, accessed June 28, 2013, http://ar.islamway.net/scholar/74. Ghoneim was imam at the Islamic Institute in California

misogynistic messages and his highly controversial encouragement of female genital mutilation.[36] In response to his contentious visit, a group of secular feminists led by prominent lawyer Bochra Bel Haj Hamida brought a lawsuit against Ghoneim on "charges of inciting hatred as well as the unauthorized use of public spaces for the purpose of worship."[37] Additionally, Abd al-Fattah Muru, also a lawyer and a former member of Ennahda, has criticized Ghoneim and other visiting religious figures for imposing their narrow religious dogma in Tunisia.

Interestingly, most secular opponents, Islamists, and Salafis seem to agree on limiting the public manifestations of sexually free individuals. This consensus came to light in the case of Amina Tyler. In March 2013, Amina Tyler, a nineteen-year-old Tunisian and a member of the Ukrainian feminist group FEMEN,[38] posted nude photos of herself on Facebook, with the slogans "my body is my own" and "f*** your morals" written on her chest. She was forced into hiding for two months because of the controversy surrounding her posting. Tyler was later arrested in May 2013 after painting graffiti onto a mosque in Kairouan. She was charged and convicted of carrying an incendiary object – a can of pepper spray – which included a $182 fine.[39] She remained in jail pending hearing on more serious charges (e.g., violating indecency laws). The incident brought issues of gender, religion, and morality to the fore. In a statement after Tyler's arrest, a spokesman for the Interior Ministry defended

---

and has published numerous articles, including several commentaries on political affairs in the global Islamic world. الموقع الرسمي للدكتور وجدي غنيم *Official Website of Dr. Wagdi Ghoneim,* accessed June 28, 2013, http://www.wagdighoneim.net/catplay.php?catsmktba=4. He received a bachelor's degree in business administration from the business school at Alexandria University in 1973, followed by a master's degree in Islamic studies from Cairo's Islamic Studies College in 1988, and a PhD from Indiana's Graduate Theological Foundation in 2006.

[36] Charles Baeder, "Controversial Cleric, Advocate of Female Genital Mutilation, Challenges Tunisian Critics," *Tunisia Live,* February 15, 2012, accessed July 18, 2012, http://www.tunisia-live.net/2012/02/15/controversial-cleric-advocate-of-female-genital-mutilation-challenges-tunisian-critics/. "Sheikh Wagdi Ghoneim and a response on female circumcision," accessed June 28, 2013, (video), http://www.youtube.com/watch?v=KouyF5u_4MQ (video)

[37] Baeder, "Controversial Cleric."

[38] FEMEN is a feminist activist group that originated in Ukraine. It describes itself as a "new ideology of the women's sexual protest [movement] presented by extreme topless campaigns of direct action ... democracy watchdogs attacking patriarchy, in all its forms: the dictatorship, the church, the sex industry." It has staged several topless protests across Europe. *Sextremism, Women Movement,* accessed May 29, 2013, http://femen.org/en.

[39] Bouazza Ben Bouazza, "Amina Tyler Trial: Tunisians Protest Outside Of FEMEN Activist Court Case," *Associated Press* May 30, 2013, accessed August 9, 2013, http://www.huffingtonpost.com/2013/05/30/amina-tyler-trial-tunisians-protest-outside-femen-activist-court-case_n_3358736.html.

authorities' actions, saying, "Our society is Muslim and we do not accept this marginal behaviour."[40]

In the same vein, when it comes to freedom of speech or freedom of sexual minorities, discrimination surfaces both in behavior and in the law.

Heated Debate on Freedom of Expression

Individual freedom of expression has also been in the spotlight since the Jasmine Revolution. For example, two bloggers received seven-year prison sentences in March 2012 after they wrote about atheism and criticized Islam. Their crimes included "public order offenses," "moral transgressions," and "harming a third party." The court based its sentencing on the Tunisian Penal Code's Article 121 (3), which prohibits the dissemination of materials "liable to cause harm to the public order and to public morals."[41] Significantly, Article 121 (3) was adopted under Ben Ali in 2001, and it was notoriously used as a tool for stifling political opposition and repressing freedom of expression of individuals or groups.

In the same vein, the LGBT community in Tunisia has increasingly vocalized its presence through Internet activity, including publishing the online *Gay Day Magazine* and displaying Facebook pages. On January 28, 2012, it led a public demonstration to demand that the state protect by law the rights of homosexual groups. Yet, in February of the same year, Minister of Human Rights and Transitional Justice Samir Dilou, an Ennahda member, publicly refused to recognize sexual orientation as a human right, calling homosexuality an illness.[42] Then, when he met with the Human Rights Council (HRC) in Geneva in June 2012, he rejected the council's two suggestions, which called for legal protection from discrimination based on sexual orientation and the decriminalization of same-sex relations inscribed in Article 230 of the Tunisian Penal Code. Dilou argued that sexual orientation is a Western-specific concept, and as such the HRC's recommendations don't align with the values of Tunisian society.

Artists' freedom of expression has also been in the spotlight. For example, Salafis protested the October 2011 broadcast of the French-Iranian

[40] "Tunisia FEMEN activist arrested for 'immoral gestures,'" *Ahram Online*, May 20, 2013, accessed June 22, 2013, http://english.ahram.org.eg/NewsContent/2/8/71923/World/Region/Tunisia-Femen-activist-arrested-for-immoral-gestur.aspx.

[41] Henda Hendoud and Olfa Riahi, "Tunisie: 'l'illusion de l'Islam' dévoile l'illusion de la liberté" ("The Illusion of Islam shed light on the illusion of freedom") *Nawaat*, April 5, 2012, accessed July 17, 2012, http://nawaat.org/portail/2012/04/05/tunisie-lillusion-de-lislam-devoile-lillusion-de-la-liberte/.

[42] Charles Baeder, "Tunisian Human Rights Minister's Remarks Spark Debate on Homophobia," *Tunisia Live*, February 9, 2012, accessed July 21, 2012, http://www.tunisia-live.net/2012/02/09/tunisian-human-rights-ministers-remarks-spark-debate-on-homophobia/.

film *Persepolis*[43] for its portrayal of God, who in one scene speaks to the protagonist when she is a little girl. Salafis attacked the headquarters of the private station that broadcast the movie, and messages circulated on Facebook calling for the destruction of the station and the death of its journalists.[44] Nessma TV has been known for its provocative series and broadcasts such as debates on sexuality and a controversial BBC-produced biopic of Saddam Hussein. Thus, by broadcasting this film, which was met with religious resistance across Muslim countries, Nessma TV seemed to be taking a stand against the rigid cultural rules followed by the Salafis. Moreover, the timing of the broadcast, just before Tunisia's first postrevolutionary, democratic elections, also seemed to make a political stand against the risk of a Salafi-influenced election.[45] Since the broadcast, Nessma TV has been brought to trial for airing a film contrary to Islamic values.

In June 2012, thousands of Salafis took to the streets of Tunis and clashed with local police to protest a contemporary art exhibition in an upscale neighborhood, which displayed works such as veiled women as punching bags, veiled women in a pile of stones, and a piece that spelled out "Glory to God" in ants. These works sparked Salafi ire, as they believed these displays insulted Islam. In response, the chairman of the Zaytuna mosque, Houcine Laabidi, called for the death of the artists for their blasphemous work,[46] and Minister of Culture Mahdi Mabrouk also condemned the artwork as sacrilegious.[47]

Laabidi has since been suspended, and the judicial officer who started the controversy by putting incendiary comments on Facebook was arrested for inciting social unrest. Additionally, the Union of Tunisian Artists not only demanded the resignation of Mahdi Mabrouk but also sued the Ministry of Culture, the Ministry of Religious Affairs, and representatives of the

---

[43] *Persepolis* is based on the autobiographical graphic novel with the same title by Iranian-born French author and illustrator Marjane Satrapi. The story revolves around a child growing up during the Iranian Islamic Revolution in 1979. The novel was published in 2000 by L'Association and Pantheon Books, and the film was released in 2007 by Sony Pictures Classics.

[44] "Tunisian Salafists attack TV station for screening film on Iran revolution," *Al Arabiya*, October 9, 2011, accessed July 21, 2012, http://www.alarabiya.net/articles/2011/10/09/170965.html.

[45] Yves Gonzalez-Quijano, "Tunisie. Les 'salafistes' a l'attaque de Nessma TV?" *Kapitalis*, October 12, 2011, accessed July 21, 2012, http://www.kapitalis.com/afkar/68-tribune/6285-tunisie-les-lsalafistesr-a-lattaque-de-nessma-tv.html.

[46] Pesha Magid, "Union to Sue Tunisian Government over Endangerment of Artists," *Tunisia Live*, June 27, 2012, accessed July 19, 2012, http://www.tunisia-live.net/2012/06/27/union-to-sue-tunisian-government-over-endangerment-of-artists/.

[47] Ikram Lakhdhar, "Union of Tunisian Artists Calls for Minister of Culture to Resign," *Tunisia Live*, June 15, 2012, accessed July 19, 2012, http://www.tunisia-live.net/2012/06/15/union-of-tunisian-artists-calls-for-minister-of-culture-to-resign/.

Zaytuna mosque for endangering the lives of the artists involved in the exhibition. At the same time, the Ministry of Culture decided to prosecute the organization responsible for hosting the event for property damage caused by the protests.[48]

Thus, while the Ministry of Culture officially asserts respect for freedom of speech, it seems that such freedoms may ultimately be curbed in one way or another if they are perceived as an attack on what the state decides is sacred. At the same time, the "Salafist muscle" could swing the state toward a more Islamist perspective. Much of the future of Tunisian freedom of expression lies with the draft constitution and the direction it adopts, which at the time of this writing remains unclear.

To summarize, tensions have been mounting not only between Ennahda and the Salafis but also between secularists and the Salafis. On one hand, secular forces have complained that Ennahda has been too lenient and too slow to react to Salafi violent protests. On the other hand, Salafis demand a more Islamic Tunisia.[49] Rached Ghannouchi has attempted to tread the fine middle line, pleasing the secularists by refusing to instate Shari'a, but then asserting that he is "a Salafist of sorts." Yet Ghannouchi also affirms that the Salafi movement in Tunisia can bring Tunisia into a civil war.[50] Similarly during a June 2012 press conference, he specifically denounced "extreme secularist" Jalel Brick[51] for insulting Islam in order to incite Salafi anger and to create tension in postrevolutionary Tunisia. Ghannouchi then called on Tunisians "to protect the revolution and things considered sacred."[52]

However, the excess of the protests against the film *The Innocence of Muslims* in September 2012, led to a stronger position in favor of freedom of speech.[53] Although Ennahda called for the constitutional criminalization of attacks on the sacred, the National Constituent Assembly speaker announced that no such blasphemy law would be put in place because of vagueness in terms.[54] But Salma Bakkar, an independent member of the

---

[48] Magid, "Union to Sue Tunisian Government over Endangerment of Artists."

[49] Ridha Bougerra, "Ghannouchi's Indulgence vis-à-vis the Salafi Intransigence," *Kapitalis*, March 8, 2012, accessed July 19, 2012, http://www.kapitalis.com/afkar/68-tribune/8650-tunisie-lindulgence-de-ghannouchi-vis-a-vis-de-lintransigeance-salafiste.html.

[50] "Tunisian Islamist Rached Ghannouchi: I'm a Salafist, of sorts & Why No Shari'a?"

[51] Jalel Brick is a very vocal member of the RCD, the former ruling party.

[52] Sana Ajmi, "Ennahdha Leader Rached Ghannouchi Calls Upon Followers to Protest on Friday," *Tunisia Live*, June 13, 2012, accessed July 19, 2012, http://www.tunisia-live.net/2012/06/13/ennahdha-leader-rached-ghannouchi-calls-upon-followers-to-protest-on-friday/.

[53] Four people died during a violent protest at the American embassy in Tunis, prompting the U.S. government to evacuate embassy personnel and call for citizens to leave the country.

[54] "No blasphemy clause in Tunisia's new constitution: Speaker," *Al Arabiya*, October 12, 2012, accessed October 24, 2012, http://english.alarabiya.net/articles/2012/10/12/243289.html.

Constituent Assembly, revealed in an interview that the blasphemy article was still there but had been moved to the preamble of the constitution under general principles.[55] While the issue remains somewhat unclear until a public version of the draft constitution is released, in early June 2013 Rached Ghannouchi stated at an event in Washington, DC, that "[b]lasphemy is not a crime. Freedom of choice is very clear in the Qur'an; it says 'let there be no compulsion in religion.'"[56]

To sum up, despite the positive steps Tunisia has taken toward democratization (such as free and regular elections, the development of an independent bureaucracy, and freedom of the press), uncertainty regarding the status of religious minorities and women's rights may put Tunisia in the same category as Turkey; that is, competitive authoritarianism. If this uncertainty is lifted, but restrictions on freedom of speech remain, Tunisia could become an unsecular democracy.

EGYPT: TOWARD A PRAETORIAN REGIME

Since the ousting of Mubarak, political developments in Egypt have shown an oscillation between a praetorian regime à la Pakistan and competitive authoritarianism centered on the presidential figure.

Until Mohamed Morsi's victory in the 2012 presidential election, the military elite, represented by the SCAF under Field Marshal Muhammad Hussein Tantawi, appeared as the main incumbent of power. This was made clear on June 17, 2012, when the SCAF issued a constitutional addendum[57] granting it sole responsibility over the armed forces and preeminence over the president elect for declaring war.[58]

From Morsi's ascent to power until the June 30, 2013, unrest, the army stepped back from the spotlight but still held the upper hand on the foreign policy and defense forces of the country. In these conditions, Egypt's army maintained, at the beginning of the revolution, a strong relationship with the United States, from which it received in 2013 $1.3 billion, accounting for approximately 80 percent of the Egyptian Defense Ministry's weapons

---

[55] Megan Radford, "Blasphemy Article Moved to Constitution Preamble," *tunisialive*, 2012, accessed January 24, 2013, http://www.tunisia-live.net/2012/10/13/blasphemy-article-moved-to-constitution-preamble/.

[56] "Leader of Tunisia's Ruling Party: Blasphemy is Not a Crime," *Human Rights First*, June 7, 2013, accessed June 23, 2013, http://www.humanrightsfirst.org/2013/06/07/leader-of-tunisia%E2%80%99s-ruling-party-blasphemy-is-not-a-crime/.

[57] Interview with Steven A. Cook by Bernard Gwertzman, "Military Power Play in Egypt," *Council on Foreign Relations*, June 18, 2012, accessed July 20, 2012, http://www.cfr.org/egypt/military-power-play-egypt/p28531.

[58] "English text of SCAF amended Egypt Constitutional Declaration," *Ahram Online*, June 18, 2012, accessed July 20, 2012, http://english.ahram.org.eg/NewsContent/1/64/45350/Egypt/Politics-/English-text-of-SCAF-amended-Egypt-Constitutional-.aspx.

procurement costs.[59] However, the international outcry against the military assault on pro-Morsi protesters in August 2013 has exacerbated the uncertainty of U.S. aid to Egypt.[60] As already mentioned, the fall of the Morsi regime and the harsh repression of Islamists since July 2013 are pivotal events in the consolidation of a praetorian regime, which has faced mounting critiques from Europe and the United States, not to mention other Muslim countries like Turkey or Tunisia.

Besides the nature of the future regime, it seems that the redefinition of state-Islam relations will primarily involve some competition between the Salafis and Al-Azhar university, which emerged as a major political actor during the brief Morsi regime.

The question of state-Islam relations was brought to the fore by the religious establishment itself, when a coalition of hundreds of scholars from Al-Azhar and the Ministry of Religious Endowments organized a march in May 2011 to the headquarters of the SCAF calling for the independence of Al-Azhar from the state. Grand Shaykh Ahmed al-Tayyeb released a document in June 2011 that set out a list of principles and demands, with an overall theme of the compatibility of Islamic values and democracy, lending legitimacy to its claims of independence from the state. Similarly, in the early stages of the transition, Al-Azhar was very active on the question of civil liberties.

In January 2012, al-Tayyeb released the Basic Freedom Document intended to serve as a reference for Egypt's new constitution and that aimed to demonstrate the compatibility of Islamic and democratic principles. The document insisted on the necessity of inscribing the principles of freedom of belief and freedom of expression in the new constitution, while emphasizing that all political, religious, and civil groups should benefit from these rights. It was at the time embraced by many political and religious movements, including the April 6 Youth Movement, the Freedom and Justice Party, the evangelical community, the Catholic Church, and the late Pope Shenouda III of the Coptic Orthodox Church. *SCAF – Supreme Council Armed Force*

---

[59] "Egypt: Background and U.S. Relations," *Congressional Research Service*, February 26, 2013, accessed June 24, 2013, http://www.fas.org/sgp/crs/mideast/RL33003.pdf. However, U.S. lawmakers have questioned this military aid, citing concerns over Islamism, the Muslim Brotherhood's stance on Israel, and security in the Sinai. "U.S. lawmakers question military aid to Egypt, citing concerns about Israel," *The Washington Post*, March 2, 2013, accessed June 24, 2013, http://articles.washingtonpost.com/2013-03-02/ world/37388565_1_military-aid-conservative-islamist-group-muslim-brotherhood. In the same vein, after the ultimatum of July 1, 2013, given by the army to the political actors, CNN claimed that on the following day, the Obama administration warned the Egyptian military that it risked losing U.S. financial assistance if it carried out a military coup against Egypt's first-ever freely elected head of state. But the U.S. Department of State denied such an initiative. Nevertheless, in July 2013, the United States House voted 315–109 to prohibit military funding for Egypt.
[60] "House Passes Defense Spending Bill Prohibiting Egypt Funds," *Business Week*, July 24, 2013, accessed August 11, 2013, http://www.businessweek.com/ news/2013-07-24/u-dot-s-dot-house-passes-pentagon-spending-bill-with-no-aid-to-egypt.]

The SCAF to a certain extent acknowledged Al-Azhar's political demands for independence, announcing in June 2012 the formation of an Islamic scholars, committee to appoint the head of Al-Azhar – a responsibility previously held by the president.[61] Additionally, in a separate initiative, Grand Shaykh Ahmed al-Tayyeb formed a specialized legal committee to work on amending Law 103/1961 regarding the organization of Al-Azhar. The committee was charged with researching a transparent way for electing the grand imam, and the possibility of having three deputies.[62]

The status of Al-Azhar was strengthened by the fact that Salafis implicitly acknowledged its arbitration on issues related to the status of Islam in the constitution (see Chapters 3 and 5). For example, Article 2 in the 2012 constitution remained intact after Grand Shaykh al-Tayyeb stated that Article 2 is "untouchable."[63]

It is worth noting that while traditional religious figures such as al-Tayyeb and Grand Mufti Ali Gomaa (2003–13) publicly supported religious freedom and protection of religious minorities, none of the presidential candidates' platforms included concrete measures to implement such rights. Instead, they vaguely stated their support for these principles. For instance, at the time presidential candidate Amr Moussa, the secretary-general of the Arab League from 2001 to 2011, presented himself as the antithesis of the Islamist candidates but did not really address the question of religious freedom or rights of religious minorities. Former Muslim Brotherhood member Abdel Moneim Fotouh also provided in his platform a general and vague assertion on freedom of worship – an assertion that came into question after the Salafis announced their support of his candidacy.[64] Similarly, Mohamed Morsi's platform lacked references to minority rights and religious freedoms.[65]

In these conditions, it seems that the question of civil liberties and freedom of expression will remain more symbolic than defined by the rule of law.

In the same vein, since the election of President Morsi and the vote of the new constitution, the Al-Azhar's discourse about independence and freedom has receded because the establishment has appeared as the major institution

---

[61] "US State department denies calling for early Egypt elections," accessed July 2, 2013, http://english.ahram.org.eg/NewsContent/1/64/75518/Egypt/Politics-/US-State-Department-denies-calling-for-early-Egypt.aspx.

[62] "SCAF orders formation of scholars panel to elect Al-Azhar leader," *Egypt Independent*, June 27, 2012, accessed July 19, 2012, http://www.egyptindependent.com/news/scaf-orders-formation-scholars-panel-elect-al-azhar-leader.

[63] "Al-Azhar, Salafis clash over Article 2," *Egypt Independent*, July 10, 2012, accessed July 20, 2012, http://www.egyptindependent.com/news/al-azhar-salafis-clash-over-article-2.

[64] Noha El-Hennawy, "Women and Salafi rank-and-file sit uneasy under Abouel Fotouh's big tent," *Egypt Independent*, May 17, 2012, accessed July 21, 2012, http://www.egyptindependent.com/news/women-and-salafi-rank-and-file-sit-uneasy-under-abouel-fotouhs-big-tent.

[65] Amir Zaky, "In Egypt's presidential race, cultural policy is absent," *Egypt Independent*, June 17, 2012, accessed July 20, 2012, http://www.egyptindependent.com/news/egypt%E2%80%99s-presidential-race-cultural-policy-absent.

that can counter the Salafi claims. For example in the 2012 constitution (now suspended), Article 44 stated, "Al-Azhar senior scholars are to be consulted in matters pertaining to Islamic law." Similarly, a new article criminalizing blasphemy, proposed by Al-Azhar, was inscribed in the 2012 constitution and did not provoke any reactions from the SCAF.[66] Since the military coup, Al-Azhar has aligned itself with the new contenders for political power. For example, Al-Azhar Grand Imam Sheikh Ahmed Al-Tayyeb[67] issued a statement supporting the new government, its plan for early elections, and its roadmap for the country. He also issued a fatwa in July 2013 declaring that "peaceful opposition against a ruler is permissible according to Sharia," which many interpreted as condoning the anti-Morsi movement.[68] In the post-Morsi context, it is reasonable to think that Al-Azhar will probably maintain its buffer role, this time between secular and Salafis.

On another note, it seems that the advancement of minority rights and freedom of expression is improbable both under Islamist and praetorian rule. For example, Article 8 of the 2012 constitution on freedom of belief stated: "Freedom of belief is absolute, and religious rights are practiced if not in contradiction with public order." The opponents to the constitution decried the article as worse than the one in the constitution under Mubarak, which lacked the public order clause. Although the clause on public order was dropped in the adopted 2012 constitution, it did not abate the concern for freedom of belief. That is why Article 64 of the 2013 draft of the constitution reasserts the principle of freedom of belief as absolute.[69] Additionally, critics pointed to the inclusion of religious rights for the Abrahamic religions as both a step forward for Christians and a loss for other religious minorities.[70]

As experienced in other Muslim countries, Egypt saw mass demonstrations against the film *The Innocence of Muslims*, with thousands

---

[66] For example, in April 2012, Adel Imam, the most popular Egyptian comedian, was sentenced to three months in jail and a fine under charges of contempt of religion, which is criminalized under Article 98(f) in the Egyptian Penal Code. For more examples, see Chapter 5. "Egyptian court upholds sentence against comedian for offending Islam," *Egypt Independent*, April 24, 2012, accessed July 21, 2012, http://www.egyptindependent.com/news/court-upholds-sentence-against-%E2%80%8Ecomedian-offending-islam.

[67] Sheikh Ahmed Al-Tayyeb has been the grand imam and president of Al-Azhar University since 2010. Al-Tayyeb was a member of Mubarak's National Democratic Party (NDP) and has been criticized for being a remnant of the old regime. He supported the ouster of Morsi in July 2013 and is perceived as an anti-Muslim Brotherhood figure.

[68] See "Azhar Grand Imam allows peaceful opposition," *State Information Service*, June 24, 2013, accessed June 24, 2013, http://www.sis.gov.eg/En/Templates/Articles/tmpArticleNews.aspx?ArtID=68643.

[69] Osman El Sharnoubi, "New Egyptian constitution offers fewer religious freedoms, critics allege," *Ahram Online*, October 2, 2012, accessed October 24, 2012, http://english.ahram.org.eg/NewsContent/1/64/54582/Egypt/Politics-/New-Egyptian-constitution-offers-fewer-religious-f.aspx.

[70] "Constituent Assembly proposes article criminalizing blasphemy," *Egypt Independent*, July 17, 2012, accessed July 22, 2012, http://www.egyptindependent.com/news/constituent-assembly-proposes-article-criminalizing-blasphemy.

gathering at the American embassy in Cairo to protest the unflattering depiction of the Prophet Muhammad. Seventy people were injured in the protests, which escalated into violence between protestors and police. Furthermore, a Cairo court sentenced, *in absentia*, seven Egyptian Christians to death for insulting the Islamic religion through their role in making the movie.

Morsi, seeking to mend his relationship with the United States, issued his condolences to America regarding embassy deaths in Libya and denounced violence in response to the film, but defended Egyptians' right to protest peacefully against what he referred to as crossing a "red line."[71] Morsi also called on the Egyptian embassy in Washington to take any and all legal measures against the makers of the film.[72]

Controversy has also surrounded the status of women's rights under the new Egyptian constitution, with concerns centering on the state's duty to enforce gender equality "without contradicting the rulings of shar'ia." A statement issued by a coalition of opposition parties and public figures decried the vague wording of the article, blaming it on Islamist domination of the drafting process, which "endangers the democracy that everyone aspired for and sacrificed for." Women's rights activists, including Heba Morayef of Human Rights Watch, lobbied for the phrasing to be changed to the more inclusive "principles of Islamic shar'ia," akin to Article 2.[73] As mentioned in Chapter 8, similar concerns about equality between Muslims and Christians were raised by opponents to the 2012 constitution.

Although the SCAF was secular in nature, as soon as 2012, it relinquished politics of freedom of expression to religiously motivated political actors. This is important to keep in mind at a time when the military has reasserted its control on Egyptian politics after the ousting of President Morsi in July 2013.

As a case in point, the declaration issued July 9, 2013, to replace the suspended constitution indirectly confirmed that there will be no major change on the status of Islam in the near future. Article 2 of the new document has been merged with Article 1 (about principles of democracy and citizenship),

[71] "Innocence of Muslims participants sentenced to death in Egypt," *The Guardian*, November 28, 2012, accessed July 4, 2013, http://www.guardian.co.uk/world/2012/nov/28/innocence-of-muslims-death-sentence.

[72] Bradley Hope, "Egypt's Morsi calls for peaceful protests over anti-Islam film," *The National*, September 24, 2012, accessed October 24, 2012, http://www.thenational.ae/news/world/egypts-morsi-calls-for-peaceful-protests-over-anti-islam-film. Mohamed Kemal, "Political responses to film that spurred embassy raid call for legal action and protests," *Egypt Independent*, September 12, 2012, accessed October 24, 2012, http://www.egyptindependent.com/news/political-responses-film-spurred-embassy-raid-call-legal-action-and-protests.

[73] "Egypt draft constitution raises fears for women's rights," September 23, 2012, accessed October 24, 2012, http://english.ahram.org.eg/NewsContent/1/64/53598/Egypt/Politics-/Egypt-draft-constitution-article-raises-fears-for-.aspx.

but the content about Shariʿa remains. The restriction of the freedom of religious worship to Christianity, Islam and Judaism is also maintained, though Al-Azhar's role in new legislation has been dropped. In the same vein, one of the first reactions to the military's repression of pro-Morsi protestors in August 2013 was the burning of Copt churches across the country.[74]

IRAQ: EVOLUTION TOWARD A COMMUNAUTARIST FEDERATION

In contrast to the exclusive or Jacobinist republic, the communautarist federation acknowledges religious diversity yet is unable to reach a point of equilibrium because certain groups are tempted to maintain the status quo. This was evident in Saddam's treatment of the Shiʿis in Iraq as a functional minority in addition to the forceful suppression of the Kurds, and is still relevant today in the political rivalry between the Sunnis, Shiʿis, and Kurds.

We described in Chapter 6 how since 2005 reforms in religious education have so far failed in providing a consensual narrative for a more pluralistic Iraqi society emphasizing tolerance for all religious and ethnic groups. For instance, many Sunnis claim the new textbooks promote a Shiʿi version of Islam at the expense of the Sunni group. At the same time, Shiʿis assert that not enough has been done to address the previous Sunni bias against the Shiʿa. Vocal Sunni opposition to textbook revision on a Shiʿi basis is paralleled by Shiʿi accusations of Sunnis fomenting sectarianism. This is one of several examples of mutual distrust between the communal elites, which has prevented Iraq from being a democracy despite its extreme levels of linkage with the United States (see Chapter 11).

Thus behaving according to Islamic norms is instrumental in defining the public space. For example, the closure of nightclubs and bars and the non-renewal of liquor licenses have been on the rise.[75] In January 2011, a ban on alcohol was imposed in the capital by the head of the Baghdad Provincial Council, Kamil al-Zaidi, who explained, "[w]e are a Muslim country, and everyone must respect that."[76] In the same vein, Shiʿi groups attempted to

---

[74] Ayat Al-Tawy, "Churches torched across Egypt in anti-Coptic violence by Morsi loyalists," *Ahram Online*, August 15, 2013, accessed August 15, 2013, http://english.ahram.org.eg/NewsContent/1/64/79124/Egypt/Politics-/Churches-torched-across-Egypt-in-antiCoptic-violen.aspx.

[75] Translated from Arabic: "Minister Tamim, will you be like the ministers that preceded you?" *Al-Hewar* blog post, 2010, retrieved July 10, 2010 from http://www.ahewar.org/debat/show.art.asp?aid=239652

[76] Ernesto Londoño, "Crackdown on alcohol seen as part of conservative moment in Iraq," *The Washington Post*, January 4, 2010, accessed August 15, 2013, http://www.washingtonpost.com/wp-dyn/content/article/2010/01/03/AR2010010302228.html. See also Mushreq Abbas, "New Religious Campaign Targets Baghdad's Cafes," *Al-Monitor*, July 19, 2013, accessed August 18, 2013, http://www.al-monitor.com/pulse/originals/2013/07/religious-campaign-targets-cafes-baghdad-iraq.html.

ban nonveiled women from the Kadhimiya neighborhood north of Baghdad in October 2012.[77]

Such impositions of "moral codes" are not particular to Shi'i groups – a 2005 example is a Sunni religious group affiliated with al-Qa'ida that prohibited women from leaving their homes in Al-Anbar. Mushreq Abbas writes for *Al-Monitor* that such activities contradict Iraqi constitution Articles 40 and 17, which state respectively that "each individual shall have the freedom of thought, conscience, and belief" and "every individual shall have the right to personal privacy so long as it does not contradict the rights of others and public morals."[78]

It is worth emphasizing, however, that these tensions over behavior happen most frequently within each sect and not across them. In other words, Islam as believing or behaving is not the main point of political contention between political groups. That is why one will be hard pressed to find in the following pages any debate over the Islamic nature of the Iraqi nation or over what it means to be Muslim and Iraqi, as we have discussed in Tunisia or Egypt. Instead, belonging to Islam is taken for granted. What is at stake is whose Islam shapes Iraq. In this regard, Iraq can be compared to a certain extent to Lebanon, in which the power sharing among communities has divided the country for so long. The other related challenge is the institutional reform to facilitate power sharing between religious and ethnic groups.

Since 2005, Iraq has followed a federal system, which provides for regional and provincial autonomy: Kurdistan is a federal territory with control over its internal administration, and Arabic and Kurdish are both official languages of Iraq. The government is not completely decentralized and the potential for regional autonomy along sectarian lines is under debate, but the 2005 constitution allows for the formation of new autonomous regions from an unlimited number of provinces (governorates). Post-2005 Iraq is thus an example of a nation-state based on a bounded plurality, which emerged after the demise of the authoritarian, homogeneous conception of the nation imposed by Saddam Hussein.

---

[77] Tim Arango, "In Iraq, Bottoms Up For Democracy," *The New York Times*, April 16, 2011, accessed August 15, 2013, http://www.nytimes.com/2011/04/17/weekinreview/17booze.html.

[78] A month after the June 2013 departure of Baghdad governor Salah Abdul Razzaq, responsible for the campaigns against liquor and nightclubs, his replacement, Ali al-Tamimi, banned and shut down cafes frequented by young people in central Baghdad on the basis of "religious violations," specifically the employment of "underage women." Many in Baghdad were shocked, especially after al-Tamimi, who represents Muqtada al-Sadr's political bloc, had repeatedly voiced his group's commitment to a civil state. Al-Tamimi formed an "emergency unit" task force and employed the help of volunteers to systematically shut down several cafes in the city center, including even those that did not employ women at all. *Al-Kufa News Agency*, June 24, 2013, accessed August 18, 2013, http://www.alkufanews.com/news.php?action=view&id=9935.

In this sense, Iraq's political system is a communautarist federation because of the deep fragmentation of the communal elites who struggle to forge bonds of trust and equality with each other. It is worth mentioning that while the Sunni elites initially opposed a federal system, they did, in 2011, express more and more frustration with the central government to the point that some leaders claimed to desire creation of a Sunni province. As a result of Prime Minister al-Maliki's failure to share power, Iraqi parliamentary speaker Osama al-Nujaifi is quoted as saying, "This should be treated wisely and quickly before things develop to where they [Sunnis] think of a kind of separation to guarantee rights."[79] This political frustration was exacerbated by the withdrawal of U.S. troops on December 16, 2011, as the government coalition in Baghdad collapsed with the walkout by Iraqiyya from parliament, the arrest warrant for Vice President al-Hashemi, and the firing of Deputy Prime Minister Saleh al-Mutlaq.[80] Protestors in Ramadi, Anbar, Mosul, Saladin, Diyala, and South Kirkuk in May 2012 called for an independent Sunni province, stating, "The Sunnis have no other recourse in Iraq except armed confrontation and the formation of independent provinces."[81]

It is important to note that the Shiʻa and the Sunni are not the only contenders for power nor do they disagree on everything. Importantly, the Kurds are a major third player in Iraqi politics, and sharing the experience of repression with the Shiʻis, the two sometimes form a political coalition against the Sunni. At the same time, the Kurds seek effective independence from Iraq with territorial autonomy, yet neither the Sunni nor Shiʻi Arabs are willing to compromise the territorial integrity of Iraq. The Kurds control the only confederated area currently in Iraq, having formed the Kurdistan Regional Government (KRG). The KRG, according to its website, exercises "executive power according to the Kurdistan Region's laws, as enacted by the Kurdistan Parliament."[82] It acts as a body largely independent from the main government in Baghdad, with its own security force and its own foreign diplomatic negotiations.

The Iraqi army post-Saddam is one of the major sites of contention between groups. Saddam held the key position of controlling the security apparatus of the state from the beginning, which allowed him to gain totalitarian power without needing the backbone of an army. The security apparatus replaced the army by subjugating it under the authority of the

[79] "Risks to Al-Azhar?," *Al-Ahram Weekly*, July 17, 2013, accessed August 9, 2013, http://weekly.ahram.org.eg/News/3403/32/Risks-to-Al-Azhar-.aspx.

[80] July 17, 2011, *World Tribune*, http://www.worldtribune.com/worldtribune/WTARC/2011/me_iraqo887_07_17.html, accessed January 5, 2012.

[81] "A 'Stable' Country Teetering on the Brink," *Qantara*, December 28, 2011, accessed January 5, 2012, http://en.qantara.de/wcsite.php?wc_c=18174.

[82] "Iraq More Divided Than Ever," *Al-Monitor*, May 20, 2013, accessed June 24, 2013, http://www.al-monitor.com/pulse/politics/2013/05/iraq-protests-saadi-initiative-divided.html.

Republican Guard and the more elite Special Guard, the members of which were largely recruited from Tikrit and "provided the regime with a crucial shield against the officer corps of the army."[83]

After the fall of Saddam, in order to foster the de-Ba'thification of the state, the U.S. government disbanded the Iraqi military, with the consequence of bolstering violence between communal groups. Sultan Barakat argues,

> Possibly the most disastrous mistake of the US administration was dismantling the army by decree .... Soldiers had their pay cancelled and were never asked to surrender weapons they had taken home with them when they abandoned the war; the officer core was humiliated by being debarred not only from holding rank in the army but from any public employment, on the grounds that it was by definition Ba'thist.[84]

By disbanding the army in this way, not only was the military left with a deep sense of betrayal, but the wider public was resentful of the association of the army, which had been "a symbol of national pride," with outlaws.[85] Military expertise and weapons lay in the hands of a disgruntled military – largely Sunni – elite and insurgent groups, while also paving the way for organized Sunni militant groups like the Jaysh Rijal al-Tariqa al-Naqshabandia (JRTN).[86] Iraq's government blamed the JRTN for April 2013 attacks in Kirkuk.[87] It is also allegedly responsible for other "highly accurate small-arms attacks" in other parts of northern Iraq, including Mosul[88] and the greater Ninawa region.[89]

---

[83] Mackey, *The Reckoning*, 318. Saddam had been cultivating the state's security apparatus since the 1968 Ba'thist coup as the head of state security under Bakr's leadership. This security apparatus included *Jihāz al-Amn al-Khāṣ* (special security); *al-Amn al-'Amm* (general security); *al-Mukhābarāt* (general intelligence); *al-Istikhbarāt* (military intelligence); and *al-Amn al-'Askarī* (military security) in addition to party security agencies, police forces, paramilitaries, and special units.

[84] Stansfield, "The transition to democracy in Iraq," 141.

[85] Sultan Barakat, "Post-Saddam Iraq: Deconstructing a Regime, Reconstructing a Nation," *Third World Quarterly* 26.4–5 (2005): pp, accessed August 10, 2011, http://www.jstor.org/stable/3993709, pp. 571–91, 579.

[86] The JRTN was established in 2007 as a result of "general discontent about the apparent chaos and corruption since the end of Ba'thist rule." It is best described as a hybrid of Islamist themes and nationalist military expertise, as it "prefers to use former members of elite military units such as the Special Republican Guard or Republican Guard as operational affiliates." Michael Knights, "The JRTN Movement and Iraq's Next Insurgency," *CTC Sentinel* 4.7 (2011), accessed August 15, 2011, http://washingtoninstitute.org/html/pdf/ Knights20110700.pdf, p. 4.

[87] Knights, "The JRTN Movement and Iraq's Next Insurgency," p. 4.

[88] "Worse and worse: Sectarian bloodshed looks set to persist," *The Economist*, May 25, 2013, accessed June 24, 2013, http://www.economist.com/news/ middle-east-and-africa/21578442-sectarian-bloodshed-looks-set-persist-worse-and-worse.

[89] Kimberly Kagan, "The Iraq War is Not Over," *The Weekly Standard*, July 1, 2013, http:// www.weeklystandard.com/articles/iraq-war-not-over_736876.html.

In sum, the biggest issue plaguing the Iraqi army has been the influence of ethno-sectarian parties. Najim Abed al-Jabouri, the former governor of Tal-Afar, declared, "The majority of these [Iraqi army] divisions are under the patronage of a political party. For example the 8th IA division in Kut and Diwanya is heavily influenced by the Dawa party; the 4th IA division in Salahadeen is influenced by President Jalal Talabani's Patriotic Union of Kurdistan; the 7th IA division in Anbar is influenced by the Iraqi Awakening Party, and the 5th IA division in Diyala is heavily influenced by the Islamic Supreme Council of Iraq."[90] This, of course, directly contradicts the Iraqi constitution, which states in Part A, Section 1, Article 9 that "the Iraqi armed forces and security services ... shall not be used as an instrument to oppress the Iraqi people [and] shall not interfere in political affairs."[91]

Moreover, "[s]ome provincial authorities, local councils, and sectarian and ethnic leaders have been concerned by the withdrawal of US troops because they feel that without US support, power may become more centralized in the hands of the few."[92] For instance, security in the Kurdistan region and the disputed territories is contentious, "particularly in Ninewa province, where a plan was put forth to invite Kurdish Peshmerga forces to patrol joint checkpoints with Iraqi Security Forces (ISF).... This proposal prompted an outcry from Arab provincial officials in Ninewa who opposed allowing the Peshmerga to operate these checkpoints with the Iraq Security Force (ISF)."[93] Since January 2010, many point out that general progress has been made toward full integration of the Peshmerga forces into the Iraqi army: about half of Peshmerga forces are paid by the central government in Baghdad, and half by the Kurdistan Regional Government (KRG).[94] In April 2013, the move by Peshmerga to deploy troops in Kirkuk, however, was largely viewed, in the words of an Iraqi ground forces general, as a "dangerous development" performed "to reach (Kirkuk's) oil wells and fields." Peshmerga defended its actions in a statement claiming its troops deployed with the consent of the governor of Kirkuk and in response to

---

[90] Ibid., 278.
[91] *English translation of the Iraqi Constitution*, United Nations Mission in Iraq, http://www.uniraq.org/documents/iraqi_constitution.pdf.
[92] Anthony Cordesman, *Iraq and the United States, creating Strategic Partnership* , June 2010, 2010, accessed August 15, 2011, http://csis.org/files/publication/100622_Cordesman_IraqUSStrategicPartner_WEB.pdf, p. 243.
[93] "Special Inspector General for Iraq Reconstruction (SIGIR)," *Quarterly Report to the United States Congress*, October 30, 2009, Public Law 108–106, as amended, and Public Law 95–452, 106–7.
[94] "Iraq: Politics, Governance, and Human Rights," *Congressional Research Service*, June 3, 2013, accessed June 24, 2013, http://www.fas.org/sgp/crs/mideast/RS21968.pdf.

"information that terrorist groups have plans to launch terrorist attacks in these regions."[95]

In addition, al-Qaʿida in Iraq and various neo-Baʿthist groups have tried to take advantage of the withdrawal of U.S. troops with renewed bombings and attacks.[96] Al-Qaʿida in Iraq (AQI) is still credited with being the most important Sunni insurgent group. AQI's leaders are largely Iraqi, and it is considered more of a national Sunni movement. It "has capitalized on Iraq's economic problems, poverty, and widespread underemployment to keep recruiting 'expendable' part-time volunteers." While "experts disagree over the level of coordination among AQI and other movements," JRTN "has increasingly joined AQI in conducting bomb attacks in the Mosul area and other parts of Iraq."[97] The increase in activity has even prompted a trend in the direction of "radicalization and mobilization of Shiʿa militants to oppose al-Qaʿida in Iraq," according to Kimberly Kagan, founder and president of the Institute for the Study of War.

Another security concern in Iraq, as mentioned in Part II, is the civil war in neighboring Syria and its influence on regional stability. The Iraqi government has moved forces to the Syrian border and continues to watch for Iraqis crossing the border to fight in Syria. Therefore, there is a strong risk that the Syrian conflict will fuel ongoing sectarian clashes in Iraq.

While concerns over Islamist influence, especially with military support from Iran and al-Qaʿida, have led to cross-sectarian calls to bolster the secular identity of Iraq especially with the 2009–10 elections, political leadership has, since the first post-Saddam elections in 2005, remained for the most part unchanged. For example, prior to the March 2010 parliamentary elections, Prime Minister al-Maliki removed his own group, the State of Law Coalition, from of the Shiʿa National Iraqi Alliance (NIA), to create an all-Shiʿa coalition.[98] Ultimately, the Sunni coalition al-Iraqiyya (Iraqi National Movement), which stresses itself to be secular and non-sectarian under the leadership of Ayad Allawi, won a plurality of 91 out of 325 parliamentary seats; the SLC won 89, the NIA won 70, and the Kurdistan Alliance won 43 seats. Despite the narrow margin of loss, al-Maliki retained his premiership, and there has been a rise in religious

---

[95] "Army: Kurdish move in disputed Iraqi province 'dangerous,'" *Al Arabiya*, April 27, 2013, accessed June 28, 2013, http://english.alarabiya.net/en/News/middle-east/2013/04/27/Kurdish-forces-deploy-near-Iraq-s-disputed-Kirkuk.html.

[96] Anthony H. Cordesman, Adam Mausner, and Elena Derby, "Iraq and the United States: Creating a Strategic Partnership," 62.

[97] See: Reidar Visser, "As the Deadline for Forming Coalitions Expires, al-Maliki Creates a Shiite Alliance for Iraq's Local Elections in April 2013," Iraq and Gulf Analysis, December 21, 2012, http://gulfanalysis.wordpress.com/2012/12/21/as-the-deadline-for-forming-coalitions-expires-maliki-creates-monster-shiite-alliance-for-iraqs-local-elections-in-april-2013/.

[98] Ibid., 87.

influence as well as an increase in religious leaders playing more influential roles in politics. Certainly, a primary example of this phenomenon is the power of Muqtada al-Sadr, although the most influential Shi'i cleric in Iraq, Ali al-Sistani, has been reluctant to delve fully into Iraqi politics, despite calls for him to do so.[99]

CONCLUSION: UNSECULAR DEMOCRACY AND THE THREE LEVELS OF SECULARITY

In sum, in light of the ongoing political transitions in Egypt, Tunisia, and Iraq, the most plausible scenarios for future regimes seem to be either praetorian regimes or competitive authoritarianism. The latter is embodied in different forms: Jacobinist republic (Egypt) or communautarist federation (Iraq). In the case that all domains of democracy are fully operational and all religions are treated equally, maybe the future of Tunisia holds possibility for unsecular democracy.

As discussed in Part I, secularity has to be evaluated at the institutional, social, and individual level. These levels refer to the interactions between state and religion, the treatment of all religions by law, and the recognition of individual freedom of the self, respectively. The challenge for most Muslim countries is to dismantle Islam as the hegemonic religion at levels one and two of secularity, in the institutions and social legitimacy of religions. Our review in this chapter of the current discussions about Islam in Tunisia and Egypt shows that this goal is not yet on the agenda. Even if it is broached, the limit still remains at the third level – that is, limits on the self, which is at risk across all Muslim countries. That is what I have called "unsecular democracy," toward which Tunisia may head.

What would it take to move toward a greater recognition of the rights of individuals, to greater freedom of expression? Is it even possible? These questions are addressed in the next chapter.

---

[99] "Could Sistani Be Iraq's Last Hope?," *Al-Monitor*, May 2, 2013, accessed June 24, 2013, http://www.al-monitor.com/pulse/originals/2013/05/iraq-political-crisis-solution-sistani.html.

The Way Forward: The Role of Islam in Democratization

As noted earlier, according to mainstream political analysis, if elections, rule of law, and the disappearance of tutelary authorities were to occur, this would create the institutional guarantees that must be in place for the functioning of a democracy. Even though secularism is not part of the minimal democratic "kit," Alfred Stepan rightly argues that some separation between state and religious institutions is needed in any operational democracy.[1] As I have argued in Part I, this institutional differentiation is a necessary but not sufficient condition of secularity, because it does not address the level of freedom of self (as a specific component of the freedom of the individual). In this regard, the experiences of Indonesia and Senegal, the two Muslim countries with an equidistance of state and religion, can illustrate a possible path toward democratization that would not entail the adoption of the Western paradigm of separation of church and state. It will also allow us to illustrate that even in these secular regimes of Indonesia and Senegal, the rights of the self are not a given.

MULTIPLE IMPLEMENTATIONS OF STATE-RELIGION EQUIDISTANCE

To understand how a shift toward democratization might occur, I consider Alfred Stepan's "twin tolerations"[2] paradigm, coupled with the "principled distance" model advanced by Rajeev Bhargava.[3] These two approaches help redefine secularization without borrowing from the Western experience. In other words, they allow us to discuss the conditions for secularization without

---

[1] Alfred Stepan, "Religion, Democracy and the 'Twin Tolerations,'" *Journal of Democracy* 11.4 (October 2000): 37–57.

[2] Ibid.

[3] Rajeev Bhargava, "States, religious diversity, and the crisis of secularism," *Open Democracy*, March 22, 2011, accessed March 23, 2011, http://www.opendemocracy.net/rajeev-bhargava/states-religious-diversity-and-crisis-of-secularism-0.

equating it with secularism. "Twin tolerations" refers to a clear demarcation between the respective spheres of influence of religious and state institutions, where neither religious nor political establishments impinge unduly on the other's jurisdiction and set of rights.[4] This demarcation does not have to translate into a complete separation. The concept of "principled distance" between religion and state introduced by Barghava, unlike neutrality, allows for state intervention in religious affairs to provide assistance to particular groups and to assure that everyone's rights within a group are upheld. This "principled distance" provides a more nuanced and flexible understanding of equality that takes into account the social needs of different religious groups and therefore entails the state's active intervention.

In these conditions, secularization can be evaluated through the following legal and political procedures: positive cooperation between state and religion; and implementation of a "principled distance."[5]

I will discuss this modus operandi in Indonesia and Senegal in order to explain how they could apply to Muslim emerging democracies. It appears that in the best case scenario where these two procedures are at work, there are still limits on some individual rights related to the freedom of the self.

Positive Cooperation between the State and Religion

None of the countries examined in this book has adopted a strategy of positive cooperation between the state and all religions, and it is not realistic to expect them to do so in the near future. Indonesia and Senegal are two notable exceptions that display a positive cooperation between state and religion in Muslim-majority nations.

Indonesia's national motto, "Unity in Diversity," epitomizes a constitutional commitment to religious, ethnic, and political diversity and equality. The *Pancasila*, the bedrock of the country's legal neutrality in religious matters, enshrines the values of social justice and consensus. Pancasila means "five pillars" and consists of five principles included in the preamble to the 1945 constitution: (1) belief in God; (2) a just and civilized humanitarianism; (3) national unity; (4) Indonesian democracy through consultation and consensus; and (5) social justice.[6]

---

[4] Alfred Stepan, "Religion, Democracy and the 'Twin Tolerations,'" 37–57.

[5] Alfred Stepan, Juan J. Linz, and Yogendra Yadav, *Crafting State-Nations: India and other Multinational Democracies* (Baltimore, MD: Johns Hopkins University Press, 2011). See also Alfred Stepan, "The Multiple Secularisms of Modern Democracies and Autocracies," in Craig Calhoun, Mark Juergensmeyer, and Jonathan van Antwerpen (eds.), *Rethinking Secularism* (New York: Oxford University Press, 2011).

[6] Kikue Hamayotsu, "Islam and Nation Building in Southeast Asia: Malaysia and Indonesia in Comparative Perspective," *Pacific Affairs* 75.3 (2002): 355.

The positive cooperation between state and religions is well illustrated by the shaping of the elementary and secondary Islamic educational curriculum[7] through a joint project between the state's education planners and religious leaders. It resulted in Islamic education becoming only one part of a broader curriculum, which upheld constitutional ideals of a pluralist and democratic Indonesia.

In multiethnic Senegal, the French-rooted republican form of democracy has persisted since Senegal gained independence in 1960. Islam is highly visible in the public sphere, especially through Sufi fraternities, whereby spiritual leaders rooted in a maraboutic hierarchical lineage also command political authority by mediating between the state and citizens at the local level. At the same time, political parties based on religion are forbidden. The first president, Leopold Senghor, was Catholic, and many high-level Muslim leaders have had Catholic spouses. Along with Islamic holidays, Christmas and Easter are national holidays, and Christians as well as Muslims have access to education in their respective religious traditions in public schools.[8]

Principled Distance between the State and Religions

Equal treatment for groups is distinct from the principle of equal treatment for individuals because there may be differential legal treatment between groups. Such a differential treatment is based on the recognition of specific provisions a group needs to operate within the national community. For example, in Senegal, the state has used differential treatment to counter conservative attacks on the Muslim family code, upholding the principle of equality between husbands and wives even as polygamy remains legal. Local laws give both sexes equal rights to property, ban forced marriages, and set stringent punishments for physical violence against women.

In Indonesia, there is no implementation of principled distance. In fact, police and judicial responses to the increasing discrimination against minorities have been mild at best.[9] Tensions among religious communities have been growing, as seen in the wake of anti-Chinese legislation and the transmigration program, which have favored Western Indonesian and Muslim citizens. Additionally, the status of Shi'is has grown increasingly precarious. For example, in July 2012, a Shi'i leader, Tajul Muluk, was sentenced

---

[7] Azyumardi Azra, Dina Afrianty, and Robert W. Hefner, "Pesantren and Madrasa: Muslim Schools and National Ideals in Indonesia," in Robert W. Hefner and Muhammad Qasim Zaman (eds.), *Schooling Islam: The Culture and Politics of Modern Muslim Education* (Princeton, NJ: Princeton University Press, 2007).

[8] International Religious Freedom Report for Senegal 2008, accessed January 8, 2012, http://www.state.gov/g/drl/rls/irf/2008/108388.htm.

[9] The government has affirmed the 2008 decree defining the Ahmadiyya as non-Muslims.

to two years in prison under charges of blasphemy for his deviant teachings that caused public anxiety.[10] While Muluk denied any deviant teachings, observers argue that his arrest reflects the growing attacks on religious minorities in Indonesia by hard-line Sunni Muslims and the state alike. In November 2012, Indonesian officials witnessed the forced conversion of eighteen Shi'a in Sampang. Sectarian violence in East Java in August 2012 left two dead.[11] Also in East Java, authorities gave 165 Shi'is living in temporary shelters (after an attack on their homes) the option to convert to Sunni Islam or remain in deteriorating living conditions without state protection. Ahmadis in Lombok lived in similar conditions for six years, after their homes were attacked, without government assistance.[12] In brief, even in Indonesia we can see political forces at work to elevate the dominant Islamic group to a hegemonic status.

Finally, neither Indonesia nor Senegal take into account the principle of self in the granting of individual freedoms.

THE CONTESTED PRINCIPLE OF SELF

The principle of self is the third dimension of secularity that is not really addressed in any approach that centers exclusively on state-religion relations. This third dimension relates to the freedom of the individual not only in the sociopolitical and economic domains but also in sexual and spiritual matters. In other words, the principle of self entails the recognition of the individual's right to make lifestyle choices that do not conform to the dominant cultural or political norm and do not obey religious principles. The same-sex marriage debate in the United States reflects exactly this tension between the preeminence of the self and a religiously constrained interpretation of the individual. For example, on June 28, 2013, the Supreme Court struck the 1996 Defense of Marriage Act (DOMA) that prevented federal recognition of same-sex marriage by defining marriage as the union between a man and woman. According to the Supreme Court decision, DOMA introduced inequality into federal law and therefore violated the Fifth Amendment's protection of equal liberty. "DOMA's principal effect is to identify a subset of state-sanctioned marriages and make them unequal."[13]

[10] Ahmad Pathoni, "Shiite's Conviction Raises Concerns about Intolerance," *Wall Street Journal*, July 16, 2012, accessed July 21, 2012, http://blogs.wsj.com/searealtime/2012/07/16/shiites-conviction-raises-concerns-about-intolerance/?blog_id=203&post_id=987.

[11] "Indonesia," *International Freedom Report*, 2012, accessed June 18, 2013, http://www.state.gov/documents/organization/208444.pdf.

[12] "Indonesia: Religious freedom under attack as Shi'a villagers face eviction," *Amnesty International*, January 15, 2013, accessed June 25, 2013, http://www.amnesty.org/en/news/indonesia-religious-freedom-under-attack-shia-villagers-face-eviction-2013-01-15.

[13] http://communities.washingtontimes.com/neighborhood/stimulus/2013/jun/27/doma-and-prop-8-supreme-courts-radical-conservatis/#ixzz2XS6zIeLt, accessed June 28, 2013.

The argument of the Supreme Court illustrates the principle of the self: if the equality of individuals is a principal value, no moral or religious argument can limit this equality. The fact that this principle challenges the beliefs of some segments of American society is by itself a testimony of the intrinsic tensions between the moral or communal limit of individualism and the limitless empowerment of the self. Although this tension is inherent to all democracies, it has become particularly acute in the Western ones where religious limitations of the self are increasingly illegitimate.

In other words, the fundamental issue is the tension between a relativistic culture that defines morality by what is good for the individual and a religiously based form of morality. The resistance of Muslim countries to grant the self total freedom is a good example of such tension. Case in point: although Indonesia is defined by the twin toleration principle, it has not acknowledged the principle of the self. Blasphemy is outlawed in article 156a of the Penal Code, which reads: "A maximum imprisonment of five years shall punish any person who deliberately in public gives expression to feelings or commits an act, a) which principally have the character of being at enmity with, abusing or staining a religion, adhered to in Indonesia; b) with the intention to prevent a person to adhere to any religion based on the belief of the almighty God."[14]

The law was upheld in April 2010 by the Indonesian Supreme Court, which stated that it "was vital to religious harmony."[15] In 2008, the government banned proselytizing by Ahmadis under the aegis of blasphemy law.[16]

Interestingly, the Indonesian government does not have an official law regarding the legality or illegality of homosexuality and transsexuality. While this is different from the laws of many Muslim-majority countries, some Indonesian advocates call for the government to take an official stance condoning LGBT status as a way of countering still-stiff societal objections to the practices.[17] The magnitude of social rejection, however, should not be underestimated; in 2013, a Pew Research Center poll found that 93 percent of Indonesians believed homosexuality should not be accepted by society.[18]

---

[14] "Indonesia upholds blasphemy law," *Al-Jazeera*, April 20, 2010, accessed June 28, 2013, http://www.aljazeera.com/news/asia-pacific/2010/04/201042081011575962.html.

[15] "Indonesia," *International Religious Freedom Report*, 2012, accessed June 28, 2013, http://www.state.gov/documents/organization/208444.pdf.

[16] Ibid.

[17] It's OK to be gay in Indonesia so long as you keep it quiet," *Deutsche Welle*, March 2, 2013, accessed June 28, 2013, http://www.dw.de/its-ok-to-be-gay-in-indonesia-so-long-as-you-keep-it-quiet/a-6456222.

[18] "The Global Divide on Homosexuality," *Pew Research Center*, June 4, 2013, accessed June 28, 2013, http://www.pewglobal.org/files/2013/06/Pew-Global-Attitudes-Homosexuality-Report-FINAL-JUNE-4-2013.pdf.

This figure is even higher in Senegal, where 96 percent of the population believed society should reject homosexuality. In contrast to Indonesia, the Senegalese government officially outlaws homosexuality. Article 319 of the Senegalese Penal Code reads in part: "Whoever will have committed an improper or unnatural act with a person of the same sex will be punished by imprisonment of between one and five years and by a fine of 100,000 to 1,500,000 francs."[19]

The social stigma against homosexuality in Senegal is also associated with discrimination against persons with HIV or AIDS because of the belief that such a status indicates homosexuality. LGBT Senegalese also face police persecution.[20] At the same time, again in contrast with Indonesia, Senegal has no laws prohibiting blasphemy or proselytizing. In 2012, the United States Department of State declared, that "There were no reports of abuses of religious freedom" in Senegal.[21] The Senegalese constitution, in Article 10, guarantees "everyone ... the right to express and diffuse their opinions freely in words, in writing, in images, [and] in peaceful marching."[22]

In sum, Senegal and Indonesia are unsecular democracies because the former outlaws homosexuality while the latter bans blasphemy. Both cases show that the respect of the principle of self constitutes another facet of secularity that is not automatically reached through "twin toleration."

A word of caution about interpreting my analysis above as a normative and teleological evaluation of non-Western political experience. My goal is not to apprehend the principle of self as the ultimate achievement of democracy that all countries should reach. It is to show instead that secularity is at play at different political levels, including the social legitimacy of religion and the definition of the individual. In this regard, all democracies differ in the ways institutional, social, and individual levels of secularization interact.

Nevertheless, most of the time non-Western democracies are evaluated through the implicit or explicit assumption that because the self is not recognized, no significant secularization has been attained. The discourse on women's rights is a case in point: in some societies like Iran, women are submitted to a strict dress code, leading to the assumption that they are deprived of all rights, when in fact they have gained significant social, economic, and

[19] "Submission in the UPR [Universal Periodic Review] review of: Senegal," *Office of the High Commissioner for Human Rights*, 2009, accessed June 28, 2013, http://lib.ohchr.org/HRBodies/UPR/Documents/Session4/SN/ILGA_SEN_UPR_S4_2009_ILGA_Etal_JOINT.pdf.

[20] "Senegal," *International Religious Freedom Report*, 2012, accessed June 28, 2013, http://www.state.gov/documents/organization/208400.pdf.

[21] Ibid.

[22] French original text reads in part: "Chacun a le droit d'exprimer et de diffuser librement ses opinions par la parole, la plume, l'image, la marche pacifique."

political rights. In other words, focusing on the self in public space does not reflect the ongoing secularization at the institutional and social levels.

On the opposite side of potential objections to my argument, it would also be misleading to read it as a relativistic defense of cultural limitations that are "essential" to Muslim societies. As a testimony of the contrary, I have described through all the chapters the never-ending adaptation and reshaping of norms and cultures since at least the emergence of the nation-state. Generally speaking, successful democracies, while meeting fundamental requirements such as free elections or rule of law can differ from European and North American models by capitalizing on their religious cultures' multivocality and democracy-concordant values.

As already mentioned, Egypt and Tunisia seem poised to evolve into praetorian regime or unsecular democracy, respectively. Tunisia lacks the pressures for acknowledgment of pluralism that diversity engenders, and Egypt's politics are unlikely to move toward a twin toleration model because of the political weakness of the Coptic minority. In fact, under the SCAF administration, the impetus to remain religiously exclusivist is only one of the challenges of the new regime. The other even more immediate risk concerns the role of the military as the tutelary authority over the new political institutions. In other words, Egypt is becoming a praetorian regime along the lines of what is found in Pakistan.

Another type of regime that does not adhere to the conditions of twin tolerations is the communautarist federation, which has characterized Iraq since 2003. This regime acknowledges religious diversity but is unable to reach a point of equilibrium because Sunni groups (previously in power) feel threatened by the redistribution of power toward Shi'is, and because some Shi'is would like to act as the dominant group. Unlike what Alfred Stepan, Juan J. Linz, and Yogendra Yadav[23] argue, the Iraq case shows that federalism is not sufficient to guarantee power-sharing mechanisms and equality. When it comes to religion, a more relevant rule is the recognition and protection of all religions by the state, or what I call legal neutrality (see Part 1). Such a principle has not yet been implemented in most Muslim-majority countries, with the notable exceptions of Senegal and to a certain extent Indonesia.

[23] Stepan, Linz, and Yadav, *Crafting State-Nations*. Also see Alfred Stepan, Juan J. Linz, and Yogendra Yadav, "The Rise of 'State-Nations,'" *Journal of Politics* 21.3 (2010): 5.

Conclusion of Part III

The Unexplored Role Of
The State In The Democratization Process

The multiple forms of demarcation between state and religion bring the role of the state into the analysis of democratization. My approach spotlights the influence of state institutions on democratic changes, an emergent topic within the vast body of literature on democratization.[1] The reshaping of state institutions toward more democratic structures has several aspects: building a strong and independent judiciary, protection of civil liberties, and the legal and political guarantees of the rule of law. This book focuses solely on secularism and the role of Islam in new regimes. In this sense, the perspective developed here echoes the work of Stepan, Linz, and Yadav, who posit that democratization involves "crafting a sense of belonging with respect to the state-wide political community, while simultaneously creating institutional safeguards for respecting and protecting politically-salient sociocultural diversities."[2] In their opinion, federalism is the only viable system to allow recognition of cultural and religious pluralism.

Providing examples of politically successful multicultural (and multinational) nation-states in India and Ukraine,[3] Stepan and colleagues convincingly argue that the nation-state is not the only viable form of democratic polity. Indeed, it cannot be viable in situations where preexisting sociocultural divisions undermine the conventional democratic prerequisite of a homogenous national identity. In such cases, deliberate actions must be taken to foster recognition of diverse identities while shaping collective norms to mobilize a broader national identity. In other words, the state is a prerequisite for nation building and remains key to the management of democratization, contrary to the popular wisdom that a sense of national community is the key ingredient of the state-building enterprise.

[1] *Perspectives on Politics* 9:2, February 2011.
[2] Stepan, Linz, and Yadav, *Crafting State-Nations*, 5.
[3] It can be objected that both India and Ukraine are currently undergoing serious economic, ethnic, and religious strife, hampering any serious progress toward greater democratization.

As discussed for Indonesia and Senegal, a "principled distance"[4] between the state and Islam is possible in heterogeneous societies, and in this sense, both countries conform to Stepan and Yadav's conception of the nation-state. But I do not think that the federal system is relevant for all Muslim countries because in the cases of Tunisia, Turkey, and Egypt, the homogeneity of society does not allow for such recognition of diversity. Instead of pluralism, some sort of legal arrangement and/or changes in the political culture are required to accommodate religious diversity and freedom of religion. In other words, when religious diversity is combined with ethnic and cultural diversity, a federal system based on the recognition of linguistic, ethnic, or regional entities can be a solution. But in the case of a greater cultural homogeneity, legal protection of religion and freedom of expression are the ways to foster democratization. In both options, the state is a prerequisite for nation building and remains key to the management of democratization, contrary to the popular wisdom that a sense of national community is the core ingredient of the state-building enterprise.[5] In the cases where there is no real diversity to foster these legal and political changes, can external influence play this role?

External Influence on Secularization: From the West or from the Diaspora

What role will Western influence play in the democratization of the Arab Spring countries? For instance, Steven Levitsky and Lucan A. Way have demonstrated that democratization is more likely to occur when a country is connected to the West through linkage or leverage. In the case of Muslim countries, linkage refers to the various economic, geopolitical, social, communication, and civil society ties between the United States and the European Union on one hand, and Muslim states on the other.[6] Leverage connotes the states' relatively limited bargaining power and their desire to avoid the potentially detrimental impact of Western action against them.[7] As a caveat to Levistky and Way's approach, it is important to keep in mind that leverage may be initiated by actors other than the state, such as religious figures, members of the diaspora, and so on. In the same vein, leverage is not exclusively Western-centric: it also comes from regional actors like Iran or Turkey. Finally, leverage is not always positive.

Extreme cases of linkage such as war can facilitate the collapse of authoritarian regimes, as in the case of Iraq under American occupation.

---

[4] Bhargava, "States, religious diversity, and the crisis of secularism."
[5] Ibid, 7–9.
[6] Steven Levitsky and Lucan A. Way, *Competitive Authoritarianism: Hybrid Regimes after the Cold War* (New York: Cambridge University Press, 2005), 23.
[7] Ibid.

Western intervention in Libya, through a coalition of multinational NATO blockades and air strikes starting in March 2011, is another extreme case of linkage leading to regime change. Needless to say, these interventions do not automatically lead to democracy or to the adoption of secular principles.

In the specific context of the transitions in Tunisia and Egypt, another possibility for external influence could come from their diasporas. For instance, one million Tunisian residents abroad were eligible to vote in the country's 2011 elections and for the first time elected eighteen representatives to the Constituent Assembly. Egyptians abroad were also granted the right to vote in the 2011 parliamentary elections as well as in the 2012 presidential elections.[8] To the dismay of Western policy makers, it is not certain, however, that the influence of these diasporas will translate into a greater "liberalization" of domestic politics.[9]

Additionally, when international actors get involved because of minorities demanding the enforcement of human rights conventions, external action can exacerbate domestic tensions. That is why in many cases, Christian groups in the Middle East have been portrayed as the "Trojan Horse" of the West, thus justifying their further exclusion from key public positions. It is probably in the interest of maintaining the Copts' nationalist image among Muslims that in the aftermath of the Maspero incidents, Pope Shenouda III rejected constituents' demands for an international investigation.[10] Even more interestingly, Copts and secular forces were the most critical of Secretary of State Hillary Clinton's July 2012 visit to Egypt, accusing the United States of interfering in domestic affairs and of concocting an alleged secret deal with Egypt's Islamist parties – namely, the Muslim Brotherhood's FJP – concerning Israel's security.[11] Moreover, a number of Christian politicians, including well-known business tycoon Naguib Sawiris and representatives of Egypt's Coptic Orthodox and evangelical churches, declined invitations to meet with the secretary of state.[12]

---

[8] Interestingly, while the mobilization of Egyptians overseas was very high in order to obtain this right, the majority of them did not go to vote.

[9] Philippe Fargues, "Demography, Migration and Revolt in the South of the Mediterranean," in C. Merlini and O. Roy (eds.), (Washington, DC: Brookings Institute Press, 2012), 17, 46.

[10] "Pope Shenouda rejects international investigation into Maspero violence," *Egypt Independent*, October 21, 2011, accessed July 21, 2012, http://www.egyptindependent.com/news/pope-shenouda-rejects-international-investigation-maspero-violence.

[11] Zeinab El Gundy, "Liberal and Christian figures, groups protest Clinton's Egypt visit," *Ahram Online*, July 15, 2012, accessed July 22, 2012, http://english.ahram.org.eg/NewsContent/1/64/47782/Egypt/Politics-/Liberal-and-Christian-figures,-groups-protest-Clin.aspx.

[12] "Egypt Orthodox, Evangelical church reps refuse meeting with Clinton," *Ahram Online*, July 15, 2012, accessed July 22, 2012, http://english.ahram.org.eg/NewsContent/1/64/47767/Egypt/Politics-/Egypt-Orthodox,-Evangelical-church-reps-refuse-mee.aspx.

Nonetheless, the political evolution of Turkey over the past three decades is an example of successful leverage by the European Union, culminating in constitutional amendments in 2004 that cemented growing civilian control over the military. Turkey has also granted increased rights to improve parity between Kurds and ethnic Turks, legalizing the use of the Kurdish language in broadcasts and educational settings in 2002.[13] In the same vein, the international community's critiques of the repression of the protests in Taksim Square in May 2013 have certainly prompted the Erdogan regime's strategy for a broader political inclusion of Kurds (see Chapter 8).

More significantly, new forms of electronic communication and social media intensify possibilities for leverage. Such technologies play a part in the dissemination of political values, norms, and ideals – including equality, social justice, and so forth – beyond the active participation of state-level actors, and this flow of information is increasingly significant in building the political consciousness of the urban middle class. The impact of transnational communication networks will definitively alter processes of social mobilization, as seen in the Egyptian and Tunisian uprisings, and will potentially transform the relationships between regimes, elites, and the middle class. This type of external influence requires a more systematic approach beyond the scope of this book. It is possible that in the long term, such influence may change the status of Islam from hegemonic to dominant.

As it stands at the time of this writing, however, Egypt is oscillating between a praetorian regime and competitive authoritarianism, while Tunisia seems poised to become an unsecular democracy. Unless we adopt a normative stance, there is no reason to think that recognition of the principle of self is in the political future of any of the countries discussed in this volume. But it will remain one of the most heated sites of contestation for decades to come.

---

[13] Turkey's first Kurdish language and literature department in a university opened in 2011. "First undergrad Kurdish department to be established in E Turkey," *Hurriyet Daily News*, January 6, 2011, accessed July 21, 2012, http://www.hurriyetdailynews.com/default. aspx?pageid=438&n=the-first-kurdish-department-will-be-founded-in-mus-2011-01-06.

General Conclusion

The Tragedy of Modernity

The making of Muslim-majority countries into nation-states has also been the making of Islam into a modern religion. This means that political and cultural actors adopted, pruned, and grafted Western concepts (the nation-state and secularism) to make them acceptable within their respective cultural contexts. However, instead of purging religion from both political power and public space, the outcome was quite the opposite: the embedding of Islam within the state apparatus.

Contradicting most modernization theories, the exportation of the Western political project to the new Muslim nations led to a counter secularization of sorts, even in the most secularly oriented states such as Turkey, Egypt, Iraq, or Tunisia. In other words, the confessionalization of Islam led to its politicization.

Confessionalization refers to the premodern period between the Peace of Augsburg (1555)[1] and the Thirty Years' War (1618–49), during which European Protestant and Catholic clergy started to enforce certain rules to distinguish their specific religious identities. Importantly, during this premodern period, state and religion remained deeply intertwined because the churches controlled and influenced social behaviors.[2] This confessionalization later developed into a religious domain separate from the state. However, the state ultimately took over control and punishment of improper behavior, so ultimately confessionalization of Christianity led to its depoliticization

---

[1] The Peace of Augsburg of 1555 was a treaty signed by Holy Roman Emperor Charles V establishing the principle of *cuius regio, eius religio* ("whose region, his religion"). In other words, this treaty acknowledged that the princes of the states in the Holy Roman Empire had the right to choose either Lutheranism or Catholicism for the people under their domain.

[2] Heinz Schilling, "Confessionalization in the Empire: Religious and Societal Change in Germany between 1555 and 1620," in *Religion, Political Culture and the Emergence of Early Modern Society: Essays in German and Dutch History* (Leiden: Brill, 1992), 208.

with greater interference of the state in social domains previously under the guidance of the church.[3]

In stark contrast, the confessionalization of Islam described in Part I of this book went hand in hand with its nationalization, as it became inscribed within the boundaries of the state.[4] This inscription of Islam within the nation and state institutions can be explained by the simultaneous processes of nation and state building, unlike the historical Western experience. As documented by much historical and political scholarship, national sentiment in its earlier forms, as a new sense of collective identity based on language and history, predated the state. Beginning in the fifteenth century, the term *nation* increasingly began to take on a political meaning to describe "a people who shared certain common laws and political institutions of a given territory."[5] This emergence of national political identities occurred at the same time as the confessionalization of Christianity, which in modern times would lead to the separation of church and state. This specific historical experience has served as the model to measure or evaluate all other secularization experiences.

As discussed in Part I of this book, the concept of the nation was foreign to the vast majority of Muslim populations, and it was adopted only by a small Westernized elite in contact with the colonial power. This elite became the rulers of the new nation-states and implemented very authoritarian and intrusive policies to transform Islam into a confession by inscribing it into the constitution, restructuring Shari'a, nationalizing Islamic institutions and clergy, and making Islam a component of the curriculum in public schools. This is how Islam as a modern religion became deeply embedded in the *habitus* of the new citizens.

To capture this simultaneous adaptation and modification of Islam as a modern religion first it was necessary in this book to move away from the dominant approaches of political Islam, which operate on the dichotomy of state and religion. Consequently, I examined the role of multiple actors (religious associations, clergy, educators etc.) and their different levels of interaction with the state.

Second, unlike most of the approaches that consider state-religion interactions antagonistic, in this book, conflict is only *one* way of interaction, used or combined with competition, adaptation, and cooperation between state agents and various social groups. Such a multiplicity of processes shows that religion, although an imported concept, was not simply forcefully imposed on social actors, but was actually enacted and appropriated by diverse local Islamic actors.

[3] See Charles Taylor, *A Secular Age* (Cambridge, MA: Belknap of Harvard University Press, 2007).
[4] See Chapter 6 on teaching Islam in public schools.
[5] John Keane, "Nations, Nationalism and European Citizens," in Sukumar Periwal (ed.), *Notions of Nationalism* (Budapest: Central European University Press, 1995), 182–3.

Finally, this book also shows that religion is not confined to beliefs or ideas but also materializes in organizations, bureaucracies, and social practices of different sorts. In this sense, the state's bureaucratic-legal structures in charge of implementing the Islamic religion have profoundly modified the religious tradition to make it modern. These modifications have affected the status and training of the religious authorities, their methodology of work, and their independence vis-à-vis political power. More specifically, as a result, religious thinking has lost its independence from politics.

RELIGIOUS THINKING HAS LOST ITS INDEPENDENCE FROM POLITICS

Since the advent of the nation-state, the dilemma of any reformist movement in Islam can be subsumed in the following formula: either serving the state or combating the state. On one hand, traditional institutions of learning have lost their independence and have produced religious interpretations justifying major national issues initiated by the state. On the other, they have focused on the *minutiae* of daily individual practices disconnected from major collective interests, for example, by issuing more and more religious opinions on grooming, dress code, or proper gender relations.

Contemporary fatwas (Islamic legal opinions) bear the clear mark of these changes. They can be public statements serving a political purpose or specific rulings sanctioning or permitting very trivial practices. The fatwa issued by Khomeini against Salman Rushdie in 1998 and the Egyptian fatwa against the use of nuclear weapons in 2010 illustrate the use of religious rulings as public statement. In both cases they are neither private nor specific but rather are highly generalized public pronouncements.[6] Simultaneously, the proliferation of so-called fatwas prohibiting certain types of behavior, such as the ban on unmarried women riding bicycles in Pakistan, points to a certain trivialization of this genre within Islamic discourse and is often decried as the fatwa crisis.[7] This double movement of politicization and trivialization underscores the shift from traditional religious authorities toward public Islamic voices including political figures and social activists.

---

[6] A fatwa, in classical legal theory, would be issued by a jurist (a mufti) or a judge (a qadi) in response to a particular query. Thus, the fatwa would be tailored to fit an individual case in a precise and highly specific way. However, the current proliferation and commodification of fatwas in the public realm reflect a change that cheapen them to fit most and satisfy all.

[7] Case in point: A 2007 fatwa issued in Egypt allowed a female to breastfeed her male coworkers in order to share the same workspace. Such a ruling created a heated debate on the nature of fatwas and led to the suspension of the Al-Azhar cleric who issued it, although he was later reinstated. See "Breastfeeding fatwa sheikh back at Egypt's Azhar," *Al-Arabiya*, May 18, 2009, accessed August 13, 2013, http://www.alarabiya.net/articles/2009/05/18/73140.html.

On the other hand, as described in Part II of this book, Islamic and Islamist groups have monopolized legitimate political opposition to the authoritarian state, at least until the Arab Spring revolutions. These religious and political agents operate on the political and religious platform created by the nation-state, even if their initial goal was to combat or destroy it.

A case in point is the theological work of political actors like Sayyid Qutb and Mawdudi. Although their main goal was political, they both produced a commentary (*Tafsir*) of the Qur'an, which is a very classical exercise, usually reserved for established religious authorities. Their interpretations, however, do not follow the traditional rules of Tafsir and actually reveal a very individualized and politicized approach to the religious text. For example, their interpretation of jihad gives preeminence to the individual's obligation to fight, hence moving the traditional interpretation of war into the realm of personal religious duty.[8] Such contemporary interpretations have been very popular among several generations of Muslims across countries who find these commentaries more accessible and meaningful than the more traditional versions. Therefore, these recent Tafsirs perpetuate and increase the modernized and politicized version of the Islamic tradition initiated by state policies while simultaneously widening the gap between traditional expressions of Islam and its modern interpretations. In this regard, the loss of diversity and pluralism in modern religious thinking, decried by scholars such as Mona Siddiqi or Khaled Abu Al Fadel,[9] can be partially explained by this nationalization of Islam.

THE DIALECTICS OF POLITICIZATION AND SECULARIZATION

At a deeper level, the complex interactions between modernization, secularization, and democratization shed light on several unexpected features of modern Muslim societies. First and foremost, the modern state has been the major agent of implementing the secular principle and, by the same token, of modernizing Islam. Second, this process has deeply affected the religious experience of Muslim citizens across societies. While this does not necessarily mean that the state can decide on matters of religious doctrine, it does mean that it has the authority to decide which parts of Islamic doctrine are relevant to modern society.

---

[8] In Islamic tradition, jihad is a collective effort of war (not an individual one), sanctioned by the caliph and the religious establishment.
[9] Mona Siddiqi, *The Good Muslim, Reflection on Classical Islamic Law and Theology* (Cambridge: Cambridge University Press, 2012); Khaled Abou El Fadel, *The Great Theft: Wrestling Islam from the Extremists* (San Francisco, CA: Harper, 2005).

In this sense, I have described in this book how the adoption of Western political concepts such as nation, public order, and legal system led to the creation of politicized versions of Islam. More generally, it appears that the sovereign authority of the state decisively influences what counts as religious and what scope of influence it has on the social order. Ultimately, this points to the fact that secularism supremacy has been a principle of state power, engineered by the state system with the consequence of redefining the Islamic tradition. This engineering of Islam is a never-ending process related to social and political changes. For example, as shown in Parts II and III, religious and political transnational influences have, in the past decades, weakened the preeminence of the state.

The politicization of Islam is, therefore, the tragic outcome of the construction of Islam as a modern religion. Spirituality and religious identities have become embedded in nationality and regimes of citizenship, thereby influencing the definition of religious minority and the conditions for apostasy and conversion (discussed in Part I). As a result, Islam as a modern religion has become far more reaching and controlling of the religious self than it was in premodern Muslim polities. In these conditions, the problem is not that "Islam needs to be reformed or modernized," as we often hear in political or scholarly circles. The problem is that this reform and modernization became part and parcel of the nation-state building and led to an unprecedented politicization of Islam.[10]

Far from being politically deliberate, this outcome was the result of multiple processes of modernization involving various social and cultural groups. It also explains why the current antimodern discourses of some religio-political actors come from people and groups that have been deeply modernized and in some ways cut from the teachings of the religious tradition. In other words, Sayyid Qutb or Osama Bin Laden are the illegitimate children of the nationalized versions of Islam and therefore disconnected from traditional forms of religious learning. At the same time, it also means that religiously based political actors will continue to influence political change. That is why we are in dire need of a path-dependent approach to secularity and religion that can be relevant to all non-Western political experiences. This requires taking into account the specific interactions between belonging, behaving, and believing and their connections with the institutional, social, and individual levels of secularization.

---

[10] Current Shi'i reformists, such as Abdol Karim Soroush, are particularly aware of such a situation, advocating a strict disentanglement of Islam and the state as the necessary step for the survival of Islamic spirituality. See Abdolkarim Surūsh, *Reason, Freedom, & Democracy in Islam: Essential Writings of 'Abdolkarim Soroush*, ed. and trans. Mahmoud Sadri and Ahmad Sadri (New York: Oxford University Press, 2000).

Appendix I

Religious Violence Index

Incidents of Religiously Based Political Violence in Muslim-majority Countries 2006–11

SCORE OF 5	State and Nonstate Violence Descriptions

Egypt

1. From 2006 to 2011, several thousand persons were imprisoned during the reporting period because of alleged support for – or membership in – Islamist groups seeking to overthrow the government. Total number unknown.
2. On October 9, 2011, military police and civilian thugs killed approximately 25 persons and wounded an estimated 330 during a demonstration in Cairo by Coptic Christians.
3. On September 30, 2011, a mob burned down the Mar Girgis Church in Marinab, Aswan.
4. On August 18, 2011, a series of cross-border attacks with parallel attacks and mutual cover was carried out in southern Israel on Highway 12 near the Egyptian border by a squad of presumably twelve militants in four groups.
5. In May 2011, sectarian violence outside a church in Imbaba, a neighborhood of Cairo, left twelve dead.
6. On March 8, 2011, Christians in the eastern Cairo suburb of Muqattam protested the burning of a church four days earlier in Atfih, thirteen miles south of Cairo, and clashed with Muslims. Twelve people died in the ensuing violence and shootings, and several Christian homes and businesses were torched.
7. In March 2011, in the Upper Egypt town of Qena, a group of extremists cut off the ear of a Coptic Christian man.
8. In March 2011, Islamist militants clashed with Muslim villagers south of Cairo over demands to close a liquor store and coffee shops. One villager was killed and eight others injured in Kasr

(continued)

SCORE OF 5	State and Nonstate Violence Descriptions

el-Bassil, in Fayoum province, in fighting that broke out after militants ordered the owner to close the shops based on their strict interpretation of Islam.

9. In late February 2011, one monk and six church workers were injured when the Egyptian military reportedly used excessive force and live ammunition at the Anba Bishoy monastery in Wadi Natroun.

10. On January 4 or 5, 2011, NSS officers reportedly tortured Salafist preacher Sayed Bilal to death. Bilal's death came within twenty-four hours of his arrest on January 4 for alleged involvement in the January 1 bombing of the Two Saints Church in Alexandria.

11. On January 1, 2011, a bomb attack at the Coptic Orthodox Church of the Two Saints in Alexandria killed at least twenty-two and injured ninety-six.

12. On November 24, 2010, clashes occurred between police and mostly Coptic rioters in Giza neighborhood in Omraniya.

13. As of November 18, 2010, Egyptian security officers had arrested 487 members of the Muslim Brotherhood.

14. On October 31, 2010, the Saydat al-Najat Church in Baghdad was attacked and Al Qaeda made threats against Copts.

15. On September 7, 2010, security forces clashed with monks at the Coptic Orthodox monastery of St. Macarius of Alexandria in Wadi Rayan.

16. In September and October 2010, the government detained approximately 100 Shia Muslims.

17. On June 27, 2010, in al Gafransh, unidentified assailants detonated an improvised explosive device on a natural gas pipeline, causing only minimal damage and no casualties.

18. On May 22, 2010, twelve young persons associated with an evangelical church were arrested after being accused of distributing evangelistic books and pamphlets.

19. In March 2010, SSI arrested Muslim Brotherhood member Nasr al-Sayed Hassan Nasr, detained him incommunicado for three months, and tortured him for forty-five days during interrogation.

20. In March 2010, SSI arrested at least nine members of the Ahmadi faith and detained them for eighty days on charges of "showing contempt for the Islamic faith."

21. On March 20, 2010, thirty individuals attacked Coptic facilities.

22. Beginning on March 15, 2010, government security officials arrested eleven members of the country's Ahmadiyya Muslim community.

SCORE OF 5	State and Nonstate Violence Descriptions

23. On February 21, 2010, in Cairo, a man threw an improvised explosive device at a Cairo synagogue, causing a fire and damaging the synagogue but causing no casualties.

24. On February 15, 2010, a U.S. citizen accused of evangelizing in Egypt was reportedly arrested upon his arrival to Cairo International Airport and deported overnight.

25. In January 2010, gunmen shot dead six Coptic Christians as they left a Christmas Mass in Nag' Hammadi.

26. Jehovah's Witnesses leadership reported the continuation of government harassment and interrogation of members during 2010.

27. On November 18, 2009, security officials at Cairo International Airport detained Quranist Abdel Latif Said.

28. In October 2009, a criminal court convicted Einas Refaat Muhamed Hassan, a convert from Islam to Christianity, of forgery for possessing a forged national identity card indicating her religion was Christianity.

29. On September 23, 2009, police officers reportedly arrested Abd al-Masih Kamel Barsoum, who is associated with an evangelical church in Minya, while he was distributing Christian religious materials in downtown Cairo.

30. Between April and July 2009, government security forces arrested 200–300 Shias.

31. On July 2, 2009, Egypt detained prominent Shi'a cleric Hassan Shehata on charges of forming an organization for the purpose of propagating Shi'ite ideas that disparage Islam and Sunni confessions.

32. In July 2009, police in Mansoura arrested a Coptic Christian woman while she was applying for birth certificates for her two children on charges of possessing false documents.

33. In June 2009, state security and police forces reportedly instigated a sectarian clash in Boshra, near Beni Suef, when they prevented Christians from praying in an unlicensed church.

34. On May 11, 2009, a small homemade bomb exploded near a church in the Egyptian capital of Cairo.

35. In June 2009, in Beni Suef, south of Cairo, a woman who was born Christian, converted to Islam to marry a Muslim man, and later reasserted her Christian identity, was charged with forgery for allegedly trying to obtain an identification document indicating one of her children was Christian.

36. On April 13, 2009, police arrested Christian convert Raheal Henen Mussa, reportedly for possession of a false identification document.

(*continued*)

SCORE OF 5	State and Nonstate Violence Descriptions

37. In March 2009, Muslim villagers attacked the homes of seven Baha'i families in the village of al-Shuraniya in Sohag Governorate.

38. On February 22, 2009, a bomb targeted a Cairo bazaar on a street lined with cafes and restaurants. One French student was killed in the blast, and at least twenty-five other civilians were injured.

39. On February 1, 2009, police arrested two citizens at the Cairo International Book Fair for distributing Bibles.

40. In January 2009, six Christian brothers were sentenced to three years in prison on charges of "resisting arrest" and "assaulting authorities."

41. In 2008, a Giza criminal court sentenced Coptic priest Mita'us Wahba to five years in prison with "forced labor" for officiating at a wedding between a Copt and a Muslim convert to Christianity.

42. In 2008, security officials in the governorate of Sharqiya arrested Quranist blogger Reda Abdel-Rahman and reportedly subjected him to physical and mental abuse in detention.

43. In 2008, airport security officials arrested a convert from Islam to Christianity, along with her husband and their two sons, ages two and four, while they were trying to board a flight to Russia.

44. In 2008, in Al Fayoum, police arrested a woman and two men on suspicion that they had distributed Christian tapes and publications.

45. In 2008, police arrested six Copts who had been assisting with renovations on the Archangel Michael Church in Deshasha.

46. In 2008, the Esna Court sentenced a Coptic shopkeeper to one month in prison for impersonating a police officer and trying to remove the veil of a woman he suspected of shoplifting.

47. In 2008, the Shubra Criminal Court sentenced three people to three years in prison each for helping a Muslim woman obtain a counterfeit national identity card that indicated her religion as Christian to facilitate her marriage to a Christian.

48. On November 11, 2008, twenty-five members of the central police force were kidnapped and later freed in Shamal Sina', Egypt.

49. In October 2008, a male convert from Islam to Christianity claimed that agents of state security had detained him on multiple occasions over several years.

50. On May 31, 2008, police located within one mile of the Abu Fana Monastery in Upper Egypt reportedly took three hours to respond to a request for help when a monk's cell at the monastery was under attack.

51. In 2007, authorities arrested five men affiliated with the Quranist movement.

SCORE OF 5 State and Nonstate Violence
Descriptions

52. In 2007, twenty-five members of the Islamic Al-Ahbash sect were charged with membership in an illegal organization and contempt for religion.

53. In 2007, police detained Siham Ibrahim Muhammad Hassan al-Sharqawi, a Muslim convert to Christianity, on the outskirts of Qena.

54. On November 21, 2007, Shadia Nagy Ibrahim was sentenced to three years in prison for allegedly falsely claiming to be Christian.

55. On November 5, 2007, authorities arrested three MECA affiliates under investigation for a variety of alleged offenses, including denigrating Islam.

56. On August 8, 2007, police detained Adel Fawzi Faltas Hanna, a retired doctor and president of the Middle East Christian Association's (MECA) Egyptian branch, and Peter Ezzat Hanna, a photographer for MECA and the Copts United website.

57. In May 2006, public prosecutor Maher Abdul Wahid ordered two Azharites, Abdul Sabur al-Kashef and Mohammed Radwan, to be tried by a low-level criminal court on charges of blaspheming Islam.

58. On April 24, 2006, three explosives hidden in bags detonated in the Dahab tourist resort in southern Sinai, Egypt. The first two explosions were successive and occurred in front of a bar and cafeteria while the third was less powerful and occurred in front of a supermarket. The blasts killed eighteen people, including five foreigners, and injured eighty-seven others.

59. On April 14, 2006, an attacker armed with sharp objects entered Saints Church in Alexandria, Egypt, and killed one person and injured two.

60. On April 14, 2006, an attacker deemed mentally unstable entered Mary Girgis Church in Al-Hadra area of Alexandria, Egypt, armed with sharp objects and injured three people with a knife.

61. On April 1, 2006, Noaman Gomaa, the estranged leader of the opposition al-Wafd Party, and some of his supporters stormed the party's headquarters in Dokki district, Cairo, Egypt. The perpetrators were attempting to occupy the premises when one of the perpetrators shot at party employees and journalists after being angered by their refusal to accept Gomaa's orders to leave the place.

62. In March 2007, the Alexandria Court of Appeal upheld the conviction of twenty-two-year-old student blogger Abdel Karim Nabil Suleiman. In February 2007, the Alexandria Criminal Court had convicted him of denigrating Islam and insulting the president through his blog entries and sentenced him to four years in prison.

(*continued*)

SCORE OF 5	State and Nonstate Violence Descriptions

Saudi Arabia

1. From 2006 to 2011, the government continued to prohibit public, non-Muslim religious activities and non-Sunni activities in predominantly Sunni areas. Many of the reported related abuses were difficult to corroborate because of witnesses' or victims' fears that disclosing such information might cause harm to themselves or to others. Total number imprisoned unknown.

2. From 2006 to 2011, police detained and imprisoned an unknown number of persons on charges of sorcery, black magic, or witchcraft.

3. On September 19, 2011, Abdul Hamid bin Hussain bin Moustafa al-Fakki, a Sudanese man, was beheaded in Medina. He had been arrested in 2005 then charged and convicted of sorcery after he allegedly agreed to cast a spell at the behest of a man working for the religious police.

4. In March 2011, a small group of Sunni Saudis demonstrated in Riyadh, the capital, calling for the release of thousands of people detained for years without charge or trial on suspicion of involvement in militant activity. Police arrested several, including three women as well as lawyer Mubarak bin Zu'air and rights activist Muhammad Bajadi, both of whom remain in detention.

5. In February 2011, small, peaceful protests by Shia took place in the Eastern Province, demanding the release of nine "forgotten" Shia detained for over thirteen years without charge or trial on suspicion of involvement in a 1996 attack on a United States military installation in Khobar, which killed nineteen. Saudi authorities detained 160 protesters.

6. In February 2011, Sheikh Tawfiq Jaber Ibrahim al-Amer, a Shi'a cleric, was arrested in February after he called for political reforms in a sermon. He was held incommunicado for a week, then released. He was re-arrested on August 3 and charged with "inciting public opinion" after persisting in his call for reform.

7. On October 26, 2010, police in Qatif detained Sheikh Saeed al Bahhar, the imam of Imam Reza Mosque in Tarot Island, and Mohammad Hassan al Hubail, the administrator of the mosque, for allegedly establishing a ceremony marking the anniversary of the death of Ayatollah Khomeini.

8. On October 1, 2010, members of the Commission for the Promotion of Virtue and Prevention of Vice (CPVPV) disrupted a private Catholic religious service and detained thirteen foreign nationals overnight before releasing them the next day.

9. On August 2, 2010, the investigation service authority in Medina raided the ranch of Shiite preacher Mohamed Ali Al-Emary. Al-Emary's son Kazim had been arrested ten days earlier.

SCORE OF 5	State and Nonstate Violence
	Descriptions

10. On March 29, 2010, security authorities reportedly detained three Shia, including the brother of Abdullah Saleh al-Muhanna, a prominent Shia and former city mayor of Khobar, who was himself detained in May 2009. In August 2010, an arrest warrant was again issued for Al-Muhanna and another Shiite cleric, Sayed Mohammad Bager Al-Nasser, who on January 14, 2010 had been detained for performing Friday prayer in a Sunni mosque. On November 29, 2010, the arrest warrant for Al-Nasser was enforced.

11. On March 19, 2010, four CPVPV officers and one uniformed police officer raided an Indian Christian prayer service being held in a private residence. Police arrested the pastor and two worshippers and detained them in the local police station until their release on March 23.

12. On March 10, 2010, Rasid.com reported the arrest of Mohammad Jasim Al-Hofoufi, a Saudi Shiite teacher accused of reading polytheistic Shiite supplements at Al-Baqi'a cemetery. Sources indicate that Al-Hofoufi was sentenced to three months' detention and sixty lashes.

13. On January 14, 2010, authorities released prominent Shiʻa figure, Sayed Mohammad Baqer al-Nasser, after detaining him for an hour for having performed Friday prayer in a Sunni mosque.

14. From November 1 to 30, 2009, at least five Shiite men from al-Ahsa were reportedly arrested for taking part in the preparations for the remembrance day of Imam Al-Mahdi in August.

15. On November 9, 2009, Ali Hussain Sibat, a Lebanese presenter on a Beirut-based satellite television channel, was sentenced to death on charges related to sorcery.

16. On November 7, 2009, intelligence officers arrested Shiite activist Munir Jassas.

17. On November 3, 2009, in Jizan, Saudi Arabia, armed assailants fired on a Saudi Arabian border patrol, killing one guard and wounding eleven others.

18. On November 2, 2009, the *Al-Heyad* e-newspaper reported that authorities arrested 118 men and women in Makkah Province and charged them with practicing sorcery.

19. On October 27, 2009, authorities reportedly arrested Shia Sayed Yusif al-Hashim for hosting Friday prayers in his house in Khobar.

20. On October 14, 2009, terrorists in a car at a security checkpoint in Darb, Jazan, Saudi Arabia opened fire on the officers at the checkpoint.

(*continued*)

SCORE OF 5	State and Nonstate Violence Descriptions

21. On September 20, 2009, the government released Naif al-Baqshi, the brother of a prominent Shiite cleric in al-Ahsa, after he spent eighteen months in prison.

22. On September 3, 2009, Hadi al-Mutif, a Sulaimaniya Isma'ili Shia who has been on death row for sixteen years for an offhand remark "insulting the Prophet Mohammad," received an additional five-year sentence for criticizing the government's justice system and human rights record.

23. Between August and October 2009, at least eight Shiite men from al-Ahsa were reportedly arrested for taking part in religious activities during Ashura in January 2009.

24. On August 27, 2009, in Jiddah, a suicide bomber detonated a suicide improvised explosive device near the Saudi Arabian Assistant Minister of the Interior of Security Affairs, wounding the government official and damaging his office.

25. On August 24, 2009, King Abdullah ordered the release of seventeen Sulaimaniya Isma'ili Shi'a men jailed after riots in Najran Province in 2000.

26. In May 2009, Rasid.com reported the arrest of prominent religious figure Sheikh Ali Hussein Al-Amar for collecting and spending money on *hussainyat* (Shiite places of worship).

27. In May 2009, police in Khobar arrested Hajj Abdullah Saleh Al-Muhanna, a Shia, for leading prayer services in his home. Without facing trial, Al-Muhanna was released from prison on June 30, 2009.

28. In March 2009, a Shi'a cleric from Awamiya Village in Qatif gave a controversial sermon wherein he raised the possibility of a separate Shi'a state. Following this sermon, the cleric reportedly went into hiding to avoid arrest. On March 19, 2009, several hundred Shi'a conducted a sit-in protest in Awamiya in support of the cleric; reports indicated more than a dozen Shi'a were arrested.

29. In February 2009, a group of Shia trying to visit the Baqi'a cemetery in Medina clashed with police and the CPVPV.

30. In January 2009, Yemane Gebriel, an Eritrean pastor, fled the country to an undisclosed location after multiple threats from the CPVPV.

31. On January 12, 2009, Rasid.com reported that students and government employees who missed school or work on a Shi'a holiday, the Tenth of Muharram, without an acceptable excuse were "punished."

32. In August 2008, Rasid.com reported that authorities arrested Shiite religious figure and reformer Sheikh Nemer Baqer Al-Nemer after a series of declarations in which he demanded religious freedom reforms.

SCORE OF 5	State and Nonstate Violence Descriptions

33. In June 2008, the government arrested Naif al-Baqshi, the brother of a prominent Shiite cleric in al-Ahsa.

34. On June 22, 2008, prominent Shi'a Sheikh in al-Ahsa was arrested by authorities after calling a previous anti-Shi'a statement by twenty-two Salafi clerics an incitement that invited violence, and demanding greater rights and political representation for the Shi'a of al-Ahsa.

35. On June 5, 2008, government authorities in the city of Khobar closed three "unofficial" Shi'a mosques operating out of private residences, detaining each mosque's imam and other attendees until the accused parties signed agreements pledging not to engage in holding such unlicensed prayer services in the future.

36. On May 23, 2008, government officials arrested fifteen Indian Christians in Qassim Province for private religious worship.

37. On May 13, 2008, Ahmad Turki al-Saab was detained in Riyadh. Al-Saab is a leading Sulaimaniya Isma'ili activist who organized a petition campaign demanding the removal from office of Najran's governor for his alleged discrimination against the minority community.

38. On May 5, 2008, the government charged Ra'if Bedawi al-Shammary, a lawyer and businessman, with "setting up an electronic site that insults Islam."

39. In April 2008, government officials arrested sixteen Asian Christians, including three women, a three-year-old child, and a one-year-old child, for conducting a worship service in the Western Province.

40. In April 2008, an Indian Christian residing in the Western Province reported that his sponsor began receiving daily phone calls from local authorities demanding the Christian's immediate deportation on the basis of a previous MOI order. The Christian was one of twenty-eight Indians arrested in a December 2003 CPVPV raid on a private religious gathering.

41. In March 2008, Bogday was sentenced to death after two men reported to authorities that he blasphemed God and the Prophet Muhammad in his barber shop.

42. On February 25, 2008, Al-Madina reported that a Mecca public court sentenced a Saudi academic to eight months of imprisonment and 180 lashes for privately meeting with a female colleague not related to him.

43. On February 21, 2008, CPVPV members arrested and later released a Saudi-American woman and a Syrian-American man at a Jeddah mall for being in a state of seclusion with an unrelated member of the opposite gender and for his not having a residency card.

(*continued*)

SCORE OF 5	State and Nonstate Violence Descriptions

44. On February 4, 2008, several dailies reported that a forty-year-old Saudi-American businesswoman and her male Syrian colleague were arrested by a *mutawwa'in* in a Riyadh coffee shop on charges of seclusion with an unrelated member of the opposite gender.

45. On January 27, 2008, CPVPV members arrested four Sulaimaniya Isma'ili activists in a Najran hotel on charges of consuming alcohol.

46. On November 2, 2007, Mustafa Ibrahim, an Egyptian pharmacist, was executed in the northern town of Ar'ar on charges of "sorcery," desecrating the Qur'an, and adultery.

47. On October 27, 2007, a young al-Ahsa man was detained on charges of having attended gatherings at a *husseiniya* and later released.

48. On October 21, 2007, two al-Ahsa men were detained. One was accused of holding a private religious gathering on his farm, and the other, a Shi'a teacher, was detained without a specific reason.

49. In September 2007, a Uighur Muslim from China was detained in a Mecca prison awaiting forcible return to China.

50. On August 18, 2007, Okaz reported that four government departments were investigating the death of a Bangladeshi laborer after CPVPV members arrested him for washing cars at prayer time in Medina.

51. On August 5, 2007, seven British and one American Shi'a performing *umra* rituals at the Grand Mosque in Mecca were harassed and detained by CPVPV members for fourteen hours before being released.

52. In July 2007, officials detained another Chinese Uighur Muslim named Habibula Ali and sent him back to China.

53. On July 27, 2007, Arab News reported the CPVPV arrested an African national for practicing "black magic" near Medina.

54. On June 27, 2007, an employee of a Shi'a mosque and husseiniya in al-Ahsa was reportedly detained for holding prohibited religious gatherings.

55. On June 1, 2007, Ahmad Al-Bulawi, a fifty-year-old retired border patrol guard, died at a CPVPV center in the northern town of Tabuk, allegedly of a heart attack. Al-Bulawi's family demanded an autopsy to determine the cause of his death. The mutawwa'in arrested Al-Bulawi and brought him to their center because he had a Saudi woman who was not his relative in his car.

56. On May 23, 2007, twenty-eight-year-old Salman Al-Huraisi, a security guard, died in a CPVPV office in Riyadh. According to his father and brother, at least eighteen mutawwa'in raided

SCORE OF 5	State and Nonstate Violence Descriptions

their home in Riyadh on suspicion of alcohol production, and then arrested ten family members.

57. On February 26, 2007, militants shot dead three French travelers in the Saudi Arabian desert north of Medina.

58. In January 2007, the government arrested and detained a Shiʿa cleric in Al-Ahsa for operating a *hussainiya* without a license.

59. In 2006, there were reports of several raids on Filipino Christian services in Riyadh.

60. On December 29, 2006, the mutawwaʾin raided a private gathering of the Ahmadiyya religious group.

61. In October 2006, police arrested a Filipino Christian man in Jeddah and falsely charged him with drug possession.

62. On October 30, 2006, *Al Hayat* reported that the mutawwaʾin chased a car containing a girl and her boyfriend, which led to an accident and the girl's death.

63. On October 15, 2006, the mutawwaʾin raided a Christian worship service in the western region of the country.

64. On June 9, 2006, police arrested two Ethiopian and two Eritrean church leaders at a private Christian worship service in Jeddah.

65. On May 27, 2006, an unidentified perpetrator, using an automatic weapon, opened fire on the headquarters of the CPVPV in Riyadh, injuring no one.

66. On May 12, 2006, an unidentified gunman opened fire on guards at the U.S. consulate in Jeddah, Saudi Arabia.

67. In April 2006, Fawza Falih Muhammad Ali received the death penalty for allegedly bewitching a man in Quraiyat.

68. In April 2006, the government arrested an Indian Roman Catholic priest.

69. In April 2006, the mutawwaʾin arrested a female Shiʿa student in Riyadh, allegedly for proselytizing to other students.

70. On February 24, 2006, al-Qaʿida claimed responsibility for an attempted suicide attack on the world's largest oil-producing center in Saudi Arabia's oil-rich Eastern Province that left at least four people dead and eight more wounded.

Pakistan

1. In 2011, members of the Ahmadi religious community remained a major target for blasphemy prosecutions, subject to specific anti-Ahmadi laws across Pakistan.

2. In 2011, there were approximately 467 major terrorist attacks in Pakistan.

3. In 2011, three people were sentenced to death for blasphemy.

4. On September 24, 2011, Faryal Bhatti, a thirteen-year-old Christian schoolgirl from Abbottabad, was expelled from school for misspelling an Urdu word, resulting in accusations of blasphemy. Her family was forced to go into hiding.

(continued)

SCORE OF 5	State and Nonstate Violence Descriptions

5. On March 2, 2011, Federal Minister for Minorities Shahbaz Bhatti was shot dead for supporting an amendment to Pakistan's blasphemy laws (section 295(C) of Pakistan's penal code).

6. On January 4, 2011, Punjab Governor Salmaan Taseer was assassinated by a member of his security detail for supporting an amendment to Pakistan's blasphemy laws (section 295(C) of Pakistan's penal code).

7. In 2010, there were approximately 699 terrorist attacks in Pakistan, including on November 5, 2010, when more than 60 persons were killed and nearly 100 injured in a suicide bomb attack on a mosque in northwest Pakistan; on September 3, 2010, TTP attacked a Shia protest in Quetta, killing over 70 people and wounding at least 100; and on July 1, 2010, at least 44 persons were killed and 175 others injured when three suicide attackers blew themselves up inside the shrine of Lahore's patron saint, Syed Ali Hajwairi.

8. According to the National Commission for Justice and Peace (NCJP), between July 1 and December 31, 2010, a total of twenty-four cases were registered under blasphemy laws. Of these, ten were Christians, seven were Hindus, three were Ahmadis, and four were Muslims.

9. As of December 2010, according to Ahmadiyya leaders, seven Ahmadis were in prison; three have been sentenced to death after being convicted of murder and are awaiting a hearing of their appeal, while four others were charged with murder in a religion-based incident.

10. In December 2010, an Ismaili doctor, Naushad Valiyani, was arrested for insulting the Prophet Mohammed in Hyderabad, Sindh.

11. On November 8, 2010, a Christian woman, Aasia Bibi, was sentenced to death for blasphemy, the first such sentence of a woman in the country.

12. In May 2010, police illegally detained three Christians, Atif Masih, Kamran Masih, and Naveed Gill, on false charges of alcohol possession in Sialkot, Punjab.

13. On May 6, 2010, according to Assist News Service, at least five Christian boys, including Shoaib Ilyas, Chaman Ashraf, Ashar Masih, Neeta Masih, and Sunny, were forced to leave their homes in Lahore after being accused of committing blasphemy.

14. In March 2010, according to ICC, Qamar David, a Christian man, was sentenced to life imprisonment and fined 101,000 rupees ($1,187) for making blasphemous remarks about the Qur'an and the Prophet Mohammad.

SCORE OF 5	State and Nonstate Violence Descriptions

15. On March 28, 2010, police filed false charges of alcohol possession against forty-seven Christians, including two children and eight women, in an attempt to intimidate and extort money from them.

16. On March 2, 2010, according to Assist News Service, Munir Masih and Ruqqiya Bibi, a Christian couple, were sentenced to twenty-five years in prison for defiling the Qur'an after touching it with unwashed hands.

17. In 2009, there were approximately 668 terrorist attacks in Pakistan, including in December 2009, when a suicide bomber attacked a Shia religious procession in Muzaffarabad, Azad Jammu, and Kashmir, killing eight persons and injuring eighty; in August 2009, militants shot and killed six Christians and injured seven others in Quetta, Balochistan.

18. In 2009, 112 cases were registered under the blasphemy laws. Of the 112 persons, 57 were identified as Ahmadis, 47 Muslims, and 8 as Christians.

19. On September 16, 2009, a young Christian man, Robert Fanish, who had been accused of blasphemy, died while in police custody.

20. In June 2009, CDN reported that police imprisoned Arshad Masih, a Christian man from Gujranwala, in a Sialkot jail and reportedly abused him while in custody because his father was a Christian preacher.

21. In March 2009, authorities in Sarghoda District in Punjab charged fifteen Ahmadis under Section 298c of the penal code for calling their place of worship a mosque and offering Eid prayers there.

22. In January 2009, police arrested four Ahmadi teenagers and an adult in Layyah, Punjab, on charges of blasphemy.

23. In January 2009, police arrested Hector Aleem in Rawalpindi on charges of sending a blasphemous text message from his cell phone.

24. In 2008, there were approximately 565 terrorist attacks in Pakistan.

25. In 2008, authorities arrested at least twenty-five Ahmadis, eleven Christians, and seventeen Muslims on blasphemy charges.

26. In September 2008, authorities arrested ten Ahmadis under Ahmadi-specific sections of the penal code. On October 11, 2008, eight more Ahmadis were added to the same case. All individuals arrested were released on bail.

27. In May 2008, Pastor Frank John was charged with blasphemy as he was conducting a religious convention in Lahore, Punjab.

(continued)

SCORE OF 5	State and Nonstate Violence Descriptions

28. On April 9, 2008, in the Karachi Korangi Industrial Area, employees beat to death Jagdesh Kumar, a Hindu employee, after he allegedly made blasphemous comments against Islam.
29. On March 6, 2008, police arrested eighty-year-old Ahmadi Altaf Husain in Kabeerwala for desecrating the Qur'an.
30. In January 2008, police in Nankana Sahib, Punjab charged an Ahmadi businessman, Manzur Ahmed, with destroying pages that included religious inscriptions.
31. In January 2008, authorities arrested an Ahmadi in Wazirabad, Punjab, on charges of distributing Ahmadi-related pamphlets.
32. In 2007, there were approximately 255 terrorist attacks in Pakistan.
33. In December 2007, Larkana police arrested twenty-one Ahmadis on charges of gathering and worshipping like Muslims after neighbors claimed to police that they heard Islamic verses coming from the home of one of the members.
34. In November 2007, three Ahmadis were arrested in Sargodha, Punjab on charges of proselytizing when they invited other locals to their places of worship.
35. In September 2007, police accused Mumtaz Ali, an Ahmadi, of subscribing, receiving, and subsequently distributing the newsletter of the local Ahmadiyya community.
36. In July 2007, the government detained a Uyghur Muslim Chinese national in Islamabad and forcibly returned him to China at the request of the government of China.
37. In May 2007, authorities arrested eighty-four-year-old Christian Walter Fazal Khan for blasphemy.
38. In April 2007, a mob tortured a Catholic man, Sattar Masih, before police arrived and arrested him for allegedly writing blasphemous words against the Prophet Muhammad.
39. In April 2007, officials accused Salamat Masih, a Christian in Toba Tek Singh, and four members of his family of desecrating papers bearing the Prophet Muhammad's name.
40. In March 2007, a mob of Muslims attacked Amanat Masih, a Christian, for allegedly desecrating the Qur'an.
41. In January 2007, Christian Martha Bibi was accused of blasphemy and imprisoned.
42. In January 2007, Shahid Masih, a seventeen-year-old Christian arrested on blasphemy charges four months earlier, was released on $1,650 bail and immediately went into hiding, afraid of the reaction of local radical Muslims who had been following the case.
43. In 2006, there were approximately 163 terrorist attacks in Pakistan.

SCORE OF 5	State and Nonstate Violence Descriptions

44. In November 2006, Catholics James Masih and Buta Masih were convicted of blasphemy and sentenced to ten years in prison for allegedly burning a Quran.

45. In October 2006, police arrested Ahmadi Mohammed Tariq and charged him under blasphemy laws for allegedly tearing off anti-Ahmadiyya stickers inside a bus.

46. In August 2006, Mian Mohammed Yar, the president of the local Ahmadiyya community in the Okara District of the Punjab, was arrested under the anti-Ahmadi laws on the charge of preaching.

47. On June 24, 2006, a mob attacked an Ahmadi locality in Jhando Sahi Village in Daska near Sialkot and injured two persons following allegations that Ahmadis had desecrated the Qur'an. The mob also set fire to vehicles, two shops, and houses belonging to Ahmadis. The district police arrived at the scene and arrested seven Ahmadis.

48. On April 7, 2006, two prison staff members at the central jail in Sahiwal, Punjab joined Muslim inmates in attacking four Christian prisoners who had gathered for prayer and Bible study.

Algeria

1. On October 10, 2011, two people in a car were injured after a roadside bomb exploded near a railway crossing in the town of Beni Amrane. The roadside bomb was planned by terrorists trying to kill police and military in the country.

2. On August 26, 2011, an AQIM attack on a military barracks at Cherchell reportedly killed two civilians and sixteen soldiers.

3. On August 14, 2011, a suicide bomber exploded outside a police station in the city of Tizi Ouzou. No one was killed, but twenty-nine were wounded in the bombing.

4. On May 25, 2011, an Oran court convicted Abdelkarim Siaghi, a convert to Christianity, of "offending" the Prophet Muhammad under the penal code and sentenced him to five years in prison and a fine.

5. On March 9, 2011, a bomb exploded in the city of Djelfa, hitting a vehicle and killing five people.

6. In 2010, there were approximately eight terrorist attacks in Algeria, including on June 25, 2010, when gunmen – whom Algerian media linked to terrorists – fired on a wedding party in the eastern *wilaya* (province) of Tebessa, killing the bridegroom, a young soldier, and four guests.

7. In 2009, there were approximately twenty-one terrorist attacks in Algeria.

8. In 2008, there were approximately ninety-nine terrorist attacks in Algeria.

(*continued*)

SCORE OF 5	State and Nonstate Violence Descriptions

9. In July 2008, a court in Tissemsilt gave Christian converts Rachid Seghir and Djammal Dahmani six-month suspended prison sentences and fines of 100,000 Algerian dinars each on charges of proselytizing and illegally practicing a non-Muslim faith.

10. In June 2008, Rachid Seghir was convicted on charges of evangelism. The courts in Tiaret and Djilfa charged five other Christian converts, Jillali Saidi, Abdelhak Rabih, Chaaban Baikel, Mohamed Khan, and Abdelkader Hori, on the same grounds.

11. In March 2008, Habiba Kouider, a convert to Christianity, was charged with "practicing a non-Muslim religion without a permit."

12. In February 2008, Youssef Ourahmane, Rachid Seghir, and another convert to Christianity were charged with blasphemy.

13. In 2007, there were approximately 124 terrorist attacks in Algeria.

14. In 2006, there were approximately 152 terrorist attacks in Algeria.

Morocco

1. On April 28, 2011, a bomb exploded in a Marrakesh cafe frequented by foreign tourists, killing seventeen persons and wounding dozens.

2. In 2010, the government expelled or declared persona non grata approximately 150 Christian foreign residents from nineteen countries for allegedly violating the proselytizing statute, without benefit of trial or other due process.

3. On February 4, 2010, security forces raided a meeting attended by sixteen Christian citizens and one foreign resident in the town of Amizmiz.

4. During the 2010 and 2009 reporting periods, authorities conducted three raids of Christian meetings attended by Moroccan Christians and resident foreigners.

5. In December 2009, police summarily deported four expatriates for alleged proselytizing and detained fourteen Christian citizens from whom they confiscated Bibles and other personal property in Saidia.

6. In March 2009, authorities detained four Spanish, one German, and seven other women and broke up their Bible study meeting.

7. In March 2008, the media reported the arrests of two French tourists who were in possession of Bibles and compact discs on suspicion of proselytizing in Zagora.

8. On February 23, 2008, the media reported the arrest of fifty-three members of the JCO in Essaouira for holding an unauthorized meeting at the house of a regional leader.

SCORE OF 5	State and Nonstate Violence Descriptions

9. On August 14, 2007, a Moroccan suicide attacker attempted to board a bus of tourists in the city of Meknes in the Meknes-Tafilalet (Region), Morocco. The driver refused to let him on the bus and instead shut the door, leaving the bomb to detonate outside. Only the attacker was injured.

10. On April 14, 2007, two brothers wearing belts packed with explosives blew themselves up within moments of each other outside the consulate and the American Language Center. Apart from the two dead perpetrators, the only casualty was a bystander who was reported slightly injured. No claim of responsibility was reported.

11. On April 11, 2007, one policeman was killed and twenty-one other people were wounded when three suspected terrorists blew themselves up after police discovered their place of hiding in Casablanca, Morocco.

12. On April 10, 2007, an unknown number of suicide bombers detonated explosives while engaging in a firefight with an unknown number of Casablanca police. No group claimed responsibility.

13. On March 12, 2007, two men got into an argument at a Moroccan Internet cafe in the Sidi Moumen slum of Casablanca, who were blocked from viewing radical materials on the Internet. Reports indicate that the argument resulted in a negligent/accidental detonation. Three people wounded, the bomber was killed, and his accomplice was injured and fled to be caught an hour later.

14. On March 11, 2007, in Casablanca, suicide bomber Abdelfettah Rayid detonated an explosive attached to his person after the owner of the busy Internet cafe asked him to stop looking at jihadist websites.

15. On November 28, 2006, a foreign Christian was fined $50 (500 dirhams) and given a six-month prison sentence for attempting to convert a Muslim to Christianity.

Malaysia

1. In October 2011, police investigated law professor Aziz Bari under the Sedition Act for an online posting that criticized the sultan of Selangor's support for a church raid by the state Islamic religious police.

2. On August 3, 2011, Selangor state religious authorities raided a Methodist church where an annual charity dinner was being held.

3. On December 16, 2010, JAIS raided a Shiite congregation in Gombak, Selangor and arrested 128 followers, including an Iranian who was giving a sermon.

4. In May 2010, the same court sentenced two men to caning and imprisonment for drinking alcohol in public in February.

(continued)

SCORE OF 5 State and Nonstate Violence
Descriptions

5. In April 2010, a Pahang Shariʻa court sentenced a man to six strokes of the cane and one year's imprisonment for drinking alcohol.

6. On February 17, 2010, the Home Ministry announced that three Muslim women and four Muslim men who had been found guilty of illicit sex under Shariʻa law had been caned on February 9.

7. On November 1, 2009, JAIS arrested former Perlis Mufti Mohd Asri Zainul Abidin, a progressive Muslim leader, for giving a religious talk without proper accreditation issued by JAIS.

8. On October 21, 2009, a Shariʻa court sentenced a Muslim sect leader to the maximum penalty of ten years in prison and six strokes of the cane for claiming to be God's prophet.

9. In September 2009, the Pahang State Shariʻa Court sentenced the Muslim waitress who served alcohol to Kartika Sari Dewi Shukanro to six strokes of the cane and a fine.

10. In September 2009, the Selangor Shariʻa High Court sentenced an unmarried couple to fines and six strokes of the cane each for the offense of *khalwat* for engaging in sexual activities.

11. On July 20, 2009, a Pahang State Shariʻa court sentenced Kartika Sari Dewi Shukarno to a $1,560 (RM 5,000) fine and six strokes of the cane for consuming alcohol in July 2008.

12. On October 7, 2008, unknown assailants placed an improvised explosive device containing petrol at the Srijenka Express bus ticket counter in the Jalan Kuala Ketil bus station in Kota, Kuala Muda district, Kedah province, Malaysia. The ticket counter was destroyed from the fire that erupted following the bomb blast, however no casualties resulted from the attack.

13. In June 2008, JAIS arrested a man who claimed to be a "messenger from the sky" that had lived for "more than 3,000 years." The man had used his home as a gathering place for his followers.

14. On May 15, 2008, two homemade petrol bombs were hurled at the Wisma DAP building in Ipoh, Perak, Malaysia. No group claimed responsibility for the attack and no casualties were reported.

15. On April 28, 2007, officers from the Selangor Islamic Affairs Department (JAIS) raided the home of a Muslim woman and Hindu man who were married in July 2006 in a Hindu temple.

16. On March 1, 2007, JAIS raided the homes of twenty-eight individuals with links to the Rufaqa Corporation to gather further evidence against the company. JAIS also raided several business premises of Rufaqa Corporation on March 2, 2007, tearing down posters and signs bearing the word *Rufaqa* and seizing books and other materials featuring Ashaari.

SCORE OF 5	State and Nonstate Violence Descriptions

17. On November 14, 2006, JAIS detained 107 persons, including several children, during a raid in Kuala Lumpur against suspected followers of the banned al Arqam Islamic group.

Bangladesh
1. On September 20, 2011, Bangladeshi police detained about 300 members of the country's biggest religious party.
2. On September 19, 2011, 150 people were injured after protesting to demand the release of Jemaat-e-Islami's top leaders, who have been held in prison for months.
3. In July 2011, fifty people were injured by police after the main opposition Bangladesh Nationalist Party (BNP) and various Islamist parties called for a nationwide strike to demand the vow in "absolute faith in Allah" be reinstated as a pillar of the constitution.
4. On January 19, 2011, a bomb exploded on a bus in Feni District. No one was killed, but five people were wounded in the blast.
5. In 2010, there were approximately nineteen terrorist attacks in Bangladesh.
6. In 2009, there were approximately twenty-seven terrorist attacks in Bangladesh.
7. In 2008, there were approximately nineteen terrorist attacks in Bangladesh.
8. On March 15, 2008, the Special Branch of police in Brahmanbaria prevented the Ahmadiyya community from holding a religious convention. Following an intervention by higher authorities, the Special Branch lifted its objections and the event was held peacefully. A similar incident occurred at Shalshiri in Panchagarh district on March 21, 2008.
9. In 2007, there were approximately nine terrorist attacks in Bangladesh.
10. On September 17, 2007, *Alpin*, the satirical weekly magazine of the newspaper *Prothom Alo*, published a cartoon that some considered blasphemous against Islam. After demonstrations in several cities, the government banned the sale of the edition, ordered copies to be seized and destroyed, and detained the cartoonist, Arifur Rahman, who was eventually released by the court.
11. In 2006, there were approximately twenty-four terrorist attacks in Bangladesh.

Jordan
1. On April 15, 2011, several hundred persons demonstrated in Zarqa for the application of Islamic law and the release of prisoners. In an ensuing brawl with government supporters, in which police participated, numerous police and demonstrators

(continued)

SCORE OF 5	State and Nonstate Violence Descriptions

were injured. The police arrested around 100 demonstrators and charged 150 others, though no government supporters or police, with "carrying out terrorist acts," "assault," "rioting," and "unlawful gathering."

2. On August 2, 2010, in Aqaba, Jordan, unknown assailants fired four rockets, killing one person and injuring four others.

3. On January 14, 2010, in Amman, Jordan, a roadside bomb targeting the convoy of Israeli Ambassador Danny Nevo detonated, but caused no casualties or damages.

4. In 2009, a court charged a literary figure with defamation of Islam, sentencing him to fines and time in jail.

5. On April 22, 2008, the Sweilih Islamic law court found Muhammad Abbad Abbad, a convert from Islam to Christianity, guilty of apostasy, annulled his marriage, and declared him to be without any religious identity. He was accused of "contempt of court" and sentenced to one week's imprisonment.

6. In late 2007 and early 2008, approximately thirty foreign resident members of evangelical churches, many of whom were longtime residents of the country, were deported, refused renewal of residency permits, or denied reentry after exiting the country.

7. In April 2007, authorities deported Pastor Mazhar Izzat Bishay of the Aqaba Free Evangelical Church, an Egyptian national and twenty-eight-year resident married to a Jordanian, to Egypt.

8. In late 2006, authorities deported Wajeeh Besharah, Ibrahim Atta, Raja Welson, and Imad Waheeb, four Coptic Egyptians living in Aqaba, to Egypt.

9. On September 4, 2006, an unknown gunman shot foreigners in Amman, Jordan, killing one and wounding six. No group claimed responsibility for the attack.

10. In January and February 2006, Jihad Al-Momani, former chief editor of the weekly newspaper *Shihan*, and Hussein Al-Khalidi of the weekly Al *Mihar*, were arrested, released, and then re-arrested for printing controversial cartoons depicting the Prophet Muhammad.

Kuwait

1. In September 2011, exiled Kuwaiti Shia cleric Yasser al-Habib disparaged the wife and companions of the Prophet Muhammad, all of whom Sunnis revere. In response the Kuwaiti government revoked al-Habib's citizenship. The government briefly detained, but did not charge, Sunni Islamist Mubarak al-Bathali, who, in response to al-Habib's statements, advocated violence against the Shia community.

SCORE OF 5	State and Nonstate Violence Descriptions

2. On June 7, 2011, online activist Nasser Abul was arrested and charged with breaching "state security," "damaging the country's interests," and "severing political relationship with brotherly countries" because of messages he posted on Twitter. On September 24, he was convicted of writing derogatory remarks about Sunni Muslims and sentenced to three months' imprisonment, but immediately released because of the time he had already been detained.

Somalia

1. Between 2006 and 2011, fighting between Islamic militants and TFG was continuous. Al-Shabaab regularly fired mortars indiscriminately from densely populated areas toward TFG/ AMISOM positions, often unlawfully placing civilians at risk. TFG and AMISOM forces frequently responded with indiscriminate counterattacks, notably in and around Bakara market.

2. On December 6, 2011, Somali police stopped a car at a checkpoint in the city of Mogadishu, Somalia; the driver detonated a bomb inside the car. The blast killed one police officer and five people.

3. In October 2011, an outburst of renewed fighting between Raskamboni and other TFG-affiliated militias against al-Shabaab in Dhobley resulted in at least eleven civilian deaths.

4. On October 30, 2011, a suicide bomber attacked the Somalia's army headquarters in the city of Mogadishu. The bombing killed four soldiers and wounded twelve more.

5. On October 4, 2011, a suicide bombing in Mogadishu, claimed by al-Shabaab, occurred outside a compound housing several government ministries, including the Ministry of Education. At least 100 civilians were killed.

6. On August 23, 2011, al-Shabaab publicly executed three men accused of spying for the TFG in the Daynile district of Mogadishu.

7. On August 21, 2011, al-Shabaab arrested twenty men in Kismayu for chewing *khat*, smoking cigarettes, or eating before sunset during the month of Ramadan. Al-Shabaab made similar arrests in Dinsoor, Bay Region; those arrested were each given twenty-five strokes with a cane for nonobservance of the fasting period.

8. On November 10, 2011, al-Shabaab militia beheaded four persons in Waradhumale in Galgaduud Region for their association with ASWJ.

9. On November 22, 2011, al-Shabaab flogged a young woman and man in the central Somali town of Jalalqsi for allegedly eloping.

(continued)

SCORE OF 5	State and Nonstate Violence Descriptions

10. In 2010, there were approximately 117 terrorist attacks in Somalia, including the August 24, 2010 al-Shabaab suicide attack on the Muna Hotel and the September 9, 2010 al-Shabaab attack on Mogadishu's airport.
11. On July 11, 2010 al-Shabaab attacked a pub in Uganda.
12. On February 21, 2011, a suicide car bomb exploded outside a police station in Mogadishu, killing eight and wounding thirty-five more.
13. In 2009, there were approximately 121 terrorist attacks in Somalia.
14. In 2009, fighting occurred between al-Shabaab and militias associated with Ahlu Sunna wal Jamaa (a Sufi nationwide organization aligned with the TFG).
15. In February 2009, Abdi Welli Ahmed, a Kenyan citizen and Christian convert from Islam, was detained and assaulted as he tried to cross the border from Ethiopia.
16. In 2008, there were approximately 168 terrorist attacks in Somalia.
17. In 2007, there were approximately 148 terrorist attacks in Somalia.
18. In 2006, there were approximately sixteen terrorist attacks in Somalia.
19. In May 2006, a sixteen-year-old boy stabbed to death his father's killer in a public execution ordered by an Islamic court.

Qatar

1. In 2011, at least six men and women, all foreign nationals, were sentenced to floggings of either 40 or 100 lashes for offenses related to alcohol consumption or "illicit sexual relations." Only Muslims considered medically fit were liable to have such sentences carried out.
2. In February 2011, a forty-one-year-old Qatari man reportedly received a five-year prison term after a court in Doha convicted him of blasphemy.
3. In 2009, six Lebanese mechanics were sentenced to three years imprisonment each and subsequent deportation for "uttering blasphemous words."
4. In February 2009, the Doha Criminal Court sentenced a Christian Lebanese expatriate to three years in prison and eventual deportation for blasphemy.

UAE

Sudan

1. In 2011, systematic, ongoing, and egregious violations of freedom of religion or belief continued in Sudan. Violations included: efforts by the Arab Muslim-dominated government in Khartoum to impose its version of Shari'a law and enforce

religiously based morality laws through corporal punishment to limit the fundamental freedoms of Muslims and non-Muslims alike; the criminalization of conversion from Islam, a crime punishable by death, and the intense scrutiny, intimidation, and torture of suspected converts by government security personnel; the denial of the rights of non-Muslims to public religious expression and persuasion, while allowing Muslims to proselytize; and the difficulty in obtaining permission to build churches, as compared to government funding of mosque construction.

2. Between 2006 and 2011, in Darfur and other areas of conflict, government forces, rebel groups, and tribal factions committed torture, killing, and abuse.

3. On October 11, 2011, an ambush killed three United Nations peacekeepers in the Zam Zam camp near the city of Al-Fashir.

4. On January 11, 2011, fighters from the Misseriya ambushed eleven people on their way to vote.

5. In 2010, there were approximately twenty-seven terrorist attacks in Sudan.

6. In 2009, there were approximately twenty-four terrorist attacks in Sudan.

7. In November 2009, police reportedly arrested sixteen-year-old Silva Kashif for indecent dress and lashed her fifty times.

8. On March 27, 2009, local officials in Chat, a Nuba Mountains village, allegedly led a mob that razed a building used by the Evangelical Presbyterian Church and the Sudanese Church of Christ.

9. On March 1, 2009, PDF members interrupted a church service and threatened further destruction after breaking the cross on the church's roof.

10. On February 1, 2009, the GNU's Humanitarian Affairs Commission (HAC) expelled the U.S. nongovernmental organization (NGO) Thirst No More from Darfur on the basis that it was not a legitimate humanitarian aid organization. Authorities accused the NGO of engaging in Christian proselytizing among Muslims in Darfur, an act forbidden by law.

11. In 2008, there were approximately thirty-two terrorist attacks in Sudan.

12. In 2007, there were approximately twenty-three terrorist attacks in Sudan.

13. In November 2007, a British national teaching at a Christian school in Khartoum was held briefly and threatened with imprisonment and corporal punishment for acceding to her students' suggestion to name a class teddy bear after the Prophet Muhammad.

(*continued*)

SCORE OF 5	State and Nonstate Violence Descriptions

14. In July 2007, a Catholic priest was jailed and held without charges for three days in connection with an investigation regarding a Khartoum woman who had planned to convert to Christianity.
15. On January 1, 2007, police raided the seat of the Episcopal Church of Sudan Diocese of Khartoum with tear gas, injuring six worshippers.
16. In 2006, there were approximately twenty-three terrorist attacks in Sudan.
17. In May 2006, officers of the National Intelligence and Security Service detained and beat Christian leaders who met with a Muslim woman who wanted to convert to Christianity.

Yemen

1. From 2006 to 2011, the government held an unknown number of Islamists who returned to Yemen from fighting in Afghanistan.
2. On October 8, 2011, a bomb exploded outside a police station headquarters in the city of Aden, injuring at least nine people.
3. On September 15, 2011, two bombs exploded in the city of Aden, hitting two security buildings. Two people were killed and two wounded in the blasts.
4. On September 3, 2011, a car bomb exploded at a military checkpoint in the city of Aden. The blast killed five soldiers and wounded eight more.
5. On July 24, 2011, five soldiers were killed and two wounded after a car bomb exploded in the city of Aden.
6. In February 2011, detainees at the Political Security prison in Sana'a, including alleged al-Qa'ida members or supporters, were reported to have been beaten by guards and held in solitary confinement after going on hunger strike to protest against their prolonged detention without charge or trial, ill treatment, and denial of adequate medical care. At least ten detainees were said to have required hospital treatment as a result of the beatings.
7. On January 7, 2011, fifteen suspected Al Qaeda gunmen ambushed army vehicles that were escorting a lorry with food supplies to an army base using rocket-propelled grenades.
8. In 2010, there were approximately 111 terrorist attacks in Yemen.
9. On November 26, 2010 (AQAP) a suicide bomber attacked a funeral procession for a prominent Houthi leader, leaving two dead and eight wounded.
10. On November 24, 2010, (AQAP) a suicide bomber attacked a group of Zaydis in the Jawf Governorate during celebrations of a Shia holiday, killing twenty-one.
11. In October 2010, militants in San'a fired a rocket-propelled grenade at a car carrying five British Embassy staff members.

SCORE OF 5	State and Nonstate Violence Descriptions

12. In September 2010, a bus ambush in San'a AQAP killed fourteen senior officers who had recently completed a U.S. counterterrorism intelligence course.

13. In June 2010, four AQAP gunmen attacked a post of the Political Security Organization in Aden, killing eleven intelligence officers and soldiers and freeing several suspected militants.

14. In April 2010, a suicide bomber tried unsuccessfully to kill British Ambassador Tim Torlot.

15. In 2009, there were approximately twenty-three terrorist attacks in Yemen.

16. Following numerous incidents and threats, Jewish children in Reyda reportedly stopped attending school in 2009. The community also closed its two synagogues, reportedly for fear of violence. As a result of the unprecedented level of violence in 2008 and 2009, many Jewish residents of Amran Governorate left the country during the reporting period.

17. In August 2009. the National Security Bureau arrested UN employee Walid Sharafuddin along with Mumar al-Abdali, Sadiq al-Sharafi, and Abdullah al-Dailami on charges of supporting the Houthi insurrection and spying for Iran.

18. In August 2009, an armed confrontation in Saada Governorate between alleged Houthi supporters, Zaydi Muslims, and Salafi Muslims left fifteen dead and five injured.

19. In June 2009, armed men kidnapped nine foreign workers at a hospital in Saada. Three of the hostages were killed immediately. Two hostages were transferred to Saudi Arabian authorities in May 2010 after eleven months in captivity. The remaining four hostages remained missing at the end of the reporting period. An investigation was ongoing, but observers reported that violent extremists may have targeted the foreigners because of rumors that they were Christian missionaries proselytizing in Saada.

20. In 2008, there were approximately twenty-two terrorist attacks in Yemen.

21. In June 2008 according to independent reports, police arrested seven Baha'is (two Yemeni citizens, four Iranians, and one Iraqi) in their homes during raids and detained them without filing charges.

22. In June 2008, a convert to Christianity and two of his associates were reportedly arrested in Hodeida for "promoting Christianity and distributing the Bible."

23. In May 2008, Imam Mohammed Ahmed Miftah disappeared after his car was attacked by gunmen from two other vehicles. Previously, Miftah was sentenced to eight years of

(*continued*)

SCORE OF 5	State and Nonstate Violence Descriptions

imprisonment, but later pardoned, for allegedly establishing contacts with Iran for the purpose of harming the country.

24. In 2007, there were approximately seven terrorist attacks in Yemen.
25. In 2007, a credible newspaper report claimed security officials harassed and detained a Muslim carrying Christian missionary publications in Taiz.
26. In 2006, there were approximately five terrorist attacks in Yemen.

Iran

1. In 2011, seventy-five Baha'is remained in prison on account of their religious beliefs.
2. In 2011, arrests and harassment of Sufi Muslims increased significantly.
3. In 2011, the number of incidents of Iranian authorities raiding church services, harassing and threatening church members, and arresting, convicting, and imprisoning worshippers and church leaders increased significantly. More than 250 Christians have been arbitrarily arrested throughout the country.
4. In September and October 2011, up to 100 Gonabadi Dervishes (a Sufi religious order), three of their lawyers, as well as twelve journalists for *Majzooban-e Noor*, a Gonabadi Dervish news website, were arrested in Kavar and Tehran in September and October.
5. In March 2011, six Baha'is were arrested in Kerman, four for allegedly providing education for young children and the other two for unknown reasons.
6. In January 2011, three Iranian lawyers who defended Sufi Dervishes were sentenced to prison terms.
7. In January 2011, Navid Khanjani, a twenty-four-year-old Baha'i who began advocating for human rights after he was denied access to higher education, was sentenced to twelve years in prison after being convicted of engaging in human rights activities, illegal assembly, and disturbance of the general public's opinion.
8. In January 2011, Sayed Mohammad Movahed Fazeli, the Sunni prayer leader of the city of Taybad, was detained following protests in Taybad against his enforced resignation as prayer leader.
9. In 2010, there were approximately thirteen terrorist attacks in Iran. The most notable ones included the December 15 attack in Tehran by an unknown militant who detonated a suicide improvised explosive device close to an emergency car of the Red Crescent Society when people were gathering in front of the governor's office building. A total of thirty-nine

SCORE OF 5	State and Nonstate Violence
	Descriptions

people were killed, while fifty others were wounded. Also, on July 15, in Zahedan, two suicide bombers, Mohammad Rigi and Abdolbasset Rigi, detonated suicide improvised explosive devices near the Grand Zahedan Shiite Mosque targeting a Revolutionary Guards gathering, killing twenty-eight people and injuring more than three hundred others.

10. In 2010, authorities regularly detained and harassed bloggers who wrote anything critical of the country's Islamic revolution.

11. In early 2010, the government started convicting and executing reformers and peaceful protestors on the charge of *moharebeh* (enmity against God). Reportedly, more than ten individuals have been charged, convicted, and sentenced to death as moharebeh. At least three are known to have been executed.

12. At the end of 2010, at least fifty-six Baha'is remained in detention because of their religious beliefs.

13. In 2010, the seven leaders of the Baha'i community – Fariba Kamalabadi, Jamaloddin Khanjani, Afif Naeimi, Behrouz Tavakkoli, Saeid Rezaie, Vahid Tizfahm, and Mahvash Sabet – remained in detention since their arrests in spring 2008.

14. Between July and December 2010, 161 additional arrests of Christians were reported. Of those arrested, thirty-three remained in jail or with an unknown status at the end of the year.

15. Between June 2008 and June 2010 more than 115 Christians were reportedly arrested on charges of apostasy, illegal activities of evangelism, antigovernment propaganda, and activities against Islam, among other charges.

16. In a December 7, 2010 report, the International Campaign for Human Rights in Iran reported that at least seventeen Baha'i were barred or expelled from universities in 2010 on political or religious grounds.

17. On November 13, 2010, following his October 2009 arrest, Youcef Nadarkhani, a pastor of a house church in Gilan, reportedly received a death sentence for apostasy and evangelism. He was held in Lakan prison, and the case was on appeal at the end of the year.

18. In June 2010, Behrouz Sadegh-Khandjani, the pastor of a house church in Shiraz, reportedly received a death sentence for apostasy following his arrest on an unknown date.

19. According to the Baha'i International Community's United Nations Office, Intelligence Ministry officers raided the home of Fakhroddin Samimi on May 31, 2010. After searching his home and confiscating personal belongings, including his computer and material related to his religious beliefs, the officers arrested him.

(*continued*)

SCORE OF 5 State and Nonstate Violence
Descriptions

20. On April 14, 2010, government agents raided Christian pastor Behnam Irani's home in Karaj and confiscated personal belongings such as cameras, computers, and Bibles.
21. On April 11, 2010, government agents arrested nineteen-year-old Daniel Shahri, a Christian, on the basis of insulting Islam.
22. In March 2010, intelligence agents in Sari reportedly arrested Shirin Foroughian Samimi, a Baha'i.
23. On March 7, 2010, government officials imprisoned a Christian convert on charges of starting a home-based fellowship and promoting Christian doctrine.
24. On February 28, 2010, Hamid Shafiee, a Christian priest, and his wife, Reyhaneh Aghajari, were arrested in the central city of Isfahan.
25. On February 20, 2010, plainclothes security agents in Tehran arrested an Armenian Christian pastor, Vahik Abrahamian.
26. On February 2, 2010, state security agents arrested Reverend Wilson Issavi, the pastor of the Evangelical Church of Kermanshah in Isfahan, on charges of "converting Muslims."
27. On January 8, 2010, the Fars Provincial Ministry of Intelligence detained an unknown number of persons who were reportedly Christians.
28. Since January 1, 2010, at least fifty Baha'is have been arbitrarily arrested.
29. In January 2010, chief prosecutor of Tehran Abbas Jafari-Dolatabadi publicly stated that the Baha'is arrested during the December 2009 demonstrations had played a role in organizing the Ashura riots.
30. In 2009, there were approximately seventeen terrorist attacks in Iran.
31. Since his arrest in December 2009 for allegedly participating in Ashura protests, Heshmatollah Tabarzadi remains in solitary confinement in Evin prison.
32. On December 24, 2009, Pakdasht security forces raided a home church gathering and arrested the fifteen members who were in attendance.
33. On December 17, 2009, security officers raided a Christian worship gathering in Karaj and arrested the two leaders, Kambiz Saghaee and Ali Keshvar-Doost.
34. On December 16, 2009, security officers on orders from the Revolutionary Court of Mashhad searched the home of and arrested Hamideh Najafi, a Christian woman residing in Mashhad.
35. In October 2009, MOIS officers searched the home of Baha'i member Ali Bakhsh Bazrafkan, confiscated items linked to his faith, and arrested him.

SCORE OF 5	State and Nonstate Violence Descriptions

36. In October 2009, MOIS officers arrested Behnam Rouhanifard for producing and distributing Baha'i music.

37. In October 2009, the government threatened the pastor of the largest church that holds public services to stop Friday worship services or face the consequence of shutting down the entire Central Assemblies of God Church in Tehran.

38. In September 2009, MOIS officers in Yazd searched the home of Soheil Rouhanifard, brother of Behnam Rouhanifard, and confiscated belongings and materials related to the Baha'i faith. The next day Soheil Rouhanifard appeared at the local MOIS office in response to a summons. Authorities interrogated and released him. He was summoned again on October 19 and arrested without charge.

39. Between June and August 2009, at least thirty Christians were arrested and detained across the country, mostly during church gatherings.

40. In July 2009, twenty Sufi practitioners were arrested after gathering to protest the arrest of Hossein Zareya, a local leader.

41. In May 2009, security officials arrested five Christian converts in Karaj who had gathered in a home for Bible study and worship.

42. In May 2009, in Bandar Manshahr, authorities arrested Abdul Zahra Vashahi, father of a prominent Christian-Iranian human rights activist in the United Kingdom, after warning him that he would be held accountable for his son's activities.

43. In March 2009, a Shiraz court sentenced three Christian converts – Seyed Allaedin Hussein, Homayoon Shokouhi, and Seyed Amir Hussein Bob-Annari – to eight-month prison terms with five years' probation.

44. In March 2009, a representative of the Gonabadi Sufi Dervishes reported that authorities were holding forty-one dervishes in Evin prison for practicing their religion.

45. In March 2009, security forces reportedly arrested Baha'i Pooya Tebyanian in his home in Semnan.

46. In February 2009, authorities razed the house of worship of Gonabadi Dervishes at Takht-e-Foulad, in Isfahan, with bulldozers. All Sufis present were arrested and had their mobile phones confiscated.

47. In February 2009, at least forty Sufis in the central city of Isfahan were arrested after protesting the destruction of a Sufi place of worship; all were released within days.

48. In January 2009, security forces in Tehran arrested five Baha'is and took them to Evin prison.

49. In January 2009, security forces in Ghaemshahr in Mazandaran Province detained four Baha'is after raiding their homes.

(*continued*)

SCORE OF 5	State and Nonstate Violence Descriptions

50. In January 2009, Jamshid Lak, a Sufi of the Gonabadi Dervish order, was flogged seventy-four times.

51. In January 2009, several Baha'i women were reportedly arrested for performing missionary work on Kish Island and later released.

52. In January 2009, authorities arrested three Christians – Hamik Khachikian (an Armenian Christian), Jamal Ghalishorani, and Nadereh Jamali (both Christian converts) – in Tehran.

53. In 2008, there were approximately eight terrorist attacks in Iran.

54. In 2008, plainclothes security officers raided the home of Isfahan Iranian Christians Abbas Amiri and his wife, Sakineh Rahnama, during a meeting. Amiri and Rahnama died of injuries suffered during the raid.

55. In late December 2008, after the closure of a Sufi Muslim place of worship, authorities arrested without charge at least six members of the Gonabadi Dervishes on Kish Island and confiscated their books and computer equipment.

56. In November 2008, Amir Ali Mohammad Labaf of the Gonabadi Sufi order was sentenced to seventy-four lashes, five years in prison, and internal exile to the town of Babak for "spreading lies."

57. In November 2008, well-known Iranian-Canadian blogger Hossein Derakhshan was arrested in Tehran while visiting the country and remained in Evin prison in the northwestern part of the country.

58. In November 2008, authorities arrested two Baha'is in Sari, Mazandaran Province, after searching their homes and confiscating Baha'i materials.

59. In November 2008, a Baha'i was arrested in Ghaemshahr.

60. In October 2008, at least seven Sufi Muslims in Isfahan and five Sufis in Karaj were arrested because of their affiliation with the Gonabadi Sufi order.

61. On August 21, 2008, Ramtin Soodmand, a Christian, was charged with spreading antigovernment propaganda.

62. In May 2008, two officials of the Baha'i community in Isfahan and one other member of the Baha'i community were arrested.

63. In May 2008, Christian convert Mojataba Hussein remained in detention.

64. On May 31, 2008, authorities arrested Christian Mohsen Namvar from his home in Tehran.

65. On May 27, 2008, security officials arrested two officials of the Baha'i community in Isfahan and one other member of the Baha'i community, reportedly on charges of burying their dead at a particular site that had been used for the past fifteen years.

SCORE OF 5 State and Nonstate Violence
Descriptions

66. In April 2008, a man and a pregnant woman, believed to be Christian converts, were arrested in the city of Amol, north of Tehran.
67. On March 17, 2008, the Intelligence Ministry detained a Baha'i man, Mohammad Ismael Forouzan. Forouzan had a pending appeal against a one-year prison sentence for unknown charges.
68. On May 14, 2008, authorities arrested six leaders of the Baha'i community at their homes in Tehran and detained them in an unknown location.
69. On March 9, 2008, authorities arrested Touraj Amini, Iraj Amini, and Payman Amoui on charges of teaching the Baha'i faith.
70. On January 31, 2008, Intelligence Ministry authorities arrested Foad Ettehadolhagh and interrogated him about the activities of the Baha'i community in Shiraz, for which he coordinated affairs on an ad hoc basis. He was released following the interrogation.
71. On January 31, 2008, police in Hamedan arrested and detained Aziz Pourhamzeh, Kamran Aghdasi, and Fathollah Khatbjavan.
72. On January 27, 2008, Pouriya Habibi and Simin Mokhtari were arrested and detained on charges of teaching the Baha'i faith.
73. On January 15, 2008, Foad Agah was arrested and detained by the Intelligence Ministry, reportedly in the process of collecting photocopies of Baha'i pamphlets.
74. In 2007, there were approximately ten terrorist attacks in Iran.
75. In 2007 there were three reported killings of senior Sunni clerics, including the June 24, 2007, killing of Hesham Saymary in the ethnically Arab-dominated province of Khuzestan
76. On December 25, 2007, Hormoz Hashemi was arrested in Shiraz for having distributed informational materials about the Baha'i faith.
77. On December 13, 2007, the Intelligence Ministry arrested and detained Shahreza Abbasi.
78. On November 18, 2007, a Baha'i man, Fayzullah Rowshan, began serving his one-year prison sentence for "teaching activities against the system of the Islamic Republic of Iran."
79. On November 13, 2007, authorities arrested Diyanat Haghighat, reportedly for seeking redress for expelled Baha'i students, including his daughter, Nasim Haghighat.
80. On November 11, 2007, authorities arrested 180 Sufis in the city of Boroujerd, following clashes with police.
81. On September 25, 2007, Jamaloddin Khanjani, a member of a group that coordinates the affairs of the Iranian Baha'i

(*continued*)

SCORE OF 5	State and Nonstate Violence Descriptions

community, was detained by the Intelligence Ministry for five days and interrogated.

82. On May 21, 2007, security forces arrested the leader of the Nematollahi Gonabadi Sufi order, Nurali Tabandeh.

83. On January 1, 2007, two Baha'i men, Riaz Heravi and Siamak Ebrahimi, were arrested and detained for twenty and thirty days, respectively.

84. In 2006, there were approximately fourteen terrorist attacks in Iran.

85. In 2006, fifty-one Baha'i were arrested during their involvement in projects in and around the city of Shiraz that focused on teaching literacy and social skills to children.

86. In 2006, Iranian Shiite Ayatollah Seyed Hossein Kazemeini Boroujerdi, along with seventeen of his followers, was imprisoned for espousing religious views incongruent with the official religious views of the government.

87. On November 1, 2006, a Baha'i man, Fayzullah Rowshan, was reportedly arrested by order of the Ministry of Information, following a search of his home.

88. On September 26, 2006, authorities arrested evangelical Christians Fereshteh Dibaj and Reza Montazami at their home in the northeastern part of the country.

89. On September 21, 2006, the Court of Appeal in Semnan province denied the appeal of eight Baha'is arrested in May 2005.

90. On August 17, 2006, a Baha'i man, Babak Roohi, was reportedly arrested in Mashhad for making fifty photocopies of a Baha'i book for a Baha'i function.

91. On July 24, 2006, authorities arrested Issa Motamedi Mojdehi, a Muslim convert to Christianity, following his attempt to register the birth of his son.

92. On June 28, 2006, a Baha'i was taken into custody and held in the Ministry of Information's detention center.

93. On June 21, 2006, a Baha'i man, Shokrollah Rahmani, was reportedly abducted in broad daylight in Khash in southeastern Iran.

94. On June 21, 2006, a Baha'i from Baluchistan province was reportedly abducted, and authorities said they suspected criminal elements were involved.

95. On June 18, 2006, the government arrested three Baha'is from Hamadan after government officials confiscated books, computers, and Baha'i documents.

96. On May 19, 2006, the government raided six Baha'i homes in Shiraz and arrested fifty-four Baha'is.

SCORE OF 5	State and Nonstate Violence Descriptions

97. Between May 9 and May 11, 2006, the government raided eleven Baha'i homes in Shahinshahr, Najafabad, and Kashan with no arrests made.

98. On May 2, 2006, a Muslim convert to Christianity, Ali Kaboli, was taken into custody in Gorgan, after several years of police surveillance, and threatened with prosecution if he did not leave the country.

99. In May 2006, fifty-four other Baha'i individuals were charged with teaching the Baha'i faith indirectly through their participation in a community education program.

100. On February 14, 2006, security forces demolished a husseiniya, as well as neighboring houses, and arrested more than twelve hundred persons, according to several sources.

101. On February 5, 2006, the government arrested three Baha'is from Esfahan for coordinating Baha'i activities.

102. On January 15, 2006, the government arrested three Baha'is from Kermanshah on charges of "involvement in Baha'i activities and insulting Islam."

Afghanistan

1. Data for 2011 terrorist attacks has yet to be released by the Global Terrorism Database.

2. In 2010, there were approximately 530 terrorist attacks in Afghanistan.

3. Numerous killings of religious leaders and attacks on mosques were attributed to al-Qa'ida and Taliban members throughout 2010.

4. Insurgent-targeted killings in violation of international humanitarian law increased, particularly in the south. The UN estimates 183 assassinations in the first six months of 2010, up 95 percent compared to 2009.

5. Between March and October 2010, twenty schools were attacked using explosives or arson, and insurgent attacks killed 126 students.

6. In October 2010 an individual was arrested in Mazar-e-Sharif for reportedly converting away from Islam.

7. on September 28, 2010, election staff members in Baghlan were kidnapped and two were killed in Balkh.

8. In May 2010, police arrested two Afghan citizens for converting away from Islam.

9. In 2009, there were approximately 470 terrorist attacks in Afghanistan.

10. In 2008, there were approximately 392 terrorist attacks in Afghanistan.

11. In 2008, a local court sentenced Sayed Perwiz Kambakhsh to death for "insolence to the Holy Prophet," after he allegedly

(*continued*)

SCORE OF 5	State and Nonstate Violence Descriptions

	downloaded and distributed information from the Internet regarding the role of women in Islamic societies. He was pardoned by President Karzai in August 2009.
	12. In September 2008, Ghaus Zalmai and Mullah Qari Mushtq were sentenced to twenty years' imprisonment for publishing a Dari-language translation of the Qur'an without the accompanying Arabic verses for comparison. President Karzai pardoned them in March 2010.
	13. In 2007, there were approximately 325 terrorist attacks in Afghanistan.
	14. On April 9, 2007, police arrested a citizen who was born a member of the Baha'i faith, after his religious beliefs were exposed to authorities by his wife.
	15. In 2006, there were approximately 262 terrorist attacks in Afghanistan.
	16. In 2006, Abdul Rahman, who was detained after converting to Christianity, highlighted the extreme cultural sensitivities surrounding religious freedom in the country.
Libya (under Qadaffi)	1. From 2006 to 2011, numerous armed clashes occurred between security forces and Islamic groups that oppose the government and advocate the establishment of an Islamic government that would enforce a more conservative form of Islam. Total arrested or killed is unknown.
	2. On June 18, 2010, authorities arrested a South Korean evangelical Christian pastor and a South Korean farmer, allegedly working as his assistant, on charges of proselytizing, according to press reports.
	3. In June 2010, authorities in Benghazi arrested an Egyptian man for proselytizing after he allegedly distributed Bibles and religious pictures to adolescents.
	4. In April 2009, the government reportedly released several converts to Christianity after allegedly detaining them for three months without charge.
	5. In March 2009, the ICC reported that converts from Islam were held without access to assistance in Tripoli in a state security prison where they were allegedly interrogated, abused, and pressured to reveal the names of other converts.
	6. On August 26, 2008, three members of the Sudanese Liberation Movement hijacked Sun Air flight 611 en route to Khartoum. No casualties were reported and two hijackers surrendered.
Bahrain	1. On December 11, 2011, a bomb exploded on a bus outside the British Embassy in the city of Manama. No one was killed or injured in the blast.
	2. By the end of 2011, at least forty-seven people had died in protests, including five police officers. More than one thousand

SCORE OF 5	State and Nonstate Violence Descriptions

people were arrested in connection with the protests; some were Sunni Muslims but the vast majority were Shi'a Muslims.

3. On March 15, 2011, as demonstrations and strikes continued, the king declared a three-month state of emergency. This came a day after around twelve hundred Saudi Arabian troops in armored vehicles had arrived in the country to buttress Bahrain's security forces. By the end of March, the main protests had been crushed, although sporadic protests in predominantly Shi'a villages continued for the rest of the year.

4. On February 14, 2011, mass pro-reform protests began. Most demonstrators were from the majority Shi'a community, who believe they are discriminated against by the ruling Sunni minority. The protests centered on Pearl Roundabout in the capital, Manama, where a protest camp was established. Police and other security forces dispersed the protesters on February 17 using excessive force.

5. In December 2010, there were clashes between Shia villagers and police officers in and around Karranah and Malikiyah villages after police officers removed Muharram-related black banners from entrances to at least two villages – actions considered provocative to many in the Shia community.

6. On September 14, 2010, in Hamad town, Manama city, in Al Manamah, Bahrain, unidentified assailants detonated an improvised explosive device.

7. On March 16, 2010, in Manama, Al Manamah, Bahrain, a seventeen-year-old male assailant, threw a Molotov cocktail at the Embassy of the United Kingdom.

8. In 2010, twenty-three detained Shia activists reported torture and other mistreatment, including beatings, deprivation of sleep, electrocution, and being subjected to forced standing for long periods of time.

9. On April 9, 2008, a Bahranian police patrol was attacked with stones and Molotov cocktails by unknown attackers in the village of Karzakan south of Manama, Al Manamah.

Comoros	1. On May 29, 2006, four men were convicted to three months in prison for "evangelizing Muslims."

2. In February 2006, the International Church of Moroni received permission to distribute gift boxes of toys for Comoran children. After promising the boxes would not contain any Bibles or religious literature, the church distributed boxes in four villages, two schools, and two hospitals. On March 27, the minister of education demanded to meet with the pastor of the International Church. During the meeting, the minister revealed that a children's Bible storybook and two necklaces with crosses

(continued)

SCORE OF 5	State and Nonstate Violence Descriptions

were found during the toy distribution. The minister demanded that the church stop all gift distribution; the church complied. On April 1, one of the church leaders was arrested for his involvement in the toy distribution. He spent one night in prison, and his house was searched. Other church leaders were similarly detained and their houses were searched.

Brunei

1. Authorities continued to arrest persons for offenses under Shari'a, such as khalwat (close proximity between the sexes) and consumption of alcohol. According to statistics released by religious authorities, fifty-one khalwat cases were reported during 2010.

2. According to statistics released by religious authorities, fifty-four khalwat cases were reported during 2009.

3. According to statistics released by religious authorities, 691 khalwat cases were recorded during 2008.

4. According to statistics released by religious authorities, thirty-one khalwat cases were reported during 2007.

5. According to statistics released by religious authorities, 389 khalwat cases were reported during the period of July 2005 to April 2006.

Mauritania

1. In 2011, at least twelve people, including Mohamed Lemine Ould Mballe, were arrested on suspicion of being members of AQIM. At least eighteen people were tried and sentenced to prison terms or to death. Although the detainees alleged that they had been tortured, the court did not order any inquiry.

2. In May 2011, fourteen prisoners who had been sentenced for terrorism activities were taken at night from a Nouakchott central prison to an unknown location.

3. On August 25, 2010, in Nema, Hodh Ech Chargui, Mauritania, an unidentified militant attempted to drive an improvised explosive device into a military barrack, but was shot and killed before he could reach the gate.

4. On December 18, 2009, in the village of Mneyssiratt in a unknown area of Mauritania, armed gunmen kidnapped two Italian nationals and an Ivorian national; no material damage or casualties were reported.

5. On November 29, 2009, in Chelkhet Legtouta, 170 miles north of Nouakchott, Trarza, Mauritania, armed assailants fired on a convoy, injuring one humanitarian worker and damaging one vehicle.

6. On September 14, 2009, Police Commissioner Abdel Vettah Ould Hababa closed three churches frequented by West Africans in the Sebkha district of Nouakchott. According to press reports, the police confiscated Bibles and furniture and briefly arrested eighty-one persons.

SCORE OF 5	State and Nonstate Violence Descriptions

7. On August 31, 2009, police in Nouakchott arrested approximately ten individuals who possessed a large quantity of Christian books, including Bibles.
8. On August 8, 2009, a suicide attacker detonated a bomb near the French embassy in the Mauritanian capital of Nouakchott.
9. On June 23, 2009, in Nouakchott, Trarza, Mauritania, two armed assailants unsuccessfully tried to kidnap, then fired on and killed a United States citizen who was the director of a computer science school.
10. On February 9, 2009, in northern Mauritania, assailants kidnapped several local Mauritanian civilians.
11. In late December 2008. authorities arrested a Norwegian woman in Ouadane for distributing Christian materials. She was released with a warning but was subsequently expelled from the country on January 2, 2009, after she continued her activities in Atar.
12. On September 15, 2008, twelve Mauritanian soldiers were abducted after their patrol was attacked by al Qaeda's Islamic Maghreb (AQIM) gunmen in Zouerate, Tiris Zemmour province.
13. In March 2008, security forces briefly detained a man at a vehicle check point between Nouakchott and Rosso for carrying large amounts of undeclared currency and Christian proselytizing material
14. On January 31, 2008, six unknown gunmen opened fire on the Israeli embassy in Mauritania, killing no one and wounding an unknown amount of people.
15. On or about August 21, 2007, Nouakchott police arrested a Christian convert on charges of proselytizing.
16. In May 2006, the transitional government arrested six Ghanaian, Guinean, and Nigerian Protestant pastors in Nouakchott, seized their religious materials, and padlocked their unauthorized churches, which were run in private houses.

SCORE Of 4

Syria	1. From 2006 to 2011, the government continued to hold an unknown number of members of the Muslim Brotherhood and other individuals associated with illegal political Islamic groups as political detainees and prisoners.

2. On December 23, 2011, two suicide car bombers attacked the city of Damascus. The bombings killed 44 and wounded 166 people.
3. On October 1, 2011, a bomb exploded in a neighborhood of Damascus, killing three Syrian military officers and wounding two more.

(continued)

SCORE Of 4

4. In 2010, human rights organizations documented the arrests of dozens of persons for alleged ties to political Islamic groups. Many persons were charged, convicted, and imprisoned for "membership in a Salafist organization" and for spreading "Wahabist/Takfiri" ideology. Total number unknown.

5. On October 10, 2010, eight alleged Islamists were sentenced to terms ranging from three to five years in jail.

6. On May 10, 2010, after several preliminary trial dates, the First Criminal Court in Damascus charged Imam Salah al-Din Kuftaro, the son of late Grand Mufti Ahmad Kuftaro, with embezzlement, operating an organization without appropriate permissions, exploiting relations with the Al-Ansar Charity, and attempting to bribe government officials. Kuftaro, however, has reportedly stated his prosecution stems from public statements he made regarding the dangers inherent in permitting Shi'as to pay Sunnis to convert and for suggesting the Iranian ambassador, at the time, was actively promoting these paid conversions at Tehran's direction.

7. On May 7, 2010, Nader Nseir, a Syrian Jehovah's Witness, was arrested and pressured to inform on fellow Jehovah's Witnesses in the country. The general counsel for Jehovah's Witnesses reported that he was tortured and experienced other ill treatment.

8. On February 10, 2010, Sheikh Abdulrahman Koki was sentenced to one year in prison for insulting the state and the president.

9. On June 29, 2009, Sheikh Salah Kuftaro, a prominent religious figure who spoke against extremism and supported interfaith dialogue, was charged with operating an institution without permission, operating an institution without an accounting system, exploiting "sisterly" relations with another foundation, exploiting the foundation's finances for personal benefit, and attempting to bribe government and state security officials (later acquitted because of lack of evidence).

10. In June 2009, security services detained a Chinese Uighur imam and his family in Damascus for approximately three weeks before releasing them.

11. In mid-May 2009, the government closed the Center for Islamic Studies for four weeks and detained Islamic scholar and Imam Mahmud Kuftaro, brother of Salah al-Din Kuftaro, for ten days.

12. In February 2009, according to the Jehovah's Witnesses' 2009 country report on Syria, government authorities interrogated a Jehovah's Witness, asking that he sign a document forswearing participation in Jehovah's Witnesses' activities.

SCORE Of 4

13. In February 2009, according to Jehovah's Witnesses' reporting, a Syrian Witness living in Lebanon returned to his home city of Latakia.

14. In January 2009, according to Jehovah's Witnesses' reporting, government authorities beat a Jehovah's Witnesses elder and demanded he sign a pledge that he would cease attending religious meetings, reading Jehovah's Witnesses' publications, and "sharing his faith with others."

15. On September 27, 2008, a suicide car bomb carrying more than 200 kg of explosives detonated in a residential neighborhood, Sayeda Zeinab, on the outskirts of Damascus, Syria, killing seventeen people and wounding fourteen others.

16. In July 2008, Muslims, whom the government alleged to be terrorists and held at Sednaya prison, began a series of riots that continued into late December. Although dependable statistics were not available, many human rights activists and diplomats believe that more than fifty prisoners thought to have ties to al-Qa'ida were killed in the fighting. Witnesses in the area of the prison reported hearing the sound of gunfire coming from the prison on multiple occasions.

17. On February 12, 2008, Imad Mughniyah, the top leader of Hezbollah, was killed by a bomb as he traveled by car through Damascus, Syria.

18. In 2007, the Supreme State Security Court sentenced at least eighty alleged Islamists to lengthy prison sentences.

19. At the end of the reporting period there were unconfirmed reports that on May 14, 2007, journalist Adel Mahfoudh was sentenced to six months in prison. On February 7, 2006, Syrian authorities arrested him after he published an article encouraging dialogue between Muslims and the cartoon artists who created caricatures of the Prophet Muhammad for the Danish newspaper *Jyllands-Posten*. He was released on bail om March 12, 2006, re-arrested on May 17, 2006, and re-released on bail in September 2006.

20. In 2006, human rights organizations documented the arrest of at least seventy persons for alleged ties to Islamist groups.

21. On September 12, 2006, Islamic militants attacked the U.S. embassy in Damascus, Syria with hand grenades, rifles, and a vehicle rigged with explosives; one guard died while the four attackers died.

Iraq

1. In 2011, many serious sectarian abuses were attributed to actors from the Shi'a-dominated Ministries of Interior and Defense and armed Shi'a groups with ties to the Iraqi government or elements within it. Data for 2011 terrorist attacks has yet to be released by the Global Terrorism Database.

(*continued*)

SCORE Of 4

2. In 2010, there were approximately 1,276 terrorist attacks in Iraq.
3. In 2009, there were approximately 1,134 terrorist attacks in Iraq.
4. In 2008, there were approximately 1,003 terrorist attacks in Iraq.
5. On February 17, 2008, KRG authorities allegedly arrested and held incommunicado for four days an Assyrian blogger, Johnny Khoshaba Al-Rikany, based on articles he had posted attacking corruption in the church.
6. In 2007, there were approximately 1,033 terrorist attacks in Iraq.
7. On April 10, 2007, during a raid on a neighborhood mosque, the Iraqi army killed two men in front of other worshippers during morning prayers.
8. In 2006, there were approximately 737 terrorist attacks in Iraq.

Tunisia

1. In October 2011, police were accused of failing to intervene effectively when religious militants attacked the headquarters of Nesma TV after it aired the animated film *Persepolis*, which they considered blasphemous.
2. Throughout 2010 reports emerged that police harassed or detained men with long beards or who wore traditional Islamic-style clothing. According to human rights lawyers, the government regularly questioned and detained Muslims observed praying frequently in mosques. Total number unknown.
3. In 2007 and 2008, according to allegations by human rights groups and defense lawyers, the government arrested men because of their Islamic appearance, their frequent attendance at mosques, or other actions related to their practice of Islam. Total number unknown.
4. On January 3, 2007, more than twenty-five Islamic extremists engaged in a firefight with authorities in Soliman, Tunisia. Twelve assailants were killed and another fifteen were arrested.
5. According to international NGOs and domestic human rights organizations, scores of persons were arrested by police beginning in late December 2006 following exchanges of gunfire between security forces and members of a Salafist armed group. Total number unknown.
6. In 2006, credible sources estimated that approximately 200 persons were serving prison sentences because of their suspected membership in the illegal Islamist political party An-Nahdha or for their alleged Islamist sympathies; however, there were no reports of cases in which the government arrested or detained persons based solely on their religious beliefs.

Oman

1.

SCORE OF 3

Turkey

1. On November 11–12, 2011, a lone hijacker attacked a ferry in the Sea of Marmara west of Istanbul. The ferry departed the port town of Izmit. The hijacker was believed to be a PKK member.
2. On October 16, 2011, a bomb exploded in the city of Adana during a PKK rally; four people were wounded in the blast.
3. On October 5, 2011, a suicide bomber exploded outside a police station in the city of Kemer. The blast caused damage to the building and cars in the area. The bomb blast killed one and wounded two others.
4. On September 30, 2011, one person was killed and two others wounded after a bomb exploded outside a Turkish military police headquarters near Antalya.
5. On September 25, 2011, PKK rebels killed six police officers after rockets were launched at their police station in the city of Siirt. Eight others were wounded in the attack.
6. On September 21, 2011, three people were killed and fifteen wounded after a bomb exploded in the city of Ankara. The PKK is being blamed for the bombing.
7. On September 20, 2011, a car bomb exploded in the city of Ankara, killing three and injuring more than thirty other people. At least five of the wounded were in critical condition.
8. On September 17, 2011, a bomb exploded next to a police bus in the city of Diyarbakır. Five people were injured in the blast.
9. On August 17, 2011, two roadside bombs exploded in Çukurca, killing eight Turkish soldiers. The PKK was blamed for the attack.
10. On May 27, 2011, a bike bomb exploded at a Turkish military housing area in the city of Diyarbakır. No one was killed, but two were wounded in the blast.
11. On January 5, 2011, a Turkish-speaking man attempted to hijack a Turkish Airlines flight and threatened to blow up the plane. Istanbul police arrested the man.
12. In 2010, there were approximately twenty terrorist attacks in Turkey.
13. According to Jehovah's Witnesses officials, at the end of 2010, twenty-one members faced prosecution and fines for their refusal in accordance with their beliefs to serve in the military.
14. In late 2010, two converts to Christianity from Islam were convicted of secretly compiling data on private citizens for a Bible correspondence course and sentenced to nine months in prison.
15. In June 2010, a foreign citizen performing missionary work and his family were deported and charged by the Ministry of Interior with threatening public order and national security.

(continued)

SCORE Of 3

16. In 2009, there were approximately thirteen terrorist attacks in Turkey.
17. In 2008, there were approximately thirty-two terrorist attacks in Turkey
18. On December 12, 2008, police in Rize detained several South Africans and charged them with missionary activities.
19. In 2007, there were approximately twenty-nine terrorist attacks in Turkey.
20. In 2006, there were approximately thirty-nine terrorist attacks in Turkey.
21. In October 2006, two Muslim converts to Christianity were charged with "insulting Turkishness," in violation of article 301 of the penal code, inciting hatred against Islam, and secretly compiling data on private citizens for a Bible correspondence course.

Uzbekistan

1. From 2006 to 2011, the government committed serious abuses of religious freedom in its campaign against extremists or those participating in underground Islamic activity. In many cases, authorities severely mistreated persons arrested on suspicion of extremism, using torture, beatings, and harsh prison conditions. The government imprisoned a significant number of individuals for membership in prohibited Muslim groups. Total number unknown. Includes the December 27, 2010, conviction of twelve persons of membership in a "jihadist extremist group" sentencing them to between three and thirteen years in prison; on January 18, 2010, human rights activist Gaybullo Jalilov and three others were sentenced to nine years in prison for membership in an extremist religious group that allegedly planned terrorist attacks against a regional airport; and in 2009, at least thirty-one persons, including twelve women, were imprisoned for HT membership.
2. In 2010, twenty-two members of religious minorities received jail terms of three to fifteen days, including nineteen Protestants and three Jehovah's Witnesses.
3. In June 2011, twenty-eight Uzbekistani men were extradited from Kazakhstan (see Kazakhstan entry) on charges of religious extremism and alleged membership in the Jihadchilar (Jihadists) Islamist organization.
4. In 2010, police arrested at least 103 more persons for Nur membership.
5. In 2010, Forum 18 reported seven separate cases against Protestants for possessing or distributing religious materials.
6. On November 29, 2010, customs officials detained three persons suspected of attempting to bring in illegal religious literature.
7. On August 4, 2010, police raided a meeting of members of an unregistered church in Tashkent.

SCORE Of 3

8. On July 29, 2010, thirteen members of an unregistered Baptist group were found guilty of charges related to attending an unauthorized public gathering.

9. On July 15, 2010, Nigmat Zufarov was found dead in prison, officially due to suicide. Zufarov had conducted a six-day hunger strike in May 2009 demanding that he be allowed to pray in prison and reportedly was mistreated by guards following the incident.

10. On June 23, 2010, police raided a house in Chirchik where members of the unregistered Full Gospel Church were present.

11. On June 17, 2010, Sunnatillo Zaripov died in prison, where he had been serving a fifteen-year term. Relatives reported to the press that he died as a result of torture, but the report could not be confirmed.

12. On June 3, 2010, a Ferghana City court sentenced seventeen men to five to eight years in prison for membership in Tabligh Jamoat, marking the first time such a large group was convicted for Tabligh Jamoat membership.

13. In June 2010, police raided a youth meeting held by an unregistered Pentecostal congregation in Chirchik.

14. On May 16, 2010, police raided the Tashkent City Church of Christ during its Sunday service.

15. On May 10, 2010, the Tashkent Regional Criminal Court sentenced eight men to unknown sentences for membership in banned religious organizations.

16. In April 2010, police raided two programs organized by Tashkent-based Protestant churches.

17. In April 2010, police raided a private home in Tashkent where ten Pentecostal women were celebrating a birthday.

18. In April 2010 an Andijon court sentenced Muhammadjon Yusupov to seven years in prison for keeping ten illegal religious books in his home.

19. On April 27, 2010, the Tashkent Regional Criminal Court sentenced twenty-five men to between three and six years for membership in banned religious organizations.

20. On April 23, 2010, a Termez court sentenced Protestants Azamat Rajapov and Abdusattor Kurbonov to fifteen days in jail for unauthorized religious activity.

21. On April 15, 2010, the Jizzakh regional criminal court sentenced twenty-five men to between two and ten years in prison (with one suspended sentence) for membership in banned religious organizations.

22. On April 12, 2010, a Kashkadarya Regional court sentenced Mehrinisso Hamdamova to seven years in a labor camp for attempting to overturn the constitutional order and distribution of materials threatening public order.

(continued)

SCORE Of 3

23. In March 2010, police raided eleven houses in Kagan belonging to Jehovah's Witnesses during the commemoration of the death of Jesus Christ.
24. On March 12, 2010, the Syrdarya Regional Criminal Court sentenced ten persons for membership in banned organizations and other crimes related to the Tashkent killings.
25. On February 23, 2010, a court convicted thirteen members of an unregistered Baptist church located in Almalyk of the unauthorized teaching of religion and fined them each 3.2 million soums ($1,939) following a police raid on a private home.
26. In January 2010, police raided a Christmas celebration of the registered Holiness Full Gospel Protestant Church held in a private home in Tashkent.
27. In January 2010, eight members of the unregistered Greater Grace Protestant Church in Samarkand were found guilty of teaching religion illegally.
28. In 2009, twenty-five members of religious minorities received jail terms of three to fifteen days.
29. NGOs reported that in 2009, forty-seven individuals were imprisoned for Nur membership, and at least twenty-six others were arrested.
30. In October 2009, an Evangelical Baptist Union's chairman, a camp director, and the camp's accountant were convicted of criminal charges related to the operation of a summer camp for children.
31. In August 2009, police raided the worship service at the registered Donam Protestant Church in Tashkent.
32. On June 28, 2009, Golib Mullajonov died in prison after reportedly being beaten by other inmates. Mullajonov had been serving a prison sentence for membership in HT.
33. In July 2009, police raided the officially registered Tashkent Baha'i Center and took six adults and fifteen youth into custody for questioning.
34. In the summer of 2009, approximately 200 persons in connection with three violent incidents were alleged by the government to have religious links and arrested.
35. On May 26, 2009, in Andijon, a suicide bomber detonated an improvised explosive device on Fitrat Street, killing one police officer and wounding three civilians.
36. On May 26, 2009, in Khonobod, assailants fired rocket-propelled grenades and small arms at a police station, killing one police officer and wounding three others
37. In an April 2009 report, the Moscow-based Memorial human rights group cited forty-three individuals in 2006, eighteen in 2007, and ten in 2008 that were prosecuted by officials on

SCORE Of 3

allegedly politically motivated charges. Nearly 95 percent of them were charged with religious extremism, many for alleged HT membership. It was impossible to verify the number of prisoners in detention for alleged HT membership; estimates from previous reporting periods were as high as forty-five hundred between 2004 and 2008.

38. On April 8, 2009, the Sergeli District Criminal Court sanctioned the police raid on the home of Pavel Nenno, a deacon of an officially registered Baptist church, in Tashkent and convicted him of violating the Code of Administrative Offences by illegally teaching religion at his home to children and gave him a fifteen-day prison sentence.

39. On April 3, 2009, a court in the town of Almalyk in Tashkent province found thirteen Baptists guilty of proselytism and fined them each fifty times the monthly minimum wage.

40. On March 3, 2009, the Kurgantepe District Criminal Court in Andijon Province convicted three members of an unregistered Protestant church – Mahmudjon Turdiev, Mahmudjon Boynazarov, and Ravshanjon Bahramov – of illegally teaching religion and sentenced them to fifteen-day jail terms.

41. In 2008, at least sixteen individuals were imprisoned for Nur membership, and at least twenty-six other individuals were arrested.

42. In 2008, at least thirty-seven persons were convicted of membership in the HT and other banned groups.

43. On December 22, 2008, law enforcement officials in Bukhara raided the home of Ikrom Merajov, a university lecturer, and confiscated religious literature.

44. In November 2008, alleged Akromiya member Khoshimjon Kadirov was arrested in Andijon and transferred to Ministry of Interior custody in Tashkent, where he was reportedly beaten to death.

45. On October 10, 2008, the Mirabad District Criminal Court in Tashkent convicted seven members of an unregistered Pentecostal church of holding an illegal religious meeting on October 4 and sentenced them to fifteen-day prison terms.

46. On July 23, 2008, authorities sentenced two Jehovah's Witnesses from Margilan, Abdubanob Ahmedov and Sergei Ivanov, to four years and three and one-half years' imprisonment respectively for allegedly teaching religion illegally.

47. On July 8, 2008, a Navoi court fined Jehovah's Witnesses Guldara Artykova and Tursuna Yuldasheva for allegedly refusing to testify in court. On May 30, police in Navoi had come to Artykova's home and detained her and Yuldasheva

(continued)

after seizing religious literature. The women were brought to a police station, where officers beat Yuldasheva, reportedly causing numerous bruises and a concussion.

48. In June 2008, four members of the unregistered Friendship Baptist Church were sentenced to ten days' administrative detention and fines of approximately $32 each for organizing illegal religious meetings, violating the Religion Law, and teaching religion illegally.

49. On June 14, 2008, Forum 18 reported that Aitmurat Khayburahmanov, a Protestant from Nukus, was beaten by authorities after his arrest for teaching religion illegally and participating in a "religious extremist" organization.

50. In May 2008, members of Navoi's unregistered Baptist Church were sentenced for holding illegal meetings.

51. In May 2008, members of Mubarak's unregistered Baptist church were sentenced following a March 2008 raid on the church.

52. In April 2008, four Seventh Day Adventists from Guliston were sentenced for holding unregistered meetings in their homes.

53. In April 2008, Olim Turayev was sentenced in Samarkand to four years' imprisonment on criminal charges of illegally teaching religion and organizing an illegal religious organization.

54. In March 2008, Mamur Tursunkulov and Nabi Kipchakov were sentenced to five days' imprisonment and Arslan Suvankulov to three days' imprisonment for illegal religious activity in Jizzakh.

55. In 2007, at least seventy-seven persons, and possibly many more, were convicted of membership in HT.

56. In 2007, Pastor Dmitry Shestakov, leader of a registered Full Gospel Pentecostal congregation, was sentenced to four years at a Navoi labor camp after being convicted of "organizing an illegal religious group," "inciting religious hatred," and "distributing extremist religious literature."

57. On November 29, 2007, the Pap District Criminal Court in Namangan Province sentenced Nikolai Zulfikarov, the leader of a small unregistered Baptist church in Khalkabad, to two years of corrective labor for illegally teaching religion.

58. In June 2007, Dilafruz Arziyeva, a member of the Jehovah's Witnesses Samarkand congregation, was convicted of illegally teaching religion.

59. On June 12, 2007, Hudoer Pardaev and Igor Kim, members of God's Love Pentecostal Church from the Jizzak region, were sentenced to ten days in prison for "illegally" teaching religion by the Yangiabad District Court.

60. On April 7, 2007, police raided the service of the unregistered Baptist Church of Guliston and detained its pastor, Victor

SCORE Of 3

Klimov, who was charged under several articles of the Administrative Code.

61. On February 8, 2007, Samarkand police arrested a Kazakh citizen pastor affiliated with the Greater Grace Church and held him in detention for eleven days.

62. On January 15, 2007, police in Nukus reportedly raided a Presbyterian church service held in a private home and arrested eighteen worshippers.

63. On August 24, 2006, police raided a house in the village of Uch-kiliz (near Termez) and detained seventeen members of the Union of Independent Churches, many of whom were subsequently beaten.

64. On May 29, 2006, authorities deported a member of Jehovah's Witnesses to Kazakhstan.

65. On April 30, 2006, 160 congregants from the formerly sanctioned Emmanuel Full Gospel Church in Nukus were celebrating Easter in a local hotel when approximately fifty policemen stormed the premises, arresting at least eight individuals, including the pastor.

66. On April 27, 2006, authorities arrested and sentenced a member of Jehovah's Witnesses to ten days in prison for illegal religious activity.

67. On April 24, 2006, numerous press reports indicated that Urgench City criminal investigators raided the home of the pastor of the Union of Independent Churches as twelve of his congregants met for lunch.

68. On April 21, 2006, in the Shaikhantahur District of Tashkent, government authorities arrested three members of the Jesus Christ Charismatic Church who were engaged in humanitarian activities at a children's hospital.

69. On April 20, 2006, authorities arrested and charged six women with possession and dissemination of HT materials.

70. On April 12, 2006, authorities coordinated countrywide raids of homes of Jehovah's Witnesses during their annual holy day, which commemorates the death of Jesus, and detained more than 500 people.

71. On April 11, 2006, government authorities raided a local Protestant's apartment while she was meeting with two other church members. Authorities took all three members along with one small child to Tashkent's Yunusobod District police headquarters, where officers attempted to force them to sign confessions of illegal religious activity.

Sources: Amnesty International; BBC News; U.S. State Department annual reports on International Religious Freedom; U.S. State Department Country Reports on Human Rights Practices; National Consortium for the Study of Terrorism and Responses to Terrorism Global Terrorism Database; Human Rights Watch World Reports.

SCORE OF 5	State and Nonstate Violence Descriptions
Sri Lanka	

1. From 1983 to 2009, the government battled the Liberation Tigers of Tamil Eelam (LTTE), a terrorist organization fighting for a separate state for the country's Tamil, and mainly Hindu, minority. Adherence to a specific set of religious beliefs did not play a significant role in the conflict, which was rooted in linguistic, ethnic, and political differences. The conflict affected Buddhists, Hindus, Muslims, and Christians. Estimates vary widely, but many believe approximately one hundred thousand persons died during the nearly thirty-year war. The government, paramilitaries, and Tamil Tigers were accused of involving religious facilities in the conflict or putting them at risk through shelling in conflict areas.

2. On October 10, 2010, a group of approximately thirty-five persons, led by six Buddhist monks, entered the premises of the Church of the Four Square Gospel in Kalutara. The intruders disrupted a worship service, threatened and assaulted the pastor, and destroyed furniture and musical instruments.

3. On June 25, 2010, approximately 100 police officers, reportedly on instructions from the Urban Development Authority, arrived at the Calvary Church in Rajagiriya. They assaulted the pastor and demolished the church, saying it was an unauthorized structure.

4. In April 2010, Sarah Malanie Perera, a Sri Lankan resident who had lived in Bahrain for nineteen years, was arrested under the Prevention of Terrorism Act because of a book she had written entitled *From Darkness to Light*. The book described her conversion to Islam and was deemed offensive to Buddhism by the Ministry of Defense.

5. On March 6, 2010, a mob of more than 100 persons, led by several Buddhist monks and individuals with reportedly close links to a local politician, disrupted the dedication of the pastor's residence of the Church of the Four Square Gospel at Kalutara in the Kalutara District.

6. On January 27, 2010, in the Kandy district of Sri Lanka's Central province, two civilians, including a Buddhist monk, were killed and four others were wounded when unidentified militants threw a grenade at a political gathering in the Thambiligala area of Gampola.

7. On January 26, 2010, in the Valvatithurai area of Jaffna district in Sri Lanka's Northern Province, unidentified militants detonated two bombs near the residence of Subramaniam Sharma, an organizer for President Rajapakse's Sri Lanka Freedom Party.

SCORE OF 5	State and Nonstate Violence Descriptions

8. On January 22, 2010, unidentified militants attacked the home of a businessman and opposition activist, Tiran Alles, with a petrol bomb.

9. In 2009, there were approximately thirty-eight terrorist attacks in Sri Lanka.

10. In May 2009, security forces conducted a raid on the offices of the National Christian Evangelical Alliance of Sri Lanka, in Colombo.

11. In 2008, there were approximately ninety-four terrorist attacks in Sri Lanka.

12. In September 2008, a group of approximately sixty persons led by a Buddhist monk and a local politician arrived at the Prayer Tower Church at Maliankulam in the Puttalam District. They set fire to the partially constructed hall the congregation used as a Sunday school.

13. In February 2008, Pastor Huthin Manohar from Mannar was arrested for transporting LTTE equipment and explosives in his van.

14. In 2007, there were approximately 138 terrorist attacks in Sri Lanka.

15. In September 2007, the chief monk of the Boddhirukkaramaya Temple led a protest against expansion work being performed on a Catholic church just north of Colombo. Protesters demanded that construction stop immediately, warning lives would be otherwise lost. A judge told Father Susith Silva to suspend the church expansion. In October 2007 police interrupted mass at the same church and sent worshippers home.

16. In April 2007, an exchange of fire between the Sri Lanka navy and a group of youths during a cordon and search operation killed Hindu priest Ratnasabapathy Aiyar Somaskantha in Velanai, Jaffna.

17. In January 2007, government security forces shot and killed Reverend Nallathamby Gnaseelan of the Tamil Mission Church of Jaffna.

18. In 2006, there were approximately 219 terrorist attacks in Sri Lanka.

19. In August 2006, government troops were accused of firing into Philip Nerean Church in Allapiddy, Kayts Island (Northern Province), Father Jim Brown's church. Approximately thirty civilians died.

20. On June 17, 2006, in Pesalai, government troops were accused of storming a church, Our Lady of Victory, and opening fire where hundreds of civilians, including Christians and Hindu Tamils, were seeking shelter from an exchange of fire between the government and the LTTE.

SCORE Of 4

Israel	1. As of October 31, 2011, the UN reported 377 attacks by settlers that damaged Palestinian property, including almost 10,000 olive trees, and injured 167 Palestinians.

2. On August 18, 2011, a series of cross-border attacks between Israel and Egypt killed twenty-three and wounded forty.
3. On March 23, 2011, a bomb exploded at a bus stop in Jerusalem killing one and wounding thirty-nine people.
4. On March 6, 2011, a pipe bomb exploded in the city of Jerusalem, wounding one person.
5. On January 9, 2011, three rockets fired from Gaza hit the Ashkelon region.
6. On January 8, 2011, a rocket fired from Gaza hit a farm near the border injuring two Thai agricultural workers. Palestinian Islamic Jihad claimed responsibility.
7. On January 7, 2011, two armed men crossed the buffer zone between Gaza Strip and Israel before opening fire on soldiers.
8. In 2010, there were approximately fourteen terrorist attacks in Israel.
9. In an April 4, 2010 *Yediot Ahronot* newspaper article, 30 percent of the more than one hundred ten thousand tourists detained in 2009 at the airport for rigorous security interrogations were on an MOI watch list, while the others were on security watch lists. There are no clearly publicized regulations as to how the MOI places a person on the watch list or on what grounds, but the questioning of such individuals often relates to their religious beliefs.
10. In March 2010, an article in *Yediot Ahronot* reported that police arrested two Haredi men at the Western Wall on suspicion that they threw chairs at a group of praying women from the Women of the Wall organization, a group occasionally targeted by religious groups for practicing its religion at holy sites.
11. In 2009, there were approximately thirty-five terrorist attacks in Israel.
12. On November 18, 2009, Israeli police temporarily detained a woman because she donned a Jewish *talith* (prayer shawl) during a ceremony in the traditional women's prayer area, rather than in the designated area.
13. In 2008, there were approximately 131 terrorist attacks in Israel.
14. In 2008, during Jewish holidays, following terrorist attacks, and in response to other potential threats, the government imposed closures to restrict travel in the country and the Occupied Territories for security purposes. These closures impeded access to holy sites in the country for Arab Muslims and Christians as well as Israeli-Arabs and Palestinians who

SCORE Of 4

possessed Jerusalem identification cards. The construction of the separation barrier also impeded access to holy sites throughout the country and the Occupied Territories during the reporting period.

15. On April 28, 2008, immigration police arrested German student Barbara Ludwig and prepared to deport her for failing to maintain a valid student visa to continue her graduate studies at Hebrew University. According to Ludwig and her attorneys at the Jerusalem Institute of Justice (JIJ), she made repeated attempts to renew her student visa but was denied because the Interior Ministry determined that she was a Messianic Jew.

16. In 2007, there were approximately fifty-three terrorist attacks in Israel.

17. In 2006, there were approximately seventy-eight terrorist attacks in Israel.

Laos

1. On April 15, 2011, troops from the Lao People's Army attacked and killed several Christians in Xiengkhouang Province.

2. In October 2010, local officials in Katin Village, Ta-Oy District, Saravan Province, reportedly threatened seven families with expulsion for converting to Christianity. Authorities had previously forced out a group of families from Katin Village in January 2010.

3. In September 2010, a group of Christians traveled to Vientiane Province to plant trees for recently relocated villagers. Some of the group also distributed religious tracts. Local authorities detained five members of the group on charges of acting without permission, causing social division, and distributing material calling for a new kingdom.

4. In August 2010, three Christian families reportedly renounced their faith in response to threats of expulsion from the village.

5. In May 2010, local authorities in Vientiane Province reportedly threatened two Christian families to renounce their faith or face ostracism from the village. The families did not recant.

6. In January 2010, local officials reportedly forced Christians out of Katin Village, Ta-Oy District, Saravan Province, when they would not renounce their faith. In March, the provincial governor interceded and instructed local officials that Decree 92 gave everyone the right to believe.

7. In early 2009, eight heads of families from a group of ten Hmong and Khmu Christian families were reportedly returned to Vietnam.

(*continued*)

SCORE Of 4

8. In September 2009, a Christian man traveling with two children from Luang Namtha to Luang Prabang, reportedly for a Christian retreat, was arrested and charged with trafficking because, according to government authorities, he did not have the parents' permission to travel with the children.

9. In September 2009, in Jinsangmai village, Luang Namtha Province, all Christian believers reportedly recanted their faith, including a man previously jailed for refusing to do so.

10. In September 2009, inhabitants of Bansai village, Savannakhet Province, reportedly pressured a Christian man to renounce his faith or leave the village. Other Christians in the same area reported difficulty in holding worship services, because there was no authorized building for worship, and the police harassed them for worshipping in houses.

11. In August 2009, the pastor was detained again along with two other church members; they were released in October. Reportedly, fifty-five Christians were expelled from the village during this period.

12. In July 2009, local officials reportedly confiscated livestock from the Christians in Katin Village as a punitive measure, after the officials attempted to ban Christianity in the village.

13. In April 2009, the final two pastors from a group of eight Khmu pastors jailed in the Oudomsai provincial prison were reportedly released.

14. In March 2009, district officials banned Christians gathering to worship at a home in Nonsomboon village in Bolikhamsai Province, where an unapproved church had been destroyed.

15. In August 2008, officials of Burikan District in Bolikhamsai Province reportedly banned approximately 150 members from gathering at a home in the village for worship services, declaring that services could be held only in a church building. Earlier in the reporting period, officials reportedly destroyed the group's church in Toongpankham village.

16. In July 2008, police authorities of Ad-Sapangthong District of Savannakhet Province reportedly interfered with worship by Christians in Boukham village and detained a pastor and four church members for two days; during this period they were reportedly held in foot stocks.

17. In July 2008, in Katan village, in Ta-Oy District, Salavan Province, a local Christian man died after local authorities reportedly forced him to drink alcohol; his relatives were reportedly fined after conducting a Christian burial service. A few days later local authorities reportedly detained eighty Christians from seventeen families and forced them, apparently including by withholding food, to publicly renounce their faith.

SCORE Of 4

18. In July 2008, more than 500 Christians in villages in several villages in Luang Prabang Province, including Huay An in Jomphet District, reportedly came under pressure to deny their faith by judicial and police officials.

19. In July 2008, two Christian leaders were arrested in Khongnoy village in Vieng Phukha District and another person was arrested in Sing District, all in Luang Namtha Province.

20. In March 2008, Khmu pastors were stopped, searched, and arrested while attempting to cross the border illegally from Bokeo Province into Thailand.

21. In February 2008, authorities reportedly arrested fifty-eight persons from fifteen families during raids on Sai Jareun and Fai villages in Bokeo Province. Those arrested were described as Hmong Christians who had fled persecution in Vietnam possibly as early as 2002 and were apparently part of the Sai Jareun Village Christian congregation.

22. In August 2007, three local Protestant leaders from Namoon Village of Long District were reportedly falsely accused of various offenses including receiving money from foreign Christian organizations to pursue underground Christian ministries. They were incarcerated for more than two months before being released in October 2007.

23. In July 2007, attacks by the authorities led to the deaths of thirteen Hmong Christians and arrests of others from Bokeo's Sai Jareun Village, reportedly because of a perception of some possible connection to the dwindling but still ongoing insurgency.

24. In May 2007, seven of the ten Christian families in Nakun Village were reportedly forced to resettle in another village after refusing to renounce their Protestant beliefs.

25. In March 2007, Protestants in Nakun Village of Bolikhamsai Province were reportedly harassed, subjected to "reeducation," and asked to sign statements indicating that they had engaged in proselytizing.

26. In March 2007, more than 100 Protestants in Nam Deua Village of Bolikhamsai Province's Pakading District were reportedly told by village and district officials that they could not believe in Christianity because it was an "American religion."

27. In February 2007, Bolikhamsai Province officials indicated that two Buddhist monks had been arrested for being ordained without government approval and for celebrating inappropriately following the ordination ceremony.

28. After a February 2007 insurgent attack on an army camp near Vang Vieng in northern Vientiane Province, which reportedly killed two Lao Army soldiers, Vang Vieng officials were said to

(continued)

SCORE Of 4

have allowed ten local Hmong and Khmu Christian families
to move from Vientiane Province to neighboring Bokeo,
Luang Namtha, and Oudomsay provinces, although the Vang
Vieng officials did not provide the legal documents required
for such a move. After a short period, the Vang Vieng officials
reportedly required the families to return to Vang Vieng, where
the male heads of family – seven Hmong and three Khmu –
reportedly were detained at Vientiane Province's Thong Harb
Prison. In August 2007 three men said to be pastors went to
the prison to ask why the men were being held. The pastors
themselves were then imprisoned but released in October after
each paid a fine of $100 (960,000 kip). Of the original ten
detainees, one reportedly died in late 2007 and another in May
2008. The other eight remained in Thong Harb Prison.

29. In January 2007, Khamsone Baccam, an ethnic Thai Dam man
    described as a Protestant leader, was arrested in Oudomsai
    Province.

30. In 2006, Nyoht was sentenced to twelve years in prison and
    died in prison. Thongchanh, whose fifteen-year sentence was
    reduced to ten years at the end of 2006, remained in prison in
    Oudomsai at the end of the reporting period.

31. In December 2006, five ethnic Yao Protestants were arrested
    in Luang Namtha Province for constructing a church building
    without appropriate authorization.

32. In November 2006, two ethnic Khmu U.S. Legal Permanent
    Residents who were visiting Khon Khen Village in Vientiane
    Province's Hinheup District were detained after participating
    in and videotaping a Protestant celebration in the village.

33. In August 2006, two LEC members in Saveth Village,
    Savannakhet Province, were arrested, reportedly for being
    outspoken about their faith.

34. From June through July 2006, a Protestant man in Nam
    Heng Village of Oudomsai Province was reportedly jailed for
    possessing ammunition at his residence.

35. In April 2006, district officials in Salavan Province placed
    Adern, an LEC member who refused the village chief's order
    to renounce his faith, under house arrest.

Sources: Amnesty International; BBC News; U.S. State Department annual reports on
International Religious Freedom; U.S. State Department Country Reports on Human Rights
Practices; National Consortium for the Study of Terrorism and Responses to Terrorism Global
Terrorism Database; Human Rights Watch World Reports

Appendix II

Egyptian Constitution, Ratified on December 26, 2012. Suspended on July 3, 2013

Source: http://www.egyptindependent.com/news/egypt-s-draft-constitution-translated

CONSTITUTION PREAMBLE

We, the people of Egypt,
In the name of the merciful God and with his aid,
declare this to be

Our Constitution, the document of the 25th of January revolution, which was started by our youth, embraced by our people, supported by our Armed Forces;

Having rejected, in Tahrir Square and all over the country all forms of injustice, oppression, tyranny, despotism, exclusion, plunder and monopoly;

Proclaimed our full rights to "bread, freedom, social justice, and human dignity," paid for by the blood of our martyrs, the pain of our injured, the dreams of our children, the strife of our men and women;

Recovered the spirit of our great civilization and our luminous history, for on the banks of the timeless Nile we established the oldest state that has always known the meaning of citizenship and equality, gave humanity the first alphabet, opened the way to monotheism and the knowledge of the Creator, embraced God's prophets and messages, and adorned the pages of history with parades of creativity;

And in continuation of our virtuous revolution which has unified all Egyptians on the path of building a modern democratic state, we declare our adherence to the following principles:

One –
The people are the source of all authorities. Authorities are instituted by and derive their legitimacy from the people, and are subject to the people's will.

The responsibilities and competencies of authorities are a duty to bear, not a privilege or a source of immunity.

Two –
A democratic system of government, establishing the grounds for peaceful transfer of power, supporting political pluralism, ensuring fair elections and the people's contribution in the decision-making process.

Three –
The individual's dignity is an extension of the nation's dignity. Further, there is no dignity for a country in which women are not honored; women are the sisters of men and partners in all national gains and responsibilities.

Four –
Freedom is a right: freedom of thought, expression and creativity; freedom in housing, property and travel; its principles laid down by the Creator in the motion of the universe and human nature.

Five –
Equality and equal opportunities are established for all citizens, men and women, without discrimination or nepotism or preferential treatment, in both rights and duties.

Six –
The rule of law is the basis of the individual's freedom, the legitimacy of authority, and the state's respect of the law. No power shall override that of righteousness, and the judiciary shall be independent, bearer of the honorable mission of defending the Constitution, upholding justice, and preserving rights and freedoms.

Seven –
Upholding national unity is an obligation, and the cornerstone of building a modern Egypt and the path to progress and development. To that end, the values of tolerance and moderation shall be spread, and the rights and freedoms of all citizens shall be protected without discrimination.

Eight –
Defending the nation is a duty and an honor. Our Armed Forces form a professional and neutral national institution that does not interfere in political affairs. It is the protective shield of the country.

Nine –
Security is a great blessing; it falls on the shoulders of a police force which works in the service of the people, for their protection and to enforce the measures of justice. For there can be no justice without protection, and no protection without security institutions that respect the rule of law and human dignity.

Ten –
Unity is the hope of the Arab nation; it is history's call, the future's bid, and destiny's demand. Such unity is to be reinforced through the integration and fraternity with countries of the Nile Valley and of the Muslim world, both a natural extension borne out of the distinctiveness of Egypt's position on the global map.

Eleven –
Egypt's pioneering intellectual and cultural leadership is an embodiment of its soft power, and a model of the free generosity of original creators and thinkers, universities, science centers, linguistic and research centers, the press, the arts, literature and mass media, the national church, and Al-Azhar with its history as a mainstay of national identity, the Arabic language and Islamic Sharia, and as a beacon for moderate enlightened thought.

We, the people of Egypt,
Out of faith in God and His heavenly messages,
In recognition of the right of the country and the nation,
With awareness of our responsibilities toward the nation and humanity,
Pledge to stay committed to the principles laid out in this Constitution, which we accept and grant to ourselves, affirming our determination to uphold and defend it, and asserting that it shall be protected and respected by the State's authorities and the general public.

PART I: STATE AND SOCIETY

Chapter One: Political principles

Article 1

The Arab Republic of Egypt is an independent sovereign state, united and indivisible, its system democratic. The Egyptian people are part of the Arab and Islamic nations, proud of belonging to the Nile Valley and Africa and of its Asian reach, a positive participant in human civilization.

Article 2

Islam is the religion of the state and Arabic its official language. Principles of Islamic Sharia are the principal source of legislation.

Article 3

The canon principles of Egyptian Christians and Jews are the main source of legislation for their personal status laws, religious affairs, and the selection of their spiritual leaders.

Article 4

Al-Azhar is an encompassing independent Islamic institution, with exclusive autonomy over its own affairs, responsible for preaching Islam, theology and the Arabic language in Egypt and the world. Al-Azhar Senior Scholars are to be consulted in matters pertaining to Islamic law.

The post of Al-Azhar Grand Sheikh is independent and cannot be dismissed. The method of appointing the Grand Sheikh from among members of the Senior Scholars is to be determined by law.

The State shall ensure sufficient funds for Al-Azhar to achieve its objectives.

All of the above is subject to law regulations.

Article 5

Sovereignty is for the people alone and they are the source of authority. The people shall exercise and protect this sovereignty, and safeguard national unity in the manner specified in the Constitution.

Article 6

The political system is based on the principles of democracy and shura (counsel), citizenship (under which all citizens are equal in rights and duties), multi-party pluralism, peaceful transfer of power, separation of powers and the balance between them, the rule of law, and respect for human rights and freedoms; all as elaborated in the Constitution.

No political party shall be formed that discriminates on the basis of gender, origin or religion.

Article 7

Defense of the motherland and its soil is a sacred duty, and conscription is obligatory in accordance with the law.

Chapter Two: Social and ethical principles

Article 8

The State guarantees the means to achieve justice, equality and freedom, and is committed to facilitating the channels of social charity and solidarity between the members of society, and to ensure the protection of persons and property, and to working toward providing for all citizens; all within the context of the law.

Article 9

The State shall ensure safety, security and equal opportunities for all citizens without discrimination.

Article 10

The family is the basis of the society and is founded on religion, morality and patriotism.

The State is keen to preserve the genuine character of the Egyptian family, its cohesion and stability, and to protect its moral values, all as regulated by law.

The State shall ensure maternal and child health services free of charge, and enable the reconciliation between the duties of a woman toward her family and her work.

The State shall provide special care and protection to female breadwinners, divorced women and widows.

Article 11

The State shall safeguard ethics, public morality and public order, and foster a high level of education and of religious and patriotic values, scientific thinking, Arab culture, and the historical and cultural heritage of the people; all as shall be regulated by law.

Article 12

The State shall safeguard the cultural and linguistic constituents of society, and foster the Arabization of education, science and knowledge.

Article 13

The institution of civil titles shall be prohibited.

Chapter Three: Economic principles

Article 14

National economy shall be organized in accordance with a comprehensive, constant development plan, ensuring the increase of national income, enhancement of standard of living, elimination of poverty and unemployment, increase of work opportunities, and increase of production.

The development plan shall establish social justice and solidarity, ensure equitable distribution, protect consumer rights, and safeguard the rights of workers, dividing development costs between capital and labor and sharing the revenues justly.

Wages shall be linked to production, bridging income gaps and establishing a minimum wage that would guarantee decent living standards for all citizens, and a maximum wage in civil service positions with exemptions regulated by law.

Article 15

Agriculture is an essential asset of the national economy. The State shall protect and increase farmland, work on the development of crop and plant varieties, develop and protect animal breeds and fisheries, achieve food security, provide the requirements of agricultural production, its good management and marketing, and support agricultural industries.

The law regulates the use of land, in such a way as to achieve social justice, and protect farmers and agricultural laborer from exploitation.

Article 16

The State is committed to the development of the countryside and the desert, working to raise the standard of living of the farmers and the people of the desert.

Article 17

Industry is an essential asset of the national economy. The State shall protect strategic industries, support industrial development, and import new technologies and their applications.

The State shall foster small handicraft industries.

Article 18

The natural resources of the State belong to the people, who have a right to their revenues. The State is committed to preserving such resources for future generations and putting them to good use.

State property is not to be disposed of. The franchise to use, or the commitment to a public utility, can only be granted according to legal regulations.

All money with no owner belongs to the State.

Article 19

The Nile River and water resources are a national wealth. The State is committed to maintaining and developing them, and preventing abuse. The use of such resources shall be regulated by law.

Article 20

The State shall protect its coasts, seas, waterways and lakes, maintain monuments and nature reserves, and remove any encroachments.

Article 21

The State guarantees and protects legitimate ownership of all kinds of public, cooperative and private property and endowments, as shall be regulated by law.

Article 22

Public funds are inviolable. It is a national duty of the State and society to safeguard them.

Article 23

The State shall support cooperatives in all forms and ensure their independence.

Article 24

Private property is inviolable and has a function in the service of national economy without deviation or monopoly. The right of inheritance shall be safeguarded. Private property may not be placed under sequestration except in cases specified by law, and with a court order. Ownership of property may not be removed except in cases where the public good requires and with just compensation paid in advance.

All of the above shall be regulated by law.

Article 25

The State is committed to reviving and encouraging the system of charitable endowments. The way an endowment is established, the management of its funds, their investment and the distribution of proceeds to the beneficiaries, shall all be regulated by law, according to the terms of the trustee.

Article 26

Social justice is the foundation of taxation and other public finance duties.

Public taxes shall not be established, modified or repealed except by law. There shall be no exemptions except in the cases prescribed by law. No one shall be required to pay additional taxes or fees except within the limits of the law.

Article 27

Workers shall have a share of the management and profits of enterprises. They shall be committed in turn to the development of production, to protecting its means and to the implementation of plans in their production units, in accordance with the law.

Workers shall be represented on the boards of directors of public sector units within the limit of 50 percent of the number of members of these boards. The law shall guarantee for small farmers and small craftsmen 80 percent of membership on the boards of directors of agricultural and industrial cooperatives.

Article 28

Saving is encouraged and protected by the State. The State shall also safeguard insurance and pension funds, in accordance with legal regulations.

Article 29

Nationalization shall not be allowed except for in consideration of public interest, in accordance with the law and against fair compensation.

Article 30

Public sequestration of property shall be prohibited.

Private sequestration shall not be allowed except under a court judgment.

PART II: RIGHTS AND FREEDOMS

Chapter One: Personal rights

Article 31

Dignity is the right of every human being, safeguarded by the State.

Insulting or showing contempt toward any human being shall be prohibited.

Article 32

Egyptian nationality is a right, regulated by law.

Article 33

All citizens are equal before the law. They have equal public rights and duties without discrimination.

Article 34

Individual freedom is a natural right, safeguarded and inviolable.

Article 35

Except in cases of flagrante delicto, no person may be arrested, inspected, detained or prevented from free movement except under a court order necessitated by investigations.

Any person arrested or detained must be informed of the reasons in writing within 12 hours, be presented to the investigating authority within 24 hours from the time of arrest, be interrogated only in the presence of a lawyer, and be provided with a lawyer when needed.

The person arrested or detained, and others, have the right of appeal to the courts against the measure of arrest. If a decision is not provided within a week, release becomes imperative.

The law regulates the rules for temporary detention, its duration and its causes, and cases of entitlement to compensation, whether for temporary detention or for a sentence carried out that a court final ruling has revoked.

Article 36

Any person arrested, detained or whose freedom is restricted in any way, shall be treated in a manner preserving human dignity. No physical or moral harm shall be inflicted upon that person.

Only places that are humanely and hygienically fit, and subject to judicial supervision, may be used for detention.

The violation of any of the above is an offense punishable by law.

Any statement proved to have been made by a person under any of the aforementioned forms of duress or coercion or under the threat thereof, shall be considered invalid and futile.

Article 37

Prison is a place of discipline and reform, subject to judicial supervision, where anything that is contrary to human dignity or a person's health is prohibited.

The State is responsible for the rehabilitation of convicts and facilitating a decent life for them after their release.

Article 38

The private life of citizens is inviolable. Postal correspondence, wires, electronic correspondence, telephone calls and other means of communication shall have their own sanctity and secrecy and may not be confiscated or monitored except by a causal judicial warrant.

Article 39

Private homes are inviolable. With the exception of cases of immediate danger and distress, they may not be entered, searched or monitored, except in cases defined by law, and by a causal judicial warrant which specifies place, timing and purpose. Those in a home shall be alerted before the home is entered or searched.

Article 40

All residents have a right to security which is safeguarded by the State, and are protected by law against criminal threats.

Article 41

The sanctity of the human body is inviolable, and the trafficking of human organs prohibited. No person may be subjected to any medical or scientific experiment without free, documented consent, and in accordance with the established foundations of medical science, in the manner regulated by law.

Article 42

Freedom of movement, residence and immigration shall be safeguarded.

No citizen may be deported from or prevented from returning to the country.

No citizen shall be prevented from leaving the country, nor placed under house arrest, except by a causal judicial warrant, and for a definite period.

Chapter Two: Moral and political rights

Article 43

Freedom of belief is an inviolable right.

The State shall guarantee the freedom to practice religious rites and to establish places of worship for the divine religions, as regulated by law.

Article 44

Insult or abuse of all religious messengers and prophets shall be prohibited.

Article 45

Freedom of thought and opinion shall be guaranteed.

Every individual has the right to express an opinion and to disseminate it verbally, in writing or illustration, or by any other means of publication and expression.

Article 46

Freedom of creativity in its various forms is the right of every citizen.

The State shall advance science, literature and the arts, care for creators and inventors, protect their creations and innovations, and work to apply them for the benefit of society.

The State shall take the necessary measures to preserve the nation's cultural heritage and promote cultural services.

Article 47

Access to information, data, documents and statistics, and the disclosure and circulation thereof, is a right guaranteed by the state, in a manner that does not violate the sanctity of private life or the rights of others, and that does not conflict with national security.

The law regulates the rules for filing and archiving public documents, the means of access to information, the means of complaint when access is refused, and the consequent accountability.

Article 48

Freedom of the press, printing, publication and mass media shall be guaranteed. The media shall be free and independent to serve the community and to express the different trends in public opinion, and contribute to shaping and directing in accordance with the basic principles of the State and society, and to maintain rights, freedoms and public duties, respecting the sanctity of the private lives of citizens and the requirements of national security. The closure or confiscation of media outlets is prohibited except with a court order.

Control over the media is prohibited, with the exception of specific censorship that may be imposed in times of war or public mobilization.

Article 49

Freedom to publish and own newspapers of all kinds is a guaranteed subject of notification for every natural or juridical Egyptian person.

The establishing of radio stations, television broadcasting and digital media is regulated by law.

Article 50

Citizens have the right to organize public meetings, processions and peaceful demonstrations, unarmed and based on the notification regulated by law.

The right to private assembly is guaranteed without the need for prior notice. Security personnel shall not attend or intercept such private meetings.

Article 51

Citizens have the right to establish associations and civil institutions, subject to notification only. Such institutions shall operate freely, and be deemed legal persons.

Authorities may not disband them or their administrative bodies without a court order, in the manner prescribed by the law.

Article 52

The freedom to form syndicates, unions and cooperatives is a right guaranteed by law. They shall be deemed legal persons, be formed on a democratic basis, operate freely, participate in the service of community service, raising the standard of productivity among their members, and safeguarding their assets.

Authorities may not disband them or their boards except under a court order.

Article 53

Professional syndicates are regulated by law and managed on a democratic basis, the accountability of their members subject to professional codes of ethics. One trade union is allowed per profession.

Authorities may not disband the boards of professional syndicates except with a court order, and may not place them under sequestration.

Article 54

Every individual has the right to address public authorities in writing and under his own signature.

Addressing public authorities should not be in the name of groups, with the exception of juridical persons.

Article 55

Citizen participation in public life and a national duty: Every citizen shall have the right to vote, run for elections, and express opinions in referendums, according to the provisions of the law.

The State is responsible for the inclusion of the name of every citizen who is qualified to vote in the voters' database without waiting for an application.

The State shall ensure the fairness, validity, impartiality and integrity of referendums and elections. Interference in anything of the above is a crime punishable by law.

Article 56

The State shall safeguard the interests of Egyptians living abroad, protect them and protect their rights and freedoms, help them perform their public duties toward the Egyptian State and society, and encourage their contribution to the development of the nation.

Their participation in elections and referendums is regulated by law.

Article 57

The right to political asylum shall be granted by the State to every foreigner deprived in their country of public rights and freedoms guaranteed by the Constitution.

Extradition of political refugees is prohibited.

All of the above shall be subject to law regulations.

Chapter Three: Economic and social rights

Article 58

High-quality education is a right guaranteed by the State for every citizen. It is free throughout its stages in all government institutions, obligatory in the primary stage, and the State shall work to extend obligation to other stages.

The State supports and encourages technical education, and oversees education in all its forms.

All educational institutions, public and private, local and otherwise shall abide by the State educational plans and goals, and realize the link between education and the needs of society and production.

Article 59

The State shall guarantee the freedom of scientific and literary research. The autonomy of universities, scientific and linguistic academies, and research centers shall be safeguarded; the State shall provide them with a sufficient percentage of the national revenue.

Article 60

The Arabic language is a primary subject in all stages of education in all educational institutions.

Religious education and national history are core subjects of pre-university education in all its forms.

Universities shall be committed to the teaching of ethics pertaining to the various disciplines.

Article 61

The State shall develop a comprehensive plan to eradicate illiteracy across ages, for males and females, to be executed with social participation within 10 years from the date of the constitution.

Article 62

Healthcare is a right of every citizen, and the State shall allocate a sufficient percentage of the national revenue.

The State shall provide healthcare services and health insurance in accordance with just and high standards, to be free of charge for those who are unable to pay.

All health facilities shall provide various forms of medical treatment to every citizen in cases of emergency or life danger.

The State shall supervise all health facilities, inspect them for quality of services, and monitor all materials, products and means of health-related publicity. Legislation to regulate such supervision shall be drafted.

Article 63

Work is a right, duty and honor for every citizen, guaranteed by the State on the basis of the principles of equality, justice and equal opportunities.

There shall be no forced labor except in accordance with law.

Public sector employees shall work in the service of the people. The State shall employ citizens on the basis of merit, without nepotism or mediation. Any violation is a crime punishable by law.

The State guarantees for every worker the right to fair pay, vacation, retirement and social security, healthcare, protection against occupational hazards, and the application of occupational safety conditions in the workplace, as prescribed by law.

Workers may not be dismissed except in the cases prescribed by law.

The right to peaceful strike is regulated by law.

Article 64

With regards to the martyrs and the injured of wars, of the 25 January revolution, and of national duty, the State shall honor them and support their families, as well as war veterans and the injured, the families of those missing at war, and similar cases.

They, their children and their wives shall have priority in employment opportunities.

All of the above shall be regulated by law.

Article 65

The State shall provide social insurance services.

All citizens unable to support themselves and their families in cases of incapacity, unemployment and old age have the right to social insurance guaranteeing a minimum sustenance.

Article 66

The State shall provide an adequate pension for small-scale farmers, agricultural workers, casual workers, and all who do not have access to the social insurance system.

All are subject to law regulations.

Article 67

Adequate housing, clean water and healthy food are given rights.

The state adopts a national housing plan, its basis in social justice, the promotion of independent initiatives and housing cooperatives, and the regulation of the use of national territory for the purposes of construction, in accordance with public interest and with the rights of future generations.

Article 68

Everyone has the right to play sports.

State and social institutions shall strive to discover talented athletes and support them, and take the necessary measures to encourage exercise.

Article 69

All individuals have the right to a healthy environment. The State shall safeguard the environment against pollution, and promote the use of natural resources in a manner that prevents damage to the environment and preserves the rights of future generations.

Article 70

Every child, from the moment of birth, has the right to a proper name, family care, basic nutrition, shelter, health services, and religious, emotional and cognitive development.

The State shall care and protect the child in the case of the loss of family. The State also safeguards the rights of disabled children, and their rehabilitation and integration into society.

Child labor is prohibited before passing the age of compulsory education, in jobs that are not fit for a child's age, or that prevent the child from continuing education.

A child may only be detained for a specified period, must be provided with legal assistance, and be held in a convenient location, taking into account separation according to gender, ages and type of crime, and be held away from places of adult detention.

Article 71

The State shall provide care for children and youth; shall support their development spiritually, morally, culturally, educationally, physically, psychologically, socially and economically; and shall empower them for active political participation.

Article 72

The State shall provide for people with disabilities health, economic and social care, and shall provide them with employment opportunities, raise social awareness toward them, and adapt public facilities to suit their needs.

Article 73

All forms of oppression, forced exploitation of humans and sex trade are prohibited and criminalized by law.

Chapter Four: Guarantees for the protection of rights and freedoms

Article 74

Sovereignty of the law shall be the basis of rule in the State.

The independence and immunity of the judiciary are two basic guarantees to safeguard rights and freedoms.

Article 75

The right to litigation is inalienable and guaranteed for all.

The State shall guarantee accessibility of judicature for litigants, and rapid decision on cases.

Any stipulation of immunity of any act or administrative decision from the control of the judicature is prohibited.

No person shall be tried except before their natural judge; exceptional courts are prohibited.

Article 76

Penalty shall be personalized. There shall be no crime or penalty except in accordance with the law of the Constitution. No penalty shall be inflicted except by a judicial sentence. Penalty shall be inflicted only for acts committed after a law has come into force.

Article 77

No criminal action shall be made except under an order from a judiciary body, save for cases defined by law.

A defendant is innocent until proven guilty in legal trial, and granted the right of defense. Every person accused of a felony shall be provided with a defense lawyer. Minor offenses, in which a defense lawyer is also required, are determined by law.

The law regulates the rules of appeal for felonies and offenses.

The state shall provide protection for victims of crime, witnesses, defendants and informants where necessary.

Article 78

The right of defense in person or by proxy is guaranteed.

The law secures, for financially incapable citizens, means to resort to justice and to defend their rights.

Article 79

Sentences shall be issued and enforced in the name of the people. Abstention from or obstruction of enforcing such sentences on the part of the concerned civil servants is considered a crime punishable by law. In such case, a person issued a sentence in his favor shall have the right to lodge a direct criminal action before the competent court.

Article 80

Any encroachment on any of the rights and freedoms guaranteed by the Constitution shall be considered a crime for which criminal and civil lawsuit shall not be forfeited by prescription. The State shall grant a fair compensation to the victim of such encroachment.

The injured party shall have the right to lodge a direct criminal action.

The National Council for Human Rights shall inform the Public Prosecution of any violation of these rights, may join the injured party in a civil action, and may appeal on their behalf.

Article 81

Rights and freedoms pertaining to the individual citizen shall not be subject to disruption or detraction.

No law that regulates the practice of the rights and freedoms shall include what would constrain their essence.

Such rights and freedoms shall be practiced in a manner not conflicting with the principles pertaining to State and society included in Part I of this Constitution.

PART III: PUBLIC AUTHORITIES

Chapter One: Legislative authority

Section 1: Common provisions

Article 82

The legislative power shall consist of the House of Representatives and the Shura Council.

Each shall exercise their respective authorities as set out in the Constitution.

Article 83

Membership of the House of Representatives and the Shura Council may not be combined.
Other cases of incompatibility may be specified by law.

Article 84

Save in exceptional cases defined by law, members of either the House of Representatives or the Shura Council are to be fully devoted to their offices, with any other job or post kept open for their return, in accordance with the provisions of the law.

Article 85

A Member of a Legislative House is unconditionally representative of the population as a whole.

Article 86

Prior to the start of his or her tenure, a Member shall take the following oath before his or her Council: "I swear by Almighty God to loyally uphold the republican system, to respect the Constitution and the law, to fully look after the interests of the people, and to safeguard the independence and territorial integrity of the motherland."

Article 87

The Court of Cassation shall have final jurisdiction over the validity of memberships in both Houses. Challenges shall be submitted to the court within a period not exceeding 30 days from the announcement of the final election results, and a verdict shall be passed within 60 days from the date of receipt of the challenge.

Where a membership is deemed invalid, it becomes void from the date the verdict is reported to Parliament.

Article 88

Throughout his or her tenure, no Member of a Legislative House may, in person of through an intermediary, purchase or rent any State property, lease or sell to or barter with the State any part of their own property, or conclude a contract with the State as vendor, supplier or contractor.

Members shall provide financial disclosures and present them to their Council, at the start and at the end of their tenure, as well as at the end of each year.

If, in relation to their membership in a Legislative House, Members should receive cash or in-kind gifts, such gifts shall go into the Public Treasury.

All of the above is subject to regulation by law.

Article 89

Members of the Legislative Houses shall not be held to account for any opinions pertaining to their tasks in Parliament.

Article 90

It is prohibited, except in cases of flagrante delicto, to take criminal action against Members of the Legislative Houses without prior permission from their Council. If not in session, permission must be granted by the Council Office, and the House of Representatives or Shura Council notified at the first subsequent session of any measures taken.

In all cases, if a request for permission to take legal action against a Member of Parliament does not receive a response within 30 days, the permission is to be considered granted.

Article 91

Members shall receive a remuneration determined by the law.

Article 92

The seats of both the House of Representatives and the Shura Council are in Cairo.

However, in exceptional circumstances, either of them may hold meetings elsewhere, at the request of the President of the Republic or one-third of the members of the House or Council.

Any meetings otherwise shall be deemed illegitimate and the resolutions passed therein shall be considered void.

Article 93

The sessions of the House of Representatives and the Shura Council shall be held in public.

However, closed sessions may be held at the request of the President of the Republic, the Prime Minister, or at least 20 of its members. The House of Representatives or Shura Council shall then decide whether the debate on the question submitted thereto shall take place in public or closed sessions.

Article 94

The President of the Republic shall convoke the House of Representatives and the Shura Council for their ordinary annual sessions before the first Thursday of October. If not convoked, the Councils are prescribed by the Constitution to meet on the said day.

The ordinary meeting session shall continue for at least eight months. The President of the Republic shall bring each session to a close with the approval of the Councils, and in the case of the House of Representatives, only after the general budget of the State has been adopted.

Article 95

When necessary, the House of Representatives or the Shura Council may be called to an extraordinary meeting, by the President of the Republic, by the Cabinet, or upon a request signed by at least 10 Shura Council or House of Representatives members.

Article 96

The meetings of the House of Representatives or Shura Council, and the resolutions they pass, shall not be considered valid unless attended by the majority of its members.

In cases other than those stipulating a special majority, resolutions shall be adopted based on an absolute majority of the members present. In case of a tie vote, the matter in deliberation shall be deemed rejected.

Article 97

Each Council shall elect, in the first meeting of its regular annual session, a speaker and two deputy speakers for the full legislative term in the case of the House of Representatives, and for half of the legislative term in the case of the Shura Council. If the seat of either becomes vacant, the Shura Council or House of Representatives shall elect a replacement, whose term will last until the end of its predecessor's.

In all cases, one-third of the members of either House could request a new election of the Speaker or Deputy Speakers in the first meeting of the regular annual session.

Article 98

If the presidency is temporarily assumed by the Speaker of the House of Representatives or of the Shura Council, said Council shall be chaired by the older of the two Deputy Speakers.

Article 99

Each Council shall lay down its own bylaws regulating its work and the manner of practicing its functions, to be published in the Official Gazette.

Article 100

Each Council shall maintain its internal order, a responsibility assumed by each Council's Speaker.

No armed forces may be present within or in vicinity of either of the Legislative Houses except at the request of the Council's Speaker.

Article 101

The President of the Republic, the Cabinet, and every member of the House of Representatives shall have the right to propose laws.

Every draft law shall be referred to a specialist committee of the House of Representatives, which shall study it and submit a report.

Draft laws presented by members of the House of Representatives shall not be referred to that committee before being first endorsed by the Proposals Committee and approved for consideration by the House of Representatives. Reasons for rejection must be presented if the Proposals Committee does not endorse a proposal for consideration.

A draft law proposed by a member but rejected by the House of Representatives may not be presented again during the same legislative term.

Article 102

Neither of the Legislative Houses may pass a bill without seeking consultation.

Each Council has the right to apply amendments and break down existing clauses or suggested amendments.

Each bill passed by one of the Councils shall be passed on to the other, which in turn shall not delay it for more than 60 days, excluding the legislative recess. It shall not be considered a law unless passed by both Councils.

Article 103

In case of legislative dispute between the two Councils, a joint committee of 20 members shall be formed, 10 selected by each Council from among its members and based on the nominations of its General Committee. The joint committee shall then propose the wording of the disputed clauses.

The proposals are then presented to each Council; if an agreement is not reached, the case is taken to the House of Representatives to reach a decision based on a two-thirds majority vote.

Article 104

The House of Representatives shall notify the President of the Republic of any law passed for the President to issue the new law within 15 days from the date of receiving it. In case the President objects to the draft law, it must be referred back to the House of Representatives within 30 days.

If the draft law is not referred back within this period, or if it is approved again by a majority of two-thirds of the members, it shall be considered a law and shall be disseminated as such.

If it is not approved by the House of Representatives, it may not be presented in the same session before four months have passed from the date of the decision.

Article 105

Every member of the House of Representatives or Shura Council is entitled to address questions to the Prime Minister or any of his deputies or ministers concerning matters within their respective jurisdiction. They in turn shall be obliged to answer such questions.

The Member may withdraw the question at any time, and the same question may not be transformed into an interrogation within the same session.

Article 106

Any Member of either Council may propose to the Prime Minister, one of his deputies or a minister the discussion of a public issue.

Article 107

Any 20 members of the House of Representatives, or 10 of the Shura Council, may request the discussion of a public issue to obtain clarification on the government's policy in its regard.

Article 108

Any Member of the House of Representatives or the Shura Council has the right to obtain data or information pertaining to their own performance at the Council, taking into account the provisions of Article 47 of the Constitution.

Article 109

Citizens may submit written proposals to either Council regarding public issues.

Citizens may also submit complaints to either Council to be referred to the relevant ministers. Based on the Council's request, the minister may provide a clarification, and the citizen who issued the complaint shall be kept informed.

Article 110

The Prime Minister, his deputies, ministers and their deputies may attend the sessions and committees of the Councils. Their attendance may be obligatory if requested by either Council. They may be assisted by high-ranking officials of their choice.

They shall be heard whenever they request to speak; they shall answer questions pertaining to issues in discussion, but shall have no counted vote when votes are taken.

Article 111

Each Council accepts the resignation of its members, which must be submitted in writing, and to be accepted must not be submitted after a Council has started measure of revoking membership against the resigning Member.

Article 112

Membership of either Council may only be revoked if a Member has lost trust, status or any of the membership requirements that were prerequisites for their election, or if they have violated the duties of the membership.

Decision on revoking membership shall be issued by a majority of two-thirds of the Council in question.

Article 113

If the seat of a member becomes vacant at least six months before the end of term, the vacant position must be filled in accordance with the law within 60 days from the date the vacancy is first reported.

The term of the new Member shall be complementary to that of the predecessor.

Section 2: House of Representatives

Article 114

The House of Representatives shall have at least 350 members, elected by direct, secret public balloting.

A candidate for parliamentary elections must be an Egyptian citizen, enjoying civil and political rights, holder of a certificate of basic education, and 25 years old or older at the time of candidacy.

Other requirements of candidacy, the provisions for election, the fairly representative division of constituencies, shall be defined by law.

Article 115

The term of membership is five calendar years, commencing from the date of its first session.

Elections for a new House of Representatives shall be held during the 60 days preceding the end of term for the previous House of Representatives.

Article 116

The House of Representatives shall hold the legislative power, and be responsible for approving the general policy of the State, the public plan for economic and social development and the Overall Budget of the State. It shall exercise control over the work of the executive authority, in the manner prescribed by the Constitution.

The procedures for drafting the public plan for economic and social development, and presenting it to the House of Representatives, are determined by law.

Article 117

The Overall Budget of the state must include all revenue and expenditure without exception. The draft Overall Budget shall be submitted to the House of Representatives at least 90 days before the beginning of the fiscal year. It shall not be considered in effect unless approved thereby, and it shall be put to vote on a chapter-by-chapter basis.

The House of Representatives may modify the expenditures in the draft Budget, except those proposed to honor a specific liability. Should the modification result in an increase in total expenditure, the House of Representatives shall agree with the government on means to secure revenue resources to achieve the balance between revenues and expenditures. The Budget shall be issued in a law, which may include modification in any existing law to the extent necessary to realize such balance.

If the new budget is not approved before the beginning of the new fiscal year, the earlier budget shall remain in effect until the new budget has been approved.

The specifics of the fiscal year, the method of budget preparation, the provisions of the budgets of institutions, public bodies, and their accounts, shall be defined by law.

Article 118

The approval of the House of Representatives is necessary for the transfer of any funds from one chapter of the Budget to another, as well as for any expenditure not included therein or in excess of its estimates; the approval shall be issued in a law.

Article 119

The basic rules for collection of public funds and the procedure for their disbursement shall be regulated by law.

Article 120

The rules governing salaries, pensions, indemnities, subsidies and bonuses taken from the State Treasury are regulated by law; so are the cases for exception from such rules, and the authorities in charge of their application.

Article 121

The Executive Authority shall not contract a loan, obtain a fund, or commit itself to a project entailing expenditure from the State Treasury for a subsequent period, except with the House of Representatives' approval.

Article 122

The final account of the Overall Budget shall be submitted to the House of Representatives within a period not exceeding six months from the end of the fiscal year. The annual report of the Central Auditing Organization and the latter's observations on the final account are to be attached.

The final account of the Overall Budget shall be put to vote on a chapter-by-chapter basis and shall be issued by a law.

The House of Representatives has the right to request from the Central Auditing Organization any additional data or pertinent reports.

Article 123

The House of Representatives may form a special committee or entrust one of its existing committees to examine the activities of any administrative department or institution or public enterprise, for the purpose of fact-finding regarding a specific issue and informing the House of Representatives of the actual financial, administrative or economic status, or for conducting investigations into a past activity; the House of Representatives shall decide on the appropriate course of action.

In order to carry out its mission, such a committee would be entitled to collect the evidence it deems necessary and to summon individuals for interviews. All executive and administrative bodies shall respond to demands by the committee and put under its disposal all the documents and evidence required.

Article 124

Members of the House of Representatives have the right to submit a request for information or for an urgent statement to the Prime Minister, to one of the Prime Minister's deputies, or to a minister in urgent public matters of importance.

The government is obliged to respond.

Article 125

Every Member of the House of Representatives is entitled to address interpellations to the Prime Minister, the Prime Minister's deputies, or to ministers concerning matters within their respective jurisdiction.

Debate on an interpellation shall take place at least seven days after its submission, except in cases of urgency as decided by the House of Representatives and with the government's consent.

Article 126

The House of Representatives may decide to withdraw its confidence from the Prime Minister, a deputy of the Prime Minister, or any one of the ministers.

A motion of no confidence may be submitted only after an interpellation, upon proposal by one-tenth of the House of Representatives' members. The House of Representatives should reach a decision within seven days from the date of debating the motion. Withdrawal of confidence needs a majority vote from the members of the House of Representatives.

In all case, a no confidence motion may not be passed in connection with an issue that had already been decided upon in the same juridical term.

If the House of Representatives decides to withdraw confidence from the Prime Minister or a minister, and the Cabinet announced its solidarity with him before the vote, then that Cabinet is obliged to offer its resignation. If the no confidence resolution concerns a certain member of the government, that member is obliged to resign their office.

Article 127

The President of the Republic may not dissolve the House of Representatives except by a causative decision and following a public referendum.

A House of Representatives may not be dissolved during its first annual session, nor for the same cause for which the immediately previous House of Representatives was dissolved.

To dissolve the House of Representatives, the President must issue a decision to suspend parliamentary sessions and hold a referendum within 20 days. If voters agreed with a valid majority on the dissolution, it shall be carried out. The President shall then call for early parliamentary elections to take place within 30 days from the date of the dissolution. The new House of Representatives shall convene within the 10 days following the completion of elections.

If no such majority agrees to the dissolution, the President of the Republic shall resign.

If, however, the referendum or elections do not take place within the specified time limit, the existing Parliament shall reconvene of its own accord on the day following the expiry of the time limit.

Section 3: Shura Council

Article 128

The Shura Council shall have at least 150 members, elected by direct secret ballot. The President of the Republic may appoint a number of members not exceeding one-tenth of the number of elected members.

Article 129

A candidate for the Shura Council must be an Egyptian citizen enjoying civil and political rights, a holder of a certificate of higher education, and, at the time of candidacy, at least 35 years old.

Other requirements of candidacy, the provisions for election, the division of constituencies, shall be defined by law.

Article 130

The term of membership of the Shura Council is six years, whereas renewed election and appointment of 50 percent of the total number of members, whether elected or appointed, is every three years, as defined by law.

Article 131

In the case of the dissolution of House of Representatives, the Shura Council shall carry out its joint legislative responsibilities. Any bills passed by the Shura Council during the period of House of Representatives' dissolution shall be presented to the new House of Representatives for consideration as soon as it is convened.

In the absence of both Legislative Houses, and where there is a requirement for urgent measures, the President of the Republic may issue decrees that have the force of law, which shall then be presented to the House of Representatives and the Shura Council – as the case may be – within 15 days from the start of their sessions.

If such decrees were not presented to the Councils, or if they were presented but not approved, their force of law is retrospectively revoked, unless the Council affirms their validity for the previous period, or chooses to settle the consequent effects in some other manner.

Chapter Two: Executive authority

Section 1: The President

Article 132

The President is the Head of State and chief of the executive authority. He looks after the interests of the people, safeguards the independence and territorial integrity of the motherland, and observes the separation between powers.

He carries out his responsibilities in the manner prescribed in the Constitution.

Article 133

The President of the Republic shall be elected for a period of four calendar years, commencing on the day the term of his predecessor ends. The President may be reelected only once.

The process of the presidential election begins at least 90 days before the end of presidential term. The result is to be announced at least 10 days before the end of term.

The President of the Republic may not hold any partisan position for the duration of the presidency.

Article 134

A presidential candidate must be an Egyptian citizen born to Egyptian parents, must have carried no other citizenship, must have civil and political rights, cannot be married to a non-Egyptian, and at the time of nomination cannot be younger than 40 Gregorian years.

Article 135

A prerequisite for nomination to the presidency is a recommendation by at least 20 elected members of the House of Representatives and the Shura Council, or endorsements from at least 20,000 citizens who have the right to vote, in at least 10 governorates, with a minimum of 1,000 endorsements from each governorate.

No one shall be allowed to endorse more than one candidate, as shall be regulated by law.

Article 136

The President of the Republic is elected by direct secret ballot, with an absolute majority of valid votes. The procedures for electing the President of the Republic shall be regulated by law.

Article 137

Before assuming the presidential position, the President of the Republic shall take the following oath before the House of Representatives and the Shura Council: "I swear by Almighty God to loyally uphold the republican system, to respect the Constitution and the law, to fully look after the interests of the people and to safeguard the independence and territorial integrity of the motherland."

In case the House of Representatives is dissolved, the oath is to be taken before the Shura Council.

Article 138

The finances of the President of the Republic are stipulated by law; the President shall not receive any other salary or remuneration, nor engage throughout the presidential term, whether in person or through an intermediary, in an independent profession or business, nor is the President allowed to buy or rent state property, nor lease or sell to or barter with the State any part of their own property, nor conclude a contract with the State as vendor, supplier or contractor.

The President must submit to the House of Representatives a financial disclosure upon taking office, upon leaving it, and at the end of each year.

If, in relation to the presidential post, the President should receive, in person or through an intermediary, cash or in-kind gifts, such gifts shall go into the State Treasury.

All of the above is subject to regulation by law.

Article 139

The President of the Republic appoints the Prime Minister, who shall be assigned by the President the task of forming the Cabinet and presenting it to the House of Representatives within 30 days. If the Cabinet is not granted parliamentary confidence, the President shall appoint another Prime Minister from the party that holds the majority of seats in the House of Representatives. If the Cabinet of that appointed Prime Minister does not obtain parliamentary confidence within a similar period, the House of Representatives then appoints a Prime Minister who shall be assigned by the President the task of forming a Cabinet, provided said Cabinet obtains parliamentary confidence within a similar period. Otherwise, the President of the Republic shall dissolve the House of Representatives and call the elections of a new House of Representatives within 60 days from the date the dissolution is announced.

In all cases, the sum of the periods set forth in this Article should not exceed 90 days.

In the case of dissolution of the House of Representatives, the Prime Minister shall present the Cabinet and its plan to the new House of Representatives at its first session.

Article 140

The President of the Republic, in conjunction with the Cabinet, shall lay out the public policy of the State and oversee its implementation, in the manner prescribed in the Constitution.

Article 141

The President of the Republic shall exercise presidential authority via the Prime Minister and the Prime Minister's deputies and ministers, except those authorities related to defense, national security and foreign policy, and authorities outlined in Articles 139, 145, 146, 147, 148 and 149 of the Constitution.

Article 142

The President of the Republic may delegate some of the presidential purviews to the Prime Minister, the Prime Minister's deputies, ministers or governors, in the manner regulated by law.

Article 143

The President of the Republic may call for Cabinet meetings to discuss important matters, shall preside over such meetings, and shall request reports about public affairs from the Prime Minister.

Article 144

The President of the Republic shall deliver a statement on the general policy of the State in a joint session of the House of Representatives and the Shura Council at the opening of their regular annual sessions.

The President may, when appropriate, make other statements or convey specific messages to either Council.

Article 145

The President of the Republic shall represent the State in foreign relations and shall conclude treaties and ratify them after the approval of the House of Representatives and the Shura Council. Such treaties shall have the force of law after ratification and publication, according to established procedures.

Approval must be acquired from both Legislative Houses with a two-thirds majority of their members for any treaty of peace, alliance, trade and navigation, and all treaties related to the rights of sovereignty or that make the State Treasury liable for any expenditures not included in its overall budget.

No treaty contrary to the provisions of the Constitution shall be approved.

Article 146

The President of the Republic shall be the Supreme Commander of the Armed Forces. The President is not to declare war, or send the Armed Forces outside State territory, except after consultation with the National Defense Council and the approval of the House of Representatives with a majority of its members.

Article 147

The President of the Republic shall appoint civil and military personnel and dismiss them, shall appoint diplomatic representatives and remove them, and shall confirm political representatives of foreign countries and organizations, as regulated by law.

Article 148

The President of the Republic shall declare, after consultation with the Cabinet, a state of emergency in the manner regulated by law. Such proclamation must be submitted to House of Representatives within the following seven days.

If the declaration takes place when the House of Representatives is not in session, a session is called for immediately. In case the House of Representatives is dissolved, the matter shall be submitted to the Shura Council, all within the period specified in the preceding paragraph. The declaration of a state of emergency must be approved by a majority of members of each Council. The declaration shall be for a specified period not exceeding six months, which can only be extended by another similar period upon the people's approval in a public referendum.

The House of Representatives cannot be dissolved while a state of emergency is in place.

Article 149

The President of the Republic may issue a pardon or mitigate a sentence.

General amnesty may only be granted in a law.

Article 150

The President of the Republic may call for a referendum on important issues relating to the supreme interests of the State.

The result of a referendum shall be binding to all state authorities and the general public in all cases.

Article 151

For the President of the Republic to resign, a letter of resignation must be presented to the House of Representatives.

Article 152

A charge of felony or treason against the President of the Republic is to be based on a motion signed by at least one-third of the members of the House of Representatives. An impeachment is to be issued only by a two-thirds majority of the members of the House of Representatives.

As soon as an impeachment decision has been issued, the President of the Republic shall cease all work; this shall be treated as a temporary obstacle preventing the President from carrying out presidential duties until a verdict is reached.

The President of the Republic shall be tried before a special court headed by the President of the Supreme Constitutional Court, the longest-serving Deputy of the President of the Court of Cassation and the State Council, and the two longest-serving presidents of the Court of Appeals; the prosecution to be carried out before such court by the Prosecutor General.

The prosecution, trial procedure and penalty are regulated by law. In the case of conviction, the President of the Republic shall be relieved of his post, without prejudice to other penalties.

Article 153

If on account of a temporary obstacle, the President of the Republic is rendered unable to carry out the presidential functions, the Prime Minister shall act in his place.

If the Presidential office becomes vacant, due to resignation, death, permanent inability to work or any other reason, the House of Representatives shall announce the vacancy and notify the Presidential Elections Commission. The Speaker of the House of Representatives shall temporarily assume the presidential authorities.

The Shura Council and its Speaker replace the House of Representatives and its Speaker in the above in cases in which the House of Representatives is dissolved.

In all cases, a new president must be elected during a period not exceeding 90 days from the date the office became vacant.

The person acting in place of the President is not allowed to run for office, request any amendment to the Constitution, dissolve the Parliament or dismiss the Cabinet.

Article 154

If the vacancy of the presidential office occurs at the same time that a referendum or the election of either the House of Representatives or the Shura

Council is being held, precedence shall be given to the presidential elections. The existing Parliament shall continue in place until the completion of the presidential elections.

Section 2: The Cabinet

Article 155

The Cabinet consists of the Prime Minister, the Prime Minister's deputies and the ministers.

The Prime Minister heads the Cabinet, oversees its work, and directs it in the performance of its functions.

Article 156

A person appointed to the position of Prime Minister or any other position in the Cabinet must be an Egyptian citizen, enjoying civil and political rights, over the age of 30, and not having carried the citizenship of any other country unless renounced within a year of reaching the age of eighteen.

It is prohibited hold a position in the Cabinet in addition to membership in either the House of Representatives or the Shura Council; if a House or Council Member is appointed to government, their place in Parliament is vacated and the provisions of Article 113 of the Constitution are applied.

Article 157

Before assuming their duties, the Prime Minister and members of the Cabinet shall take the following oath before the President of the Republic: "I swear by Almighty God to loyally uphold the republican system, to respect the Constitution and the law, to fully look after the interests of the people and to safeguard the independence and territorial integrity of the motherland."

Article 158

The finances of the Prime Minister and members of Cabinet are stipulated by law; they shall not receive any other salary or remuneration, nor engage throughout the term of their posts, whether in person or through an intermediary, in independent professions or business, nor are they allowed to buy or rent state property, nor lease or sell to or barter with the State any part of their own property, nor conclude a contract with the State as vendors, suppliers or contractors.

A member of Cabinet must submit a financial disclosure to the House of Representatives upon taking office, upon leaving it and at the end of each year.

If, in relation to their posts, they should receive cash or in-kind gifts, such gifts shall go into the State Treasury. All of the above is subject to regulation by law.

Article 159

The Cabinet shall exercise the following functions in particular:

1. Collaborate with the President of the Republic in laying down the public policy of the State and overseeing its implementation.
2. Direct, coordinate and follow up on the work of the ministries and their affiliated public bodies and organizations.
3. Prepare draft laws and decrees.
4. Issue administrative decisions in accordance with the law, and monitor their implementation.
5. Prepare the draft Overall Budget of the State.
6. Prepare the draft economic and social development plan of the state.
7. Contract and grant loans in accordance with the provisions of the Constitution.
8. Supervise the implementation of laws, maintain state security and protect the rights of the citizens and the interests of the State.

Article 160

The Minister shall draw up the ministry's general policy, supervise its implementation and offer guidance and control, in the framework of the State's public policy.

Article 161

A member of the Cabinet may make a statement before the House of Representatives, the Shura Council, or one of their committees, concerning any matters within the scope of his purview.

The Council or committee may discuss such a statement and convey its position regarding it.

Article 162

The Prime Minister shall issue necessary regulations for the enforcement of laws, in such a manner that does not involve any disruption, modification, or exemption from their enforcement, and shall have the right to vest others with authority to issue them, unless the law designates who should issue the necessary regulations for its own implementation.

Article 163

The Prime Minister shall issue the regulations necessary for the creation and organization of public services and facilities upon the Cabinet's approval.

The House of Representatives' approval is required, if such regulations result in new expenditures in the Overall Budget of the State.

Article 164

The Prime Minister shall issue regulations of discipline upon the Cabinet's approval.

Article 165

The authority in charge of the appointment and dismissal of civil servants, the functions of the main positions, and the responsibilities, rights and securities of employees, is regulated by law.

Article 166

The President of the Republic, the Prosecutor General, and the House of Representatives, with a motion signed by one-third of its members, have the right to accuse the Prime Minister or any of the members of the Cabinet concerning crimes committed during their term of office or in relation to their work.

In all cases, charges can only be brought with the approval of two-thirds of the members of the House of Representatives. An accused member of Cabinet is relieved of their post until a verdict is reached. The end of their term of service does not preclude the start or resumption of prosecution.

Article 167

For the Cabinet or one of its members to resign, a letter of resignation must be presented to the President of the Republic.

Chapter Three: The Judicial Authority

Section 1: General provisions

Article 168

The Judicial Authority shall be independent, vested in the courts of justice, which shall issue their judgments in accordance with the law. It's powers are defined by law. Interference in the affairs of the judiciary is a crime that is not forfeited by the passing of time.

Article 169

Every judiciary body shall administer its own affairs; each shall have an independent budget and be consulted on the draft laws governing its affairs, by the means that are regulated by law.

Article 170

Judges are independent, cannot be dismissed, are subject to no other authority but the law, and are equal in rights and duties.

The conditions and procedures for their appointment and disciplinary actions against them are defined and regulated by the law. When delegated, their delegation shall be absolute, to the destinations and in the positions defined by the law, all in a manner that preserves the independence of the judiciary and the accomplishment of its duties.

Article 171

Sessions in court shall be public, unless, in consideration of public order or morals, the court deems them confidential. In all cases, the verdict shall be given in an open session.

Section 2: *The judiciary and public prosecution*

Article 172

The judiciary adjudicates in all disputes and crimes except for matters that are to be decided by another judicial body. The judiciary settles any disputes relating to the affairs of its members.

Article 173

The Public Prosecution is an integral part of the judiciary, to investigate, press and follow charges in all criminal cases except what is exempted by law. Other competencies are defined by law.

The Public Prosecution is conducted by a Prosecutor General appointed by the President of the Republic, based on the selection of the Supreme Judicial Council from among the Deputies to the President of the Court of Cassation, the Presidents of the Court of Appeals and Assistant Prosecutor Generals, for a period of four years, or for the period remaining until retirement age, whichever comes first, and only once during a judge's career.

Section 3: *The State Council*

Article 174

The State Council is an independent judicial body that exclusively undertakes adjudicating in administrative disputes and disputes pertaining to the implementation of its decisions. It also undertakes disciplinary proceedings and appeals, adjudicates in legal issues to be determined by law, reviews and drafts bills and resolutions of legislative character referred to it, and reviews contracts to which the State is a party.

Other competencies to be determined by law.

Section 4: The Supreme Constitutional Court

Article 175

The Supreme Constitutional Court is an independent judicial body, seated in Cairo, which exclusively undertakes the judicial control of the constitutionality of the laws and regulations.

The law defines other competencies and regulates the procedures to be followed before the court.

Article 176

The Supreme Constitutional Court is made up of a president and ten members. The law determines judicial or other bodies that shall nominate them and regulates the manner of their appointment and requirements to be satisfied by them. Appointments take place by a decree from the President of the Republic.

Article 177

The President of the Republic or Parliament shall present draft laws governing presidential, legislative or local elections before the Supreme Constitutional Court, to determine their compliance with the Constitution prior to dissemination. The Court shall reach a decision in this regard within 45 days from the date the matter is presented before it; otherwise, the proposed law shall be considered approved.

If the Court deems one or more parts of the text non-compliant with the provisions of the Constitution, its decision shall be implemented.

The laws referred to in the first paragraph are not subject to the subsequent control stipulated in Article 175 of the Constitution.

Article 178

The Official Gazette shall publish verdicts issued by the Supreme Constitutional Court and decisions pertaining to preemptive control of draft laws governing presidential, legislative or local elections.

The effects of a decision on the unconstitutionality of a legislative text are regulated by law.

Section 5: Judicial bodies

Article 179

State Affairs is an independent judicial body; it undertakes legal representation of the State in disputes, and technical supervision of legal affairs departments within State Administration.

It shall be responsible for the drafting of contracts and the settling of disputes to which the State is a party, in the manner regulated by law.

Other competencies shall be defined by law.

Its members share immunities, securities, rights and duties assigned to other members of the judiciary.

Article 180

The Administrative Prosecution is an independent judicial body; it investigates financial and administrative irregularities, raises disciplinary proceedings before the courts of the State Council and follows up on them, and takes legal action to address deficiencies in public facilities. Other competencies shall be defined by law.

Its members share immunities, securities, rights and duties assigned to other members of the judiciary.

Section 6: Judicial officers

Article 181

The legal profession is a free profession and a cornerstone of justice. Lawyers shall be autonomous in practicing their profession and shall be safeguarded by guarantees that protect them and enable them to carry out their work, in the manner regulated by law.

Article 182

Officers at the Real Estate Publicity Department, forensic experts and judicial experts shall enjoy technical autonomy in their work.

Chapter Four: Local administration

Section 1: Local administrative division of the State

Article 183

The State is divided into administrative units that are considered as judicial persons and include governorates, provinces, cities, districts and villages. One administrative unit may comprise more than one village or district. Other administrative units that are judicial persons may be established, all as regulated by law, in a manner that supports decentralization, empowering administrative units in providing local services and facilities, improving them and managing them well.

Article 184

The State shall provide what the Local Unit should need in terms of technical, administrative and financial assistance, shall ensure equitable distribution of facilities, services and resources, and shall work to bring development levels and living standards in these units to a common standard, as regulated by law.

Article 185

The income of Local Units shall include additional taxes and fees of local nature. The Unit shall follow the same rules and procedures in the collection of public funds as followed by the State. All of the above shall be regulated by law.

Article 186

The law regulates cooperation between Local Units in matters of mutual benefit and means of cooperation between Local Units and the state apparatus.

Article 187

The law regulates the manner of selecting governors and heads of other local administrative units, and defines their jurisdiction.

Section 2: Local councils

Article 188

Every Local Unit shall elect a Local Council by direct, secret ballot for a term of four years.

Representatives from the executive apparatus of the Local Unit shall form part of the Council but have no counted vote.

Every Council elects its President and Deputy from among its elected members.

Conditions and procedures for nomination and election are regulated by law.

Article 189

The Local Council shall be concerned with the issues that matter in the Unit it represents and shall create and manage local facilities – economic, social and health-related – and other activities, in the manner regulated by law.

Article 190

The Local Council decisions issued within the limits of its jurisdiction are final and not subject to interference from the executive authorities, except to prevent the Council from overstepping limits, or causing damage to public interest or the interests of other Local Councils.

Any dispute over the jurisdiction of a Local Council shall be dealt with as a matter of urgency by the Legislation Department of the State Council, all in the manner regulated by law.

Article 191

Every Local Council shall be in charge of its own budget and final accounts, in the manner regulated by law.

Article 192

It is prohibited to dissolve Local Councils as part of a comprehensive administrative procedure. The manner to dissolve and reelect any one of them shall be regulated by law.

Chapter Five: National security and defense

Section 1: The National Security Council

Article 193

The National Security Council shall be created, presided over by the President of the Republic and including in its membership the Prime Minister, the Speakers of the House of Representatives and the Shura Council, the Minister of Defense, the Minister of Interior, the Minister of Foreign Affairs, the Minister of Finance, the Minister of Justice, the Minister of Health, the Chief of the General Intelligence Services, and the Heads of the Committees of Defense and National Security in the House of Representatives and the Shura Council.

The Council shall invite whoever is seen as being of relevant expertise to attend its meetings without having their votes counted.

The Council adopts strategies for establishing security in the country; facing disasters and crises of all kinds and taking necessary measures to contain them; and identifying sources of threat to Egyptian national security, whether at home or abroad, and undertaking necessary actions to address them on the official and popular levels.

Other competencies and regulations are defined by law.

Section 2: The Armed Forces

Article 194

The Armed Forces shall belong to the people. Their duty is to protect the country, and preserve its security and territories. It is the State alone that shall create these forces. No individual, entity, organization or group is allowed to create military or para-military structures, bands, or organizations.

The Armed Forces shall have a Supreme Council as regulated by law.

Article 195

The Minister of Defense is the Commander in Chief of the Armed Forces, appointed from among its officers.

Article 196

The law regulates public mobilization and defines the conditions of service, promotion and retirement in the Armed Forces.

The Judicial Committees for the officers and personnel of the Armed Forces are alone responsible for adjudicating in all administrative disputes pertaining to decisions affecting them.

Section 3: The National Defense Council

Article 197

A National Defense Council shall be created, presided over by the President of the Republic and including in its membership the Speakers of the House of Representatives and the Shura Council, the Prime Minister, the Minister of Defense, the Minister of Foreign Affairs, the Minister of Finance, the Minister of Interior, the Chief of the General Intelligence Service, the Chief of Staff of the Armed Forces, the Commander of the Navy, the Air Forces and Air Defense, the Chief of Operations for the Armed Forces and the Head of Military Intelligence.

The President of the Republic may invite whoever is seen as having relevant expertise to attend the Council's meetings without having their votes counted.

The Council is responsible for matters pertaining to the methods of ensuring the safety and security of the country and to the budget of the Armed Forces. It shall be consulted about draft laws related to the Armed Forces. Other competencies are to be defined by law.

Section 4: The Military Judiciary

Article 198

The Military Judiciary is an independent judiciary that adjudicates exclusively in all crimes related to the Armed Forces, its officers and personnel.

Civilians shall not stand trial before military courts except for crimes that harm the Armed Forces. The law shall define such crimes and determine the other competencies of the Military Judiciary.

Members of the Military Judiciary are autonomous and cannot be dismissed. They share the immunities, securities, rights and duties stipulated for members of other judiciaries.

Section 5: The Police

Article 199

The Police force is a statutory civil body with the President of the Republic as its Supreme Chief. It shall perform its duty in the service of the people, its loyalty being to the Constitution and the law, and its responsibilities to preserve order, public security and morality, to implement laws and regulations, and to safeguard the peace, dignity, rights and freedoms of citizens, all as regulated by law and in a manner that enables Police personnel to carry out their duties.

PART IV: INDEPENDENT BODIES AND REGULATORY AGENCIES

Chapter One: Common Provisions

Article 200

Independent bodies and regulatory agencies that are defined in the Constitution have judicial personality, neutrality, and technical, administrative and financial autonomy.

Additional independent bodies and regulatory agencies are defined by the law.

These independent bodies and agencies shall be consulted about draft laws and regulations that relate to their fields of operation.

Article 201

Reports from independent bodies and regulatory agencies are to be presented to the President of the Republic, the House of Representatives and Shura Council within 30 days from the date they are issued.

The House of Representatives shall consider such reports and take appropriate action within a period not exceeding six months from the date of receipt. The reports shall be presented for public opinion.

Regulatory agencies shall notify the appropriate investigative authorities with any evidence of violations or crime they may discover.

All of the above shall be regulated by law.

Article 202

The President of the Republic shall appoint the heads of independent bodies and regulatory agencies upon the approval of the Shura Council, for a period of four years, renewable once. They shall not be dismissed except with the consent of a majority of the members of the Council; the same prohibitions apply to them that apply to ministers.

Article 203

For the creation of each independent body or regulatory agency, a law shall be issued defining competencies other than those outlined in the Constitution, regulating the agency's work and stipulating the necessary securities to enable its personnel to carry out that work.

The Law shall define details of appointment, promotion, accountability and dismissal, and other conditions of employment, to ensure the impartiality and autonomy of personnel.

Chapter Two: Regulatory Agencies

Section 1: The National Anti-Corruption Commission

Article 204

The National Anti-Corruption Commission combats corruption, deals with conflicts of interest, promotes and defines the standards of integrity and transparency, develops the national strategy concerned with such matters, ensures the implementation of said strategy in coordination with other independent bodies, and supervises the concerned agencies specified by law.

Section 2: Central Auditing Organization

Article 205

The Central Auditing Organization has control over state funds and any other body specified by law.

Section 3: The Central Bank

Article 206

The Central Bank stipulates monetary, credit and banking policies, supervises their implementation, monitors the performance of the banking system, works to establish price stability, and has exclusive rights to issue currency.

All of the above shall be in accordance with the overall economic policy of the State.

Chapter Three: The Economic and Social Council

Article 207

The Economic and Social Council supports the participation of social groups in the preparation of economic, social and environmental policies, and promotes social dialogue.

The Cabinet, the House of Representatives and the Shura Council shall consult the Economic and Social Council on those policies and any related draft laws.

The Council shall consist of at least 150 members, selected by their elected organizations of trade unions, syndicates, associations of farmers, workers and professionals, and other social groups, provided the representation of workers and farmers makes up for at least 50 percent of the Council members.

Membership of this Council may not be combined with membership of the Cabinet or any of the Legislative Houses.

The details of forming the Council, electing its President, the regulations governing its work, and the means of presenting its recommendations to the state authorities shall be defined by law.

Chapter Four: The National Electoral Commission

Article 208

The National Electoral Commission is exclusively responsible for managing referendums and presidential, parliamentary and local elections, which shall include the preparation of a database of voters, input on the division of constituencies, control over electoral funding and expenditure, electoral campaigns and other procedures, up to the announcements of results.

The Commission may be entrusted with supervising the elections of trade unions and other organizations.

All of the above shall be regulated by law.

Article 209

The National Electoral Commission shall be administered by a board made up of 10 members selected evenly from among the Deputies of the Court of Cassation, the Courts of Appeal, the State Council, the State Affairs and Administrative Prosecution, and elected by their respective assemblies from outside their board members, to be fully delegated for exclusive work at the Commission for one term of six years. The presidency of the Commission shall go to its longest-serving member from the Court of Cassation.

Elections shall be held to renew half of the Commission members every three years.

The Commission may refer to public figures or specialists deemed to have relevant expertise in the field of elections. The Commission shall have an executive body.

All of the above shall be regulated by law.

Article 210

Voting and counting of votes in referendums and elections run by the Commission shall be administered by its affiliated members under the overall supervision of the Board. Members shall be furnished with the necessary securities that enable them to perform their role with impartiality and autonomy.

As an exceptional measure, the Commission shall delegate the overseeing of voting and counting of votes to members of the judiciary for at least 10 years from the date the constitution is ratified, all as regulated by law.

Article 211

The Supreme Administrative Court shall adjudicate on appeals brought against the decisions of the National Electoral Commission pertaining to referendums and parliamentary or presidential elections and their results. Appeals pertaining to local elections shall be brought before an administrative court.

The law regulates the procedure for appeals and the timeline for adjudication in a manner that does not disrupt the electoral process or the announcement of final results. The final results of referendums or presidential elections may not be challenged after their announcement.

In all cases, the announcement of results must take place within a period not exceeding eight days from the ballot date.

Chapter Five: Independent Bodies

Section 1: The Supreme Authority for Endowment Affairs

Article 212

The High Authority for Endowment Affairs regulates, supervises and monitors public and private endowments, ensures their adherence to sensible administrative and economic standards, and raises awareness about endowments in society.

Section 2: The Supreme Authority for Heritage Conservation

Article 213

The Supreme Authority for Heritage Conservation regulates the means of protecting the cultural and architectural heritage of Egyptians, supervises its collection and documentation, safeguards its assets, and revives awareness of its contributions to human civilization.

This Authority shall undertake the documentation of the 25 January revolution.

Section 3: The National Council for Education and Scientific Research

Article 214

The National Council for Education and Scientific Research develops the national strategy for education in all its forms and all its stages, ensures integration between the stages, promotes scientific research, develops national standards for the quality of education and scientific research, and monitors the implementation of such standards.

Section 4: Independent press and media organizations

Article 215

The National Media Council regulates the affairs of radio, television, and printed and digital press, among others.

The Council shall ensure the freedom of media in all its forms, safeguard plurality, fight centralization and monopoly, protect the interests of the public, and establish controls and regulations ensuring the commitment of media to adhere to professional and ethical standards, to preserve the Arabic language, and to observe the values and constructive traditions of society.

Article 216

The National Press and Media Association manages State-owned press and media institutions and undertakes the development of them and their assets to maximize their national investment value and ensure their adherence to sensible professional, administrative and economic standards.

PART V: FINAL AND TRANSITIONAL PROVISIONS

Chapter One: Amendments to the Constitution

Article 217

The amendment of one or more of the Constitution articles may be requested by the President of the Republic or the House of Representatives. The request shall specify the articles to be amended and the reasons for the amendments, and if initiated by the House of Representatives shall be signed by at least five House of Representatives Members.

In all cases, the House of Representatives and Shura Council shall debate the request within 30 days from the date of its receipt; each council shall issue its decision to accept the request in whole or in part by two-thirds majority of its members.

If the request is rejected, the same amendments may not be requested again before the next legislative term.

Article 218

If the amendment request is approved by both Houses, each of them shall discuss the text of the articles to be amended within 60 days from the date of approval; if approved by a two-thirds majority of each House, the amendment shall be put to public referendum within 30 days from the date of approval.

The amendment shall be effective from the date of announcement of the referendum result.

Chapter Two: General Provisions

Article 219

The principles of Islamic Sharia include general evidence, foundational rules, rules of jurisprudence, and credible sources accepted in Sunni doctrines and by the larger community.

Article 220

Cairo is the capital of the State. The capital may be moved by law.

Article 221

The National Flag, the State's emblem, decorations, insignia, seal and the National Anthem are defined by law.

Article 222

Provisions stipulated by laws and regulations prior to the proclamation of this Constitution shall remain valid and in force. They may not be amended or repealed except in accordance with the regulations and procedures prescribed in the Constitution.

Article 223

Laws shall be published in the Official Gazette within 15 days from the date of their issuance, to be effective 30 days from the day following the date of publication, unless the law has specified a different date.

Provisions of the laws shall apply only from the date of their enforcement and shall have no retroactive effect. However, with the approval of a two-thirds majority of the members of the House of Representatives, provisions to the contrary may be made in articles pertaining to non-criminal and non-tax-related matters.

Article 224

Elections of the House of Representatives, Shura Council and local councils shall be held in accordance with the system of individual candidacy, a list-based system, a combination of the two, or any other electoral system defined by law.

Article 225

This Constitution shall be in force as of the date of announcing the public approval of it in a referendum, based on a majority of valid votes of the referendum participants.

Chapter Three: Transitional provisions

Article 226

The current presidential term comes to an end four years from the date of the President taking office. He may only be re-elected only once.

Article 227

Every position for which a limited term is stipulated in the constitution or by law, whether a non-renewable or renewable once, is calculated from the date the position was assumed. The term of office shall also expire if the person in office reaches the retirement age as prescribed by law.

Article 228

The High Elections Commission, existing at the time this Constitution comes into effect, shall undertake the full supervision of the first parliamentary elections. The funds of the Committee and of the High Presidential Elections Committee are transferred to the National Electoral Commission, as soon as the latter is formed.

Article 229

Procedures for the first parliamentary elections shall begin within 60 days of this Constitution coming into effect, the first legislative term held within 10 days from the date of announcing the final result of the elections.

In this House of Representatives, farmers and workers shall have a minimum of 50 percent representation.

A worker refers to anyone who is hired by another for a fee or salary. A farmer refers to anyone who has taken agriculture as a profession for a minimum of 10 years preceding parliamentary nomination.

The standards and regulations required for a candidate to be considered a farmer or a work shall be determined by law.

Article 230

The existing Shura Council shall assume full legislative authority until the new House of Representatives is formed. Full legislative authority will then be transferred to the House of Representatives, until the election of a new Shura Council, which shall occur within six months from the start of the House of Representatives' session.

Article 231

The first legislative elections following the adoption of this Constitution shall be held in the following manner: Two-thirds of the seats are to be won by a list-based electoral system and one-third by individual candidacy, with parties and independent candidates allowed to run in each.

Article 232

Leaders of the dissolved National Democratic Party shall be banned from political work and prohibited to run for presidential or legislative elections for a period of 10 years from the date of the adoption of this Constitution. Leadership includes everyone who was a member of the Secretariat of the Party, the Policies Committee or the Political Bureau, or was a member of the People's Assembly or the Shura Council during the two legislative terms preceding the 25 January revolution.

Article 233

The first Supreme Constitutional Court, once this Constitution is applied, shall be formed of its current President and the 10 longest-serving judges among its members. The remaining members shall return to the posts they occupied before joining the court.

Article 234

The provision concerning appeals on verdicts issued on crimes stated in the third part of Article 77 shall be valid starting a year after the Constitution has come into effect.

Article 235

The existing Local Administration system shall remain in place, and the system laid down in this Constitution applied gradually over the 10 years following the date of its adoption.

Article 236

Constitutional declarations issued by the Supreme Council of the Armed Forces and by the President of the Republic from 11 February 2011 to the date of the adoption of this Constitution are hereby repealed, while their consequent effects shall remain valid and in force and may not in any way be appealed against.

Edited by Lindsay Carroll and Sara Edmunds

Bibliography

Abbas, Mushreq. "Iraqi Federal Court Delays Ruling on Term-Limit Law." *Al-Monitor.* July 3, 2013. Accessed August 8, 2013. http://www.al-monitor. com/pulse/originals/2013/07/iraq-federal-court-ruling-delay-term-limit-law. html.

Abbas, Mushreq. "New Religious Campaign Targets Baghdad's Cafes." *Al-Monitor.* July 19, 2013. Accessed August 18, 2013. http://www.al-monitor.com/pulse/ originals/2013/07/religious-campaign-targets-cafes-baghdad-iraq.html.

Abd-al-Amir, Ali. "Maliki's Sectarian Populism Working Among Iraqi Shiites." *Al-Monitor.* May 17, 2013. Accessed June 25, 2013. http://www.al-monitor. com/pulse/politics/2013/05/shiite-opposition-maliki-iraq-challenges.html.

Abdelmassih, Mary. "Egypt's President Approves 17 Year-old Church Building Permit." *Assyrian International News Agency.* June 8, 2013. Accessed August 9, 2013. http://www.aina.org/news/20130607192710.htm.

Abed-Kotob, Sana. "The Accommodationists Speak: Goals and Strategies of the Muslim Brotherhood in Egypt." *International Journal of Middle East Studies* 27 (1995): n. p.

Abi-Mershed, Osama. *Trajectories of Education in the Arab World: Legacies and Challenges.* New York: Routledge, 2007.

Abou El Fadel, Khaled. *The Great Theft: Wrestling Islam from the Extremists.* San Francisco: Harper, 2005.

Aboul Enein, Ahmed. "Electoral monitors report referendum violations." *Daily News Egypt.* December 15, 2012. Accessed January 28, 2013. http://www.dailynews-egypt.com/2012/12/15/electoral-monitors-report-referendum-violations/.

"About the Kurdistan Regional Government." *The Kurdistan Regional Government.* Accessed June 24, 2013. http://www.krg.org/p/p. aspx?l=12&s=030000&r=314&p=224.

Acharya, Amitav. "How Ideas Spread: Whose Norms Matter? Norm Localization and Institutional Change in Asian Regionalism." *International Organization* 58.02 (2004): 239–75.

"After Tahrir: Egyptians Assess Their Government, Their Institutions, and Their Future." *Zogby Research Service.* June 2013. Accessed June 24, 2013. http:// www.zogbyresearchservices.com/zrs/Zogby_Research_Services_ZRS_Home_ files/Egypt%20June%202013%20FINAL.pdf.

Agrama, Hussein Ali. "Secularism, Sovereignty and Indeterminacy: Is Egypt a Secular or a Religious State?" *Comparative Studies in Society and History* 52.3 (2010): 495–523.

"'Ahl Al-Bayt' yaslam risala ila Sheikh Al-Azhar wal-Mufti wal-Baba Shenouda." *Al-Youm Al-Saabi'*. April 17, 2011. Accessed June 18, 2013. http://www.youm7. com/News.asp?newsID=392970.

Ahmed, Akbar S. *Jinnah, Pakistan and Islamic Identity: The Search for Saladin*. London: Routledge, 1997.

Ahmed, Amir. "Islamists claim victory in 1st round of Egypt referendum." *CNN*. December 16, 2012. Accessed January 28, 2013. http://www.cnn. com/2012/12/16/world/meast/egypt-referendum/index.html.

Ahram, Ariel. "Iraq and Syria: The Dilemma of Dynasty." *Middle East Quarterly* 9.2 (2002): n. p.

"Ahram Online Editor Says Brotherhood Drove Him Out of Institution." *Jadaliyya*. February 17, 2013. Accessed June 25, 2013. http://www.jadaliyya.com/pages/ index/10236/ahram-online-editor-says-brotherhood-drove-him-out.

"Alaa Abul Azayem." *Islamopedia Online*. Accessed June 20, 2013. http://www. islamopediaonline.org/profile/alaa-abul-azayem.

"Al Ahram sends editor into early retirement; Brotherhood to blame?" *Egypt Independent*, January 18, 2013. Accessed January 28, 2013. http://www.egyptin- dependent.com/news/al-ahram-sends-editor-early-retirement-brotherhood-blame.

"Al Qaeda and the faltering Sahwa movement." *Islamopedia*. Accessed January 28, 2013. http://www.islamopediaonline.org/country-profile/iraq/transnational- influence/al-qaeda-and-faltering-sahwa-movement.

Alam, A. "Islam and Post-Modernism: Locating the Rise of Islamism in Turkey." *Journal of Islamic Studies* 20.3 (2009): 352–75.

Alami, Mona. "Egypt constitution will be bad news for women, activists say." *USA Today*. January 11, 2013. Accessed January 13, 2013. http://www.usatoday. com/story/news/world/2013/01/11/egypt-constitution-women-rights/1784135/.

Ali, Ahmed. "The Revival of the Islamic Supreme Council of Iraq: 2013 Iraq Update #28." *Institute for the Study of War*. July 2013. Accessed August 6, 2013. http:// iswiraq.blogspot.com/2013/07/the-revival-of-islamic-supreme-council.html.

"Ali Laarayedh." *Tunisia Live*. December 17, 2011. Accessed June 24, 2013. http:// www.tunisia-live.net/whoswho/ali-laarayedh/.

Aliriza, Fadil. "Future of women's rights in Tunisia remains in doubt." *Egypt Independent*, July 12, 2012. http://www.egyptindependent.com/news/future- womens-rights-tunisia-remains-doubt.

"Al-Gamaa Al-Islamiya Rejects Egypt's Interim Constitution." *Ahram Online*. July 9, 2013. Accessed August 5, 2013. http://english.ahram.org.eg/ NewsContentP/1/76081/Egypt/AlGamaa-AlIslamiya-rejects-Egypts-interim- constitu.aspx.

"Al-intikhaabaat fii 21 jaam'a: 34% lil-ikhwaan wa 66% lit-tayyaaraat al-madaniya wal-mustaqilliin." *Al-Masry Al-Yawm*. March 21, 2013. Accessed June 24, 2013, http://www.almasryalyoum.com/node/1583896.

Al-Kufa News Agency. June 24, 2013. Accessed August 18, 2013. http://www.alku- fanews.com/news.php?action=view&id=9935.

Al-Masry Al-Youm. Accessed October 6, 2012. http://www.almasry-alyoum.com/ article2.aspx?ArticleID=231189&IssueID=1573.

Al-Tawy, Ayat. "Churches Torched across Egypt in Anti-Coptic Violence by Morsi loyalists." *Ahram Online*. August 15, 2013. Accessed August 15, 2013. http:// english.ahram.org.eg/NewsContent/1/64/79124/Egypt/Politics-/Churches-torched-across-Egypt-in-antiCoptic-violen.aspx.

"Al-qabad 'ala al-salafi Abu Zaid Al-Tounsi." *BBC News Arabic*. April 3, 2013. Accessed June 22, 2013. http://www.bbc.co.uk/arabic/middlee-ast/2013/04/130403_tunisian_salafist_abou_zeid.shtml.

"Al-Wasat Party calls for urgent 'national reconciliation' meeting." *Al-Ahram*. June 15, 2013. Accessed June 20, 2013. http://english.ahram.org.eg/NewsContent/1/64/74054/Egypt/Politics-/AlWasat-Party-calls-for-urgent-national-reconcilia.aspx.

"Religious Freedom and Persecution in Egypt." *American Center for Law and Justice*. June 4, 2009. Accessed January 23, 2013. http://media.aclj.org/pdf/egypt_memo.pdf.

Amir Arjomand, S. "Axial Civilizations, Multiple Modernities, and Islam." *Journal of Classical Sociology* 11.3 (2011): 327–35.

el-Amrani, Issandr. "When Protest Serves Power." *International Herald Tribune*, October 23, 2012. http://latitude.blogs.nytimes.com/2012/10/23/a-first-protest-against-the-muslim-brotherhood-consecrates-its-hold-on-power/.

Anderson, J. N. D. "The Tunisian Law of Personal Status." *International and Comparative Law Quarterly* 7.2 (1958): 262–79.

Anderson, Liam D. and Gareth R. V. Stansfield. *The Future of Iraq: Dictatorship, Democracy, or Division?* New York: Palgrave Macmillan, 2004.

"Anti-Islam film: US Condemns Pakistan minister's bounty." *BBC Online*, September 23, 2012. Accessed January 23, 2013. http://www.bbc.co.uk/news/world-asia-19692971.

Ant, Onur. "Erdogan Facing Elections Can't Count on Basci Aid: Turkey Credit." *Bloomberg*. July 17, 2013. Accessed August 9, 2013. http://www.bloomberg.com/news/2013-07-16/erdogan-facing-elections-can-t-count-on-basci-aid-tur-key-credit.html.

Antlöv, Hans, Derick W. Brinkerhoff, and Elke Rapp. "Civil Society Organizations and Democratic Reform: Progress, Capacities, and Challenges in Indonesia." *37th Annual Conference, Association for Research on Nonprofit Organizations and Voluntary Action*. November 2008. http://www.rti.org/pubs/antlov_csos_in_indo_arnova.pdf.

Arango, Tim. "In Iraq, Bottoms Up For Democracy." *The New York Times*. April 16, 2011. Accessed August 15, 2013. http://www.nytimes.com/2011/04/17/weekinreview/17booze.html.

"Syrian war's spillover threatens a fragile Iraq." *New York Times*, September 24, 2012. Accessed January 28, 2013. http://www.nytimes.com/2012/09/25/world/middlee-ast/iraq-faces-new-perils-from-syrias-civil-war.html?pagewanted=all&_r=0.

"Army: Kurdish move in disputed Iraqi province 'dangerous'." *Al-Arabiya*. April 27, 2013. Accessed June 28, 2013. http://english.alarabiya.net/en/News/middle-east/2013/04/27/Kurdish-forces-deploy-near-Iraq-s-disputed-Kirkuk.html.

Asad, Talal. *Genealogies of Religion: Discipline and Reasons of Power in Christianity and Islam*. Baltimore, MD: Johns Hopkins University Press, 1993.

Formations of the Secular: Christianity, Islam, Modernity. Stanford, CA: Stanford University Press, 2003.

Ashiwa, Yoshiko and David L. Wank. *Making Religion, Making the State: The Politics of Religion in Modern China*. Stanford, CA: Stanford University Press, 2009.

Aslan, Reza. "The Islam debate Egypt needs." *The Washington Post*. August 4, 2011. Accessed August 19, 2013. http://www.washingtonpost.com/blogs/on-faith/post/the-islam-debate-egypt-needs/2011/08/04/gIQAw47Hui_blog.html.

Atty, Mohamed Abdel. "International institutions offered to finance Egypt economy, says minister," *Al-Masry Al-Youm*, February 16, 2011. Accessed January 28, 2013. http://www.egyptindependent.com/news/international-institutions-offered-finance-egypt-economy-says-minister.

Awan, Jawad R. "Alliance between PPP, PML-Q unofficially over." *The Nation*. June 6, 2013. Accessed June 20, 2013. http://www.nation.com.pk/pakistan-news-newspaper-daily-english-online/national/06-Jun-2013/alliance-between-ppp-pml-q-unofficially-over.

Aydin, Cemil. *The Politics of Anti-Westernism in Asia: Visions of World Order in Pan-Islamic and Pan-Asian Thought*. New York: Columbia University Press, 2007.

Ayoob, Mohammed. *The Many Faces of Political Islam*. Ann Harbour, University of Michigan Press, 2008.

Azak, Umut. *Islam and Secularism in Turkey: Kemalism, Religion and the Nation State*. London: I. B. Tauris, 2010.

"Azhar Grand Imam allows peaceful opposition." *State Information Service*. June 24, 2013. Accessed June 24, 2013. http://www.sis.gov.eg/En/Templates/Articles/tmpArticleNews.aspx?ArtID=68643.

"Azhar, U.S. join condemnation over Shia murders." *Egypt Independent*. June 24, 2013. Accessed June 24, 2013. http://www.egyptindependent.com/news/azhar-us-join-condemnation-over-shia-murders.

Aziz, T. M. "The Role of Muhammad Baqir Al-Sadr in Shii Political Activism in Iraq from 1958–1980." *International Journal of Middle East Studies* 25.2 (1993): 207–22.

Bacha, Ali Hazrat. "PML-Q wants end to drone strikes." *Dawn.com*, December 20, 2012. Accessed June 21, 2013. http://dawn.com/news/772808/pml-q-wants-end-to-drone-attacks.

Bahadur, Kalim. *The Jama'at-i-Islami of Pakistan: Political Thought and Political Action*. New Delhi: Chetana Publications, 1977.

"Bahais cannot enroll in public schools, education minister says." *Egypt Independent*. January 6, 2013. Accessed June 18, 2013. http://www.egyptindependent.com/news/bahais-cannot-enroll-public-schools-education-minister-says.

Bahgat, Hossam. "Criminalizing Incitement to Religious Hatred – Egypt Case Study." *Office of the High Commissioner on Human Rights*. Accessed June 18, 2013. http://www2.ohchr.org/english/issues/opinion/articles1920_iccpr/docs/Hossam_Nairobi.pdf.

Bale, Tim and Aleks Szczerbiak. "Why Is There No Christian Democracy in Poland – and Why Should We Care?" *Party Politics*, May 30, 2008. http://ppq.sagepub.com/content/14/4/479.

Barakat, Sultan. "Post-Saddam Iraq: Deconstructing a Regime, Reconstructing a Nation." *Third World Quarterly* 26.4–5 (2005): 571–91.

Barber, Matthew. "Clerics In Egypt Call For Global Jihad Against Regime's Shiite Allies." *Eurasia Review*. June 18, 2013. Accessed June 18, 2013. http://www.eurasiareview.com/18062013-clerics-in-egypt-call-for-global-jihad-against-regimes-shiite-allies-oped/.

Batatu, Hanna. "Iraq's Underground Shi'a Movements: Characteristics, Causes and Prospects." *Middle East Journal* 35.4 (1981): 578–94.

The Old Social Classes and the Revolutionary Movements of Iraq: A Study of Iraq's Old Landed and Commercial Classes and of Its Communists, Ba'thists, and Free Officers. Princeton, NJ: Princeton University Press, 1978.

Batnitzky, Leora Faye. *How Judaism Became a Religion: An Introduction to Modern Jewish Thought.* Princeton, NJ: Princeton University Press, 2011.

Bayat, Asef. "Revolution without Movement, Movement without Revolution: Comparing Islamic Activism in Iran and Egypt." *Comparative Studies in Society and History* 40.1 (1998): 136–69.

"The Coming of a Post-Islamist Society," *Critique: Critical Middle East Studies.* 1996. Accessed January 21, 2013. https://openaccess.leidenuniv.nl/bitstream/handle/1887/9768/12_606_020.pdf?sequence=1.

Bayoumi, Alaa. "Egypt's Salafis split ahead of elections." *Al-Jazeera.* January 14, 2013. Accessed June 18, 2013. http://www.aljazeera.com/indepth/features/2013/01/201311410504796074 9.html.

Beaman, Lori G. "The Myth of Pluralism, Diversity, and Vigor: The Constitutional Privilege of Protestantism in the United States and Canada." *Journal for the Scientific Study of Religion* 42.3 (2003): 311–25.

Behuria, Ashok K. "Sects within Sect: The Case of Deoband-Barelvi Encounter in Pakistan." *Strategic Analysis* 32.1 (2008): 57–80.

Bell, Daniel. "The Return of the Sacred? The Argument on the Future of Religion." *British Journal of Sociology* 28.4 (1977): 420–49.

Bellin, Eva. "The Robustness of Authoritarianism Reconsidered: Lessons of the Arab Spring." *Comparative Politics* 44. 2 (2012): 127–149.

Ben Bouazza, Bouazza. "Amina Tyler Trial: Tunisians Protest Outside Of FEMEN Activist Court Case." *Associated Press.* May 30, 2013. Accessed August 9, 2013. http://www.huffingtonpost.com/2013/05/30/amina-tyler-trial-tunisians-protest-outside-femen-activist-court-case_n_3358736.html.

"Tunisia security blocks salafi conference." *Salon.* May 19, 2013. Accessed June 22, 2013. http://www.salon.com/2013/05/19/tunisia_security_blocks_salafi_conference_3/.

Beneke, Chris and Christopher S. Grenda (eds.). *The First Prejudice: Religious Tolerance and Intolerance in Early America.* Philadelphia: University of Pennsylvania Press, 2011.

Benoit-Lavelle, Mischa. "New Tunisian Government Faces Old Challenges." *Al-Monitor.* March 10, 2013. Accessed June 22, 2013. http://www.al-monitor.com/pulse/originals/2013/03/tunisia-new-government-technocrat-challenges.html.

Berger, Maurits. "Apostasy and Public Policy in Contemporary Egypt: An Evaluation of Recent Cases from Egypt's Highest Courts." *Human Rights Quarterly* 25.3 (2003): 720–40.

Berlinski, Claire. "Turkey's agony – how Erdogan turned a peaceful protest into a violent nightmare." *The Spectator.* June 15, 2013. Accessed June 20, 2013. http://www.spectator.co.uk/features/8934351/turkeys-agony-the-view-from-taksim-square/.

Bhargava, Rajeev. "States, religious diversity, and the crisis of secularism." *Open Democracy.* March 22, 2011. Accessed March 23, 2011. http://www.opendemocracy.net/rajeev-bhargava/states-religious-diversity-and-crisis-of-secularism-o.

"Biography." *Office of Sayed Mahdi Almodarresi.* Accessed June 20, 2013. http://www.modarresi.org/english/biography.htm.

Boulby, Marion. "The Islamic Challenge: Tunisia since Independence." *Third World Quarterly* 10.2 (1988): 590–614.

Blair, David. "April Iraq's deadliest month in almost five years." *The Telegraph.* May 2, 2013. Accessed June 24, 2013. http://www.telegraph.co.uk/news/worldnews/middleeast/iraq/10032814/April-Iraqs-deadliest-month-in-almost-five-years.html.

Bradley, Allan. "Tunisian Election Results Tables." *Tunisia Live.* October 24, 2011. Accessed July 22, 2012. http://www.tunisia-live.net/2011/10/24/tunisian-election-results-tables/.

"Breastfeeding fatwa sheikh back at Egypt's Azhar." *Al-Arabiya.* May 18, 2009. Accessed August 13, 2013. http://www.alarabiya.net/articles/2009/05/18/73140.html.

"Brotherhood puts forward three members for governorships." *Egyptian Independent.* January 13, 2013. Accessed January 28, 2013. http://www.egyptindependent.com/news/brotherhood-puts-forward-three-members-governorships.

"Brotherhood's FJP condemns violent protests over new Islamist governors." *Ahram Online.* June 19, 2013. Accessed June 21, 2013. http://english.ahram.org.eg/NewsContent/1/64/74430/Egypt/Politics-/Brotherhoods-FJP-condemns-violent-protests-over-ne.aspx.

Brown, Nathan, J., "Islam and Politics in the New Egypt." *The Carnegie Papers.* Washingtion, DC: Carnegie Endowment for International Peace, 2013.

"Post-Revolutionary Al-Azhar." *The Carnegie Papers.* Washington, DC: Carnegie Endowment for International Peace, 2011.

Brown, Nathan J. et al. "Inscribing the Islamic Sharia in Arab Constitutional Law." In *Islamic Law and the Challenges of Modernity.* Edited by Yvonne Yazbeck Haddad and Barbara Freyer Stowasser. Walnut Creek, CA: Altamira Press, 2004.

Brown, Nathan J. and Amr Hamzawy. "The Draft Party Platform of the Egyptian Muslim Brotherhood: Foray into Political Integration or Retreat into Old Positions? – Carnegie Endowment for International Peace." *Carnegie Endowment for International Peace.* N.p., 2008. Accessed July 24, 2012. http://www.carnegieendowment.org/2008/01/14/draft-party-platform-of-egyptian-muslim-brotherhood-foray-into-political-integration-or-retreat-into-old-positions/4va.

Brumberg, Daniel. "Foreign Policy Magazine." *Foreign Policy.* December 19, 2011. Accessed July 23, 2012. http://mideast.foreignpolicy.com/posts/2011/12/19/sustaining_mechanics_of_arab_autocracies.

Bruton, F. Brinley and Ammar Cheikhomar. "Syrian refugees targeted in Turkish town." *NBC News.* May 27, 2013. Accessed June 21, 2013. http://worldnews.nbcnews.com/_news/2013/05/27/18473267-syrian-refugees-targeted-in-turkish-town?lite.

Bunzel, Cole. "Jihadism's Widening Internal Divide: Intellectual Infighting Heats Up." *Jihadica.* January 29, 2013. Accessed June 27, 2013. http://www.jihadica.com/jihadism%E2%80%99s-widening-internal-divide-intellectual-infighting-heats-up.

Burgat, François and William Dowell. *The Islamic Movement in North Africa.* Austin: Center for Middle Eastern Studies, University of Texas, 1993.

Burgis, Michelle. "Faith in the State? Traditions of Territoriality, International Law and the Emergence of Modern Arab Statehood." *Journal of the History of International Law* 11.1 (2009): 37–79.

Byman, Daniel. "After the Hope of the Arab Spring, the Chill of an Arab Winter." *Washington Post.* December 1, 2011. December 20, 2011.

Calabrese, John. "The Regional Implications of the Syria Crisis." *Middle East Institute*. December 21, 2012. Accessed June 21, 2013. http://www.mei.edu/content/regional-implications-syria-crisis.

Calhoun, Craig J., Mark Juergensmeyer, and Jonathan van Antwerpen. *Rethinking Secularism*. Oxford: Oxford University Press, 2011.

Camau, Michel and Vincent Geisser. *Le Syndrome Autoritaire: La Politique En Tunisie De Bourguiba a Ben Ali*. Paris: Presses De Sciences-po, 2004.

Carré, Olivier. "L'Ideologie Politico-religieuse Nasserienne a La Lumiere Des Manuels Scolaires." *Politique Etrangere* 37 (1972): 535–53.

La Légitimation islamique des socialismes arabes. Analyse conceptuelle combinatoire de manuels scolaires égyptiens, syriens et irakiens. Paris: Presses FNSP (Sciences Po), 1979.

Casanova, José. "Religion, European Secular Identities, and European Integration." In *Religion in an Expanding Europe*. Edited by Timothy Byrnes and Peter Katzenstein, 65–92. Ithaca, NY: Cornell University Press, 2006.

Cavdar, Gamze. "Islamist New Thinking in Turkey: A Model for Political Learning?" *Political Science Quarterly* 121.3 (2006): 477–97.

Cesari, Jocelyne. *Why the West Fears Islam: An Exploration of Muslims in Liberal Democracies*. New York: Palgrave Macmillan, 2013.

Chandra, Siddharth and Douglas Kammen. "Generating Reforms and Reforming Generations: Military Politics in Indonesia's Democratic Transition and Consolidation." *World Politics* 55:1. October 2002. 96–136.

Charrad, Mounira. *States and Women's Rights: The Making of Postcolonial Tunisia, Algeria, and Morocco*. Berkeley: University of California Press, 2001.

Chaves, Mark, Peter J. Schraeder, and Mario Sprindys. "State Regulation of Religion and Muslim Religious Vitality in the Industrialized West." *The Journal of Politics* 56.4 (1994): 1087–97.

Cheviron, Nicolas. "Acclaimed Turkish pianist Say on trial for blasphemy." *AFP*. October 18, 2012. Accessed January 24, 2013. http://www.google.com/hostednews/afp/article/ALeqM5iiooqomrIJRW3FpzK1e6XDEtHSYw?d>ocId=CNG. b7490d699f872ba1c830ddc9ac429b95.31.

Chishti, Faiz Ali. *Betrayals of Another Kind: Islam, Democracy and the Army in Pakistan*. Cincinnati, OH: Stosius, 1990.

Chulov, Martin. "Qais al-Khazali: from kidnapper and prisoner to potential leader." *The Guardian*. December 31, 2009. Accessed June 25, 2013. http://www.guardian.co.uk/world/2009/dec/31/iran-hostages-qais-al-khazali.

Churchill, Erik. "Tunisia's Electoral Lesson: The Importance of Campaign Strategy." *Carnegie Endowment*. October 27, 2011. Accessed July 22, 2012. http://carnegieendowment.org/2011/10/27/tunisia-s-electoral-lesson-importance-of-campaign-strategy/6b7g.

"Clashes break out at Egyptian church over kidnapping rumours." *Ahram Online*. February 28, 2013. Accessed June 18, 2013. http://english.ahram.org.eg/NewsContent/1/64/65830/Egypt/Politics-/Clashes-break-out-at-Egyptian-church-over-kidnappi.aspx.

Cline, Lawrence E. "The Prospects of the Shi'a Insurgency Movement in Iraq." *Journal of Conflict Studies* 20.20 (n.d.): n. p.

Cockburn, Patrick. "Iraqi army losing hold on north to Sunni and Kurdish forces as troops desert." *The Independent*. April 28, 2013. Accessed June 24, 2013.

http://www.independent.co.uk/news/world/middle-east/iraqi-army-los-ing-hold-on-north-to-sunni-and-kurdish-forces-as-troops-desert-8591762 .html.

Cole, Juan Ricardo and Nikki R. Keddie. *Shi'ism and Social Protest*. New Haven, CT: Yale University Press, 1986.

"Consensus Urged on Tunisia Constitution." *Maghrebia*. July 25, 2013. Accessed August 4, 2013. http://magharebia.com/en_GB/articles/awi/features/2013/07/25/ feature-01.

"Contested Sufi Electoral Parties: The Voice of Freedom Party and the Liberation of Egypt Party." *Islamopedia Online*. Accessed January 28, 2013. http://www. islamopediaonline.org/country-profile/egypt/islam-and-electoral-parties/ contested-sufi-electoral-parties-voice-freedom-par.

"Coptic Church submits demands to Morsy." *Egypt Independent*. April 10, 2013. Accessed June 21, 2013. http://www.egyptindependent.com/news/coptic-church-submits-demands-morsy.

"Coptic tourism minister denies offer of Egypt vice-presidency." *Ahram Online*. July 8, 2012. Accessed June 21, 2013. http://english.ahram.org.eg/ NewsContent/3/12/47134/Business/Economy/Coptic-tourism-minister-denies-offer-of-Egypt-vice.aspx.

Corbett, Michael and Julia Corbett Mitchell. *Politics and Religion in the United States*, first edition. Abingdon: Taylor and Francis, 1999.

Coskun, Orhan and Nick Tattersall. "Erdogan's ambition weighs on hopes for new Turkish constitution." *Reuters*. February 18, 2013. Accessed June 21, 2013. http://www.reuters.com/article/2013/02/18/us-turkey-constitution-idUSBRE91H0C220130218.

"Crime Rates in Post-Revolutionary Egypt Soar Amid Security Woes." *Al-Arabiya*. May 4, 2013. Accessed August 9, 2013. http://english.alarabiya.net/en/News/ middle-east/2013/05/04/Crime-rate-soars-in-post-revolutionary-Egypt-amid-security-woes.html.

"Crowds in Cairo praise Morsi's army overhaul." *Al-Jazeera*. August 13, 2012. Accessed January 28, 2013. http://www.aljazeera.com/news/middlee-ast/2012/08/201281215511142445.html.

Dabash, Hamdi and Usama Al-Mahdi. "Balagh lil-Na'ib al-'Am yatahim Hasan wal-Huweiny wa Borhamy wa rumuz 'al-Salafiyya' bitharat al-fatna al-Ta'ifiyya bi-tamwiil sa'udi." *Al-Masry Al-Youm*. June 6, 2011. Accessed June 18, 2013. http://today.almasryalyoum.com/article2.aspx?ArticleID=298862.

Danchev, Alex and John MacMillan. *The Iraq War and Democratic Politics*. London: Routledge, 2005.

Danopoulos, Constantine P. "Religion, civil society, and democracy in Orthodox Greece." *Journal of Southern Europe and the Balkans* 6.1 (April 2004): 41–55.

Daoud, Hussein Ali. "Iraq More Divided Than Ever." *Al-Monitor*. May 20, 2013. Accessed June 18, 2013. http://www.al-monitor.com/pulse/politics/2013/05/ iraq-protests-saadi-initiative-divided.html.

Daragahi, Borzou. "Tunisia: Economic revival depends on banking reconstruc-tion." *Financial Times*. May 28, 2013. Accessed June 22, 2013. http:// www.ft.com/intl/cms/s/0/7a8978c4-c196-11e2-9767-00144feab7de. html#axzz2X0BFyg4T.

Al-Darwish, Qusayy Salih. "Yahduthu fi Tunis." In *The Politicization of Islam: A Case Study of Tunisia*. Edited by Mohamed Elhachmi Hamdi. Boulder, CO: Westview Press, 1998.

Davie, Grace, Linda Woodhead, and Paul Heelas. *Predicting Religion: Christian, Secular, and Alternative Futures*. Aldershot, England: Ashgate Publishers, 2003.

Deeb, Lara and Mona Harb. "Politics, Culture, Religion: How Hizbullah Is Constructing an Islamic Milieu in Lebanon." *Review of Middle East Studies* 43.2 (2010): 198–206.

Devlin, John F. "The Baath Party: Rise and Metamorphosis." *The American Historical Review* 96.5 (1991): 1396.

"Discrimination against Sunnis and the question of federalism revived." *Islamopedia Online*. Accessed January 28, 2013. http://www.islamopediaonline.org/country-profile/iraq/islam-and-major-political-movements/discrimination-against-sunnis-and-question-.

Dombey, Daniel. "Alcohol laws spark renewed religious debate in Turkey." *The Financial Times*. May 29, 2013. Accessed June 21, 2013. http://www.ft.com/intl/cms/s/0/161dddae-c870-11e2-8cb7-00144feab7de.html#axzz2WpIujkmF.

Doumato, Eleanor Abdella and Gregory Starrett. *Teaching Islam: Textbooks and Religion in the Middle East*. Boulder, CO: Lynne Rienner Publishers, 2007.

Duara, Prasenjit. *Rescuing History from the Nation: Questioning Narratives of Modern China*. Chicago, IL: University of Chicago Press, 1995.

Duits, Linda and Liesbet van Zoonen. "Headscarves and Porno-Chic: Disciplining Girls' Bodies in the European Multicultural Society." *European Journal of Women's Studies* 13 (2006): 103–17.

Durrani, Naureen and Mairead Dunne. "Curriculum and National Identity: Exploring the Links between Religion and Nation in Pakistan." *Journal of Curriculum Studies* 42.2 (2010): 215–40.

Earle, Edward Mead. "The New Constitution of Turkey." *Political Science Quarterly* 40.1 (1925): 73–100.

Eddin, Mohamed Hossan. "Wafd Party considers pulling out of NSF." *Egypt Independent*. April 19, 2013. Accessed August 15, 2013. http://www.egyptindependent.com/news/wafd-party-considers-pulling-out-nsf.

"Wafd Party says Brotherhood wants civil war." *Egypt Independent*. July 16, 2013. Accessed August 15, 2013. http://www.egyptindependent.com/news/wafd-party-says-brotherhood-wants-civil-war.

"Egypt." *International Freedom Report*. 2012. Accessed June 18, 2013. http://www.state.gov/documents/organization/208598.pdf.

"Egypt: Al-Gamaa Al-Islamiya Demands Interim President Resignation." *Aswat Masriya*. July 7, 2013. Accessed August 5, 2013. http://allafrica.com/stories/201307070139.html.

"Egypt budget deficit reaches $29 bn in 1st 11 months of 2012/13." *Ahram Online*. June 21, 2013. Accessed June 22, 2013. http://english.ahram.org.eg/NewsContent/3/12/74591/Business/Economy/Egypt-budget-deficit-reaches--bn-in-st--months-of-.aspx.

"Egypt churches withdraw from Morsi's national dialogue." *Al-Ahram Online*. January 24, 2013. Accessed January 28, 2013. http://english.ahram.org.eg/NewsContent/1/64/63180/Egypt/Politics-/Egypt-churches-withdraw-from-Morsis-national-dialo.aspx.

"Egypt destroys textbooks praising Mursi, Brotherhood," *Gulf News*, September 16 2013. Accessed September 13, 2013. http://gulfnews.com/news/region/egypt/egypt-destroys-textbooks-praising-mursi-brotherhood-1.1232182

"Egypt Islamist Figures Set 3 Demands in Meeting with El-Sisi." *Ahram Online*. August 4, 2013. Accessed August 16, 2013. http://english.ahram.org.eg/NewsContent/1/64/78256/Egypt/Politics-/Egypt-Islamist-figures-set–demands-in-meeting-wit.aspx

"Egypt New Interim President: Judge Adly Mansour." Accessed July 3, 2013. http://english.ahram.org.eg/NewsContent/1/64/75638/Egypt/Politics-/Egypts-new-interim-president-Judge-Adly-Mansour.aspx

"Egypt's Morsi 'will not attend' Coptic pope ceremony," *AFP*, November 12, 2012, Accessed October 1 2013. http://www.google.com/hostednews/afp/article/ALeqM5hpUR4Y2wpRHcyuplpEh9ZBpiCsMg?docId%3DCNG.cddd441c7c4ca34f51e4e1f72f107e16.1e1

"Egypt Opinion Polls Reveal Dissatisfaction with Morsi." *Ahram Online*. July 2, 2013. Accessed August 18, 2013. http://english.ahram.org.eg/NewsContent/1/64/75491/Egypt/Politics-/Egypt-opinion-polls-reveal-dissatisfaction-with-Mo.aspx

"Egypt Opinion Poll Reveals Dissatisfaction with Morsi." Accessed July 3, 2013. http://english.ahram.org.eg/NewsContent/1/152/75491/Egypt/Morsi,-one-year-on/Egypt-opinion-polls-reveal-dissatisfaction-with-Mo.aspx

"Egypt Protesters Breach U.S. embassy over 'insulting' film." *BBC Online*, September 11, 2012. Accessed January 23, 2013. http://www.bbc.co.uk/news/world-middle-east-19562688

"Egypt Says Sinai Patrols Kill 60 Militants since Morsi Ouster." *The Jerusalem Post*. August 7, 2013. Accessed August 9, 2013. http://www.jpost.com/Middle-East/Egypt-says-Sinai-patrols-kill-60-militants-since-Morsi-ouster-322352

"Egypt: Use of Blasphemy-like Charges Must End." *USCIRF*. April 5, 2013. Accessed June 18, 2013. http://www.uscirf.gov/news-room/press-releases/3967.html

"Egypt villagers 'proud' of killing Shiites." *Global Post*. June 24, 2013. Accessed June 25, 2013. http://www.globalpost.com/dispatch/news/afp/130624/egypt-villagers-proud-killing-shiites

"Egypt's Al-Gamaa Al-Islamiya Calls for End to Turmoil after 'Massacre'." *Ahram Online*. July 27, 2013. Accessed August 5, 2013. http://english.ahram.org.eg/NewsContent/1/64/77548/Egypt/Politics-/Egypts-AlGamaa-AlIslamiya-calls-for-end-to-turmoil.aspx

"Egypt's Al-Gamaa Al-Islamiya denies involvement in 1997 Luxor massacre." *Ahram Online*. June 19, 2013. Accessed June 20, 2013. http://english.ahram.org.eg/NewsContent/1/64/74458/Egypt/Politics-/Egypts-AlGamaa-AlIslamiya-denies-involvement-in--L.aspx

"Egypt's Constitutional Decree Crisis." *Al-Jazeera Center for Studies*. December 6, 2012. Accessed January 28, 2013. http://studies.aljazeera.net/en/positionpapers/2012/12/2012126742876179.htm

"Egypt's Coptic pope criticises Morsi over cathedral attacks." *Ahram Online*. April 9, 2013. Accessed June 21, 2013. http://english.ahram.org.eg/NewsContent/1/64/68830/Egypt/Politics-/Egypts-Coptic-pope-criticises-Morsi-over-cathedral.aspx

"Egypt's Draft Constitution Translated." *Egyptian Independent*. December 2, 2012. Accessed January 21, 2013. http://www.egyptindependent.com/news/egypt-s-draft-constitution-translated

"Egypt's Interim Constitutional Declaration Draws Criticisms." *Ahram Online.* July 9, 2013. Accessed August 4, 2013. http://english.ahram.org.eg/NewsContent/1/64/76110/Egypt/Politics-/Egypts-interim-constitutional-declaration-draws-cr.aspx.

"Egypt's Pope says Islamist rulers neglect Copts." *Ahram Online.* April 26, 2013. Accessed June 21, 2013. http://english.ahram.org.eg/NewsContent/1/64/70168/Egypt/Politics-/Egypts-Pope-says-Islamist-rulers-neglect-Copts.aspx.

"Egypt's Salafists Divide over Mursi Ouster." *Asharq Al-Awsat.* July 5, 2013. Accessed August 5, 2013. http://m.asharq-e.com/content/1373128265623311800/Top%20Stories.

"Egypt's Salafist Parties Split, Weakening Influence." Sami-Joe Abboud. Trans. Al-Khaleej. *Al-Monitor.* January 3, 2013. Accessed January 28, 2013. http://www.al-monitor.com/pulse/politics/2013/01/salafist-schism-nour-watan-egypt.html.

"Egyptian Elections." *Jadaliyya.* January 9, 2012. Accessed June 20, 2013. http://www.jadaliyya.com/pages/index/3331/egyptian-elections_preliminary-results_updated-.

"Egyptian electricity supply outstrips national demand." *Ahram Online.* June 16, 2013. Accessed June 23, 2013. http://english.ahram.org.eg/NewsContent/3/12/74183/Business/Economy/Egyptian-electricity-supply-outstrips-national-dem.aspx.

"Egyptian pope goes into seclusion." *BBC News.* December 20, 2004. Accessed June 25, 2013. http://news.bbc.co.uk/2/hi/middle_east/4110861.stm.

Eickelman, Dale F. and James P. Piscatori. *Muslim Politics.* Princeton, NJ: Princeton University Press, 1996.

Eisenstadt, Shmuel N. *The Great Revolutions and the Civilizations of Modernity.* Leiden: Brill, 2006.

"11 Dead in Blast at JUI-F Election Rally." *The Express Tribune.* May 7, 2013. Accessed August 15, 2013. http://tribune.com.pk/story/545518/blast-at-jui-f-rally-in-hangu-leaves-several-injured/.

"11 Islamist Parties Launch 'Legitimacy Support' Alliance." *Ahram Online.* June 28, 2013. Accessed August 11, 2013. http://english.ahram.org.eg/NewsContent/1/64/75145/Egypt/Politics-/-Islamist-parties-launch-Legitimacy-Support-allian.aspx.

Elhachmi Hamdi, Mohamed. *The Politicization of Islam: A Case Study of Tunisia.* Boulder, CO: Westview Press, 1998.

Eliade, Mircea. *Myths, Dreams, and Mysteries: The Encounter between Contemporary Faiths and Archaic Realities.* New York: Harper, 1961.

Enein, Ahmed Aboul. "Morsy appoints 90 members to Shura Council." *Daily News Egypt.* December 23, 2012. Accessed January 28, 2013. http://www.dailynews-egypt.com/2012/12/23/morsy-appoints-90-members-to-shura-council/.

"English translation of the Iraqi Constitution." *United Nations Mission in Iraq.* http://portal.unesco.org/ci/fr/files/20704/11332732681iraqi_constitution_en.pdf/iraqi_constitution_en.pdf.

"Erdogan cracks down." *The Economist.* June 21, 2013. Accessed June 21, 2013. http://www.economist.com/news/europe/21579873-vicious-police-tactics-have-reclaimed-taksim-square-and-other-places-protest-high.

"Erdogan Democracy Package: What does it offer minorities?" *Al Monitor,* October 1 2013. Accessed October 1, 2013. http://www.al-monitor.com/pulse/originals/2013/09/democratization-package-kurds-turkey-minorities.html?utm_source=&utm_medium=email&utm_campaign=8280

"Erdogan's Popularity Topline." *Pew Research Service.* June 5, 2013. Accessed August 9, 2013. http://www.pewglobal.org/2013/06/05/erdogan-favorability-topline/.

Esposito, John L. *Islam and Politics.* Syracuse, NY: Syracuse University Press, 1998.

The Islamic Threat: Myth or Reality? New York: Oxford University Press, 1999.

Esposito, John L. and Mogahed, Dalia. *Who Speaks for Islam? What a Billion Muslims Really Think.* New York: Gallup Press, 2007.

European Commission. "Commission Staff Working Document: Turkey 2012 Progress Report." *Communication from the Commission to the European Parliament and the Council: Enlargement Strategy and Main Challenges 2012–2013.* October 10, 2012. Accessed January 21, 2013. http://ec.europa.eu/enlargement/pdf/key_documents/2012/package/tr_rapport_2012_en.pdf.

"European Parliament resolution on the situation in Turkey." *European Parliament.* June 12, 2013. Accessed June 21, 2013. http://www.europarl.europa.eu/sides/getDoc.do?pubRef=-//EP//NONSGML+MOTION+P7-RC-2013-0305+0+DOC+PDF+V0//EN.

"EU's Ashton 'Deeply Deplores' Deaths in Egypt Protests." *Deutsche Welle.* July 27, 2013. Accessed August 9, 2013. http://www.dw.de/eus-ashton-deeply-deplores-deaths-in-egypt-protests/a-16979554.

Ewing, Katherine. "The Politics of Sufism: Redefining the Saints of Pakistan." *The Journal of Asian Studies* 42.2 (1983): 251–68.

Ezzat, Dina. "Muslim Brotherhood figures seek Egypt diplomatic posts." *Ahram Online.* January 19, 2013. Accessed June 21, 2013. http://english.ahram.org.eg/NewsContent/1/64/62823/Egypt/Politics-/Muslim-Brotherhood-figures-seek-Egypt-diplomatic-p.aspx.

"Sinai crisis heightens tension between Egypt president, army chief." *Ahram Online.* May 21, 2013. Accessed June 22, 2013. http://english.ahram.org.eg/News/72030.aspx.

Fadel, Leila. "Liberals and leftists resign from constitution-writing panel in Egypt." *The Washington Post.* March 25, 2012. Accessed June 21, 2013. http://articles.washingtonpost.com/2012-03-25/world/35448298_1_islamist-parties-free-egyptians-ghar.

"Family accused of sparking Al-Khosous religious violence turn themselves in." *Al-Ahram Online.* April 15, 2013. Accessed June 22, 2013. http://english.ahram.org.eg/NewsContent/1/64/69273/Egypt/Politics-/Family-accused-of-sparking-AlKhosous-religious-vio.aspx.

Faraj, Mohammad 'Abdus Salam. *Jihad: The Absent Obligation.* Birmingham: Maktabah al Ansaar, 2000.

Fargues, Philippe. "Demography, Migration and Revolt in the South of the Mediterranean." In *Arab Society in Revolt, the West Mediterranean Challenge.* Edited by Merlini, Cesare, and O. Roy. Washington, DC: Brookings Institute Press, 2012, 17–46.

Farouk-Sluglett, Marion and Peter Sluglett. "The Historiography of Modern Iraq." *The American Historical Review* 96.5 (1991): 1408.

Fathy, Yasmine. "On Egypt uprising's 2nd anniversary, calls for freedom have yet to be realized." *Ahram Online.* January 24, 2013. http://english.ahram.org.eg/NewsContent/1/64/62985/Egypt/Politics-/On-Egypt-uprisings-nd-anniversary,-calls-for-freed.aspx.

Feldman, Noah. *The Rise and Fall of the Islamic State*. Princeton: Princeton University Press, 2008.

"Fii istiqbaalihi as-Saamraani, as-Sayyid Ammaar al-Hakiim yad'uu ilaa 'adam tahmiish ayyi mukawwan fii tashkiil al-hakuumaat al-mahalliya." *President of the Islamic Supreme Council of Iraq*. June 20, 2013. Accessed June 22, 2013. http://bit.ly/1aE32PH.

Findley, Carter V. *Turkey, Islam, Nationalism, and Modernity: A History, 1789–2007*. New Haven, CT: Yale University Press, 2010.

Fiss, Joelle. "Leader of Tunisia's Ruling Party: Blasphemy is Not a Crime." *Human Rights First*. June 7, 2013. Accessed June 23, 2013. http://www.humanrightsfirst.org/2013/06/07/leader-of-tunisia%E2%80%99s-ruling-party-blasphemy-is-not-a-crime/.

Fleishman, Jeffrey. "Egypt Protestors Put Their Wills on Twitter, Facebook." *Los Angeles Times*. October 18, 2011. Accessed October 19, 2011. http://articles.latimes.com/2011/oct/18/world/la-fg-egypt-twitter-wills-20111019.

"Foreign currency reserves rise to US$16 billion in May." *Egypt Independent*. June 7, 2013. Accessed June 24, 2013. http://www.egyptindependent.com/news/foreign-currency-reserves-rise-us16-billion-may.

"Former Militants of Egypt's al-Gama'a al-Islamiya Struggle for Political Success." *Jamestown Foundation. Terrorism Monitor* 10.18. September 27, 2012. http://www.unhcr.org/refworld/docid/506c37e42.html.

Fox, Jonathan. "World Separation of Religion and State Into the 21st Century." *Comparative Political Studies* 39.5 (2006): 537–69.

Fox, Jonathan and Yasemin Akbaba. "Securitization of Islam and Religious Discrimination: Religious Minorities in Western Democracies, 1990 to 2008." *Comparative European Politics*, May 13, 2013, doi: 10.1057/cep.2013.8.

Fox, Jonathan and Shmuel Sandler. "Separation of Religion and State in the Twenty-First Century: Comparing the Middle East and Western Democracies." *Comparative Politics*, 37.3 (2005): 317–35.

Fox, Jonathan and A. Schandler, *Bringing Religion into International Religions*. New York: Palgrave Macmillan, 2006.

Franganillo, Jorge Fuentelsaz and Ana Belén Soage. "The Muslim Brothers in Egypt." In *The Muslim Brotherhood: The Organization and Policies of a Global Islamist Movement*. Edited by Barry Rubin, 39–57. New York: Macmillan, 2010.

"French Foreign Minister Calls on Egypt to Release Morsi." *France 24*. July 30, 2013. Accessed August 9, 2013. http://www.france24.com/en/20130730-eus-ashton-meets-morsi-amid-renewed-cairo-protests.

Fuller, Graham E. "Islamist Politics in Iraq after Saddam Hussein." *USIP Special Report* No. 108. August 2003. http://www.usip.org/sites/default/files/sr108.pdf.

"Further competition between Tamarod and Tagarod." *Daily News Egypt*. June 22, 2013. Accessed June 24, 2013. http://www.dailynewsegypt.com/2013/06/22/further-competition-between-tamarod-and-tagarod/.

"Gama'a al-Islamiya organises pro-Morsi protests to counter 'rebellion' campaign." *Al-Bawaba*. June 6, 2013. Accessed June 20, 2013. http://www.albawaba.com/news/gamaa-al-islamiya-organises-pro-morsi-protests-counter-rebellion-campaign-497409.

Gerges, Fawaz. *The Far Enemy: Why the Jihad Became Global*. New York: Cambridge University Press, 2005.

"German Foreign Minister Westerwelle Calls for Restraint in Egypt as Protests Continue." *Deutsche Welle*. August 1, 2013. Accessed August 9, 2013. http://www.dw.de/german-foreign-minister-westerwelle-calls-for-restraint-in-egypt-as-protests-continue/a-16991415.

Al-Ghannoushi, Rachid. "al-Harakat al-ittijah al-islami fi Tunis." vol. 3. In *The Politicization of Islam: A Case Study of Tunisia*. Edited by Mohamed Elhachmi Hamdi. Boulder, CO: Westview Press, 1998.

Maqalat. Paris: Dar al-Karawan, 1984.

Ghazi, Yasir. "At Least 32 People Killed in Iraq Attacks." *New York Times*. June 25, 2013. Accessed June 26, 2013. http://www.nytimes.com/2013/06/26/world/middleeast/iraq-attacks.html.

Ghazi, Yasir and Tim Arango. "Iraq Parliament votes to keep Maliki from seeking new term." *New York Times*. January 26, 2013. Accessed January 28, 2013. http://www.nytimes.com/2013/01/27/world/middleeast/iraq-parliament-votes-to-keep-maliki-from-seeking-new-term.html.

Ghoshal, Baladas. "Democratic Transition and Political Development in Post-Soeharto Indonesia." *Contemporary Southeast Asia* 26:3 (2004): 506–529.

Gjorvad, Nicholas. "The Future of Al-Wasat Party." *Daily News Egypt*, January 16, 2013. http://www.dailynewsegypt.com/2013/01/16/the-future-of-al-wasat-party/.

"Going to the dogs." *The Economist*. March 30, 2013. Accessed June 22, 2013. http://www.economist.com/news/middle-east-and-africa/21574533-unless-president-muhammad-morsi-broadens-his-government-egypts-economy-looks.

Gollmer, Anggatira. "It's OK to be gay in Indonesia so long as you keep it quiet." *Deutsche Welle*. March 2, 2013. Accessed June 28, 2013. http://www.dw.de/its-ok-to-be-gay-in-indonesia-so-long-as-you-keep-it-quiet/a-6456222.

Goudineau, Alexandre and Noha Moustafa. "Sukuk law in state of flux until Al-Azhar review." *Egypt Independent*. April 4, 2013. Accessed June 17, 2013. http://www.egyptindependent.com/news/sukuk-law-state-flux-until-al-azhar-review.

"Government postpones dissolution of Brotherhood" *Al Ahram*, September 24, 2013, Accessed September 24, 2013. http://english.ahram.org.eg/NewsContent/1/64/82409/Egypt/Politics-/Egypt-government-postpones-dissolution-of-Brotherh.aspx.

Grasso, Christopher. "The Boundaries of Toleration and Tolerance: Religious Infidelity in the Early American Republic." In *The First Prejudice: Religious Tolerance and Intolerance in Early America*. Edited by Chris Beneke and Christopher S. Grenda, 286–302. Philadelphia: University of Pennsylvania Press, 2011.

Greenslade, Roy. "Press freedom groups condemn Turkish police violence against journalists." *The Guardian*. June 6, 2013. Accessed June 20, 2013. http://www.guardian.co.uk/media/greenslade/2013/jun/06/journalist-safety-turkey.

Grim, Brian J. and Roger Finke. *The Price of Freedom Denied: Religious Persecution and Conflict in the 21st Century*. New York: Cambridge University Press, 2011.

el Gundy, Zeinab. "Salafist split brings new choices, complications for voters." *Al Ahram Online*, January 23, 2013. Accessed January 28, 2013, http://english.ahram.org.eg/NewsContent/1/64/62908/Egypt/Politics-/Salafist-splits-bring-new-choices,-complications-f.aspx.

al-Haddad, Al-Tahir. "Al-Mara'a Bein Ash-Sharii'a wal-Fuqahaa'." *Book in the Muslim thinking: For the Seventh Year Students in Secondary Education.* Ministry of Education and Training. N.D. pp. 66–7.

Hablli, Sheikh 'Uthmaan Muhammad. "The Effect of Faith in the Society, Uniformity Among the Three Heavenly Messages." In the *Book of Islamic Education for the First Year Students, in Secondary Education.* Ministry of Education, Tunisia.

Haddad, Yvonne Yazbeck and Barbara Freyer Stowasser. *Islamic Law and the Challenges of Modernity.* Walnut Creek, CA: AltaMira, 2004.

Hadiz, Vedi R. "Reorganizing Political Power in Indonesia: A Reconsideration of So-Called 'Democratic Transitions'." *The Pacific Review* 16.4: 591–611.

Hafez, Kai. *Radicalism and Political Reform in the Islamic and Western Worlds.* Cambridge: Cambridge University Press, 2010.

Hale, William M. and Ergun Özbudun. *Islamism, Democracy and Liberalism in Turkey: The Case of the AKP.* New York: Routledge, 2010.

Halime, Farah. "Egypt's Long-Term Economic Recovery Plan Stalls." *The New York Times.* May 2, 2013. Accessed June 26, 2013. http://www.nytimes.com/2013/05/02/world/middleeast/02iht-m02-egypt-renaissance.html.

Hallaq, Wael B. *An Introduction to Islamic Law.* Cambridge, UK: Cambridge University Press, 2009.

The Impossible State: Islam, Politics, and Modernity's Moral Predicament. New York: Columbia University Press, 2012.

Hamayotsu, Kikue. "Islam and Nation Building in Southeast Asia: Malaysia and Indonesia in Comparative Perspective." *Pacific Affairs* 75.3 (2002): 353–75.

Haq, Farhat. "Pakistan: A State for the Muslims or an Islamic State?" In *Religion and Politics in South Asia.* Edited by Ali Riaz, 119–46. New York: Routledge, 2010.

Haqqānī, Husain. *Pakistan: Between Mosque and Military.* Washington, DC: Carnegie Endowment for International Peace, 2005.

Harb, Ali. "Al-Khilaafa Mu'assassa Madaniya" *Book in the Muslim Thinking: For the Third Year Students in Secondary Education.* Ministry of Education, Tunisia. n.d., 50–1.

Harris, Christina Phelps. *Nationalism and Revolution in Egypt.* Stanford, CA: Mouton, 1964.

Hasab Allah, Ali. "Al-Qur'an Mu'jiza 'Aamma" *Book in the Muslim Thinking: For the Third Year Students in High School.* Ministry of Education, Tunisia. The Pedagogical National Center. 2006.

Hasanain, Sabri. "Ishti'al harb istitla'at al-ra'i fi intikhabat ar-ri'asa al-masriyya." *Elaph.com.* May 16, 2012. http://www.elaph.com/Web/news/2012/5/736077. html.

Hashemi, Kamran. "Religious Legal Traditions, International Human Rights Law and Muslim States." *Studies in Religion, Secular Beliefs and Human Rights* 7. Boston, MA: Martinus Nijhoff Publishers, 2008.

Hassan, Rios. *Faithlines: Muslim Conceptions of Islam and Society.* Karachi: Oxford University Press, 2002.

Hefner, Robert W. and Muhammad Qasim, Zaman. *Schooling Islam: The Culture and Politics of Modern Muslim Education.* Princeton, NJ: Princeton University Press, 2007.

El-Hennawy, Noha. "With Nour Party, Salafis attempt to tap into party politics." *Egypt Independent.* May 19, 2011. Accessed June 18, 2013. http://www.egypt-independent.com/news/nour-party-salafis-attempt-tap-party-politics.

Hobsbawm, Eric. *The Age of Revolution.* London: Weidenfeld & Nicolson, 1962.

Holyoake, George Jacob. *English Secularism: A Confession of Belief.* Chicago: Open Court Publishers, 1896.

Hourani, Albert Habib. *Arabic Thought in the Liberal Age: 1798–1939.* Cambridge: Cambridge University Press, 1988.

"House Passes Defense Spending Bill Prohibiting Egypt Funds." *Business Week.* July 24, 2013. Accessed August 11, 2013. http://www.businessweek.com/news/2013-07-24/u-dot-s-dot-house-passes-pentagon-spending-bill-with-no-aid-to-egypt.

Human Rights Watch. "Tunisia: 20 Human Rights Questions for Political Parties Presenting Candidates in the October 23 Constituent Assembly Election." August 9, 2011. Accessed January 23, 2013. http://www.hrw.org/news/2011/08/09/tunisia-20-human-rights-questions-political-parties-presenting-candidates-october-23.

"Hundreds protest Egypt's constitution in Alexandria in absence of Islamists." *Ahram Online.* December 28, 2012. Accessed June 20, 2013. http://english.ahram.org.eg/NewsContent/1/64/61428/Egypt/Politics-/Hundreds-protest-Egypts-constitution-in-Alexandria.aspx.

Idle, Nadia and Alex Nunns (eds.) *Tweets from Tahrir: Egypt's Revolution as It Unfolds, in the Words of the People Who Made it.* New York: OR Books, 2011.

"IMF Freezes Talks with Egypt, Awaits International Recognition of Interim Government." *Ahram Online.* July 25, 2013. Accessed August 8, 2013. http://english.ahram.org.eg/News/77366.aspx.

"IMF Loan Aims to Help Tunisia Boost Growth, Protect Poor." *IMF Survey.* June 17, 2013. Accessed June 22, 2013. http://www.imf.org/external/pubs/ft/survey/so/2013/CAR061713A.htm.

"IMF points to 'progress' in aid talks with Egypt." *Ahram Online.* June 20, 2013. Accessed June 22, 2013. http://english.ahram.org.eg/NewsContent/3/12/74556/Business/Economy/IMF-points-to-progress-in-aid-talks-with-Egypt.aspx.

Ināyat, Hamīd. *Modern Islamic Political Thought: The Response of the Shī'ī and Sunnī Muslims to the Twentieth Century.* London: I. B. Tauris, 2005.

"Indonesia." *International Freedom Report.* 2012. Accessed June 18, 2013. http://www.state.gov/documents/organization/208444.pdf.

"Indonesia: Blasphemy law should be repealed to show Indonesia's commitment to the protection of freedom of expression." *Asian Human Rights Commission.* June 7, 2012. Accessed June 28, 2013. http://www.humanrights.asia/countries/indonesia/news/alrc-news/human-rights-council/hrc20/ALRC-CWS-20-04-2012.

"Indonesia: Religious freedom under attack as Shi'a villagers face eviction." *Amnesty International.* January 15, 2013. Accessed June 25, 2013. http://www.amnesty.org/en/news/indonesia-religious-freedom-under-attack-shia-villagers-face-eviction-2013-01-15.

"Indonesia upholds blasphemy law." *Al-Jazeera.* April 20, 2010. Accessed June 28, 2013. http://www.aljazeera.com/news/asia-pacific/2010/04/20104208101575962.html.

"Innocence of Muslims participants sentenced to death in Egypt." *The Guardian*, November 28, 2012. Accessed January 23, 2013. http://www.guardian.co.uk/ world/2012/nov/28/innocence-of-muslims-death-sentence.

"Inqisaam beyn 'an-naqaabaat al-mahaniya' hawl al-mushaaraka fii muzhaahirat '30 Yunio.'" *Al-Masry Al-Youm*. June 11, 2013. Accessed June 26, 2013. http:// www.almasryalyoum.com/node/1835021.

"Interim Constitution Rejected by Church, NSF and Salafis." *Egypt Independent*. July 10, 2013. Accessed August 4, 2013. http://www.egyptindependent.com/ news/interim-constitution-rejected-church-nsf-and-salafis.

Iqbal, Muhammad. *Speeches and Statements of Iqbal*. Lahore: Al-Manâar Academy, 1948.

Iraq Legal Development Project. "The Status of Women in Iraq: Update to the Assessment of Iraq's De jure and De facto compliance with International Legal Standards." December 2006. Accessed January 23, 2013. http://apps.americanbar.org/rol/publications/iraq_status_of_women_update_2006.pdf.

"Iraq MPs to bar Maliki from third term." *The News*, January 27, 2013. Accessed January 28, 2013. http://www.thenews.com.pk/Todays-News-1-156593-Iraq-MPs-to-bar-Maliki-from-third-term.

"Iraqi Interfaith Council Tries to Protect Minorities." *Al-Monitor*. June 11, 2013. Accessed June 13, 2013. http://www.al-monitor.com/ pulse/originals/2013/06/iraq-interfaith-dialogue-council-minorities. html?utm_source=&utm_medium=email&utm_campaign=7500.

"Iraq: July Deadliest Month in Years as Violence Kills over 1,000 People, UN Reports." *UN News Service*. August 1, 2013. Accessed August 9, 2013. http:// www.un.org/apps/news/story.asp?NewsID=45546#.UgULEGTwLIw.

"Iraq's Senior Shia Clerics Prohibit Arab-Kurdish War." *Rudaw*, July 12, 2012. Accessed January 28, 2013. http://www.rudaw.net/english/kurds/5513.html.

"Islam to remain state religion in Egypt new constitution," *Ahram Online*, September 13 2013. Accessed September 15, 2013. http://english.ahram.org. eg/NewsContent/1/64/81649/Egypt/Politics-/Islam-to-remain-state-religion-in-Egypts-new-const.aspx.

"Islamist Egyptian governor of Luxor resigns." *Al-Arabiya*. June 23, 2013. Accessed June 24, 2013. http://english.alarabiya.net/en/News/middle-east/2013/06/23/ Egypt-s-hardline-Islamist-to-resign-as-Luxor-governor.html.

"Islamists and old regime men in Morsy's Shura Council appointments." *Islamopedia Online*. Accessed January 28, 2013. http://www.islamopediaonline.org/news/ islamists-and-old-regime-men-morsys-shura-council-appointments.

"Islamists: parliamentary elections will be held next year." *Egypt Independent*. July 26, 2013. Accessed June 24, 2013. http://www.egyptindependent.com/news/ islamists-parliamentary-elections-will-be-held-next-year.

"Islamists form community police militias." *Egypt Independent*. March 12, 2013. Accessed June 24, 2013. http://www.egyptindependent.com/news/islamists-form-community-police-militias.

"Islamist Nour, Wasat Parties Cautiously Positive about Egypt Military Statement." *Ahram Online*. July 1, 2013. Accessed August 5, 2013. http://english.ahram. org.eg/NewsContent/1/64/75435/Egypt/Politics-/Islamist-Nour,-Wasat-parties-cautiously-positive-a.aspx.

al-Kadhimi, Mustafa. "Political Alliances Shift in Bagdad." *Al-Monitor*. Accessed August 14, 2013. http://www.al-monitor.com/pulse/originals/2013/06/new-iraqi-government-formation.html.

"A New Iraqi Curricula." *Islamopedia Online*, November 1, 2011. http://www.islamopediaonline.org/country-profile/iraq/islam-and-education-system/new-iraqi-curricula.

"Bahais cannot enroll in public schools, Egyptian education minister says." *Islamopedia Online*, January 8, 2013. http://www.islamopediaonline.org/news/bahais-cannot-enroll-public-schools-egyptian-education-minister-says.

"In Tunisia, a rape victim is prosecuted for 'public indecency.'" *Islamopedia Online*, October 4, 2012. http://www.islamopediaonline.org/news/tunisia-rape-victim-prosecuted-public-indecency.

"Jamaat-i-Islami (JI)." *Islamopedia Online*, October 11, 2012. http://www.islamopediaonline.org/country-profile/pakistan/islam-and-politics/jamaat-i-islami-ji.

"Jamiat Ulema-e-Islam (JUI)." *Islamopedia Online*, October 11, 2012. http://www.islamopediaonline.org/country-profile/pakistan/islam-and-politics/jamiat-ulema-e-islam-jui.

"Morsi's approval ratings rise to 63 pct: poll." *Islamopedia Online*, January 14, 2013. http://www.islamopediaonline.org/news/morsis-approval-ratings-rise-63-pct-poll.

"Pakistan Muslim League-Quaid-e-Azam (PML-Q)." *Islamopedia Online*, October 11, 2012. http://www.islamopediaonline.org/country-profile/pakistan/islam-and-politics/pakistan-muslim-league-quaid-e-azam-pml-q.

"Pakistani cleric legislator threatens the destruction of the US." *Islamopedia Online*, June 22, 2011. http://www.islamopediaonline.org/news/pakistani-cleric-legislator-threatens-destruction-us.

Al-Jalassi, Mohammad Yassin. "Is the End Coming for Ennahda's Salafist Ties?" *Al-Monitor*. January 14, 2013. Accessed June 22, 2013. http://www.al-monitor.com/pulse/contents/articles/politics/2013/05/tunisia-salafist-ennahda-relations.html.

Jacobson, David. *Of Virgins and Martyrs: Women and Sexuality in Global Conflict*. Washington, DC: Johns Hopkins University Press, 2012.

Jamal, Amaney A. *Barriers to Democracy: The Other Side of Social Capital in Palestine and the Arab World*. Princeton, NJ: Princeton University Press, 2007.

"Jaysh Rijaal at-Tariiqa an-Naqashbandia – Qaati' Gharb Ninewa – Qasaf maqarr lil-'adu al-Amriikii bi-hawn 82 milimitir" or Abo al-Qeaqaa Forums. http://bit.ly/12cVonJ.

"Jihad organization accuses judges of implementing 'Zionist' scheme." Al-Masry Al-Youm. April 12, 2012. http://www.egyptindependent.com/news/jihad-organization-accusesjudges-implementing-zionist-scheme.

Jinnah, Mohammad Ali and Jamil-ud-din Ahmad. *Speeches and Writings of Mr Jinnah*. Lahore, Pakistan: Muhammad Ashraf, 1947.

Johansen, Baber. "Apostasy as Objective and Depersonalized Fact: Two Recent Egyptian Court Judgments." *Social Research: An International Quarterly* 70.3 (2003): 687–710.

Johnston, David L. "Hassan Al-Hudaybi and the Muslim Brotherhood: Can Islamic Fundamentalism Eschew the Islamic State?" *Comparative Islamic Studies* 3.1 (2007): 39–56.

Jones, Curtis F. "The New Egyptian Constitution." *The Middle East Journal* 10 (1956 summer): 3000–7.

"June 30 and beyond: What Happens after the U.S. Transfers Power to Iraq?" *The Brookings Institution.* May 24, 2004. http://www.brookings.edu/~/media/events/2004/5/24iraq/20040524.pdf.

"JUP vows to guard blasphemy law." *The Nation.* October 15, 2012. Accessed June 20, 2013. http://www.nation.com.pk/pakistan-news-newspaper-daily-english-online/national/15-Oct-2012/jup-vows-to-guard-blasphemy-law.

al-Kadhimi, Mustafa. "Sistani Calls for 'Civil State' in Iraq." *Al-Monitor.* January 16, 2013. http://www.al-monitor.com/pulse/originals/2013/01/iraq-sistani-calls-civil-state.html.

"The New Muqtada al-Sadr Seeks Moderate Image." *Iraq Business News.* March 13, 2013. Accessed June 20, 2013. http://www.iraq-businessnews.com/2013/03/13/the-new-muqtada-al-sadr-seeks-moderate-image/.

Kagan, Kimberly. "The Iraq War is Not Over." *The Weekly Standard.* July 1, 2013. http://www.weeklystandard.com/articles/iraq-war-not-over_736876.html.

Kalyvas, Stathis. "Unsecular Politics and Religious Mobilization." In *European Christian Democracy.* Edited by T. Kselman and J. A. Buttigieg. Notre Dame, IN: University of Notre Dame Press, 2003, 293–320.

Kamber, Michael. "Iraq." *The New York Times.* December 4, 2012. Accessed January 28, 2013. http://topics.nytimes.com/top/news/international/countriesandterritories/iraq/index.html.

Kamil, Muhammad. "Al-intikhaabaat fii 21 jaam'a: 34% lil-ikhwaan wa 66% littayyaaraat al-madaniya wal-mustaqilliin." *Al-Masry Al-Youm.* March 21, 2013. Accessed June 24, 2013. http://www.almasryalyoum.com/node/1583896.

Kaplan, Benjamin J. *Divided by Faith: Religious Conflict and the Practice of Toleration in Early Modern Europe.* Cambridge, MA: Belknap of Harvard University Press, 2007.

Karpat, Kemal H. *The Politicization of Islam: Reconstructing Identity, State, Faith, and Community in the Late Ottoman State.* New York: Oxford University Press, 2001.

Karsh, Efraim. *Saddam Hussein: A Political Biography.* New York: Grove, 2003.

Katzenstein, Peter J. *Civilizations in World Politics: Plural and Pluralist Perspectives.* London: Routledge, 2010.

Katzman, Kenneth. "Iraq: Politics, Governance, and Human Rights." *Congressional Research Service.* June 3, 2013. Accessed June 24, 2013. http://www.fas.org/sgp/crs/mideast/RS21968.pdf.

Keck, Margaret E. and Kathryn Sikkink. *Activists beyond Borders: Advocacy Networks in International Politics.* Ithaca, NY: Cornell University Press, 1998.

Kepel, Gilles. *Jihad: The Trail of Political Islam.* London: I. B. Tauris, 2004.

Khalaf, Roula. "Tunisia has finally turned up the heat on the Salafis." *The Financial Times.* May 20, 2013. Accessed June 20, 2013. http://www.ft.com/cms/s/0/6b4e8ab2-c14f-11e2-9767-00144feab7de.html#axzz2WpIujkmF.

Khalaf Allah, Ahmad. "Al-Qur'an wa Tahriir al-Insaan," or "Qur'an and the Liberation of Man." *Book in the Muslim Thinking: For the Third Year Students in High School.* Ministry of Education, Tunisia. The Pedagogical National Center. 2006.

Khalaji, Mehdi. "Sistani and the End of Traditional Religious Authority in Shiism." *The Washington Institute for Near East Policy.* September 2006. Accessed January 20, 2013. http://www.washingtoninstitute.org/uploads/Documents/pubs/PolicyFocus59final.pdf.

Khalidi, Rashid. *The Origins of Arab Nationalism.* New York: Columbia University Press, 1991.

Khattab, Moushira. "Women's Rights under Egypt's Constitutional Disarray." *Wilson Center.* January 21, 2013. http://www.wilsoncenter.org/sites/default/files/womens_rights_under_egypts_constitutional_disarray.pdf.

Khazan, Olga. "Meet Egypt's Jon Stewart, who is now under investigation for satire." *Washington Post.* January 2, 2013. Accessed January 28, 2013. http://www.washingtonpost.com/blogs/worldviews/wp/2013/01/02/egypt-bassem-youssef-jon-stewart-investigation/.

Khlifi, Roua. "Despite Ban and Alleged Role in Assassination, Ansar al-Sharia Continues Activities." *Tunisia Live.* August 1, 2013. Accessed August 6, 2013. http://www.tunisia-live.net/2013/08/01/ansar-al-sharia-continues-activities-despite-ban-and-alleged-role-in-assassination/.

Kingsley, Patrick. "Egypt 'suffering worst economic crisis since 1930s.'" *The Guardian.* May 16, 2013. Accessed June 22, 2013. http://www.guardian.co.uk/world/2013/may/16/egypt-worst-economic-crisis-1930s.

Kirkpatrick, David D. and Mayy El Sheikh. "Egypt Opposition Gears Up After Constitution Passes." *New York Times.* December 23, 2012. Accessed June 20, 2013. http://www.nytimes.com/2012/12/24/world/middleeast/as-egypt-constitution-passes-new-fights-lie-ahead.html.

"Kitlat al-Matalak tahtij alaal-hakuuma wa tatakhawwaf min 'tahdiidat Asaa'ib Ahl al-Haqq'" or *Shafaaq News.* May 8, 2013. Accessed June 21, 2013. http://www.shafaaq.com/sh2/index.php/news/iraq-news/57302--qq.html.

Klausen, Jytte. *The Cartoons That Shook the World.* New Haven, CT: Yale University Press, 2009.

Knights, Michael. "The JRTN Movement and Iraq's Next Insurgency." *CTC Sentinel* 4.7 (2011): n. p.

Koplow, Michael. "Turkey's War on Journalists." *The Atlantic,* October 24, 2012. Accessed January 28, 2013. http://www.theatlantic.com/international/archive/2012/10/turkeys-war-on-journalists/264049/#.

Kortam, Hend. "Blame and Condemnation after Rabaa Violence." *Daily News Egypt.* July 28, 2013. Accessed August 5, 2013. http://www.dailynewsegypt.com/2013/07/28/blame-and-condemnation-after-rabaa-violence/.

Koundinya, Satyoki. "The Concept of Mutah Marriage: Is it a Social Evil?" RGSOIPL. 2010.

Krueger, Katherine and Ayesha Shug. "Constitutional Reform in Turkey." *Muftah.* July 8, 2013. Accessed August 5, 2013. http://muftah.org/constitutional-reform-in-turkey-and-the-recent-protests/.

Kselman, Thomas and Joseph A. Buttigieg (eds). *European Christian Democracy. Historical Legacies and Comparative Perspectives,* 293–320. Notre Dame, IN: University of Notre Dame Press, 2003.

Kuru, Ahmet T. *Secularism and State Policies toward Religion: The United States, France, and Turkey.* Cambridge: Cambridge University Press, 2009.

Lamboley, Carolyn. "Tunisia's Leading Party Reaffirms Commitment to Arab-Muslim Identity." *Tunisialive.net*, March 26, 2012. Accessed January 22, 2013. http://www.tunisia-live.net/2012/03/26/tunisias-leading-party-reaffirms-commitment-to-arab-muslim-identity/.

Landau, Jacob M. *The Politics of Pan-Islam: Ideology and Organization.* Oxford, England: Clarendon, 1990.

Lapidus, Ira M. *A History of Islamic Societies.* Cambridge: Cambridge University Press, 2002.

Lawrence, Bruce B. *Defenders of God: The Fundamentalist Revolt against the Modern Age.* San Francisco. CA: Harper & Row, 1989.

Letsch, Constanze. "Turkish composer and pianist convicted of blasphemy on Twitter." *The Guardian.* April 15, 2013. Accessed June 25, 2013. http://www.guardian.co.uk/world/2013/apr/15/turkish-composer-fazil-say-convicted-blasphemhy.

Levitsky, Steven and Lucan A. Way. "Elections without Democracy: The Rise of Competitive Authoritarianism." *Journal of Democracy* 13.2 (April 2002): 51–65.

Competitive Authoritarianism: Hybrid Regimes after the Cold War. New York: Cambridge University Press, 2005.

"Labor Organization Accuses FJP of Hindering Trade Union Freedoms Law." *Al-Masry Al-Youm.* May 30, 2012. Accessed June 26, 2013. http://www.egyptindependent.com/news/labor-organization-accuses-fjp-hindering-trade-unions%E2%80%99-freedom-law-nehal-news-1.

Loehr, Daniel. "The Palestine Clause in Tunisia's Constitution: For Whom?" June 20, 2012. Accessed January 22, 2013. http://akio.tumblr.com/post/25525886161/the-palestine-clause-in-tunisias-constitution-for.

Londoño, Ernesto. "Crackdown on Alcohol Seen as Part of Conservative Moment in Iraq." *The Washington Post.* January 4, 2010. Accessed August 15, 2013. http://www.washingtonpost.com/wp-dyn/content/article/2010/01/03/AR2010010302228.html

"U.S. lawmakers question military aid to Egypt, citing concerns about Israel." *The Washington Post.* March 2, 2013. Accessed June 24, 2013. http://articles.washingtonpost.com/2013-03-02/world/37388565_1_military-aid-conservative-islamist-group-muslim-brotherhood.

Louër, Laurence. *Transnational Shia Politics: Religious and Political Networks in the Gulf.* New York: Columbia University Press, 2008.

Loveluck, Louisa. "Egypt court rules upper house of parliament elected illegally." *The Guardian.* June 2, 2013. Accessed June 20, 2013. http://www.guardian.co.uk/world/2013/jun/02/egypt-court-rules-parliament-illegally.

Luizard, Pierre-Jean. "The Sadrists in Iraq: Challenging the United States, the Marja'iyya and Iran." In *The Shi'a Worlds and Iran.* Edited by Sabrina Mervin. New York: SAQI Books, 2010, 255–81.

"Luxor protests against Al-Gamaa Al-Islamiya govenor continue." *Ahram Online.* June 20, 2013. Accessed June 21, 2013. http://english.ahram.org.eg/NewsContent/1/64/74515/Egypt/Politics-/Luxor-protests-against-AlGamaa-AlIslamiya-govenor-.aspx.

Mackey, Sandra. *The Reckoning: Iraq and the Legacy of Saddam Hussein.* New York: Norton, 2002.

al-Mahdi, Kamaal 'Abd-Allah. "Athaar al-Imaan fiil-mujtama' 3." *Book of Islamic Education for the First Year Students in Secondary Education*. Ministry of Education, Tunisia.

"Al-Hurria Qa'idat al-Hukm." *Book in the Muslim Thinking: For the Third Year Students in High School*. Ministry of Education, Tunisia. The Pedagogical National Center. 2006.

"Al-Mahkama al-Ittihaadiya al-'Iraaqiya turudd shakilan ta'an i'tilaaf al-Maaliki bi-tahdiid wilaayaat ar-ru'saa'" or *Al-Iraq lil-Jamii'*, March 14, 2013. Accessed June 25, 2013, http://www.iraq4allnews.dk/ShowNews.php?id=51089.

Makiya, Kanan. *Republic of Fear: The Politics of Modern Iraq*. Berkeley: University of California Press, 1989.

Malik, S. Jamal. "Waqf in Pakistan: Change in Traditional Institutions." *Die Welt Des Islams* 30.1/4 (1990): 63.

al-Malky, Aly. "Salafis slam FJP over female candidate requirements in draft elections law." *Al-Masry al-Youm*, January 19, 2013. Accessed January 28, 2013. http://www.egyptindependent.com/news/salafis-slam-fjp-over-female-candidate-requirements-draft-elections-law.

"Muqaabila | Qais al-Khazali: Hizballah abraz harakat muqaawama fii al-mintaqa wal-'aalam" *Al-Akhbar*. June 20, 2012. Accessed June 24, 2013. http://www.al-akhbar.com/node/32660.

Mardin, Şerif. *Religion and Social Change in Modern Turkey: The Case of Bediuzzaman Said Nursi*, Albany: State University of New York Press, 1989.

Markey, Patrick and Samia Nakhoul. "Iraq says proxy war over Syria threatens its neutrality." *Reuters*. June 20, 2013. Accessed June 22, 2013. http://www.reuters.com/article/2013/06/20/us-iraq-syria-zebari-idUSBRE95J0B220130620.

Martini, Jeffrey et al. *The Muslim Brotherhood, Its Youth, and Implications for U.S. Engagement*. RAND National Defense Research Institute. 2012. Quoting "Rub' A'adaa' Hizb al-Hurriya wal-'Adaala Laiso Akhwaan" *Al-Youm Al-Sabi'*. May 17, 2011. http://bit.ly/18jx2kB.

Mashhour, Amira. "Islamic Law and Gender Equality: Could There Be a Common Ground?: A Study of Divorce and Polygamy in Sharia Law and Contemporary Legislation in Tunisia and Egypt." *Human Rights Quarterly* 27.2 (2005): 562–96.

"Al-Mashruu' as-siyaasi lil-hizb al-Islaami al-Iraqi" The Iraqi Islamic Party. Accessed June 22, 2013, http://www.iraqiparty.com/page/our-project/.

Masood, Wajahat. "Pakistani cleric legislator threatens the destruction of the US." *Islamopedia Online*, June 22, 2011. Accessed January 28, 2013. http://www.islamopediaonline.org/news/pakistani-cleric-legislator-threatens-destruction-us.

"Mass resignations at Al-Wasat party." *Daily News Egypt*. June 29, 2013. Accessed August 5, 2013. http://www.dailynewsegypt.com/2013/06/29/mass-resignations-at-al-wasat-party/.

"Mass resignations in Egypt's Salafist Al-Watan Party." *Ahram Online*. June 15, 2013. Accessed June 20, 2013. http://english.ahram.org.eg/NewsContent/1/64/74006/Egypt/Politics-/Mass-resignations-in-Egypts-Salafist-AlWatan-Party.aspx.

"Mawqa' Fadiilat ash-Sheikh Abi Ishaaq al-Hiweini." Accessed June 25, 2013. http://www.alheweny.org/aws/play.php?catsmktba=661.

Mayer, Ann Elizabeth. "Reform of Personal Status Laws in North Africa: A Problem of Islamic or Mediterranean Laws?" *Middle East Journal* 49.3 (1995): 432–46.

McAdam, Doug and David A. Snow. *Readings on Social Movements: Origins, Dynamics and Outcomes.* New York: Oxford University Press, 2010.

McEvers, Kelly. "Abuse of Temporary Marriages Flourishes in Iraq." *National Public Radio.* October 19, 2013. Accessed June 18, 2013. http://www.npr.org/templates/story/story.php?storyId=130350678.

McGraw, Barbara A. and Jo-Renee Formicola. *Taking Religious Pluralism Seriously: Spiritual Politics on American Sacred Ground.* Waco, TX: Baylor University Press, 2005.

Mcleod, Ross H. "The Struggle to Regain Effective Government under Democracy in Indonesia." *Bulletin of Indonesian Economic Studies* 41.3 (2005): 367–386.

"Media Use in the Middle East: an Eight-Nation Survey." *Northwestern University in Qatar.* June 2013. Accessed June 26, 2013. http://qatar-news.northwestern.edu/wp-content/uploads/6-18-13-MenaMediaUse_Regional-AR.pdf.

Melki, Wiam. "Salafists Take Over Kram Mosque." *Tunisia Live.* October 16, 2011. Accessed July 22, 2012. http://www.tunisia-live.net/2011/10/16/salafist-taking-over-the-area-of-kram/.

Menza, Mohamed Fahmy. *Patronage Politics in Egypt: The National Democratic Party and Muslim Brotherhood in Cairo.* London, Routledge Press, 2013.

Meric, Ali Berat. "Turkey's Kurtulmus Sets July Deadline for New Constitution." *Bloomberg.* May 10, 2013. Accessed June 21, 2013. http://www.bloomberg.com/news/2013-05-10/turkey-s-kurtulmus-sets-july-deadline-for-new-constitution.html.

Mervin, Sabrina. *The Shia Worlds and Iran.* New York: Saqi Books 2010.

El-Meshmeshy, Sarah. "Al Kasaby: 'Any reformation starts with morals and ethics; no reformation without righteousness.'" *Twenty.7 Magazine.* May 11, 2013. Accessed June 20, 2013. http://twentysevenmag.com/13/?p=690.

Meziou, Dorra Megdiche. "Tunisian Opposition Unites against Islamist Government." *Al-Monitor.* April 9, 2013. Accessed June 22, 2013. http://www.al-monitor.com/pulse/politics/2013/04/tunisia-opposition-unites-against-islamist-government.html.

Mietzner, Marcus. "The Politics of Military Reform in Post-Suharto Indonesia: Elite Conflict, Nationalism, and Institutional Resistance." *East–West Center Policy Studies* 23 (2006).

Mitchell, Richard P. *The Society of the Muslim Brothers.* London: Oxford University Press, 1969.

"Missing Christian girl may spark sectarian strife in Egypt." *Al Aribiya News,* November 3, 2012. http://english.alarabiya.net/articles/2012/11/03/247401.html.

Moaddel, Mansoor. *Jordanian Exceptionalism: A Comparative Analysis of State-religion Relationships in Egypt, Iran, Jordan, and Syria.* Houndmills, Basingstoke, Hampshire: Palgrave, 2002.

Moore, Clement Henry. *Tunisia since Independence: The Dynamics of One-party Government.* Berkeley: University of California Press, 1965.

"Morcos: Morsy's constitutional declaration hinders democratic transition." *Egypt Independent.* October 24, 2012. Accessed June 21, 2013. http://www.egypt-independent.com/news/morcos-morsy-s-constitutional-declaration-hinders-democratic-transition.

"Morsi's advisory team less diverse after months of walkouts." *Ahram Online.* February 19, 2013. Accessed June 21, 2013. http://english.ahram.org.eg/NewsContent/1/64/65135/Egypt/Politics-/Morsis-advisory-team-less-diverse-after-months-of-.aspx.

Moustafa, Tamir. "Conflict and Cooperation between the State and Religious Institutions in Contemporary Egypt." *International Journal of Middle East Studies* 32.1 (2000): 3–22.

"The Islamist Trend in Egyptian Law." *Politics and Religion* 3 (2010): 610–30.

"MQM says no action being taken against terrorists." *Geo TV*. June 22, 2013. Accessed June 23, 2013. http://www.geo.tv/GeoDetail.aspx?ID=106400.

Mufti, Malik. *Sovereign Creations: Pan-Arabism and Political Order in Syria and Iraq*. Ithaca, NY: Cornell University Press, 1996.

Munson, Henry. "Islamic Revivalism in Morocco and Tunisia." *The Muslim World* 76.3–4 (1986): 203–18.

"Muslim Brotherhood Statement 2 in Response to General Shafiq's Allegations, Black Propaganda." *Ikhwan Web*. June 11, 2012. Accessed July 22, 2012. http://www.ikhwanweb.com/article.php?id=30084.

Mustafa, Hamza. "Iraq: Sadr and Hakim Demand Maliki Resignation." *Asharq Al-Awsat*. July 31, 2013. Accessed August 6, 2013. http://www.aawsat.net/2013/07/article55311805.

"Iraq: Sadr and Hakim Form New 'Strategic' Alliance." *Asharq Al-Awsat*. July 11, 2013. Accessed August 8, 2013, http://www.aawsat.net/2013/07/article55309198.

"Sadr–Maliki Political Crisis Heats Up." *Asharq Al-Awsat*. April 11, 2013. Accessed June 20, 2013. http://www.aawsat.net/2013/04/article55298421.

Nadelmann, Ethan A. "Global Prohibition Regimes: The Evolution of Norms in International Society." *International Organization* 44.4 (1990): 479–526.

Nakash, Yitzhak. *The Shi'is of Iraq: With a New Introduction by the Author*. Princeton, NJ: Princeton University Press, 2003.

Nasr, Seyyed Vali Reza. *Forces of Fortune: The Rise of the New Muslim Middle Class and What It Will Mean for Our World*. New York: Free, 2009.

National Consortium for the Study of Terrorism and Responses to Terrorism. Accessed August 14, 2013. http://www.start.umd.edu/start/data_collections/tops/terrorist_organization_profile.asp?id=40.

Naylor, Phillip Chiviges. *North Africa: A History from Antiquity to the Present*. Austin: University of Texas, 2009.

Nazemroaya, Mahdi Darius. "Egypt's Constitutional Referendum: Did President Morsi Hijack Democracy?" *Global Research*, January 22, 2013. http://www.globalresearch.ca/statistically-examining-cairos-constitutional-referendum-did-morsi-hijack-democracy/5320067.

Nasrawi, Salah. "Setback for Al-Maliki." *Al-Ahram Weekly*. June 19, 2013. Accessed June 25, 2013. http://weekly.ahram.org.eg/News/3073/19/Setback-for-Al-Maliki.aspx.

Nexon, Daniel. *The Struggle for Power in Early Modern Europe: Religious Conflict, Dynastic Empires, and International Change*. Princeton, NJ: Princeton University Press, 2009.

Nguyen, Virginie. "Salafi leader criticizes Brotherhood for excluding other groups." *Al-Masry Al-Youm*, January 24, 2013. Accessed January 28, 2013. http://www.egyptindependent.com/news/salafi-leader-criticizes-brotherhood-excluding-other-groups.

Nisman, Daniel. "Egypt Elections: The SCAF's Window of Opportunity." *Middle East Online* (2011): n. p. December 4, 2011. Accessed December 23, 2011. http://www.middle-east-online.com/english/?id=49636.

Norell, Magnus. "The Taliban and the Muttahida Majlis-e-Amal (MMA)." *China and Eurasia Forum Quarterly* 5.3 (2007): 61–82.

"Nour Party Changes Position on Article 219." *Egypt Independent,* September 16 2013. Accessed September 18 2013. http://www.dailynewsegypt. com/2013/09/16/al-nour-party-changes-position-on-article-219.

"Nour Party Criticises Proposed Egypt Cabinet." *Ahram Online.* July 16, 2013. Accessed August 5, 2013. http://english.ahram.org.eg/NewsContent/1/64/76599/ Egypt/Politics-/Nour-Party-criticises-proposed-Egypt-cabinet.aspx.

Oday, Hatem. "Sistani Warns against Sectarianism in Iraq." *Al-Monitor.* Naria Tanoukhi. trans. January 14, 2013. Accessed January 28, 2013. http://www.al-monitor.com/pulse/politics/2013/01/iraqi-dialogue-sectarianism.html.

Okail, Nancy. "Two Years after Mubarak's Fall, Torture and Denial Continue Unabated in Morsi's Egypt." February 11, 2013. Accessed August 18, 2013. http://www.freedomhouse.org/blog/two-years-after-mubarak%E2%80%99s-fall-torture-and-denial-continue-unabated-morsi%E2%80%99s-egypt.

"Two Years after Mubarak's Fall, Torture and Denial Continue Unabated in Morsi's Egypt." *Freedom House Egypt.* February 11, 2013. Accessed June 24, 2013. http://www.freedomhouse.org/blog/two-years-after-mubarak%E2%80%99s-fall-torture-and-denial-continue-unabated-morsi%E2%80%99s-egypt.

O'Kane, Joseph P. "Islam in the New Egyptian Constitution: Some Discussions in Al-Ahram." *Middle East Journal* 26 (1972): 137–48.

Okeke-Ibezim, Felicia. *Saddam Hussein: The Legendary Dictator.* New York: Ekwike, 2006.

Öniş, Ziya. "The Political Economy of Islamic Resurgence in Turkey: The Rise of the Welfare Party in Perspective." *Third World Quarterly* 18.4 (1997): 743–766.

Otmazgin, Nissim and Eyal Ben-Ari. *Popular Culture and the State in East and Southeast Asia.* Abingdon, Oxon: Routledge, 2012.

Otto, Jan Michiel. *Sharia Incorporated: A Comparative Overview of the Legal Systems of Twelve Muslim Countries in past and Present.* Leiden: Leiden University Press, 2010.

Otto, Jan Michiel. "Towards comparative conclusions on the role of sharia in national law." In *Sharia incorporated: A Comparative Overview of the Legal Systems of Twelve Muslim Countries in Past and Present.* Edited by Jan Michiel Otto. Leiden: Leiden University Press, 2010.

Owen, Roger, *State, Power and Politics in the Making of the Modern Middle East,* London: Routledge, 2004 (revised).

Ozel, Isik. "The Politics of De-Delegation: Regulatory (In)dependence in Turkey." *Regulation and Governance* 6.1 (2012): 119–129.

Ozer, Veda. "Will the Gezi effect rehabilitate Turkish democracy?" Accessed July 2, 2013. http://www.hurriyetdailynews.com/will-the-gezi-effect-rehabilitate-turk-ish-democracy.aspx?pageID=449&nID=49827&NewsCatID=466.

"Pakistan." *International Freedom Report.* 2012. Accessed June 18, 2013. http:// www.state.gov/documents/organization/208650.pdf

"Pakistan Film Protests: 19 Die in Karachi and Peshawar." *BBC Online,* September 21, 2012. Accessed January 23, 2013. http://www.bbc.co.uk/news/world-asia-19678412.

"Pakistan's Medieval Constitution." *Wall Street Journal*, June 22, 2010: A21. http://online.wsj.com/news/articles/SB10001424052748704198004575311043 6322 37762

Paley, Amit R. "In Iraq's Provincial Elections, Main Issue Is Maliki Himself." *The Washington Post*. January 17, 2009. Accessed August 16, 2013. http://articles.washingtonpost.com/2009-01-17/world/36921869_1_maliki-state-of-law-coalition-kurdish-bloc.

Pape, Robert Anthony. *Dying to Win: The Strategic Logic of Suicide Terrorism*. New York: Random House, 2005.

Paris, Jonathan. "Prospects for Pakistan." *Legatum Institute*. January, 2010. Accessed June 20, 2013. http://www.li.com/docs/publications/2010-publications-prospects-for-pakistan.pdf.

Parker, Emily. "Final Draft of Constitution Announced, but Approval Remains Questionable." *Tunisia Live*. June 3, 2013. Accessed June 21, 2013. http://www.tunisia-live.net/2013/06/03/final-draft-of-constitution-announced-but-approval-remains-questionable/.

Payne (ed.). "Rights Group: Police Rape woman in Tunisia, then charge her with indecency." *CNN*, October 2, 2012. http://www.cnn.com/2012/10/02/world/africa/tunisia-rape-protest/index.html.

Periwal, Sukumar. *Notions of Nationalism*. Budapest: Central European University Press, 1995.

Perkins, Kenneth J. *A History of Modern Tunisia*. New York: Cambridge University Press, 2004.

Pew Research Center. "Overall, do you think women will have more rights, fewer rights, or about the same rights under the Freedom and Justice Party-led government as they had in the past?" May 8, 2012. http://poll.orspub.com/document.php?id=quest12.out_3161&type=hitlist&num=1&action=addfav&%3C?ph p%20echo%20;%20?%3E.

"Egyptians Increasingly Glum." May 16, 2013. Accessed June 20, 2013. http://www.pewglobal.org/files/2013/05/Pew-Global-Attitudes-Egypt-Report-FINAL-May-16-2013.pdf.

"The Global Divide on Homosexuality." June 4, 2013. Accessed June 28, 2013. http://www.pewglobal.org/files/2013/06/Pew-Global-Attitudes-Homosexuality-Report-FINAL-JUNE-4-2013.pdf.

Rising Tide of Restrictions on Religion, September 2012. Washington, DC, Pew Forum on Religion and Public Life.

Pew Forum on Religion and Public Life, Global Attitudes. Accessed June 6, 2013. http://www.pewglobal.org/files/2012/05/Pew-Global-Attitudes-2012-Egypt-Report-Topline.pdf p.27.

Global Attitudes and Arab Spring. Accessed June 6, 2013. http://www.pewglobal.org/files/2012/07/Pew-Global-Attitudes-Project-Arab-Spring-TOPLINE-Tuesday-July-10-2012.pdf p.56.

Phillips, Christopher. "The impact of Syrian refugees on Turkey and Jordan." *The World Today (Chatham House)* 68.8/9 (2012). Accessed June 21, 2013. http://www.chathamhouse.org/publications/twt/archive/view/186289.

Pioppi, Daniela. "Is There an Islamist Alternative in Egypt?" *IAI Working Paper* (2011).

Piscatori, James P. *Islam in a World of Nation-states*. Cambridge [Cambridgeshire]: Cambridge University Press, 1986.

"PM Qandil says experts will amend Egypt's constitution." *Ahram Online.* April 9, 2013, Accessed June 20, 2013. http://english.ahram.org.eg/ NewsContent/1/64/68826/Egypt/Politics-/PM-Qandil-says-experts-will-amend-Egypts-constitut.aspx.

"PM warns Muslims of provocation over film." *Hurriyet Daily News,* September 15, 2012. Accessed January 23, 2013. http://www.hurriyetdailynews.com/pm-warns-muslims-of-provocation-over film.aspx?pageID=238&nID=30196&Ne wscatID=338.

"PML-Q presents 6-point budget proposals in Senate." *Daily Times.* June 19, 2013. Accessed June 21, 2013, http://www.dailytimes.com.pk/default.asp?page=2013 %5C06%5C19%5Cstory_19-6-2013_pg7_20.

Polat, Necati. "Regime Change in Turkey." *International Politics* 50 (2013). 435–454.

"Poll: 40% Do Not Know Interim President, 70% Do Not Know PM." *Egypt Independent.* July 23, 2013. Accessed August 5, 2013. http://www.egyptindependent.com/news/poll-40-do-not-know-interim-president-70-do-not-know-pm.

"Polling the Nations." *ORS Publishing,* May 8, 2012. Accessed January 28, 2013. http://poll.orspub.com/document.php?id=quest12.out_3161&type=hitlist&nu m=1&action=addfav&%3C?php%20echo%20;%20?%3E.

Pratt, Nicola Christine. *Democracy and Authoritarianism in the Arab World.* Boulder, CO: Lynne Rienner Publishers, 2007.

"Pro-Morsi Group Compares El-Sisi to Syria's Assad." *Ahram Online.* July 25, 2013. Accessed August 5, 2013. http://english.ahram.org.eg/NewsContent/1/64/77344/ Egypt/Politics-/ProMorsi-group-compares-ElSisi-to-Syrias-Assad.aspx.

"Pro-Morsi Wasat Party Leaders Arrested." *Ahram Online.* July 29, 2013. Accessed August 5, 2013. http://english.ahram.org.eg/NewsContent/1/64/77678/Egypt/ Politics-/ProMorsi-Wasat-Party-leaders-arrested.aspx.

"Q&A: Israeli deadly raid on aid flotilla." *BBC News Middle East.* March 22, 2013. Accessed June 21, 2013. http://www.bbc.co.uk/news/10203726.

Qur'an Verse 49:13, Sahih International Translation, http://quran.com/49/13.

Rabasa, Angel and F. Stephen Larrabee. "The Rise of Political Islam in Turkey." *RAND National Defense Research Institute* (2008). http://www.rand.org/content/dam/rand/pubs/monographs/2008/RAND_MG726.pdf.

Rabie, Dalia. "Abu Ismail builds on support by launching a new party in a turbulent political scene." *Egypt Independent.* March 14, 2013. Accessed June 20, 2013. http://www.egyptindependent.com/news/abu-ismail-builds-support-launching-new-party-turbulent-political-scene.

Radford, Megan. "Blasphemy Article Moved to Constitution Preamble." *Tunisia Live.* October 13, 2012. Accessed January 24, 2013. http://www.tunisia-live.net/2012/10/13/blasphemy-article-moved-to-constitution-preamble/.

Raheem, Kareem. "Bomb attacks kill more than 70 Shi'ites across Iraq." *Reuters.* May 20, 2013. Accessed June 26, 2013. http://www.reuters.com/article/2013/05/20/ us-iraq-violence-idUSBRE94I0DU20130520.

"More than 70 killed in wave of Baghdad bombings." *Reuters.* May 27, 2013. Accessed June 26, 2013. http://www.reuters.com/article/2013/05/27/us-iraq-violence-idUSBRE94Q0D620130527.

Rahimi, Babak. "The Sadr-Sistani Relationship." *The Jamestown Publication,* 2007. Accessed January 20, 2013. http://www.jamestown.org/ single/?no_cache=1&tx_ttnews%5Btt_news%5D=1055.

Ur-Rahman, Javaid. "JUI-F may get ministerial slot next week." *The Nation*, June 20, 2013. Accessed June 20, 2013. http://www.nation.com.pk/pakistan-news-newspaper-daily-english-online/editors-picks/20-Jun-2013/jui-f-may-get-ministerial-slot-next-week.

"Reactions to Egyptian Crackdown on Pro-Morsi Camps." *Associated Press.* August 15, 2013. Accessed August 15, 2013. http://abcnews.go.com/International/wireStory/reactions-egyptian-crackdown-pro-morsi-camps-19966083.

Rejeb, Khaled Ben. "Economic Profile of Ennhada: Diversification of Banking System and 'Open Sky' Membership." *Tunisialive*, November 5, 2011. http://www.tunisia-live.net/2011/11/05/economic-profile-of-ennahda-diversification-of-banking-system-and-open-sky-membership.

"Results of Shura Council elections." *Carnegie Endowment for International Peace.* February 29, 2012. Accessed June 20, 2013. http://egyptelections.carnegieendowment.org/2012/02/29/results-of-shura-council-elections.

Riedel, Bruce. "U.S.-Pakistan Relationship and the Future of Afghanistan." *Brookings Institute.* June 5, 2013. Accessed June 22, 2013. http://www.brookings.edu/blogs/up-front/posts/2013/06/05-us-pakistan-relationship-future-afghanistan-riedel.

"Risks to Al-Azhar?" *Al-Ahram Weekly.* July 17, 2013. Accessed August 9, 2013. http://weekly.ahram.org.eg/News/3403/32/Risks-to-Al-Azhar-.aspx.

Risse-Kappen, Thomas, Steve C. Ropp, and Kathryn Sikkink. *The Power of Human Rights: International Norms and Domestic Change.* New York: Cambridge University Press, 1999.

Rogan, Eugene L. *The Arabs: A History.* New York: Basic, 2009.

Ross, Michael. *The Oil Curse: How Petroleum Wealth Shapes the Development of Nations.* Princeton, NJ: Princeton University Press, 2012.

Rowley, Charles and Nathanael Smith. "Islam's Democracy Paradox: Muslims Claim To Like Democracy, So Why Do They Have So Little?" *Public Choice,* 3–4 (2009): 273–99.

Roy, Olivier. "Post-Islamic Revolution." *The European Institute,* 2011. Accessed January 21, 2013. http://www.europeaninstitute.org/February-2011/qpost-islamic-revolutionq-events-in-egypt-analyzed-by-french-expert-on-political-islam.html.

Rubin, Barry. *Islamic Fundamentalism in Egyptian Politics.* Basingstoke: Palgrave Macmillan, 2002.

Ruedy, John. *Islamism and Secularism in North Africa.* New York: St. Martin's, 1994.

Sabry, Bassem. "Will Egypt Have Its Second Revolution on June 30?" *Al-Monitor.* June 9, 2013. Accessed June 24, 2013. http://www.al-monitor.com/pulse/originals/2013/06/egypt-second-revolution-morsi-anniversary.html.

"Only Politics Can Save Egypt's Economy." *Al-Monitor.* June 13, 2013. Accessed June 24, 2013. http://www.al-monitor.com/pulse/originals/2013/06/egypt-economy-political-crisis-stagnant.html.

Sachsenmaier, Dominic and S. N. Eisenstadt. *Reflections on Multiple Modernities: European, Chinese, and Other Interpretations.* Leiden: Brill, 2002.

Sadah, Ali Abel. "Could Sistani Be Iraq's Last Hope?" *Al-Monitor.* May 2, 2013. Accessed June 24, 2013. http://www.al-monitor.com/pulse/originals/2013/05/iraq-political-crisis-solution-sistani.html.

"Iraq's Anbar Province Struggles To Form Government." *Al-Monitor.* July 17, 2013. Accessed August 15, 2013. http://www.al-monitor.com/pulse/originals/2013/07/anbar-difficulty-forming-local-government.html.

Sadek, Sameer. "Jama'a al-Islamiya to celebrate constitution, Morsy on revolution's anniversary." *Al-Masry Al-Youm*, January 11, 2013. Accessed January 28, 2013. http://www.egyptindependent.com/news/jama-al-islamiya-celebrate-constitution-morsy-revolution-s-anniversary

"Sadr visits Baghdad church, site of 2010 attack." *Al-Arabiya*, January 4, 2013. Accessed January 28, 2013. http://english.alarabiya.net/articles/2013/01/04/258618.html.

"Iraq Moves Troops To Syrian Border." *Al-Monitor.* June 18, 2013. Accessed June 22, 2013. http://www.al-monitor.com/pulse/originals/2013/06/iraq-moves-troops-syria-border.html.

"Maliki Scrambles to Address Deteriorating Iraqi Security." *Al-Monitor.* May 23, 2013. Accessed June 20, 2013. http://www.al-monitor.com/pulse/originals/2013/05/iraq-security-breakdown-crisis-baghdad.html.

"Muqtada al-Sadr: Staying In Iraqi Government a 'Sin.'" *Al-Monitor.* March 22, 2013. Accessed June 22, 2013. http://www.al-monitor.com/pulse/originals/2013/03/sadr-letter-against-maliki.html.

"Sadr Gives Maliki 'Final Warning.'" *Al-Monitor.* May 29, 2013. Accessed June 21, 2013. http://www.al-monitor.com/pulse/originals/2013/05/sadr-maliki-iraq-warning.html.

"Sectarian Violence Erupts Again across Iraq." *Al-Monitor.* May 21, 2013. Accessed June 20, 2013. http://www.al-monitor.com/pulse/originals/2013/05/iraq-violence-truce-efforts-saadi.html.

Saeed, Abdullah and Hassan Saeed. *Freedom of Religion, Apostasy, and Islam.* Aldershot, Hants, England: Ashgate, 2004.

Saeed, Javaid. *Islam and Modernization: A Comparative Analysis of Pakistan, Egypt, and Turkey.* Westport, CT: Praeger, 1994.

Safah Al-Din, Mohammad. "Mamduuh al-Waali.. Rajul as-Sulta Yas'i li-Akhwinat as-Sahaafa" or "Mamdouh al-Wali: A man in authority seeks to Brother-ize the press." *Al-Badeel.* December 26, 2012. Accessed June 25, 2013. http://elbadil.com/hot-issues-cases/2012/12/26/89368.

Sakaoglu, Emre Tunc. "USAK Report: Violence Against Women in Turkey." *The Journal of Turkish Weekly.* March 8, 2012. Accessed June 21, 2013. http://www.turkishweekly.net/news/132146/.

"Salafi Da'wa calls on Egyptians to Unite." *Daily News Egypt.* July 7, 2013. Accessed August 5, 2013. http://www.dailynewsegypt.com/2013/07/07/salafi-dawa-calls-on-egyptians-to-unite/.

"Salafi Groups in Egypt." *Islamopedia Online.* http://www.islamopediaonline.org/country-profile/egypt/salafists/salafi-groups-egypt.

"Salafi Leader: Morsy Should Step Down if Millions Protest." *Egypt Independent.* June 6, 2013. Accessed June 20, 2013. http://www.egyptindependent.com/news/salafi-leader-morsy-should-step-down-if-millions-protest.

"Salafist Nour Party head confirms rift with Brotherhood." *Al Ahram Online,* January 12, 2013. http://english.ahram.org.eg/NewsContent/1/64/62250/Egypt/Politics-/Salafist-Nour-Party-head-confirms-rift-with-Brothe.aspx.

"Salafist Call and Nour Party call for early presidential elections." Accessed July 3, 2013. http://english.ahram.org.eg/newsContent/1/64/75456/Egypt/Politics-/Egypts-Salafist-Call,-Nour-Party-calls-for-early-p.aspx.

Salih, Mohammed A. "Syrian conflict threatens to fracture Iraq." *Christian Science Monitor*, December 27, 2012. Accessed January 28, 2013. http://www.csmonitor.com/World/Middle-East/2012/1227/Syrian-conflict-threatens-to-fracture-Iraq.

Salvatore, Armando. *Islam and the Political Discourse of Modernity*. UK: Garnet Limited, 1999.

"Samaahat As-Sayyid Al-Qaa'id Yuwajjih Nadaa'an Ilaa Ash-Sha'bi wal-Hakuumati Ba'ad Mawjati At-Tafjiiraati Al-Mustamirra" or *The Office of Muqtada al-Sadr*. May 27, 2013. Accessed June 21, 2013. http://jawabna.com/index.php/permalink/6505.html.

"Satirical show host Youssef under investigation for alleged Morsi insult." *Al-Ahram Online*. January 1, 2013. Accessed January 28, 2013. http://english.ahram.org.eg/NewsContent/1/64/61620/Egypt/Politics-/Satirical-show-host-Youssef-under-investigation-ov.aspx.

Sattar, Omar. "Ahzab sunniyya wa shi'aiyya 'iraqiyya tabdhal juhudan li-tashkil jabha jadida yatz'amuha Al-Maliki wal-Mutlaq." *Al-Hayat*. June 6, 2013. Accessed June 20, 2013. http://alhayat.com/Details/521175.

Sayyid, Bobby S. *A Fundamental Fear: Eurocentrism and the Emergence of Islamism*. London: Zed, 2003.

Schilling, Heinz. *Religion, Political Culture and the Emergence of Early Modern Society: Essays in German and Dutch History*. Leiden: Brill, 1992.

Schwedler, Jillian. "Can Islamists Become Moderates?: Rethinking the Inclusion-Moderation Hypothesis." *World Politics* 63.2 (2011): 347–76.

Sen, Mustafa. "Transformation of Turkish Islamism and the Rise of the Justice and Development Party." *Turkish Studies* 11.1 (2010): 59–84.

"Senegal." *International Religious Freedom Report*. 2012. Accessed June 28, 2013. http://www.state.gov/documents/organization/208400.pdf.

Sethi, Ali. "One Myth, Many Pakistans." *New York Times*. June 2, 2010. Accessed October 23, 2011. http://www.nytimes.com/2010/06/13/opinion/13sethi.html?scp=1&sq=%22one%20myth,%20many%20pakistans%22&st=cse#.

"Seven of 17 new regional governors from Egypt's Muslim Brotherhood." *Ahram Online*. June 16, 2013. Accessed June 21, 2013. http://english.ahram.org.eg/NewsContent/1/64/74184/Egypt/Politics-/Seven-of--new-regional-governors-from-Egypts-Musli.aspx.

Sfeir, George N. "The Abolition of Confessional Jurisdiction in Egypt: The Non-Muslim Courts." *Middle East Journal* 10.3 (1956): 248–56.

Shafak, Elif. "Rape, abortion and the fight for women's rights in Turkey." *The Guardian*. September 9, 2012. Accessed June 21, 2013. http://www.guardian.co.uk/commentisfree/2012/sep/09/reape-abortion-fight-womens-rights-turkey.

Shanahan, Rodger. "Shi'a Political Development in Iraq: The Case of the Islamic Dawa Party." *Third World Quarterly* 25.5 (2004): 943–54.

Shapiro, Ian, Rogers M. Smith, and Tarek E. Masoud. *Problems and Methods in the Study of Politics*. Cambridge: Cambridge University Press, 2004.

el-Sharnoubi, Osman. "President's dialogue talks yield promise to form committee to study constitutional change." *Al Ahram Online.* January 29, 2013. http://english.ahram.org.eg/NewsContent/1/64/63569/Egypt/Politics-/Constitutional-amendments-committee-formed-at-Mors.aspx.

Sharp, Jeremy M. "Egypt: Background and U.S. Relations." *Congressional Research Service.* February 26, 2013. Accessed June 24, 2013. http://www.fas.org/sgp/crs/mideast/RL33003.pdf.

"Ash-sheikh Wagdi Ghoneim." *Islam Way.* Accessed June 28, 2013. http://ar.islamway.net/scholar/74.

"Ash-sheikh Wagdi Ghoneim wa radd 'alaa khitaan al-anaath" or *Al-Hayaa biga lown Salafii* or *Life in Salafi Colors* (Facebook group). Accessed June 28, 2013. http://bit.ly/19E12pd (Facebook) and http://www.youtube.com/watch?v=KouyF5u_4MQ (video).

Shuaib, Farid Sufian. "Constitutional Restatement of Parallel Jurisdiction between Civil Courts and Syariah Courts in Malaysia: Twenty Years on (1988–2008)." *Malaysan Law Journal* 5 (2008).

Siddiqi, Mona. *The Good Muslim, Reflection on Classical Islamic Law and Theology.* Cambridge: Cambridge University Press, 2012.

Sil, Rudra and Peter J. Katzenstein. *Beyond Paradigms: Analytic Eclecticism in the Study of World Politics.* Houndmills, Basingstoke, Hampshire: Palgrave Macmillan, 2010.

Silverstein, Brian. *Islam and Modernity in Turkey.* New York: Palgrave Macmillan, 2011.

Siman, Bernard. "The Islamist Government Experiments in Egypt and Turkey." *World Review.* July 30 2013. Accessed August 7 2013. http://www.worldreview.info/content/islamist-government-experiments-turkey-and-egypt.

Simon, Joel. "For Turkey, world's leading jailer, a path forward." *Committee to Protect Journalists.* December 11, 2012. Accessed June 20, 2013. http://www.cpj.org/blog/2012/12/for-turkey-worlds-leading-jailer-of-the-press-a-pa.php.

Skovgaard-Petersen, Jakob. *Defining Islam for the Egyptian State: Muftis and Fatwas of the Dār Al-Iftā.* Leiden: Brill, 1997.

Slama, Nissaf. "Ongoing Operations Around Chaambi Mountain Target Armed Fighters." *Tunisia Live.* August 5, 2013. Accessed August 6, 2013. http://www.tunisia-live.net/2013/08/05/ongoing-operations-around-chaambi-mountain-target-armed-fighters/.

Slater, Dan. "Revolutions, Crackdowns, and Quiescence: Communal Elites and Democratic Mobilization in Southeast Asia." *American Journal of Sociology* 115.1 (2009): 203–54.

Slavin, Barbara. "Obama Sent a Secret Letter to Iraq's Top Shiite Cleric." *Foreign Policy,* August 5, 2010. http://www.foreignpolicy.com/articles/2010/08/05/obama_sent_a_secret_letter_to_iraqs_top_shiite_cleric?page=0,1.

Springborg, Robert. "Sisi's Islamist Agenda for Egypt: The General's Radical Political Vision." *Foreign Policy.* July 28, 2013. Accessed August 13, 2013. http://www.foreignaffairs.com/articles/139605/robert-springborg/sisis-islamist-agenda-for-egypt.

Starrett, Gregory. *Putting Islam to Work: Education, Politics, and Religious Transformation in Egypt.* Berkeley: University of California Press, 1998.

Steinvorth, Daniel. "Erdogan the Misogynist: Turkish Prime Minister Assaults Women's Rights." *Spiegel Online.* June 19, 2012. Accessed June 21, 2013. http://www.spiegel.de/international/europe/turkish-prime-minister-erdogan-targets-women-s-rights-a-839568.html.

Stepan, Alfred C. "Religion, Democracy, and the 'Twin Tolerations.'" *Journal of Democracy* 11.4 (2000): 37–57.

Stepan, Alfred, Juan J. Linz, and Yogendra Yadav. "The Rise of 'State-Nations.'" *Journal of Democracy* 21.3 (2010): 50–68.

Crafting State-Nations: India and Other Multinational Democracies. Baltimore, MD: Johns Hopkins University Press, 2011.

Stowasser, Barbara F. *The Islamic Impulse.* London: Croom Helm U.a., 1987.

"Stressing that Iraq's value and wealth lie in its diversity, Sayyid Ammar al-Hakim receives a delegation from the Alliance of Turkmen Political Forces headed by Sheikh al-Mawla." President of the Islamic Supreme Council of Iraq. January 22, 2013. http://www.almejlis.org/eng/more/4181-1/Stressing-that-Iraqs-value-and-wealth-lie-in-its-diversity,-Sayyid-Ammar-al-Hakim-receives-a-delegation-from-the-Alliance-of-Turkmen-Political-Forces-headed-by-Sheikh-al-Mawla.

Stuster, J. Dana. "Pakistan demands end to U.S. drone strikes – for the ninth time." *Foreign Policy.* June 5, 2013. Accessed June 22, 2013. http://blog.foreignpolicy.com/posts/2013/06/05/pakistan_calls_for_end_to_us_drone_strikes_again.

"Submission in the UPR [Universal Periodic Review] review of: Senegal." *Office of the High Commissioner for Human Rights.* 2009. Accessed June 28, 2013. http://lib.ohchr.org/HRBodies/UPR/Documents/Session4/SN/ILGA_SEN_UPR_S4_2009_ILGA_Etal_JOINT.pdf.

Surūsh, ʿAbd Al-Karīm, Mahmoud Sadri, and Ahmad Sadri. *Reason, Freedom, & Democracy in Islam: Essential Writings of ʿAbdolkarim Soroush.* New York: Oxford University Press, 2000.

"Survey of Textbook and Curricular Content," *Islamopedia Online.* Accessed August 4, 2013, http://www.islamopediaonline.org/country-profile/egypt/islam-and-education-system/survey-textbook-and-curricular-content.

"Survey reveals growing public apprehension over democratic process." *Today's Zaman.* June 16, 2013. Accessed June 24, 2013. http://www.todayszaman.com/news-318446-survey-reveals-growing-public-apprehension-over-democratic-process.html.

Syed, Anwar Hussain. *Pakistan: Islam, Politics, and National Solidarity.* New York: Praeger, 1982.

Tait, Robert. "Egypt: Doubts cast on Turkish claims for model democracy." *The Guardian,* February 13, 2011. Accessed January 28, 2013. http://www.guardian.co.uk/world/2011/feb/13/egypt-doubt-turkish-model-democracy.

"Taking a stand: Joint resolution against drone strikes submitted." *The Express Tribune,* June 5, 2013. Accessed June 20, 2013. http://tribune.com.pk/story/559362/taking-a-stand-joint-resolution-against-drone-strikes-submitted/.

Tarrow, Sidney G. *Power in Movement: Social Movements and Contentious Politics.* Cambridge, England: Cambridge University Press, 1998.

Taşpınar, Ömer. "Turkey: The New Model?" *Brookings Institution*. April 2012. http://www.brookings.edu/research/papers/2012/04/24-turkey-new-model-taspinar.

El-Tawy, Ayat. "Skepticism over new Egypt Cabinet reshuffle." *Ahram Online*. January 6, 2013. Accessed June 21, 2013. http://english.ahram.org.eg/NewsContent/1/64/61906/Egypt/Politics-/Skepticism-over-new-Egypt-Cabinet-reshuffle.aspx.

"April 6 movement to mark 5th anniversary with 'outcry.'" *Ahram Online*. April 6, 2013. Accessed June 20, 2013. http://english.ahram.org.eg/NewsContent/1/64/68457/Egypt/Politics-/April--movement-to-mark-th-anniversary-with-outcry.aspx.

Taşpınar, Ömer. "Turkey: The New Model?" *Brookings Institution*. April 2012. Accessed August 19, 2013. http://www.brookings.edu/research/papers/2012/04/24-turkey-new-model-taspinar.

Taylor, Charles. *A Secular Age*. Cambridge, MA: Belknap of Harvard University Press, 2007.

el-Tabei, Haitham. "First Christmas for Egypt Copts under Islamist Rule." January 6, 2013. http://www.google.com/hostednews/afp/article/ALeqM5h5wpgVO5Tre2UgXUF1SoV8sYrzYw?docId=CNG.be14a436685537a4e41bae07031bf8f4.5e1.

Tepe, Sultan. *Beyond Sacred and Secular: Politics of Religion in Israel and Turkey*. Stanford University Press, 2008.

"The Egyptian mass media are leading the fight against Morsi's power grab." *Postaljazeera*, December 2, 2012. http://postaljazeera.wordpress.com/2012/12/02/the-egyptian-mass-media-are-leading-the-fight-against-morsis-power-grab/.

"The Turkish economy: Strong but vulnerable." *The Economist*. June 15, 2013. Accessed June 22, 2013. http://www.economist.com/news/europe/21579491-turkey-remains-highly-exposed-loss-confidence-foreign-investors-strong-vulnerable.

Tibi, Bassam. *The Sharia State: Arab Spring and Democratization*. Abingdon: Routledge, 2013.

Tohid, Owais. "Pakistan's Frontier Passes Islamic Law, Ranking Islamabad." *Christian Science Monitor*. N.p., June 10, 2003. Accessed October 12, 2011. http://www.csmonitor.com/2003/0610/p07s02-wosc.html.

Toor, Saadia. *The State of Islam: Culture and Cold War Politics in Pakistan*. London: Pluto, 2011.

Trew, Bel. "The Brotherhood needs us more than we need them: Salafist Nour Party spokesman." *Al Ahram Online*, October 15, 2012. Accessed January 28, 2013. http://english.ahram.org.eg/NewsContent/1/64/55616/Egypt/Politics-/The-Brotherhood-needs-us-more-than-we-need-them-Sa.aspx.

"Tunisia: Constitution Will Not Criminalise Blasphemy." *Allafrica*, October 15, 2012. Accessed January 24, 2013. http://allafrica.com/stories/201210161420.html.

"Tunisia: Country Specific Information." U.S. *State Department*. January 23, 2013. http://travel.state.gov/travel/cis_pa_tw/cis/cis_1045.html.

"Tunisia Crisis: Tens of Thousands Join Protest." *BBC News*. August 6, 2013. Accessed August 9, 2013. http://www.bbc.co.uk/news/world-africa-23597308.

"Tunisia death toll rises to four in U.S. embassy attack." *AlertNet*, September 15, 2012. Accessed January 23, 2013. http://www.trust.org/alertnet/news/tunisia-death-toll-rises-to-four-in-us-embassy-attack/.

"Tunisia draft constitution not based on Sharia." *Middle East Online*. June 6, 2013. Accessed June 23, 2013. http://www.middle-east-online.com/english/?id=59160.

"Tunisia Femen activist arrested for 'immoral gestures.'" *Ahram Online*. May 20, 2013. Accessed June 22, 2013. http://english.ahram.org.eg/NewsContent/2/8/71923/World/Region/Tunisia-Femen-activist-arrested-for-immoral-gestur.aspx.

"Tunisia NGO accuses pro-Islamist group of attack," *AFP*, January 9, 2013. Accessed January 28, 2013. http://www.moroccoworldnews.com/2013/01/73295/tunisia-ngo-accuses-pro-islamist-group-of-attack/.

"Tunisia Poll Shows Nidaa Tunis More Popular Than Ennahda." *Al-Monitor*. May 15, 2013. Accessed August, 15, 2013. http://www.al-monitor.com/pulse/politics/2013/05/tunisian-poll-ennahda-popularity-declines-nidaa-tunis.html.

"Tunisia vendor dies after self-immolation." *Al-Jazeera*. March 13, 2013. Accessed June 26, 2013. http://www.aljazeera.com/news/middleeast/2013/03/201331385433367799.html.

"Tunisians Find Facebook Number One Source of News, Says New Study." *Tunisia Live*. June 20, 2013. Accessed June 24, 2013. http://www.tunisia-live.net/2013/06/20/tunisians-find-facebook-number-one-source-of-news-says-new-study/.

"Tunisia begins landmark discussion on draft constitution." Accessed July 1, 2013. http://www.globalpost.com/dispatch/news/afp/130701/tunisia-begins-landmark-debate-draft-constitution-0.

"Tunisia's Tamarod Gathers Steam: Another Domino Effect?" *Middle East Online*. July 4, 2013. Accessed August 6, 2013. http://www.middle-east-online.com/english/?id=59892

"Tunisian ruling islamists accept to stand down." BBC September 28 2013. Accessed October 1 2013, http://www.bbc.co.uk/news/world-asia-24315192

"Tunisians loose faith in Ennahda, Revolution." *Al-Monitor*, October 1, 2013, Accessed October 1, 2013. http://www.al-monitor.com/pulse/originals/2013/09/ennahda-tunisia-resign-missteps-revolution.html?utm_source=&utm_medium=email&utm_campaign=8280#ixzz2gUBt7rMP.

"Turkey." *Amnesty International Annual Report 2013*. 2013. Accessed June 21, 2013. http://www.amnesty.org/en/region/turkey/report-2013.

"Turkey." *International Religious Freedom Report*. 2012. Accessed June 21, 2013. http://www.state.gov/documents/organization/208588.pdf.

"Turkey Plans Legal Reform to Prevent Coup." *Deutsch Welle*. Accessed August 5, 2013. http://www.dw.de/turkey-plans-legal-reform-to-prevent-coups/a-16927618.

"Turkey's AKP plans to consolidate power in local administrations ahead of 2014 presidential election." COSPP. January 24, 2013. http://www.cospp.com/news/2013/01/24/turkey-s-akp-plans-to-consolidate-power-in-local-administrations-ahead-of-2014-presidential-election.html.

"Two days of protests and violence leave Egypt on the edge." *Ahram Online*. January 26, 2013. Accessed January 28, 2013, http://english.ahram.org.eg/NewsContent/1/64/63378/Egypt/Politics-/Two-days-of-protests-and-violence-leave-Egypt-on-e.aspx.

"Two Iraq Sunni Ministers Quit after Deadly Clashes." *Ahram Online*. April 23, 2013. Accessed August 9, 2013. http://english.ahram.org.eg/newsContent/2/8/69990/World/Region/Two-Iraq-Sunni-ministers-quit-after-deadly-clashes.aspx.

"Two years on since revolution, Tunisia struggles with new political realities." *Ahram Online*. January 14, 2013. Accessed January 28, 2013. http://english.ahram.org.eg/newsContent/2/8/62468/World/Region/Two-years-on-since-revolution,-Tunisia-struggles-w.aspx.

"UN: Iraq sectarian violence worst in years." *Deutsche Welle*. June 1, 2013. Accessed June 26, 2013. http://www.dw.de/un-iraq-sectarian-violence-worst-in-years/a-16853048.

United States Commission on International Religious Freedom. "USCIRF Annual Report 2012 – Countries of Particular Concern: Iraq." March 20, 2012. Accessed January 22, 2013. http://www.unhcr.org/refworld/docid/4f71a67526.html.

"US State department denies calling for early Egypt elections." Accessed July 2, 2013. http://english.ahram.org.eg/newsContent/1/64/75518/Egypt/Politics-/US-State-Department-denies-calling-for-early-Egypt.aspx.

Vela, Justin. "'Abortions Are like Air Strikes on Civilians': Turkish PM Recep Tayyip Erdogan's Rant Sparks Women's Rage." *Independent*. N.p., May 30, 2012. Accessed July 14, 2012. http://www.independent.co.uk/life-style/health-and-families/health-news/abortions-are-like-air-strikes-on-civilians-turkish-pm-recep-tayyip-erdogans-rant-sparks-womens-rage-7800939.html.

Vella, Matthew. "Blasphemy? It's not criminal—Council of Europe." *Malta Today*, March 8, 2009. Accessed January 24, 2013. http://www.maltatoday.com.mt/2009/03/08/t13.html.

Vikor, Knut, *Between God and the Sultan, an History of Islamic Law*. Oxford: Oxford University Press, 2006.

Visser, Reidar. "As the Deadline for Forming Coalitions Expires, Maliki Creates a Shiite Alliance for Iraq's Local Elections in April 2013." *Iraq and Gulf Analysis*. December 21, 2012. Accessed August 18, 2013. http://gulfanalysis.wordpress.com/2012/12/21/as-the-deadline-for-forming-coalitions-expires-maliki-creates-monster-shiite-alliance-for-iraqs-local-elections-in-april-2013/.

"From Quietism to Machiavellianism?" *Norwegian Institute of International Affairs*, 2006. Accessed January 20, 2013. http://historiae.org/documents/Sistani.pdf.

Volpi, Frédéric. *Political Islam Observed: Disciplinary Perspectives*. New York: Columbia University Press, 2010.

von Luebke, Christian. "Post-Suharto Indonesia." *Stanford Program on International and Cross-Cultural Education*. Fall 2009. Accessed July 26, 2013. http://iis-db.stanford.edu/docs/381/Post-Suharto.pdf.

Waltz, Susan. "Islamist Appeal In Tunisia." *Middle East Journal* 40.4 (1986): 651–70.

Ware, L. B. "Ben Ali's Constitutional Coup in Tunisia." *Middle East Journal* 42, no. 4 (1988): 587–601.

"Wasat Party to suggest new national dialogue." *Egypt Independent*. April 17, 2013. Accessed June 20, 2013. http://www.egyptindependent.com/news/wasat-party-suggest-new-national-dialogue.

White, Jenny B. *Islamist Mobilization in Turkey: A Study in Vernacular Politics*. Seattle: University of Washington, 2002.

Wiktorowicz, Quintan. "Anatomy of the Salafi Movement." *Studies in Conflict & Terrorism* 29.3 (2006): 207–39.

Willis, John. "Debating the Caliphate: Islam and Nation in the Work of Rashid Rida and Abul Kalam Azad." *The International History Review* 32.4 (2010): 711–32.

Wendt, Nathan. "Turks Grew Discontent with Leaders, Freedom Before Unrest." *Gallup*. June 14, 2013. Accessed August 9, 2013. http://www.gallup.com/poll/163061/turks-grew-discontent-leaders-freedom-unrest.aspx.

"Worse and worse: Sectarian bloodshed looks set to persist." *The Economist*. May 25, 2013. Accessed June 24, 2013. http://www.economist.com/news/middle-east-and-africa/21578442-sectarian-bloodshed-looks-set-persist-worse-and-worse.

Wyer, Sam. "The Resurgence of Asa'ib Ahl al-Haq." *The Institute for the Study of War*, December 2012.

Yavuz, M. Hakan. *Islamic Political Identity in Turkey*. Oxford: Oxford University Press, 2003.

Younis, Mohamed. "Egyptians' Views of Government Crashed Before Overthrow." *Gallup*. August 2, 2013. Accessed August 9, 2013. http://www.gallup.com/poll/163796/egyptian-views-government-crashed-overthrow.aspx.

Youssef, Nariman. *Egypt's Draft Constitution Translated*. 2012. Accessed January 21, 2013. http://www.egyptindependent.com/news/egypt-s-draft-constitution-translated.

"Zanjeer or Qama Zani on Ashura During Muharram." *Mazloom Hussain*, December 7, 2012. Accessed January 28, 2013, http://www.ezsoftech.com/mazloom/zanjeer.asp.

Zeghal, Malika. *Gardiens de l'Islam. Les oulémas d'al-Azhar dans l'Egypte contemporaine*. Paris: Presses de Sciences Po, 1996.

Zeidan, David. "Radical Islam in Egypt: A Comparison of Two Groups." *Middle East Review of International Affairs* 3.3 (1999): 1–10.

"Zitouna Mosque to resume Religious Teaching." *Magharebia*, April 18, 2012. Accessed September 17, 2013. http://magharebia.com/en_GB/articles/awi/features/2012/04/18/feature-02.

Zollner, Barbara H. E. *The Muslim Brotherhood: Hasan Al-Hudaybi and Ideology*. London: Routledge, 2009.

Zubaida, Sami. *Islam, the People and the State: Political Ideas and Movements in the Middle East*, third edition. London: I. B. Tauris, 2009.

Al-Zubaidi, Layla. "The Struggle over Women's Rights and the Personal Status Law: A Test Case for Iraqi Citizenship?" *Orient* 52:2 (2011): 39–51.

Index